W9-BCS-001

RAGAN

STUDY GUIDE PAUL T. DICKINSON   GUSTAVO INDART

MICROECONOMICS

FOURTEENTH CANADIAN EDITION

ISBN: 978-0-321-82840-8

Acquisitions Editor: Claudine O'Donnell
Developmental Editor: Suzanne Schaan
Project Manager: Andrea Falkenberg

10 9 8 7 6 5 4 3 2 1 WC

Printed and bound in Canada.

PEARSON

CONTENTS

TO THE STUDENT

The contents of this book will help you reinforce and test your understanding of the analytical and theoretical concepts in each chapter of *Microeconomics,* Fourteenth Canadian Edition, by Christopher T. S. Ragan. In this new edition of the *Study Guide,* we have tailored the questions and exercises to the contents of the new edition of the text.

Our teaching experience has led us to believe that students often have the most trouble comprehending theoretical concepts and applying them to specific economic situations. The textbook covers a broad range of policy issues and real-world examples and applications. You will find excellent discussions of issues and policy applications in the body of the text, in the boxes entitled *Applying Economic Concepts* and *Extensions in Theory*, and in some of the *Additional Topics* posted online. Consequently, the role of the *Study Guide* is twofold—to help you better understand and apply the economic concepts you will meet in the text, and to give you a means to check your understanding. Many *Study Guide* questions, therefore, stress the application of economic theory using hypothetical and often numerical examples.

Each chapter in the *Study Guide* corresponds to a text chapter and is divided into nine sections, ordered as follows. The LEARNING OBJECTIVES are identical to those appearing at the beginning of each textbook chapter. The CHAPTER OVERVIEW provides a brief overview of the important concepts and issues addressed in the chapter. The HINTS AND TIPS section provides our suggestions and tips for how to study effectively and how you might avoid some common errors on examinations. It will be interesting for you to compare our list with yours after you have received your midterm results. Good luck!

The CHAPTER REVIEW section is divided into the same major subsections as each chapter of the text. Each subsection begins with a review of the main issues and concepts and then provides some multiple-choice questions that are primarily non-quantitative in nature. These questions are intended to give you quick feedback on your awareness and understanding of the basic concepts covered in the subsection. When you answer multiple-choice questions, avoid the temptation to leap at the first answer that seems plausible. There is one best answer for each question. You should be able to explain why any other answer is not as satisfactory as the one you have chosen.

The SHORT-ANSWER QUESTIONS have two functions. First, they give you practice formulating your economic reasoning in written form. We often discover what we don't understand only when we try to write an explanation. Second, the questions help you to check your understanding of the broad theoretical concepts before attempting applied questions with more technical content.

In many ways, the EXERCISES section has been the main distinguishing feature of this *Study Guide* since its first edition. We believe the greatest reinforcement to learning economics comes from doing the questions in this section. Not only do they solidify and enhance your understanding, but they also give you the tools on which to rely when memory fails in exams! We urge you not to make the mistake of avoiding the exercise questions just because your examinations may consist entirely of multiple-choice questions. Even in multiple-choice examinations, you need the understanding and the ability to analyze, which you will get from doing the exercises. Wherever mathematics is used, it does not require you to know more than the basic skills you learned in Chapter 2. We firmly believe that these exercises will enhance your ability to do well on all examinations, including those consisting entirely of multiple-choice questions. Do not be discouraged if you have difficulty with certain exercises. The most effective learning often comes from seeing how and why you got the wrong answer to a problem. We have also provided some more challenging problems in the section entitled EXTENSION EXERCISES.

The ADDITIONAL MULTIPLE-CHOICE QUESTIONS section focuses on additional applications of the concepts and analysis from the text, and some questions require numerical or algebraic solutions. In the SOLUTIONS section, we have provided brief explanations for more than 70 percent of these questions, which are identified by an asterisk next to the question number.

Unlike other study guides, the SOLUTIONS section provides answers for all questions. Please note that the written explanations are intended to guide you through the economic reasoning only, and should not be viewed as sample answers for examination purposes. In many cases your instructors may require fuller explanations on midterm and final examinations. A full appreciation of the issues can be achieved only after you have participated in lectures, carefully read the textbook, and thought your way through the concepts and economic applications with the assistance of this *Study Guide*.

Economic Issues and Concepts

Chapter Overview

This introductory chapter discusses some of the major issues that confront all economies. An economy is endowed with **scarce resources**, while human wants are unlimited. Choices must therefore be made regarding **production** and **consumption**. A central element of choice is the concept of **opportunity cost**, which measures the benefit of the best forgone alternative when making a choice. An economy's opportunity cost in production is illustrated through its **production possibilities boundary**. In addition to production and consumption choices, economies must also address how to avoid unemployment and how to ensure adequate growth over time. Different types of economic systems make these choices through different processes. This chapter reviews the main features of *command* economies, *free-market* economies, and *mixed* economies.

Economists focus on three sets of decision makers in a market economy: individuals (consumers), firms (producers), and government. Consumers are assumed to have the objective of maximizing their well-being (utility), while firms' decisions are made with the goal of maximizing their profits. (The objectives of government are discussed later.) The interactions between households and firms through markets are best illustrated in a diagram depicting the **circular flow** of income and expenditure.

One of the great economic debates of the twentieth century concerns the relative merits of **centrally planned economies** versus **free-market economies**. The pros and cons of each are reviewed, as are the main reasons why practically all communist countries have moved from command systems to mixed systems. The central lesson from this chapter is that the market economy is a self-organizing entity that coordinates millions of decentralized, independent decisions made by self-interested consumers and producers.

Chapter 1 concludes with *A Refresher on Graphing*, which reviews some basic concepts from high-school graphing used in the text.

LO **LEARNING OBJECTIVES**

After studying this chapter, you will be able to

1 explain the importance of scarcity, choice, and opportunity cost, and how all three concepts are illustrated by the production possibilities boundary.

2 view the market economy as self-organizing in the sense that order emerges from a large number of decentralized decisions.

3 explain how specialization gives rise to the need for trade, and that trade is greatly facilitated by money.

4 identify the economy's decision makers and see how their actions create a circular flow of income and expenditure.

5 see that all actual economies are mixed economies, having elements of free markets, tradition, and government intervention.

Hints and Tips

The following may help you avoid some of the most common errors on examinations.

✓ Understand that the opportunity cost of one commodity is the amount of other commodities you could have instead. For example, a major part of the opportunity cost of your education is the amount of income you could have earned had you not been studying (hence the goods and services you could have bought with it).

✓ Recognize that existing resources are fully employed at all points on the production possibilities boundary (PPB), so reallocating resources to produce more of one commodity means less of other commodities must be produced. The slope of the PPB, therefore, measures the economy's opportunity cost of one commodity in terms of another.

✓ Don't dismiss the notion that you make **marginal** decisions simply because you believe you "don't think that way." Recall that third pair of designer jeans (or whatever it was) that you *didn't* buy because you already had two pairs and you "didn't need" another pair? Would you have bought the item if it were on sale for $1? Yes? So perhaps you didn't buy the third pair because you "couldn't afford" it? Let's translate what you're saying. You bought your first and second pair because you "needed them" and/or "could afford them" and/or "they were worth the money," which is not what you thought for the third pair. All these are your own ways of saying the first two pairs were "worth" their opportunity costs to you, while the third pair wasn't. You made a marginal decision!

✓ Understand the difference between the causes and consequences of a movement along the PPB and a shift of the PPB.

✓ This hint applies to all of the multiple-choice questions in this *Study Guide* and in examinations. You are expected to choose the best answer, so it is advisable to read all answers even when you think you have found the correct one. Sometimes one answer is partially correct (e.g., the moon gives off light), but another is better (e.g., the moon gives off light by reflecting the sun's rays). Sometimes one answer will apply only in certain circumstances (e.g., individuals increase utility by buying more of a good that gives extra satisfaction), while another will apply in all circumstances (e.g., individuals increase utility by buying more of a good that gives extra satisfaction in excess of marginal cost). Take a little time to make sure you choose the best answer.

Chapter Review

What Is Economics?

After studying this section you should understand the problem of scarcity, the need for choice, and why choice creates opportunity cost. You should be able to illustrate the relationships among scarcity, choice, and opportunity cost using a production possibilities boundary (PPB); to explain why growth in a country's productive capacity can be represented by an outward shift in its PPB; and to describe why unemployment of resources can be represented by points inside a country's PPB.

1. **The fundamental problem of economics is, in short,**
   (a) too many poor people.
   (b) finding jobs for all.
   (c) the scarcity of resources relative to wants.
   (d) constantly rising prices.
   (e) the relative inefficiency that results when no single authority has control over the selfish decisions of consumers and producers.

2. **Scarcity is a problem that**
   (a) more efficient production would eliminate.
   (b) is non-existent in wealthy economies.
   (c) exists due to finite amounts of resources and unlimited human wants.
   (d) arises when productivity growth slows down.
   (e) exists in command economies but not market economies.

3. **Which of the following is *not* an example of a factor of production?**
   (a) A bulldozer.   (b) A mechanic.
   (c) A farmhand.   (d) A tractor.
   (e) A haircut.

4. **Opportunity cost measures the**
   (a) different opportunities for spending money.
   (b) monetary cost of purchasing a commodity.
   (c) alternative means of producing output.
   (d) amount of one good forfeited to obtain a unit of another good.
   (e) market price of a good.

5. **If a DVD costs $20 and a videocassette costs $10, then the opportunity cost of five DVDs is**
   (a) 50 videocassettes.   (b) 10 videocassettes.
   (c) 5 videocassettes.   (d) 2 videocassettes.
   (e) $25.

6. **Assuming that the alternative is employment, the opportunity cost of a university education is**
   (a) tuition costs only.
   (b) tuition and book costs only.
   (c) the forgone salary only.
   (d) tuition costs plus book costs plus forgone salary.
   (e) all items in (d) plus university residence fees and the cost of cafeteria meals.

7. **A downward-sloping production possibilities boundary that is also a straight line implies**
   (a) constant opportunity costs.
   (b) zero opportunity costs.
   (c) only one good is produced.
   (d) rising opportunity costs.
   (e) all goods are produced in equal quantities.

8.   **Which of the following causes an outward shift in the production possibilities boundary?**
     (a)   A decrease in unemployment.
     (b)   A loss in the productive capacity of agricultural acreage caused by a prolonged drought.
     (c)   An increase in the productivity of all factors of production.
     (d)   Shifting resources away from the production of one good toward another.
     (e)   Both a decrease in unemployment and an increase in productivity.

9.   **Putting currently unemployed resources to work can be illustrated by**
     (a)   shifting the production possibilities boundary outward.
     (b)   a movement along a given production possibilities boundary.
     (c)   moving from a point on the boundary to a point outside it.
     (d)   moving from a point inside the boundary to a point on it.
     (e)   moving from a point on the boundary to a point inside it.

The Complexity of the Modern Economy

Modern economies involve a countless number of economic decisions by self-interested individual consumers and producers. These independent decisions must be coordinated for the economy to use its scarce resources to produce the things people want to buy in the amounts that they want to purchase. This section sets the stage for subsequent study of how self-organizing free markets perform this coordination in modern economies, of the types of government actions that help or hinder efficient coordination, and of the issues that arise when economic efficiency seems to conflict with social values. It enables you to visualize the market interactions of consumers and producers through the circular flow of income and expenditure. The fundamental concept, used throughout the text, of maximization through decisions made "on the margin" is first introduced. You will also better understand how modern economies are based on the specialization and division of labour; as well as the causes and impact of economic globalization and the areas of disagreement over its consequences.

10. **One of the great insights of Adam Smith was that**
     (a)   modern economies require central planning.
     (b)   benevolence is the foundation of economic order.
     (c)   the rich will get richer and the poor will get poorer in a market economy.
     (d)   central coordination is required for any modern economy.
     (e)   by acting in their own self-interest, people produce a spontaneous economic order.

11. **Which of the following is one of the main characteristics of a market economy?**
     (a)   The objective of individuals is to maximize society's well-being.
     (b)   Firms must meet production quotas.
     (c)   Sellers can sell all they want to, regardless of price.
     (d)   Private property.
     (e)   People ignore financial incentives.

12. **Broadly speaking, a major reason why a relatively *efficient* economic order arises in a market economy is that**
    - (a) producers and consumers face different prices.
    - (b) pricing decisions are coordinated by producers, because they have better knowledge of the availability of resources than consumers.
    - (c) consumers determine the price structure, since they know best what they want.
    - (d) government manipulates prices in the best interests of society as a whole.
    - (e) prices respond to overall conditions of scarcity or plenty.

13. **In economics, the term *market economy* refers to**
    - (a) institutions such as the Toronto Stock Exchange.
    - (b) a place where buyers and sellers physically meet, such as at farmers' markets.
    - (c) a society where individuals specialize in productive activities and enter voluntary trades.
    - (d) a society where most economic decisions are made by marketing analysts.
    - (e) an economy in which advertising is central to the marketing of goods and services.

14. **In a barter economy, individuals**
    - (a) haggle over the money price of each and every commodity.
    - (b) trade goods directly for other goods.
    - (c) use money to lubricate the flow of trades.
    - (d) must each produce all of the goods and services he or she consumes.
    - (e) do not require factors of production.

15. **The introduction of production lines where individuals specialize in performing specific tasks is known as**
    - (a) the division of labour.
    - (b) the concentration of labour.
    - (c) the market economy.
    - (d) the advent of labour as a factor of production.
    - (e) lean production.

16. **Economic theory assumes that individuals**
    - (a) make choices to maximize their utility.
    - (b) seek to maximize profits.
    - (c) are the principal buyers of the factors of production.
    - (d) specialize their labour.
    - (e) are the only buyers of goods and services in a mixed economy.

17. **A central assumption in economic theory regarding firms is that they**
    - (a) are each owned by a single individual.
    - (b) must be incorporated.
    - (c) seek to maximize profits.
    - (d) must all be making profits.
    - (e) are the principal owners of the factors of production.

18. **Individual consumers maximize their well-being by**
    (a)   not wasting time making marginal decisions.
    (b)   comparing the total satisfaction received from one good with the total satisfaction received from another good.
    (c)   buying more of a good for which the marginal benefit is positive.
    (d)   buying more of a good for which the marginal benefit exceeds the marginal cost.
    (e)   comparing the average satisfaction received from various goods.

19. **The two major types of markets in the circular flow of income are**
    (a)   public markets and private markets.
    (b)   product markets and factor markets.
    (c)   free markets and controlled markets.
    (d)   markets for goods and markets for services.
    (e)   regulated markets and open markets.

20. **The circular flow of income and expenditure shows the flow of**
    (a)   goods and services from firms to consumers.
    (b)   payments for goods and services from consumers to firms.
    (c)   factor services from consumers to firms.
    (d)   payments for factor services from firms to consumers.
    (e)   All of the above.

21. **The use of money when buying and selling**
    (a)   makes exchange easier.
    (b)   makes barter more difficult.
    (c)   makes specialization of labour more difficult.
    (d)   increases the opportunity costs of exchange.
    (e)   makes the division of labour more difficult.

22. **Specialization of labour leads to a more efficient allocation of resources because of**
    (a)   more self-sufficiency.
    (b)   the use of barter.
    (c)   the principle of comparative advantage.
    (d)   a decrease in scarcity.
    (e)   both increased self-sufficiency and decreased scarcity.

23. **The market in which an individual sells labour services is called a**
    (a)   product market.
    (b)   factor market.
    (c)   foreign-exchange market.
    (d)   mixed market.
    (e)   goods market.

24. **A major cause of the recent move toward globalization is**
    (a)   international trade is a new phenomenon.
    (b)   a big reduction in the costs of transportation and information.
    (c)   a recognition that each country must produce what it consumes.
    (d)   increased living standards in developing countries.
    (e)   a growing concern about achieving equity among countries.

25. **The process of globalization tends to**
    (a)   reduce the incidence of layoffs and retraining.
    (b)   increase the influence of national governments over large firms.
    (c)   create greater similarity of consumer tastes among countries.
    (d)   reduce the need for concern over human rights.
    (e)   reduce productive efficiency by "exporting" jobs.

Is There an Alternative to the Market Economy?

This section emphasizes the remarkable achievement of the market economy in creating order out of millions of independent and decentralized decisions. After reading this section, you will develop a better appreciation of the twentieth century's great economic debate on the relative merits of a market (or mixed) economy versus a command economy, and why practically all command economies have become mixed economies. (See *Lessons from History 1-1.*) While there is no practical alternative to a mixed economy, there remains ample room for discussion and disagreement as to the appropriate depth and breadth of government intervention.

26. **Which of the following would be a source of similarity among alternative types of economic systems?**
    (a)   The ownership of resources (private and public).
    (b)   The process for making economic decisions.
    (c)   The need to determine what is to be produced and how to produce it.
    (d)   The role that tradition plays in determining production and employment.
    (e)   The role of government in determining what is produced.

27. **In the Canadian economy, the majority of decisions on resource allocation are made by**
    (a)   consumers and firms through the price system.
    (b)   the various levels of government.
    (c)   negotiation between unions and firms.
    (d)   business firms only.
    (e)   legal contract.

28. **Complex economic plans for many sectors of the economy are most associated with**
    (a)   a market system.
    (b)   the Canadian economy.
    (c)   a command economy.
    (d)   a feudal system.
    (e)   a traditional economy.

29. **There is general agreement among economists that government intervention in modern market economies**
    (a)   is not needed.
    (b)   should be restricted to enforcing the law.
    (c)   creates unacceptable reductions in work incentives.
    (d)   is appropriate when private markets create externalities and fail to produce public goods.
    (e)   creates the appropriate distribution of income.

30. **The failure of central planning (*Lessons from History 1-1*) was caused by**
    (a)   production bottlenecks, shortages, and gluts.
    (b)   lack of incentive to produce goods of high quality.
    (c)   a failure to protect the environment.
    (d)   poor incentives that didn't reward hard or efficient work.
    (e)   All of the above.

Short-Answer Questions

1.   What was Karl Marx's basic argument against free markets? How did most centrally planned economies' attempts to address this actually contribute to their failure?

2.   Explain the reasoning process that links scarcity and opportunity cost.

3.   Why is the production possibilities boundary (PPB) typically drawn concave to the origin, and what does this imply for opportunity costs?

Exercises

1.   **The Key Economic Problems**
       Four key economic problems are identified in Chapter 1.
       (1)   What is produced and how? (resource allocation)
       (2)   What is consumed and by whom? (distribution)
       (3)   Why are resources sometimes idle? (unemployment)
       (4)   Is productive capacity growing? (economic growth)

For each of the following topics, identify which of the four types of economic problem applies. Use each classification only once.

(a) Rises in oil prices during the 1970s encouraged a switch to alternative energy sources. 1

(b) The standard of living in Canada, measured by real output per capita, has risen steadily over the past century. 4

(c) Large harvests worldwide cause lower grain prices, thereby helping consumers but hurting farmers. 2

(d) The unemployment rate decreased in the late 1990s. 3

2. **The Production Possibilities Boundary (PPB)**
This exercise gives you practice in constructing and interpreting a production possibilities boundary (PPB).

The economy of Islandia produces only two consumer goods, *necklaces* and *fish*. Only labour is required to produce both goods, and the economy's labour force is fixed at 100 workers. The table below indicates the daily outputs of necklaces and fish that can be produced with various quantities of labour.

Number of Workers	Daily Necklace Production	Number of Workers	Daily Fish Production (kg)
0	0	0	0
20	10.0	20	150
40	20.0	40	250
60	25.0	60	325
80	27.5	80	375
100	30.0	100	400

(a) Draw the PPB for this economy, using the grid in Figure 1-1. [*Hint:* The labour force is always fully employed along the PPB.]

Figure 1-1

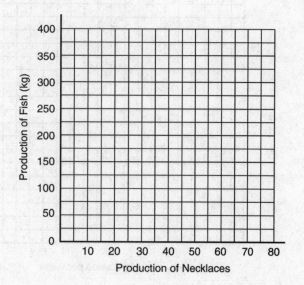

(b) What is the opportunity cost of producing the first 10 necklaces? What is the opportunity cost of producing the next 10 necklaces (i.e., from 10 to 20)? What happens to the opportunity cost of necklaces as their production is continuously increased?

(c) Suppose that actual production levels for a given period were 20 necklaces and 250 kg of fish. What can you infer from this information?

(d) Suppose a central planner in this economy were to call for an output combination of 35 necklaces and 150 kg of fish. Is this plan attainable? Explain.

(e) New technology is developed in necklace production, so that each worker can now produce double the daily amount indicated in the schedule. What happens to the PPB? Draw the new boundary on the grid. Can the planner's output combination in (d) now be met?

3. **Individual Choice and Opportunity Cost**
This exercise illustrates the concept of opportunity cost for an individual who faces fixed prices and has a fixed income.

Junior gets a weekly allowance of $10. He spends all of his allowance on only two commodities: video games at the arcade and chocolate bars. Assume that the price of a video game is 50 cents and the price of a chocolate bar is $1.

Figure 1-2

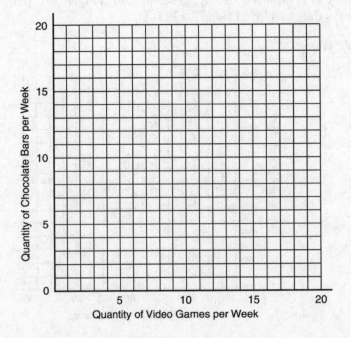

(a) Plot Junior's weekly attainable combinations of consumption.

(b) Can Junior attain the following consumption combinations?
   (i)   15 video games and 2 chocolate bars.
   (ii)   4 video games and 8 chocolate bars.
   (iii)   7 video games and 7 chocolate bars.

(c) What is the opportunity cost of Junior's first chocolate bar? His second? His third?

(d) By visual inspection of Junior's consumption possibility boundary, what could you say about his opportunity cost of consuming each of these commodities?

Linear = constant opportunity cost

4.   **The Opportunity Cost of University Education**
   This question also explores opportunity cost but without diagrams. It is a variant of *Applying Economic Concepts 1-1*.

   Pamela, a first-year student at Lakehead University, is considering whether or not to advance her studies by taking summer courses. Her monetary expenses would be tuition, $1000; books, $350; and living expenses, $1500. Her alternative is to work as a lifeguard, which would earn her $3500 for the summer. What is Pamela's opportunity cost of taking summer courses?

   doesn't count! constant no matter which choice

Extension Exercises

E1.   A Specific PPB
   This exercise addresses an economy's production possibilities algebraically. In the upcoming chapters you will be asked to make more use of algebra.

   An economy's production possibilities boundary is given by the mathematical expression $20 = 4A + B$, where A is the quantity of good A and B is the quantity of good B.

(a) If all resources in the economy were allocated to producing good A, what is the maximum level of production for this good? What is the maximum level of production for good B?

   $B = 0 \Rightarrow A = 5$
   $A = 0 \Rightarrow B = 20$

(b) Suppose that the production of B is increased from 12 to 16 units and that the economy is producing at a point on the production possibilities boundary. What is the opportunity cost per unit of good B? What is the opportunity cost per unit of good B if the production of this good were increased from 16 to 20?

   $B = 12 \Rightarrow 20 = 4A + 12$
   $\qquad 8 = 4A$
   $\qquad 2 = A$

   $B = 16 \Rightarrow 20 = 4A + 16$
   $\qquad 4 = 4A$
   $\qquad 1 = A$

   $\dfrac{1A}{4B}$

   $B = 20 \Rightarrow 20 = 4A + 20$
   $\qquad 0 = 4A$
   $\qquad A = 0$

   $\dfrac{1A}{4B}$

(c) In what way is this production possibilities boundary different from that in Exercise 2 in terms of opportunity costs?

This is constant vs. increasing in Exercise 2.

(d) In what way does the combination of four units of good *A* and five units of good *B* represent the problem of scarcity?

More resources req'd than are currently available
→ 4A + 4B is unattainable

E2. **A Conceptual PPB**
This problem is conceptually challenging. The ability to solve it would reflect an excellent understanding of the production possibilities concept.

Consider the production possibilities for two totally dissimilar goods, such as apples and machine tools. Some resources are suitable for apple production and some for the production of machine tools. There is, however, no possibility of shifting resources from one product to another. In this case, what does the production possibilities boundary look like? Explain and show graphically.

Additional Multiple-Choice Questions

*1. **If the factors of production available to an economy were unlimited,**
(a) the opportunity cost of producing more goods would be zero.
(b) the price of cars would be infinitely high.
(c) there would be no unemployment.
(d) scarcity would become the most serious economic problem.
(e) All of the above.

2. **If a 12-month membership in a fitness club costs as much as tickets for 24 Montreal Expos baseball games, the opportunity cost of a one-month membership in the fitness club is**
(a) 1/2 a baseball game.
(b) 1 baseball game.
(c) 2 baseball games.
(d) 12 baseball games.
(e) 24 baseball games.

$$\frac{24 \text{ games}}{12 \text{ moths}}$$

Questions 3 to 6 refer to Figure 1-3.

Figure 1-3

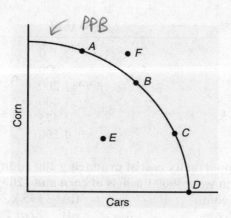

*3.   **If the market economy moves from Point *A* to Point *C*,**
    (a)   there is unemployment in the corn industry.
    (b)   the opportunity cost of the marginal car increases.
    (c)   technological change has made the production of cars more efficient.
    (d)   the central planner values cars more than corn.
    (e)   All of the above are true.

*4.   **Point *E* represents a situation that**
    (a)   is currently unattainable and can be expected to remain so.
    (b)   will be attainable only if there is economic growth.
    (c)   results from inefficient use of resources or failure to use all available resources.
    (d)   has a higher opportunity cost than points on the boundary itself.
    (e)   can never occur in a market economy.

*5.   **With currently available resources, point *F* represents a situation that**
    (a)   results if resources are not fully employed.
    (b)   can be achieved if consumers demand fewer cars than at point *C*.
    (c)   is currently attainable.
    (d)   can be achieved if all resources were allocated to the production of cars.
    (e)   None of the above.

6.   **Assuming that the initial situation is point *B*, which one of the following represents a reallocation of resources away from car production to corn production?**
    (a)   Point *A*.   (b)   Point *C*.
    (c)   Point *E*.   (d)   Point *D*.
    (e)   Point *F*.

Questions 7 to 14 refer to the following schedule of production possibilities for combinations of corn and beef, produced on a land tract of a given size and fertility.

Corn (bushels)	Beef (kg)
10 000	0
8 000	900
6 000	1 200
4 000	1 400
2 000	1 475
0	1 500

(handwritten annotations: next to corn column 2000, 2000, 2000, 2000, 2000, 2000; next to beef column 900, 1300, 200, 75, 25)

*7. **What would be the opportunity cost of producing 200 additional kilograms of beef if the current production were 4000 bushels of corn and 1200 kg of beef?**
(a) 6000 bushels of corn.
(b) 175 kg of beef.
(c) 2000 bushels of corn.
(d) Zero.
(e) None of the above.

*8. **What would be the opportunity cost of producing 2000 additional bushels of corn if the current production were 6000 bushels of corn and 1200 kg of beef?**
(a) 900 kg of beef.
(b) 1200 kg of beef.
(c) 300 kg of beef.
(d) Zero.
(e) None of the above.

(handwritten: 1200 − 900 =)

*9. **Which of the following combinations represent unattainable production levels with the current tract of land?**
(a) 8000 bushels of corn and 500 kg of beef.
(b) 8000 bushels of corn and 1200 kg of beef.
(c) 200 bushels of corn and 1475 kg of beef.
(d) 6000 bushels of corn and 1300 kg of beef.
(e) Both 8000 bushels of corn and 1200 kg of beef and 6000 bushels of corn and 1300 kg of beef.

*10. **The production possibilities shown for corn and beef mean the PPB**
(a) is a straight line because the change in corn is 2000 bushels all along.
(b) is concave because the total amount of beef increases as less corn is produced.
(c) is concave because the opportunity cost of beef increases as more beef is produced.
(d) is concave because the opportunity cost of corn falls as more corn is produced.
(e) is concave both because total beef increases as less corn is produced and the opportunity cost of corn falls as more corn is produced.

*11. **The opportunity cost of increasing corn production from 4000 to 6000 is**
(a) the same as the opportunity cost of increasing corn production from 8000 to 10 000.
(b) the same as the opportunity cost of increasing corn production from 2000 to 4000.
(c) 0.1 kg of beef per bushel of corn.
(d) 1200 kg of beef.
(e) None of the above.

(handwritten: $\frac{200}{2000}$)

*12. **Which of the following events is likely to lead to an outward shift of the production possibilities boundary?**
   (a) A reallocation of land use such that corn production increases from 6000 bushels to 8000 bushels while beef production decreases from 1200 kg to 900 kg.
   (b) Some of the land is lost due to a flood.
   (c) Twenty of the existing acres are not used for either beef or corn production.
   (d) Corn prices fall relative to beef prices.
   (e) None of the above.

*13. **The opportunity cost per bushel of corn is 0.15 kg of beef when**
   (a) corn production is increased from 8000 to 10 000.
   (b) corn production is increased from 6000 to 8000.
   (c) corn production is increased from 4000 to 6000.
   (d) beef production is decreased from 1500 to 1475 kg.
   (e) None of the above.

*14. **Assuming that land is fully utilized and that corn production continually increases by 2000 bushels, the opportunity cost of beef**
   (a) increases.
   (b) decreases.
   (c) is zero.
   (d) remains constant.
   (e) is undefined.

15. **In a command economy, where to produce on the production possibilities boundary is determined by**
   (a) the preferences of consumers, who spend their income accordingly.
   (b) a central plan established by the government.
   (c) traditional patterns of spending that change little from year to year.
   (d) the preferences of workers, who vote to indicate their preferences.
   (e) relative prices of goods.

16. **Decisions regarding resource allocation are**
   (a) necessary only in centrally planned economies.
   (b) made by central planners in traditional economies.
   (c) necessary only in economies that are not industrialized.
   (d) decentralized, but coordinated by the price system, in market economies.
   (e) primarily determined by traditional customs in market economies.

*17. **In a free-market economy, the allocation of resources is determined by**
   (a) the government and its marketing boards.
   (b) the various stock exchanges in the country.
   (c) a central planning agency.
   (d) the millions of independent decisions made by individual consumers and firms.
   (e) the sobering discussions at the annual convention of the Canadian Economics Association.

*18. **The main coordinating device in a self-organizing economy is**
  (a)   the way that government spends its tax revenues.
  (b)   government intervention to correct market failures.
  (c)   the economy's system of market-determined prices.
  (d)   the degree of income redistribution by government.
  (e)   the overall coordinated system of taxation and spending to achieve multiple objectives of government.

19. **A barter economy**
  (a)   refers to the direct trading of goods.
  (b)   does not require the use of money.
  (c)   requires a double coincidence of wants.
  (d)   involves costly searches for satisfactory exchanges.
  (e)   All of the above are true.

20. **Utility-maximizing decisions of individuals are part of the study of _____ and changes in the unemployment rate are part of the study of _____.**
  (a)   microeconomics; macroeconomics
  (b)   the theory of choice; microeconomics
  (c)   the production possibilities boundary; a centrally planned economy
  (d)   economic aggregates; the objectives of individual firms.
  (e)   None of the above.

Solutions

Chapter Review

1.(c) 2.(c) 3.(e) 4.(d) 5.(b) 6.(d) 7.(a) 8.(c) 9.(d) 10.(e) 11.(d) 12.(e) 13.(c) 14.(b) 15.(a) 16.(a) 17.(c) 18.(d) 19.(b) 20.(e) 21.(a) 22.(c) 23.(b) 24.(b) 25.(c) 26.(c) 27.(a) 28.(c) 29.(d) 30.(e)

Short-Answer Questions

1.   Marx argued that although a market system would produce high total output, it could not be relied on to ensure a just distribution of that output. (He argued that the rich would get richer and the poor would get poorer.) In addressing this by measures to create a more even distribution of income (e.g., by guaranteeing complete job security), centrally planned economies did not provide the incentives for diligent and efficient work that are created by the "punishment and reward" forces of free markets.

2.   *Scarcity* implies choice; *choice* means you must give up something to have something else, and what you give up is the opportunity cost of that something else. In essence, this implies that anything that has an opportunity cost is "scarce."

3.   All factors of production are not equally adaptable to producing all goods. As more and more of one good is produced, the economy transfers resources from more efficient uses to progressively less efficient uses. As this happens, more and more resources must be transferred from the production of one good to get a constant increase in the amount of another good. In other words, the opportunity cost of producing a good increases as more of it is produced. This is reflected in the changing slope of the PPB, which makes the PPB concave to the origin.

4. **(a)** <u>Developing countries:</u> Activists argue that free trade reduces the standard of living in developing countries, and does so largely at the expense of the poorest members (i.e., the poor get poorer). Defenders argue that free trade increases the average standard of living in both developed and developing countries. While there may be less disagreement that the poorest members of developing countries do get poorer, defenders may still argue that free trade at least gives developing countries the *opportunity* to internally redistribute the overall gains in a socially just way.

    (b) <u>Democracy:</u> Activists argue that free trade agreements are made in an undemocratic manner "behind closed doors." Defenders argue that the process is not undemocratic because the agreements must be passed by the governments of participating countries—specifically, by the *elected* bodies (parliaments) of the democratic countries.

Exercises

1. **(a)** 1 **(b)** 4 **(c)** 2—redistribution from farmers to consumers **(d)** 3—while (4) could also apply, this item is specifically talking about a fall in the proportion of the labour force (a resource) that is idle (i.e., wanting a job but not having one). It is possible for this to happen even without any economic growth.

2. **(a)** **Figure 1-4**

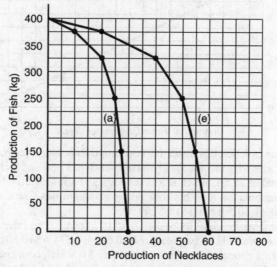

    (b) It takes 20 workers to produce the first 10 necklaces, and these 20 could have been used to increase fish production from 375 (with the other 80 workers) to 400. So the opportunity cost of these 10 necklaces is 25 (= 400 − 375) kg of fish, or 2.5 kg for each necklace (= 25/10). Similarly, the next 10 necklaces need another 20 workers, further reducing fish production from 375 to 325—an opportunity cost of 50 kg of fish, or 5 kg per necklace (= 50/10). Thus, the opportunity cost of producing necklaces is increasing (i.e., from 2.5 kg of fish per necklace to 5 kg per necklace), and if you continue transferring 20 more workers from fish to necklaces, you see the opportunity cost per necklace continue rising (i.e., (325 − 250)/(25 − 20) = 15 kg, (250 − 150)/(27.5 − 25) = 40 kg, (150 − 0)/(30 − 27.5) = 60 kg). This continually rising opportunity cost per necklace is reflected in the slope of production possibilities boundary (a) in Figure 1-4 getting continually steeper as more and more necklaces (and fewer and fewer fish) are produced.

    (c) This production combination lies <u>inside</u> the production possibilities boundary, so <u>some workers are unemployed or inefficiently used.</u> In this case, using unemployment as the example, 20 necklaces should require 40 workers and 250 kg of fish should also require 40 workers, for a total of only 80 workers, leaving 20 of the full 100 workers unemployed.

    (d) This combination is outside the production possibilities boundary and is therefore unattainable with current resources and technology. The maximum number of necklaces it is possible to make using all 100 workers is only 30. With 20 workers producing 150 kg of fish, the remaining 80 could produce only 27.5 necklaces (not 35).

(e) The production possibilities boundary moves to the right in the manner shown in Figure 1-4. The planner's output combination is now attainable: with 20 workers producing fish, the remaining 80 could produce 55 necklaces. The combination of 150 kg of fish and 35 necklaces is therefore inside the new boundary, implying that the economy would be using its resources inefficiently if it produced this combination.

3. (a) **Figure 1-5**

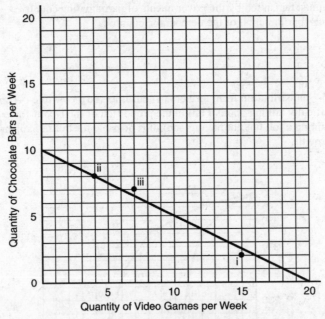

(b) (i) Yes, this combination lies inside his consumption possibilities boundary and is therefore affordable with $10. (15 videos at 50 cents each is $7.50 and 2 chocolate bars at $1 each is $2, for a total of $9.50, which is less than his $10 allowance.)

(ii) Yes, this combination is on his consumption possibilities boundary and therefore costs exactly $10. (4($0.50) + 8($1) = $10)

(iii) No, this combination costs more than his $10 allowance and therefore lies outside his consumption possibilities boundary. (7($0.50) + 7($1) = $10.50)

(c) To purchase the first chocolate bar, Junior must pay $1, which could have been used to purchase two video games. Thus, the opportunity cost of the first chocolate bar is two video games. The opportunity cost of the second and third bars is also two video games each.

(d) Since the consumption possibilities boundary is linear (i.e., a straight line), the opportunity cost is constant.

4. Pamela's opportunity cost of taking summer courses is $4850 ($1000 tuition + $350 books + forgone earnings of $3500). Her living expenses are not counted since they would have to be incurred regardless of which alternative she chooses.

Extension Exercises

E1. (a) If all resources were allocated to the production of good A, there would be no production of good B. So, according to the mathematical expression, the maximum production of good A is five units. (Convert $20 = 4A + B$ to $A = 5 - 0.25B$, so $A = 5$ when $B = 0$.) If all resources were used to produce good B, then $B = 20$ and the production of good A is zero. ($B = 20 - 4A$, so $B = 20$ when $A = 0$.)

(b) The increase from 12 to 16 units of B requires a loss in production of good A of one (from two to one). An increase in B from 16 to 20 requires a loss in production of good A of one (from one to zero). Therefore, the opportunity cost *per unit* of good B is 0.25 units of A in each case. (From $A = 5 - 0.25B$, you see A changes by 0.25 whenever B changes by 1.)

(c) The opportunity cost is constant, whereas it was increasing in Exercise 2 above.

(d) According to the equation, four units of A and four units of B are possible. The combination of four units of A and five units of B is not feasible. Scarcity is indicated by the fact that more resources are required than are currently available.

E2. When all resources suitable to apple production are employed, the resulting apple output is A′ in Figure 1-6. When all resources suitable to machine tool production are employed, the resulting quantity of machine tools is M′. Since there is no possibility of shifting resources between these two outputs, the production possibilities boundary is simply the point corresponding to the coordinates (A′, M′). Any combination of apples and machine tools either inside or on the dashed lines implies unemployed or inefficiently used resources, and any combination outside the dashed lines is unattainable.

Figure 1-6

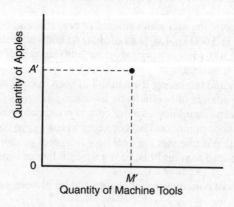

Quantity of Machine Tools

Additional Multiple-Choice Questions

1.(a) 2.(c) 3.(b) 4.(c) 5.(e) 6.(a) 7.(c) 8.(c) 9.(e) 10.(c) 11.(c) 12.(e) 13.(b) 14.(b) 15.(b) 16.(d) 17.(d) 18.(c) 19.(e) 20.(a)

Explanations for the Asterisked Multiple-Choice Questions

1.(a) Unlimited resources means that having more of one good does not require having less of another, hence no opportunity cost. Since scarcity requires that there be an opportunity cost, no opportunity cost means no scarcity. Having resources available does not necessarily mean they are all used, so it does not rule out unemployment. (Indeed, technically speaking, "unlimited" means it is impossible to use them all.) Finally, in the absence of scarcity it is likely that prices would be very low rather than very high (and, again technically speaking, "infinity" can't be achieved anyway).

3.(b) The slope of the PPB (looking from the horizontal axis) shows how much corn must be given up for each extra car. The concave PPB is steeper at C than at A because more corn must be given up to get the extra car, hence a higher opportunity cost of a car. (Prove this for yourself by drawing a little right-angled triangle at each point, with equal horizontal axis and the PPB as the hypotenuse. Now compare the height of their vertical axes.) Both points are on the PPB, so there is no unemployment. Technological change would cause a shift of the PPB, not a movement along it. The relative quantities produced tell us nothing about prices, so nothing about values.

4.(c) The text defines the PPB as all combinations of commodities which can be produced when *efficiently* using *all available resources*. Point E is inside the PPB, so does not meet this condition (as answer (c) says). This can be a temporary situation (so (a) is wrong). Economic growth will shift the PPB out to the right—it changes what is *feasible* to produce, not necessarily what is *actually* produced (so (b) is wrong). Unemployment of resources often exists in a market economy (so (e) is wrong). Since the slope of the PPB changes, there are many potentially very different opportunity costs along the boundary changes (so (d) is not a valid comparison). [*Note:* Some texts will say that the opportunity cost of having more (say) cars at E is zero because you do not have to reduce the amount of corn. BUT see the answer to Question 7 below.]

5.(e)   With currently available resources, point F is unattainable.

7.(c)   It is tempting to say that the opportunity cost is zero, since it is possible to produce 1400 kg of beef with no reduction in corn. This would be incorrect, however, since it is also possible to produce 6000 bushels of corn with no reduction in beef. The economy has a choice, and by choosing to have 200 additional kilograms of beef, it is choosing *not* to have the 2000 extra bushels of corn. Despite the fact that the economy is inside its PPB, therefore, the opportunity cost of the extra beef is the extra corn that could have been produced (i.e., another 2000 bushels, from 4000 to 6000).

8.(c)   Contrast this with Question 7, where the economy was **inside** the PPB and so could produce more of either beef or corn. In Question 8, however, the economy is **on** the PPB, so producing more of one good requires producing less of another (or others). The extra benefit from producing these 2000 more bushels (from 6000 to 8000) can be had only at the cost of producing 300 fewer kilograms of beef (from 1200 to 900). This opportunity cost can't be avoided when the economy is on its PPB.

9.(e)   With 8000 bushels of corn, the maximum amount of beef that can be produced is 900 kg, so 1200 kg, (b), is unattainable and 500 kg, (a), is attainable. At 6000 bushels of corn the maximum amount of beef is 1200 kg, so 1300, (d), is unattainable. At 2000 bushels of corn, the maximum amount of beef is 1475 kg, so (c) is attainable.

10.(c)   Starting from zero corn and increasing the amount of corn in constant increments of 2000 bushels, the maximum possible amount of beef falls by increasing amounts (25, 75, 200, 300, 900). Thus, the slope of the PPB keeps increasing as more corn is produced, making the PPB concave (so (a) is incorrect) because the opportunity cost of more corn keeps increasing (so (c) is correct but (d) and (e) are incorrect). While it is true that the total beef increases as more corn is produced, this would happen with any downward-sloping PPB, be it a straight line or concave or even convex (so (b) and (e) are incorrect).

11.(c)   The extra 2000 bushels of corn requires giving up 200 kg of beef, so 200/2000 = 0.1 units of beef per extra unit of corn.

12.(e)   Answer (a) involves a movement along the PPB. Answer (b) causes an inward shift of the PPB. Answer (c) is a point inside the PPB. Answer (d) gives an incentive to change the combination of corn and beef produced (i.e., a movement along the PPB), but does not change the combinations that it is possible to produce with current technology.

13.(b)   Numbers are usually easy when you know what you are looking for. The schedule shows corn changing in increments of 2000. To find where the change in beef per bushel of corn is 0.15 kg, multiply the 2000 total change in corn by 0.15 and get 300. This is the change in beef between 6000 and 8000 bushels of corn.

14.(b)   The production of more and more corn requires moving resources out of beef production that are progressively less adaptable to the production of corn, so the quantity of beef forgone per extra unit of corn (the opportunity cost of corn) increases. If the opportunity cost of corn increases, then the opportunity cost of beef decreases. For example, if an extra 20 corn means giving up 5 beef, the opportunity cost per unit of corn is 5/20 = 0.25 units of beef and the opportunity cost per unit of beef is 20/5 = 4 units of corn. But if an extra 20 corn means giving up 10 beef instead of 5, the opportunity cost per unit of corn *increases* to 10/20 = 0.5 units of beef (i.e., up from 0.25) and the opportunity cost per unit of beef *decreases* to 20/10 = 2 units of corn (i.e., down from 4).

17.(d)   Answer (d) refers to Adam Smith's "invisible hand," but answers (a), (b), and (c) are also present in our economy, so why aren't these correct too? First, (b) is only one example of the "invisible hand" of a market, whereas (d) covers all such markets and thus is a better answer. Answers (a) and (c) warn you about sloppy use of terminology! They are present in a *mixed* economy, but not in a *free-market* economy.

18.(c)   All answers other than (c) refer to the actions of government that, although they may be desirable (e.g., answer (b)), are "organized" by specific individuals (politicians and civil servants) in line with the policies of the government in power. The self-organizing force in a market or even a mixed economy is the actions of masses of individuals (producers and consumers) in line with their self-interest, which in turn is heavily influenced by the prices of the various goods and services.

Economic Theories, Data, and Graphs

Chapter Overview

Chapter 1 provided an overview of the types of issues economists consider. Chapter 2 presents some important distinctions made by economists and discusses the approaches used to analyze economic questions.

Economists evaluate statements or relationships that purport to explain economic behaviour. An important distinction is made between **positive statements**, which concern what is, was, or will be, and **normative statements**, which are judgements about what should be done. Disagreements over positive statements can, in principle, be settled by an appeal to the facts (i.e., they are testable). Disagreements over normative statements cannot be settled in this way.

Theories (or **models**) are designed to give meaning to observed sequences of events. A theory typically consists of definitions of **variables** and assumptions about how things behave. Any theory has certain logical implications that must hold if the theory is not to be rejected. These are the theory's **predictions** or **hypotheses**. Theories are tested by checking their predictions against the evidence. In economics the evidence most often comprises **data** drawn from the real world.

The relationships among variables in economic theories are usually presented in tables, graphs, or equations. These provide compact summaries of a large number of data observations and play an important role in economic modelling.

LO LEARNING OBJECTIVES

After studying this chapter, you will be able to

1 distinguish between positive and normative statements.

2 explain why and how economists use theories to help them understand the economy.

3 understand the interaction between economic theories and empirical observation.

4 identify several types of economic data, including index numbers, time-series and cross-sectional data, and scatter diagrams.

5 see that the slope of a line on a graph relating two variables shows how one responds to a small change in the other.

Hints and Tips

The following may help you avoid some of the most common errors on examinations.

✓ Understand the difference between endogenous (dependent) and exogenous (independent) variables. Changes in the exogenous variables cause changes in the endogenous variables, not the other way around. That is, the *direction of causation* is from the exogenous variables to the endogenous variables. For example, cold weather causes more people to wear scarves, but more people wearing scarves will not cause cold weather.

✓ Recognize that assumptions must be made to create a hypothesis relevant for use in the real world, and that the predictive or explanatory powers of theory need not depend on the accuracy of the assumptions. Generally, it is the simplifying assumptions that give a theory its ability to make predictions and explain its major implications, rather than merely describe all possible situations.

✓ Don't mentally reject a theory because its predictions do not conform to the way *you* behave or explain why *you* choose to behave that way. As with all social sciences, the purpose of a theory in economics is to predict and explain the behaviour of an entire group, not of specific individuals within that group. Some individuals like to take big risks, but *on average* people as a group are willing to pay to reduce the risks they take (i.e., they pay insurance premiums).

✓ Understand how to draw and read graphs, and how to construct, solve, and interpret simple equations. These are valuable tools that will improve your understanding of the material and, in so doing, significantly reduce the extent to which you have to rely on memory.

Chapter Review

Positive and Normative Advice

The objective of this section is to distinguish between positive and normative statements. Positive statements are assertions of fact that can be tested, in principle even if not always in practice. Normative statements refer to what ought to be; they are based on personal opinion (i.e., on *value judgements*) and cannot be tested by appealing to facts. This section also explains why there is less disagreement among economists on many issues than may appear to be the case in public discussions.

1. **Normative statements**
   (a)   concern an individual's beliefs about what ought to be.
   (b)   are based on value judgements.
   (c)   cannot be subjected to empirical scrutiny.
   (d)   cannot be deduced from positive statements.
   (e)   All of the above.

2. **"Capital punishment deters crime" is an example of**
   (a)   a positive statement.   (b)   a value judgement.
   (c)   a normative statement.   (d)   an analytic statement.
   (e)   an untestable statement.

3. **"Capital punishment should be reintroduced in Canada" is an example of**
   (a)   a positive statement.   (b)   a normative statement.
   (c)   an analytic statement.   (d)   a testable hypothesis.
   (e)   None of the above.

4. **Which of the following is probably the main reason why economists are often seen to disagree in public discussions?**
   (a)   Economists like to stimulate debate.
   (b)   Different economists make different value judgements.
   (c)   Most economists disagree on positive statements.
   (d)   Economists fail to distinguish between theories and models.
   (e)   Economists are the only people who realize that the world is a very complex place.

Building and Testing Economic Theories

This section contains a non-technical discussion of the basic structure and building blocks of economic theories (sometimes called *models*); the roles of variables, assumptions, and predictions in developing theories; and the purpose and usefulness of an economic model as an illustrative abstraction or as a quantitative specification of one or more components of a complex economic world. Economic theories adopt a scientific approach, whereby hypotheses and predictions are developed and then tested against data, taking care to distinguish between a *correlation* among variables and a *causal* relationship. When the testing process shows that a theory does not give predictions that are reasonably consistent with the empirical evidence, it signals that the theory needs to be amended and/or a better alternative theory needs to be developed. The usefulness of a theory depends on how well it can predict group behaviour, not the behaviour of a particular individual in the group.

5. **If the assumptions imposed in an economic theory are unrealistic, then the theory**
   (a)   will always be refuted by the evidence.
   (b)   is incorrect and should be rejected.
   (c)   will not predict well and should be rejected.
   (d)   will require more complex statistical techniques for testing.
   (e)   may nonetheless predict better than any alternative theory.

6. **The role of assumptions in theory is to**
   (a)   represent the world accurately.
   (b)   improve understanding of a complex world by reasonably abstracting from reality.
   (c)   avoid simplifications of the real world.
   (d)   ensure that the theory considers all features of reality, no matter how minor.
   (e)   None of the above.

7. **A theory may contain all *except* which of the following?**
   (a)   Predictions about behaviour that are deduced from the assumptions.
   (b)   A set of assumptions defining the conditions under which the theory is operative.
   (c)   Hypotheses about how the world behaves.
   (d)   A normative statement expressed as a functional relation.
   (e)   Hypothesized relationships among variables.

8. **Direction of causation refers to**
   (a) the effect of an exogenous variable on an endogenous variable.
   (b) the effect of a variable determined outside the theory on the value of a variable determined within the theory.
   (c) whether the value of one variable rises or falls when another variable rises.
   (d) whether an assumption increases or decreases the accuracy of a prediction.
   (e) Both (a) and (b).

9. **The statement that the quantity produced of a commodity is positively related to its price is**
   (a) a normative statement.
   (b) a testable hypothesis.
   (c) not testable as currently worded.
   (d) a value judgement.
   (e) both a testable hypothesis and a value judgement.

10. **Statistical analysis in economics**
   (a) uses data generated in controlled laboratory experiments.
   (b) is mainly designed to prove or disprove the validity of assumptions.
   (c) must use techniques that take account of simultaneous changes in many variables.
   (d) should look only for evidence that confirms a theory.
   (e) uses correlation as proof of causality.

11. **Economic predictions are intended to**
   (a) forecast the behaviour of each consumer.
   (b) forecast the behaviour of groups of individuals.
   (c) test normative statements.
   (d) anticipate the irrational behaviour of certain odd individuals.
   (e) identify value judgements.

12. **The theory that extraterrestrials exist and visit Earth in flying saucers**
   (a) has been disproved by scientific evidence.
   (b) is inconsistent with scientific observation.
   (c) can never be disproved.
   (d) has been refuted.
   (e) has not been scientifically proved, but can't be disproved.

Economic Data

Economists use data drawn from real-world observations to test their theories. This section reviews two ways in which data can be examined: index numbers and graphs.

13. **If a particular index number in 2013 is 159 and the base year is 2010, then the index shows an increase of**
   (a) 5.9 percent between 2010 and 2013.
   (b) 59 percent between 2010 and 2013.
   (c) 159 percent between 2010 and 2013.
   (d) 0.59 percent between 2010 and 2013.
   (e) an indeterminable amount, since the value of the index in the base year is unknown.

14. **Index numbers are useful because**
    (a) identifying trends is easier using relative rather than absolute numbers.
    (b) each component can be weighted to reflect its relative importance.
    (c) they can all be given the same value in the base year.
    (d) All of the above are true.
    (e) Only (a) and (c) are true.

15. **Which of the following is an example of cross-sectional data?**
    (a) Annual unemployment rates for Canada.
    (b) Vancouver housing prices for the period 1963 to 2012.
    (c) Last year's crime rates for all Canadian cities.
    (d) A series of this year's daily interest rates.
    (e) None of the above—they are all examples of time-series data.

16. **Observations drawn repeatedly from successive months are**
    (a) cross-sectional data.
    (b) time-series data.
    (c) unweighted data.
    (d) logarithmic data.
    (e) scattered data.

17. **A scatter diagram can be used to plot**
    (a) time-series data but not cross-sectional data.
    (b) cross-sectional data but not time-series data.
    (c) neither cross-sectional nor time-series data.
    (d) either cross-sectional or time-series data.
    (e) only endogenous variables.

Graphing Economic Theories

The relationship between schedules of numbers for two (or more) variables can be more easily seen when the functional form is expressed mathematically and displayed graphically. After completing this section, you should be comfortable reading functional relationships, translating equations into graphs, and interpreting graphs.

18. **The slope of a straight line is**
    (a) always positive.
    (b) calculated by dividing the value of the variable measured on the horizontal axis by the value of that measured on the vertical axis.
    (c) zero.
    (d) constant.
    (e) increasing or decreasing, depending on whether the slope is positive or negative, respectively.

19. **Suppose that economic analysis estimates the following relationship between imports (*IM*) and national income (*Y*): *IM* = 100 + 0.15*Y*. This means that**
    (a) imports are negatively related to national income.
    (b) when national income is zero, imports are zero.
    (c) imports are 15 percent of national income.
    (d) imports are 15 times greater than national income.
    (e) other things remaining constant, for every increase of $1 in national income, imports will rise by 15 cents.

20. Still use $IM = 100 + 0.15Y$ from Question 19. The equation is graphed with IM on the vertical axis and Y on the horizontal axis; if the value of Y is 200

  (a) the line is horizontal, meeting the vertical axis at $IM = 130$.
  (b) the line is vertical, meeting the horizontal axis at $Y = 130$.
  (c) the line is upward-sloping, meeting the horizontal axis at $Y = 130$.
  (d) the line is upward-sloping, meeting the vertical axis at $IM = 100$.
  (e) because we know only one value for Y, we can't draw any line.

Short-Answer Questions

1. In each case, write P or N to indicate whether it is a <u>positive</u> or a <u>normative</u> statement.

  (a) A statement of fact that is factually wrong. _____P_____
  (b) A value judgement. _____N_____
  (c) A prediction that an event will happen. _____N C_____
  (d) A statement about what the author thinks ought to be. _____N_____
  (e) A statement that can be tested by evidence. _____P_____
  (f) A value judgement based on evidence known to be correct. _____N_____
  (g) A hurricane forecast. _____P_____
  (h) An opinion survey that indicates a majority of Canadians believe taxes ought to be reduced. _____P N_____

2. In each case, identify the direction of causality by classifying the italicized variable(s) as <u>endogenous</u> (EN) or <u>exogenous</u> (EX).

  (a) *Market price and equilibrium quantity* of a commodity are determined by demand and supply. _____EN_____
  (b) The number of sailboats sold annually is a function of *national income*.
      _____EX_____
  (c) The *condition of forest ecosystems* can be affected by regional air pollutants.
      _____EN_____
  (d) The quantity of housing services purchased is determined by the *relative price of housing, income, and housing characteristics*. _____EX_____
  (e) Other things being equal, an increase in interest rates reduces *consumer expenditures*.
      _____EN_____

3. It is very important for theory, for empirical research, and often for economic and social policy to identify whether a <u>correlation</u> between variables is also a <u>causal</u> relationship. State whether the correlation between *each pair* of variables is positive or negative, whether or not it is also a causal relationship, and, if causal, explain the direction of causality.

  (a) Average income and the number of TV sets purchased both increase.

      +, causal →

      can afford more TVs.

  (b) The number of people who want to go to university falls, and the income that can be earned without a university degree rises.

      −, causal

      ←

(c)   As winter approaches in Canada, (i) more birds fly south, (ii) electricity consumption increases, and (iii) the number of trees with leaves declines. [*Hint:* There are three pairs of variables: (i) and (ii), (i) and (iii), (ii) and (iii).]

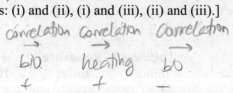

(d)   During the same period, (i) more children are sent to daycare, (ii) income tax deductions for daycare increase, and (iii) the price of potatoes falls. [*Hint:* Again, there are three pairs of variables.]

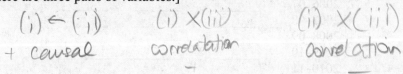

Exercises

1.   **Constructing Index Numbers**

This exercise asks you to construct a price index for the out-of-pocket cost of attending university, and illustrates how data can be used differently to support different points of view. You may want to review the section on index numbers in the text, along with Tables 2-2 and 2-3, before doing this exercise.

The table below presents a decade's data on three components of the annual out-of-pocket expenses for the University of Northern Labrador: tuition fees, the amount it costs to live in the university's hall of residence, and the cost of a full meal plan in the residence. [*Note:* This is <u>not</u> a question on the opportunity cost of a university education—see *Applying Economic Concepts 1-1* in Chapter 1 of the text.]

Year	Tuition	Residence	Food
2003–04	$2748	$3420	$3320
2004–05	3036	3820	3520
2005–06	3276	4100	4000
2006–07	3540	4384	4500
2007–08	3788	4704	4800
2008–09	4052	4924	5040
2009–10	4456	4924	5200
2010–11	4902	5164	5320
2011–12	5860	5344	5340
2012–13	6446	5344	5520

(a) Using 2003–04 as the base year, construct individual price indices for each of the three expense items. [*Note*: Students familiar with a spreadsheet software program may wish to use it in answering this question.]

Year	Tuition Index	Residence Index	Food Index
2003–04	_____	_____	_____
2004–05	_____	_____	_____
2005–06	_____	_____	_____
2006–07	_____	_____	_____
2007–08	_____	_____	_____
2008–09	_____	_____	_____
2009–10	_____	_____	_____
2010–11	_____	_____	_____
2011–12	_____	_____	_____
2012–13	_____	_____	_____

(b) Which of these three items increased the most in percentage terms for the period 2003–04 to 2004–05? Over the entire decade, 2003–04 to 2012–13?

(c) What was the percentage increase in residence fees between 2006–07 and 2007–08?

The next three questions together illustrate how the same data can be used to argue for different points of view—something that often happens in the world around us.

(d) Construct an *unweighted* (i.e., equal weight) index of total out-of-pocket expenses. Put the values in the following table.

Year	Unweighted Index	Weighted Index	Year	Unweighted Index	Weighted Index
2003–04	_____	_____	2008–09	_____	_____
2004–05	_____	_____	2009–10	_____	_____
2005–06	_____	_____	2010–11	_____	_____
2006–07	_____	_____	2011–12	_____	_____
2007–08	_____	_____	2012–13	_____	_____

(e) Construct a *weighted* index of total out-of-pocket expenses. Put the values in the table. [*Note*: The text discusses a weighted index in the section on *More Complex Index Numbers* but does not construct one. A weighted index takes account of the relative importance of each component expense, as measured by the component's percentage share of total expenses *in the base year*, 2003–04. These base-year percentages are the "weights." For subsequent years, multiply each component's index number by its base-year weight, and add the resulting three numbers to get the weighted index of total expenses for each year.]

(f)   Assume that the university wants to increase tuition fees for 2012–13. Looking over the entire decade, if you were president of the university, which of the five indices would you use to argue in favour of the fee increase? If you were president of the student council, which index would you use to argue against the fee increase? Explain.

2.   Linear Relationships
This exercise gives you practice in interpreting and graphing linear relationships.

Suppose that an economist hypothesizes that the annual quantity demanded of a specific manufacturer's personal computers (Q^D) is determined by the price of the computer (P) and the average income of consumers (Y). The specific functional relationship among these three variables is hypothesized to be the expression $Q^D = Y - 4P$.

(a)   Which of these variables are endogenous and which are exogenous?

Q^D Y, P

(b)   What does the negative sign before the term $4P$ imply about the relationship between Q^D and P? What does the implicit positive sign before the term Y tell you about the relationship between income and quantity demanded?

inverse correlation   +

(c)   Suppose for the moment that average income equals $8000. Write a simplified expression for the demand relationship [i.e., the relationship for $Q^D = f(P)$].

$Q^D = f(P) = 8000 - 4P$

(d)   Assuming that $Y = \$8000$, calculate the values of Q^D when $P = 0$, $P = \$500$, $P = \$1000$, and $P = \$2000$.

solve eqⁿ

(e)   Plot the relationship between P and Q^D (assuming that $Y = \$8000$) on the graph in Figure 2-1. Indicate the intercept value on each axis.

Figure 2-1

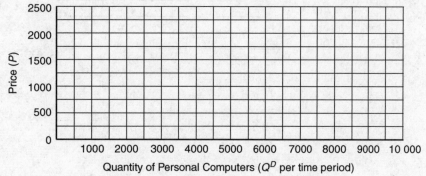

(f)   Calculate the slope of the relationship in (e).

(g)   Assuming that $Y = \$8000$, calculate the change in the quantity demanded when the price increases from $1000 to $2000. Do the same for a price increase from $500 to $2000. Call the change in the quantity demanded ΔQ^D and the change in the price ΔP. Determine the ratio $\Delta Q^D/\Delta P$. Is this ratio constant? [*Note:* Δ means "change in."]

(h)   Now suppose that evidence indicates that in subsequent time periods, the average income of consumers changed to $9000 per period. Plot the new relationship between P and Q^D. What are the intercept values and the slope?

Extension Exercises

The following exercises review two methods for solving a system of linear equations. The first exercise works through the diagrammatic method while the second uses the algebraic approach. Although they are not used until Chapter 3 of the text when the demand and supply model is presented, it is useful to review these methods now while we are covering linear relationships. When you have competence in both approaches you will find that the algebraic approach is easier and takes less time than drawing scale diagrams.

E1.   Using Scale Diagrams
    Consider the following two linear equations:

$$(1) \qquad N_1 = 5 + 0.5X$$
$$(2) \qquad N_2 = 55 - 0.5X$$

(a)   Complete the following table using the N_1 column for equation 1 and the N_2 column for equation 2.

X	N_1	N_2	N_3
0			
10			
20			
30			
40			
50			
60			

(b) Plot the relationships between X and N_1 and N_2 in the graph provided below.

Figure 2-2

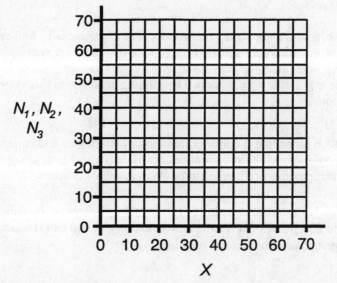

(i) The linear curve relating variables X and N_1 has a (positive/negative) _____ slope of _____.

(ii) The linear curve relating variables X and N_2 has a (positive/negative) _____ slope of _____.

(c) The equations are "simultaneously" solved at the value of X where $N_1 = N_2$ (which is where the two lines on the graph intersect). What are the values of X and N?

(d) Assume that the constant term in equation (1) increases from 5 to 25. Complete column N_3 in (a), and plot the new relationship on the graph in (b). The curve in equation (1) has shifted _____ (direction) by _____ (amount). The slope is _____.

(e) What is the new solution to this system of equations? [*Hint*: Replace N_1 with N_3 and repeat (c).]

E2. Using the Algebraic Method
This exercise takes you step-by-step through the algebraic method for solving a system of simultaneous equations. The algebraic method is extremely useful in both microeconomics and macroeconomics.

Consider two equations describing the relationships between two variables x and y

$$x_1 = a + by, \qquad (1)$$

$$x_2 = c - dy. \qquad (2)$$

where a, b, c, and d are positive constants. The objective is to find values of x and y for which both equations are satisfied. First, note that there are two equations and three unknowns—the unknowns are the solution values to x_1, x_2, and y. Thus, if a unique solution exists, there is a missing equation. The missing equation to this system simply states that in the solution:

$$x_1 = x_2 \qquad (3)$$

The solution procedure requires elimination of unknowns and equations by means of substitution. Each substitution reduces the system by both an unknown and an equation, until all that remains is a single unknown in a single equation.

(a) Step 1: Eliminate equation (1) and x_1 from the system by substituting equation (1) into equation (3). Write the new equation (3), and call it equation (3 ′). How many equations and unknowns remain?

(b) Step 2: Eliminate equation (2) and x_2 from the system by substituting equation (2) into equation (3 ′) you derived in (a). Write the new equation (3 ′), and call it equation (3 ″). How many equations and unknowns remain?

(c) Step 3: Solve equation (3 ″) you derived in (b), to create the equation for the solution value of y.

(d) Step 4: Substitute into equation (1) the expression for the solution value of y that you found in part (c). You now have the equation for the solution values of both x_1 and x_2 (since the two are the same value at the solution). [*Hint*: Check your answer by also substituting the expression for the solution value of y into equation (2). If you get the same value for x_1 and x_2 your answer is correct, but if you get different values you have the wrong answer.]

(e) Having done the exercise using the general algebraic equations, you will find it very easy to solve the system for any specific numerical values of the constants in equations (1) and (2). Let us suppose that a = 200, b = 2, c = 400, and d = 3. Repeat Steps 1 through 4 to solve for the numerical values of x and y.

Additional Multiple-Choice Questions

*1. **Which of the following is the best example of a positive statement?**
   (a) Equal distribution of national income is a desirable goal for society.
   (b) Foreign ownership is undesirable for Canada and should therefore be eliminated.
   (c) Although free trade may have caused some Canadians to lose their jobs, it has significantly increased the income of the average Canadian.
   (d) Taxes should be lowered.
   (e) Deficit reduction should be the government's priority.

*2. **With respect to agriculture, weather is an example of**
   (a) an exogenous factor of production.   (b) an endogenous input.
   (c) a dependent variable.   (d) an induced input variable.
   (e) a positive statement.

3. **If annual per capita consumption expenditure decreases as average annual income decreases, these two variables are then said to be**
   (a) negatively related.   (b) positively related.
   (c) randomly related.   (d) independent of each other.
   (e) None of the above.

*4. **Which of the following statements about economic theories is most appropriate?**
   (a) The most reliable test of a theory is the realism of its assumptions.
   (b) The best kind of theory is worded so that it can pass any test that is applied to it.
   (c) The most important aspect of the scientific approach is that it uses mathematics and diagrams.
   (d) We expect our theories to hold only with some margin of error.
   (e) Economic theories are based on normative statements and can therefore never be refuted.

*5. **A scientific prediction is a conditional statement because it**
   (a) takes the form "if that occurs, then this will result."
   (b) is conditional on being correct.
   (c) is impossible to test.
   (d) is true in theory but not in practice.
   (e) is derived from normative statements.

6. **The term *economic model* may refer to**
   (a) an application of a general theory in a specific context.
   (b) a specific quantitative formulation of a theory.
   (c) a particular theory or subset of theories in economics.
   (d) an illustrative abstraction of some real-world phenomenon.
   (e) All of the above.

*7. **Economic hypotheses are generally accepted only when**
   (a) the evidence indicates that they are true with a high degree of probability.
   (b) they have been proved beyond a reasonable doubt.
   (c) they have been established with certainty.
   (d) the evidence supports the hypotheses in all cases.
   (e) Both (c) and (d) are correct.

*8. Suppose that a scatter diagram indicates that imports are, on average, positively related to national income over time. If in one year imports fall when national income increases, the observation
   (a) disproves the positive relationship between the two variables.
   (b) suggests that other factors also influence the quantity of imports.
   (c) proves a negative relationship between the two variables.
   (d) suggests that a measurement error has necessarily been made.
   (e) suggests that the two variables are independent of each other.

*9. Which of the following equations is consistent with the hypothesis that federal income tax payments (T) are positively related to family income (Y) and negatively related to family size (F)?
   (a) $T = -733 + 0.19Y + 344F$.
   (b) $T = -733 - 0.19Y - 344F$.
   (c) $T = -733 + 0.19Y - 344F$.
   (d) $T = +733 - 0.19Y + 344F$.
   (e) None of the above.

Questions 10 to 12 refer to the following graph:

Figure 2-3

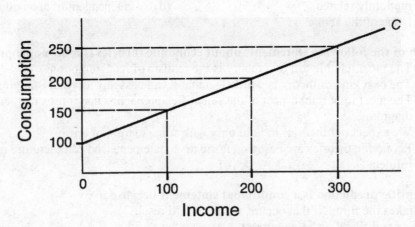

10. In the graph above, the slope of the line showing the relationship between consumption and income is
   (a) –2.
   (b) 0.5.
   (c) 2.
   (d) 2.5.
   (e) 150.

11. According to the graph above, when an individual has no income, consumption is
   (a) –200.
   (b) –100.
   (c) 0.
   (d) 100.
   (e) None of the above.

*12. The line showing the relationship between consumption (C) and income (Y) can be represented mathematically as
   (a) $C = 0.5Y$.
   (b) $C = 2Y$.
   (c) $C = 100 + 0.5Y$.
   (d) $C = 100 + 2Y$.
   (e) $C = -100 + Y$.

Questions 13 to 18 refer to the following graph, which depicts the relationship between performance on an economics examination and hours spent studying late the night before the early-morning exam!

Figure 2-4

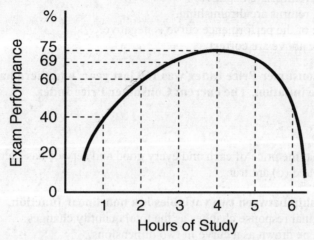

13. **Exam performance is a(n) _____ variable and hours of study is a(n) _____ variable.**
    (a) non-linear; non-linear
    (b) marginal; contour
    (c) exogenous; endogenous
    (d) endogenous; exogenous
    (e) slope; marginal

*14. **The slope of this curve between one and two hours of study is calculated by**
    (a) 60/2.
    (b) (60 – 30)/2.
    (c) (60 – 40)/2.
    (d) (60 – 40)/(2 – 1).
    (e) (60 + 40)/(2 + 1)

15. **The marginal return (that is, the change in exam performance) to the third hour of study is**
    (a) 69 percent.
    (b) 9 percent.
    (c) 23 percent.
    (d) 6 percent.
    (e) 3 percent.

*16. **As study time increases from one hour to four hours the marginal return to study time is _____ and the total return to study time is _____.**
    (a) diminishing; increasing
    (b) increasing; increasing
    (c) diminishing; diminishing
    (d) increasing; diminishing
    (e) diminishing; zero

*17. **At four hours of study, the marginal return to a minute of study more or less is (approximately)**
    (a) 75 percent.
    (b) increasing.
    (c) diminishing.
    (d) zero.
    (e) cannot be determined with the information provided.

*18. Due to a lack of sleep, exam performance suffers from a fifth and sixth hour of study. For this range of study hours, one can say that
  (a) total returns are diminishing.
  (b) marginal returns are negative.
  (c) marginal returns are diminishing.
  (d) the slope of the performance curve is negative.
  (e) All of the above are correct.

*19. Suppose the Consumer Price Index was 160 last year, and there has since been a 2 percent price inflation. The current Consumer Price Index
  (a) is 162.0.
  (b) is 163.2
  (c) is 160.02.
  (d) shows that the price of each and every good and service has increased by 2 percent.
  (e) Both (a) and (d) are true.

*20. If the relationship between two variables is a non-linear function,
  (a) the marginal response changes as the total quantity changes.
  (b) it cannot be drawn as a curve in two dimensions.
  (c) the slope of the curve at a specific point is the slope of the tangent to the curve at that point.
  (d) the slope at a specific point is the value on the vertical axis divided by the value on the horizontal axis.
  (e) Both (a) and (c) are true.

Solutions

Chapter Review

1.(e) 2.(a) 3.(b) 4.(b) 5.(e) 6.(b) 7.(d) 8.(e) 9.(b) 10.(c) 11.(b) 12.(e) 13.(b) 14.(d) 15.(c) 16.(b) 17.(d) 18.(d) 19.(e) 20.(d)

Short-Answer Questions

1. (a) P (b) N (c) P (d) N (e) P (f) N (g) P (h) N

2. (a) EN (b) EX (c) EN (d) EX (e) EN

3. (a) Positive correlation (i.e., both move in the same direction). Probably also causal, with causality running from income (exogenous) to TV sets (endogenous)—higher income causes an increase in the number of TVs purchased.
    (b) Negative correlation (i.e., the variables move in opposite directions). Also causal, with causality running from higher alternative incomes to lower attendance—the higher alternative incomes cause lower attendance (via the increase in the opportunity cost of attending university).
    (c) Positive correlation between birds flying south and electricity consumption, negative correlation between birds flying south and trees with leaves, and negative correlation between electricity consumption and trees with leaves. There is no *causal* relationship among any of the three variables; they are all caused by a fourth variable: the fall in temperature as winter approaches.
    (d) Positive correlation between children in daycare and the tax deductions, and a negative correlation between each of these and the price of potatoes. Causality runs from the size of the

tax deduction to the number of children in daycare, since the tax deduction reduces the cost of daycare. There is no causal relationship between either of these and the price of potatoes.

Exercises

1. **(a)** For any specific year the index is found by taking the cost in that year, dividing by the cost in the base year (2003–04, in this case), and multiplying the result by 100. For example, the tuition index in year 2007–08 is $(3788/2748) \times 100 = 137.8$ (which is rounded to 138 in the table below).

Year	Tuition Index	Residence Index	Food Index
2003–04	100	100	100
2004–05	110	112	106
2005–06	119	120	120
2006–07	129	128	136
2007–08	138	138	145
2008–09	147	144	152
2009–10	162	144	157
2010–11	178	151	160
2011–12	213	156	161
2012–13	235	156	166

(b) The cost of residence increased by 12 percent for the period 2003–04 to 2004–05, while that of tuition and food increased by 10 percent and 6 percent, respectively. During the decade from 2003–04 to 2012–13, the fees for tuition, residence, and food increased 135 percent, 56 percent, and 66 percent, respectively.

(c) Residence fees increased by 7.8 percent between 2006–07 and 2007–08. (The index increased by 10, from 128 to 138, which is 10 percent of the *base year* costs but only $(10/128) \times 100 = 7.8\%$ of the costs in 2006–07.)

(d) The unweighted index is obtained by taking the average of the three indexes. For example, the unweighted index for 2012–13 is $(235 + 156 + 166)/3 = 186$.

Year	Unweighted Index	Weighted Index	Year	Unweighted Index	Weighted Index
2003–04	100	100	2008–09	148	148
2004–05	109	109	2009–10	154	154
2005–06	120	120	2010–11	163	162
2006–07	131	131	2011–12	177	174
2007–08	140	140	2012–13	186	182

(e) The weighted index is a weighted average of the three separate indexes, with the weights being the proportions of total cost *in the base year*. In the base year 2003–04, the total fee was $2748 + $3420 + $3320 = $9488. Thus the weights are: 0.29 on tuition ($2748 is 29 percent of $9488), 0.36 on residence ($3420 is 36 percent of $9488), and 0.35 on food ($3320 is 35 percent of $9488). These weights are applied to the three indices in each year to create the single weighted average index for each year. For example, in 2012–13 the weighted index is $0.29(235) + 0.36(156) + 0.35(166) = 182$. See the table above for the index values in other years.

(f) The university president would cite one of the total expenses indices in (d) to justify higher fees. The weighted index of total expenses shows that the cost of a university education increased by only 82 percent over the decade, and even the unweighted index shows an increase of only 86 percent. [*Note:* The unweighted index treats each component as one-third of total costs, while the weighted index treats tuition as only 29 percent of total costs, with residence and food as 36 percent and 35 percent, respectively.] The president of the student council would cite the tuition price index in (a) to argue that fees have already increased enough (or too much). This index shows tuition fees increased by 135 percent over the decade—far more than the 82 percent and 86 percent increases in the indices of total expenses. [*Note:* The residence costs and food costs increased by much smaller percentages (56 percent and 66 percent, respectively) than tuition, thereby holding down the percentage increase in total expenses.]

2. **(a)** Since both price and average income affect quantity demanded, Q^D is endogenous, while P and Y are exogenous. [*Note:* If you are revising after having already done Chapter 4, recall that P is exogenous in the demand curve but endogenous in the overall market for computers.]

(b) Q^D and P are negatively related; as P increases, Q^D falls. Q^D and Y are positively related; as Y increases, Q^D increases.

(c) The *equation* becomes $Q^D = 8000 - 4P$.

(d) $Q^D = 8000 - 4(0) = 8000$; $Q^D = 8000 - 4(500) = 6000$; $Q^D = 8000 - 4(1000) = 4000$; $Q^D = 8000 - 4(2000) = 0$.

(e) As shown in Figure 2-5, the intercept on the P axis is 2000, and the intercept on the Q^D axis is 8000. (That is, at a price of $2000 no computers would be demanded, and if computers were free 8000 would be demanded.)

Figure 2-5

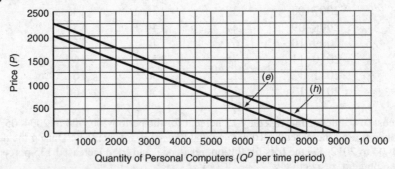

(f) The slope is calculated as $\Delta P/\Delta Q^D$; for example, $-2000/8000 = -1/4$. Since the relationship is linear, the slope is the same all along the line.

(g) The change in quantity demanded is -4000 when P increases from 1000 to 2000. When P increases from 500 to 2000, quantity demanded falls by 6000. In both cases the ratio $\Delta Q^D/\Delta P$ is equal to -4. It is the inverse of the slope.

(h) The intercept on the P axis is $2250, and the intercept on the Q^D axis is 9000. The slope remains $-1/4$ because the coefficient on P remains unchanged at 4. See Figure 2-5.

Extension Exercises

E1. **(a)**

X	N_1	N_2	N_3
0	5	55	25
10	10	50	30
20	15	45	35
30	20	40	40
40	25	35	45
50	30	30	50
60	35	25	55

(b) **Figure 2-6**

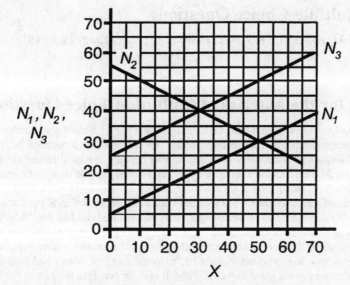

(i) positive; +1/2 (e.g., between $X = 10$ and $X = 20$, $\Delta N_1 / \Delta X = +5/+10 = +1/2$)

(ii) negative; −1/2 (e.g., between $X = 10$ and $X = 20$, $\Delta N_2 / \Delta X = -5/+10 = -1/2$)

(c) $N_1 = N_2$ where the two curves intersect. $N = 30$ and $X = 50$ solves this system of equations.

(d) The **curve** has shifted <u>leftward</u> by <u>40</u> (or equivalently, upward by 20); the slope is unchanged at +1/2.

(e) $N = 40$ and $X = 30$.

E2. **(a)** <u>Step 1</u>: Substitute equation (1) into equation (3) for x_1. This gives

$$a + by = x_2. \qquad (3')$$

There remain two equations, (2) and (3′), and two unknowns, x_2 and y.

(b) <u>Step 2</u>: Substitute equation (2) into (3′) for x_2. This yields

$$a + by = c - dy. \quad (3'')$$

There is only one equation remaining, (3″), and only one unknown, y.

(c) <u>Step 3</u>: Rearranging terms in (3″) yields: $by + dy = c - a$, or equivalently, $(b + d)y = c - a$.

Dividing both sides by $(b + d)$ yields $y^* = (c - a)/(b + d)$, which is the solution value for y.

(d) <u>Step 4</u>: Substitute y^* into equation (1), which yields $x_1^* = a + b(c - a)/(b + d)$

Multiply both sides by $(b + d)$ and cancel, which gives:

$$(b + d)x_1^* = a(b + d) + b(c - a) = ab + ad + bc - ab = ad + bc$$

Divide both sides by $(b + d)$ and cancel, giving the solution value for x_1^* (and for x_2^*, since $x_1^* = x_2^*$ from equation (3)).

$$x_1^* = (ad + bc)/(b + d).$$

(e) Inserting the numerical values gives $x_1 = 200 + 2y$ and $x_2 = 400 - 3y$

Setting $x_1 = x_2$ gives $200 + 2y = 400 - 3y$.

Rearranging gives $5y = 200$, so $y = 200/5 = 40$

Substituting $y = 40$ into $x_1 = 200 + 2y$ gives $x_1 = 200 + 2(40) = 280$

Check by substituting $y = 40$ into $x_2 = 400 - 3y$, which gives $x_2 = 400 - 3(40) = 280$

Additional Multiple-Choice Questions

1.(c) 2.(a) 3.(b) 4.(d) 5.(a) 6.(e) 7.(a) 8.(b) 9.(c) 10.(b) 11.(d) 12.(c) 13.(d) 14.(d) 15.(b) 16.(a) 17.(d) 18.(e) 19.(b) 20.(e)

Explanations for the Asterisked Multiple-Choice Questions

1.(c) All other answers are statements of value judgements (as with *desirable, undesirable, should be*), none of which contain any testable hypothesis. For example, if (d) were to be reworded to say "Equal distribution of national income is desirable because it would create greater work incentives for all," it would then include a testable hypothesis about income distribution/redistribution and incentives.

2.(a) The direction of causality runs from weather conditions to agricultural production, making agriculture the dependent variable endogenously determined (within the "theory") and weather being an exogenous factor of production (an input into agricultural production and determined outside the "theory"). There is no positive statement because no testable hypothesis has been made; for example, the hypothesis could be "extreme weather causes bad harvests" (yes) or "extreme weather causes good harvests" (no). It is even possible to reverse the direction of causality by making a highly specific positive statement— for example, changes in agricultural methods have contributed to global warming—but in the absence of such specificity the "best" answer is the one that obviously applies to the general case.

4.(d) Human behaviour, even as a group, can't be predicted with certainty. Every economic theory will predict with a margin of error, though the "best" theories will minimize that margin. The validity of a theory's assumptions is not as important as it may initially seem, since the objective is to provide reasonable explanations/predictions. For example, the ancient navigation system used by sailing ships to get from one part of the world to another was based on the (now apparent) highly unrealistic assumption that the earth was flat, and one could drop off the edge! Nevertheless, it worked (i.e., gave accurate predictions)!

5.(a) Guard against ignoring (or failing to express) an applicable condition, whether because you are unfamiliar with it or because you are so familiar with it that it becomes "too obvious to bother with." For example, in this chapter you have looked at relationships between two variables (e.g., consumption and income) under the *condition* that other influences on consumption do not change (e.g., the prices of consumption goods).

7.(a) "A high degree of probability" says the hypothesis is acceptable until and unless a better one is found. "Beyond a reasonable doubt" says it is highly unlikely that a better hypothesis will be found. The two interpretations are very different.

8.(b) This answer follows from (i) the recognition that the relationship is positive *on average*, and (ii) the explanation for Question 5 reminding us of the "other things constant" condition. If other influences on imports changed in that year (such as an unusual increase in the prices of some imports), the effect of higher incomes increasing the demand for imports could have been more than offset by the effect of higher import prices reducing the quantity of imports demanded. And while it is *possible* that a measurement error was made in that year, it is not *necessarily* the reason for the overall negative relationship between imports and national income in that year (so answer (d) is incorrect).

9.(c) The positive sign on the coefficient of Y shows a direct (i.e., positive) relationship between T and Y. The negative sign on the coefficient of F shows an inverse (i.e., negative) relationship between T and F. A positive or negative sign on the constant term (733) shows only whether the intercept on the T axis on a graph is positive or negative, and says nothing about how the variables are related.

12.(c) Using $C = 100 + 0.5Y$, if $Y = 0$ then $C = 100 + 05(0) = 100$, being the intercept on the C axis. The line also shows that for each \$100 *increase* in Y (ΔY), C increases by \$50 (ΔC). Thus there is a positive relationship between C and Y (i.e., both move in the same direction, indicated by the "plus" sign), and the increase in C is *one-half* of the increase in Y. Thus the slope of the line (rise/run = $\Delta C/\Delta Y$) = 50/100 = 0.5.

14.(d) This is nothing more than calculating the slope over the segment as "rise-over-run." Rise is the change in performance (60 – 40 = 20) and run is the change in hours of study (2 – 1 = 1), giving the slope of 20/1 = 20. You see that the *marginal* return to the second hour of study is 20 units of performance, which is the slope between the first and second hours of study.

16.(a) You will come across the relationship between marginal and total many times in your study of economics. As long as the marginal is positive, regardless of whether it is rising or falling, the total will be rising.

17.(d) The data do not give changes in performance *per minute* of extra study. A minute is so small an increment, however, that the question can be interpreted as asking "What is the slope **at** four hours of study?" Since the curve is upward-sloping below four hours and downward-sloping above four hours, then at four hours it is neither upward- nor downward-sloping (i.e., it is **flat** at four hours, meaning that at that point it has a slope of zero). Alternatively, you can calculate the *average* slope between three hours and five hours using rise-over-run. Rise is performance at three hours (69) minus performance at five hours (69) equals zero. Run is 5 –3 = 2, and like any number divided into zero, the result is zero.

18.(a) Between four and five hours of study, performance falls (answer (a)) from about 75 to 70—a *negative marginal return* (answer (b)) of <u>minus</u> 5 to the *extra* hour of study (indicated by the negative slope of the total performance curve). Adding the sixth hour of study reduces performance even more (from about 70 to 40), and by an even greater amount than for the fifth hour (the drop of 30 marks is a bigger drop than 5 marks). Thus as you study more (beyond the fourth hour), your *marginal* returns to each extra hour diminish (answer (c)). [*Practical application:* Don't stay up all night studying—you will need an active mind in your economics exams!]

19.(b) If the increase had been 2 percent *of the base year level,* the index would have risen from 160 to 162. In this question, however, prices rose by 2 percent *since last year,* when the index was 160. The index this year, therefore, is 102 percent of 160 = 163.2.

20.(e) For example, the extra (i.e., marginal) response can get less and less, but as long as it is positive the total response will be increasing. As the marginal gets less, the slope of the curve showing the total response gets flatter. Furthermore, the tangent to a curve at any specific point has the same slope as the curve at that point.

Demand, Supply, and Price

Chapter Overview

This chapter introduces you to the economic model of **demand** and **supply**, which describes how the interactions of buyers and sellers determine the **equilibrium** price and quantity exchanged in competitive markets for goods and services.

A downward-sloping **demand curve** shows the relationship between price and **quantity demanded**. From a buyer's perspective, the lower the (relative) price of a product, the more attractive it is to purchase. A **supply curve** shows the relationship between price and **quantity supplied**. From a seller's perspective, a higher (relative) price for a product makes it more attractive to sell. If quantity supplied does not equal quantity demanded (a disequilibrium situation), the model predicts that market pressures will cause changes in price, which change both quantity demanded and quantity supplied, until **quantity demanded equals quantity supplied** at the **equilibrium price**.

Using the method of **comparative statics**, the effects on equilibrium of a shift in either demand or supply can be determined. The equilibrium price and quantity exchanged respond to changes in the determinants of demand (consumers' income, tastes, population, prices of other products, and expectations about the future) and the determinants of supply (prices of inputs, technology, government taxes or subsidies, prices of other products, and the number of firms).

LO LEARNING OBJECTIVES

After studying this chapter, you will be able to

1. list the factors that determine the quantity demanded of a good.

2. distinguish between a shift of the demand curve and a movement along the demand curve.

3. list the factors that determine the quantity supplied of a good.

4. distinguish between a shift of the supply curve and a movement along the supply curve.

5. explain the forces that drive market price to equilibrium, and how equilibrium price is affected by changes in demand and supply.

Hints and Tips

The following may help you avoid some of the most common errors on examinations.

✓ Understand the difference between changes in quantity demanded (supplied) and changes in demand (supply). A change in quantity demanded (supplied) is a response to a change in the price of the good, while a change in demand (supply) is a response to a change in some other exogenous variable.

✓ Understand how and why demand and supply curves shift in response to changes in the exogenous variables. For example, with a fall in production costs, suppliers are willing to provide more at each price, so supply increases (i.e., the supply curve shifts to the right).

✓ Understand how and why a change in an exogenous variable may shift the demand in different directions depending on the type of good (normal or inferior) and the relationship between goods (substitutes or complements). For example, an increase in the price of automobile parking downtown increases the opportunity cost of driving to work. The higher opportunity cost of driving to work can increase the demand for public transportation (a substitute for driving to work) but reduce the demand for gasoline (a complement to downtown parking, because downtown parking and gasoline are linked through the use of automobiles).

✓ Recognize that the pressures of demand and supply will not give accurate predictions of equilibrium prices in some types of markets (as explained in *Applying Economic Concepts 3-1*). Nevertheless, even in these markets, the forces of demand and supply can have substantial effects over long periods of time and often indicate the direction of change in prices over shorter periods.

✓ Practise doing freehand sketches of demand and supply diagrams to show how equilibrium price and quantity change when an exogenous variable changes. When two (or more) exogenous variables change, sketch the diagrams for each change individually and compare the results. If both sketches show (say) an increase in price, you can conclude that equilibrium price will rise. But if one sketch shows an increase in price while the other shows a decrease, the net effect on equilibrium price is uncertain—it depends on the relative magnitudes of the two changes.

Chapter Review

Demand

Understanding the difference between the concepts of quantity demanded and demand is an important objective in this section. Remember that quantity demanded refers to the amount of a product consumers desire to purchase at a *specific price*, whereas demand refers to the *entire relationship* between price and quantity demanded. Consumers' response to a change in the product's own price is a *movement along* a demand curve, but a change in any of the other determinants of demand causes a *shift* in the entire demand curve. This section explains how and why the demand curve shifts, and the direction in which it shifts.

1. **The term *quantity demanded* refers to the**
    (a) amount of a good that consumers are willing to purchase at some price during some given time period.
    (b) amount of some good that consumers would purchase if they only had the income to afford it.
    (c) amount of a good that is actually purchased during a given time period.
    (d) minimum amount of a good that consumers require and demand for survival.
    (e) amount of a good that consumers are willing to purchase regardless of price.

2.   **An increase in quantity demanded refers to** *movement along curve*
    (a) rightward shifts in the demand curve only.
    (b) a movement up along a demand curve.
    (c) a greater willingness to purchase at each price.
    (d) an increase in actual purchases.
    (e) a movement down along a demand curve.

3. **The demand curve and the demand schedule**
    (a) each reflect the relationship between quantity demanded and price, *ceteris paribus*.
    (b) show the impact of changes in income or tastes.
    (c) are constructed on the assumption that price is held constant.
    (d) illustrate that in economic analysis, only two variables are taken into account at any one time.
    (e) characterize the relationship between price and actual purchases.

4.   **An increase in demand means that** *shift of curve*
    (a) consumers actually buy more of the good.
    (b) at each price, consumers desire a greater quantity.
    (c) consumers' tastes have necessarily changed.
    (d) price has decreased.
    (e) consumers buy more of the good specifically <u>because</u> its price has decreased.

5. **If goods *A* and *B* are complements, an increase in the price of good *A* will lead to**
    (a) an increase in the price of good *B*.
    (b) a decrease in the quantity demanded of good *B*.
    (c) a decrease in demand for good *B*.
    (d) no change in demand for good *B* because *A* and *B* are not substitutes.
    (e) a rightward shift in the demand for good *B*.

6. **Increased public awareness of the adverse health effects of smoking**
    (a) is a non-economic event that cannot be incorporated into the demand-and-supply model.
    (b) is characterized as a change in tastes that leads to a leftward shift in the demand curve for cigarettes.
    (c) will lead to an eventual increase in the price of cigarettes due to shifts in the demand curve for cigarettes.
    (d) induces a decrease in the supply of cigarettes.
    (e) decreases the quantity demanded of cigarettes.

7. **In economics, the term *inferior good* means that**
    (a)   the good is of low quality.
    (b)   an increase in income shifts its demand curve inward to the left.
    (c)   one of its complementary goods has a significantly higher price.
    (d)   demand does not change when the price of a substitute good changes
    (e)   the good is of low quality <u>and</u> has many substitutes of equally low quality.

Supply

As with demand, it is important to understand the difference between quantity supplied and supply. A movement along a supply curve is a response to a change in the good's own price and is referred to as a **change in quantity supplied**. A shift in the entire curve is a response to a change in one of the other determinants of supply and is referred to as a **change in supply**. An occurrence that makes production of a commodity more (less) profitable will cause firms to want to increase (decrease) supply—but you must also understand (1) the various occurrences that can <u>cause</u> such changes in profitability, and (2) how and why each occurrence <u>shifts</u> the supply curve of that commodity.

8. **A shift in the supply curve may be caused by any of the following *except***
    (a)   an improvement in technology.
    (b)   an increase in the wage paid to labour.
    (c)   an increase in average consumer income.
    (d)   an increase in the number of firms in the industry.
    (e)   Both (b) and (c) are correct—neither will shift the supply curve.

9. **A rightward shift in the supply curve indicates**
    (a)   a decrease in price.
    (b)   an increase in demand.
    (c)   an increase in quantity supplied.
    (d)   that at each price quantity supplied has increased.
    (e)   an increase in consumers' desire for a product.

10. **An increase in the price of an input will**
    (a)   decrease quantity supplied.
    (b)   decrease quantity supplied at each price.
    (c)   decrease supply.
    (d)   cause the supply curve to shift to the left.
    (e)   Answers (b), (c), and (d) are all correct.

11. **A movement along a supply curve could be caused by**
    (a)   an improvement in technology.
    (b)   a government subsidy to producers.
    (c)   a change in the price of the product.
    (d)   a change in the number of producers.
    (e)   a decrease in production costs.

12. **When two goods are complements *in production*,**
    (a) a fall in the price of one will increase demand for the other.
    (b) an increase in the price of one will increase the supply of the other.
    (c) an increase in the production of one must be offset by a decrease in production of the other.
    (d) they have identical supply curves.
    (e) they must also be complements in consumption.

The Determination of Price

This section puts the demand and supply curves together to show the **market** for a product. If, at a particular market price, quantity demanded is not equal to quantity supplied, pressures are exerted on price to change until the market clears—i.e., until quantity demanded is equal to quantity supplied. You should understand **how** these pressures of **excess demand** and **excess supply** bring the market to this **equilibrium**. (For the mathematically inclined, *Extensions in Theory 3-2* explains how to use simultaneous equations to derive the equilibrium price and quantity.) Further, you should be able to show how equilibrium price and quantity exchanged are affected by changes in demand and supply—i.e., by which curve shifts and in what direction. Finally, understand the important distinction between *absolute* and *relative* prices. [*Note: Lessons from History 3-1* explains how markets responded to recent weather events that changed demand and supply. *Applying Economic Concepts 3-1* explains how and why three simple conditions allow the demand-and-supply model to reasonably determine market price: the implications when these are *not* satisfied are examined in later chapters.]

13. **Excess demand exists whenever**
    (a) price exceeds the equilibrium price.
    (b) quantity supplied is greater than quantity demanded.
    (c) the equilibrium price is above the existing price.
    (d) there is downward pressure on price.
    (e) there is surplus production.

14. **If government increased everyone's income tax rates to finance more generous benefits for seniors, the demand-and-supply model would predict (*ceteris paribus*) a change in equilibrium price and quantity for some commodities because of**
    (a) a change in supply.
    (b) a change in quantity demanded by consumers.
    (c) a change in average income with no change in the distribution of income.
    (d) a change in demand caused by a change in average income changes.
    (e) a change in the distribution of income with no change in average income.

15. **An increase in both equilibrium price and quantity exchanged is consistent with**
    (a) an increase in supply.
    (b) a decrease in supply.
    (c) a decrease in quantity supplied.
    (d) an increase in demand.
    (e) a decrease in demand.

16. **Assuming a downward-sloping demand curve, an improvement in production technology is predicted to lead to**
    (a) a decrease in supply.
    (b) an increase in both equilibrium price and quantity exchanged.
    (c) a decrease in equilibrium price and an increase in equilibrium quantity exchanged.
    (d) a decrease in equilibrium price but no change in equilibrium quantity exchanged.
    (e) an increase in equilibrium price and a decrease in equilibrium quantity exchanged.

17. **Comparative statics**
    (a) is the analysis of market equilibria under different sets of conditions.
    (b) is the analysis of demand without reference to time.
    (c) refers to constant equilibrium prices and quantities.
    (d) describes the path by which equilibrium price changes.
    (e) refers to disequilibrium prices and quantities.

18. **When price exceeds its equilibrium value, the quantity actually bought and sold**
    (a) is the quantity demanded.
    (b) is the quantity supplied.
    (c) is unknown because the market is not in equilibrium.
    (d) is different for consumers than for producers.
    (e) is the quantity at equilibrium.

19. **A change in the money price of a product, other things constant, is**
    (a) a change in its absolute price but not a change in its relative price.
    (b) a change in its relative price but not a change in its absolute price.
    (c) a change in both its relative price and its absolute price.
    (d) a change in its opportunity cost.
    (e) Both (c) and (d) are correct.

Short-Answer Questions

1. What is meant by *equilibrium*? How is it related to the concept of excess demand or excess supply being a "market force"?

2. Explain the negative slope of a demand curve in terms of the concept of opportunity cost first encountered in Chapter 1.

3. Why is the price of a product an exogenous variable in the demand and supply curves separately, but endogenous to the market as a whole?

4. In the late 1990s, the prices of company shares on stock markets rose to levels which, for many firms, were much higher than warranted by the values of their assets and their profits. How can demand and supply analysis explain why this "bubble" in stock market prices was caused by expectations that share prices would continue to rise?

Exercises

1. **Market Equilibrium Using Demand and Supply Schedules**
The demand and supply schedules for athletic shoes sold at Trendy Shoes Inc. at the local mall are hypothesized to be as follows (in pairs of shoes per week):

(1) Price	(2) Quantity Demanded		(3) Quantity Supplied	(4) Excess Demand (+) Excess Supply (−)
	D	D'		
$120	40	_____	130	_____
110	50	_____	110	_____
100	60	_____	90	_____
90	70	_____	70	_____
80	80	_____	50	_____
70	90	_____	30	_____
60	100	_____	10	_____

(a) Using the grid provided in Figure 3-1, plot the demand and supply curves. Indicate the equilibrium levels of price and quantity.

Figure 3-1

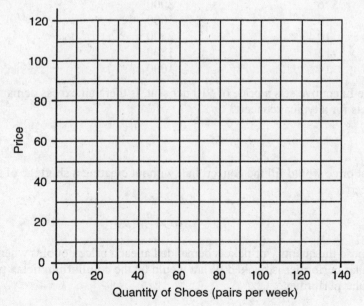

(b) Fill in column 4 in the table on the previous page for values of excess demand and excess supply. What is the value of excess demand (supply) at equilibrium? _____

(c) Suppose there is a change in teenage fashion such that a substitute shoe, Block Mardens, becomes trendy. As a result, the quantity demanded of athletic shoes at Trendy Shoes Inc. decreases by 30 units per week at each and every price. Put the new quantities demanded in column (2) on the previous page, and draw the new demand curve D' on the grid.

(d) At the initial equilibrium price you reported in answer (b), what market pressure on price is created by this change in tastes? How does price respond to this pressure? How do quantities demanded and supplied react?

(e) After price has adjusted to the new equilibrium, what is the equilibrium price and the equilibrium quantity?

2. **"Fair Pricing" and Black Markets**
The Executive of the Students' Association at the University of Equality has recently announced that "in the interests of fairness" all seats for on-campus concerts will sell at the same price regardless of the popularity of the performer. The campus concert hall has a seating capacity of 5000. Suppose the demand schedule for tickets for a *typical* concert or performer is as follows:

Price	Quantity Demanded
$ 6	8000
8	5000
10	2500
12	1500
14	1000

(a) If the Executive sets a price of $10 per seat, is there an excess demand or supply of tickets for a typical concert?

(b) What price would fill the concert hall without creating a shortage of seats at a typical concert?

(c) Suppose the quantity of tickets demanded at each price doubles when a particularly popular performer is booked. What would be the equilibrium ticket price for a popular performer?

(d) If the Executive set the price for all concerts at the equilibrium price for a typical concert, how will ticket scalping (a type of "black market" where some people buy tickets at the box-office price and resell them at higher prices) affect the achievement of the "fairness" objective?

3. **Practising with Demand and Supply**

Read the description of events (2nd column of the table below) in each market (1st column). Predict the impact on each market of these events by drawing the appropriate shifts of curves in the accompanying diagram. Use + and – to indicate whether there will be an increase or a decrease in demand (*D*), supply (*S*), equilibrium price (*P*), and equilibrium quantity (*Q*). If there is no change, use 0. If the change can't be predicted, use *U* for uncertain. [*Note*: See "Hints and Tips" for finding the answer when two events occur simultaneously.]

Figure 3-2

	Market	Event		*D*	*S*	*P*	*Q*
(a)	Canadian wine	Early frost destroys a large percentage of the grape crop in British Columbia	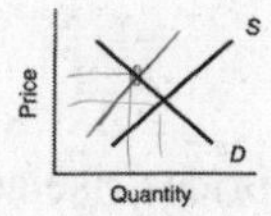	0	−	+	−
(b)	Wood-burning stoves	The price of heating oil and natural gas triples	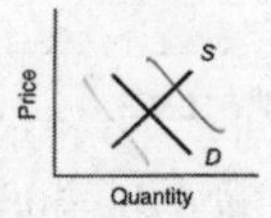	+	0	+	+
(c)	Cell phones	Technological advances reduce the costs of producing cell phones	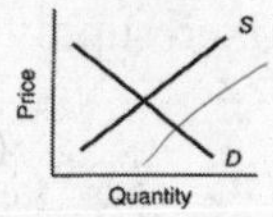	0	+	−	+
(d)	Gold	Large gold deposits are discovered in northern Ontario	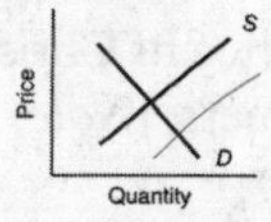	0	+	−	+
(e)	Fast foods	The public show greater concern over high sodium and cholesterol in fast foods; also, there is an increase in the minimum wage	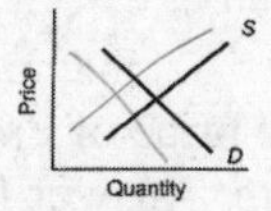	−	−	U	−
(f)	Bicycles	There is increasing concern by consumers about physical fitness; also, the price of gasoline falls	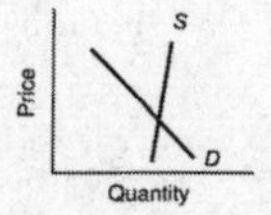	U	0	U	U

	Market	Event	D	S	P	Q
(g)	Beer	The population of drinking age increases; also, brewery unions negotiate a big increase in wages	 $+$	$-$	$+$	u
(h)	Housing	House prices are expected to rise significantly in the near future	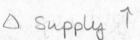 $+$	$-$	$+$	$+$

4. **Movements along Curves versus Shifts of Curves**

For each of the following, determine if the sentence is referring to a change in demand, a change in quantity demanded, a change in supply, or a change in quantity supplied. If applicable, indicate the resulting change in equilibrium price and quantity.

(a) In August 2005, Hurricane Katrina caused an increase in the world price of oil.

Δ supply ↓

(b) Prices of personal computers fall despite a substantial increase in the number sold.

Δ supply ↑ S

(c) Apartment rental prices rise as student enrollment swells.

Δ demand ↑

(d) Lower airfares reduce the number of empty seats on regularly scheduled flights. [*Hint*: There is a fixed supply of seats on regularly scheduled flights.] vertical supply curve.

Δ quantity demanded →

(e) Increases in the price of Christmas trees cause trees to be planted on land previously used by dairy farmers. [*Note*: Answer for both the market for Christmas trees and the market for milk.]

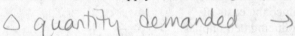
Xmas trees: Δ quantity supplied →
Dairy farmers: Δ supply ↓

(f) An increase in the price of Pacific salmon is linked to a reduction in fishing for Atlantic cod. [*Note*: Answer for both the market for Atlantic cod and the market for Pacific salmon.] [*Hint*: The two types of fish are substitutes in consumption.]

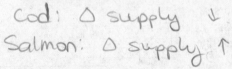
Cod: Δ supply ↓
Salmon: Δ supply ↑

(g) The 1998 ice storm in Quebec affected the market for portable gas-powered generators not only in Quebec but also in other regions of Canada.

Δ demand ↑

5. **Changes in Exogenous Variables**

This question demonstrates how changes in exogenous variables impact market equilibrium. It takes you through the process of making a scale diagram from simple functional relationships for demand and supply, and then finding equilibrium on the diagram. [*Note:* A similar question is given in Extension Exercise E2, using algebra instead of a scale diagram to find equilibrium.]

The quantity demanded of gadgets (Q^D) depends on the price of gadgets (P) and the price of a substitute good *(Py)* according to the following relationship.

$$Q^D = 10 - 1P + 0.5Py$$

The quantity of gadgets supplied (Q^S) is positively related to the price of gadgets and negatively related to the price of some input *(Pn)* according to

$$Q^S = 30 + 1P - 0.1Pn$$

(a) Assume initially that $Py = \$40$ and $Pn = \$200$. Substitute these values into the equations to obtain the equations for the demand and supply curves.

(b) Using the equations you obtained in (a), find Q^D and Q^S when $P = \$0$, and locate these quantities on the grid in Figure 3-3. Using the demand curve equation in (a), find the P at which $Q^D = 0$, and locate this price on the grid.

(c) For every \$5 increase in the price of gadgets, what is the change in Q^D and Q^S? What are the slopes of the demand and supply curves? Draw the demand and supply curves on the grid in Figure 3-3, and label them D_1 and S_1, respectively. [*Hint:* The demand and supply curves are straight lines.] What is the equilibrium price and quantity?

Figure 3-3

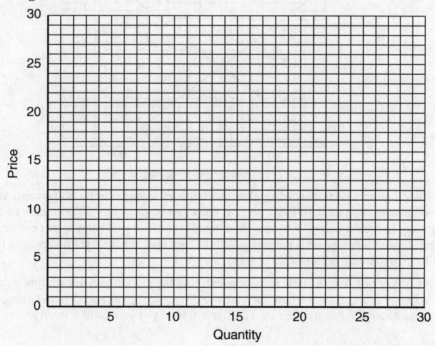

(d) Now Py falls from \$40 to \$20, and Pn rises from \$200 to \$300. What are the new equations for the demand and supply curves? Draw these new curves in Figure 3-3, and label them D_2 and S_2, respectively.

(e) By how much have equilibrium price and quantity changed as a result of the simultaneous shifts in the demand and supply curves? What do you see when you compare the change in equilibrium quantity with the horizontal shifts in the demand and supply curves? Why?

(f) What would happen to equilibrium price and quantity if Py fell by more than \$20? Why? What if Py fell by less than \$20?

6. **An Unexpected Government Budget Deficit?**
This question illustrates why it is important to take account of market reactions when calculating the cost to taxpayers of some types of government policy. [*Note:* This question is repeated as Extension Exercise E3, which uses algebra instead of a scale diagram.]

Figure 3-4 shows the supply curve and (private-sector) demand curve of a hypothetical market for farm machinery in Canada (with quantity in thousands of units).

Figure 3-4

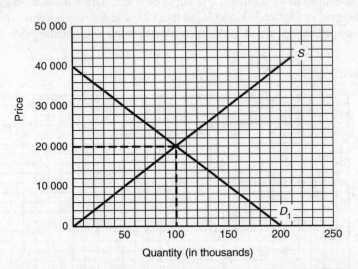

The federal government wants output in this industry to increase by 50 percent. With current industry output at 100 000 units, it therefore plans to buy 50 000 units of farm machinery (which it will give to less-developed countries) at whatever price is set by the market. Since market price is currently \$20 000 per unit, it estimates this program will cost \$1 billion (excluding administrative costs).

(a) Considering that the government is entering the market and demanding an extra 50 000 units, draw the new (private sector <u>plus</u> government) demand curve for farm machinery. What are the new equilibrium levels of price and quantity?

(b) How much does the government actually pay for the 50 000 units? What is the percentage increase in industry output? Why does this increase fall short of the government's target of 50 percent?

(c) How many units would the government have to purchase in order to meet its objective of increasing industry output to 150 000 units? How much would this cost the government?

(d) What wrong assumption did the government make about the supply of farm machinery when it predicted that buying 50 000 units would cost $1000 million and would increase production by 50 percent?

Extension Exercises

These Extension Exercises use the algebraic method of simultaneous equations to find market equilibrium and changes in equilibrium. (See *Extensions in Theory 3-2* in the text.)

E1. Equilibrium by Algebra
In this exercise you solve for equilibrium price and quantity using the algebraic method. As you go through the exercise, sketch your own demand and supply diagram—not to scale—and compare it with Figure 3-11 in the Solutions section when you have finished.
The demand and supply curves of widgets are given by

	General Form	This Exercise
Demand:	$Q^D = a - bP$	$Q^D = 300 - 1.0P$
Supply:	$Q^S = c + dP$	$Q^S = 0 + 0.5P$

(a) For each curve, find the value of the price axis intercept (i.e., where $Q = 0$) and quantity axis intercept (where $P = 0$). Show these points on your diagram.

(b) Impose the equilibrium condition, $Q^D = Q^S$, and solve algebraically for the equilibrium price and quantity. Show the equilibrium values on your diagram.

(c) Using the values for this exercise, divide the difference between the quantity axis intercepts of the demand and supply curves $(a - c)$ by the sum of the (absolute values) of the inverse of the slopes of the two curves $(b + d)$. Where have you seen the resulting number before? Divide the difference between the price axis intercepts of the demand and supply curves $(a/b - c/d)$ by the sum of the (absolute values) of the slopes of the two curves $(1/b + 1/d)$. Where have you seen this number before?

(d) Now suppose the supply curve is unchanged, but the demand curve changes to

$$Q^D = 300 - 1.5P$$

Find the price and quantity axis intercepts for this demand curve. Add this curve to your diagram (and label it D_2).

(e) At the initial equilibrium price you found in (b), is there now any excess demand or excess supply in the market? How much? Show this on your diagram.

(f) Apply the equilibrium condition, $Q^D = Q^S$, and solve for the new equilibrium price and quantity. Show the new equilibrium values on your diagram.

(g) Repeat part (c) using the supply curve and the new demand curve. Where have you seen these numbers before?

E2. Changes in Exogenous Variables: The Algebraic Approach
This question takes you through the algebraic method of solving for the effect of changes in exogenous variables on equilibrium price and quantity.

The quantity demanded of gadgets (Q^D) depends on the price of gadgets (P) and average household income (Y) according to the following relationship:

$$Q^D = 30 - 10P + 0.001Y$$

The quantity of gadgets supplied (Q^S) is positively related to the price of gadgets and negatively related to W, the price of some input (e.g., labour) according to

$$Q^S = 5 + 5P - 2W$$

(a) Assume initially that $Y = \$40\ 000$ and $W = \$5$. Substitute these values into the equations to obtain the equations for the demand and supply curves.

(b) Now use the equilibrium condition $Q^D = Q^S$ to solve the demand and supply equations simultaneously for the equilibrium price.

(c) Substitute the equilibrium price into either the demand or supply equation to obtain the equilibrium quantity. [*Hint*: Use both the demand and the supply equations. If they do not give the same Q, your P is wrong.]

(d) Draw a diagram on the grid in Figure 3-5 showing the demand and supply curves and the equilibrium values of price and quantity. Label these curves D_1 and S_1. For each curve, show the values of the price axis intercept (where $Q = 0$) and the quantity axis intercept (where $P = 0$). [*Note:* At very low prices the supply equation gives negative quantities. Negative quantities can't be produced, so draw the supply curve as a broken line in this range.]

Figure 3-5

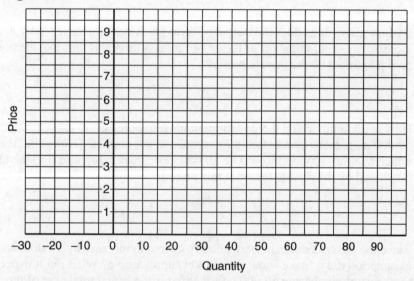

(e) Now suppose average household income increases to $55 000 but W remains unchanged. Derive the equation for the new demand curve and calculate the new levels of equilibrium price and quantity. Add the new curve to your diagram (label it D_2), and show the new equilibrium values.

(f) Next, assume that the input price W increases to $12.50. Using the demand curve you derived in (e), determine the new equilibrium price and quantity. Add the new curve to your diagram (label it S_2), and show the new equilibrium values.

E3. Government Intervention in the Market
This repeats Exercise 6 but uses the algebraic method to find equilibrium. Draw your own demand and supply diagram—not to scale—as you go along. When you have finished the question, compare your diagram with the diagram in the solution to Exercise 6.
The government wants the output of farm machinery to increase by 50 000 units. It therefore plans to purchase 50 000 units (which it will donate to less-developed countries) at whatever price is set by the market. The supply curve and the private-sector demand curve equations (with quantity expressed in thousands of units) are

$$Q^D = 200 - 0.005P$$
$$Q^S = 0 + 0.005P$$

(a) Impose the equilibrium condition, $Q^D = Q^S$, and solve for the equilibrium price and quantity.

(b) Now the government intervenes as an additional demander, wanting to purchase 50 000 units. What is the equation for the new (private sector <u>plus</u> government) demand curve for farm machinery? What are the new equilibrium levels of price and quantity?

(c) By how many units does the output of farm machinery increase? Why does the increase in output fall short of the government's target? [*Hint*: How many units are now purchased by the private sector?]

(d) How many units would the government have to purchase to cause production to be 50 000 units more than before it intervened in the market? [*Hint*: Find the price at which quantity supplied would be 50 000 more than in (a), and find the quantity purchased by the private sector at this price.]

(e) Since the government expected industry output to increase by 50 000, what wrong assumption did it make about the market supply curve? What did it expect to be the total cost of purchasing 50 000 units? What is the actual total cost of the 50 000 units it purchased in (b)? What would be the total cost in (d) if government bought the number of units necessary to increase industry output by 50 000?

Additional Multiple-Choice Questions

*1. **When the Multiple Listing Service (MLS) reports that in the month of April at an average selling price of $350 000, total sales of homes in Toronto were 2000 units, they are referring to**
   (a) quantity demanded.
   (b) quantity supplied.
   (c) equilibrium quantity.
   (d) actual purchases, which may or may not equal quantity demanded or quantity supplied.
   (e) actual purchases, which must be the equilibrium quantity.

2. **A decrease in the price of iPods will result in**
   (a) an increase in demand for iPods.
   (b) a decrease in supply of iPods.
   (c) an increase in the quantity demanded of iPods.
   (d) a movement up along the demand curve for iPods.
   (e) a rightward shift in the demand curve for iPods.

*3. **A decrease in the price of DVD players will cause**
    (a)   a leftward shift in the demand curve for videocassette tape players.
    (b)   an increase in demand for videocassette tapes.
    (c)   a rightward shift in the demand curve for DVDs.
    (d)   an increase in demand for DVD players.
    (e)   Both (a) and (c) are correct.

*4. **Which of the following would *not* cause a change in demand?**
    (a)   A decrease in average income.
    (b)   An increase in the price of a substitute good.
    (c)   A decrease in the cost of producing the good.
    (d)   An increase in population.
    (e)   A government program that redistributes income.

5. **Which of the following would *not* cause an increase in the supply of broccoli?**
    (a)   A decrease in the price of broccoli.
    (b)   A decrease in the price of labour employed in harvesting broccoli.
    (c)   An improvement in pesticides, thereby decreasing the variability in broccoli output.
    (d)   An increase in the number of producers.
    (e)   An improvement in harvesting technology.

Questions 6 and 7 refer to the following diagram.

Figure 3-6

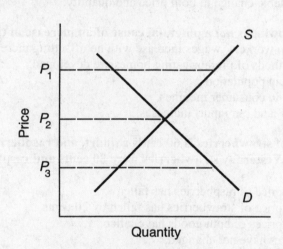

6. **At a price of P_1,**
    (a)   there is upward pressure on price.
    (b)   demand will rise to restore equilibrium.
    (c)   quantity supplied is greater than quantity demanded.
    (d)   the market has reached an equilibrium price.
    (e)   a shortage exists.

7. **When price equals P_3,**
    (a)   quantity exchanged equals quantity demanded.
    (b)   there is excess supply.
    (c)   there is a tendency for price to rise.
    (d)   the market is in equilibrium.
    (e)   a surplus exists.

8. **As consumer preferences change in favour of organically grown vegetables, other things constant, economic theory predicts which of the following will occur in the market for these vegetables?**
   (a) A decrease in price and an increase in the quantity exchanged.
   (b) An increase in both equilibrium price and quantity.
   (c) A shift in the supply curve to the right.
   (d) An increase in equilibrium price and a decrease in equilibrium quantity.
   (e) A leftward shift of the demand curve.

*9. **Simultaneous increases in both demand and supply are predicted to result in**
   (a) increases in both equilibrium price and quantity.
   (b) a higher equilibrium price but a smaller equilibrium quantity.
   (c) a lower equilibrium price but a larger equilibrium quantity.
   (d) a larger equilibrium quantity but no predictable change in price.
   (e) a higher price, but no predicable change in equilibrium quantity.

*10. **A decrease in input prices as well as a simultaneous decrease in the price of a good that is substitutable in consumption will lead to**
   (a) a lower equilibrium price and a larger equilibrium quantity.
   (b) a lower equilibrium price but no change in equilibrium quantity.
   (c) a lower equilibrium price and an uncertain change in quantity.
   (d) a lower equilibrium price and a smaller equilibrium quantity.
   (e) an unpredictable change in both price and quantity.

*11. **Which of the following is *not* a potential cause of an increase in the price of housing?**
   (a) Construction workers' wages increase with no offsetting increase in productivity.
   (b) Cheaper methods of prefabricating homes are developed.
   (c) An increase in population.
   (d) An increase in consumer incomes.
   (e) The price of land (an input) increases.

*12. **Today the price of strawberries is 60 cents a quart, and raspberries are priced at 75 cents a quart. Yesterday strawberries were 80 cents and raspberries $1. Thus, for these two goods,**
   (a) the relative price of raspberries has fallen.
   (b) the relative price of strawberries has fallen by 20 cents.
   (c) the relative prices of both goods have fallen.
   (d) relative prices have not changed.
   (e) the relative price of strawberries has risen.

*13. **For an inferior good, an increase in average incomes and a simultaneous increase in production costs will**
   (a) increase equilibrium price and quantity.
   (b) decrease equilibrium price and increase equilibrium quantity.
   (c) increase equilibrium price but may increase or decrease equilibrium quantity.
   (d) decrease equilibrium price but may increase or decrease equilibrium quantity.
   (e) decrease equilibrium quantity but may increase or decrease equilibrium price.

Questions 14 to 20 refer to the following diagram of the market for hamburgers in Collegeville.

Figure 3-7

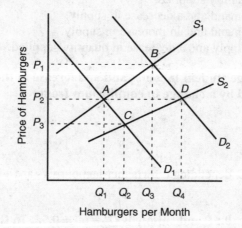

*14. A change in Collegeville's market equilibrium from *A* to *B* may be caused by
  (a) a decrease in wages of part-time workers.
  (b) a decrease in the price of hot dogs.
  (c) an increase in the student population of Collegeville.
  (d) an increase in the price of hamburgers.
  (e) Both (c) and (d) are correct.

15. An increase in the price of hot dogs may be depicted in the hamburger market by a change in equilibrium from
  (a) *A* to *D*.   (b) *A* to *C*.
  (c) *C* to *D*.   (d) *A* to *B*.
  (e) Both (c) and (d) are correct.

*16. A change in equilibrium from *A* to *D* may be explained by
  (a) an increase in Collegeville's student population.
  (b) a decrease in the price of beef patties.
  (c) an increase in the price of hot dogs coupled with an increase in the wages of restaurant employees.
  (d) a technological improvement in the production of hamburgers coupled with consumer concern about mad cow disease.
  (e) a decrease in the price of fries (a complement to hamburgers) coupled with a reduction in the wages of restaurant employees.

*17. Which event would best explain a decrease in equilibrium quantity from Q_4 to Q_3?
  (a) An increase in the price of beef patties.
  (b) A decrease in Collegeville's student population.
  (c) A decrease in the price of fries (a complement to hamburgers).
  (d) An increase in the supply of hamburgers due to entry of new firms.
  (e) Consumer concern about the effects of a cattle disease.

*18. If equilibrium changes from *A* to *B*, one could say
  (a) there has been an increase in demand.
  (b) quantity supplied has increased.
  (c) price has increased.
  (d) supply has not changed.
  (e) All of the above are correct.

*19. **A decrease in equilibrium price from P_1 to P_3 may be explained by**
  (a) a decrease in supply.
  (b) a decrease in quantity supplied.
  (c) a decrease in demand and a decrease in supply.
  (d) a decrease in demand and an increase in supply.
  (e) an increase in supply and a decrease in quantity supplied.

*20. **An increase in average student incomes and an increase in the number of hamburger firms can be depicted by a change in equilibrium from**
  (a) D to B.
  (b) C to D.
  (c) D to A.
  (d) C to B.
  (e) A to D or B to C, depending on whether hamburgers are a normal or an inferior good, respectively.

*21. **Demand is $Q^D = 200 - 0.5P$ and supply is $Q^S = 60 + 0.5P$. In this market, equilibrium quantity is _____ units and equilibrium price is _____.**
  (a) 160, \$80   (b) 105, \$90
  (c) 140, \$130   (d) 130, \$140
  (e) 200, \$140

*22. **In the demand function for Good X, $Q^D{}_X = 400 - 0.25P_X + 0.01P_Z - 0.001Y$, where P_Z is the price of another good and Y is average income,**
  (a) Goods X and Z are normal goods.
  (b) Good X is an inferior good, and Goods X and Z are complementary goods.
  (c) Good X is a normal good, and Goods X and Z are substitute goods.
  (d) Good X is an inferior good, and Goods X and Z are substitute goods.
  (e) Good X is a normal good, and Goods X and Z are complementary goods.

Solutions

Chapter Review

1.(a) 2.(e) 3.(a) 4.(b) 5.(c) 6.(b) 7.(b) 8.(c) 9.(d) 10.(e) 11.(c) 12.(b) 13.(c) 14.(e) 15.(d) 16.(c) 17.(a) 18.(a) 19.(e)

Short-Answer Questions

1. Equilibrium is a condition of stability, with no existing pressures for change. New pressures arise from changes in the exogenous variables that shift the demand and supply curves. Such shifts create excess demand or excess supply at the old equilibrium price, which are market forces that put pressure on price and quantity until a new position of stability (i.e., equilibrium) is reached.

2. Because of the "other things constant" (i.e., *ceteris paribus*) condition, prices of other goods are constant all along a demand curve. Consequently, as the dollar price (i.e., the <u>absolute</u> price) of a good falls, its price <u>relative</u> to the price of other goods is also falling. The fall in relative price is a fall in the good's opportunity cost, to which demanders react by increasing quantity demanded (i.e., a movement along the demand curve).

3. When demanders (suppliers) move along a demand (supply) curve, they are *reacting* to a change in the product's own price, other things constant. Along the demand (supply) curve in a competitive market, therefore, quantity is endogenous and price is exogenous—neither demanders nor suppliers *by themselves* determine the price. In the market as a whole, however, both the equilibrium price and the equilibrium quantity are determined by the *interaction* of demand and supply—i.e., both price and quantity are endogenous.

4. The stock market "bubble" was an example of inflation as a *self-fulfilling prophecy*—the prices of stocks and shares rose because people expected them to rise. Expectations of higher prices shifted the demand curve for stocks and shares to the right as demanders anticipated making big capital gains (i.e., "Buy now and sell for a higher price later"). For the very same reason, the supply curve of shares offered for sale shifted to the left (i.e., "Why sell at today's prices when more money can be made by selling later at higher prices?"). Both the increase in demand and the decrease in supply created excess demand at existing prices, causing prices to rise and creating the "bubble" in the stock market. [*Note*: Eventually the bubble "burst" when expectations of rising prices changed to expectations of falling prices. Demand fell and supply increased, prices of stocks and shares plunged, and many people lost a great deal of wealth!]

Exercises

1. (a) **Figure 3-8**

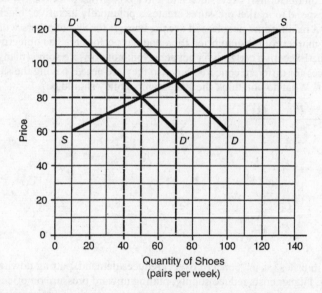

Equilibrium price is $90 and equilibrium quantity is 70 pairs per week.

(b) At each price, subtract quantity supplied from quantity demanded to get:

Price	Excess Demand (+) or Excess Supply (−)
$120	−90
110	−60
100	−30
90	0
80	+30
70	+60
60	+90

Equilibrium occurs where quantity demanded equals quantity supplied, at $P = \$90$. There is no excess demand or excess supply in equilibrium.

(c) The change in tastes (as in "fashion") shifts the demand curve for athletic shoes to the left by 30 pairs at each price. At each price, the value in the D' column of the question's table is the value in the D column, minus 30. See Figure 3-8 in (a).

(d) After tastes change, quantity demanded at $90 is (70 – 30) 40 units per week. Quantity supplied remains at 70 units. There is excess supply of (70 – 40) 30 units per week, which puts downward pressure on price. Demanders react to the falling price by increasing the quantity of athletic shoes demanded each week (i.e., moving down D' in Figure 3-8). Trendy reacts by reducing quantity supplied (i.e., moving down S in Figure 3-8).

(e) Subtracting 30 (the fall in demand) from the excess demand/excess supply column gives zero excess demand or supply at $P = \$80$, which is the new equilibrium price. At $P = \$80$, the quantity in the D' column is 50 and the quantity in the S column is 50, so the new equilibrium quantity at $P = \$80$ is 50.

2. (a) Excess supply of 2500 seats. (5000 seats supplied minus 2500 demanded.)

(b) At $P = \$8$, quantity demanded equals the 5000 seats supplied.

(c) The equilibrium price for a popular performer is $10, where quantity demanded equals quantity supplied equals 5000.

(d) At the $8 equilibrium price for a typical concert, 10 000 seats are demanded for a popular performer; there is excess demand of 5000 seats. Many people are willing to pay more than $8 to see a popular performer. For example, 2000 people are willing to pay $14 to see one. If 1000 of them failed to get an $8 ticket, scalpers buying at $8 and selling at $14 would gain $6(1000) = $6000. The combination of excess demand and a box-office price (below equilibrium) that is not allowed to respond to market pressures creates a potentially lucrative "black market" for ticket scalping. As a result, some people will see the concert for $8 but others will have paid even more than the $10 market equilibrium price for a popular performer. The objective of "fairness" as defined by the Executive certainly is not achieved: not only are some (many?) students paying different prices for different concerts, but also they are not all paying the same price to see the same concert! What do you think the Executive's policy should be?

3.

	D	S	P	Q
(a)	0	–	+	–
(b)	+	0	+	+
(c)	0	+	–	+
(d)	0	+	–	+
(e)	–	–	U	–
(f)	U	0	U	U
(g)	+	–	+	U
(h)	+	–	+	U

Selected explanations

(e) The change in tastes (as in "concern over") reduces demand, putting downward pressure on price and quantity. Higher costs reduce supply, putting upward pressure on price and downward pressure on quantity. Both reduce quantity, but have opposing effects on price. The net effect on price, therefore, is uncertain. (The net effect depends on the relative size of the shifts in the demand and supply curves—see Exercise 5 for more on this.)

(f) The change in tastes (as in "concern about") increases demand, but the fall in price of gasoline reduces demand (because the cost of using automobiles falls). The net effect on the demand curve, and therefore on equilibrium P and Q, can't be predicted without empirical evidence on the relative size of the two effects.

(h) Expectations of higher future prices increase demand (upward pressure on P and Q) and reduce supply (upward pressure on P and downward pressure on Q). Price rises (same prediction for each event), but equilibrium quantity may rise or fall (opposing predictions for the two events).

4. (a) World supply of oil fell (a leftward shift of the supply curve). Hurricane Katrina badly damaged some large oil rigs in the Gulf of Mexico, as well as the pipelines that carried oil from Gulf ports to refineries. Because most other oil producers were operating close to capacity, they did not have the flexibility to quickly increase their output to offset the reduction in supply caused by Katrina. (See *Lessons from History 3-1* for more detail.)

(b) Change (increase) in supply. The combination of a lower price and an increase in quantity sold is consistent with a rightward shift of the supply curve.

(c) Change (increase) in demand. The demand curve for apartments shifts to the right, resulting in higher rents and an increase in the quantity of apartments supplied.

(d) Lower airfares increase quantity demanded—a movement along (down) the demand curve for air travel. The supply of seats on regularly scheduled flights is unchanged (a vertical supply curve). Neither curve shifts, so the equilibrium values do not change but the market moves closer to the equilibrium.

(e) Change (increase) in quantity supplied in the market for Christmas trees. Higher prices cause a movement along (up) the supply curve, moving closer to equilibrium. Change (decrease) in supply in the market for milk. The supply curve of milk shifts left, increasing equilibrium price and reducing equilibrium quantity. [*Note:* The wording of the question implies that Christmas trees and milk are substitutes *in production*—if more land is used for Christmas trees, less is available for the cattle that produce milk.]

(f) Change (reduction) in supply of Atlantic cod. The supply curve of Atlantic cod shifts left, raising equilibrium price and reducing equilibrium quantity. Because Atlantic cod and Pacific salmon are substitutes *in consumption*, the higher price of cod changes (increases) the demand for salmon. The demand curve for salmon shifts right, increasing both equilibrium price and equilibrium quantity.

(g) In Quebec, the increase in demand pushed up the price and quantity sold. Because the generators are portable, generators in other parts of the country were brought to Quebec, attracted by the higher price. Thus supply also increased in Quebec, moderating the increase in price and further increasing the quantity sold (i.e., a new equilibrium caused by rightward shifts in both the demand and supply curves). The price in Quebec still increased somewhat, however, because the rightward shift of the demand curve exceeded the rightward shift of the supply curve. In other regions of the country, demand was unchanged but supply decreased as generators were diverted to Quebec, so in these regions price increased while quantity sold fell (i.e., a movement along the demand curve in these regions as the supply curve shifted leftward). (See *Lessons from History 3-1* for more detail.)

5. **(a)** The demand and supply curves show quantity as a function of the good's own price, other things constant (i.e., *ceteris paribus*). With Py constant at \$40, the demand equation reduces to $Q^D = 30 - 1P$ (i.e., $10 - 1P + 0.5(40) = 30 - 1P$). With Pn constant at \$200, the supply equation reduces to $Q^S = 10 + 1P$ (i.e., $30 + 1P - 0.1(200) = 10 + 1P$.) Thus the equations for the demand and supply <u>curves</u> are $Q^D = 30 - 1P$ and $Q^S = 10 + 1P$.

(b) At $P = 0$, $Q^D = 30$ and $Q^S = 10$ (the quantity axis intercepts of D_1 and S_1 in Figure 3-9). At $Q^D = 0$, $P = \$30$ (the price axis intercept of D_1).

Figure 3-9

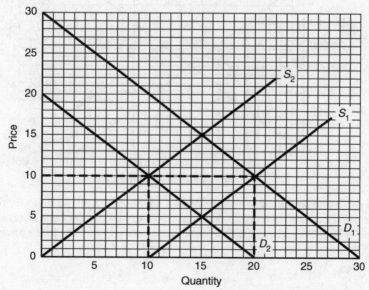

(c) For both demand and supply, every $5 change in P changes Q by 5. Both have a slope of 1 (i.e., rise/run = $\Delta P/\Delta Q = 5/5 = 1$). [*Note*: Δ means "change in."] You now have the information needed to draw S_1 and D_1. The market is in equilibrium where S_1 and D_1 intersect, at $P = \$10$ and $Q = 20$.

(d) With Py constant at $20, $Q^D = 10 - 1P + 0.5(20) = 20 - 1P$. With Pn constant at $300, $Q^S = 30 + 1P - 0.1(300) = 0 + 1P$. The equations for the new demand and supply curves are $Q^D = 20 - 1P$ and $Q^S = 0 + 1P$. Repeating parts (b) and (c) using these new equations gives you the information needed to draw S_2 and D_2.

(e) S_2 and D_2 intersect (i.e., the new equilibrium) at $P = \$10$ and $Q = 10$. Thus P is unchanged and Q has fallen by 10 units (from 20 to 10). Because both curves shift horizontally by the *same amount* in the *same direction*, no excess demand or supply is created at the old equilibrium P of $10. Consequently, the equilibrium price is unchanged and the equilibrium quantity changes by the amount of the (equal) leftward shift in the two curves.

(f) If Py fell by more than $20, demand would shift left by more than 10 units. The leftward shift of D would be greater than the leftward shift of S, creating excess supply at $P = \$10$. Equilibrium price would fall and equilibrium quantity would fall by more than in (e). If Py fell by less than $20, demand would shift left by less than 10 units. The leftward shift of D would be less than the leftward shift of S, creating excess demand at $P = \$10$. Equilibrium price would rise and equilibrium quantity would fall by less than in (e). [*Note:* What you see from this exercise is that when the demand and supply curves shift in the <u>same</u> direction, the effect on equilibrium quantity is predictable but the effect on equilibrium price depends on the relative magnitudes of the shifts. If you experiment by increasing Py and decreasing Pn you will find that, when the two curves shift in <u>opposite</u> directions, the outcome is reversed—the effect on equilibrium price is now predictable, but the effect on equilibrium quantity now depends on the relative magnitudes of the shifts in the demand and supply curves.]

6. (a) D_1 shifts to the right by the additional 50 000 units demanded by government. The new demand curve D_2 intersects the S curve (i.e., equilibrium) at $P = \$25\ 000$ and $Q = 125\ 000$ units. [*Note:* The government will buy 50 000 units at whatever price is set *by the market*, but the maximum price the private sector will pay is $40 000. Consequently, the market price will not exceed $40 000, so D_2 does not extend beyond $P = \$40\ 000$.]

Figure 3-10

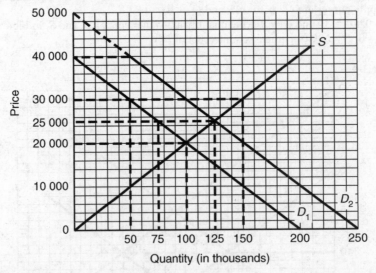

(b) Purchasing 50 000 units at $25 000 each costs a total of $1.25 billion. Industry output increases by 25 percent (from 100 000 to 125 000 units). Industry output does not increase by the full 50 000 units bought by government because the private sector reacts to the price increase by reducing its quantity demanded (i.e., moving along D_1) by 25 000 units.

(c) Price would have to rise to $30 000 to get $Q^S = 150\ 000$. At $30 000 the private sector would buy only 50 000 units, so the government would have to buy 100 000 units at a price of $30 000 per unit for a total cost of $3 billion—three times the initial estimate!

(d) Government erroneously assumed the supply curve of farm machinery to be horizontal at $P = \$20\ 000$. Only with a horizontal supply curve would there be no increase in price when demand increased, so there would be no fall in quantity demanded by the private sector.

Extension Exercises

E1. (a) At $P = 0$, $Q^D = 300 - 1.0(0) = 300$ and $Q^S = 0.5(0) = 0$. So $Q^D = 300$ and $Q^S = 0$ are the quantity axis intercepts for D_1 and S, respectively, in your diagram (Figure 3-11). At $Q = 0$ the demand equation solves for $P = \$300$ and the supply equation solves for $P = \$0$. These are the price axis intercepts for D_1 and S in your diagram.

Figure 3-11

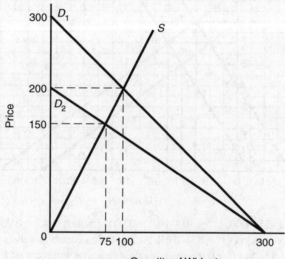

(b) Setting $Q^D = Q^S$ gives $300 - 1.0P = 0.5P$, so $1.5P = 300$ and $P = \$200$.
Putting $P = \$200$ in the demand equation gives the equilibrium quantity $Q^D = 300 - 1.0(200) = 100$. [*Note:* Putting $P = \$200$ into the supply equation also gives $Q^S = 0.5(200) = 100$. Since both Q^D and $Q^S = 100$ at $P = \$200$, you know you have the correct values for equilibrium because there is neither excess demand nor excess supply.]

(c) The equation $(a - c)/(b + d)$ gives $(300 - 0)/(1 + 0.5) = 300/1.5 = \$200$. You have seen this before in part (b); it is the equilibrium price. The equation $(a/b - c/d)/(1/b + 1/d)$ gives $(300/1 - 0/0.5)/(1/1 + 1/0.5) = 300/3 = 100$. You have seen this before in part (b); it is the equilibrium quantity. [*Note:* $P = (a - c)/(b + d)$ is the P^* equation in *Extensions in Theory 3-2* in the text, and $Q = (a/b - c/d)/(1/b + 1/d)$ is an alternative expression for the Q^* equation in *Extensions in Theory 3-2*.]

(d) For D_2 in the diagram, the quantity axis intercept (i.e., Q^D at $P = \$0$) remains at $Q^D = 300 - 1.5(0) = 300$. The price axis intercept (i.e., P at $Q^D = 0$) falls to $0 = 300 - 1.5P$, so $P = 300/1.5 = \$200$.

(e) At $P = \$200$, $Q^S = 0.5P = 0.5(200) = 100$, but $Q^D = 300 - 1.5P = 300 - 1.5(200) = 0$.
There is excess supply $(Q^S - Q^D)$ of $(100 - 0 =)$ 100 widgets.

(f) Setting $Q^D = Q^S$ gives $300 - 1.5P = 0.5P$, so $2P = 300$ and $P = 300/2 = \$150$. Putting $P = \$150$ in the demand equation gives the equilibrium quantity $Q^D = 300 - 1.5(150) = 300 - 225 = 75$ widgets. [*Note:* Similarly, putting $P = \$150$ in the supply equation gives $Q^S = 0.5(150) = 75$.]

(g) The equation $P^* = (a - c)/(b + d)$ gives $(300 - 0)/(1.5 + 0.5) = 300/2 = \$150$. The equation $Q^* = (a/b - c/d)/(1/b + 1/d)$ gives $(300/1.5 - 0/0.5)/(1/1.5 + 1/0.5) = 200/2.67 = 75$ widgets. You have seen these before in part (f); they are the new equilibrium price (P^*) and equilibrium quantity (Q^*).

E2. **(a)** The demand and supply curves show quantity as a function of the good's own price, other things constant (i.e., *ceteris paribus*). With Y constant at \$40 000, $Q^D = 30 - 10P + 0.001(40\ 000) = 70 - 10P$. With W constant at \$5, $Q^S = 5 + 5P - 2(5) = -5 + 5P$. Thus the equations for the demand and supply <u>curves</u> are $Q^D = 70 - 10P$ and $Q^S = -5 + 5P$.

(b) Setting $Q^D = Q^S$ gives $70 - 10P = -5 + 5P$, $15P = \$75$, $P = 75/15 = \$5$.

(c) Using the demand curve equation, equilibrium $Q^D = 70 - 10(5) = 20$ gadgets.
Using the supply curve equation, equilibrium $Q^S = -5 + 5(5) = 20$ gadgets.

(d) At $P = 0$, $Q^D = 70 - 10(0) = 70$ and $Q^S = -5 + 5(0) = -5$. These are the quantity axis intercepts for D_1 and S_1 in Figure 3-12. At $Q = 0$ the demand equation solves for $P = \$7$ and the supply equation solves for $P = \$1$. These are the price axis intercepts for D_1 and S_1 in Figure 3-12.

Figure 3-12

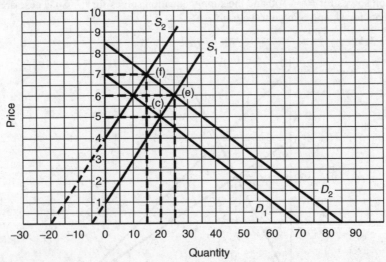

(e) With Y constant at \$55 000, $Q^D = 30 - 10P + 0.001(55\ 000) = 85 - 10P$. So the equation for the new demand curve (D_2) is $Q^D = 85 - 10P$. At $P = 0$ this equation solves for the quantity axis intercept of $Q^D = 85$. At $Q^D = 0$ it solves for the price axis intercept of $P = \$8.50$.
Setting $Q^D = Q^S$ for equilibrium gives $85 - 10P = -5 + 5P$, $15P = 90$, $P = \$6$. Setting $P = \$6$ in either the demand or supply equation solves for the new equilibrium quantity of 25.

(f) With W constant at \$12.50, $Q^S = 5 + 5P - 2(12.50) = -20 + 5P$. So $Q^S = -20 + 5P$ is the equation for the new supply curve (S_2). The price and quantity axis intercepts are \$4 and –20, respectively.
Setting $Q^D = Q^S$ for equilibrium gives $85 - 10P = -20 + 5P$, $15P = 105$, $P = 105/15 = \$7$.
Substituting $P = \$7$ into the demand curve equation gives equilibrium $Q^D = 85 - 10(7) = 15$.
[*Note:* Doing the same with the supply curve equation also gives equilibrium $Q^S = -20 + 5(7) = -20 + 35 = 15$.]

E3. Your illustrative diagram should show the curves and values in Figure 3-10 above. The note in the answer to Exercise 6(a) explains why D_2 does not extend above $P = \$40\ 000$.

(a) Setting $Q^D = Q^S$ for equilibrium gives $200 - 0.005P = 0 + 0.005P$, which solves for $P = 200/0.01 = \$20\ 000$. Substituting $P = \$20\ 000$ in the supply curve equation gives equilibrium $Q^S = 0 + 0.005(20,000) = 100$ (i.e., 100 000 units). [*Note:* Doing the same using the demand curve equation, $Q^D = 200 - 0.005(20,000) = 100$.]

(b) The private-sector <u>plus</u> government demand is $Q^D = 200 - 0.005P + 50 = 250 - 0.005P$.
Setting $Q^D = Q^S$ for equilibrium gives $250 - 0.005P = 0 + 0.005P$, which solves for $P = 250/0.01 = \$25\ 000$—i.e., a price increase of \$5000. Substituting $P = \$25\ 000$ into either the Q^D or Q^S equation (and multiplying by 1000) gives equilibrium quantity of 125 000 units.

(c) Comparing (a) and (b) shows production of farm machinery increases by only 25 000, not the full 50 000 purchased by the government. This is because the private sector reacts to the increase in price by reducing quantity demand by 25 000 units, from 100 000 in (a) to $Q^D = 200 - 0.005(25\ 000) = 75\ 000$ in (b).

(d) Because output was 100 000 before government intervened, industry output would have to be 150 000 to meet the government's objective of a 50 000 increase. The supply curve tells us that 150 000 would be produced only when $150 = 0 + 0.005P$, which solves for $P = 150/0.005 = $30 000$. At this price the private sector would purchase only $Q^D = 200 - 0.005(30\ 000) = 50$ (i.e., 50 000 units). Government would have to buy $150\ 000 - 50\ 000 = 100\ 000$.

(e) Government erroneously assumed the supply curve of farm machinery to be horizontal at $P = $20\ 000$. Only with a horizontal supply curve would there be no increase in price when demand increases, and so no fall in quantity demanded by the private sector. The government expected to buy 50 000 units for a total cost of $20\ 000(50\ 000) = 1 billion. At the new market price of $25 000, the actual cost of 50 000 units is $1.25 billion. To achieve its objective by purchasing 100 000 units at $30 000 each would cost the government $3 billion!

Additional Multiple-Choice Questions

1.(d) **2.**(c) **3.**(e) **4.**(c) **5.**(a) **6.**(c) **7.**(c) **8.**(b) **9.**(d) **10.**(c) **11.**(b) **12.**(d) **13.**(e) **14.**(c) **15.**(e) **16.**(e) **17.**(a) **18.**(e) **19.**(d) **20.**(e) **21.**(d) **22.**(d)

Explanations for the Asterisked Multiple-Choice Questions

1.(d) For a trade to take place in free markets, demanders must be willing to buy and suppliers must be willing to sell. At the equilibrium price, the quantity sold equals both the quantity demanded and the quantity supplied. If price is not at the equilibrium level, however, the quantity sold (or "traded") is the *lesser of* quantity demanded or quantity supplied. When price is above equilibrium, the amount that demanders are willing to buy is less than the amount that suppliers want to sell— so only the quantity demanded will be sold. When price is below equilibrium, the amount that demanders want to buy is more than the amount that suppliers are willing to sell—so only the quantity supplied will be sold.

3.(e) Videocassettes and DVDs are substitute goods, so a fall in the price of DVD players reduces demand for videocassettes and videocassette players. DVDs and DVD players are complementary goods, so a fall in the price of DVD players increases the demand for DVDs.

4.(c) All answers with the exception of (c) actually refer to a change in the *ceteris paribus* conditions underlying a <u>demand</u> curve, and hence would cause the demand curve to shift. Only answer (c) refers to a change in the conditions underlying a <u>supply</u> curve—in this case the fall in costs of production. This would make it more profitable to produce the good at each price, thus increasing the supply at each price (i.e., shifting the supply curve to the right).

9.(d) Do this by sketching a demand and supply diagram for each change separately, starting both from the old equilibrium. In your first diagram, the increase in demand creates excess demand at the old equilibrium price, increasing both price and quantity (along the supply curve). In your second diagram, the increase in supply creates excess supply at the old equilibrium price, reducing price but increasing quantity (along the demand curve). Since both changes increase quantity, then equilibrium quantity will definitely increase. But the two changes have opposing effects on price, so the change in the equilibrium price is not predictable; it depends on the relative magnitudes of the two changes. If the (horizontal) shift in the demand curve is greater than the (horizontal) shift in the supply curve, equilibrium price will increase. If the reverse is true, equilibrium price will fall. If the two shifts are the same size, equilibrium price will remain unchanged. (Sketch a different diagram for each of these three cases.)

10.(c) Unlike Question 9, the demand and supply curves shift in *different* directions; the decrease in input prices increases supply but the fall in price of a substitute in consumption reduces demand. Follow the method suggested in the answer to Question 9—i.e., sketch a diagram for each change separately—to see that this time the direction of change in equilibrium price is predictable but the direction of change in equilibrium quantity is not. The increase in supply puts upward pressure on quantity and downward pressure on price. The decrease in demand puts downward pressure on both price and quantity. Since both changes put downward pressure on price, equilibrium price will fall. But since they put opposing pressures on quantity, the net effect on equilibrium quantity is ambiguous (it depends on which curve shifts more).

11.(b) Answers (a) and (e) increase production costs, reducing supply (i.e., a vertical upward shift of the supply curve at each Q) and raising price. Answers (c) and (d) increase demand (given that, for (d), housing is a normal good), again raising price. Answer (b), however, increases supply by reducing production costs (i.e., a vertical downward shift of the supply curve at each Q), thus reducing price.

12.(d) Yesterday the relative price of strawberries to raspberries was $0.8/1.0 = 0.8$ (i.e., price of strawberries was 80 percent of the price of raspberries), and today it is $0.6/0.75 = 0.8$—so no change. Conversely, the relative price of raspberries to strawberries went from $1.0/0.8 = 1.25$ yesterday to $0.75/0.6 = 1.25$ today—again no change. So while the *absolute* prices fell by different amounts (20 cents for strawberries 25 cents for raspberries), the *percentage* fall was the same for both ($20/80 = 0.25 = 25$ percent and $25/100 = 0.25 = 25$ percent). Because each had the same percentage fall in its own price, their relative price (hence the opportunity cost) did not change.

13.(e) As in Question 9, both demand and supply shift in the *same* direction (though here they shift to the left while in Question 9 they shift to the right), so the effect on equilibrium quantity is predictable but the effect on equilibrium price is uncertain. The increase in production costs shifts the supply curve to the left, putting upward pressure on price and downward pressure on quantity. The increase in average incomes shifts the demand curve *for an inferior good* to the left, putting downward pressure on both price and quantity. Both shifts cause quantity to decrease, but one shift pushes price up while the other pushes price down. The net effect on equilibrium price is ambiguous (it depends on which curve shifts more—see Question 9).

14.(c) The change in the equilibrium position from A to C leaves the market for hamburgers on the same supply curve (S_1) but a higher demand curve (a shift from D_1 to D_2). So you must look for a change in an "other things constant" condition that shifts the demand curve out to the right (i.e., an increase in demand). Answer (a) would lower the cost of production and thus increase supply, not demand. Answer (b) would be a fall in the price of a substitute in consumption, reducing the demand for hamburgers. Answer (d) is a *result* of the shift in demand, not its *cause*—so both (d) and (e) are wrong. Answer (c) gives an increase in population, thereby increasing the number of demanders and causing demand to increase from D_1 to D_2.

16.(e) Only (a) and (e) have changes that increase demand (since a decrease in the price of beef patties increases *quantity demanded*, not demand). Only (d) and (e) have changes that increase supply. Since <u>both</u> demand and supply increase, the answer is (e).

17.(a) The move from Q_4 to Q_3 is along the same demand curve D_2, caused by a reduction in supply from S_2 to S_1. An increase, as in the price of beef patties in answer (a), raises the costs of production, which is reflected in that shift of the supply curve. Answers (b), (c), and (e) would have shifted the demand curves, so are false. Answer (c) would shift the supply curve but would cause an increase in supply when Q_4 to Q_3 is a *reduction* in supply.

18.(e) In this case, the equilibrium point stays on the same supply curve (S_1) but moves to a new point on it because demand increases from D_1 to D_2. Supply has not changed (so answer (d) is correct), but the increase in demand (answer (a)) created excess demand of $Q_4 - Q_1$ at P_2, pushing the new equilibrium point to B at a higher equilibrium price (answer (c)) and a higher equilibrium quantity (answer (b)).

19.(d) See that the new equilibrium P_3 is on different demand <u>and</u> supply curves than the initial equilibrium P_1. Demand has *fallen* from D_2 to D_1 and supply has *increased* from S_1 to S_2. Answers (a) and (c) have wrong descriptions about the direction of shift of at least one curve. Answers (b) and (e) accurately describe part of what has happened but are incomplete because they look at only what has happened to the supply side of the market and ignore the shift in the demand curve. Answer (d) is the *best* of the five options.

20.(e) The increase in the number of hamburger firms will increase supply, shifting the curve from S_1 to S_2. This says that the initial equilibrium was on S_1 (either A or B) and the final equilibrium must be on S_2 (either C or D). The increase in average incomes will reduce demand for a normal good (shifting the curve from D_1 to D_2) but reduce demand for an inferior good (shifting the curve from D_2 to D_1). For a normal good, therefore, the initial equilibrium was on S_1 and D_1 (at point A) and the final equilibrium on S_2 and D_2 (at point D). For an inferior good, however, the initial equilibrium was on S_1 and D_2 (at point B) and the final equilibrium on S_2 and D_1 (at point C). Since the question gives no information as to whether hamburgers are normal or inferior goods, we can't say whether the equilibrium point moved from A to D (a normal good) or from B to C (an inferior good).

21.(d) Setting $Q^D = Q^S$ gives $200 - 0.5P = 60 + 0.5P$, so $P = 200 - 60 = \$140$. Putting $P = \$140$ into either the demand equation ($Q^D = 200 - 0.5(140) = 200 - 70 = 130$) or the supply equation ($Q^S = 60 + 0.5(140) = 60 + 70 = 130$) gives an equilibrium quantity of 130 units.

22.(d) The minus sign on Y says that an increase in income reduces the demand for X (a negative or inverse relationship), so X is an inferior good. The plus sign on P_z says that an increase in the price of Z increases the demand for X (a positive or direct relationship), so X and Z are substitute goods.

Elasticity

Chapter Overview

The interaction of demand and supply was shown to determine equilibrium price and quantity in the previous chapter. The present chapter examines another important aspect of the interaction of demand and supply: the **responsiveness** of quantity demanded (or supplied) to changes in price, and the responsiveness of demand and supply to changes in other exogenous variables. **Elasticity** is the economic term for this type of responsiveness or sensitivity.

Price elasticity of demand is measured as the percentage change in quantity demanded divided by the percentage change in the commodity's own price. Demand is said to be **elastic** when the percentage change in quantity demanded exceeds (in absolute terms) the percentage change in price and **inelastic** when the reverse holds. Demand is said to be **unit elastic** when the two percentage changes are of equal magnitude. If the price elasticity of demand for a product is known, one can predict the percentage change in quantity demanded that would result from a given percentage price change. The magnitude of a product's elasticity of demand also allows us to predict whether an increase in its price will result in an increase, a decrease, or no change in **total expenditure** on the product. An important influence on the elasticity of demand is the availability of substitute products.

Similarly, the **price elasticity of supply** is the percentage change in quantity supplied divided by the percentage change in the commodity's own price. The same classifications—elastic, inelastic, or unit elastic—also apply, again determined by the relative magnitudes of the percentage changes in quantity (supplied) and price.

Tax incidence refers to how the *burden* of a tax on goods and services is distributed between consumers and producers. This chapter shows that tax incidence is independent of whether producers or consumers *nominally* pay the tax. Rather, the distribution of the burden of a sales tax critically depends on the relative magnitudes of the elasticities of demand and supply.

LO LEARNING OBJECTIVES

After studying this chapter, you will be able to

1 explain what price elasticity of demand is and how it is measured.

2 explain the relationship between total expenditure and price elasticity of demand.

3 explain what price elasticity of supply is and how it is measured.

4 see how demand and supply determine the effects of an excise tax.

5 measure the income elasticity of demand and be able to distinguish between normal and inferior goods.

6 measure cross elasticity of demand and be able to distinguish between substitute and complement goods.

Additional elasticity measures are relevant when consumer income or the price of another good changes the **income elasticity** and **cross-price elasticity**, respectively. The sign of the income elasticity (positive or negative) indicates whether the good is **normal** or **inferior**, while the sign of the cross-price elasticity indicates whether the goods are **substitutes** or **complements** in consumption.

Hints and Tips

The following may help you avoid some of the most common errors on examinations.

✓ Don't let the term *elasticity* overwhelm you. It is nothing more than a technical name for a measurement of responsiveness or sensitivity.

✓ The relationship between a change in price and a change in total expenditure (positive or negative) on a commodity depends on the magnitude of the *absolute value* of its price elasticity of demand. This is why the terms *more elastic* and *less elastic* refer to the absolute value of price elasticity of demand, despite the fact that it is actually a negative number on a downward-sloping demand curve (since price and quantity demanded move in opposite directions). Thus, for example, when demand has a price elasticity of –2, it is *more elastic* than when it has an elasticity of –1 (since the absolute value 2 exceeds the absolute value 1).

✓ Don't confuse slope with elasticity. For example, although a linear demand curve has a constant slope, it does not have a constant elasticity. The ratio of the *absolute* change in quantity to the *absolute* change in price is constant all along a linear demand curve, but the ratio of the *percentage* changes is not.

✓ There are different elasticities (price elasticity, income elasticity, cross elasticity) and there can be different ways of writing the formula for calculating an elasticity. It is easy to get confused if you lose sight of the fact that they are all doing the same thing. They are all comparing the percentage change in the quantity of a commodity (demanded or supplied) with the percentage change in one of the exogenous variables (the price of the commodity, income, the price of another commodity).

Chapter Review

Price Elasticity of Demand

This section focuses on the responsiveness of quantity demanded to changes in the commodity's own price. This responsiveness can be referred to as the own-price elasticity of demand, the price elasticity of demand, or simply the elasticity of demand. Because the absolute change in price or quantity is a different percentage of the value before the change than the value after the change, elasticity takes the change as a percentage of the *average* of the two values. Depending on its magnitude, elasticity is classified as elastic, inelastic, or unit elastic. Make certain you understand the implications of this classification for the effect of a change in the commodity's price on the change in consumers' total expenditure on the commodity, particularly along a linear (i.e., constant slope) demand curve. The section also explains why the elasticity of demand depends on the availability and closeness of substitutes, on how broadly or narrowly the product is defined, and on the length of the time span being considered.

1. **The price elasticity of demand refers to a measure that shows the**
    (a) responsiveness of quantity demanded of a good to changes in its price.
    (b) variation in prices due to a change in demand.
    (c) size of price changes caused by a shift in demand.
    (d) degree of substitutability across commodities.
    (e) magnitude of the shifts in a demand curve.

2. **The price elasticity of demand is measured by the**
    (a) change in quantity demanded divided by the change in price.
    (b) change in price divided by the change in quantity demanded.
    (c) slope of the demand curve.
    (d) percentage change in quantity demanded divided by the percentage change in price.
    (e) average quantity demanded divided by the average price.

3. **If the percentage change in price is greater than the percentage change in quantity demanded, demand**
    (a) is elastic.   (b) is inelastic.
    (c) is unit-elastic.   (d) shifts outward to the left.
    (e) shifts to the right.

4. **An increase in the price of a good and a decrease in total expenditure on this good are associated with**
    (a) inferior goods.   (b) substitute goods.
    (c) normal goods.   (d) elastic demand.
    (e) inelastic demand.

5. **The price elasticity of demand for a good will be greater**
    (a) the less available are suitable substitutes for this good.
    (b) the longer the time period considered.
    (c) for a group of related goods as opposed to an element of that group.
    (d) the greater is income.
    (e) All of the above are correct.

6. **If a 10 percent increase in the price of ski lift tickets causes a 5 percent decrease in total expenditure on lift tickets, then demand is**
    (a) elastic.   (b) inelastic.
    (c) perfectly inelastic.   (d) normal.
    (e) inferior.

7. **Which of the following commodities is most likely to have an elastic demand?**
    (a) Toothpicks.   (b) Cigarettes.
    (c) Heart pacemakers.   (d) Broccoli.
    (e) Vegetables.

8. **When price falls along a straight-line demand curve, the (absolute value of) elasticity**
    (a) first rises and then falls.   (b) is the same at all prices.
    (c) first falls and then rises.   (d) continually rises as price falls.
    (e) continually falls as price falls.

9. **As price rises along a straight-line demand curve, total expenditure on the commodity**
    (a) first rises and then falls.   (b) is the same at all prices.
    (c) first falls and then rises.   (d) continually rises as price falls.
    (e) continually falls as price falls.

Price Elasticity of Supply

The responsiveness of quantity supplied to a change in price can also be classified as elastic, inelastic, or unit elastic. As with demand, the price elasticity of supply is calculated at the average values of price and quantity. As with demand, the price elasticity of supply ranges from zero (perfectly inelastic) to infinity (perfectly inelastic). A linear supply curve through the origin has unit elasticity throughout its entire length (a special case). The price elasticity of supply is affected by the ease with which producers can shift production to or from other products, by how production costs change with output, and by how quickly producers can change their *productive capacity*.

10. **A value of zero for the elasticity of supply of some product implies that**
    (a) the supply curve is horizontal.
    (b) supply is highly responsive to price.
    (c) the supply curve is vertical.
    (d) the product will not be supplied at any price.
    (e) None of the above.

11. **The elasticity of supply for a product will tend to be larger**
    (a) the higher is the elasticity of demand for the product.
    (b) the lower is the elasticity of demand for the product.
    (c) the harder it is for firms to shift from the production of one product to another product.
    (d) the easier it is for firms to shift from the production of one product to another product.
    (e) the shorter the time period involved.

12. **In the short run, a shift in demand will generally cause**
    (a) the price to overshoot its long-run equilibrium value.
    (b) the price to undershoot its long-run equilibrium value.
    (c) the quantity exchanged to overshoot its long-run equilibrium value.
    (d) both price and quantity exchanged to overshoot their long-run equilibrium values.
    (e) None of the above.

13. **Suppose that the short-run demand for a good is relatively more inelastic than its long-run demand. A given rightward shift in the supply curve will lead to a**
    (a) smaller decrease in price in the long run than in the short run.
    (b) smaller increase in quantity in the long run than in the short run.
    (c) larger decrease in price in the long run than in the short run.
    (d) smaller decrease in both price and quantity in the long run than in the short run.
    (e) larger decrease in both price and quantity in the long run than in the short run.

An Important Example Where Elasticity Matters

This section looks at the importance of elasticity for the effects of an *excise tax* on "price." (A *sales tax* such as the GST is a percentage of the price of a good or a service, while an *excise tax* is the same dollar amount regardless of price. The principles of the analysis are the same in both cases, but the excise tax is easier to explain and calculate.) When government imposes a tax on a good, there is no longer a single price since the price paid by the consumer (*consumer price*) exceeds the price retained by the seller (*seller price*) by the amount of the tax. The *tax incidence*, otherwise called the *burden of the tax*, refers to the shares of the tax "paid" by sellers (via a fall in the seller price) and by consumers (via an increase in consumer price). Tax incidence depends on the relative elasticities of demand and supply, and is unaffected by whether the tax is included in the price charged by sellers or paid by consumers as an add-on at the till. The more elastic is demand relative to supply, the smaller the consumers' share of the burden of taxation and the greater the sellers' share. This section shows why.

14. **Tax incidence refers to**
    (a) who is legally responsible for paying the tax revenue to the government.
    (b) the legislative process taxes must pass through.
    (c) the economic costs of avoiding taxes.
    (d) who ultimately bears the burden of the tax.
    (e) None of the above.

15. **Suppose the market supply curve for some good is upward sloping. If the imposition of a sales tax causes no change in the equilibrium quantity sold in the market, the good's demand curve must be _____, meaning that the burden of the tax has fallen completely on the _____.**
    (a) vertical; firms
    (b) vertical; consumers
    (c) horizontal; firms
    (d) horizontal; consumers
    (e) Not enough information is provided to answer this question.

16. **Since the goods and services tax (GST) or harmonized sales tax (HST) is added to the price a consumer must pay for a commodity, the**
    (a) entire burden of the tax is borne by consumers.
    (b) consumer price increases by the amount of the tax.
    (c) seller price is unaffected.
    (d) entire burden is borne by sellers who must collect the tax.
    (e) distribution of the burden depends on the elasticities of demand and supply.

17. **Consumers bear a greater share of the burden of the tax the more**
    (a) inelastic is supply.
    (b) elastic is supply.
    (c) inelastic is demand.
    (d) elastic is demand.
    (e) Both (b) and (c) are correct.

Other Demand Elasticities

The *income elasticity* of demand and the *cross-price elasticity* of demand measure the responsiveness of demand to income and to the prices of other goods, respectively. Just as price elasticity is measured holding all other exogenous variables constant (thus referring to the responsiveness of quantity demanded to price *along* a demand curve), so income elasticity and cross elasticity also hold all other exogenous variables constant, including the product's price (thus referring to how the demand curve *shifts* when income or other prices change). The sign on the income elasticity (positive or negative) shows the *direction* of the shift (i.e., whether the good is normal or inferior), and the magnitude of the income elasticity shows *by how much* the demand curve shifts when income changes. Similarly, the sign on the cross elasticity shows the *direction* of the shift (i.e., whether the two goods are substitutes or complements), and the magnitude of the cross elasticity shows *by how much* the demand curve shifts when the price of the other good changes. Review the terminology of elasticity in *Extensions in Theory 4-2* in the text to ensure a thorough understanding of the classification of the various elasticities.

18. **Which of the following pairs of commodities is most likely to have a cross elasticity of demand that is positive?**
    (a) Hockey sticks and pucks.
    (c) Cassettes and compact discs.
    (e) Hamburgers and french fries.
    (b) Bread and cheese.
    (d) Perfume and garden hoses.

19. **Margarine and butter are predicted to have**
    (a) the same income elasticities of demand.
    (b) very low price elasticities of demand.
    (c) negative cross elasticities of demand with respect to each other.
    (d) positive cross elasticities of demand with respect to each other.
    (e) elastic demands with respect to price.

20. **Which of the following pairs of commodities is most likely to have a cross elasticity of demand that is negative?**
    (a) Cornflakes and raisin bran.
    (c) CD players and compact discs.
    (e) Hamburgers and hot dogs.
    (b) Orange juice and apple juice.
    (d) Perfume and garden hoses.

21. **Inferior commodities have**
    (a) zero income elasticities of demand.
    (b) negative cross elasticities of demand.
    (c) negative elasticities of supply.
    (d) highly elastic demands.
    (e) negative income elasticities of demand.

22. **Which of the following goods is most likely to have an income elasticity of demand that is positive but less than one?**
    (a) Ground beef.
    (c) Perfume.
    (e) Sailboats.
    (b) Microwave ovens.
    (d) Winter vacations.

Short-Answer Questions

1. Why is the cross elasticity of demand positive for substitute goods and negative for complementary goods?

2. If a $100 fall in the price of television sets and a $100 fall in the price of automobiles each increased quantity demanded by 50 000, would the price elasticity of demand be the same for both? Why/why not?

3. What would you expect to see when comparing the price elasticity of demand for Kit-Kat bars with the price elasticity of demand for candy as a whole? Why?

4. What does a "necessity" commonly mean in everyday language? What is the economic definition of a necessity? Can you think of a good that is a necessity according to the economic definition but not in everyday language?

The answers to the remaining questions in this section are "short," but answering these questions requires more thought. Also, Question 7 requires an understanding of the equation for a straight-line demand curve.

5. Mr. Quitit from Quaffalot wants to increase the sales tax on beer. He argues it would be good social policy because the price paid by consumers would increase by almost all the extra tax, which would substantially reduce purchases of beer and so leave low-income families with more money to spend on food and clothing. Can you see why Mr. Quitit's reasoning may be inconsistent? [*Hint:* What is the condition for consumers to bear the "burden" of a tax? What is the condition for an increase in price to reduce total expenditure on a commodity?]

6. This question reviews your understanding of the relationships between elasticity of demand and total expenditure when price changes. Complete the following table:

	Price Elasticity	Change in Price	Change in Total Expenditure
(a)	2.0	up	↓
(b)	1.0	down	○
(c)			up	none
(d)	0.0	down	↓
(e)	0.6	↑	up

7. The daily demand curve facing the City Transit Authority (CTA) is given by $Q^D = 46 - 0.2P$, where quantity is in thousands of riders per day (i.e., 46 = 46 000) and price (the fare) is in cents. The current fare is $1.30 (i.e., $P = 130$) and there are 20 000 riders per day. The CTA hires you to advise it on how much it should increase the fare in order to maximize its revenues (i.e., the total expenditure of its riders). What advice will you give the CTA? [*Hint:* You do not need to actually *calculate* any elasticities. Review Figure 4-5 in the text, then find the expenditure-maximizing price from the equation.]

Midpoint, where elasticity=1 maximizes revenue.

Exercises

1. **Calculating and Classifying the Price Elasticity of Demand**
   This exercise reviews your ability to calculate and classify elasticity. In each of the following scenarios, categorize the price elasticity of demand as *elastic*, *perfectly elastic*, *inelastic*, *perfectly inelastic*, or *unit elastic*. Where calculations are required, use average price and quantity. [*Hint:* There are two cases where categorization is not possible with the information provided.]

   (a) The price of personal computers falls from $2750 to $2250, and the quantity demanded increases from 40 000 units to 60 000 units.

   (b) Canada Post increases the price of a stamp from 61 cents to 63 cents, but expenditure on postage stamps remains the same.

   (c) The price of a book of matches doubles from 1 cent to 2 cents, but the quantity purchased does not change.

   (d) An increase in the demand for blue jeans causes the price to increase from $45 to $55 and the amount purchased to increase from 1 million to 1.1 million.

   (e) A sudden decline in the supply of avocados leads to an increase in price by 10 percent and an accompanying reduction in quantity demanded by 20 000 units from the original level of 90 000 units.

   (f) A 5 percent decrease in the price of gasoline results in a decrease in gasoline expenditure of 5 percent.

   (g) A 10 percent increase in consumer income results in a 15 percent increase in the price of snowboards as well as a 15 percent increase in purchases.

   (h) Canadian farmers increase their output of wheat by 25 percent, and there is no change in the price of wheat.

2. Elasticity and Total Expenditure

This exercise reviews the relationship between the price elasticity of demand and total expenditure. Two alternative demand curves are shown in the upper panels of Figure 4-1.

Figure 4-1

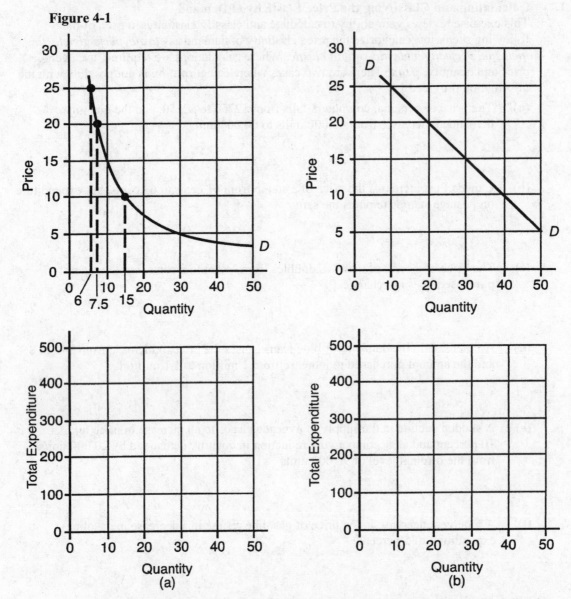

(a) Calculate the total expenditure associated with each demand curve at the following prices: $25, $20, $15, $10, and $5. Graph the respective total expenditure curves in the grids provided in the lower panels of Figure 4-1.

(b) By inspection of these expenditure curves, what can you say about the price elasticity of demand along each of the demand curves?

3. **Linear Demand and Elasticity**
This exercise establishes the point that elasticity is not constant along a straight-line demand curve. [*Note:* Extension Exercise E4 establishes the same point using a different method.]

(a) Calculate the numerical values of price elasticity along the linear demand curve in Figure 4-2, using the four price–quantity segments indicated by the dots (i.e., the arcs *A* to *B*, *B* to *C*, *C* to *D*, and *D* to *E*). Confirm that elasticity declines as price decreases even though the slope is constant.

Figure 4-2

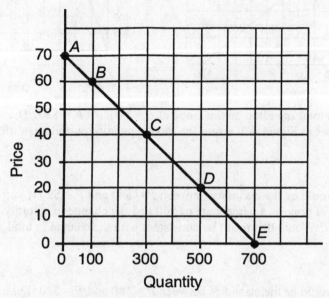

(b) What is the elasticity of demand when the price falls from $40 to $30? What would happen to total expenditure on this good if the price fell further?

4. **Why Elasticity Uses Average Values**
This exercise shows why it is necessary to calculate elasticity of demand using average price and quantity. It also shows that, along a *straight-line* demand curve, the magnitude of changes around the same averages does not affect the elasticity of demand. [*Note:* This conclusion does *not* necessarily apply to non-linear demand curves.]

Figure 4-3

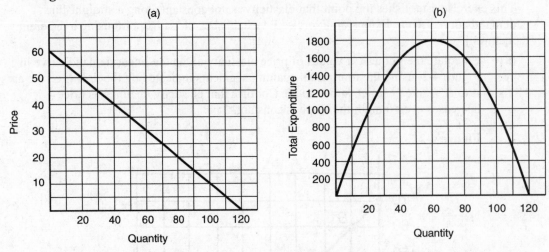

(a)

(b)

(a) What is total spending on this good at $P = \$40$? At $P = \$20$? Draw the prices and quantities in Figure 4-3(a) and the total expenditures and quantities in Figure 4-3(b).

(b) What would be the elasticity between $P = \$40$ and $P = \$20$ if you calculated the change in price as a percentage of $40 and the change in quantity as a percentage of 40 units? Would this result be consistent with the change in total spending?

(c) What would be the elasticity between $P = \$40$ and $P = \$20$ if you calculated the change in price as a percentage of $20 and the change in quantity as a percentage of 80 units? Would this result be consistent with the change in total spending?

(d) What is the elasticity of demand between $P = \$40$ and $P = \$20$ when correctly calculated using the average price and average quantity? Is this consistent with the change in total spending? What can you conclude about the reason for using average price and quantity in the calculation of elasticity?

(e) What is total expenditure at $P = \$50$? At $P = \$10$? Draw these points in Figure 4-3. What is elasticity of demand between these two prices? Is this elasticity consistent with the change in total expenditure?

(f) Comparing what you found in (d) with what you found in (e), fill in the blanks in the following statement: On a *straight-line* demand curve, any changes that have the same ___average___ price and quantity give ___same___ elasticity.

5. **A "Quick Method" for Use with Linear Demand Curves**
   This exercise teaches a quicker way to calculate elasticity once the slope of the demand curve is known. In the process you will find another way to write the formula for elasticity.

   (a) In Figure 4-3(a) in Exercise 4 above, what is the elasticity of demand between $P = \$45$ and $P = \$35$?

   (b) What is the slope of the demand curve (i.e., $\Delta P/\Delta Q$)?

   (c) What is the ratio of price to quantity *at the midpoint* of the range between $P = \$45$ and $P = \$35$ (i.e., P_{AVE}/Q_{AVE})? Divide this ratio by the slope of the demand curve. How does the result compare with the elasticity you calculated in (a)?

   Notice that in (c) you actually calculated elasticity *at a point* on the demand curve using the formula $(P/Q)/(\Delta P/\Delta Q)$. Use this formula for (d). [*Hint:* You do not have to recalculate $\Delta P/\Delta Q$ since it is constant all along a linear demand curve.]

   (d) What is the elasticity of demand at $P = \$20$? Would this be the elasticity of demand if price changed from \$25 to \$15? From \$30 to \$10? Why?

6. **A Ray of Light on a Straight-Line Demand Curve**
   In Exercise 5 you saw that the formula for elasticity can be written as $(P/Q)/(\Delta P/\Delta Q)$. On a diagram, P/Q is the slope of the *ray from the origin* (i.e., the line from the "zero" point) to a point on the demand curve. Since the slope of the curve ($\Delta P/\Delta Q$) is constant all along a straight-line demand curve, the value of elasticity falls as the ray gets flatter (i.e., $(P/Q)/(\Delta P/\Delta Q)$ gets smaller as P/Q falls). This makes it very easy to see how elasticity changes along a straight-line demand curve. [Very useful in exams!]

   Draw for yourself any straight-line demand curve. For each of the following questions, draw the ray from the origin to the relevant point on the demand curve and compare the slope of the ray to the slope of the curve. The answers come easily.

   (a) The slope of the ray to the *midpoint* on the demand curve equals the (absolute value of) the slope of the curve. What is elasticity at the midpoint?

   (b) Pick a price *above* the midpoint, and draw the ray. How does the slope of the ray compare to the slope of the curve? What does this say about elasticity?

   (c) Pick a price *lower* than the midpoint, and draw the ray. What do you see now? What does this say about elasticity?

(d) What is the slope of the ray to the point on the demand curve where quantity demanded = 0? What is elasticity?

(e) What is the slope of the ray to the point on the demand curve at price = $0? What is elasticity?

7. **The Elasticity of Supply**
   This exercise reviews the calculation of the elasticity of supply, and compares elasticities of supply for straight-line supply curves. Find the answers by computing the elasticities between the points indicated on the supply curves in Figure 4-4.

   Figure 4-4

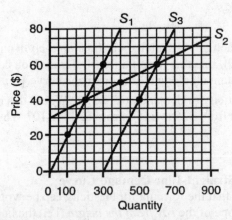

(a) Demonstrate that the elasticity of supply equals 1 all along S_1. How is this result related to the fact that this supply curve passes through the origin?

b/c it goes through origin, then P&Q always increase by same proportion.

(b) Demonstrate that elasticity falls as price increases along S_2.

(c) Compare the elasticities on S_1 and S_3 between $P = \$40$ and $P = \$60$. What does this comparison tell you about the effect on elasticity when a linear supply curve takes a parallel shift to the right (an increase in supply)? *elasticity falls.*

(d) What does your conclusion in (c) imply about the effect on elasticity when a linear supply curve takes a parallel shift to the left (a reduction in supply)?

∴ must increase

8. **Tax Incidence**
    Tax incidence depends on the elasticities of demand and supply. This exercise illustrates the relationship. [*Note:* For the mathematically inclined, the Extension Exercise on tax incidence proves the relationship.]

    The following diagrams show the demand and supply curves in the markets for beer and orange juice. Suppose a sales tax of $t per litre is imposed in each of these markets.

    Figure 4-5

    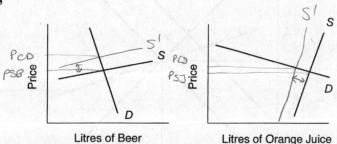

    Litres of Beer   Litres of Orange Juice

    (a) Shift the appropriate curve to show the impact of the tax in each market. Label the new consumer price and seller price in the beer market P_{CB} and P_{SB}, respectively. In the market for orange juice, label them P_{CJ} and P_{SJ}, respectively.

    (b) In which market is most of the burden of the tax borne by consumers? What do you see when you compare the elasticities of demand and supply in this market?

    Consumer Beer: Demand inelastic, supply elastic
    produce OJ: Demand elastic, supply inelastic

    (c) In which market is most of the tax borne by producers? What do you see when you compare the elasticities of demand and supply in this market?

    (d) In which market is the difference between the consumer price and the seller price greater?

    Neither — $t in both

9. **Tax Incidence, Elasticity, and Overshooting**
    This exercise expands on Exercise 8 to demonstrate why policymakers may need to take a longer-term perspective. In the example used here, the objective is to reduce smoking without reducing the standard of living of lower-income families. The exercise combines the relationship between tax incidence and elasticity with the relationship between elasticity and time.

In Figure 4-6, D_{SR} is the short-run demand curve for cigarettes and D_{LR} is the long-run demand curve. Government puts an excise tax on cigarettes of $\$t$ per pack. Before the tax, equilibrium is at P^* per pack and Q^* packs per week.

Figure 4-6

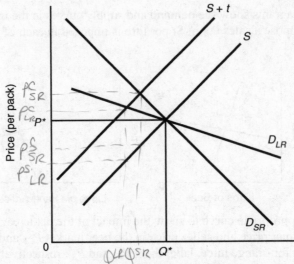

(a) Locate the short-run equilibrium and draw the quantity (Q_{SR}), the price paid by consumers (P^C_{SR}), and the price retained by suppliers (P^S_{SR}). Locate the long-run equilibrium and draw Q_{LR}, P^C_{LR}, and P^S_{LR}.

(b) How does the effect of the tax on equilibrium quantity differ between the short run and the long run? Why?

Greater in LR b/c demand is more elastic in LR

(c) How does the incidence of the tax differ between the short run and the long run? Why?

Greater on consumer in SR than LR
SR prices "overshoot" LR eqm values

(d) How does the effect of the tax on total consumer spending on cigarettes differ between the short run and the long run? Why?

SR demand inelastic ∴ expenditure ↑
LR demand less inelastic ∴ smaller ↑ in expenditure
if LR isolastic, expenditure ↓

(e) Does this policy meet the policymakers' objective in the short run? Why/why not?

NO - small ↓ smoking, ↑ price ⇒ less $ for low-income families

(f) Does this policy meet the policymakers' objective in the long run? Why/why not?

yes. large ↓ smoking, ∴ tax incidence on consumers falls

Extension Exercises

E1. **Elasticities and *Ceteris Paribus***

Calculating the elasticity of one variable in response to changes in another requires holding all other variables constant (i.e., *ceteris paribus*). This exercise establishes the point. [*Note:* Successful completion of this exercise would indicate that you have a very good understanding of elasticity.]

The following table provides data on income as well as prices and quantity demanded of goods *x* and *y* for five different periods (or observations). You are asked to calculate different elasticities of demand (price elasticity, income elasticity, and cross elasticity) between periods that satisfy the "other things constant" condition.

Period	Income	P_x	Q^D_x	P_y	Q^D_y
(1)	$10 000	$25	10	$10	42
(2)	10 000	28	9	10	40
(3)	10 000	28	8	15	35
(4)	11 000	28	9	15	36
(5)	11 500	34	7	20	32

(a) Why should no elasticities be calculated between periods 4 and 5?

More than 1 variable has changed

(b) For each of the following, calculate the relevant elasticity from the changes that occur between the two appropriate periods:

price elasticity for *x* is _____, based on periods _1_ and _2_ ;
price elasticity for *y* is _____, based on periods _2_ and _3_ ;
income elasticity for *x* is _____, based on periods _3_ and _4_ ;
income elasticity for *y* is _____, based on periods _3_ and _4_ ;
cross elasticity of demand for *y* with respect to the price of *x* is _____, based on periods _1_ and _2_ ; *↑constant* *↑changes*
cross elasticity of demand for *x* with respect to the price of *y* is _____, based on the periods _2_ and _3_ . *↑constant* *↑changes*

E2. **Diagrammatic Features of Elasticity**

The classification of elasticity can often be determined by diagrammatic features of the relevant curves. The six diagrams in Figure 4-7 represent different combinations of elasticities of demand and supply at the equilibrium price P_E. Indicate which diagrams correspond to each of the following statements. (η_d refers to elasticity of demand, and η_s refers to elasticity of supply).

(a) η_d is greater than one and η_s is unity _1&6_
(b) η_d is unity and η_s is infinity _4_
(c) η_d is unity and η_s is unity _5_
(d) η_d is greater than one and η_s is zero _2_
(e) η_d is zero and η_s is unity _3_
(f) η_d is infinity and η_s is unity _6_

Figure 4-7

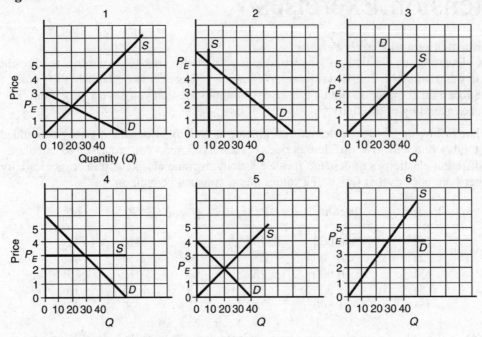

E3. **Tax Incidence Using Equations**

This exercise takes you step-by-step to the results of *Extensions in Theory 4-1* in the text. Draw an illustrative diagram—not a scale diagram—as you go along, to give a visual perspective on what is happening. [*Note:* This exercise is intended only for students covering *Extensions in Theory 4-1* in their course.]

(a) Using P_C for the price paid by consumers and P_S for the price retained by suppliers, the equations for the (linear) demand and supply curves are

	General Form	This Exercise
Demand:	$Q^D = a - bP_C$	$Q^D = 200 - 0.5P_C$
Supply:	$Q^S = c + dP_S$	$Q^S = 20 + 0.25P_S$

[*Hint:* To draw your diagram, recall that (1) 200 and 20 are the quantity axis intercepts of the demand and supply curves, respectively, and (2) –0.5 and 0.25 are the *reciprocals* (the inverse) of the slopes of the curves.]

At first there is no tax, so $P_C = P_S$. Calculate equilibrium price (P_E) and quantity (Q_E) with no tax.

(b) Introduce an excise tax (t) of $60 per unit sold. Now, $P_C = P_S + t$ and $P_S = P_C - t$. In the supply equation, replace P_S with $P_C - t$ and rewrite the equation to get the tax-inclusive supply function as a relationship between Q^S and P_C.

(c) Use the demand equation in (a) and the tax-inclusive supply equation derived in (b) to solve for the new equilibrium P_C. What is the change in P_C ($= \Delta P_C$) caused by the tax? Since $P_S = P_C - 60$, what is the change in P_S ($= \Delta P_S$)? What is the tax incidence on consumers and suppliers (i.e., the change in each price as a proportion of the tax)?

(d) Put the tax-inclusive P_C from (c) in the demand equation from (a) to find the new quantity demanded. Put the after-tax P_S from (c) in the supply equation from (a) to find the new quantity supplied. Does quantity demanded equal quantity supplied? [*Hint:* If not, the prices found in (c) are wrong.] What is the change in equilibrium quantity (ΔQ_E) as a result of the tax?

You have now found *what* the effects of the tax are. The next steps show you *why*.

(e) Take the (absolute value) of the slope of the demand curve (i.e., the value of $1/b$) and divide it by the sum of the (absolute values) of the demand and supply curve slopes (i.e., $1/b + 1/d$). Where have you seen this number before? Multiply it by the amount of the tax ($t = \$60$). Where have you seen this number before?

Now write the general form (i.e., using the letters instead of the numbers) of the equation for the effect of the tax on P_C. [*Hint:* It does not look the same as the equation in the text, but it means the same.]

$\Delta P_C =$

(f) Repeat section (e) using the slope of the supply curve (i.e., $1/d$) as the numerator.

Write the general form of the equation for the effect of the tax on P_S.

$\Delta P_S =$

(g) How would ΔP_C and ΔP_S change if you increased the slope of the demand curve (i.e., made demand less elastic) and reduced the slope of the supply curve (i.e., made supply more elastic)?

Now fill in the blanks to complete the following statement: The less elastic is supply relative to demand, the greater is the tax incidence on _____ and the _____ it is on _____.

(h) Finally, divide the tax ($t = \$60$) by the denominator you used in (e) and (f). Where have you seen this number before?

Write the general form of the equation for the change in equilibrium quantity.

$\Delta Qe =$

Would ΔQe change if you increased the slope of the demand curve ($1/b$) and reduced the slope of the supply curve ($1/d$) by exactly the same amount?

Fill in the spaces to complete the following statement: The effect of a sales tax on the equilibrium quantity depends solely on the amount of the tax and the _____ the slopes of the demand and supply curves, regardless of their _____ slopes.

Exercises E4 and E5 are based on material in *Additional Topics: Some Further Details About Demand Elasticity* on the text's MyEconLab website for Chapter 4. They use elasticity at a point on the demand curve (the *point elasticity* of demand) rather than the elasticity between two points (the *arc elasticity* of demand).

The point elasticity of demand is calculated as the ratio of price to quantity (P/Q) at a point on the demand curve, divided by the slope of the demand curve. On a linear demand curve, the slope ($\Delta P/\Delta Q$) is the same at all points. [*Note:* The slope is $\Delta P/\Delta Q$ because price is measured on the vertical axis and quantity on the horizontal axis.] Dividing by the slope, $\Delta P/\Delta Q$, is the same as multiplying by the reciprocal of the slope, $\Delta Q/\Delta P$. Thus

$$\eta_d = (P/Q)/(\Delta P/\Delta Q) \quad \text{or} \quad \eta_d = (P/Q) \times (\Delta Q/\Delta P)$$

For the linear demand curve $Q = a - bP$, $\Delta P/\Delta Q = 1/b$, so the point elasticity formula is

$$\eta_d = (P/Q)/(1/b) \quad \text{or} \quad \eta_d = (P/Q) \times b$$

E4. Point Elasticity Along a Straight-Line Demand Curve
Using the point elasticity formula and the linear demand curve equation, $Q^D = 200 - 2P$, complete the table below. [*Note:* An example row is done for you.] Sketch your own illustrative diagram to give a visual perspective as you go through the exercise.

Price	Quantity	η_d	Description	Expenditure as Price Falls	Rises
$100					
$ 80	40	4	elastic	increases	decreases
$ 60	___	___	_____	_____	_____
$ 50	___	___	_____	_____	_____
$ 40	___	___	_____	_____	_____
$ 20	___	___	_____	_____	_____
$ 0	___	___	_____	_____	_____

E5. Point Elasticity on Different Demand Curves

This exercise again shows that elasticity is more than just slope, this time by comparing elasticities (at the same price) *between* linear demand curves rather than *along* a curve. The equations for the demand curves in Figure 4-8 are

$D_0: Q = 30 - P$ $D_1: Q = 40 - 2P$ $D_2: Q = 60 - 2P$ $D_3: Q = 80 - 2P$

Figure 4-8

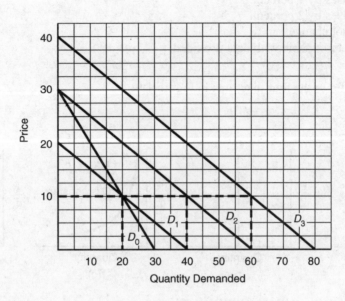

(a)   Complete the following table:

Curve	Price	Quantity	Slope	Elasticity
D_0	$10	_____	_____	_____
D_1	$10	_____	_____	_____
D_2	$10	_____	_____	_____
D_3	$10	_____	_____	_____

(b)   Complete the following statements using the results found in (a). In all cases the comparison is between price elasticities at *the same price* on different *straight-line* demand curves.

(i)   When two demand curves intersect at a positive quantity, the one with the _____ slope is _____ elastic.

(ii)   When two demand curves with different slopes have the same price–axis intercept, the elasticity of demand of the flatter curve is _____ that of the steeper curve.

(iii)   When demand increases with no change in slope, elasticity _____.

(iv)   When two demand curves with different slopes do not intersect at any price, elasticity on the outer curve is _____ than on the inner curve _____ slope.

Additional Multiple-Choice Questions

*1. **If the price elasticity of demand for a good is 2 and price increases by 2 percent, the quantity demanded**

    (a)   decreases by 4 percent.

    (b)   decreases by 1 percent.

    (c)   decreases by 2 percent.

    (d)   does not change.

    (e)   is indeterminable with data provided.

$$2 = \frac{x}{2}$$

Questions 2 to 5 refer to the four diagrams in Figure 4-9.

Figure 4-9

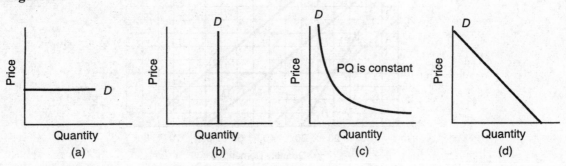

      (a)   (b)   (c)   (d)

*2. **The demand curve with an elasticity of zero is**

    (a)   a.   (b)   b.

    (c)   c.   (d)   d.

    (e)   None of the above.

*3. **The demand curve with an elasticity of unity is**

    (a)   a.   (b)   b.

    (c)   c.   (d)   d.

    (e)   None of the above.

*4. **The demand curve with an elasticity of infinity is**

    (a)   a.   (b)   b.

    (c)   c.   (d)   d.

    (e)   None of the above.

*5. **The demand curve with an elasticity that is variable is**

    (a)   a.   (b)   b.

    (c)   c.   (d)   d.

    (e)   Both (c) and (d).

*6. **The price elasticity of demand for snowmobiles is estimated to be 1.2; thus an increase in price**

    (a)   always decreases quantity demanded by 12 percent.

    (b)   always decreases quantity demanded by 1.2 percent.

    (c)   increases total expenditure.

    (d)   decreases total expenditure.

    (e)   decreases total expenditure by 1.2 percent.

*7. **If the demand for some commodity has an elasticity of unity, a decrease in price**
- (a) causes a 1 percent decrease in quantity demanded.
- (b) induces no change in quantity demanded.
- (c) results in no change in total expenditure.
- (d) is matched by a unit increase in quantity demanded.
- (e) Both (a) and (c) are correct.

Questions 8 to 10 refer to the following schedule. (Use average prices and quantities in your calculations.)

Price per Unit	Quantity Offered for Sale
$10	400
8	350
6	300
4	200
2	50

8. **As price increases from $4 to $6, the elasticity of supply is**
- (a) 1.0.
- (b) 50.
- (c) 0.5.
- (d) 5.0.
- (e) 2.0.

*9. **As price rises from $6 to $10 per unit, the supply response is**
- (a) elastic.
- (b) of unit elasticity.
- (c) of zero elasticity.
- (d) inelastic.
- (e) infinitely elastic.

*10. **The supply curve implied by the schedule is**
- (a) elastic for all price ranges.
- (b) inelastic for all price ranges.
- (c) of zero elasticity for all price ranges.
- (d) of variable elasticity, depending on the initial price chosen.
- (e) of constant elasticity.

11. **A perfectly inelastic demand curve means that**
- (a) a percentage decrease in price increases quantity demanded by the exact same percentage.
- (b) an increase in price reduces quantity demanded.
- (c) the price elasticity of demand is infinity.
- (d) any change in price is perfectly matched by a change in quantity demanded.
- (e) quantity demanded does not change in response to any price change.

12. **A decrease in income by 10 percent leads to a decrease in quantity demanded by 5 percent; the income elasticity of demand is therefore**
- (a) –0.5.
- (b) 2.0.
- (c) 0.5.
- (d) 50.0.
- (e) 15.0.

*13. A commodity is classified as a normal good if
  (a) a decrease in consumer income results in a decrease in demand.
  (b) it is consumed by a majority of the population.
  (c) its price and quantity demanded are negatively related, *ceteris paribus*.
  (d) an increase in its price leads to an increase in quantity supplied.
  (e) a decrease in consumer income results in an increase in demand.

14. If an individual allocates $200 as monthly expenditure on compact discs and decides to spend no more and no less regardless of price, this individual's demand for compact discs is
  (a) perfectly inelastic.   (b) perfectly elastic.
  (c) of unit elasticity.   (d) less than one but greater than zero.
  (e) of zero elasticity.

15. A shift in demand would not affect price when supply is
  (a) perfectly inelastic.   (b) perfectly elastic.
  (c) of unit elasticity.   (d) a straight line through the origin.
  (e) of zero elasticity.

*16. The producers' share of the burden of a sales tax will be greater
  (a) the more elastic is supply.   (b) the more inelastic is supply.
  (c) the more elastic is demand.   (d) the more inelastic is demand.
  (e) Both (b) and (c) are correct.

*17. Suppose the market supply curve is upward sloping. If the imposition of a sales tax causes no change in the price consumers pay, the good's demand curve must be _____, implying that the burden of the tax is _____.
  (a) vertical; entirely borne by producers
  (b) horizontal; entirely borne by consumers
  (c) perfectly inelastic; shared equally by consumers and producers
  (d) perfectly elastic; entirely borne by producers
  (e) downward sloping; shared by consumers and producers

18. If two goods have a negative cross-price elasticity of demand, we know that
  (a) they are both inferior goods.
  (b) they are substitutes.
  (c) they are both normal goods.
  (d) they are complementary goods.
  (e) one is inferior and the other is normal, but we can't determine which is which.

*19. Pizza and hamburgers are likely to have
  (a) a positive cross elasticity of demand.
  (b) positive income elasticities of demand.
  (c) a negative cross elasticity of demand.
  (d) price elasticities of demand greater than one.
  (e) a cross elasticity of demand equal to zero.

*20. A commodity with an income elasticity equal to –0.5
    (a)   is said to have an inelastic demand.
    (b)   is an inferior good.
    (c)   is a complementary good.
    (d)   has a downward sloping demand curve.
    (e)   has a demand curve with a constant slope of 0.5 in absolute terms.

Elasticity at a Point on the Demand Curve

Questions 21 to 24 are mainly intended for students covering material in *Additional Topics: Some Further Details About Demand Elasticity* on MyEconLab. They use elasticity at a point on the demand curve (the *point elasticity* of demand) rather than the elasticity between two points (the *arc elasticity* of demand). Point elasticity is very useful for showing how elasticity changes along a straight-line demand curve (as in Exercise 6) and for comparing elasticities between different demand curves (as in Extension Exercise E4).

The elasticity formula in the text can be rearranged to give $\eta_d = (P/Q)/(\Delta P/\Delta Q)$, which is the price/quantity ratio at a point divided by the slope of the demand curve. It can also be written as $\eta_d = (P/Q) \times (\Delta Q/\Delta P)$, which is the P/Q ratio multiplied by the inverse of the slope.

Use the following figure to answer Questions 21 to 23.

Figure 4-10

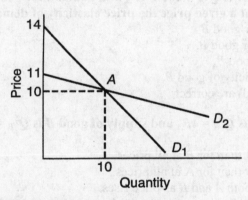

Example Question: What is the elasticity for D_1 at point A?
At A both P and $Q = 10$, so $P/Q = 1$. The constant slope along the straight-line demand curve D_1 is the change in price from \$14 to \$10 (so $\Delta P = 4$) divided by the change in quantity from 0 to 10 (so $\Delta Q = 10$), giving the slope $(\Delta P/\Delta Q) = 4/10 = 0.4$. At point A, therefore, $\eta_d = (P/Q)/(\Delta P/\Delta Q) = 1/0.4 = 2.5$.

21. The point elasticity of demand for D_2 at point A is
    (a)   0.1.   (b)   2.5.
    (c)   1.0.   (d)   10.0.
    (e)   4.0.

*22. At a price of \$10, demand curve D_1
    (a)   has the same elasticity as any other point along D_1.
    (b)   is more elastic than at any other price below \$10.
    (c)   is more elastic than D_2.
    (d)   is inelastic.
    (e)   None of the above.

23. **Starting from point *A*, a 10 percent reduction in price along D_1 will result in an increase in quantity demanded of**
   (a)   25 percent.   (b)   100 percent.
   (c)   10 percent   (d)   1 percent.
   (e)   2.5 percent.

*24. **If two demand curves have the same price–axis intercept but different slopes, then at a given price**
   (a)   the one with the flatter slope is more elastic.
   (b)   they have the same elasticity.
   (c)   the one with the steeper slope is more elastic.
   (d)   they are both unit elastic regardless of price.
   (e)   the relative elasticities are unknown, because elasticity is different at each price.

Elasticity Using Equations

These questions are intended for courses that use equations to describe the demand and supply functions, and Questions 25 to 27 use point price elasticity (explained before Question 21 above). For demand equation $Q^D = a - bP$, the slope is 1/b and price elasticity of demand at a specific price is $\eta = (P/Q)/(1/b)$ or $\eta = (P/Q) \times (b)$. For supply equation $Q^S = c + dP$, the slope is 1/d and price elasticity of supply is $\eta = (P/Q)/(1/d)$ or $\eta = (P/Q) \times (d)$.

*25. **If demand for good *A* is $Q^D_A = 200 - 1P_A$ and demand for good *B* is $Q^D_B = 100 - 0.5P_B$, at a given price the price elasticity of demand for good *A* is**
   (a)   the same as for good *B*
   (b)   greater than for good *B*.
   (c)   less than for good *B*.
   (d)   twice the elasticity of good *B*.
   (e)   Both (b) and (d) are correct.

*26. **If supply of good *A* is $Q^S_A = 4P_A$ and supply of good *B* is $Q^S_B = 2P_B$, the price elasticity of supply**
   (a)   is greater for *A* than for *B* at all prices.
   (b)   is greater for *B* than for A at all prices.
   (c)   decreases for both *A* and *B* as price rises.
   (d)   equals unity at all prices on both supply curves.
   (e)   increases for both *A* and *B* as price rises.

*27. **Along the same linear demand curve, elasticity of demand (i) between *P* = \$10 and *P* = \$8, (ii) between *P* = \$12 and *P* = \$6, and (iii) at *P* = \$9**
   (a)   is the same for all three cases.
   (b)   is greater between *P* = \$12 and *P* = \$6 than for the other two cases.
   (c)   is smaller at *P* = \$9 than for the other two cases.
   (d)   is the same at *P* = \$9 as between *P* = \$10 and *P* = \$8, but both are greater than between *P* = \$12 and *P* = \$6.
   (e)   cannot be compared, because quantity demanded and change in quantity demanded are unknown.

*28. The demand function for widgets is $Q^D = a - b_1P - b_2Y - b_3P_A$, where P is the price of widgets, Y is average household income, and P_A is the price of ayogs. This function says

(a) widgets are a Giffen good.

(b) widgets are an inferior good, and ayogs and widgets are substitute goods.

(c) widgets are a normal good, and ayogs and widgets are substitute goods.

(d) widgets are a normal good, and ayogs and widgets are complementary goods.

(e) widgets are an inferior good, and ayogs and widgets are complementary goods.

Solutions

Chapter Review

1.(a) 2.(d) 3.(b) 4.(d) 5.(b) 6.(a) 7.(d) 8.(e) 9.(a) 10.(c) 11.(d) 12.(a) 13.(a) 14.(d) 15.(b) 16.(e) 17.(e) 18.(c) 19.(d) 20.(c) 21.(e) 22.(a)

Short-Answer Questions

1. For substitutes, price and demand move in the same direction (e.g., an increase in the price of cola increases demand for Sprite). For complements, they move in opposite directions (e.g., an increase in price of CDs reduces demand for CD players).

2. No. These are the same absolute changes but different percentage changes. $100 is a much smaller percentage change in the price of automobiles than in the price of TV sets, and 50 000 is a bigger percentage of automobile sales than of TV sales. Thus there would be a bigger percentage change in quantity demanded and a smaller percentage change in price for automobiles than TV sets, hence a larger elasticity of demand for automobiles. [*Note:* Since these numbers are purely hypothetical, so are the conclusions about relative elasticities of automobiles and TV sets in the real world.]

3. Kit-Kat bars have a significantly bigger price elasticity of demand, since there are many more close substitutes for a particular type of candy than for candy as a whole.

4. In everyday language, a necessity is something a person "can't do without." In economics, it is a commodity with an income elasticity of demand that is positive but less than unity: a likely example is eggs or some other food staple. People can do without eggs, but the income elasticity of demand likely is quite small.

5. For consumers to bear such a high burden of the tax, demand would have to be much less elastic than supply. If demand were *inelastic* (i.e., price elasticity less than 1), spending on beer would increase, leaving *less* money to spend on food and clothing. [*Note:* The policy could work in the longer term if the long-run demand curve for beer were more elastic than the short-run demand, but this would not change the inconsistency in Mr. Quitit's reasoning.]

6. **(a)** down; **(b)** none; **(c)** 1; **(d)** down; **(e)** up

7. On the demand curve $Q^D = 46 - 0.2P$, the midpoint at which elasticity = 1 and revenue is maximized is at 23 (000) riders. The revenue-maximizing price is $0.2P = 23$ cents, $P = 115$ cents ($1.15). The current fare of $1.30 is greater than $1.15, so it is on the *elastic* part of the demand curve. Raising price would reduce revenue (i.e., expenditure of riders), not increase it. You should advise the CTA to *reduce* the fare to $1.15.

Exercises

1. **(a)** $\eta = 2.0 = (20\ 000/500 \times 2500/50\ 000)$; elastic demand (i.e., >1).

   (b) Elasticity of unity – constant expenditure means $\%\Delta Q = \%\Delta P$.

(c) Perfectly inelastic demand (elasticity = 0). The percentage change in Q is zero, and zero divided by anything is zero.

(d) η cannot be determined because the demand curve has shifted—i.e., other things are <u>not</u> constant (*ceteris paribus* condition violated).

(e) The 20 000 change (from 90 000 to 70 000) is 25 percent of the 80 000 average. $\eta = (\%\Delta Q/\%\Delta P) = 25/10 = 2.5$. Since $2.5 > 1$, demand is elastic.

(f) Perfectly inelastic demand. For a 5 percent fall in price to reduce expenditure by 5 percent, quantity must be unchanged. $\eta = (\%\Delta Q/\%\Delta P) = 0/5 = 0$.

(g) η can't be determined because the demand curve shifts—so all other things are *not* constant (i.e., the *ceteris paribus* condition is violated).

(h) $\eta = (\%\Delta Q/\%\Delta P) = 25/0 = $ infinity (undefined). Demand is perfectly elastic.

2. (a) **Figure 4-11**

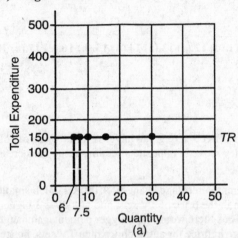
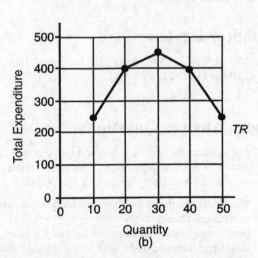

(b) <u>Panel (a):</u> Multiplying P by Q at each price gives the same total expenditure at every point on the demand curve. A constant expenditure means that the percentage rise in Q equals the percentage fall in P, so the price elasticity of demand ($\%\Delta Q/\%\Delta P$) must equal unity all along this demand curve.

<u>Panel (b):</u> Since total expenditure increases as price falls from $25 to $20 to $15, demand is elastic over this range. Total expenditure is at its maximum value of $450 when price equals $15; this corresponds to unit elasticity. As price decreases from $15 to $10 and then to $5, total revenue falls so demand is inelastic along this portion of the demand curve.

3. (a) The following measures express elasticity as $(\Delta Q/\Delta P) \times (P_A/Q_A)$, where Q_A and P_A are the average quantity and price, respectively, and $(\Delta Q/\Delta P)$ is the reciprocal (inverse) of the slope.
$A–B$, $\eta = (100/10)(65/50) = (10)(1.3) = 13.0$;
$B–C$, $\eta = (200/20)(50/200) = (10)(0.25) = 2.5$;
$C–D$, $\eta = (200/20)(30/400) = (10)(0.075) = 0.75$;
$D–E$, $\eta = (200/20)(10/600) = (10)(0.0167) = 0.167$.
[*Note:* In all cases the reciprocal of the slope is 10, so the slope = 1/10 = 0.1.]

(b) $\eta = (\Delta Q/\Delta P)(P_A/Q_A) = (100/10)(35/350) = 1.0$. Over this price range, demand is unit elastic so total expenditure is constant. With further reductions in price, total expenditure will decline as we move into the inelastic portion of the demand curve.

4. **Figure 4-12**

(a)

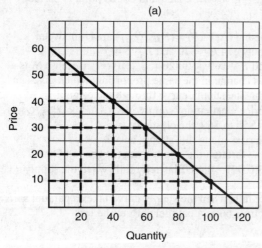

(b)

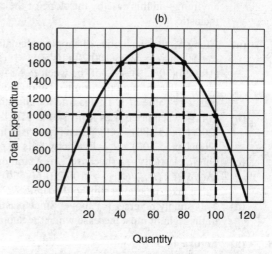

(a) At $P = \$40$ and $Q = 40$, TE $= P \times Q = 40(40) = \$1600$. At $P = \$20$ and $Q = 80$,
TE $= P \times Q = 20(80) = \$1600$. [*Note:* TE is constant because the average $P = (40 + 20)/2 = 30$,
and $P = \$30$ is the midpoint of the demand curve, where $\eta = 1$. Similarly, the average
$Q = (40 + 80)/2 = 60$, which is the midpoint of the demand curve read from the quantity axis.]

(b) Calculating elasticity this way would give $\eta = (\Delta Q/Q)/(\Delta P/P) = (40/40)/(20/40) = 1(0.5) = 2$.
This would imply an elastic demand, meaning that expenditure would increase when price fell
from \$40 to \$20. But this is not consistent because expenditure remains constant at \$1600.

(c) This method would give $\eta = (\Delta Q/Q)/(\Delta P/P) = (40/80)/(20/20) = 1(0.5) = 0.5$. This would imply
an inelastic demand, meaning that expenditure would decrease when price increased from \$20 to
\$40. Again, this is not consistent with a constant expenditure of \$1600.

(d) In this case $\eta = (\Delta Q/Q_{AVE})/(\Delta P/P_{AVE}) = (40/60)/(20/30) = 0.67/0.67 = 1$. This says demand is unit
elastic between \$40 and \$20, meaning expenditure should remain unchanged, which it does. This
is consistent. Elasticity calculated using the average values of P and Q, therefore, gives the
correct prediction for the change in total expenditure.

(e) At $P = \$50$, $Q = 20$ and TE $= 50 \times 20 = \$1000$. At $P = \$10$, $Q = 100$ and TE $= 10 \times 100 = \$1000$.
Total expenditure is constant, which is consistent with $\eta = (\Delta Q/Q_{AVE})/(\Delta P/P_{AVE}) =$
$(80/60)/(40/30) = 1.33/1.33 = 1$.

(f) average; the same

5. (a) $\eta = (\Delta Q/Q_{AVE})/(\Delta P/P_{AVE}) = (20/40)/(10/40) = 0.5/0.25 = 2$

(b) $\Delta P/\Delta Q = (45 - 35)/(30 - 50) = 10/-20 = (-) 0.5$. [*Note:* The negative sign in parentheses shows
the demand curve has a negative slope, but we are using absolute values for elasticity.]

(c) $P_{AVE}/Q_{AVE} = 40/40 = 1$. $(P_{AVE}/Q_{AVE})/(\Delta P/\Delta Q) = 1/0.5 = 2$. This is exactly the same as the value of
elasticity calculated in (a).

(d) $(P/Q)/(\Delta P/\Delta Q) = (20/80)/0.5 = 0.25/0.5 = 0.5$. Yes. Elasticity of demand *between* \$25 and \$15, or
between \$30 and \$10, is exactly the same as elasticity *at* \$20. This is because (i) the slope
$(\Delta P/\Delta Q)$ is the same at all points on the linear demand curve, and (ii) the average price and
quantity (i.e., \$20 and 80, respectively) are the same over both price ranges.

6. (a) Since the slope of the ray $(P/Q) =$ the slope of the curve $(\Delta P/\Delta Q)$, elasticity $= (P/Q)/(\Delta P/\Delta Q) = 1$.

(b) Above the midpoint, the slope of the ray is greater than the slope of the curve, so $(P/Q)/(\Delta P/\Delta Q)$
is greater than unity, and demand is elastic.

(c) Below the midpoint, the slope of the ray is less than the slope of the curve, so $(P/Q)/(\Delta P/\Delta Q)$ is
less than unity, and demand is inelastic.

(d) Quantity demanded is zero when price is at the value where the demand curve meets the vertical
axis. Here, the ray from the origin is the vertical axis, with a slope of infinity (undefined).
Dividing infinity by anything—in this case the slope of the curve—gives infinity. Demand at this
point is perfectly elastic.

(e) Here, the ray from the origin is the horizontal axis, with a slope of zero. Dividing zero by anything—in this case by the slope of the curve—gives zero. Demand at this point is perfectly inelastic.

7. (a) Along S_1, the elasticities of supply calculated using $(\Delta Q/\Delta P) \times (P_{AVE}/Q_{AVE})$ are (i) between $P = \$0$ and $P = \$20$, $(100/20)(10/50) = 1$; (ii) between $P = \$20$ and $P = \$40$, $(100/20)(30/150) = 1$; (iii) between $P = \$40$ and $P = \$60$, $(100/20)(50/250) = 1$. Because S_1 is a straight line through the origin, P and Q always change in the same proportion, which gives an elasticity value of 1. This is true for any straight-line supply curve through the origin.

(b) For S_2, when price rises from $40 to $50, the price elasticity of supply is $(\Delta Q/\Delta P) \times (P_{AVE}/Q_{AVE}) = (200/10)(45/300) = 3.0$. When price rises from $50 to $60, the elasticity is $(200/10)(55/500) = 2.2$. Elasticity falls as price rises along this supply curve.

(c) On S_1, elasticity = 1 (because S_1 is a straight line through the origin—see (a) above). On S_3, $(\Delta Q/\Delta P) \times (P_{AVE}/Q_{AVE}) = (100/20)(50/550) = 5(0.09) = 0.45$. Elasticity falls when the supply curve takes a parallel shift to the right.

(d) This simply reverses (c) above. Since elasticity falls when the supply curve takes a parallel shift to the right, it must increase when the supply curve takes a parallel shift to the left.

8. (a) **Figure 4-13**

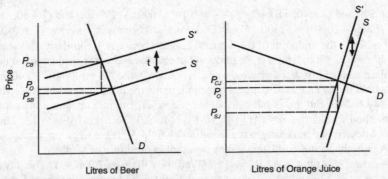

Litres of Beer   Litres of Orange Juice

(b) The tax on beer is borne primarily by consumers. The relative slopes of the demand and supply curves in this market suggest that the demand for beer is relatively inelastic, while its supply is relatively elastic.

(c) The tax on orange juice is borne primarily by producers. Demand in this market is relatively elastic, while supply is relatively inelastic.

(d) Neither. The difference between consumer and seller prices is the same $\$t$ in each market.

9. **Figure 4-14**

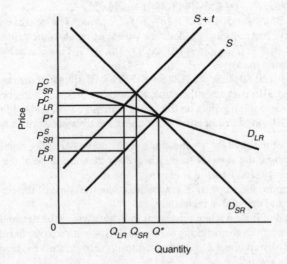

(a) See Figure 4-14.

(b) The effect on equilibrium quantity is greater in the long run, because demand is more elastic in the long run than in the short run (so quantity demanded is more sensitive to changes in price in the long run).

(c) Incidence is greater on the consumer in the short run than in the long run. Because the short-run demand curve is less elastic (or more inelastic) than the long-run demand curve, short-run prices "overshoot" their long-run equilibrium values.

(d) Because the short-run demand is inelastic over the relevant range, the increase in consumer price increases expenditure on cigarettes. The long-run demand curve is less inelastic, causing a smaller increase in consumer spending on cigarettes. If the long-run demand actually is elastic, consumer spending on cigarettes will fall (i.e., less spending on cigarettes than at the pre-tax equilibrium).

(e) No. There is a relatively small reduction in smoking, and the increase in spending on cigarettes will leave less money available to spend on other things, thereby reducing the standard of living of families with smokers.

(f) Likely it will. Because long-run demand is more elastic, there is a bigger fall in smoking and the tax incidence on consumers falls too. If the long-run demand is actually elastic (e.g., because it takes smokers some time to "kick the habit," and the higher prices deter the start of smoking among new younger generations), spending on cigarettes will fall.

Extension Exercises

E1. **(a)** Elasticity measures are calculated under the *ceteris paribus* assumption that other factors affecting demand are unchanged. Between periods 4 and 5, not only has income changed, but so have the prices of x and y.

(b) Periods (1) to (2), price elasticity for

$$x = -\frac{9-10}{28-25} \times \frac{(28+25)/2}{(9+10)/2} = 0.93$$

Periods (2) to (3), price elasticity for

$$y = -\frac{35-40}{15-10} \times \frac{(15+10)/2}{(35+40)/2} = 0.33$$

Periods (3) to (4), income elasticity for

$$x = \frac{9-8}{11\ 000-10\ 000} \times \frac{(11\ 000+10\ 000)/2}{(9+8)/2} = 1.24$$

Periods (3) to (4), income elasticity for

$$y = \frac{36-35}{11\ 000-10\ 000} \times \frac{(11\ 000+10\ 000)/2}{(36+35)/2} = 0.30$$

Periods (1) to (2), cross elasticity of demand for y with respect to the price of

$$x = \frac{40-42}{28-25} \times \frac{(28+25)/2}{(40+42)/2} = -0.43$$

Periods (2) to (3), cross elasticity of demand for x with respect to the price of

$$y = \frac{8-9}{15-10} \times \frac{(15+10)/2}{(8+9)/2} = -0.29$$

E2. **(a)** 1 and 6.　　　　　　　**(b)** 4.

　　　(c) 5.　　　　　　　　　　**(d)** 2.

　　　(e) 3.　　　　　　　　　　**(f)** 6.

E3. **(a)** Setting $Q^D = Q^S$ makes $200 - 0.5P = 20 + 0.25P$, so $0.75P = 180$ and $P = \$240$

$Q_E = 200 - 0.5(240) = 200 = 120 = 80$, and $Q_E = 20 + 0.25(240) = 80$

(b) $Q_S = 20 + 0.25(P_C - 60) = 20 - 0.25(60) - 0.25P_C = 5 + 0.25P_C$

(c) $200 - 0.5P_C = 5 + 0.25P_C$, $0.75P_C = 195$, $P_C = 195/0.75 = \$260$

$\Delta P_C = 260 - 240 = \$20$. $P_S = P_C - t = 260 - 60 = \$200$. $\Delta P_S = 200 - 240 = (-)\$40$

$\Delta P_C/t = 20/60 = 1/3$ (incidence of tax on consumers)

$\Delta P_S/t = 40/60 = 2/3$ (incidence of tax on suppliers)

(d) $Q^D = 200 - 0.5(260) = 200 - 130 = 70$, and $Q^S = 20 + 0.25(200) = 70$. Since $Q^D = Q^S = 70$, this is the new equilibrium. The change in equilibrium quantity is $\Delta Q_E = 70 - 80 = -10$ (i.e., a reduction of 10 units as a result of the tax).

(e) $(1/b)/(1/b + 1/d) = (1/0.5)/(1/0.5 + 1/0.25) = 2/6 = 1/3$. You have seen this before in (c) above—it is the incidence of the tax on consumers. Multiplying by the amount of the tax gives $1/3(t) = 1/3(\$60) = \$20$. You also saw this in (c)—it is the increase in the price paid by consumers (ΔP_C). The general equation for ΔP_C is

$$\Delta P_c = \frac{\dfrac{1}{b}}{\dfrac{1}{b} + \dfrac{1}{d}} \bullet t$$

(f) $(1/d)/(1/b + 1/d) = (1/0.25)/(1/0.5 + 1/0.25) = 4/6 = 2/3$. Multiplying by the tax gives $2/3(t) = 2/3(\$60) = \$40$. You also saw these values in (c) above: \$40 is the fall in price retained by suppliers (ΔP_S), and 2/3 is the incidence of the tax on suppliers. The general form of the equation for ΔP_S is

$$\Delta P_s = \frac{\dfrac{1}{d}}{\dfrac{1}{b} + \dfrac{1}{d}} \bullet t$$

(g) The easiest way to show the effect is to increase 1/b (the slope of the demand curve) and decrease 1/d (the slope of the supply curve) by exactly the same amount. Thus, the denominator in the ΔP_C and ΔP_S equations (i.e., 1/d + 1/b) is unchanged. Looking only at the numerators, therefore, the increase in 1/b increases ΔP_C and the decrease in 1/d reduces ΔP_S. The incidence of the tax on consumers rises and the incidence on suppliers falls. The blanks in the statement are: suppliers; smaller; demanders.

(h) $\$60/6 = 10$. You saw this number in (d) above—it is the change in equilibrium quantity as a result of the tax. The general form of the equation for this change is

$$\Delta Q_E = \frac{t}{\dfrac{1}{b} + \dfrac{1}{d}}$$

From this equation you see ΔQ_E would *not* change because 1/b + 1/d would be unchanged. The spaces in the statement should be filled in with "sum of" and "relative."

E4. $Q^D = 200 - 2P$; $\eta = (P/Q) \times 2$;

Price	Quantity	η_d	Description	Expenditure as Price Falls	Expenditure as Price Rises
$100	0	Infinite	perfectly elastic	increases	P can't rise
$ 80	40	4	elastic	increases	decreases
$ 60	80	1.5	elastic	increases	decreases
$ 50	100	1	unit-elastic	decreases	increases
$ 40	120	2/3	inelastic	decreases	increases
$ 20	160	0.25	inelastic	decreases	increases
$ 0	200	0	perfectly inelastic	P can't fall	increases

E5. D_0: $Q = 30 - P$ D_1: $Q = 40 - 2P$ D_2: $Q = 60 - 2P$ D_3: $Q = 80 - 2P$

    (a) The completed table is:

Curve	Price	Quantity	Slope	Elasticity
D_0	\$10	20	1	$(10/20)1 = 0.5$
D_1	\$10	20	$1/2 = 0.5$	$(10/20)2 = 1$
D_2	\$10	40	$1/2 = 0.5$	$(10/40)2 = 0.5$
D_3	\$10	60	$1/2 = 0.5$	$(10/60)2 = 0.33$

    b)   (i) flatter; more (or steeper; less) (ii) the same as (iii) falls (iv) less; regardless of

Additional Multiple-Choice Questions

1.(a) **2.**(b) **3.**(c) **4.**(a) **5.**(d) **6.**(d) **7.**(c) **8.**(a) **9.**(d) **10.**(d) **11.**(e) **12.**(c) **13.**(a) **14.**(c) **15.**(b). **16.**(e) **17.**(d) **18.**(d) **19.**(a) **20.**(b) **Point Elasticity:** **21.**(d) **22.**(b) **23.**(a) **24.**(b) **Using Equations:** **25.**(a) **26.**(d) **27.**(a) **28.**(e)

Explanations for the Asterisked Multiple-Choice Questions

1.(a)   Since $\%\Delta Q^D/\%\Delta P = 2$, then $\%\Delta Q^D/2 = 2$, so $\%\Delta Q^D = 2 \times 2 = 4$.

2.(b)   Moving up or down this vertical demand curve, P changes but Q^d does not. Since the absolute $\Delta Q^d = 0$ then the $\%\Delta Q^d = 0$ too, so $\eta = \%\Delta Q^d/\%\Delta P = 0/\%\Delta P = 0$ (zero).

3.(c)   Moving down the demand curve, a constant <u>absolute</u> change in P is a bigger <u>percentage</u> change of the lower price. Since the level of Q gets higher and higher as P falls, the absolute ΔQ^d must increase to get the higher $\%\Delta Q^d$ needed to match the higher $\%\Delta P$ and keep $\%\Delta Q^d = \%\Delta P$. Thus the constant ΔP requires an increasing ΔQ^d to keep $\eta = 1$, so $\Delta P/\Delta Q^d$ must get smaller and smaller. Since $\Delta P/\Delta Q^d$ is the slope, then the slope must get less and less—i.e., the curve gets flatter and flatter. [*Note:* Not all demand curves with variable slopes will *necessarily* have $\eta = 1$, so how do we know this one does? Notice that the area under the curve is the same at each and every combination of P and Q. The area under the curve is (desired) consumer expenditure on the product (i.e., P multiplied by Q). A fall in P and a rise in Q will cause no change in expenditure <u>*only when*</u> the percentage changes are equal—i.e., only when $\%\Delta Q^d = \%\Delta P$.]

4.(a)   Moving right or left along this horizontal demand curve, Q^d changes but P does not. Since the absolute $\Delta P = 0$ then the $\%\Delta P = 0$ too, so $\eta = \%\Delta Q^d/\%\Delta P = \%\Delta Q^d/0 = \infty$ (infinity, or "undefined").

5.(d)   Since the demand curve is downward-sloping with a constant slope, a constant *absolute* ΔP generates a constant *absolute* ΔQ. Moving down the demand curve, however, a constant absolute ΔP at lower and lower levels of P gives <u>a higher and higher</u> *percentage* ΔP. Conversely, a constant absolute ΔQ at higher and higher levels of Q gives a <u>lower and lower</u> *percentage* ΔQ. To see what happens to price elasticity as price continues to fall along the demand curve, divide the lower and lower $\%\Delta Q^d$ by the higher and higher $\%\Delta P$ and you see that $\eta = \%\Delta Q^d/\%\Delta P$ must fall. [*Note:* Along the straight-line demand curve, elasticity falls from ∞ (infinity) where the demand curve intersects the price axis to 0 (zero) where it intersects the quantity axis. To understand why, check the <u>percentage</u> increase in Q^d when it increases from zero to positive, and the <u>percentage</u> increase in P when it increases from zero to positive, and then see what $\%\Delta Q^d/\%\Delta P$ must be in each case.]

6.(d)   Because 1.2 exceeds unity, demand is elastic. An increase in price reduces total expenditure when demand is elastic, because the percentage fall in quantity demanded exceeds the percentage rise in price.

7.(c)   With unit elasticity the percentage increase/decrease in price equals the percentage decrease/increase in quantity demanded, so total spending on the good is unchanged—e.g., any reduction in spending attributable to the lower price is *exactly offset* by the increase in spending attributable to the increase amount demanded (so (b) is wrong). To have unit elasticity with a 1 percent *decrease* in quantity (answer (a)) would require both an increase in price (whereas the question says price *falls*) and the price increase to be by 1 percent (which the question does not specify), so (a) is wrong for two reasons (hence (e) is also wrong). Finally, elasticity requires comparing *percentage* changes, not *unit* changes, so (d) is wrong.

9.(d) The $4 price change is 50 percent of the average price of $8. The 100 increase in Q^S is 28.6 percent of the average of 350. So $\%\Delta Q^S/\%\Delta P = 28.6/50 = 0.57$ is less than 1, so supply is inelastic.

10.(d) The $2 reduction in price from $10 to $8 is 22 percent of the $9 average, and the resulting 50 fall in quantity supplied is 13 percent of the 375 average, for an elasticity of $13/22 = 0.59$, which is less than 1 so supply is inelastic here (so answers (a) and (c) are wrong). The $2 reduction in price from $4 to $2 is 67 percent of the $3 average, and the resulting 150 fall in quantity supplied is 120 percent of the 125 average, for an elasticity of $120/67 = 1.8$, which exceeds 1 so demand is elastic here (so answer (b) is wrong). Comparing the two price ranges, not only does the value of elasticity change (so answer (e) is wrong) but it varies between elastic and inelastic depending on the price range chosen (as answer (d) states).

13.(a) Income and demand move in the same direction for a normal good, so a decrease in income decreases demand. Answers (b), (c), and (d) are obviously wrong, because they refer to a change in price rather than a change in income.

16.(e) First, for a <u>given supply curve</u>, the more elastic (i.e., the less inelastic) is *demand* then the greater the reduction in quantity demanded as consumer price rises because of the tax. The greater reduction in quantity demanded means a bigger movement <u>along the supply curve</u> and so a bigger fall in the associated supplier price—i.e., *a greater "burden" of the tax on suppliers when demand is more elastic/less inelastic.* So answer (c) is correct, while answer (d) is wrong. [*Note:* On Figure 4-14 in the answer to Exercise 9, see that the fall in the supplier price between the equilibrium with and without the tax is greater using the *flatter* D curve.] Next, for a <u>given demand curve</u>, the less elastic (i.e., the more inelastic) is *supply* then the less the reduction in quantity supplied as supplier price falls because of the tax. The smaller reduction in quantity supplied means a smaller movement <u>along the demand curve</u> and so a smaller rise in the associated consumer price. Since the sum of the fall in supplier price plus the rise in consumer price must equal the amount of the tax at the new equilibrium, then a smaller rise in the consumer price must also mean a bigger fall in the supplier price—i.e., *a greater "burden" of the tax on suppliers when supply is less elastic/more inelastic.* So answer (a) is wrong and answer (b) is correct. [*Note:* On Figure 4-13 in the answer to Exercise 8, see that the fall in the supplier price between the equilibrium with and without the tax is greater using the *steeper* S curve.] Thus, as answer (e) states, both answers (c) and (d) are correct. [*Note:* For students covering *Extensions in Theory 4-1,* Extension Exercise E3 gives a mathematical proof of the answer.]

17.(d) The incidence depends on the relative elasticities of demand and supply, so there are only two cases where the entire incidence is on suppliers (i.e., no change in the price paid by demanders). One case is where supply is sufficiently inelastic as to be perfectly inelastic, but this is ruled out because the question says that the supply curve is upward-sloping. The other case is where demand is sufficiently elastic as to be perfectly elastic. The combination of the upward-sloping supply curve and no change in consumer price, therefore, means demand must be perfectly elastic.

19.(a) Since the two fast foods are substitutes in consumption, an increase in the price of one will increase demand for the other. Since price and demand both move in the same direction, the ratio of their percentage changes is a positive number. The cross elasticities of demand between pizzas and hamburgers, therefore, are positive.

20.(b) The negative sign on the income elasticity of –0.5 says that an *increase* in income *reduces* demand for the good—i.e., it is an inferior good. "Inelastic demand" is shorthand for *price* elasticity being inelastic, so answer (a) is wrong. When *two* goods are complementary to each other they have a negative *cross elasticity* of demand, so answer (c) is wrong. A downward-sloping demand curve requires a negative *price* elasticity of demand, so answer (d) is wrong. A demand curve with a constant slope of 0.5 in *absolute* terms simply describes a *straight-line* downward-sloping demand curve, hence a negative but varying *price* elasticity, so answer (e) is also wrong. Thus, while all answers other than (b) refer to situations of *negative* elasticity, they say nothing at all about *income-elasticity* of demand.

22.(b) On a straight-line downward-sloping demand curve, the (absolute value of) price elasticity of demand falls continually as price falls, so answer (b) is correct and answers (a) and (e) are wrong. [Using $\eta_d = (P/Q)/(\Delta P/\Delta Q)$, as price falls the slope $\Delta P/\Delta Q$ is unchanged but P/Q falls, so $(P/Q)/(\Delta P/\Delta Q)$ falls.] Answer (c) is wrong because at point A the ratio P/Q is the same on both curves but the slope $\Delta P/\Delta Q$ is greater on D_1 than on D_2, so $\eta_d = (P/Q)/(\Delta P/\Delta Q)$ is *less* on D_1 than D_2. Finally, since D_1 is a straight-line downward-sloping demand curve, it is *price-elastic* at all points above the midpoint ($P = \$5.50$) so answer (d) is wrong. [*Note:* Practise this with Exercise 6.]

24.(b) *Additional Topics: Some Further Details About Demand Elasticity* on MyEconLab proves that, for a straight-line downward-sloping demand curve, a "quick method" for finding the point price elasticity is to divide the price by the difference between that price and the price–axis intercept of the demand curve—i.e., at any given P_X, $\eta_d = P_X / (P_{INTERCEPT} - P_X)$. If P_X is the same on both D curves and $P_{INTERCEPT}$ is the same on both, then η_d is the same *regardless* of differences in slope. [*Note:* The flatter demand curve *would* be more elastic if, as in Figure 4-10, the two crossed at a *positive Q*. The flatter demand curve would then have a smaller $P_{INTERCEPT}$ than the steeper one, giving a smaller ($P_{INTERCEPT} - P_X$) and so a bigger $P_X / (P_{INTERCEPT} - P_X)$: more elastic at P_X. In this question, however, because the two demand curves have the same price intercept they cross at $Q = 0$. If you are confused by this, review Extension Exercise E5.]

25.(a) The two linear demand curves ($Q^D = a - bP$) have the same price–axis intercept (a/b)—i.e., $200/1 = 200$ for Q^D_A and $100/0.5 = 200$ for Q^D_B, and in such cases the elasticity is the same at a given price. To prove this, take any P and calculate both point price elasticities using $\eta = (P/Q) \times (b)$. For example, at $P = \$150$ then $\eta_A = (P/Q^D_A) \times (b) = (150/50) \times 1 = 3$ and $\eta_B = (P/Q^D_B) \times (b) = (150/25) \times 0.5 = 3$. Alternatively, applying the formula $\eta_d = P_X / (P_{INTERCEPT} - P_X)$ explained in the answer to Question 24 above, at $P = \$150$ you get $\eta_d = 150/(200 - 150) = 3$ in both cases.

26.(d) Both supply curves are straight lines through the origin (i.e., have a *zero* price–axis intercept), so price and quantity always change in the same proportion—i.e., elasticity is unity all along each curve. (See Exercise 7(a)) To prove this, if you choose any P and apply the formula for the point elasticity of supply, $\eta = (P/Q)/(1/d)$, you will see that the ratio (P/Q) always equals the slope $(1/d)$.

27.(a) All three cases have the same average price (\$9) and, therefore, the same average quantity. Along a linear demand curve, elasticity at the average price and quantity is unaffected by the magnitude of the change around the average. Elasticity $= (\Delta Q / \Delta P) \times (P_{AVE}/Q_{AVE})$ and $\Delta Q / \Delta P$ is the same all along the straight line. Since P_{AVE}/Q_{AVE} is also the same in all three cases, then elasticity must be the same. The arc elasticities in cases (i) and (ii) are the same as the point elasticity in case (iii). (See Exercise 5.)

28.(e) The negative sign on P means that the demand curve is downward-sloping, so widgets are not a Giffen good. The negative sign on Y means that an increase in income reduces the demand for widgets, so widgets are an inferior good. The negative sign on P_A means that an increase in P_A reduces the demand for widgets, so the two are complementary goods.

Markets in Action

Chapter Overview

This chapter gives you practice in applying the basic principles of supply and demand that were developed in Chapters 3 and 4. The chapter begins with a brief introduction to interactions that occur between markets. The remainder of the chapter extends supply and demand analysis to examine the effects on market efficiency of government intervention in the form of price controls and quotas to restrict output.

Analysis of one market in isolation is called **partial equilibrium analysis**. As you have already seen in your analysis of complementary goods and substitute goods, however, events in one market can impact demand or supply in other markets. But **linkages** between markets can go beyond this; there can be **feedback effects** from the linked market to the market in which the change first occurred, and the supplies of some commodities can be linked in production. Full consideration of all linkages across all markets is called **general equilibrium analysis**, but for most markets partial equilibrium analysis is a legitimate approach and is widely used in introductory economics courses.

Government **price controls** are policies that attempt to hold prices at some disequilibrium value. A *price floor* is a minimum permissible price; when *binding* (or *effective*), price floors result in excess supply. A *price ceiling* is a maximum permissible price; when binding, price ceilings result in excess demand. Price ceilings may also lead to **black markets**.

The effects of strict rent controls (which have been made less strict in recent years) provide a vivid example of the potential effects of a price ceiling. The impacts of rent controls are best understood by distinguishing between the short-run effects and the long-run effects. Not only were the short-run problems created by strict rent controls intensified in the long run, but other problems arose too.

The final section of the chapter explains and applies the concept of **market efficiency** using **economic surplus** as a measure of an individual market's benefit *to society as a whole*. You should understand not only the basic theory and its implications for the types of government intervention in competitive markets that are used as examples, but also its role as one input into the decision-making process. [*Note:* In later chapters this basic analysis of market efficiency is extended to cover producers and consumers separately, market structures other than competitive markets, and situations where government intervention may be desirable and sometimes even necessary.]

Hints and Tips

The following may help you avoid some of the most common errors on examinations.

✓ Recognize that a price control may or may not be *binding*, depending on the type of control and where it is located relative to the uncontrolled market equilibrium. If it is not binding, it will have no effect. For example, a minimum allowable price will have an effect only if it is set above the equilibrium price, while a maximum allowable price will be effective only if set below the equilibrium price.

✓ Understand that a policy that raises the price paid by consumers can increase or decrease total expenditure on the product depending on the elasticity of demand. If demand is inelastic the policy increases consumer spending on the product, but if demand is elastic then consumer spending falls even though price rises. Obviously this has important implications for producers as well as consumers.

✓ Whenever there are forces preventing market pressures from allocating available supply among the demanders, the allocation will be done by other methods. A fundamental issue is whether these other methods give better or worse results, and for whom.

✓ You need to understand the basic analysis of economic surplus and market efficiency in this chapter in order to properly understand its extensions and applications in later chapters. Some of you may be tempted to develop only a superficial understanding of this analysis because the implications of government interventions you see here conflict with your personal views about what should be the role and objectives of government in society. Do *not* succumb to this temptation! Bear in mind that what you are learning here is a first step in the economics of policy analysis: subsequent extensions and applications later in the text will interest you and may even surprise you. Carefully read the final section in the text (*A Cautionary Word*).

Chapter Review

The Interaction Among Markets

Events in one market are often linked to events in other markets. As shown by the cross elasticities of demand in Chapter 4, a change in one market can have an impact on other markets. But *feedback* from these other markets may then alter effects of the change in the first market. This section introduces you to these linkages and feedback effects. In order to predict the effects of the interactions between markets, it is important to understand how and why the markets are linked.

1. **The market for public transportation in Winnipeg is likely to be linked to which of the following markets?**
   (a) Mass transit in Toronto.
   (b) Winnipeg Stock Exchange.
   (c) Mortgage rates in Canada.
   (d) Parking costs in downtown Winnipeg.
   (e) World market for wheat.

2. **Partial equilibrium analysis refers to**
   (a) shifts in the demand curve only.
   (b) shifts in the supply curve only.
   (c) the study of markets where equilibrium can be only partially reached because of government controls.
   (d) the study of all markets together.
   (e) the analysis of a single market in isolation.

3. **Which of the following best describes a major difference between partial-equilibrium and general-equilibrium analysis?**
   (a) In a partial equilibrium, some excess demand or supply remains.
   (b) General-equilibrium analysis generally applies to all commodities, because it assumes all commodities are identical.
   (c) Partial-equilibrium analysis recognizes the impact of changes in exogenous variables but ignores the feedback effects.
   (d) Partial-equilibrium analysis considers only the effect of a change in a good's own price.
   (e) General-equilibrium analysis does not study private markets.

4. **Assume that there is a fixed amount of land suitable for growing vegetables and the demand for squash increases while the demand for carrots remains unchanged. Which of the following is most likely to occur?**
   (a) The price of squash increases, and the price of carrots falls.
   (b) The prices of squash and carrots both increase.
   (c) Farmers produce more carrots to compensate for a lower price of carrots.
   (d) The demand for carrots will eventually increase because carrots and squash are complements in consumption.
   (e) The price of squash will remain unchanged while the price of carrots falls.

Government-Controlled Prices

This section considers two generic forms of price controls: price ceilings and price floors. Ceilings are maximum allowable prices, while floors are minimum allowable prices. When examining a price control you should first determine whether or not it is *binding*, and then consider which groups benefit from the control and which lose from it. After reading this section, you should be able to discuss the implications of excess supply or demand resulting from price controls, and the implications of black markets. [*Note:* The topical issue of health care in Canada is mentioned as a form of price ceiling. Since the consumer price is $0, services are rationed by people "waiting their turn." Canadians paying for treatment in the U.S. because they do not wish to wait are analytically similar to a black market.]

5. **When controls set price at some disequilibrium value, the quantity exchanged**
   (a) is determined by the quantity demanded.
   (b) is determined by the quantity supplied.
   (c) is determined by the greater of quantity demanded and quantity supplied.
   (d) is determined by the lesser of quantity demanded and quantity supplied.
   (e) cannot be determined.

6. **Holding a product's price below its equilibrium level will**
   (a) ensure that everyone obtains the quantity they desire to purchase.
   (b) encourage an increased production of the good.
   (c) result in less of the good being consumed.
   (d) eliminate the incentive for black-market profiteering.
   (e) result in an excess supply of the good.

7. **At a disequilibrium price,**
   (a) profits of sellers are eliminated.
   (b) changes in demand must be matched by changes in supply.
   (c) there are always unsold goods.
   (d) there is always excess demand.
   (e) quantity demanded may be greater than or less than quantity supplied.

8. **Price ceilings above the equilibrium price and price floors below the equilibrium price will both lead to**
   (a) a partial equilibrium but not a general equilibrium.
   (b) black markets.
   (c) an increase in production but a fall in consumption.
   (d) a reduction in quantity exchanged.
   (e) no change in production or consumption.

9. **A black market may occur whenever**
   (a) producers' prices cannot be controlled but retailers' prices can be controlled.
   (b) there is an excess supply of a commodity at the controlled price.
   (c) consumers are prepared to pay more than the ceiling price and exchange cannot be enforced at the ceiling price.
   (d) a ceiling price is maintained above the equilibrium price.
   (e) there is a binding price floor.

10. **In a free-market economy, the rationing of scarce goods is done primarily by**
    (a) the price mechanism.   (b) the government.
    (c) business firms.   (d) consumers.
    (e) marketing boards.

11. **Allocation by sellers' preferences can best be done at no loss to the seller when**
    (a) there is a disequilibrium price.
    (b) quantity supplied is less than quantity demanded.
    (c) there is a binding price floor.
    (d) there is excess supply.
    (e) the controlled price is set above the equilibrium price.

12. **Which of the following can be an objective of a government price ceiling that may be frustrated by a black market?**
    (a) To keep the price of a specific good low.
    (b) To restrict output of a specific good.
    (c) To satisfy notions of equity.
    (d) All of the above.
    (e) None of the above; each may be government objectives, but black markets cannot prevent any from being achieved.

Rent Controls: A Case Study of Price Ceilings

The analysis in this section focuses on the "first generation" of rent controls, which have since been significantly modified albeit not entirely eliminated. When well-intentioned governments first introduced rent controls, they often had adverse effects on some of the very people they were intended to benefit (i.e., tenants). In any discussion of rent controls, it is important to distinguish between short-term (or short-run) and long-term (or long-run) effects. And if the market price (i.e., rent) is prevented from determining (1) the available supply of rental units and (2) how they are allocated among demanders, other mechanisms will arise to do so.

13. **Which of the following is the least likely effect of rent controls?**
    (a) Rental housing shortage in the long run.
    (b) Development of a black market.
    (c) Short-run increases in the supply of rental housing.
    (d) Resource allocation away from the rental housing industry.
    (e) Less expenditure by landlords on upkeep and maintenance.

14. **The rental housing market is characterized by**
    (a) long-run and short-run supply elasticities of equal magnitude.
    (b) perfectly inelastic demand in both the long run and the short run.
    (c) short-run inelastic supply and long-run elastic supply.
    (d) short-run elastic supply and long-run inelastic supply.
    (e) elastic supply in both the short and the long run.

15. **Which of the following groups is likely to benefit from rent controls?**
    (a) Current tenants.
    (b) Future tenants.
    (c) Landlords.
    (d) Owner-occupiers.
    (e) Developers of rental housing.

16. **Which of the following is the main reason why the adverse effects of rent controls are greater in the long run than in the short run?**
    (a) Governments can reduce excess demand in the long run by building more public housing.
    (b) Rates of return on investment are greater in other markets.
    (c) Demand for rental apartments is more elastic in the long run than in the short run.
    (d) Rent controls give existing tenants a greater incentive to move to home ownership when their incomes increase.
    (e) Governments are better able to eliminate black markets in the long run than in the short run.

An Introduction to Market Efficiency

This section introduces the concept of *market efficiency* as a basis for analyzing whether the *overall* effects of government intervention in a specific market benefit or harm *society as a whole*. A market's "efficient" level of output is that which maximizes its total *economic surplus* by the production and consumption of each and every unit of the good for which the extra *value to consumers* exceeds the *value of resources* used to produce that unit. You should understand how these "values" are measured to calculate economic surplus, why each unit's economic surplus is represented by the vertical distance between the demand and supply curves, and why market efficiency occurs at the competitive market equilibrium. Within the overall market for the good, any potential economic surplus that is *not* generated is a *deadweight loss* to society and represents the extent of *market inefficiency*. Understand why deadweight loss exists when production and consumption is either <u>below</u> or <u>above</u> the competitive equilibrium level.

Using this concept of economic surplus within the demand-and-supply model of competitive markets, you will learn how government intervention in the form of *price controls* and *output quotas* can create deadweight loss and market inefficiency. [*Note:* Especially if you are reading this section for revision after having already covered later chapters in your course, you should recognize that there are some important caveats. First, market efficiency is not the only thing for government to consider; as noted at the end of Chapter 5 (in the section *A Cautionary Word*), the *normative values* of government and society may legitimately favour policies to change the *distribution* of economic surplus even if this reduces the *total value* of surplus. Second, in some cases where markets are *not* competitive, government intervention can actually *increase* economic surplus.]

17. **The value to consumers of a unit of a good or service is measured by**
    (a) the price they pay for it.
    (b) the maximum price they are willing to pay for it.
    (c) the vertical distance between the demand and supply curves.
    (d) its additional costs of production.
    (e) the economic surplus it generates.

18. **The value to suppliers of a unit of a good or a service is measured by**
    (a) the price they receive for it.
    (b) the minimum price they are willing to accept for it.
    (c) the vertical distance between the demand and supply curves.
    (d) its level of market inefficiency.
    (e) the economic surplus it generates.

19. **In the market for a specific good, "economic surplus" measures**
    (a) the extent to which average costs of production fall as output rises.
    (b) the degree of over-investment in the industry producing the good.
    (c) the amount of excess supply at equilibrium.
    (d) the net value to society of the amount produced.
    (e) the proportion of total output produced that is actually sold.

20. **Economic surplus from a given unit of output arises because**
    (a) firms make extra profit on that unit of output.
    (b) average costs of production fall as output increases.
    (c) resources of a lower value are transformed into a good with a higher value.
    (d) the value of resources used in its production exceeds its value to consumers.
    (e) its price is equal to the extra costs of producing that unit.

21. **Economic surplus from a given unit of output is represented by**
  (a)   the extra profits it generates for the firm.
  (b)   the height of the supply curve at that unit.
  (c)   the height of the demand curve at that unit.
  (d)   the vertical distance between the demand and supply curves at that unit.
  (e)   the difference between the actual price paid by the consumer and the maximum price that the consumer would be willing to pay for it.

22. **In a free competitive market for a particular good, market efficiency is achieved when**
  (a)   firms are making maximum profits possible.
  (b)   output exceeds the market-clearing level.
  (c)   the total quantity produced and consumed maximizes economic surplus.
  (d)   all consumers are paying the maximum price they are willing to pay.
  (e)   consumers would be unwilling to buy more of the good at a lower price.

23. **Which of the following best describes "deadweight loss"?**
  (a)   The difference between actual and equilibrium output.
  (b)   The difference between the actual price and the minimum that suppliers are willing to accept.
  (c)   The difference between actual price and the maximum that consumers are willing to pay.
  (d)   The potential economic surplus that is not created.
  (e)   All of the above; they all mean the same thing.

24. **In a competitive market**
  (a)   both a binding price floor and a binding price ceiling create market inefficiency.
  (b)   a binding price floor creates market inefficiency but a binding price ceiling does not.
  (c)   a binding price ceiling creates market inefficiency but a binding price floor does not.
  (d)   a binding price floor creates market inefficiency only when demand is inelastic.
  (e)   both a binding price floor and a binding price ceiling increase market efficiency by increasing the economic surplus on the last unit produced and consumed.

25. **The basic economic analysis of the effects of government intervention in a competitive market supports the conclusion that**
  (a)   intervention should never be undertaken.
  (b)   intervention should be undertaken only if it does not reduce economic surplus.
  (c)   both positive and normative judgements argue for non-intervention.
  (d)   intervention should be undertaken only if it benefits consumers of that good.
  (e)   intervention can be desirable on grounds other than market efficiency.

26. **Economists view an increase in economic surplus as improving market efficiency because**
  (a)   consumers are made better off.
  (b)   producers and consumers are each made better off.
  (c)   government receives more tax revenue.
  (d)   gainers can, in principle, compensate losers and still be better off than before.
  (e)   gainers will, in practice, compensate losers and still be better off than before.

Short-Answer Questions

1. When trees are cut to make timber for house construction and furniture, the smaller branches are made into wood pulp that is used to make paper. How is the market for timber linked to the market for pulp, and what would be the effect of an increase in demand for timber on the market for pulp?

   Complements in production

   timber demand ↑, price ↑, quantity ↑
   pulp supply ↑, price ↓

2. When price ceilings create excess demand by preventing a market from reaching equilibrium, what alternative methods may develop to allocate the available quantity supplied among demanders?

   - 1st come 1st served   - black market
   - seller's preference   - gov't rationing

3. Why does the economic surplus on an extra unit of a good represent that unit's "value added" to society as a whole? Starting from equilibrium in this market, and still using the notion of "value added," explain why market efficiency argues for a fall in the quantity produced if demand for the good falls.

4. Assume that the market for taxicabs starts in equilibrium, then no more taxicab permits are granted despite subsequent increases in demand for taxicab rides. That is, a *quota* is placed on taxicab permits equal to the number of permits at the initial equilibrium. Who benefits and who loses from this type of supply management? Explain your answer for both the short run and the long run. [*Hint:* Once issued, the taxicab permits become the property of the holders, to keep or sell as they please.]

Exercises

1. **Linkages Between Housing Markets**
   Half the homeowners in the city of Suburbia commute to work in the nearby city of Centreville, and the other half work in Suburbia and never go to Centreville. The city government of Centreville decides to substantially increase the property tax on its homeowners to pay for the recent increase in the wages paid to the city's employees.

   (a) In Panel (a) of Figure 5-1 show the effect of the tax on house prices in Centreville. [*Note:* Treat the tax as a component of the price of housing.]

Figure 5-1

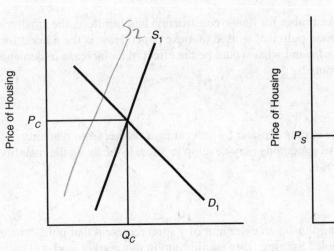

(a)   (b)

Quantity of Housing in Centreville   Quantity of Housing in Suburbia

(b) Will current homeowners in Suburbia benefit from the change in property taxes in Centreville? Why/why not? Do you need to make any changes in Panel (b) of Figure 5-1?

> Demand ↑
>
> Property value ↑

(c) In the future, will new residents who move to Suburbia from another province benefit from the change in Centreville's taxes? Explain.

> NO. Lose b/c higher prices

(d) Suppose that, instead of paying for higher wages, Centreville used the extra tax revenues to expand and speed up its underground public transportation system. Would the 50 percent of Suburbia's homeowners who work in Centreville benefit from the tax increase? Would the 50 percent who never go to Centreville benefit?

> Yes. b/c property value + subway.
>
> Yes b/c still have higher property value

2. **Minimum Wages, Employment, and Unemployment**

   Minimum wages are often used as an example of a price floor (see *Applying Economic Concepts 5-1* in the text). The purpose of this exercise is not to predict the effect of minimum wages on employment (an issue on which there are quite different viewpoints), but to show (i) how the effect of any price floor on quantity purchased depends on the elasticity of demand, and (ii) that in the labour market, an increase in unemployment (i.e., excess supply of labour) caused by a minimum wage should not be confused with a decrease in employment (i.e., the number of people actually working).

   Figure 5-2 is an illustrative diagram—not to scale—of two labour markets with the same equilibrium price (P_E) and quantity (Q_E). In Market 1 demand is inelastic and supply is elastic. Market 2 shows the reverse, with an elastic demand and inelastic supply. Draw the relevant effects in each market as you go through the question.

Figure 5-2

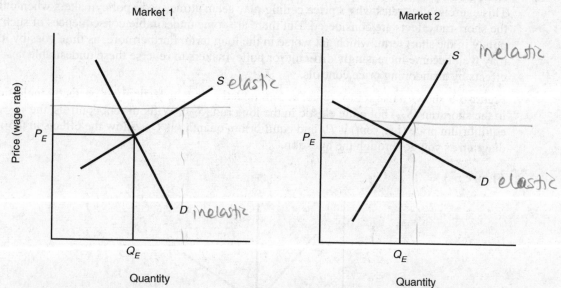

Market 1 / Market 2

Price (wage rate)

P_E

Q_E

Quantity

S elastic

D inelastic

S inelastic

D elastic

(a) The same price floor (P_{MIN})—or minimum wage—is imposed on each market. What is the necessary condition for this to be an effective price floor? Why?

Higher than equm. price

(b) Which market has the bigger reduction in employment as a result of the minimum wage? Why?

2- elastic demand

(c) Which market has the bigger increase in unemployment (i.e., excess supply)? Why? [*Hint:* The diagrams are not to scale, so you can't answer this question by inspecting the diagrams. Consider the responses of quantity demanded and quantity supplied separately before reaching a conclusion.]

Can't be determined.
2 elastic demand-bigger fall in employment
1. elastic supply- bigger increase in # of ppl in labour market (willing to work @ that wage)

(d) What happens to the total wage bill (i.e., firms' total expenditure on labour) in each market? Why?

1. ↑ ble demand inelastic
2. ↓ ble demand elastic

(e) In light of what you have discovered, comment on the following statement: "The bigger the increase in unemployment caused by a minimum wage, then the greater is the reduction in employment and in the total earnings of workers as a whole."

↳only demand   ↳both demand + supply
This statement ignores elasticity of supply

3. **Rent Controls**

This exercise illustrates why a price ceiling may seem attractive to policymakers when only the short-run effects are considered. But there are some undesirable consequences of such a policy in the short term, which get worse in the long term. Furthermore, as time goes by it may well become increasingly difficult for policymakers to reverse these undesirable effects by abandoning price controls.

Figure 5-3 shows a market for rental accommodation in which supply is perfectly inelastic in the short run (S_{SR}) but quite elastic in the long run (S_{LR}). Without rent controls, the equilibrium price (i.e., rent) is P_E and equilibrium quantity is Q_E. Show the effects in the diagram as you go through the question.

Figure 5-3

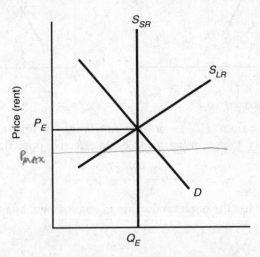

Quantity of Rental Accommodation

(a) Impose a price ceiling (P_{MAX}) on the rental market. What is the necessary condition for the control to be effective? Why?

lower than P_E

(b) Why might policymakers view this as an attractive social policy in the short run?

Decrease prices

(c) How will some young single people living in their parents' homes react to the rent controls in the short run? How does their reaction show itself in the market? Will anyone be made worse off by their reaction? Why/why not?

Move out – increase demand
some w/ greater need for apartments
won't be able to find any

(d) Will a single parent having both a full-time and a part-time job be at a disadvantage in the controlled housing market? Why/why not? Will a family with pets be at a disadvantage? Why/why not?

1st come 1st serve
disadvantage

seller's choice
disadvantage

(e) What new and undesirable effect emerges in the long run? Will this have any effect on what you found in (c) and (d)? Why?

Quantity supplied ↓.
Quality ↓
(c) & (d) made worse

(f) In the diagram, draw another short-run supply curve showing the rental accommodation that exists after quantity supplied has adjusted to its new long-run level. What would be the short-run effect of abandoning rent controls? Explain why this would be an example of "overshooting." What trade-off faces the policymaker who wants to let the market return to its pre-controls equilibrium without any overshooting?

excess demand pushes P ↑. low-income renters move out (to where?)
overshooting long-run equilibrium P.
long-run: supply ↑
– gradually increase controlled rent until it reached free market equ'm
—avoids high rents
—supply changes not fast enough: demand still in excess

4. **Price Controls, Quotas, and Market Efficiency**
In this question you investigate the effects of three types of intervention in a competitive market: a binding price ceiling, a binding price floor, and an output quota. Using Figure 5-4, you first calculate the implications for consumers, producers, and overall market efficiency of each intervention relative to the competitive market equilibrium. Then you compare and contrast the effects of each intervention with the effects of the other interventions. [*Note:* Figures 5-4(a) and 5-4(b) are identical.]

Figure 5-4

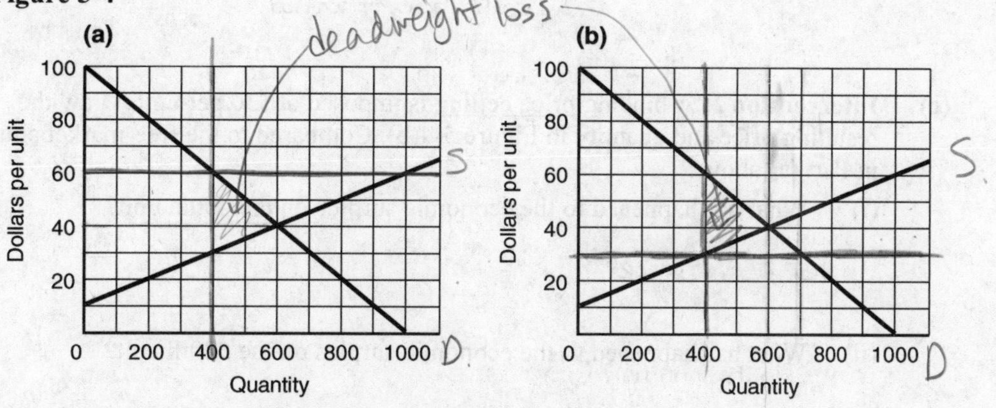

(a) At the free market equilibrium in Figure 5-4(a):

(i) Economic surplus on the 400th unit is __30__.
(ii) Economic surplus on the 600th unit is __0__.
(iii) Potential economic surplus on the 800th unit is __–30__. *deadweight loss.*
(iv) How much is total economic surplus at equilibrium? [*Hint:* Split the area of total surplus into two right-angled triangles (the one above the equilibrium price and the one below it) and, for each triangle, multiply rise by run and take half of the result. Then add the two areas together.]

Area of surplus triangle   27000

(b) **Intervention 1:** A binding <u>price floor</u> is imposed at $60 per unit. Draw the resulting price and quantity in Figure 5-4(a). Compared to the free-market situation in Part (a) above

    (i)   what has happened to the economic surplus on the 400th unit?

no change

    (ii)   what has happened to the economic surplus on the 500th unit?

    (iii)   by how much does consumer spending (and suppliers' revenues) change as a result of the price control? What does this tell you about the elasticity of demand over the relevant range in this market? Why?

unchanged at $24,000
elasticity must be unitary over this range of D

    (iv)   without calculating actual numbers, explain what has happened to suppliers' profits. How do you know?

Revenue is unchanged *} profits ↑*
Producing less → less costs

    (v)   Calculate the effect on total economic surplus. What does this tell you about the effect on market efficiency? Explain your answer. [*Hint:* Find the deadweight loss using the two-triangles method, and subtract it from the surplus you found in Part a(iv) above.]

Econ surplus not maximized
$3000 deadweight loss

(c) **Intervention 2:** A binding <u>price ceiling</u> is imposed at $30 per unit. Draw the resulting price and quantity in Figure 5-4(b). Compared to the free-market situation in Part (a) above:

    (i)   What has happened to the economic surplus on the 400th unit?

no surplus now

    (ii)   What has happened to the economic surplus on the 500th unit?

increased

    (iii)   By how much does consumer spending (and suppliers' revenues) change as a result of the price control?

fell to $900

    (iv)   Without calculating actual numbers, explain what has happened to suppliers' profits. How do you know?

1st 400 units: production cost same, lower price point ⇒ lower revenue
other 200 units: used to be produced & sold @ price higher than prod. costs

(v)   Calculate the effect on total economic surplus. What does this tell you about the effect on market efficiency? Explain your answer.

Econ surplus not maximized
$3000 deadweight loss

(d)   Comparing your answers in Parts (b) and (c), what are the <u>similarities or differences</u> between the effects of the price floor and price ceiling on the following:

(i)   Consumer spending (and suppliers' revenues)?

higher w/ price floor than price ceiling

(ii)   Economic surplus on the 400th unit and on the 500th unit of the good?

same

(iii)   Deadweight loss?

same

(iv)   Market efficiency? *same*

(e)   **Intervention 3:** A <u>quota</u> of 400 units of output is imposed.

(i)   What happens to price? Why?

prices rise to $60

(ii)   Comparing the effects of the quota and the price floor on consumers and market efficiency, what do you see? How would your answers to Part (d) change if you were comparing the effects of the price floor with the quota?

same effect: 400 units, $60 price

(iii)   If the firms in the industry that receive the quotas have an *alienable right* to them—i.e., each firm can keep or sell its quota allocation as it wishes—how will the effect on a firm's profits differ between the price floor and the quota? Explain why.

new firms want to enter industry b/c of high profits
must pay high price for allocation, reducing its profits
below price-floor levels

5.   **Taxpayer-Funded Government Interventions**
Governments often attempt to assist producers through various taxpayer-funded schemes designed to push prices received by suppliers above their equilibrium levels. In the text and in Exercise 4 above you investigated how this is done using a binding price floor and a quota system. This question now investigates two other schemes that have been used by some countries mainly to benefit farmers. (For more information, see *Additional Topics: Agriculture and the Farm Problem* on MyEconLab.) Here you will investigate the cost to taxpayers and the effects on economic surplus and market efficiency. [*Note:* This question is repeated as Extension Exercise E2, using equations instead of scale diagrams.]

A small town in Saskatchewan has the monthly demand curve (D_1) and supply curve (S_1) for kumquats shown in Figures 5-5 and 5-6. At the equilibrium price of $0.9 per bushel and sales of 2800 bushels, kumquat farmers receive $2520 per month. The local government plans to assist kumquat producers by increasing the price of kumquats. Here, you will advise it on two plans.

Figure 5-5

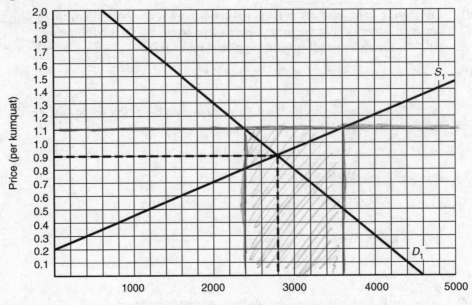

Plan 1: Government will buy, at a price of $1.10 per bushel, any amount of kumquats that are produced but not sold to consumers. Government will then destroy what it buys.

(a)   What is the new effective demand curve facing kumquat growers? [*Hint:* Will farmers sell to consumers at a price less than they can sell to government?] Draw this new demand curve in Figure 5-5 and label it D_2.

q>1.10, D_1.   y<1.10, y=1.10   1.10

(b)   How many bushels are produced? How many are purchased by consumers? How many are purchased and destroyed by government? Show these on Figure 5-5.

3600/month   ⤷3600-2400=1200
Consumer Q=2400 @ p=1.10

(c)   What is the monthly income of kumquat farmers? What is the monthly expenditure on kumquats by private consumers? What is the monthly cost to government (i.e., taxpayers) of Plan 1? [*Note:* Ignore all administrative and disposal costs.] In Figure 5-5, lightly shade the area showing the cost to government.

1.10 (3600)=3960.   cost to gov't: 1.10(1200)=1320
Consumers: 1.10(2400)=2640

Plan 2: Kumquat farmers will produce whatever amount they wish, and sell it all to private consumers. Government will then pay farmers the difference between $1.10 per bushel and the price paid by consumers.

Figure 5-6

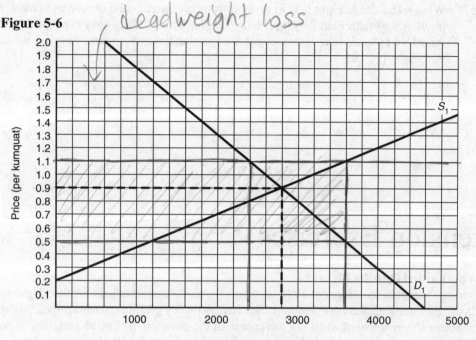

deadweight loss

Quantity of Kumquats (per month)

(d) In Figure 5-6, draw the new effective monthly demand curve facing kumquat growers and label it D_3. Show the quantity produced and the price paid by consumers. Lightly shade the area showing the cost to government (again ignoring administrative costs).

$y > 1.10, \quad y < 1.10, \quad D_2 \quad y = 1.10$
D_1

(e) How does the income of kumquat farmers differ between Plan 1 and Plan 2? How does consumer spending on kumquats differ between Plan 1 and Plan 2? Why? How does the cost to government differ between Plan 1 and Plan 2? Why?

Income same
Consumer spending ↓ even though they buy more quantity
Cost to gov't ↑ to make up the difference

(f) The local government is leaning toward adopting Plan 2, estimating that it will cost only $0.2 per bushel for 2800 bushels. What has it failed to take account of in reaching this estimate? If the government's only criterion is to minimize the cost to taxpayers, which plan would you advise it to adopt? If the government's criteria include the well-being of society as a whole, which of the two plans would you advise it to adopt? Why? Plan 2 — everything is consumed.

Plan 2

(i) higher outputs when price ↑
(ii) fall in price that induces consumers to increase spending.

(g) What is the deadweight loss in economic surplus (hence the degree of market *inefficiency*) with Plan 2? With Plan 1? [*Hint:* This is fairly easy for Plan 2, but for Plan 1 you should take into account the fact that the government destroys whatever it purchases.]

$\downarrow$ econ surplus + amount gov't destroys b/c
it has no value to society

Extension Exercises

E1. Who Turned Out the Lights?
During Quebec's Ice Storm of 1998, demand for many items such as firewood, propane, flashlights, and candles rose dramatically. Just as theory predicts, so did prices. Many businesses were accused of taking advantage of the situation by "price gouging." The *Montreal Gazette*, January 14, 1998, quoted a lawyer from the Quebec Consumers Association: "It's not illegal to increase prices when demand goes up, but we are in a crisis situation here . . . and businesses should be helping people, not abusing them." This exercise examines the implications of holding prices constant during such a crisis.

Assume that each of 100 households in the small town of Ville de Glace has an identical weekly demand for candles, and the entire town's market demand curve is $Q^D = 200 - 100P$. The supply of candles in Ville de Glace is perfectly inelastic at 100 per week.

(a) Find the equilibrium price and quantity for the entire town. How many candles does each household consume per week?

$100 = 200 - 100P$ $Q = 200 - 100(1) = 100$
$100P = 100$ 1 candle / household
$P = 1$

(b) Suppose that when the ice storm knocks out the electrical supply, the demand for candles in Ville de Glace increases to $Q^D = 1100 - 100P$. What is the new market equilibrium price and quantity? How many candles does each household consume?

$100 = 1100 - 100P$ $Q = 1100 - 100(10) = 1100 - 1000 = 100$
$100P = 1000$ 1 candle/household
$P = 10$

(c) Suppose that price controls are introduced to keep prices at their pre–ice storm levels. What is the equilibrium, and how many candles does each household consume? [*Hint:* How will the available supply be allocated among demanders?]

$Q_D = 1100 - 100(1)$ 1st come 1st serve
     $= 1000$ seller's choice
shortage of 900

(d) Why is there potential for a black market in candles? Explain how it would work. Would keeping the price at pre–ice storm levels have achieved its objective?

Buy all candles at $1, sell for $10.
So, no

E2. **The Cost to Taxpayers of Government Intervention (Using Equations)**
This question investigates two schemes designed to assist farmers by supporting prices above their equilibrium levels. [*Note:* It is the same as Exercise 5, but the solutions are found using equations rather than scale diagrams. Sketch your own diagrams as you go along and, when you have finished the question, compare them with the diagrams in the solution to Exercise 5.]

(a) A small town in Saskatchewan has the monthly demand curve for bushels of kumquats of $Q^D = 4600 - 2000P$ and supply curve of $Q^S = -800 + 4000P$. What is the price per bushel and the number of bushels at equilibrium? What is the monthly income of kumquat farmers and monthly consumer spending on kumquats?

Plan 1: The local government wants to increase the monthly income of kumquat farmers by purchasing, at a price of $1.10 per bushel, any kumquats that are produced but not sold to consumers. The government will then destroy what it buys.

(b) What does the new effective demand curve facing kumquat growers look like? [*Hint:* Will farmers sell to consumers at a price less than they can sell to government?] How many bushels are produced? How many are purchased by consumers? How many are purchased and destroyed by government?

Demand is Q_D for prices above $1.10.
Perfectly elastic at $P = \$1.10$ & thereafter

(c) What is the monthly income of kumquat farmers? What is the monthly expenditure on kumquats by private consumers? What is the monthly cost to government (i.e., taxpayers) of Plan 1? [*Note:* Ignore all administrative and disposal costs.]

Plan 2: In this plan kumquat farmers will produce whatever amount they wish, and sell it all to private consumers. The government will then pay farmers the difference, for each bushel, between $1.10 and the price paid by consumers.

(d) What does the new effective demand curve facing kumquat farmers look like? How many bushels are produced? What is the price paid by consumers?

Same Q_D

Now go to Exercise 5 above, and do sections (e), (f), and (g) to complete this exercise.

Additional Multiple-Choice Questions

*1. **If good *B* has to be jointly produced with good *A* (e.g., as a byproduct of good *A*), market linkages will create pressure for**
 (a) an increase in demand for *A* to reduce the quantity demanded of *B*.
 (b) an increase in demand for *A* to increase the price of *B*.
 (c) a reduction in the supply of *A* to reduce the price of *B*.
 (d) a reduction in the cost of producing *A* to reduce the supply of *B*.
 (e) an increase in demand for *A* to increase the quantity demanded of *B*.

movement along demand curve

*2. **Partial equilibrium analysis of the market for a particular good refers to situations where**
  (a)   the market is moving toward equilibrium, but the excess demand or supply has not yet been fully eliminated.
  (b)   some firms in the market are in equilibrium, but others are not.
  (c)   only that part of the market for which data exist is being analyzed.
  (d)   the effects on this market of induced changes in other markets are ignored.
  (e)   feedback effects from other markets are taken into account.

*3. **If X and Y are complementary goods, which of the following best represents a "feedback effect" resulting from a fall in the price of X?**
  (a)   The demand for X falls because the price of Y increases.
  (b)   The demand for Y increases because the price of X falls.
  (c)   The quantity of X demanded increases because the price of X falls.
  (d)   The demand for Y increases because purchasing power is increased by the fall in the price of X.
  (e)   Both (b) and (d); they both affect the market for Y through the fall in the price of X.

Questions 4 to 7 refer to Figure 5-7.

Figure 5-7

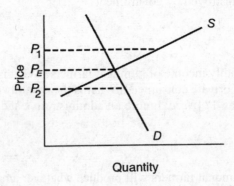

4. **A price ceiling equal to P_1**
  (a)   results in excess supply.
  (b)   results in excess demand.
  (c)   results in neither excess demand nor excess supply.
  (d)   can lead to a black market.
  (e)   has no effect.

5. **A price ceiling equal to P_2**
  (a)   leads to a level of consumption that is greater than quantity supplied.
  (b)   results in a greater quantity produced than is actually sold.
  (c)   is often justified as a means of helping producers.
  (d)   may result in allocation by sellers' preferences.
  (e)   results in unsold stocks of output.

*6. **A price floor equal to P_E would result in excess supply if**
  (a)   demand decreases due to a change in tastes.
  (b)   supply falls due to an increase in labour costs.
  (c)   the demand curve shifts to the right.
  (d)   either curve shifts in a direction that causes upward pressure on price.
  (e)   no more firms entered the industry.

7. **Suppose that the government decides P_E is too high and therefore imposes a price ceiling equal to P_2. Further suppose that a black market develops in which all output is sold at the highest attainable price. The black market price is**
    (a) equal to P_E.
    (b) greater than P_E.
    (c) greater than P_2 but less than P_E.
    (d) equal to P_2.
    (e) less than P_2.

*8. **Lineups (or queues) are one possible allocative mechanism when there is**
    (a) excess supply.
    (b) a binding price floor.
    (c) government intervention in the market that controls price above equilibrium level.
    (d) an effective price ceiling.
    (e) Both (b) and (d) are correct.

Questions 9 and 10 refer to Figure 5-8 in which the demand for rental housing increases from D_0 to D_1 (*SR* and *LR* refer to the short run and the long run, respectively).

Figure 5-8

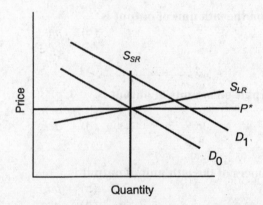

*9. **If demand increases from D_0 to D_1 and there are no rent controls,**
    (a) there will be a greater quantity increase in the short run than the long run.
    (b) the short-run price overshoots its long-run equilibrium level.
    (c) the amount of rental housing will not be affected in the long run.
    (d) rents will rise more in the long run than in the short run.
    (e) price will always equal P^*.

*10. **Assume that rents are controlled at price P^*. Which of the following best describes the likely events if demand increases from D_0 to D_1?**
    (a) There will be no shortage of rental units in either the short run or the long run.
    (b) Landlords will have less opportunity to discriminate among prospective tenants.
    (c) The apartment shortage will be eliminated in the long run.
    (d) Landlords will spend less on maintenance as well as new construction.
    (e) All consumers will have access to more affordable housing.

*11. **The size of a shortage of rental accommodation under rent controls depends on**
    (a) the elasticity of demand for rental accommodation.
    (b) the elasticity of supply for rental accommodation.
    (c) the length of time rent controls are in effect.
    (d) the amount by which the controlled price falls short of the equilibrium price.
    (e) All of the above are correct.

Questions 12 to 16 refer to Figure 5-9, showing the competitive market for a specific good.

Figure 5-9

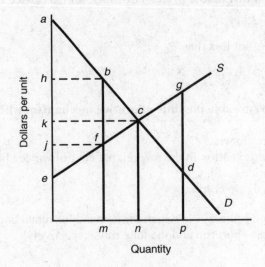

*12. Economic surplus on the *m*th unit of output is
(a) *bm.*   (b) *fm.*
(c) *bf.*   (d) *bcf.*
(e) *abfj.*

13. Total economic surplus on *m* units of output is
(a) *bm.*   (b) *acfj.*
(c) *abfe.*   (d) *ack.*
(e) *jfm.*

14. The value to consumers of the *m*th unit of output is
(a) *bm.*   (b) *fm.*
(c) *bf.*   (d) *ace.*
(e) *hbfj.*

*15. Economic surplus on the *p*th unit of output is
(a) *pg* minus *dp.*   (b) *cdpn.*
(c) *dp* plus *gd.*   (d) *dp* minus *gp.*
(e) *gp.*

*16. If area *bcf* were equal to area *cgd*, total economic surplus on *p* units of output would be
(a) *gd.*   (b) *bcf* plus *cgd.*
(c) *abfe* minus *cgd.*   (d) the same as at equilibrium.
(e) the same as on *m* units of output.

*17. The deadweight loss from government imposing a minimum price of *h* dollars is
(a) *bfc.*
(b) the same as from imposing a maximum price of *j* dollars.
(c) the same as from imposing a quota of *m* units of output.
(d) All of the above.
(e) None of the above.

*18. **Imposing an output quota below the competitive equilibrium level of output creates market inefficiency**

    (a)   because the price paid by consumers increases.

    (b)   because the price received by producers increases.

    (c)   because some extra units of output in excess of the quota have a higher value to consumers than the value of resources needed for their production.

    (d)   in a market where demand is inelastic because total consumer expenditure on the good increases, but not in a market where demand is elastic and total consumer expenditure on the good falls.

    (e)   Both (a) and (d) since consumers are adversely affected in each case.

19. **In a competitive market, a binding price ceiling causes _____ by _____.**

    (a)   market efficiency; increasing the economic surplus of the last unit of output produced and consumed

    (b)   market inefficiency; creating a deadweight loss in economic surplus

    (c)   market efficiency; increasing the amount produced and consumed

    (d)   market inefficiency; increasing the amount produced and consumed

    (e)   market efficiency; making the good more affordable for low-income households

*20. **Quotas that lead to higher profits in some industry will in the long run**

    (a)   result in more producers in the industry.

    (b)   make it more costly to enter this industry.

    (c)   result in a larger output for each producer.

    (d)   help individuals who are just entering this industry.

    (e)   reduce the price of the industry's product.

Solutions

Chapter Review

1.(d) 2.(e) 3.(c) 4.(b) 5.(d) 6.(c) 7.(e) 8.(e) 9.(c) 10.(a) 11.(b) 12.(d) 13.(c) 14.(c) 15.(a) 16.(b) 17.(b) 18.(b) 19.(d) 20.(c) 21.(d) 22.(c) 23.(d) 24.(a) 25.(e) 26.(d)

Short-Answer Questions

1. Timber and wood pulp are complements in production (like oil and natural gas in the text). An increase in the demand for timber increases the price of timber and the quantity produced. This in turn increases the supply of wood pulp, driving down the price of wood pulp.

2. Examples of allocation methods referred to in the text's section on price ceilings include first-come-first-served, sellers' preferences, black markets, and rationing by government.

3. When economic surplus exists, the maximum price consumers are willing to pay exceeds the minimum price suppliers are willing to accept for that unit. Thus the value to consumers exceeds the value of resources needed to supply the extra unit, and this difference adds value by transforming resources of lower value into output of higher value. A fall in demand (with no change in supply) reflects a reduction in the value per unit to consumers. For units produced in excess of the new equilibrium quantity, value added becomes negative—i.e., a deadweight loss in economic surplus because the value of resources used in the production of these units now exceeds these units' value to consumers. Eliminating this negative by not producing these units thus increases economic surplus in this market. Society as a whole benefits by transferring resources from the production of this good to the production of goods for which value added is positive rather than negative.

4. Even if taxi fares are fixed by government, excess demand for taxi rides makes consumers pay by longer waiting times, especially in peak periods. Permit holders benefit from more rides per day (i.e., less time spent waiting in the taxi ranks), thereby getting more income and more profit. In the long run people wanting to enter the industry push up the market price of permits, because permits now are a "passport to profit." Current permit holders benefit from an increase in their wealth (i.e., the higher value of their permits), but new entrants into the industry get no benefit at all! The expectation of higher incomes pushes up the price of permits until the higher price offsets any increase in earnings due to restricted supply. In short, the initial permit holders benefit from the increase in the market value of their permits, but new entrants do not benefit and consumers lose.

Exercises

1. **(a)** The tax is equivalent to an increase in the cost of "producing" housing, thus shifting the supply curve vertically upward (a reduction in supply) in Centreville and raising housing prices. (In Panel (a) of Figure 5-1, show a leftward shift in the supply curve, a higher equilibrium price, and a lower equilibrium quantity.)

(b) The high proportion of people living in Suburbia and commuting to work in Centreville means that housing in Centreville and Suburbia are substitute goods—i.e., the markets are linked. The increase in price in Centreville increases demand for substitute goods, raising house prices in Suburbia too. (In Panel (b) of Figure 5-1, show a rightward shift of the demand curve generating a higher equilibrium price.) Current homeowners in Suburbia benefit from an increase in wealth; the houses they previously bought at lower prices are now worth more. [*Note:* We ignore the fact that, if current homeowners move to another house in Suburbia in the future, they too will pay the higher price.]

(c) New residents coming into Suburbia in the future will not benefit, since they must pay the higher prices for housing in Suburbia.

(d) The 50 percent who commute benefit in two ways; their houses are worth more, and they can get around Centreville more easily when they are there (and perhaps reduce the time taken to get to work). The 50 percent of Suburbia residents who never go to Centreville still benefit from the higher values of their houses.

2. **(a)** To be effective, the price floor must be set above the market equilibrium price (or wage). If it is set at or below the equilibrium, the market will simply remain at equilibrium and there will be no effect.

(b) The number of people actually employed is read from the inner of the demand and supply curves—in this case, the demand curve. Since Market 2 has the more elastic demand curve, the increase in the wage rate causes a bigger reduction in employment in Market 2 than in Market 1. (On your diagram, you will see a bigger fall in quantity demanded in Market 2 than in Market 1 when you draw the same minimum wage above P_E.)

(c) Unemployment is the amount of excess supply of workers—the number of people wanting to work (read from the supply curve) minus the number of people working (read from the demand curve). In this question we cannot determine which has the bigger increase in unemployment. Because Market 2 has the more-elastic demand curve, it has the bigger fall in employment (i.e., in quantity demanded). But Market 1 has the more-elastic supply curve, so it has the bigger increase in the number of people wanting to work at the higher wage (i.e., in quantity supplied). Without knowing the equations for the demand and supply curves, it is not possible to predict which market will have the bigger excess supply. Indeed it is quite possible that the amount of unemployment caused by the minimum wage is the same in the two markets.

(d) The wage bill (i.e., wage rate multiplied by number employed) rises in Market 1 because demand for labour is inelastic: The percentage fall in employment (quantity demanded) is less than the percentage increase in the wage rate (price). The wage bill falls in Market 2 because demand for labour is elastic: The percentage fall in employment (quantity demanded) exceeds the percentage increase in the wage rate (price).

(e) As you have already seen, the reduction in employment depends *only* on the elasticity of demand while the increase in unemployment depends on the elasticities of *both* demand and supply. The statement in the question totally ignores the effect of the elasticity of supply on unemployment, implicitly assuming that the increase in unemployment equals the reduction in employment. This would be true only if the supply curve were perfectly inelastic.

3. **(a)** To be effective (or binding), the price ceiling must be set below the market equilibrium price. If the ceiling is set at or above the equilibrium price, the market will remain in equilibrium and the price ceiling will have no effect.

(b) The supply of housing is highly inelastic in the short run; it is shown in Figure 5-3 as perfectly inelastic. Thus rent controls may seem an attractive social policy in the short run by making rental accommodation more "affordable," without noticeably reducing the quantity available.

(c) Some young single people will react to the lower (or "more affordable") rents by moving out of their parents' houses and getting their own apartments. This reaction contributes to the excess demand generated in the short run (i.e., $(Q_D - Q_E)$ in Figure 5-10), as the quantity demanded increases while the quantity supplied remains unchanged. Some people who have a much greater need for apartments (e.g., because they have small children), reflected in their willingness to pay higher prices, will be unable to find apartments because they have been taken by the young singles who leave their parents' houses.

Figure 5-10

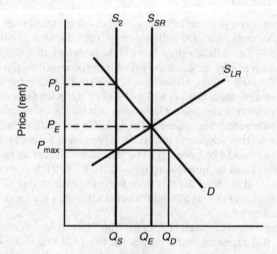

Quantity of Rental Accommodation

(d) Because market prices no longer allocate supply among demanders, other methods must do it instead. The single parent with two jobs is at a disadvantage with the first-come-first-served method because other people with more time available will get to the vacant apartments first. Families with pets will be at a disadvantage under the sellers' preferences method since many landlords will prefer to rent to families without pets.

(e) The long-run supply curve is more elastic, so quantity of rental accommodation supplied falls in the long run (indicated by a movement down the long-run supply curve in your diagram). Excess demand increases (to $Q_D - Q_S$), which intensifies all the problems in (c) and (d). Furthermore, the quality of accommodation may well fall because, as rents are held down, apartment owners can get a better return by putting their money into other investments instead of spending it on maintaining the rental properties.

(f) The new short-run supply curve is perfectly inelastic at S_2 in Figure 5-10. If rent controls are abandoned, the excess demand will push rents up to a short-run equilibrium at the price P_0. This increase in rents would significantly reduce the standard of living of low-income renters, many of whom may not have sufficient income to pay the high rents and would have to move out (but to where?). The new short-run equilibrium rent P_0 "overshoots" the long-run equilibrium rent, P_E. Over time, more rental accommodation will become available (i.e., a movement up the long-run supply curve), and the increase in quantity supplied will reduce rents to the long-run equilibrium level. To avoid overshooting, policymakers could gradually increase the controlled rent until it reached the long-run equilibrium level. Compared with the effects of immediately abandoning controls, a gradual increase would avoid the high rents caused by overshooting; but, the adjustment in supply would take longer, causing the other problems of rent control attributable to excess demand to remain for a longer time.

4.   **Figure 5-11**

   (a)

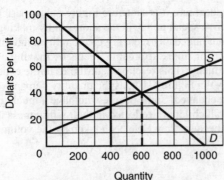

   (b)

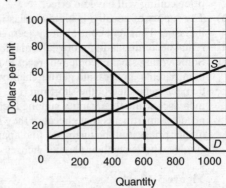

   (a) Subtracting the minimum price sellers are willing to accept (read from the S curve) from the maximum price that consumers are willing to pay (read from the D curve) gives (i) $30, (ii) $0, and (iii) <u>minus</u> $30—i.e., a deadweight loss of $30 (although this 800th unit will not be produced at equilibrium, which is why the question asks for the *potential* surplus here). Find (iv) as follows: $(100 - 40)600/2 + (40 - 10)600/2 = 60(300) + 30(300) = 90(300) = \$27\ 000$.

   (b) (i) Nothing—it remains unchanged at $30. (ii) Before the price floor the 500th unit generated $(50 - 35)$ $15 of economic surplus, which is now lost because that unit is no longer produced. (iii) Spending (and revenues) is unchanged at $24 000, so elasticity must be unitary over that range of the D curve. (iv) Suppliers' profits have increased; revenues are unchanged, but they are producing less so costs will be lower. (v) The price floor creates a deadweight loss equal to the area of the triangle of lost economic surplus—i.e., $(60 - 40)(600 - 400)/2 + (40 - 30)(600 - 400)/2 = 30(100) = \$3000$. Subtract this from the economic surplus of $27 000 at equilibrium and the resulting economic surplus is $24 000. Market efficiency no longer exists because economic surplus is not maximized.

   (c) (i) Nothing—it remains unchanged at $30. (ii) The $15 surplus is now lost because the unit is no longer produced. (iii) Spending and revenues fell from $24 000 to $30(400) = \$12\ 000$. (iv) Although revenues and costs have both fallen, we can still conclude that profits have fallen. First, costs of the 400 units still produced are unchanged, but because they sell for $30 instead of $40 the revenues on them have fallen by $4000. Second, the other 200 units previously produced sold for a price in excess of the firms' extra production costs on each unit (read from the S curve)—i.e., an addition to profits that is now no longer forthcoming. (v) Since the reduction in output (200 units) is the same as with the $60 price floor in (b)(v) above, the deadweight loss and thus the reduction in economic surplus and the degree of market efficiency are exactly the same too.

   (d) For items (ii), (iii), and (iv) the effect is <u>exactly</u> the same with the $60 price floor and the $30 price ceiling (because they both result in the same reduction in quantity and deadweight loss). The only difference between the two interventions is in item (i); both consumer spending and suppliers' revenue (and profits) are higher with the price floor than the price ceiling.

   (e) (i) Price rises to $60. (ii) See that both the price floor and the quota result in a price of $60 and a quantity of 400; they have the same effect on consumers and market efficiency. Your answers to Part (d) would not change. (iii) The initial increase in firm profits via the quota will cause other firms to want to enter the industry, but they can't do this without buying a quota. Thus a market for quotas will develop, and the price new entrants will have to pay for the quota will reduce profits below the level they would have with the price floor.

5. **Figure 5-12: Plan 1**

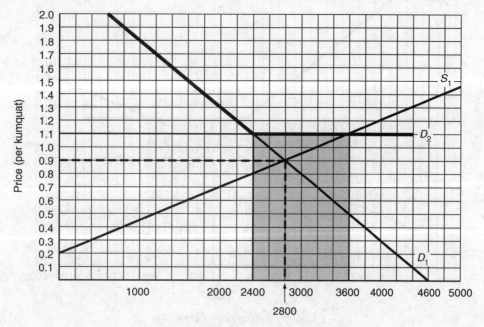

Quantity of Kumquats (per month)

(a) The demand curve facing farmers (D_2 in Figure 5-12) is the consumer demand curve D_1 for prices above $1.10, and then becomes perfectly elastic at $P = \$1.10$ (since farmers can sell as much as they want to the government at that price).

(b) Given the new demand curve, output at $P = \$1.10$ is 3600 per month at the intersection of D_2 and S_1. Reading from D_1 shows that consumers purchase $Q = 2400$ at $P = \$1.10$. Government buys and destroys 3600 – 2400 = 1200 per month.

(c) Monthly income of farmers is $1.10(3600) = \$3960$. Expenditure by consumers is $1.10(2400) = \$2640$. Cost to government (the shaded area in Figure 5-12) is $3960 – \$2640 = \$1320$ (or $1.10(1200) = \$1320$).

(d) The new demand curve facing kumquat producers (D_2 in Figure 5-13) is exactly the same as for Plan 1; they are guaranteed a price of $1.10 again, so demand is perfectly elastic at quantities above $Q = 2400$. Output is 3600 per month, as in Plan 1, but in Plan 2 it is all sold to consumers at $P = \$0.5$ (i.e., the price at which quantity demanded also is 3600, read from D_1).

(e) Income of kumquat farmers is the same in Plans 1 and 2, at $1.10(3600) = \$3960$. Consumers spend $0.50(3600) = \$1800$ in Plan 2, which is $840 less than the $2640 in Plan 1. Consumer spending falls as price falls along D_1 because consumer demand for kumquats is inelastic. Because suppliers get the same income but consumers spend less in Plan 2, the cost to government must be greater in Plan 2—i.e., ($1.10 – \$0.50)3600 = \$0.6(3600) = \$2160$ in Plan 2, which is $840 more than the $1320 in Plan 1.

Figure 5-13: Plan 2

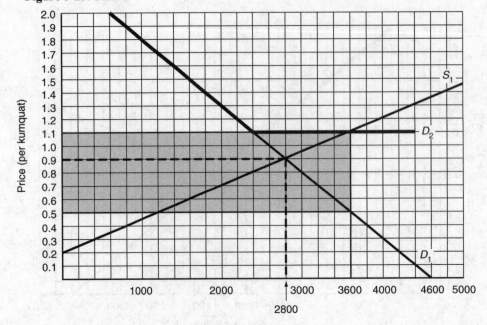

Quantity of Kumquats (per month)

(f) The local government failed to take into account (i) the higher output that would be produced when the price for producers increased from $0.90 to $1.10, and (ii) the fall in price (from $0.90 to $0.50) needed to induce consumers to increase their purchases from 2800 to 3600. If the government's objective is to minimize the cost to taxpayers it should adopt Plan 1 (costing taxpayers $1320 rather than $2160). But from the perspective of society as a whole, Plan 2 is preferable since everything that is produced is actually consumed, unlike Plan 1 where taxpayers pay farmers for some output that nobody consumes.

(g) In Plan 2 there is a deadweight loss equal to the area of the triangle above the D_1 curve and below the S curve on the 600 units produced in excess of the free-market equilibrium level (i.e., 3600 – 2800). For all these units of output resources are being transformed from something of a higher value (read from the S curve) into something of a lower value (read from the D curve). In Plan 1, the amount bought by government is destroyed and so has zero value to society. Since the resources used to produce the quantity destroyed are no longer available to use in the production of any other goods, their value too has been destroyed and becomes part of the deadweight loss. Thus the deadweight loss on what the government buys and destroys is the whole area below the S curve on the 600 units above the free-market equilibrium plus the whole area below the D curve on the 400 units below the free-market equilibrium (2800 – 2400 = 400). This area under the demand curve includes both the lost economic surplus that would have existed at equilibrium (i.e., the area above the supply curve and below the demand curve on these 400 units), and the value of society's resources that has also been destroyed (i.e., the area under the supply curve for these 400 units).

Extension Exercises

E1. (a) $Q^S = 100$, and setting $Q^D = Q^S$ and solving yields $P_E = 1$ and $Q_E = 100$. Total consumption is 100 candles per week and each of the 100 households consumes one candle per week.

(b) Setting $Q^D = Q^S$ now yields $100 = 1100 - 100P$, which solves for $P_E = 10$ and $Q_E = 100$. Again, each of 100 households consumes 1 candle per week but now pays $10 instead of $1.

(c) If price is kept at $1 during the ice storm, the quantity demanded is $Q^D = 1100 - 100P = 1000$. But there are only 100 candles available, thus there is excess demand of 900 candles per week. Since all households are assumed to have identical demand, each would like to purchase

10 candles. The first 10 households that get to the store purchase all 100 candles, leaving 90 households without any candles.

(d) The excess demand, which will persist because the regular market does not move to its new equilibrium price of $10, creates the potential for a black market. For example, the first household that gets to the store can buy all 100 candles at $1 each and sell them to other households for up to $10 per candle. Obviously, the objective to keep prices at $1 is not achieved.

E2. **(a)** With $Q^D = 4600 - 2000P$ and $Q^S = -800 + 4000P$, setting $Q^D = Q^S$ for equilibrium gives $4600 - 2000P = -800 + 4000P$, $P = 5400/6000 = \$0.9$. With $P = 0.9$, the demand and supply equations solve for $Q^D = Q^S = 2800$ bushels. Monthly income of producers = monthly spending on kumquats by consumers = $0.9(2800) = \$2520$.

(b) **Plan 1:** Effective demand is $Q^D = 4600 - 2000P$ for prices above the guaranteed price of $1.10, and perfectly elastic at $P = \$1.10$ thereafter. Output $= Q^S = -800 + 4000P = -800 + 4000(1.10) = 3600$. Consumers buy $Q^D = 4600 - 2000(1.10) = 2400$. The government buys $3600 - 2400 = 1200$ bushels.

(c) The monthly income of farmers = $1.10(3600) = \$3960$. Private consumers spend $1.10(2400) = \$2640$. Cost to government = $1.10(1200) = \$1320$.

(d) **Plan 2:** The new effective demand curve and kumquat production are exactly the same as in Plan 1. Consumers pay the price at which $Q^D = Q^S = 3600$—i.e., $3600 = 4600 - 2000P$, so $2000P = 1000$ and $P = 1000/2000 = \$0.50$ per bushel.

[Now go to the answers for Exercise 5, sections (e), (f), and (g).]

Additional Multiple-Choice Questions

1.(e) **2.**(d) **3.**(a) **4.**(e) **5.**(d) **6.**(a) **7.**(b) **8.**(d) **9.**(b) **10.**(d) **11.**(e) **12.**(c) **13.**(c) **14.**(a) **15.**(d) **16.**(e) **17.**(d) **18.**(c) **19.**(b) **20.**(b)

Explanations for the Asterisked Multiple-Choice Questions

1.(e) If goods are complements in production, an increase in the output of one means more of the other is produced as well (as the example of oil and natural gas in the text). An increase in demand for A increases the price of A, and producers react by producing more of A <u>and</u> more of its complement B. The increase in supply of B reduces the price of B, thereby increasing the quantity demanded (i.e., a movement along the demand curve for B).

2.(d) *Partial equilibrium* analysis compares equilibrium points in a *specific* market. In the comparison of *long-run* equilibrium points, firms as well as markets are in equilibrium (so answers (a) and (b) are incorrect). Furthermore, analysis may be empirical (i.e., based on data) or theoretical/conceptual: the latter does not require any data (so answer (c) is wrong). Answer (e) refers to *general* equilibrium analysis which, unlike *partial* equilibrium analysis, looks at the total effects of a change in the specific market—including *feedback effects* on that market. The partial equilibrium analysis of a fall in price encompasses both income and substitution effects within the specific market. But *general equilibrium* analysis goes further, including (for example) how the initial change in a specific market affects other markets, which in turn can have *feedback effects* on demand and equilibrium in the specific market.

3.(a) The fall in the price of X increases quantity demanded of X (a movement along the *D* curve for X) <u>and</u> the demand for Y (a rightward shift in the *D* curve for Y). The increase in demand for Y increases the price of Y which, because they are complementary goods, "feeds back" into the market for X by reducing the demand for X (an inward shift in *D* curve for X). Answers (b), (d), and (e) are wrong because they are effects of the change in the market for X on the market for Y, not feed<u>back</u> effects from Y to X caused by the initial change in X. Answer (c) is wrong because it looks only at the market for X—i.e., it is a <u>movement along</u> the demand curve for X, not a feedback effect from the change in the market for Y (which would <u>shift</u> the D curve for X) caused by the initial change in the market for X.

6.(a) Without any changes in the *D* or *S* curves, a price floor at P_E would not be binding—i.e., it would have no effect since the market would remain at its free-market equilibrium price of P_E. If the

D curve shifted in, however, market forces would try to pull the price down to its new lower free-market equilibrium level, but the price floor at P_E would prevent this from happening. At P_E the quantity supplied would remain unchanged while quantity demanded fell, thus creating excess supply. [*Note:* This points out that governments must look into the future to predict the ultimate effects of policy.] Answers (b), (c), and (d) are wrong because any of these changes would put upward pressure on price, which is not stopped from rising by a price <u>floor</u> so again the price floor would not be binding. Answer (e) is wrong because firms leaving the industry, other things constant, would shift the supply curve to the left (a decrease in supply), causing excess demand at P_E rather than excess supply.

8.(d)   In situations of *excess demand*, lining up (or "first-come, first served") is one way to allocate available supply among demanders when the market price is prevented from rising to do so. Answers (a), (b), and (c) are wrong because they refer to situations of *excess supply*: there is more than enough supply to satisfy all demanders at the current above-equilibrium price. Further, since (b) is wrong then so is (e).

9.(b)   Because the short-run supply curve is less elastic than the long-run supply curve, the new short-run equilibrium price is higher than the long-run equilibrium price (i.e., price overshoots in the short run). Suppliers react to the higher price by increasing quantity supplied in the long run, which reduces price until the long-run equilibrium is reached.

10.(d)   With rent controls the increase in *D* causes excess demand (a shortage), so answer (a) is wrong. Market price can't perform its rationing and allocative functions, so other methods will be used. Personal preferences and prejudices is one of these methods, which can be used without "costing" vacant apartments—so answer (b) is also wrong. Because rents are controlled, profits are squeezed as costs of upkeep, repairs, and construction rise—or returns to alternative investments increase—and less is invested in these activities (so answer (d) is correct). Since fewer new rental units will be built in this less-profitable market, supply will fall, thereby further increasing excess demand in the long run (so answer (c) is wrong). Finally, answer (e) is wrong because (i) the reduction in long-run supply prevents some low-income potential consumers from getting apartments, (ii) the reduction in maintenance means some will get lower-quality housing than otherwise, and (iii) the continuing excess demand creates the conditions for black-market pricing.

11.(e)   With the price held below equilibrium, the excess demand (i.e., shortage) is greater (i) the flatter (more elastic) are the demand and supply curves (so answers (a) and (b) are right), and (ii) the further below the free-market equilibrium the controlled price is imposed (so answer (d) is right). [*Note:* Draw both of these cases to convince yourself.] Furthermore, supply is more elastic in the long run than in the short run because it becomes less and less profitable to build or own rental units, and more profitable to transform existing units into owner-occupied condominiums. This creates an even bigger reduction in supply over time, and hence a more-elastic long-run supply curve results. So answer (c) is correct because of its impact through answer (b).

12.(c)   The economic surplus on any <u>single unit</u> of output is the vertical distance between the demand and supply curves at that unit (the value to consumers of that unit minus the extra cost of resources used to produce it). This is the amount at which the single unit contributes to the *total* economic surplus generated by the production and the consumption of *all* units.

15.(d)   In contrast to Question 13, where the *D* curve for a unit of output being considered lies above the *S* curve, here the *D* curve lies <u>below</u> the *S* curve and so its production and consumption creates a deadweight loss (the amount by which the value of extra resources exceeds the value to consumers). You still subtract the value of extra resources (*dp*) used in production from the value to consumers (*gp*), but now you get a <u>negative</u> value (since *gp* > *dp*) for surplus on that unit—i.e., the amount by which production and consumption of this unit <u>reduces</u> total economic surplus, hence the deadweight loss.

16.(e)   Compared to the free-market equilibrium of *n* units, which maximizes economic surplus (area *ace*), area *bcf* is the deadweight loss with *m* units while *cgd* is the deadweight loss with *p* units. Total economic surplus is *ace* minus *bcf* at *m* units and *ace* minus *cgd* at *p* units. So <u>in this case</u> the remainder (the economic surplus) would be the same for both overproduction and underproduction.

17.(d)   All three programs would result in an output of *m* units, resulting in the same deadweight loss (*bcf*) and the same economic surplus (*abfe*).

18.(c)   The reduction in output (to less than at the intersection of the *D* and *S* curves) creates the deadweight loss in economic surplus to which answer (c) refers. This would occur regardless of whether demand is elastic or inelastic (so answers (d) and (e) are wrong). And although the quota will increase the price paid by consumers and received by producers, it is the reduction in quantity, not the increase in price, that *causes* the deadweight loss (so answers (a) and (b) are wrong). Indeed, the deadweight loss would be created even if the quota were combined with a binding price ceiling that *reduced* the price paid by consumers and received by producers.

20.(b) The higher profit generated by quotas gives other firms an incentive to pay for a quota. A market for quotas develops, and new entrants will have to pay existing quota holders the resulting market price. Obviously this makes it more costly to enter the industry (so answer (d) is incorrect). Answer (a) is incorrect; the number of firms will be unchanged because, with a fixed number of quotas, a new firm can enter the industry only when another firm leaves (by selling its quota, which is a form of "licence to produce"). Answers (c) and (e) are wrong because (i) quotas are effective only when they <u>reduce</u> output supplied to a level below the free-market equilibrium, and (ii) this reduction in output supplied <u>increases</u> the price paid by consumers.

Consumer Behaviour

Chapter Overview

This chapter develops a model that explains how individuals make consumption choices and how demand curves can be derived from the model. Economic theory assumes that consumers choose among products so as to maximize the **total utility** (i.e., satisfaction) that they receive from the goods and services they consume.

A central assumption of utility theory is **diminishing marginal utility**: the utility a consumer derives from additional units of a product diminishes as more of that product is consumed. Consumers maximize utility when the utility derived from the last dollar spent on each product is the same. As a product's price changes, consumers adjust their quantity demanded so as to again maximize their total utility; this behaviour results in a downward-sloping demand curve.

Any price change induces a consumer response that results from the **substitution effect** and the **income effect**. The substitution effect is caused by a change in *relative prices* which disturbs the equilibrium condition that the marginal utility per dollar spent is equalized across goods. The income effect arises because a price change causes a change in the consumer's *purchasing power* or **real income**. The substitution effect always works to increase (decrease) consumption of a good whose price has decreased (increased). The income effect may increase or decrease consumption of a good whose price has decreased depending on whether the good is normal or inferior, respectively.

The amount that consumers actually have to pay to purchase a commodity is usually less than the maximum amount they would be willing to pay. The difference is called **consumer surplus** (which is a component of economic surplus encountered in Chapter 5).

The appendix to this chapter analyzes income and substitution effects using a more formal model of consumer behaviour: **indifference curves**.

LEARNING OBJECTIVES

After studying this chapter, you will be able to

1. describe the difference between marginal and total utility.

2. explain how utility-maximizing consumers adjust their expenditure until the marginal utility per dollar spent is equalized across products.

3. understand how any change in price generates both an income and a substitution effect on quantity demanded.

4. see that consumer surplus is the "bargain" the consumer gets by paying less for the product than the maximum price he or she is willing to pay.

5. explain the "paradox of value."

Hints and Tips

The following may help you avoid some of the most common errors on examinations.

✓ The real key to understanding this chapter is not to think of the utility-maximizing condition as some magical formula that people have to know in order to get the most satisfaction out of the time and resources available to them. Rather, think of it as a *description* of why people choose to do what they do. The following hints are examples of this.

✓ You don't have to know all about the physics of mass and momentum to know how to moderate your step and speed to avoid walking into a brick wall—you just do it! If someone were to ask "Why didn't you buy another pizza this week instead of that CD?" and you reply "Because I didn't want to" or "Because I liked the CD more," you are following the utility-maximizing condition. What you are effectively saying is "Because I had to choose one or the other, I chose the one that gave me the greater satisfaction for the money." That's what the utility-maximizing condition is saying too!

✓ Students often doubt the utility-maximizing condition because it is not possible to buy an extra dollar's worth of something that costs more than one dollar. This does not prevent us from allocating spending in a way that maximizes utility. Even though we might not be able to reach the *exact* equality you will see in the utility-maximizing condition, it does mean that we have come *as close as possible* to it.

✓ Think of diminishing marginal utility as a description of how most of us feel and behave. When you buy two new tops, why don't you buy a third since they are all the same price? A common answer is "Because two is enough" or "Because I don't need it." But if it were being given away for free, would you have taken it? What you are really saying is that you get more utility (whether you call it a "want" or a "need") from the second one than from the third one, and so on—i.e., you get diminishing marginal utility from each additional unit of the good.

✓ Understand that the sum of marginal utilities equals total utility—just as the sum of the marks you get on each individual question equals your total mark on the exam.

✓ Understand the difference between marginal and infra-marginal decisions. Many, if not most, of our decisions are not made "on the margin." They are infra-marginal decisions where we know that the items we are buying are more than "worth the money" to us—another way of saying that they give us *consumer surplus* (the difference between what we pay and the maximum we would be willing to pay). This does not alter the fact that the marginal decisions—those where we mentally (and again often automatically) assess whether something is "worth the money"—are the decisions that determine how we allocate our spending among commodities.

Chapter Review

Marginal Utility and Consumer Choice

It is important to understand the difference between total and marginal utility. Total utility may be rising while marginal utility is falling—a source of confusion for some students—because the total rises whenever a positive value is added. The condition for utility maximization for any pair of goods can be interpreted in two ways. Be certain that you can discuss each by reviewing Equations 6-1 and 6-2 in the text, as well as the relevant discussion. The condition for utility maximization and the law of diminishing marginal utility together result in a negatively sloped demand curve. An understanding of this derivation is central to this section.

1. **If the marginal utility from consuming more of a good is zero, total utility is**
   (a)   also zero.
   (b)   constant.
   (c)   negative.
   (d)   decreasing.
   (e)   increasing.

2. **Sally is allocating her expenditure between movies and cappuccinos in such a way that she is maximizing her utility. If the price of admission to the movies increases, Sally will reallocate her expenditure such that**
   (a)   the marginal utility of a movie will increase.
   (b)   her movie attendance will increase.
   (c)   her cappuccino consumption will decrease.
   (d)   the marginal utility of cappuccino will increase.
   (e)   the marginal utility per dollar spent on movies will exceed that for cappuccinos.

3. **The hypothesis of diminishing marginal utility states that**
   (a)   the less of a commodity one is consuming, the less the additional utility obtained by an increase in its consumption.
   (b)   the more of a commodity one is consuming, the more the additional utility obtained by an increase in its consumption.
   (c)   the more of a commodity one is consuming, the less the additional utility obtained by an increase in its consumption.
   (d)   the more of a commodity one is consuming, the less will be total utility.
   (e)   marginal utility cannot be measured, but total utility can.

4. **According to utility theory, a consumer will maximize total utility when goods A and B are consumed in quantities such that MU_A/MU_B**
   (a)   equals the ratio of the price of A to the price of B.
   (b)   equals the ratio of total utility of A to that of B.
   (c)   equals the ratio of the price of B to the price of A.
   (d)   equals the ratio of the quantities demanded.
   (e)   always equals unity.

5. **Another way of stating the utility-maximizing condition in Question 4 above is that consumers will purchase successive units of each product until**
   (a)   the MU of every good is the same.
   (b)   the average utility of every good is the same.
   (c)   the average utility of each good equals its marginal utility.
   (d)   the marginal utility of the last dollar spent on each is the same.
   (e)   the ratio of total to marginal utility is the same for each good.

6. **If Monique's marginal utility is positive but decreases as more of a commodity is consumed, her total utility**
   (a)   is increasing.
   (b)   is also decreasing.
   (c)   is constant.
   (d)   may be increasing, decreasing, or constant.
   (e)   increases at the same rate.

7. **The market demand curve of a good is found by**
   - (a) adding the utilities of each consumer buying the good.
   - (b) horizontally summing the demand curves of individual consumers.
   - (c) adding the prices that each consumer is willing to pay for the good.
   - (d) relating quantity demanded to the sum of incomes of all individual demanders.
   - (e) measuring how total demand changes when the price of a substitute good changes.

Income and Substitution Effects of Price Changes

The change in quantity demanded resulting from a price change (i.e., the movement along a demand curve) can be divided into substitution and income effects. A price change affects consumer behaviour through two channels. First, relative prices (i.e., opportunity costs) change, which induces a substitution effect on the quantity demanded. Second, the consumer's purchasing power (or *real income*) changes, which induces an income effect on the quantity demanded. The key to understanding this section is the ability to isolate each effect. This is achieved by conceptually holding purchasing power constant to isolate the substitution effect, and only then recognizing the change in purchasing power (while holding relative prices constant at their new value) to identify the income effect. The income and substitution effects change quantity demanded in the same direction for normal goods, but in opposing directions for inferior goods. (Although in theory it is possible for the income effect of an inferior good to generate a positively sloped demand curve, in reality this is highly unusual and very rarely seen.)

8. **The substitution effect refers to the change in quantity demanded that results from a change in**
   - (a) income.
   - (b) total utility.
   - (c) relative prices.
   - (d) the availability of substitute goods.
   - (e) marginal utility.

9. **The income effect refers to the change in quantity demanded that results from a change in**
   - (a) money income.
   - (b) purchasing power.
   - (c) total utility.
   - (d) marginal utility.
   - (e) wages.

10. **If the price of good B increases, other things constant, the substitution effect**
    - (a) decreases consumption of good B.
    - (b) increases consumption of good B.
    - (c) increases consumption of good B if it is a normal good.
    - (d) increases consumption of good B if it is an inferior good.
    - (e) decreases consumption of good B only if it is an inferior good.

11. **An increase in the absolute price of one good, other things constant, increases**
    - (a) money income.
    - (b) real income.
    - (c) purchasing power.
    - (d) the opportunity cost of buying that good.
    - (e) the relative price of other goods.

12. **A change in the price of a good currently being consumed by a household, other things constant, implies**
     (a)   a change in the household's real income.
     (b)   a change in the household's purchasing power.
     (c)   a change in the opportunity cost of buying goods.
     (d)   that the current consumption bundle no longer maximizes utility at the new prices.
     (e)   All of the above.

Consumer Surplus

After completing this section, you should be able to explain the concept of *consumer surplus* and the distinction between total and marginal valuations. Know how to measure what consumers are willing to pay for a given quantity of a commodity and what they actually have to pay—that's the key to a good understanding of this section! You should also be able to use these concepts to resolve the so-called *paradox of value*.

13. **The consumer surplus derived from consumption of a commodity**
     (a)   is the difference between the total value placed on a certain amount of consumption and the total payment made for it.
     (b)   will always be less than the total amount actually paid for the commodity.
     (c)   will always be more than the total amount consumers are willing to pay for the commodity.
     (d)   equals the total value of that commodity to consumers.
     (e)   equals the total amount actually paid for that commodity.

14. **If an individual is prepared to pay $3 for the first unit of a commodity, $2 for the second, and $1 for the third unit, and the market price is $1,**
     (a)   consumer surplus is $3.
     (b)   the individual will purchase three units of the commodity.
     (c)   the individual's demand curve for this commodity is downward-sloping.
     (d)   consumer surplus on the last unit purchased is zero.
     (e)   All of the above.

15. **The total value Mr. Wimpy places on his consumption of hamburgers equals**
     (a)   the amount he pays for them.
     (b)   price multiplied by marginal value.
     (c)   marginal value multiplied by quantity demanded.
     (d)   price multiplied by quantity demanded.
     (e)   his total expenditure on hamburgers plus his consumer surplus.

16. **Consumer surplus can be measured by the area between the demand curve and the**
     (a)   quantity axis.
     (b)   supply curve.
     (c)   horizontal line at the market price.
     (d)   vertical line at the quantity demanded.
     (e)   price axis.

17. **The "paradox of value" arises from the fact that**
    (a) people can increase total utility by consuming more of a good with a negative marginal utility.
    (b) some goods are essential for life.
    (c) there is no necessary positive relationship between households' marginal and total values of consumption.
    (d) the higher the price of a good, the greater is the total value of consumption.
    (e) not all households behave as assumed in economic theory.

Appendix to Chapter 6: Indifference Curves

Indifference curve analysis assumes that the amount of good A that a consumer is prepared to trade in return for more of good B diminishes as more of good B is obtained. This assumption causes indifference curves to be negatively sloped and of a particular curvature (i.e., bowed in toward the origin). Satisfaction is maximized by choosing a consumption bundle on the highest attainable indifference curve along the consumer's budget line. Using indifference curves, a change in quantity demanded induced by a price change can be graphically decomposed into the income and substitution effects.

18. **An indifference curve represents**
    (a) constant quantities of one good with varying quantities of another.
    (b) the prices and quantities of two goods that can be purchased for a given sum of money.
    (c) all combinations of two goods that give the same level of utility.
    (d) combinations of goods whose marginal utilities are always equal.
    (e) all combinations of goods that can be purchased with a given income and constant prices.

19. **The marginal rate of substitution between goods A and B**
    (a) shows the amount of good A that an individual would be willing to trade for one more unit of good B.
    (b) depends on the amount of goods A and B consumed.
    (c) equals relative prices at the consumer's utility maximizing choice.
    (d) always has a negative algebraic value.
    (e) All of the above.

20. **A budget line**
    (a) describes the demand for two goods.
    (b) describes the quantity demanded at each and every price.
    (c) ranks bundles of goods according to a household's preferences.
    (d) separates bundles of goods that a household can purchase at current income and prices from those that it cannot purchase.
    (e) slopes upward as income increases.

21. **At the point where the budget line is tangent to an indifference curve,**
    (a) equal amounts of goods give equal satisfaction.
    (b) the ratio of prices of the goods must equal the marginal rate of substitution.
    (c) the prices of the goods are equal.
    (d) a household cannot be maximizing its satisfaction.
    (e) the marginal rate of substitution is zero.

22. **A household's demand curve can be derived from**
    (a) a single indifference curve.
    (b) a single budget line.
    (c) a price-consumption line.
    (d) an income-consumption line.
    (e) the indifference map and a single budget line.

Short-Answer Questions

1. Explain why it is not utility-maximizing to continue buying more of a good as long as its marginal utility is positive. How does this relate to the concept of opportunity cost?

2. If utility can't be measured, how can we know that people who allocate their resources to maximize utility are consuming where the ratio of marginal utility to price is the same for all commodities?

3. You spend a total of $500 each week on commodities other than housing. You would like to go to a symphony concert every week, but a seat costs $100. You don't go every week because you "can't afford it." Since you do have $500 per week to spend, what must you *really* mean by "can't afford it"?

4. For a fall in price, why is the substitution effect similar for both normal and inferior goods, but not the income effect?

5. You currently spend a total of $10 each week on 10 cans of fruit juice, but you would be willing to spend $15 for them if you had to. What is that difference between $15 and $10 called? Since you are willing to spend $15 and a can costs $1, why don't you buy 15 cans each week?

Exercises

1. **The Utility-Maximizing Condition: Prove It for Yourself!**
    In this exercise you make decisions about what you do and do not want to consume, and reach your own conclusion about the condition for utility-maximization. You will also see that people do not have to know the condition in order to behave as it predicts.

    You have a fixed budget of $30 per month to spend on two types of chocolate bar, chocks and minties. Your (diminishing) marginal utility (MU) schedules for the two are shown below (where Q_{CH} and Q_{MI} are the quantities of chocks and minties, respectively).

Chocks		Minties	
Q_{CH}	MU_{CH}	Q_{MI}	MU_{MI}
1	20	1	40
2	18	2	36
3	16	3	32
4	14	4	28
5	12	5	24
6	10	6	20
7	8	7	19
8	6	8	18
9	4	9	17
10	2	10	16

    (a) At first the price of chocks (P_{CH}) and the price of minties (P_{MI}) are equal at $3 per bar. You are consuming two chocks and eight minties per month. What is your utility from the second chock? From the eighth minty?

    _18   18_

    (b) If you transfer $3 of spending from minties to chocks, what is your reduction in utility from losing the eighth minty? What is your increase in utility from gaining the third chock? Will you make this transfer? Why/why not?

    → its MU = 18   → its MU = 16.   _Total utility_
    No b/c loss of ³⁄₂ exceeds the gain of 2 in utility.   _falls by 2._

    (c) If you transfer $3 of spending from chocks to minties, what is your reduction in utility from losing the second chock? What is your increase in utility from gaining the ninth minty? Will you make this transfer? Why/why not?

    18.,   17   no b/c loss of 3 exceeds gain
    of ?1. Total utility falls by 1.

    (d) Given your answers to (a), (b), and (c), which combination of chocks and minties will you choose? For that option, how does the ratio of marginal utilities, MU_{CH}/MU_{MI}, for the last chock and the last minty compare with the ratio of their prices, P_{CH}/P_{MI}?

    _(= 18/18 =   = 3/3 = 1_
    Choose (a) — 2 chocks, 2 minties.
    other combos reduce total utility

    (e) Now the price of chocks falls to $2 and the price of minties rises to $4. What has happened to the opportunity cost of a chock bar? You change to buying three chocks and six minties. What is your utility from the last two chocks? From the sixth minty?

    _Original   P_CH = 3/3 = 1   NOW, P_CH = 2/4 = 1/2_
    _Op. cost   P_MI   P_MI_
    of chock

Marginal utility from the last 2 chocks = 18 + 16 = 34
Marginal utility from the 6th minty = 20

(f) If you now transfer $4 of spending from minties to chocks, how much utility do you lose from minties? How much utility do you gain from chocks? What has happened to your total utility compared to (e)? Why? Will you make this transfer?

$4 transfer. increases # chocks from 3 →5 ↑utility by 14+12=26 } yes
reduces # minties from 6→5 ↓utitity by 20

(g) If you transfer another $4 from minties to chocks, what happens to your total utility from minties and chocks combined? Why? Will you make this transfer?

minties 5→4, losing 12 y utility
chocks 5→7, gaining 10+8=18 utility } reduces total utility. so no.

(h) Given your answers to (e), (f), and (g), which combination of chocks and minties will you choose? For that option, how does the ratio of marginal utilities, MU_{CH}/MU_{MI}, $=\frac{12}{24}=\frac{1}{2}$ } equal for the last chock and the last minty compare to the ratio of their prices, P_{CH}/P_{MI}? $\frac{2}{4}=\frac{1}{2}$ Do you see any similarity between this comparison and the comparison you found in (d)? What do you conclude is the condition for utility maximization?

(f) → gives highest utility → maximized when 2 ratios are equal

2. **Utility Maximization and the Demand Curve**

This exercise asks you to apply the condition for utility maximization to determine a consumer's consumption bundle, and to then derive a demand curve from the consumer's utility maximizing behaviour.

A certain consumer spends recreation time and income on only two leisure activities: tennis and fishing. Assume the consumer has the basic equipment to pursue both activities. The price associated with these activities consists of ball replacement costs for tennis and the cost of bait for fishing. The marginal utility schedules for hours spent on these activities are shown in the table below.

	Marginal Utility Schedule	
Hours per week	**Fishing**	**Tennis**
1	20	20
2	18	19
3	16	18
4	14	17
5	12	16
6	10	15
7	8	14
8	6	13

(a) For simplicity, assume that the cost per hour of each activity is $1 (i.e., balls and bait used per hour). Further, assume that a $1 expenditure on other goods yields a marginal utility of 18. How many hours would this consumer spend on each leisure activity in order to maximize total utility?

$$\frac{MU_O}{P_O} = \frac{18}{1} = \frac{MU_F}{P_F} = \frac{MU_T}{P_T}$$

∴ 3hrs fishing
3hrs tennis

(b) Suppose that the cost of fishing decreases to $0.55 per hour. What change in the "mix" of tennis and fishing would be required to maximize utility? Explain, using marginal utility to price ratios, why this is the case.

$$\frac{MU_F}{P_F} = \frac{18}{1} = \frac{MU_F}{0.55}$$

9.9 = MU_F
≅ 10 hrs to fishing

(c) Sketch the demand curve for fishing from the above information. (Assume that it is linear.)

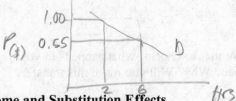

3. **Income and Substitution Effects**

In this exercise you use the utility-maximizing condition to identify the income and substitution effects along a demand curve as price changes. The table shows your marginal utility schedules for avids (MU_A) and blogs (MU_B)—the only foods you eat—where Q_A and Q_B are the quantities of each.

Q_A	MU_A	Q_B	MU_B
3	105	3	85
4	100	4	80
5	95	5	70
6	90	6	60
7	80	7	50
8	70	8	40
9	60	9	30
10	50	10	20

(a) You have a fixed budget of $90 per week. Last week the price of avids (P_A) was $12 and the price of blogs (P_B) was $6. You bought 4 avids. How many blogs could you afford to buy? Is this a utility-maximizing combination? Why/why not?

(b) This week P_A falls to $6 and P_B remains unchanged—but you lose $24 of your $90 budget for this week! Can you still buy the combination of avids and blogs you bought last week? What has happened to your real income (i.e., purchasing power) between last week and this week?

(c) At the new prices, and with only $66 to spend, you plan to increase your purchases of avids from 4 to 7. How many blogs would you buy? Is this a utility-maximizing combination? Why/why not? What would happen to your total utility compared to (a) above? [*Hint:* How much utility would you gain from the extra 3 avids? How much utility would you lose from buying fewer blogs?]

(d) On the way to the store you find the $24 you thought you had lost! When you get there you buy 9 avids. How many blogs do you buy? Is this a utility-maximizing combination?

(e) Comparing (a) and (d) you see you have the same amount of money, P_B is unchanged, P_A has fallen, and your purchases of avids have increased from 4 to 9.

    (i)   Is your increase from 4 to 9 avids a change in quantity demanded or a change in demand? Why?

    (ii)   What part of the increase in avids is your substitution effect of the fall in P_A? What was the cause of your substitution effect?

    (iii)   What part of the increase in avids is your income effect of the fall in P_A? What was the cause of your income effect?

    (iv)   Are your substitution and income effects on avids working the same direction? For you, are avids a normal good or an inferior good?

4.   **Calculating Consumer Surplus**

Consumer surplus can be calculated in two ways; the following exercise guides you through both.

The table that follows provides data on the total value that a certain student places on the consumption of different quantities of personal pan pizzas per week.

Pizzas per Week	Total Value	Marginal Value
1	$14	14
2	24	10
3	31	7
4	36	5
5	40	4

(a)   Calculate the marginal value the student places on each successive pizza consumed. Put the values in the table.

(b)   If the price of a pizza is $5, how many will this student purchase per week?

4 pizzas. Price = Marginal Value

(c)   Calculate the total consumer surplus in (b) by subtracting total expenditure from total consumption value.

$16

(d)   Calculate total consumer surplus in (b) by summing the consumer surplus derived from each individual pizza purchased.

$16

5. **Total Value, Total Expenditure, and Consumer Surplus**
A household's demand for widgets is depicted in Figure 6-1.

Figure 6-1

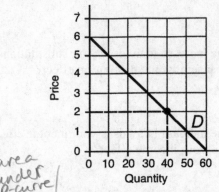

area under D-curve

If widgets have a current price of $2 per unit, the total value this household places on its consumption of widgets is __$160__. However, the household's total expenditure on widgets is __$80__, so it receives consumer surplus of __$80__. If the market price drops to $1, this household's total valuation of widgets would (increase/~~decrease~~) by __$15__ and its consumer surplus would (increase/~~decrease~~) by __$45__. The value this household places on its consumption of the twentieth widget is __$4__, and it is willing to pay __$100__ for 20 widgets.

area under D curve.   *read from D curve*

6. **"Get Me Tickets for the Playoffs!"**
A certain chief executive officer (CEO) with a large corporation instructs her personal secretary (a recent graduate of a prestigious MBA program) to purchase tickets to the Stanley Cup playoffs. Specifically, she tells him, "If the tickets are $150 each, buy one ticket for me; at $100 each, buy two; and, if the price is $50 each, buy me three." The young secretary (eager to make an impression) responds, "Madame, your instructions appear to be inconsistent. You are saying that you are *willing to pay* more in total for two tickets than for three!" Is the secretary correct in thinking that the instructions are inconsistent? Explain. [*Hint:* Sketch the CEO's demand curve for tickets.]

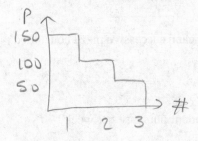

willing to pay $150 for 1st
$100 for 2nd   2 tickets: 250
$50 for 3rd.   3 tickets: $300

willing to pay = value she places on the tickets
not the price

Extension Exercise

E1. Are You a Member?

The concept of consumer surplus can be used to explain many observed pricing schemes. The following exercise addresses membership fees.

An individual's weekly demand for playing squash is given by

$$Q^D = 10 - 2P$$

where Q^D is hours of squash time demanded per week and P is the price per hour (for each player) of court time (assume that this person can always find a partner).

(a) Plot the individual's demand curve for squash.

Figure 6-2

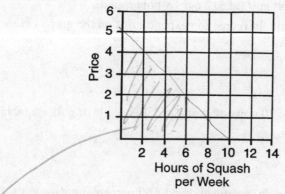

(b) The only squash courts available are at The Racquet Club, Inc., where each player is charged $2 per hour. How much squash does this person play per week?

$$Q = 10 - 2 \cdot 2 = 6.$$

(c) What is this individual's total valuation of the games consumed per week?

21

(d) How much does this person actually spend on squash each week?

$$2 \times 6 = 12$$

(e) What is this individual's consumer surplus?

$$21 - 12 = 9$$

(f) The Racquet Club, Inc., is considering a pricing scheme whereby individuals still pay $2 per hour of court time, but in addition they must also pay a mandatory membership fee. What is the largest fee The Racquet Club, Inc., could charge for a weekly membership without losing this individual as a customer? Explain.

(g) As an alternative pricing scheme, suppose that The Racquet Club, Inc., introduces a membership fee but does not charge members for court time (i.e., members are entitled to unlimited use of the facility). What is the maximum amount this individual is willing to pay for a weekly membership under these circumstances?

Appendix Exercises

The following exercises are for students covering the material in the appendix to this chapter. The appendix should be read before attempting these exercises.

A1. Budget Lines

The purpose of this exercise is to review your understanding of budget lines.

Suppose an individual has an annual budget of $600 to spend on two recreation activities: skiing (at $20 per day) and golf (at $12 per 18-hole round).

(a) Draw the budget line for recreation expenditures on the graph below. Label the budget line BL_A.

(b) Is a combination of 20 units of skiing and 20 rounds of golf attainable? Explain.

(c) Suppose an increase in income allowed a 50 percent increase in the recreation budget. Graph the new budget line and label it BL_C—assume prices are unchanged.

Figure 6-3

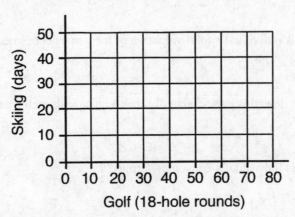

(d) Suppose now that the price of skiing increases to $30 per day, *ceteris paribus*. Draw the new budget line and label it BL_D.

(e) Finally, suppose that the price of a round of golf increases to $18. Graph the new budget line (BL_E). Compare BL_E and BL_A. Explain your findings.

A2. Indifference Curves and Equilibrium

The exercise that follows uses indifference curve analysis to solve for the consumer's equilibrium and to derive a demand curve.

(a) The following table provides information on the combinations of food and clothing that are contained on indifference curves I, II, and III. For example, indifference curve I includes a combination containing 45 units of food and zero units of clothing, as well as a combination containing 30 units of food and 5 units of clothing.

Units of Food			Units of Clothing		
I	II	III	I	II	III
45	50	55	0	10	20
30	35	40	5	15	25
20	25	30	10	20	30
15	20	25	15	25	35
10	15	20	25	35	45

(i) Graph indifference curves I, II, and III on the grid provided below.

Figure 6-4

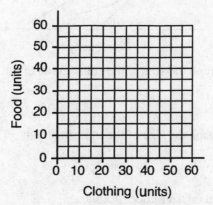

(ii) Draw a budget line on the graph that represents a budget constraint of $350 and food and clothing prices of $10 and $15, respectively.

(iii) Given (i) and (ii), what combination of food and clothing will maximize consumer satisfaction? Explain.

(b) Now extend the analysis and use the same graph to show the derivation of a demand curve for clothing (assume that "food" stands for "everything consumed except clothing"). Change the price of clothing so that a budget line with the same food intercept (35) is tangent to each of the indifference curves I, II, and III. (Extend the X axis as necessary.)

(i) The utility-maximizing quantities of clothing on indifference curves I, II, and III are _____, _____, and _____, respectively. The prices of clothing represented by the budget lines are _____, _____, and, _____, respectively.

(ii) Draw the price-consumption line on the graph. What does this line tell you about the individual's price elasticity of demand for clothing?

(iii)   Describe how the information on the price-consumption line can be used to derive a demand curve for clothing.

A3.   Income and Substitution Effects

This exercise uses indifference curve analysis to decompose the effect of a price change into income and substitution effects.

On the graph in Figure 6-5, an individual is shown to move from equilibrium E_0 to a new equilibrium E_1 in response to a decline in the price of commodity X.

Figure 6-5

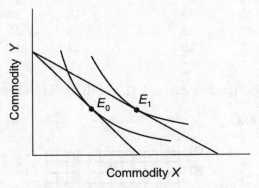

(a)   Illustrate on the graph the size of the substitution effect.

(b)   Illustrate on the graph the size of the income effect.

(c)   Is commodity X an inferior good? Explain.

A4.   "Turn Out the Lights!"

This example develops a practical application of income and substitution effects. During the 1970s, the Government of Ontario decided to promote conservation of electricity. At the same time, it did not want to adversely affect the real incomes of households. The following example illustrates how a tax-and-rebate scheme that takes advantage of income and substitution effects can achieve these twin objectives. [*Note:* The issue of electricity conservation remains relevant today.]

Assume that a typical household has $300 per month to spend on consumption of electricity and entertainment. Suppose that the price of a kilowatt hour (kwh) of electricity is $0.10, while a unit of entertainment costs $1.00. In its initial equilibrium, the household is consuming 2000 kwh of electricity and 100 units of entertainment.

(a)   Draw the household's initial budget line on the following graph, and label its initial equilibrium E_A. Draw a representative indifference curve through E_A and label it I_A.

Figure 6-6

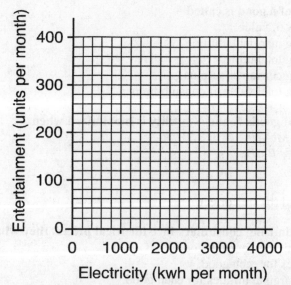

(b) Now suppose a tax of 50 percent is imposed on electricity so that the consumer price of a kwh is now $0.15. This typical household responds by changing its consumption bundle to 90 units of entertainment and 1400 kwh of electricity. Draw the new budget line and a possible indifference curve. Label the new equilibrium point E_B and the new indifference curve I_B.

(c) The government now decides to compensate households for the electricity tax by using the resulting revenue to send each household a monthly rebate that restores its real income. Draw the new budget line and label the new equilibrium E_C. Explain.

(d) Could the government have achieved its twin objectives with this tax-and-rebate scheme? Explain.

Additional Multiple-Choice Questions

*1. **If total utility is increasing, marginal utility is**
(a) increasing.   (b) decreasing.
(c) positive.   (d) negative.
(e) constant.

2. **If marginal utility is negative, total utility is**
(a) negative.   (b) positive.
(c) increasing.   (d) decreasing.
(e) constant.

3. The idea that a consumer derives less additional satisfaction from consuming successive units of a good is called
   (a) the paradox of value.
   (b) diminishing marginal utility.
   (c) diminishing total utility.
   (d) diminishing consumer surplus.
   (e) diminishing total value of consumption.

4. Given any pair of goods X and Y, utility is maximized when
   (a) $MU_X/P_X = MU_Y/P_Y$.
   (b) $MU_X/MU_Y = P_X/P_Y$.
   (c) $MU_X = MU_Y$.
   (d) $P_X = P_Y$.
   (e) Both (a) and (b) are correct.

*5. If all utility-maximizing consumers face identical prices, they will have identical
   (a) marginal utilities for each good.
   (b) total utilities for each good.
   (c) ratios of marginal utilities for each good.
   (d) ratios of total utilities for each good.
   (e) preferences.

*6. Suppose Liam is maximizing utility by allocating his expenditure between CDs and movies. If the price of movies increases, the resulting substitution effect will cause Liam to react so that
   (a) marginal utility of movies will increase and his marginal utility of CDs will decrease.
   (b) marginal utility of movies will decrease and his marginal utility of CDs will increase.
   (c) marginal utility of both movies and CDs will decrease.
   (d) total utility of both goods increases.
   (e) consumption of both goods decreases.

Questions 7 to 9 refer to the following schedule, which depicts the total value a student places on weekly restaurant meals.

Quantity of Restaurant Meals per Week	Total Value of Consumption
0	$ 0
1	30
2	50
3	66
4	74
5	80

7. The marginal value of the third restaurant meal is
   (a) $22.   (b) $16.
   (c) $146.   (d) $8.
   (e) $66.

*8. If the price of a restaurant meal were $8, how often would this student eat out per week?
(a) 0.   (b) 1.
(c) 2.   (d) 3.
(e) 4.

*9. If the price were $8, this student's consumer surplus would be
(a) zero.   (b) $66.
(c) $18.50.   (d) $42.
(e) Cannot be determined with the information provided.

*10. If I am willing to pay $50 for a particular pair of blue jeans, but when I arrive at the store they are on sale for $30,
(a) I should buy all the blue jeans in the store.
(b) the value I place on the consumption of these blue jeans is lowered by $20.
(c) I receive consumer surplus of $20 if I purchase the pair of blue jeans.
(d) my valuation of consuming the pair of blue jeans is now $70.
(e) my consumer surplus decreases by $20.

*11. Diamonds have a higher price than water because
(a) the total value placed on the consumption of diamonds is greater than that of water.
(b) the total consumption value of water is greater than that of diamonds.
(c) the marginal consumption value of diamonds is greater than that of water.
(d) households are willing to pay more in total for diamonds than for water.
(e) all necessities of life have a high marginal value in consumption.

*12. At first the city's *fixed* supply of water was sold at the market equilibrium price per litre. It then passed a law requiring that the water be provided free. This law
(a) ensures that only households with the highest marginal values will consume water.
(b) ensures that all households will consume equal quantities of water.
(c) is likely to result in some households with a low marginal value of water getting water while others with a higher marginal value do without.
(d) ensures that all households can always consume water until the marginal value of water is zero.
(e) would increase the total consumption value of water.

*13. When the price of a good declines, the income effect
(a) will be greater for products that account for a large share of the consumer's budget.
(b) implies that consumers' real income has also declined.
(c) is predicted to increase consumption of inferior goods.
(d) is predicted to decrease consumption of normal goods.
(e) Both (c) and (d) are correct.

*14. The substitution effect
(a) is always dominated by the income effect for normal goods.
(b) is caused by a change in real income.
(c) may cause demand curves to be upward sloping.
(d) is opposite in sign to the income effect for all normal goods.
(e) always increases quantity demanded of a good whose relative price has fallen.

*15. **Demand curves for normal goods slope downward because**
   (a) the substitution effect of a price change is greater than the income effect.
   (b) substitution and income effects work in the same direction.
   (c) the income effect is always greater than the substitution effect.
   (d) the income effect is always less than the substitution effect.
   (e) None of the above, because demand curves for normal goods slope upward.

*16. **The income and substitution effects of a fall in price of a good show that**
   (a) inferior goods can't have downward-sloping demand curves.
   (b) the substitution effect increases the quantity demanded of a normal good but reduces quantity demanded of an inferior good.
   (c) money income rises when price falls.
   (d) a Giffen good must be an inferior good but an inferior good need not be Giffen.
   (e) purchasing power falls when price falls.

*17. **Albert and Henri each consume some potatoes and some rice. They buy from the same store (i.e., buy the same quality and pay the same prices), and they each spend the same amount of money on potatoes and rice combined, but Albert buys more potatoes and less rice than Henri. If the price of potatoes is half the price of rice, the utility-maximization condition predicts that**
   (a) Albert's marginal utility of potatoes is bigger than Henri's. $P_P = \frac{1}{2} P_R$
   (b) Henri's marginal utility of rice is bigger than Albert's.
   (c) The ratio $MU_{rice}/MU_{potatoes}$ is 2 for both Albert and Henri. $2P_P = P_R$
   (d) All of the above are correct.
   (e) None of the above is correct.

*18. **Which of the following would most likely explain why Arabella's demand curve for high-fashion dresses is upward-sloping?**
   (a) She prefers to give up more of other goods per dress than less of other goods.
   (b) High-fashion dresses are a Giffen good.
   (c) If she could pay less than the market price without other people knowing it, she would demand fewer dresses.
   (d) A higher market price generates more units of admiration from other people.
   (e) All of the above.

*19. **The market demand curve for a conspicuous consumption good is _____ because _____.**
   (a) upward-sloping; lower prices reduce conspicuousness
   (b) upward-sloping; marginal utility per dress decreases with the number of dresses
   (c) downward-sloping; lower prices reduce conspicuousness
   (d) upward-sloping; higher prices create more consumer surplus for each individual consumer
   (e) downward-sloping; lower prices increase the number of consumers

Appendix

The following questions are for students covering material in the appendix to this chapter. Read the appendix before answering these questions.

Questions 20 to 24 refer to the four diagrams in Figure 6-7, which depict an initial budget line labelled *ab* and a new budget line *a'b'*. The new budget line results from a change in income, prices, or both.

Figure 6-7

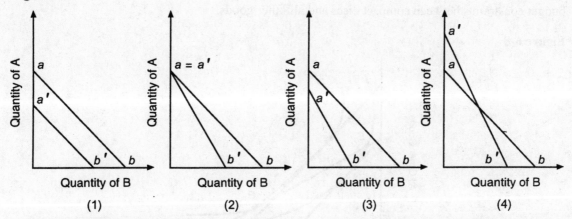

(1)   (2)   (3)   (4)

*20. Which graph (or graphs) depicts the shift in a budget line that results from a decrease in income, *ceteris paribus*?
(a) 1.   (b) 2.
(c) 3.   (d) 4.
(e) 1 and 3.

21. Which shift (or shifts) in the budget line could be explained by an increase in the price of good B, *ceteris paribus*?
(a) 1.   (b) 2.
(c) 3.   (d) 4.
(e) 2 and 3.

*22. Which shift (or shifts) could be explained by increases in the prices of both goods?
(a) 1.   (b) 3.
(c) 1 and 3.   (d) 3 and 4.
(e) 1 and 4.

*23. Which shift (or shifts) are consistent with a decrease in the price of good A and an increase in the price of good B, *ceteris paribus*?
(a) 2.   (b) 3.
(c) 4.   (d) 3 and 4.
(e) 2 and 3.

*24. Which graphs describe the shift in a budget line that results from decreases in both the price of good A and income?
(a) 2.   (b) 2 and 4.
(c) 2 and 3.   (d) 3 and 4.
(e) 2, 3, and 4.

Questions 25 to 29 refer to Figure 6-8, which shows an individual's indifference curves and budget constraints between compact discs and all other goods.

Figure 6-8

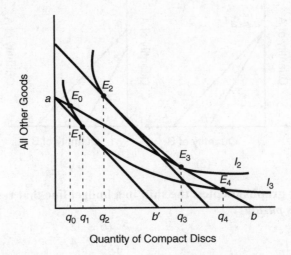

Quantity of Compact Discs

25. **Starting from budget line *ab*, which consumption bundle maximizes utility?**
   (a) E_0.
   (b) E_1.
   (c) E_2.
   (d) E_3.
   (e) E_4.

26. **Starting from budget line *ab*, assume that the price of compact discs increases such that the new budget line is *ab′*. Quantity demanded of compact discs decreases by**
   (a) q_3q_0.
   (b) q_3q_1.
   (c) q_3q_2.
   (d) q_2q_0.
   (e) q_3q_4.

*27. **The substitution effect of a rise in the price of compact discs is equal to the**
   (a) increase from q_0 to q_2.
   (b) increase from q_2 to q_3.
   (c) decrease from q_3 to q_2.
   (d) decrease from q_2 to q_1.
   (e) decrease from q_3 to q_1.

*28. **The income effect of a rise in the price of compact discs is equal to the**
   (a) increase from q_0 to q_2.
   (b) increase from q_2 to q_3.
   (c) decrease from q_3 to q_2.
   (d) decrease from q_2 to q_1.
   (e) decrease from q_1 to q_0.

*29. **From the information in Figure 6-8, one can say that compact discs are**
   (a) normal goods.
   (b) inferior goods.
   (c) Giffen goods.
   (d) conspicuous consumption goods.
   (e) Both (b) and (c) are correct.

Solutions

Chapter Review

1.(b) 2.(a) 3.(c) 4.(a) 5.(d) 6.(a) 7.(b) 8.(c) 9.(b) 10.(a) 11.(d) 12.(e) 13.(a) 14.(e) 15.(e) 16.(c) 17.(c)
Appendix: 18.(c) 19.(e) 20.(d) 21.(b) 22.(c)

Short-Answer Questions

1. The utility-maximizing condition is $MUx/Px = MUy/Py$. Focusing only on (say) MUx totally ignores the role of prices and the marginal utility of other goods. For example, assume another hamburger costs $3 and gives 4 extra units of utility. Also assume that spending the $3 on three more cups of coffee costing $1 each would increase utility by 6 units. If you have to choose between the hamburger and the coffees you will not buy the hamburger despite the fact that its marginal utility is positive. In essence, the *opportunity cost* of 4 units of utility from the hamburger is 6 units of utility from the 3 coffees. You will maximize utility by choosing the 3 coffees.

2. It is a logical inference from the conditions that (i) the objective is to maximize utility, and (ii) people will make choices consistent with achieving that objective. If the ratio MU/P were not equal across commodities, spending more on one commodity and less on another would increase total utility. Not reallocating spending in this way would be inconsistent with achieving the objective of utility maximization.

3. Since you have $500 and the concert costs $100, obviously you are *able* to go to the concert if you wish. The reason you don't go every week is because you *do not want* to give up the utility obtained from the other things you can buy with $100. So in this case "can't afford it" means "it would not be utility-maximizing."

4. The substitution effect is the reaction to a change in relative prices (i.e., opportunity cost) at a *constant* level of purchasing power. Since "normal" and "inferior" goods are defined in terms of your response to a *change* in purchasing power (or in income, *ceteris paribus*), the distinction is not relevant to the substitution effect. The opportunity cost changes regardless of what happens to purchasing power. But the fall in price does increase purchasing power too, and how you spend this *extra* purchasing power differs depending on whether the good is normal or inferior.

5. The $5 difference between what you are willing to pay and what you actually pay is your consumer surplus from the 10 cans of juice. You do not buy more than 10 cans because your *marginal value* of the next 5 cans is less than your *marginal value* from another good (or goods) that you can buy with the $5.

Exercises

1. (a) Marginal utility from the second chock = 18. Marginal utility from the eighth minty = 18.
    (b) The reduction in utility from losing the eighth minty = 18 (its *MU*). The increase in utility from gaining the third chock = 16 (its *MU*). You will not make the transfer, since the loss in utility exceeds the gain in utility and total utility would fall by 18 – 16 = 2.
    (c) The reduction in utility from losing the second chock = 18 (its *MU*). The increase in utility from gaining the ninth minty = 17 (its *MU*). You will not make the transfer, since the loss in utility exceeds the gain in utility and total utility would fall by 18 – 17 = 1.
    (d) You will choose (a), 2 chocks and 8 minties, since the other combinations would reduce your total utility. At this combination, $MU_{CH}/MU_{MI} = 18/18 = 1$ and $P_{CH}/P_{MI} = 3/3 = 1$. That is, $MU_{CH}/MU_{MI} = P_{CH}/P_{MI}$.
    (e) The opportunity cost of a chock bar falls from one minty ($P_{CH}/P_{MI} = \$3/\$3 = 1$) to one-half a minty ($P_{CH}/P_{MI} = \$2/\$4 = 0.5$). Marginal utility from the last two chocks = 18 + 16 = 34. Marginal utility from the sixth minty = 20.
    (f) The $4 transfer reduces the number of minties from 6 to 5, and increases the number of chocks from 3 to 5. Losing the sixth minty reduces utility by 20, and gaining the fourth and fifth chock increases utility by 14 + 12 = 26. You will make the transfer since it increases total utility by 26 – 20 = 6.
    (g) Transferring another $4 means reducing minties from 5 to 4, losing the *MU* of the fifth minty = 24. The $4 will buy the sixth and seventh chock, increasing utility by 10 + 8 = 18. You will not make the transfer, since it would reduce total utility by 24 – 18 = 6.
    (h) You will choose (f), because the combination of 5 minties and 5 chocks gives you the highest total utility. At this combination, $MU_{CH}/MU_{MI} = 12/24 = 1/2$ and $P_{CH}/P_{MI} = 2/4 = 1/2$. The two ratios are equal—just as they were in (d). You can therefore conclude that utility is maximized at the combination of goods where the ratio of marginal utilities equals the ratio of prices.

2. (a) Utility maximization requires that $MU_T/P_T = MU_F/P_F = MU_o/P_o$. Since $MU_o/P_o = 18/1$, utility maximization implies 3 hours on tennis (where $MU_T/P_T = 18/1$) and 2 hours on fishing (where $MU_F/P_F = 18/1$), for a total of 5 hours of leisure time.

(b) With the price of fishing reduced to $0.55, the condition that the marginal utility per dollar of expenditure is equalized across all goods is satisfied when 6 hours are allocated to fishing and 3 hours to tennis (approximately). This mix is where $MU_o/P_o = 18/1 = 18$, $MU_F/P_F = 10/0.55 = 18$ (approx.), and $MU_T/P_T = 18/1 = 18$.

(c) **Figure 6-9**

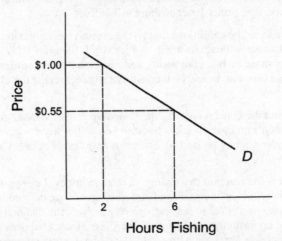

3. (a) The 4 avids at $12 each cost $48, leaving $90 – $48 = $42 to spend on $42/$6 = 7 blogs. This is a utility-maximizing combination because $MU_A/MU_B = P_A/P_B$ (i.e., 100/50 = 12/6 = 2).

(b) Yes, you can still buy last week's combination with the ($90 – $24 =) $66 you have left. At $6 each, 4 avids and 7 blogs cost $11(6) = $66. Purchasing power (or real income) is unchanged because last week's combination of avids and blogs can still be bought, with no money left over.

(c) At $6 each the 7 avids cost $42, leaving $66 – $42 = $24 to buy $24/$6 = 4 blogs. This is a utility-maximizing combination because $MU_A/MU_B = 80/80 = 1$ and P_A/P_B $6/$6 = 1. Taking the sum of the marginal utilities of the fifth, sixth, and seventh extra avids you are buying (95 + 90 + 80 = 265) and subtracting the sum of marginal utilities of the seventh, sixth, and fifth blogs that you are no longer buying (50 + 60 + 70 = 180) gives an increase in total utility of 265 – 180 = 85.

(d) The 9 avids at $6 each cost $54, leaving $90 – $54 = $36 to spend on $36/$6 = 6 blogs. This is a utility-maximizing combination because $MU_A/MU_B = 60/60 = 1$ and $P_A/P_B = $6/$6 = 1$.

(e) (i) A change in quantity demanded—i.e., a movement along the demand curve. The only change was in the price of avids—all else is constant.

(ii) The substitution effect is the increase from 4 avids in (a) to 7 in (c). Purchasing power (i.e., real income) is constant, so the change from 4 to 7 is solely a response to the fall in the opportunity cost of avids (i.e., P_A/P_B), from 2 blogs per avid to 1 blog per avid.

(iii) The income effect is the increase from 7 to 9 avids, which is the response to the increase in purchasing power of the $90 budget as the price of avids fell from $12 to $6.

(iv) Yes, the income and substitution effects of the price fall each increase the quantity of avids demanded. The increase in purchasing power caused part of the increase in quantity demanded, so avids are normal (not inferior) goods. [*Note:* Applying Panel (i) of Figure 6-2 in the text to this exercise, the two prices are $12 and $6, and the quantities of avids are $Q_0 = 4$, $Q_0^S = 7$, and $Q_1 = 9$.]

4. (a)

Pizzas per Week	Total Value	Marginal Value
1	$14	14
2	24	10
3	31	7
4	36	5
5	40	4

(b) 4 pizzas, where price ($5) equals marginal value.

(c) consumer surplus = total value minus total expenditure = $36 – ($5 × 4) = $16.

(d) Consumer surplus from each unit consumed equals the marginal value minus market price. Consumer surplus on the first unit is ($14 – $5) $9, on the second unit is ($10 – $5) $5, on the third unit is ($7 – $5) $2, and on the fourth unit is ($5 – $5) $0. Summing these yields gives $9 + $5 + $2 = $16 (the same as in (c)).

5. $160, the area under the demand curve at 40 widgets, calculated as $2 × 40 = $80 + 0.5($6 – $2) × 40 = $80, for a total of $160;

$80 ($2 × 40);

$80 ($160 – $80);

increase by $15 (from $160 to ($1 × 50) + 0.5($6 – $1) × 50 = $175);

increase by $45 (from $80 to $175 – $50 = $125);

$4 (read from the demand curve);

$100 (area under the demand curve at 20 widgets = ($4 × 20) + 0.5($6 – $4) × 20 = $80 + $20).

6. No, the secretary is not correct. The CEO's demand curve is sketched in Figure 6-10. The CEO is willing to pay $150 for the first ticket, $100 for the second, and $50 for the third. Thus, for two tickets she is willing to pay $250 ($150 + $100), and for three she is willing to pay $300 ($150 + $100 + $50). If the price is $100 per ticket, she has to pay only $200 for two, and if the price is $50, she has only to pay $150 for three. What she is *willing* to pay is determined by the value she places on the consumption of these goods, not on the cost of purchasing them.

Figure 6-10

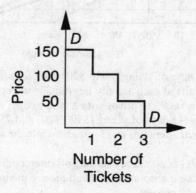

Extension Exercise

E1. (a) **Figure 6-11**

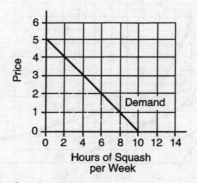

(b) Six hours per week (i.e., $Q^D = 10 – 2 × $2 = 6$).
(c) $21 (obtained by calculating the area under the demand curve up to a quantity of 6).
(d) $12 (i.e., $2 × 6).
(e) $9 (obtained by calculating the area below the demand curve and above the price line, = total valuation minus total spending = $21 – $12).

(f) For consumption of 6 hours, this person is willing to pay the total valuation of $21. At a price of $2, current payment is $12 for six hours. Therefore, this individual is willing to pay an additional $9 to play six hours of squash, which may be collected as a membership fee.

(g) By joining the club, the price per hour is zero, so as a member this person would now play 10 hours of squash each week. The value this individual places on 10 hours of squash is $25. Thus $25 could now be charged for a membership in The Racquet Club, Inc., without losing this person as a member.

Appendix Exercises

A1. Figure 6-12

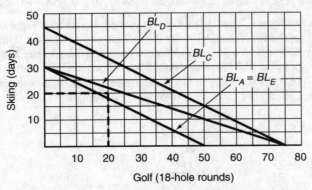

(a) Intercepts on BL_A are 30 days of skiing ($600/$20) and 50 rounds of golf ($600/$12).

(b) The combination of 20 units of each activity lies outside the budget line BL_A. It is therefore unattainable (unaffordable) at these prices with a total budget of $600.

(c) Intercepts on BL_C are now 45 days of skiing ($900/$20) and 75 rounds of golf ($900/$12).

(d) The intercept for golf on BL_D remains at 75 rounds; while the skiing intercept changes to 30 days ($900/$30).

(e) The skiing intercept on BL_E is 30 units, and the golf intercept is now 50 rounds ($900/$18). BL_E and BL_A are identical because absolute prices and money income have changed in exactly the same proportion (i.e., by 50 percent).

A2. (a) (i) The indifference curves are shown on the graph below.

Figure 6-13

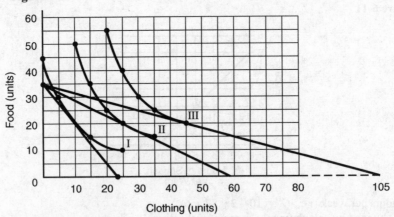

(ii) The budget constraint intercept on the food axis is $350/$10 = 35, and on the clothing axis is $350/$15 = 23.33.

(iii) Tangency occurs at 20 food and 10 clothing. Given the budget constraint, curve I is the highest indifference curve attainable.

(b) (i) Utility-maximizing quantities of clothing (i.e., at tangency) on I, II, and II are 10, 25, and 45, respectively. The prices of clothing are $15, $6, and $3.33, respectively. These prices are found as follows: the consumption of food is constant at 20 units, so spending on food is constant at $10 \times 20 = \$200$ and the spending on clothing must therefore be constant at $\$350 - \$200 = \$150$. The price of clothing on I is $\$150/10 = \$15$, on II is $\$150/25 = \$6$, and on III is $\$150/45 = \$3.33$. [*Note:* These prices give budget constraint intercepts on the clothing axis of $\$350/\$15 = \$23.33$, $\$350/\$6 = \$58.33$, and $\$350/3.33 = 105$.]

   (ii)   Connecting the points of tangency gives a horizontal price-consumption line at 20 units of food. This shows a unit-elastic demand for clothing over the price range, with constant spending on clothing at $150.

   (iii)   Plot the utility-maximizing price/quantity combinations of clothing from the price-consumption line on a separate graph, with price on the Y axis and quantity demanded on the X axis (i.e., $15 and 10 units, $6 and 25 units, and $3.33 and 45 units).

A3. **(a)** The substitution effect is AB in the graph.

    (b) The income effect is BC in the graph.

    (c) No. If X were an inferior good, there would have to be a negative income effect. The income effect is positive, so X is a normal good.

Figure 6-14

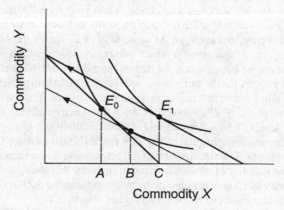

A4. **(a)** The initial budget line is ab in the following graph.

Figure 6-15

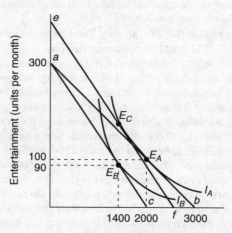

    (b) The resulting budget line is ac in the above graph.

    (c) If the household's real income (i.e., purchasing power) were restored, it would be able to purchase its initial level of utility represented by I_A at the new prices. Thus, the new budget line would be parallel to budget line ac and just tangent to I_A. Budget line ef in Figure 6-15 is the new budget line. [*Note:* The size of the rebate will vary for each answer since it depends on the curvature of I_A, which has been arbitrarily drawn by each student.] In the above diagram, the rebate will be a sum that is sufficient to increase entertainment purchases by ae, *ceteris paribus*.

(d) Yes, the government could have realized its twin objectives because bundle E_C necessarily represents a reduction in electrical consumption relative to that at E_A but the same real income (i.e., utility) as before intervention. The move from E_A to E_C is a substitution effect. The income effect of the price increase (E_C to E_B) is offset by the monthly rebate.

Additional Multiple-Choice Questions

1.(c) **2.**(d) **3.**(b) **4.**(e) **5.**(c) **6.**(a) **7.**(b) **8.**(e) **9.**(d) **10.**(c) **11.**(c) **12.**(c) **13.**(a) **14.**(e) **15.**(b) **16.**(d) **17.**(c) **18.**(d) **19.**(e) **Appendix: 20.**(a) **21.**(b) **22.**(c) **23.**(c) **24.**(e) **25.**(d) **26.**(b) **27.**(c) **28.**(d) **29.**(a)

Explanations for the Asterisked Multiple-Choice Questions

1.(c) This is a universal mathematical relationship which applies to countless more cases than economics. For example, you and a friend take an exam with four questions, each out of 10. You get marks of 8, 7.5, 6.5, and 5, and your friend gets 5, 6.5, 7.5, and 8. Thus your *marginal* ("extra") marks per question *decreased* as you went along, while your friend's marginal marks *increased*. Since both of you got a positive score for each question, however, *total* marks *increased* with each question (and, in this case, you each got the same total of 27 marks out of 40).

5.(c) Beware! This is the type of question for which you really do know the answer, but can choose an incorrect answer in exams because you are rushing and don't stop to think. Different people have different marginal utilities for the same good, and to maximize utility they will buy goods to the point where *per dollar* returns in terms of *extra utility* are equal. That is, each person maximizes utility when relative prices ($P_X/P_Y = 2$) equals the ratio of marginal utilities ($MU_X/MU_Y = 2$). This happens when the levels of MU_X/MU_Y are 4/2, 180/98, 6000/3000, etc.

6.(a) The principle of diminishing marginal utility says that MU falls as *more* is consumed, hence MU *rises as less is consumed*. The substitution effect, responding to the increase in the relative price of movies, reduces the quantity of movies demanded (thereby increasing the MU of movies) and increases the quantity of CDs demanded (thereby decreasing the MU of CDs). Restricting the question to the substitution effect rules out any other response.

8.(e) First note that the total value of consumption is not the same as total utility. It is the total amount the individual would be willing to spend. Finding the marginal values, therefore, tells you the demand curve—and along the demand curve, marginal value equals price. At a price of $8 the marginal value of the fourth meal is 8 (i.e., 74 – 66).

9.(d) At $8 four meals are demanded (see 8(e) above). Total expenditure is $8 × 4 = $32. Total value is $74. The difference, $74 – $32 = $42, is consumer surplus.

10.(c) Answer (a) is silly but is there to remind you of (i) the constraint imposed by total income/spending power, and (ii) the principle of *diminishing marginal utility*—i.e., the additional utility value to you falls as you buy more and more pairs of jeans. In the remaining answers, remember that *ceteris paribus* still applies: nothing has happened to change the prices of other goods and services, nor the value to you ($50) of consuming the new pair of jeans. You pay only $30 for something you value at $50 (i.e., the maximum you would be willing to pay), and your *consumer surplus* is the difference between the two ($50-$30=$20).

11.(c) The marginal value to consumers of the last diamond (i.e., the one at the intersection of the market D and S curves) as reflected in the market price is higher than the marginal value of the last unit of water because the far lower supply of diamonds pushes up the market equilibrium price. If a huge increase in the supply of diamonds actually lowered their price to equal that of a litre of water, the two would have the same low marginal value to consumers but the total value of water (hence the total they would be <u>willing</u> to spend on it) would still be far higher than diamonds because without water we die (so answers (a), (d), and (e) are wrong). Answer (b) is not itself an incorrect statement, but it is an incorrect answer to the question asked because it is not the *reason* why diamonds are priced higher than water.

12.(c) When the market price was charged, people would not buy any additional litres of water for which their marginal valuation was less than the market price. With water being free, however, people will continue to use it as long as it has any positive marginal valuation. Since it is in *fixed supply*, someone could use a litre for which he/she had a marginal valuation of (say) $0.05 and prevent that litre from being used by someone for whom the marginal value was $0.10—thus reducing the total consumption value, not increasing it as in (e). The fixed supply also rules out (d).

13.(a) A fall in the price of a good on which consumers spend a large share of their budget will increase purchasing power more than if it were a small share, thus generating a bigger income effect.

14.(e) The substitution effect is the reaction to the change in *opportunity cost* at a given level of purchasing power. The opportunity cost falls when the relative price of the good falls—i.e., getting a unit of the good requires giving up <u>less</u> of other goods than before. The (price-induced) income effect is the response to the change in purchasing power (at the same level of nominal money income) resulting from the change in price. The income effect of a fall in price (for example) will increase or decrease quantity demanded depending on whether it is a normal or an inferior good. The response of quantity demanded to the change in opportunity cost, however, is in the opposite direction to the price change for normal and inferior goods alike.

15.(b) Consider a fall in the price of a good. Its opportunity cost is reduced, hence an increase in quantity demanded via the *substitution effect*. The purchasing power of a nominal level of income increases, thus increasing quantity demanded via the price-induced *income effect*. Since both the income and substitution effects of the <u>fall</u> in price work to <u>increase</u> the quantity demanded of the normal good, there is a negative (inverse) relationship between P and Qd—i.e., a negatively-sloped demand curve. Whether the income effect is greater than or less than the substitution effect (answers (a), (c) and (d)) is totally immaterial to this negative relationship since both effects work in the same direction for the normal good.

16.(d) To have an upward-sloping demand curve (as a Giffen good), the income effect must be in the *opposite direction* to the substitution effect—true only for inferior goods—and be *greater than* the substitution effect, which is not true of all (if any!) inferior goods.

17.(c) Since the price of rice is twice the price of potatoes, and Albert and Henri both face the same market prices, they both maximize utility where the $MU_{rice}/MU_{potatoes} = 2$. But this says nothing whatsoever about the absolute values of their MUs. Albert could have a lower (or higher) MU for both than Henri, but still have the same *ratio*.

18.(d) For Arabella the wearing of high fashion is *conspicuous consumption*; she is buying a vehicle to get what she perceives as a form of "admiration" (or "snob appeal") value from other people. When (say) a 10 percent higher price generates more than a 10 percent increase in admiration, the price per unit of admiration actually falls. Thus, the higher price of the dress increases quantity of dresses demanded because it moves Arabella along her <u>downward-sloping</u> demand curve for admiration. Answer (a) is wrong because she would prefer to pay a lower price, thus a lower opportunity cost to her, *as long as others did not know it*—in which case she would demand even more dresses (so (c) is also wrong). Answer (b) is wrong because a Giffen good must also be an inferior good, which is certainly not the case for high-fashion dresses.

19.(e) If the price of high-quality diamond necklaces fell to $20 each, far more would obviously be sold because so many people who are unwilling to buy them at previously high prices would now enter the market as consumers of diamond necklaces. Many current high-income people likely would buy far less, if any, because they would now not be "conspicuous." That is, current consumers would move down their upward-sloping <u>individual</u> demand curves, but the influx of new consumers would still create a downward-sloping <u>market</u> demand curve.

20.(a) The decrease in income indicates a reduction in the maximum amounts of both goods that can be purchased, which is true for both Panel (1) and Panel (3). The *ceteris paribus* condition, however, says that *only* income has changed, *nothing else*. So relative (and absolute) prices must be unchanged, hence the slope of the budget line must be unchanged: a situation that exists only in Panel (1).

22.(c) To answer the question, assume money income is unchanged—so any change in the quantity at which the budget constraint intersects an axis must be caused by a change in price of the good on that axis. In Panel (1) the slope of the budget constraint (i.e., relative price) is unchanged so there has been an equal percentage increase in the prices of both goods. In Panel (3) the relative price P_B/P_A has increased, showing that the percentage increase in P_B (say 10 percent) exceeds the percentage increase in P_A (say 8 percent). The other answers are wrong because in neither case has the price of <u>both</u> goods increased: in Panel (2) P_A is unchanged and in Panel (4) P_A fell.

23.(c) Without the *ceteris paribus* condition, any budget line for which the opportunity cost of good A falls relative to that of good B would be consistent with these price changes—i.e., the budget line becomes steeper, which is the case in Panels (2), (3), and (4). The *ceteris paribus* condition, however, says that nominal income and the prices of other goods remain unchanged.

Consequently, the fall in P_A combined with the same income must increase the maximum amount of A that could be purchased, which is true only for Panel (4).

24.(e)   The fall in P_A makes the budget line steeper, which is true for Panels (2), (3), and (4). In Panel (2), the percentage fall in P_A equals the percentage fall in income, so the maximum A that can be bought is unchanged. In Panel (3) the percentage fall in income is greater than the percentage fall in P_A, reducing the maximum A. In Panel (4), the percentage fall in income is less than the percentage fall in P_A, increasing the maximum A.

27.(c)   A substitution effect leaves the consumer on the same indifference curve, which is true only of points E_2 and E_3.

28.(d)   An income effect is between points of tangency on two *parallel* budget constraints, which is true only of E_1 and E_2.

29.(a)   The income effect on CDs is the move from E_2 to E_1, which reduces the quantity of CDs purchased. Since this reduction is the result of a *fall* in purchasing power, CDs are a normal good. This also rules out (b) and (c). If CDs were a conspicuous consumption good, the total (income plus substitution) effect of the increase in price would *increase* the individual's quantity demanded. Since quantity demanded *falls* (from q_3 to q_1), this rules out (d).

Producers in the Short Run

Chapter Overview

This chapter opens with a discussion of several issues related to the nature of firms. The **proprietorship**, the **partnership**, and the **corporation** are the major forms of business organization in Canada today. Further, each has subcategories. For example, partnerships can be **ordinary** or **limited**, while corporations may be **private**, **public**, or **state-owned**. Firms have several methods of raising financial capital that comprise *equity* and *debt*.

Each firm is assumed to behave as a single, consistent decision-making unit whose goal is to maximize profit. Profit is the difference between revenue and costs. Accounting profits are the difference between revenues and **explicit costs**, but **economic profit** is defined as revenues minus the full opportunity cost of resources used, and is equal to accounting profit minus additional **implicit costs**.

Production decisions are classified into three time horizons: the **short run**, the **long run**, and the **very long run**. In the short run, one or more factors of production are fixed (e.g., plant and equipment), whereas in the long run all factors are variable. In the short run there are both **fixed costs** and **variable costs**, while in longer periods all costs are variable costs. The very long run allows for technological changes to occur. An important short run production phenomenon is the **law of diminishing returns**: as additional units of a variable factor of production are used with a given quantity of a fixed factor, the **marginal** and **average product** of the variable factor will eventually decrease.

The relationship between a firm's costs and output is depicted by its cost curves. **Total cost** is the sum of **total fixed cost** and **total variable cost**. These three total cost curves can be used to generate the associated cost curves for units of output: **average total cost**, **average fixed cost**, **average variable cost**, and **marginal cost**. The law of diminishing returns implies that, since marginal and average product eventually fall, marginal and average costs will eventually rise.

 LEARNING OBJECTIVES

After studying this chapter, you will be able to

1   identify the various forms of business organization and discuss the different ways that firms can be financed.

2   distinguish between accounting profits and economic profits.

3   understand the relationships among total product, average product, and marginal product; and the law of diminishing marginal returns.

4   explain the difference between fixed and variable costs, and the relationships among total costs, average costs, and marginal costs.

Hints and Tips

The following may help you avoid some of the most common errors on examinations.

✓ Understand that economists and accountants use different definitions of profits not because one is "right" and the other is "wrong," but because they serve different purposes. By taking account of both explicit and implicit costs, economic profit in a market system sends a "signal" that affects behaviour—specifically, whether and how society's resources will be reallocated among the different industries and products.

✓ Understand that, whether applied to product (i.e., output) or cost, the basic relationships among total, average, and marginal are the same. When marginal is less than average, the average must fall, and when marginal is greater than average, the average must rise. Do not confuse the direction of change of the marginal with its level—whether marginal is rising or falling, average will fall if marginal is less than average.

✓ Understand the relationship between product curves and cost curves, and learn how to derive the cost curves from the product curves given the price of the variable factor. For example, if you pay someone an additional $20 (the price of the variable factor) to dig four more holes (the marginal product of the variable factor), the extra cost per hole (the marginal cost of a unit of output) must be $5, on average.

✓ Understand what the shape of the product curves implies for the shape of the cost curves. For example, if the marginal product of additional units of the variable factor increases while the price of the factor is unchanged, then the marginal cost per additional unit of output falls.

✓ Read *Extensions in Theory 7-1* in the text. By taking a closer look at what is meant by a "fixed" factor of production, you will avoid a possible confusion between short-term and long-term costs for some types of firms you may see in the world around you.

Chapter Review

What Are Firms?

This section identifies the various forms of business organizations and explains equity and debt financing. It explains the important assumption generally used in economics that firms act in a manner consistent with their objective to maximize profits. [*Note: Additional Topics: Do Firms Really Maximize Profits?* on MyEconLab looks at other possible objectives and how they relate to the profit maximization assumption.] The topical issue of whether firms need to be motivated by social responsibility in addition to the pursuit of profit is also raised. [*Note: Applying Economic Concepts 7-1* in the text gives an interesting overview of the different perspectives on this issue.]

1. **One of the major differences between an ordinary partnership and a corporation is that**
   (a) the owners of a corporation always outnumber the owners of a partnership.
   (b) a corporation always has more assets.
   (c) the owners of a corporation have no personal liability for the actions of the firm, whereas partners have unlimited liability.
   (d) corporations are always more profitable.
   (e) all corporations are listed on a stock market such as the Toronto Stock Exchange.

2. Corporations can finance their operations by
    (a) reinvesting profits.
    (b) issuing bonds.
    (c) issuing new equity.
    (d) issuing bills or notes.
    (e) All of the above.

3. The assumptions of profit maximization and consistent decision making
    (a) apply to single proprietorships only.
    (b) apply to all forms of business organizations except transnational corporations.
    (c) have been observed to be always true.
    (d) imply that profit is the only factor that influences business decisions.
    (e) allow theory to ignore the firm's internal and financial structures.

4. A firm's real capital refers to
    (a) money borrowed from banks.
    (b) the value of the firm's stocks.
    (c) its start-up financing provided by the original owners.
    (d) its plant and equipment.
    (e) its undistributed profits.

Production, Costs, and Profits

This section introduces the concept of the production function, which is the relationship between inputs (*factors of production*) and the firm's output. The important and fundamental concept of economic profit also is introduced in this section, and a thorough understanding of the difference between *economic profit* and *accounting profit* is essential to understanding the economic theory of the firm. Accounting profit is revenues minus *explicit costs*, and economic profit is accounting profit minus *implicit costs*. Thus, economic profit is revenues minus opportunity costs, with opportunity costs including both explicit costs and implicit costs. Using opportunity costs allows economic profit, positive or negative, to provide important signals for the allocation of resources in the economy. The nature and role of economic profit is so important that a careful rereading of the subsection titled "Costs and Profits" in the text will prove to be an excellent investment for most students. Also, you should understand that the three time horizons faced by firms—the short run, the long run, and the very long run—can differ markedly among firms, since they are not defined by a specific number of months or years but by what is being held fixed and what is variable in each time period.

5. An example of an intermediate product is
    (a) asparagus.
    (b) bricks.
    (c) a middle manager.
    (d) the output of a clothing manufacturer.
    (e) unskilled labour.

6. A production function in economics means
    (a) any function performed by an employee when producing output.
    (b) the various functions performed by all employees when producing output.
    (c) the function performed by the person in charge of the production process.
    (d) the relationship between inputs and output.
    (e) All of the above.

7. **Economic profit is defined as the difference between**
   (a) accounting profit and explicit costs.
   (b) total revenue and opportunity costs.
   (c) total revenue and the monetary costs of hiring resources for current use.
   (d) net income before and after taxes.
   (e) total revenue and implicit costs.

8. **Opportunity cost refers to**
   (a) what must be given up to secure the next-best alternative.
   (b) unexpected costs to the firm.
   (c) the best rate of return possible on an investment.
   (d) the return to using something in the most profitable way.
   (e) the cost of hiring labour or renting equipment.

9. **Implicit costs generally have to be estimated because**
   (a) they are not paid through a market transaction.
   (b) most of a firm's costs are monetary costs.
   (c) many labour contracts include fringe benefits.
   (d) the firm uses many different types of inputs.
   (e) revenues are sometimes unknown.

10. **The implicit costs for a firm include**
    (a) the opportunity cost of the owner's time.
    (b) the riskless rate of return that can be earned on the owner's capital.
    (c) the additional rate of return required to compensate for risk.
    (d) All of the above.
    (e) None of the above.

11. **Accounting profit is**
    (a) always positive.
    (b) usually greater than economic profit.
    (c) the same as zero economic profit.
    (d) the result of technologically inefficient production.
    (e) less than zero economic profit.

12. **Zero economic profit refers to**
    (a) what all firms, on average, obtain as a return on investment.
    (b) the base used by Canada Revenue Agency to levy business taxes.
    (c) revenue just equalling the owner's opportunity costs.
    (d) the level of profits necessary to ensure that the firm covers its day-to-day operating expenses.
    (e) a return to capital that is comparable to rates of return earned on bank deposits.

13. **If economic profit is zero for all firms in an industry, then**
    (a) firms will shift resources toward alternative investments.
    (b) revenues equal the monetary costs of operation.
    (c) industry resources are earning a rate of return equal to the rate available elsewhere.
    (d) firms will cease production immediately.
    (e) firms will exit the industry.

14. **The short run is defined as a period**
    (a)   of less than a month.
    (b)   during which there is insufficient time to change the employment level of *any* factor.
    (c)   during which at least one factor of production is fixed and others are variable.
    (d)   during which new firms can enter an industry and old firms can exit.
    (e)   during which there is insufficient time to change output.

15. **The long-run time horizon**
    (a)   is the same for all firms.
    (b)   allows the impact of new inventions to be felt.
    (c)   is defined as the minimum length of time it takes to vary output.
    (d)   is a length of time that is sufficient for all factors to be variable.
    (e)   allows for changes in only labour employment levels.

16. **Positive economic profit is**
    (a)   the excess of revenues over explicit costs.
    (b)   the excess of revenues over implicit costs.
    (c)   the money income of the firm's owner.
    (d)   a signal for firms in other industries to expand their output.
    (e)   a signal for resources to enter the industry in the long run.

Production in the Short Run

The relationship between output and the variable factor, labour, is developed in this section. This input–output relationship can be presented in three ways: total product, average product, and marginal product. Make sure that you understand how all three are related to one another. The average–marginal relationship is of particular importance and will be repeated in other contexts throughout the text. It is also important that you understand the role of diminishing marginal returns in determining the shape of the marginal, average, and total product curves.

17. **The law of diminishing returns refers to**
    (a)   the effects of increases in factor costs.
    (b)   the division of labour.
    (c)   the range of output over which average product is rising.
    (d)   the eventual effect of applying more and more labour to a fixed amount of capital.
    (e)   the effect of not immediately adopting a new technology.

18. **Assuming that capital is a fixed input and that labour is variable, the total product curve relates**
    (a)   output to various levels of capital and labour employment.
    (b)   output to various levels of labour employment.
    (c)   labour cost to the level of output.
    (d)   total cost to various levels of labour employment.
    (e)   output to the cost of labour.

19. **When a firm increases employment of a variable input in the short run, it**
    (a)   shifts the production possibility curve.
    (b)   shifts its total product curve upward.
    (c)   alters its production function.
    (d)   is making a long-run decision.
    (e)   moves along its total product curve.

20. **If labour is the variable factor, average product is defined as**
    (a) total product divided by total output.
    (b) the quantity of labour divided by total product.
    (c) the additional output produced by the last unit of labour.
    (d) output per unit of labour.
    (e) total product divided by capital.

21. **The change in output that results when another unit of the variable factor is employed is referred to as the**
    (a) marginal product.
    (b) average product.
    (c) average fixed product.
    (d) total product.
    (e) average total product.

22. **If average product is falling, marginal product**
    (a) is less than average product.
    (b) is equal to average product.
    (c) is greater than average product.
    (d) can be greater than, equal to, or less than average product.
    (e) is negative.

23. **The law of diminishing returns states that**
    (a) as output increases, the rate of increase in costs will eventually decrease.
    (b) as output increases, profits will eventually decline.
    (c) the marginal product of a variable factor will eventually decrease.
    (d) as more labour is employed, the wage rate will increase and thereby increase costs.
    (e) as more labour is employed, the total product curve will eventually have a negative slope.

Costs in the Short Run

This section develops three total cost curves (*TC*, *TFC*, and *TVC*) and four unit cost curves (*ATC*, *AFC*, *AVC*, and *MC*). It is important that you understand how these curves relate to one another and to the product curves in the previous section. There is a lot of information to learn in this section that will be used repeatedly throughout a microeconomics course.

24. **"Spreading overhead" refers to**
    (a) increasing capital to spread total costs.
    (b) decreasing average fixed costs as output increases.
    (c) increasing output to decrease average total costs.
    (d) any decrease in total costs.
    (e) increasing employment of the variable factor.

25. **Using the notation in the text, *AFC* equals**
    (a) $ATC - AVC$.　　　　　　　　　　(b) $AVC + MC$.
    (c) ATC at its minimum point.　　　　(d) $TC - TVC$.
    (e) $ATC + AVC$.

26. **AVC is equal to**
    (a) MC + AFC.
    (b) TVC per unit of labour.
    (c) ATC + AFC.
    (d) MC at the minimum point of AVC.
    (e) ATC + MC.

27. **If the difference between average total cost (ATC) and average variable cost (AVC) at 100 units of output is $1, at 200 units of output the difference between ATC and AVC must be**
    (a) $2.
    (b) $1.
    (c) 50 cents.
    (d) $1.50
    (e) zero.

28. **A firm's capacity**
    (a) continuously declines as output increases.
    (b) is the output level corresponding to minimum average total cost.
    (c) is the size of its plant.
    (d) varies with its labour employment.
    (e) is the maximum output that can physically be produced with a given amount of capital.

29. **A change in the wage rate paid to the variable factor (labour) will shift**
    (a) the ATC curve.
    (b) the AVC curve.
    (c) the MC curve.
    (d) the AFC curve.
    (e) the ATC, AVC, and MC curves.

30. **When the price (i.e., wage rate) of the variable factor labour is constant,**
    (a) MC falls as marginal product of labour rises.
    (b) AVC falls as average product of labour rises.
    (c) MC = AVC when marginal product equals average product.
    (d) All of the above.
    (e) None of the above.

Short-Answer Questions

1. What is the basic difference between the definitions of profits used by economists and accountants? Why do economists use their definition?

2. After five years of working, Sally left a $50 000-a-year job to start her own business. She withdrew $40 000 from her savings account, which paid 4 percent annual interest, to pay for some equipment that she can sell at any time for $40 000 (although she could have earned 5 percent had she bought shares in another business having the same risk as her own). Her only other costs are the $30 000 per year she charges her business for her own services. In the first year her business made accounting profits of $22 000. Will other people with $40 000 savings want to leave a $50 000 job to open a business like Sally's if their only objective is money? Explain.

3. Explain how the average product of labour can be rising when the marginal product of labour is either rising or falling. How would this apply to the effect of your performance in your next two courses on your B+ grade point average?

4. Explain why the average product curve does not change when the hourly wage rate rises, but the average total cost (*ATC*) curve shifts upward. As an example, show what happens to average variable cost (*AVC*) and *ATC* at output of Q = 500, which requires 100 hours of labour input to produce, when the hourly wage rate rises from $20 to $25, and total fixed costs (*TFC*) are $5000.

5. A firm uses unskilled workers, workers with specialized skills, and specialized equipment. It can hire more unskilled workers immediately, but it takes one month to train another specialized worker, and it must order additional specialized equipment one year in advance. For this firm, what time horizons define the short run, the long run, and the very long run? Why?

Exercises

1. **Accounting Profits versus Economic Profits**
   The difference between accounting and economic profits is the emphasis of this exercise.

   The following table presents last year's annual income statement for Harry's Hardware Store. Harry worked full-time at the store. He also used $50 000 of his savings to furnish and stock the store (included in costs). At the beginning of last year, he had been offered a $40 000 annual salary to work in another hardware store.

   Annual Income Statement

Revenues		Costs	
Sales of merchandise	$194 000	Wholesale purchases	$120 000
Service revenues	10 000	Store supplies	4 000
		Labour costs (hired)	20 000
		Utilities	2 000
		Rent	10 000
		Depreciation on fixtures	4 000
Total revenues	$204 000	**Total costs**	$160 000

   (a) Calculate last year's accounting profits for Harry's Hardware Store.

   $$204\ 000$$
   $$-\ 160\ 000$$
   $$\overline{044\ 000}$$

(b) Assume an interest rate of 5 percent. What are the economic costs and economic profits of Harry's business?

forgone salary *forgone interest*

Econ costs = 160 000 + 40 000 + 2500 = 202 500

∴ Econ profits = 1500

(c) What would Harry's economic profits be if he could get an interest rate of 10 percent by investing in another business that was exactly as risky as his own?

Econ costs = 202 500 + 2500 = 205 000

Econ loss of 1000.

2. Accounting Profits, Economic Profits, and Taxes

This exercise highlights the tax implications of the difference between accounting and economic profits.

Monique, an economics student who has one more year at university to complete her degree, is considering setting up her own business for the summer. Specifically, Monique plans to provide door-to-door delivery of the *Financial Post*, the *Globe and Mail*, and the *Toronto Star* to families living in their summer cottages. Because she will be graduating and seeking permanent employment next year, this enterprise is for one summer only and is an alternative to earning a $3000 after-tax income as a lifeguard.

The following list itemizes the particulars:

- Monique expects total revenues of $24 000 for the season.
- To deliver the papers, she must purchase a van for $6000, which she is certain to sell at season's end for $4000.
- The licence for distributing newspapers in these regions costs $3000 and lasts for three years. However, it is non-transferable (i.e., it cannot be sold or used by anyone else).
- To finance the purchase of the van and the licence, Monique will withdraw $9000 from her savings account for a period of six months. This account pays an annual interest rate of 10 percent.
- It will cost $8000 to purchase the newspapers in bulk. To get this special price, Monique agrees to pay the $8000 up front (i.e., at the beginning of the season). She borrows this amount from a bank for six months at an annual interest rate of 15 percent.
- Costs of promotion, gas, and other incidentals come to $2500.
- Although Monique expects $24 000 in revenues, she may actually earn less. Thus there is some risk involved. She feels that $1000 would compensate her for taking the risk.
- The tax rate on this business is 50 percent of net income.

(a) What will be Monique's explicit costs for hired and purchased factors?

Explicit costs = 2000 + 3000 + ~~(6000)~~ + 8000 + .15(8000) + 2500. = 16 100

↳ not cost of van ↳ it's depreciation of van

(b) What will be Monique's implicit costs?

forgone earnings

Implicit costs = 450 + ⟨1000⟩ + 3000 = 4450

forgone interest *risk premium*

(c) What will be Monique's accounting profit before taxes and after taxes?

Before tax: 24000 − 16100 = 7900

After tax: 7900 − ½(7900) = 3950

(d) What will be her economic profit after taxes? Is she likely to set up this business for the summer if her only objective is to maximize her income? NO

Econ profit after taxes = 3950 − 4450 = −500

(e) If the business tax rate were applied to economic profits rather than to accounting profits, would Monique be more or less likely to undertake this enterprise?

Econ profits = 24000 - 20550 = 3450
before tax

After tax = ½(3450) = 1725 ∴ yes she will

3. The Average Product, Marginal Product, and Total Product Curves

In this exercise, you develop the relationships among the three product curves. The data in the following table relate employment levels of a variable factor to the resulting output.

Variable Factor	Total Product	Average Product	Marginal Product
1	10	10	
			150
2	160	80	
			170
3	330	110	
			150
4	480	120	
			120
5	600	120	
			70
6	670	11.67	
			10
7	680	9.7	

(a) Fill in the blanks. [*Note:* Since marginal product refers to a change in output from one level of the variable factor to another, it is shown *between* the rows.]

(b) Graph the total product curve in Panel (i) of Figure 7-1, and the average product and marginal product curves in Panel (ii). [*Note*: Plot marginal product at the *midpoint* between units of the variable factor, i.e., at 1.5, 2.5, 3.5, etc. on the horizontal axis.]

Figure 7-1

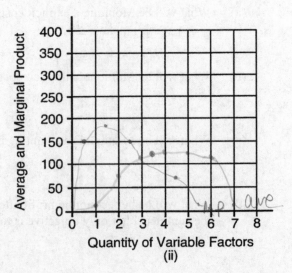

(c) At what output is the point of diminishing marginal productivity?

[handwritten: Max MP= 170 → after 3rd unit]

(d) What is the relationship between average and marginal productivity at the point of diminishing average productivity? Why is this?

[handwritten: Max AP occurs after 4th & 5th unit of variable factor. Pt of diminishing ave. product is 5th factor. MP b/w 4th & 5th units equals AP @ this point.]

[handwritten right margin: Before 5th pt. MP > AP. AP↑. After 5th pt MP < AP AP↓]

4. The Relationship Between Productivity and Cost

This exercise is designed to illustrate the relationship between productivity and cost with a minimum of figures. Assume that the cost associated with the fixed factors is $30 and the cost of each variable unit is $10.

(a) Complete the following table. [*Note:* A number divided by zero equals infinity, ∞.]

Units of Variable Factor	Total Product	Marginal Product	Average Product	Total Cost	Marginal Cost	Average Total Cost
0	0		0	$30		∞
		2			$5.00	
1	2		2	$40		$20.00
		3			3.33	
2	5		*2.5*	*$50*		*10.00*
		2			*5.00*	
3	7		*2.33*	*$60*		*8.57*
		1			*10.00*	
4	8		*2*	*$70*		*8.75*

(b) Graph the total, average, and marginal product curves in Panel (i) of Figure 7-2, and the three cost curves in Panel (ii). Remember that the "marginal" points are plotted at the midpoints of the intervals on the horizontal axis.

Figure 7-2

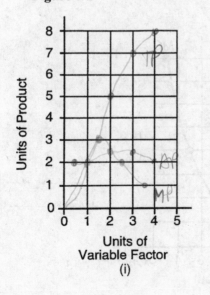

Units of Variable Factor
(i)

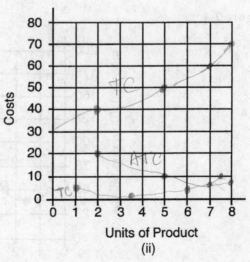

Units of Product
(ii)

5. **The Firm's Cost Structure**

This exercise gives you practice reading information from a firm's cost structure. Given the family of cost curves in Figure 7-3, answer the following questions.

(a) The capacity of this firm occurs at an output of ____8____ .

(b) The effect of diminishing marginal returns occurs after an output level of ____5____ .

(c) The effect of diminishing average returns occurs after an output level of ____7____ .

(d) As output increases, the vertical distance between the *ATC* and *AVC* curves ____falls____ because ____AFC ↓____ . [*Note:* Figure 7-3 is not drawn to scale.]

Figure 7-3

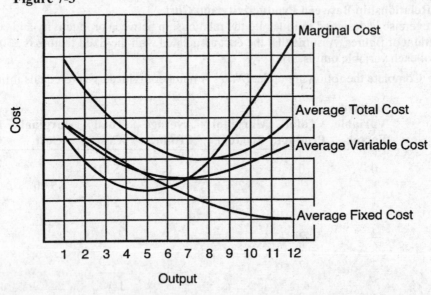

6. **The Relationship Among Marginal Cost, Average Costs, and Total Costs**

This exercise gives only the firm's total fixed costs and its marginal cost curve (in diagrammatic form). From these, you are asked to derive the firm's entire cost structure.

The marginal cost curve for a particular firm is presented in Figure 7-4. Because marginal cost is plotted at the midpoint, the marginal cost of producing (for example) the first unit of output is $50. In addition, suppose that the firm's fixed costs are $100.

Figure 7-4

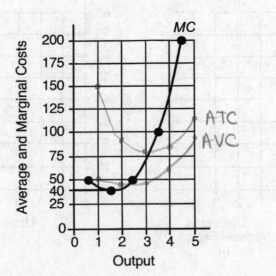

(a) Use the firm's *MC* curve together with the level of fixed costs to determine total variable costs (*TVC*), total costs (*TC*), average variable costs (*AVC*), and average total costs (*ATC*).

[handwritten, upper right] = TC/output

Output	MC	TVC	TC	AVC	ATC
0		0	100	—	—
	$50				
1		50	150	50	150
	40				
2		90	190	45	95
	50				
3		140	240	46.67	80
	100				
4		240	340	60	85
	200				
5		440	540	88	108

(b) Plot (approximately) the *AVC* and *ATC* curves on the graph.

Extension Exercises

E1. Deriving a Firm's Cost Structure from Its Algebraic Total Cost Function
Assume that you are in the business of producing a commodity for which short-run total costs are represented by the following equation:

$$TC = 30 + 3Q + Q^2$$

where Q is output of the commodity and TC is total costs.

(a) What are total fixed costs (*TFC*) equal to? How do you know?

[handwritten] $Q = 0 \Rightarrow TC = 30 + 3(0) + 0^2 = 30$

(b) What is the equation for total variable costs (*TVC*)?

[handwritten] $TVC = TC - TFC = 30 + 3Q + Q^2 - 30 = Q^2 + 3Q$

(c) What is the equation for average total costs (*ATC*)?

[handwritten] $ATC = \dfrac{TC}{Q} = \dfrac{30 + 3Q + Q^2}{Q} = Q + 3 + \dfrac{30}{Q}$

(d) Fill in the blanks in the following table.

Q	TVC	TFC	TC	ATC	MC
0	0	30	30	—	
1	4	11	34	34	4
2	10	11	40	20	6
3	18	11	48	16	8
4	28	11	58	14.5	10
5	40	11	70 ⟩ 14	14	12
6	54	11	84	14	14
7	70	11	100	14.3	16
8	88	11	118	14.8	18
9	108	11	138	15.3	20
10	130	11	160	16	22

(e) What is the capacity of this firm? Why?

b/w output levels 5+6, where ATC is at minimum

(f) What is marginal cost at this capacity output? Why?

$14 b/c MC=ATC @ min. ATC

(g) The equation for this firm's *MC* curve is

$$MC = 3 + 2Q$$

(Students familiar with calculus should note that this is the first derivative of the *TC* curve.) To understand why marginal cost is plotted at the midpoints, use the equation for *MC* to calculate *MC* at outputs of 5, 5.5, and 6. Compare these answers with the marginal cost you derived in (d), which was calculated by taking the difference in *TC* between outputs of 5 and 6.

Attempt exercises E2 and E3 only if you cover *Additional Topic: Do Firms Really Maximize Profits?* on MyEconLab.

E2. Profit Maximization, Satisficing, and Sales Maximization
This question highlights the different price–quantity implications for a profit maximizer, a satisficer, and a sales maximizer. The diagram in Figure 7-5 presents the demand and cost conditions faced by a firm.

Figure 7-5

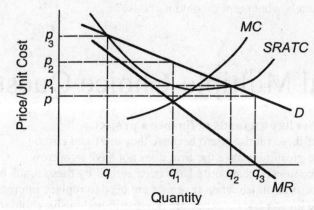

(a) What would be the choice of price and output for a profit maximizer? _____

(b) What would be the range of price and output for a profit satisficer who is content to cover opportunity costs as a minimum? _____

(c) What could be the price and output of a sales maximizer who is willing to accept losses for short periods? _____

E3. Profits Under Different Objectives

As in the previous question, this exercise emphasizes the different output decisions of firms based on their goals. In this case you are given the firm's profit function.

Assume that a firm is capable of making a reasonable projection of its profits (π) as it expands output (Q), using the following profit function:

$$\pi = 7Q - Q^2 - 6$$

(a) For values of $Q = 1, 2, 3, 3.5, 4, 5,$ and 6, plot the profit function on the grid in Figure 7-6.

Figure 7-6

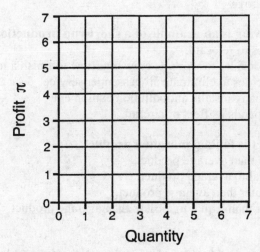

(b) If a satisficing firm has a profit target of $4, what range of output will that firm accept?

(c) What output is consistent with profit maximization?

(d)   If the firm were a sales maximizer and constrained to have profits of a least $2, approximately what output would it choose?

Additional Multiple-Choice Questions

*1.   When a firm uses its own funds to finance a project,
   (a)   the cost of these funds is zero because they are fixed costs.
   (b)   profits are greater because the firm does not have to borrow.
   (c)   the forgone interest that could have been earned by these funds is an implicit cost.
   (d)   future profits diminish when revenues are used to replace internal investment funds.
   (e)   profits are greater because they are not distributed to shareholders.

*2.   Suppose that you own a dairy store that makes and sells homemade ice cream, using an ice cream maker that has no alternative use and no resale value. It cost $1500 when it was purchased 15 years ago. The opportunity cost of its use is
   (a) $100, representing the annual depreciation.
   (b)   zero.
   (c)   some number greater than zero but under $100, representing the annual depreciation.
   (d)   the amount of interest payable on the cost of a replacement machine.
   (e)   its replacement cost.

*3.   A firm has total revenues of $100 000, total explicit costs of $75 000, and implicit costs of $25 000. It is correct to say that
   (a)   economic profits are $25 000.
   (b)   accounting profits are zero.
   (c)   accounting profits are negative.
   (d)   economic profits are zero.
   (e)   None of the above.

*4.   Which of the following is an example of a short-run production decision?
   (a)   A firm decides to relocate.
   (b)   A contractor decides to work its crew overtime to finish a job.
   (c)   A railway decides to eliminate all passenger service.
   (d)   A paper company installs antipollution equipment.
   (e)   An airline expands its fleet of aircraft.

*5.   If marginal product is falling, marginal product
   (a)   is always less than average product.
   (b)   is always equal to average product.
   (c)   is always greater than average product.
   (d)   can be greater than, equal to, or less than average product.
   (e)   is negative.

6.   For a firm using only two factors of production, capital and labour, with capital being a fixed factor, the wage bill in the short run equals
   (a)   short-run total costs.
   (b)   total variable costs.
   (c)   average total cost multiplied by output.
   (d)   marginal costs.
   (e)   All of the above, since fixed costs are constant.

*7.   Assuming that labour is the only variable factor of production and the wage rate is constant, which of the following statements is true?
    (a)   If MP_L is rising, AVC must also be rising.
    (b)   If MP_L is falling, AVC must also be falling.
    (c)   If MC exceeds AVC, ATC must be rising.
    (d) AFC falls as output rises in both the short run and the long run.
    (e)   None of the above.

Questions 8 to 13 refer to Figure 7-7, which illustrates a firm's average total cost (ATC) and average variable cost (AVC) curves.

Figure 7-7

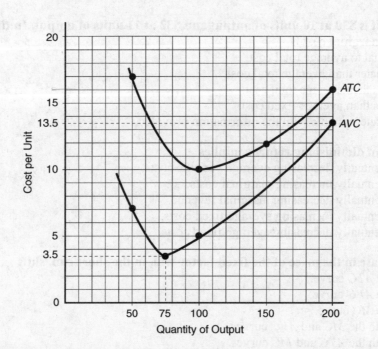

8.   **When the firm is producing 200 units of output, total costs in the short run are**
    (a) $3200.   (b) $2700.
    (c) $16.   (d) $13.50.
    (e)   Indeterminable with data provided.

*9.   **When output equals 100 units, marginal cost is**
    (a) $5.   (b) $15.
    (c) $10.   (d) $500.
    (e)   Indeterminable with data provided.

10.   **At a total product of 200 units, AFC is**
    (a) $2.50.   (b) $13.50.
    (c) $16.   (d) $2700.
    (e)   Indeterminable with data provided.

11.   **If the level of production is 50 units, TFC is**
    (a) $350.   (b) $7.
    (c) $500.   (d) $10.
    (e)   Indeterminable with data provided.

*12. **At an output of 75, *MC* is**
- (a) rising.
- (b) equal to *AVC*.
- (c) $3.50.
- (d) All of the above.
- (e) Indeterminable with data provided.

*13. **This firm's capacity is**
- (a) $10.
- (b) 75 units of output.
- (c) 200 units of output.
- (d) 100 units of output.
- (e) Indeterminable with information provided.

*14. **Total cost is $30 at 10 units of output and $32 at 11 units of output. In this range of output, marginal cost is**
- (a) equal to average total cost.
- (b) greater than average total cost.
- (c) less than average total cost.
- (d) less than average fixed cost.
- (e) indeterminable with the information provided.

*15. **The law of diminishing returns implies**
- (a) eventually decreasing average variable costs.
- (b) eventually increasing marginal costs.
- (c) eventually decreasing marginal revenue.
- (d) eventually increasing average fixed costs.
- (e) eventually decreasing average fixed costs.

*16. **An increase in the price of the fixed factor will, in the short run, shift**
- (a) the *ATC* curve.
- (b) the *AVC* curve.
- (c) the *MC* curve.
- (d) both the *MC* and *AVC* curves.
- (e) both the *ATC* and *MC* curves.

Questions 17 and 18 are intended for those covering *Additional Topics: Do Firms Really Maximize Profits?* on MyEconLab.

17. **Satisficing theory argues that**
- (a) the majority of shareholders are satisfied with their management.
- (b) the firm's objective is to attain some minimally acceptable profit level.
- (c) the firm will produce the output corresponding to maximum market share.
- (d) the most successful firms are those that produce goods that best satisfy consumers.
- (e) firms deliberately keep profits low to satisfy governments.

*18. **A basic difference between satisficing theory and the theories of profit maximization and sales maximization is that**
- (a) satisficing is based on the goals of management, whereas the others are based on the goals of shareholders.
- (b) satisficing predicts the largest level of output among the three theories.
- (c) satisficing predicts that the firm will never produce the output level corresponding to either maximum profits or maximum sales.
- (d) satisficing predicts a range of outputs; the others predict unique output levels.
- (e) shareholders are satisfied with management so long as profits are positive.

Solutions

Chapter Review

1.(c) 2.(e) 3.(e) 4.(d) 5.(b) 6.(d) 7.(b) 8.(a) 9.(a) 10.(d) 11.(b) 12.(c) 13.(c) 14.(c) 15.(d) 16.(e) 17.(d) 18.(b) 19.(e) 20.(d) 21.(a) 22.(a) 23.(c) 24.(b) 25.(a) 26.(d) 27.(c) 28.(b) 29.(e) 30.(d)

Short-Answer Questions

1. Accounting profits are revenues minus explicit costs, whereas economic profits also deduct implicit costs (which are part of total opportunity cost). Economists take this approach since their definition of profits identifies whether there is a financial incentive for resources to enter an industry (i.e., in response to positive economic profit), or to leave the industry (i.e., in response to negative economic profit), or neither (i.e., in reaction to zero economic profit, which says that resources can do no better and no worse in this industry than elsewhere).

2. Sally's income is $30 000 + $22 000 = $52 000, which is $2000 more than she made in her former job. (There are no depreciation costs because her equipment can be sold at any time for the purchase price of $40 000.) But Sally's accounting profit ignores two implicit costs: (i) the $1600 interest (i.e., 4 percent of $40 000) she no longer earns on her savings and (ii) the $400 risk premium (i.e., 1 percent of $40 000), which is the difference between the 4 percent that her savings would earn in the bank and the 5 percent they would make if she invested them in another business with the *same risk* as hers. So her equivalent total income had she remained in her job and used her $40 000 to buy shares could have been $50 000 + $1600 + $400 = $52 000. Since her revenue is $52 000 and her opportunity cost is $52 000, Sally makes zero economic profits, so other people will be indifferent as to whether they open a business like Sally's.

3. For average product of labour to be rising, marginal product of labour can be rising or falling as long as it is *greater* than the average. In this example, the "product" is the number of grade points. If the extra grade points (i.e., those you get for each additional course) are more than the average (your previous GPA), marginal exceeds average and your average will rise. Thus your GPA of B+ would rise regardless of whether you got an A- followed by an A on your next two courses (i.e., marginal grades decreasing) or an A followed by an A- (i.e., marginal grades decreasing).

4. The average product refers only to the average *quantity* of output per hour, determined by the production function *regardless* of the cost of inputs. If the wage rate rises, any given output costs more to produce and increases the average variable cost per unit of output, shifting up the *AVC* curve. Since $ATC = AVC + AFC$, and *AFC* is unchanged, the shift in the *ATC* curve equals the shift in the *AVC* curve. For 100 hours at $20 per hour, $ATC = AVC + AFC = $2000/500 + $5000/500 = $4 + $10 = $14. At a wage rate of $25, $ATC = AVC + AFC = $2500/500 + $5000/500 = $5 + $10 = $15. The *AVC* and *ATC* both increase by $1.

5. The short run lasts for up to one year, because during this period at least one factor of production can't be varied. The long run starts one year hence, because this is the period needed to change all factors of production. The very long run can't be determined from the question, because there is no information on how long it would take for a new technology to become available and, once available, how long it would take the firm to adopt it.

Exercises

1. **(a)** TR minus explicit costs = $204 000 – $160 000 = $44 000.
   (b) Harry's economic costs are the $160 000 explicit costs plus implicit costs equal to his $40 000 forgone salary plus $2500 interest forgone on the $50 000 investment (assuming no depreciation) = $202 500. Harry has economic profits of $204 000 – $202 500 = $1500.

(c) Harry's implicit costs would now include an extra risk premium of 5 percent on the $50 000 investment = $2500. This brings his economic costs to $202 500 + $2500 = $205 000, and economic profit of $204 000 – $205 000 = – $1000. That is, negative economic profits (i.e., an economic loss) of $1000.

2. (a) Explicit costs:

Licence	$3 000
Interest payments on loan	600
Bulk purchase	8 000
Promotion, gas, etc.	2 500
Depreciation of van	2 000
Total explicit costs	**$16 100**

(b) Implicit costs:

Interest forgone on savings	$ 450
Risk premium	1 000
Forgone lifeguard earnings	3 000
Total implicit costs	**$4 450**

(c) Accounting that profit before taxes = Revenue minus explicit costs = $24 000 – $16 100 = $7900. Accounting profit after taxes = $7900 × 0.50 = $3950.

(d) Economic profit after taxes = Accounting profit after taxes minus implicit costs = $3950 – $4450 = –$500 (i.e., an economic loss of $500). If Monique were to ignore the $1000 risk she would make $500 more money by setting up the business than by being a lifeguard. But being an economics student she knows about the risk factor, and so will not set up the business.

(e) Monique would set up the business if taxes were paid on economic profit instead of accounting profit. Her before-tax economic profit would be *TR* minus explicit costs minus implicit costs = $24 000 – $20 550 = $3450, on which she would pay taxes of 50 percent of $3450 = $1725, leaving her an economic profit of $1725 even after allowing for the $1000 risk factor. By taxing net income, Canada Revenue Agency does not allow Monique to deduct some real (albeit implicit) costs, so the $3950 taxes she pays on accounting profit converts her before-tax economic profit of $3450 into an after-tax economic loss of $500.

3. (a)

Variable Factor	Total Product	Average Product	Marginal Product
1	10	10	
			150
2	160	80	
			170
3	330	110	
			150
4	480	120	
			120
5	600	120	
			70
6	670	112	
			10
7	680	97	

(b) Figure 7-8

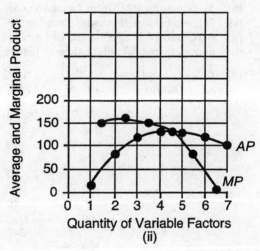

Quantity of Variable Factors
(i)

Quantity of Variable Factors
(ii)

(c) Maximum *MP* is 170, which is for the third unit of the variable factor (plotted at 2.5 units in the table). Thus diminishing marginal productivity begins after employment of the third unit of the variable factor.

(d) Maximum *AP* occurs at the fourth and fifth unit of the variable factor (so the point of diminishing average product is at the fifth unit). The *MP* between the fourth and fifth units (plotted at 4.5 units) equals the *AP* at this point. Before the fourth unit, *MP* exceeds *AP* so *AP* rises. After the fifth unit, *MP* is less than *AP* so *AP* falls.

4. (a)

Units of Variable Factor	Total Product	Marginal Product	Average Product	Total Cost	Marginal Cost	Average Total Cost
0	0		0.0	$30		∞
		2			$5.00	
1	2		2.0	40		$20.00
		3			3.33	
2	5		2.5	50		10.00
		2			5.00	
3	7		2.3	60		8.57
		1			10.00	
4	8		2.0	70		8.75

(b) Figure 7-9

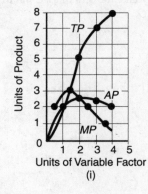

Units of Variable Factor
(i)

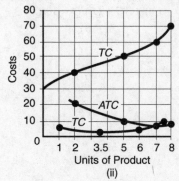

Units of Product
(ii)

5. (a) 8. (Capacity is the output level at the minimum point of the short-run *ATC* curve.)
    (b) 5. (Diminishing *MP* means increasing *MC*, which occurs after an output of 5.)
    (c) 7. (Diminishing *AP* means increasing *AVC*, which occurs after an output of 7.)
    (d) falls; average fixed costs fall. (As more output is produced, the constant level of *TFC* is spread over more units of output, thereby reducing *AFC*.)

6. (a)

Output	*MC*	*TVC*	*TC*	*AVC*	*ATC*
0		$ 0	$100	—	—
	$50				
1		50	150	$50.00	$150
	40				
2		90	190	45	95
	50				
3		140	240	46.67	80
	100				
4		240	340	60	85
	200				
5		440	540	88	108

(b) **Figure 7-10**

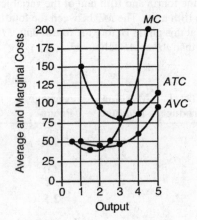

Extension Exercises

E1. (a) $30. Fixed costs are paid even at zero output. $TC = \$30$ is found by setting $Q = 0$ in the *TC* equation.
    (b) $TVC = 3Q + Q^2$. Since $TVC = TC - TFC$, simply take the $30 of *TFC* out of the *TC* equation.
    (c) $ATC = TC/Q = (30 + 3Q + Q^2)/Q = 30/Q + 3 + Q$.

(d)

Q	TVC	TFC	TC	ATC	MC
0	$ 0	$ 30	$ 30	—	
					$4
1	4	30	34	34	
					6
2	10	30	40	20	
					8
3	18	30	48	16	
					10
4	28	30	58	14.5	
					12
5	40	30	70	14	
					14
6	54	30	84	14	
					16
7	70	30	100	14.3	
					18
8	88	30	118	14.8	
					20
9	108	30	138	15.3	
					22
10	130	30	160	16	

(e) Between output levels 5 and 6, where ATC is at its minimum.

(f) $14. $MC = ATC$ at minimum ATC.

(g) The marginal costs of outputs 5, 5.5, and 6 are 13, 14, and 15, respectively. Looking at the table in (d) you see the difference in TC between outputs 5 and 6 is 14, which is precisely the MC at the midpoint of 5.5 units of output.

E2. **(a)** p_2 and q_1. (The output is chosen where $MC = MR$, and the price is read from the demand curve.)

    (b) From p_3 and q to p_1 and q_2. (Both of these price–quantity combinations are where $AR = ATC$, so total revenue just equals total cost—the latter being defined in terms of opportunity cost in economics.)

    (c) p and q_3. (This is the only price–quantity combination in the diagram where $AR < ATC$, with economic losses of $(ATC - AR)q_3$.)

E3. **(a)** **Figure 7-11**

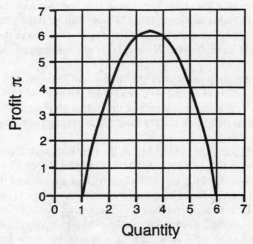

    (b) From $Q = 2$ to $Q = 5$. This can be read from Figure 7-11. Using $\pi = 7Q - Q^2 - 6$ and setting $Q = 2$ gives $\pi = 14 - 4 - 6 = 4$. Similarly, setting $Q = 5$ gives $\pi = 35 - 25 - 6 = 4$.

(c) $Q = 3.5$. Read this from the diagram. If you set $Q = 3.5$ in $\pi = 7Q - Q^2 - 6$, profit is $24.5 - 12.25 - 6 = 6.25$.

(d) $Q = 5.5$ (approximately). This gives $\pi = 38.5 - 30.25 - 6 = 2.25$.

Additional Multiple-Choice Questions

1.(c) **2.**(b) **3.**(d) **4.**(b) **5.**(d) **6.**(b) **7.**(e) **8.**(a) **9.**(c) **10.**(a) **11.**(c) **12.**(d) **13.**(d) **14.**(c) **15.**(b) **16.**(a) **17.**(b) **18.**(d)

Explanations for the Asterisked Multiple-Choice Questions

1.(c) The income that the firm could have had by investing these funds elsewhere, at an equivalent level of risk, is the opportunity cost of using these "retained earnings" to finance the project, and so must be treated as a cost of production when calculating economic profit. If there is a risk that the project may be less profitable than anticipated, the true opportunity cost should include an allowance for this risk. For example, this implicit cost could be calculated indirectly by taking the return from a riskless government bond and adding an estimated "risk premium," or directly using the rate of return that is offered on corporate bonds issued by firms with the same level of risk as the project.

2.(b) The ice cream maker has no resale value, so no opportunity cost hence no depreciation.

3.(d) Total economic costs ($100 000) is the sum of both explicit costs ($75 000) and implicit costs ($25 000). The firms total revenue is also $100 000. Subtracting total (economic) costs from total revenue gives economic profit of zero (so (d) is correct and (a) and (e) are incorrect). To the extent that the $25 000 implicit costs include (for example) *opportunity cost* and a *risk premium* that accounting costs do not, accounting costs will be less than economic costs so accounting profit will be greater than economic profit, hence greater than zero (so (b) and (c) are incorrect).

4.(b) The short run is the period of time over which at least one factor of production can't be varied. All answers other than (b) involve changes in one or more factors of production that take *more time* than simply using the *existing* labour stock more intensively. Overtime work allows the firm to get more hours worked *without delay*, since it does not even require training time for more workers. It is an example of labour (hours of work) as a highly variable factor of production relative to the others, and so is a short-run decision.

5.(d) The fall in *MP* (when diminishing marginal productivity sets in) starts when $MP > AP$. As *MP* falls, *AP* continues to rise because $MP > AP$, until $MP = AP$. Further decline in *MP* brings $MP < AP$, so *AP* now falls too.

7.(e) A rising *MP* gives a falling *MC*, and a falling *MP* gives a rising *MC*. But the implications for *AVC* in (a) and (b) depend on the *level* of *MC* compared to *AVC* (i.e., greater or less than), not on the *direction* of *change* in *MC*. This rules out (a) and (b)—neither *must* be happening. In (c), $MC > AVC$ means *AVC* must be rising, but *ATC may* still be falling because of the effect of the falling *AFC*. Choice (d) is incorrect because fixed costs are zero in the long run.

9.(c) At 100 units, *ATC* is at its minimum. When *ATC* is at its minimum, $MC = ATC$, and *ATC* read from the vertical axis is $10.

12.(d) This uses the same reasoning process as Question 9. At 75 units, *AVC* is at its minimum. When *AVC* is at minimum, $MC = AVC$, and *AVC* read from the vertical axis is $3.50.

13.(d) "Capacity" output is defined in economics as the output level that gives the minimum average total cost of production. This definition differs from the everyday (non-economic) meaning of capacity as the maximum possible level.

14.(c) Total cost rises from $30 to $32, so the *MC* of the eleventh unit of output is $2. $ATC = TC/Q = \$30/10 = \$3$ and $\$32/11 = \$2.91$. Thus the *MC* of $2 is less than *ATC*.

15.(b) Diminishing returns is a short-run concept whereby using more and more of a variable factor with a constant amount of a fixed factor eventually causes extra output (i.e., marginal product, or *MP*) to fall. Falling *MP* of the factor combined with a constant factor price means rising *MC* of output (as in answer (b)). Rising MC eventually causes average *variable* costs to rise (the opposite of answer (a)). As output rises, *AFC* falls regardless of whether there are diminishing returns or increasing returns to the variable factor; answer (d) is wrong because *AFC* falls as output rises, and answer (e) is wrong because falling *AFC* need not be accompanied by diminishing returns.

16.(a) An increase in the price of the fixed factor increases *TFC* which, since the amount is by definition unchanged, increases *AFC* at each and every level of output. Since there is no effect on either productivity (marginal or average) or price of the variable factor, there is no effect on *MC* or *AVC* (so (b), (c), (d) and (e) are wrong). The unchanged *AVC* plus an increased *AFC* causes an upward shift in the *ATC* curve (so answer (a) is correct).

18.(d) The satisficing theory is consistent with a whole range of output, with profits anywhere in that range being equal to or exceeding the "satisfactory" level (which includes but is not restricted to maximum profit). While (a) may well be true of satisficing and sales maximization, it is not necessarily true of profit maximization (so potentially creating a "principal–agent problem"). Sales maximization predicts the largest output, so answer (b) is wrong. The satisficing range of output includes the profit maximization level, among others, so answer (c) is wrong. The satisficing level of profit is a "target" level, generally based on what shareholders would regard as satisfactory. The target level will likely be set relative to the level of profit made by other firms in the industry, so if they were making a 4 percent profit rate and the specific firm was making 1 percent, it would not be "satisficing" (so answer (e) is wrong).

Producers in the Long Run

LO **LEARNING OBJECTIVES**

After studying this chapter, you will be able to

1 explain why profit maximization requires firms to equate marginal product per dollar spent for all factors.

2 explain why profit-maximizing firms substitute away from factors whose prices have risen and toward factors whose prices have fallen.

3 understand the relationship between short-run and long-run cost curves.

4 discuss the importance of technological change and why firms are motivated to innovate.

Chapter Overview

This chapter examines the behaviour of producers in both the **long run** and the **very long run**. There are no fixed factors of production in the long run, so a given output can be produced using different combinations of all inputs. Some input combinations are **technically efficient**, but not all technically efficient combinations are **economically efficient**, since economic efficiency takes the prices of factors into account while technical efficiency does not. Profit-maximizing firms will substitute among factors to achieve the combination that **minimizes long-run costs** for the level of output it wishes to produce. This occurs when inputs are used in quantities such that the marginal product per dollar of expenditure is the same for each.

A **long-run average cost (*LRAC*) curve** represents the boundary between attainable and unattainable levels of cost for a given technology. The shape of the *LRAC* curve depends on the relationship between inputs and outputs as the scale of a firm's operation changes. **Increasing**, **constant**, and **decreasing returns (to scale)** lead, respectively, to decreasing, constant, and increasing long-run average costs. Long- and short-run cost curves are related; every point on the *LRAC* curve corresponds to a different combination of factors and, therefore, to points on different **short-run average total cost (*SRATC*) curves**. The *LRAC* curve is the **envelope curve** of the *SRATC* curves.

In the very long run, **technological change** leads to increases in **productivity**. **Innovation** is the key to productivity growth. New production techniques, better inputs, and new products are types of innovations that have historically driven **productivity growth**.

The appendix to this chapter analyzes the long-run production choices using a more formal model: **isoquant analysis**.

Hints and Tips

The following may help you avoid some of the most common errors on examinations.

✓ When doing numerical calculations using the condition for efficient combinations of capital and labour, write the general condition first (using letters instead of numbers) and then insert the relevant numbers. This method avoids the common problem of confusion between the numbers applying to capital and to labour.

✓ Understand the reasoning behind the condition for the cost-minimizing factor combination. For example, if spending $100 less on labour reduces output by 50 while spending $60 more on capital increases output by 50, the same total output is produced for $40 less.

✓ Understand what causes a movement along the various cost curves and what causes a shift in them. A change in the amount of a variable factor with the same technology and at least one fixed factor causes a movement along the *SRATC* curve; a change in all factors (i.e., no fixed factor) with the same technology causes a movement along the *LRAC* curve; a change in factor prices with a constant technology shifts both the *SRATC* curves and the *LRAC* curve; a change in technology shifts both the *SRATC* curves and the *LRAC* curve.

✓ Economies (diseconomies) of scale, increasing (decreasing) returns, and decreasing (increasing) costs all refer to the same thing—a downward-sloping (upward-sloping) *LRAC* curve (or a specific portion thereof).

Chapter Review

The Long Run: No Fixed Factors

This section explains the difference between technical efficiency and economic efficiency, and the condition necessary for minimizing the costs of producing different levels of output in the long run. You should understand the following: the relationship between profit maximization and cost minimization; the role of the principle of substitution in explaining a firm's input use; and how increasing returns (economies of scale), decreasing returns (diseconomies of scale), and constant returns affect the shape of the *LRAC* curve, and why each occurs. It is important to understand the relationship between the short- and long-run cost curves: with the simplifying assumption that capital and labour are the only factors of production, a change in labour with no change in capital causes a movement along the *SRATC* curve, while a change in both labour and capital is generally required to move along the *LRAC* curve. Further, a movement along the *LRAC* curve is equivalent to a shift in the *SRATC* curve.

1. **In addition to choosing the level of output, a firm in the long run must also select**
   (a) the appropriate technology.
   (b) the amount of overtime for its labour force.
   (c) the cost-minimizing combination of inputs.
   (d) the profit-maximizing quantity of labour to employ with its fixed plant.
   (e) All of the above.

2. **The cost-minimizing factor mix is obtained when**
   (a) the marginal products of all factors are equalized.
   (b) the marginal product per dollar expended on each factor is equalized.
   (c) the marginal product of each factor divided by total expenditure on that factor is equalized across all factors.
   (d) the cost of employing an additional unit of each factor is equalized across all factors.
   (e) each factor's marginal cost is equalized.

3. **A firm's long-run average cost curve depicts**
   (a) what costs will be attainable with technological improvement.
   (b) the lowest attainable unit costs when all factors are variable.
   (c) a firm's profit-maximizing output choices.
   (d) the lowest attainable average cost when all factor prices vary.
   (e) the lowest attainable average cost when technology is variable.

4. **The long-run average cost curve is determined by**
   (a) technology and tastes.
   (b) long-run supply of output.
   (c) population growth.
   (d) technology and input prices.
   (e) All of the above.

5. **If the long-run average cost curve is upward sloping, the firm is experiencing**
   (a) decreasing returns.
   (b) diseconomies of scale.
   (c) increasing costs.
   (d) All of the above.
   (e) None of the above.

6. **One possible explanation for economies of scale is**
   (a) invention and innovation.
   (b) the introduction of new, better inputs.
   (c) a decrease in a factor price.
   (d) increased specialization of production tasks.
   (e) technological improvement.

7. **One possible cause of diseconomies of scale is**
   (a) an increase in the price of an input
   (b) using more of labour with no change in the amount of capital.
   (c) a decrease in the price of an input.
   (d) alienation of the labour force as the firm gets bigger.
   (e) total costs of production increase by the same percentage as output increases.

8. **Minimum efficient scale is**
   (a) the minimum output that can be produced with a given capital stock.
   (b) the smallest output at which *LRAC* reaches its minimum.
   (c) the minimum combination of inputs required to produce a given level of output.
   (d) the output at which the marginal product per dollar spent is equal for all inputs.
   (e) any point of technical efficiency.

The Very Long Run: Changes in Technology

In the very long run, the relationship between inputs and output changes because technology changes. The extent of technological change is reflected in productivity growth (i.e., output per unit of some input, such as labour) and is an important source of rising living standards over time. This is a non-technical section that identifies three sources of technological change.

9. **Which of the following is the best measure of productivity?**
   (a) Total output.
   (b) Total output per hour.
   (c) Total output per unit of resource input.
   (d) Total output per dollar of revenue.
   (e) Total profit per unit of output.

10. **Which of the following is *not* a type of technological change?**
    (a) Process innovation.
    (b) New production techniques.
    (c) Product innovation.
    (d) Improved inputs.
    (e) Economies of scale.

11. **The very long run**
    (a) introduces changes in factor prices.
    (b) always involves a greater range of output than the short run or the long run.
    (c) applies to a period in which new production methods can be introduced.
    (d) extends long-run analysis to higher production levels.
    (e) introduces allowance for variable plant size.

12. **An *economically efficient* method of production is one that**
    (a) uses the smallest number of resource inputs.
    (b) necessarily involves the use of multiple stages in the production process.
    (c) produces a given output at minimum cost.
    (d) cannot also be technologically efficient.
    (e) minimizes the use of scarce capital.

Appendix to Chapter 8: Isoquant Analysis

This appendix develops a formal model of cost minimization in the long run. Isoquant analysis is analytically similar to indifference curve analysis, which was covered in the appendix to Chapter 6. In reading this appendix, you should first understand the characteristics of isoquant and isocost curves, and then focus on understanding the cost-minimizing input combination. This occurs when a given isoquant is tangent to an isocost curve. The tangency implies that the marginal rate of technical substitution equals the relative prices of the factors, which is equivalent to the condition, seen in the first section of this chapter, that the marginal product per dollar spent on each factor is equal all across factors.

13. **If the marginal rate of (technical) substitution at a specific point on an isoquant is (–)2**
   (a) the price of the factor on the horizontal axis is twice the price of the factor on the vertical axis.
   (b) the price of the factor on the vertical axis is twice the price of the factor on the horizontal axis.
   (c) the marginal product of the factor on the horizontal axis is twice the marginal product of the factor on the vertical axis.
   (d) the marginal product of the factor on the vertical axis is twice the marginal product of the factor on the horizontal axis.
   (e) a movement along the isoquant will double output.

14. **An isocost line for two factors, C and B, (their respective prices are P_C and P_B) could have which of the following equations?**
   (a) $BC = \$100$.
   (b) $\$100 = P_C + P_B$.
   (c) $\$100 = P_B B + P_C C$.
   (d) $\$100 = P_B P_C$.
   (e) $BC = P_B B + P_C C$.

15. **If two factors, C and B, are graphed in the same unit scale with C on the vertical axis, and an isocost line has a slope $= -2$, then**
   (a) $P_B = 2P_C$.   (b) $P_C/P_B = 2$.
   (c) $C = 2B$.   (d) $B = 2C$.
   (e) $P_B B = 2P_c C$.

16. **At the point of tangency of the isocost line in Question 15 with an isoquant,**
   (a) the desired factor combination has $2C$ for each B.
   (b) the marginal product of factor B is twice that of C.
   (c) the desired factor combination has $2B$ for each C.
   (d) the marginal product of factor C is twice that of B.
   (e) the marginal rate of substitution is -0.5.

Short-Answer Questions

1. Why is technical efficiency a necessary condition for economic efficiency but economic efficiency not a necessary condition for technical efficiency?

2. If the price of capital is twice the price of labour and the firm is producing where the marginal product of capital is less than twice the marginal product of labour, explain in words (i.e., no equations) why the firm would not be minimizing the cost of its output.

3. For a firm with constant returns to scale, what does the *LRAC* curve look like? Why? If one of the *SRATC* curves reached its minimum point at $4 per unit of output, what can you say about the *SRATC* curves at lower levels of output? At higher levels of output?

4. Why is cost minimization a necessary condition for profit maximization?

5. The cost-minimizing combinations of capital (*K*) and labour (*L*) for different levels of output per month (*Q*) are shown in the table.

Q	*K*	*L*	*LRAC* ($)
1 000	5	100	_____
2 000	10	180	_____
4 000	18	300	_____
6 000	25	400	_____
8 000	34	650	_____
10 000	60	1 000	_____

Calculate the *LRAC* at each level of total output if the price of capital is $20 per unit and the price of labour is $4 per unit. At what output level does increasing returns to scale cease? Explain.

$$LRAC = \frac{TC}{Q} = \frac{P(K) + P(L)}{Q}$$

Exercises

1. Technical versus Economic Efficiency
This exercise explores the distinction between technical and economic efficiency.

A firm has four alternative methods of producing 100 gizmos. Each method represents different combinations of three factors: labour, lathe time, and raw materials. The inputs required by each method are given in the following table.

	Production Method			
	A	**B**	**C**	**D**
Labour hours	100	90	60	80
Lathe hours	25	75	80	70
Raw materials (kg)	160	150	120	100

(a) Assume that the price per unit of each factor is $1. Determine the cost of each production method and indicate which is economically efficient.

(b) Suppose that the price of an hour of lathe time increases to $2 (other prices remaining constant); what method(s) would a profit-maximizing firm now use?

(c) Which of these methods is not technically efficient? Explain.

2. **Cost Minimization**
The focus of this question is the condition for cost minimization given in Equations 8-1 and 8-2 of the text. Review the associated discussion in the text first.

Three firms are able to combine capital (K) and labour (L) in various ways, resulting in the marginal products shown in the following table. [*Note:* As you move to higher combination numbers, more capital is substituted for less labour thereby decreasing MP_K and increasing MP_L.] All firms face the same factor prices: the price of a unit of capital is $10, and the price of a unit of labour is $5.

Combination Number	Firm A MP_K	Firm A MP_L	Firm B MP_K	Firm B MP_L	Firm C MP_K	Firm C MP_L
1	10	1	6	3	25	2
B 2	8	2	5	4	20	4
A 3	6	3	4	6	14	7
C 4	4	4	3	8	10	8
5	2	5	2	10	5	10

(a) Firm A is currently using combination 3; Firm B is using combination 2; and Firm C is using combination 4. Which firm is minimizing its costs? Explain.

$$\frac{MP_L}{MP_K} = \frac{P_L}{P_K}$$
↳ min costs

(b) How would each firm that is not currently minimizing costs have to alter its use of capital and labour to minimize its costs of production? Explain.

3. **The Relationship Between *SRATC* and *LRAC***
This exercise highlights the relationship between short- and long-run average cost curves. It uses the simplifying assumption that technology permits only two possible short-run cost curves.

A firm is operating in an industry in which it is technologically possible to construct only two classes of plant. Class A is highly automated (i.e., more capital-intensive), requiring an initial fixed-cost investment of $1 000 000 and having a marginal cost of $3 per unit of output. Class B is less automated (i.e., more labour-intensive), requiring an initial investment of $500 000 and having a marginal cost of $4 per unit of output. Thus the total cost curve for each class of plant can be represented by the following equations:

Class A plant: $TC_A = \$1\ 000\ 000 + 3Q$
Class B plant: $TC_B = \$500\ 000 + 4Q$

(a) What is the *ATC* equation for each class of plant? Draw the two *ATC* curves in Figure 8-1, and identify the *LRAC* curve facing the firm.

Figure 8-1 $ATC = \dfrac{TC}{Q}$

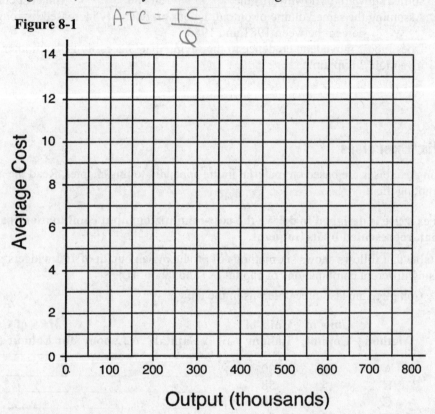

Output (thousands)

(b) If this firm plans to produce 400 000 units of output, which plant should it use? Explain.

B

(c) Over what range of output do economies of scale occur for each class of plant? Why?

4. **Innovation**

Well into the post–Second World War period, Inco (then International Nickel) possessed monopoly power based on the rich nickel ore around Sudbury, Ontario. Discoveries of nickel elsewhere, however, gradually eroded its power to control prices, and during the metal slump of the early 1980s Inco posted losses of $1 billion (1981–1984). Then, Inco developed a new method for mining nickel, and as a result it made a profit of $45 million in 1985. The increase in profit occurred despite the fact that there was little change in its output and in nickel prices. The number of employees it hired, however, fell from 35 000 in 1981 to 21 000 in 1985.

(a) Economists would term the new mining method a ___very long___ run development, which shifted (upward or downward) the ___short___ run and ___long___ run cost curves.

(b) Assuming the same volume of output, labour productivity increased by roughly _____ percent between 1981 and 1985.

(c) Does Inco's move lend credence to the saying that "necessity is the mother of invention"? Explain.

Appendix Exercises

The following exercises are based on material in the appendix to this chapter. Read the appendix before attempting them.

A1. **This exercise is designed to derive the cost-minimizing input combination for a given output, represented by its isoquant.**

The table that follows shows six methods of producing an output of 100 widgets per month by using different combinations of capital (K) and labour (L).

(a) Complete the last three columns in the table.

Method	Units of Capital	Units of Labour	Δ Capital	Δ Labour	*MRS* of Capital for Labour (ΔK/ΔL)
A	10	80	_____	_____	_____
B	15	58	_____	_____	_____
C	25	40	_____	_____	_____
D	40	24	_____	_____	_____
E	58	15	_____	_____	_____
F	80	9	_____	_____	_____

(b) On the graph in Figure 8-2, plot the isoquant defined by the data in the table. [*Note:* Assume that these are the only feasible methods, and connect points by straight line segments.]

Figure 8-2

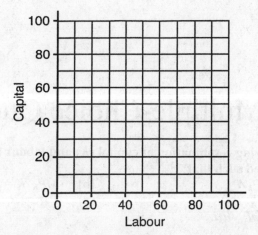

(c) For each of the following price combinations, calculate the slope of the isocost line, P_L/P_K, and determine the economically efficient method of production by drawing the minimum isocost line in the diagram in (b).

	Price of Labour	Price of Capital	P_L/P_K	Method
(1)	$1000	$ 500	_____	_____
(2)	1000	1000	_____	_____
(3)	1000	2000	_____	_____

A2. The following exercise gives you practice using isoquant analysis.
Figure 8-3 depicts isoquants for several levels of output that could be produced with different combinations of capital and labour.

Figure 8-3

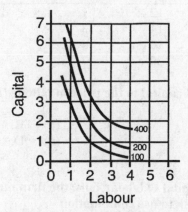

(a) If the relative price of labour to capital were 1, how many units of capital and labour would this firm employ to produce 100 units of output (at minimum cost)?

(b) If the price of capital were to change to one-half its original level, and the firm wanted to produce 200 units of output at minimum cost, how much capital and labour would it now employ? Explain.

(c)   By examination of these three isoquants, what (if anything) can be said about returns to scale?

Additional Multiple-Choice Questions

1.   **The profit-maximizing combination of capital (K) and labour (L) occurs when these factors are employed such that**
   (a) $MP_K/P_K = MP_L/P_L$.
   (b) $MP_K/K = MP_L/L$.
   (c) $MP_K/P_L = MP_L/P_K$.
   (d) $P_K K = P_L L$.
   (e) $MP_K/P_K K = MP_L/P_L L$.

*2.   **Suppose that the marginal product of capital in a particular firm is 5, the marginal product of labour is 10, the price of capital is \$2, and the price of labour is \$1. To minimize costs, this firm will**
   (a) substitute more capital for less labour.
   (b) substitute more labour for less capital.
   (c) not alter its factor mix.
   (d) hire more capital and keep labour constant.
   (e) reduce labour employment.

Questions 3 and 4 refer to the following table, which presents four possible combinations of capital (K) and labour (L) and their associated marginal products. Each combination produces exactly 100 units of output. Assume that the firm wishes to minimize production costs.

Combination	K	MP_K	L	MP_L
A	14	12	1	10
B	12	14	3	7
C	8	16	4	4
D	6	20	7	2

*3.   **If the ratio of the price of capital to the price of labour (P_K/P_L) is 2, this firm will employ combination**
   (a) A.
   (b) B.
   (c) C.
   (d) D.
   (e) Either C or D.

*4.   **If the relative price of capital to labour falls, the firm may (depending on the magnitude of the fall) wish to use combination**
   (a) A.
   (b) B.
   (c) C.
   (d) D.
   (e) Indeterminable with data provided.

*5.   **Constant long-run average costs for a firm means that**
   (a) there are greater advantages to small than to large plants.
   (b) an unlimited amount of output will be produced.
   (c) any scale of production costs the same per unit as any other.
   (d) total cost is independent of the level of output.
   (e) marginal cost equals zero.

6. **Suppose a firm doubles the amount of all of its factors of production and, as a result, output increases from 100 units to 300 units. This firm is operating under**
   (a) diseconomies of scale.
   (b) long-run decreasing returns.
   (c) decreasing costs.
   (d) decreasing total cost.
   (e) increasing costs.

*7. **A firm experiencing long-run increasing returns that decides to increase output should do so by**
   (a) substituting more labour and less capital.
   (b) employing a new technology.
   (c) employing less of each factor.
   (d) building smaller plants.
   (e) building larger plants.

*8. **An upward shift in the family of short-run cost curves as well as the long-run average cost curve could be explained by**
   (a) economies of scale.
   (b) an increase in the fixed factor such as plant size.
   (c) an increase in a factor price.
   (d) a larger capital–labour ratio.
   (e) technological improvement.

*9. **When a firm seeks to minimize the cost of producing a given output, it does *not* need to know**
   (a) the technically efficient input combinations.
   (b) the economically efficient input combinations.
   (c) its production function.
   (d) the prices of inputs.
   (e) the maximum level of profits.

10. **In a country where labour is relatively abundant and capital is scarce, it is likely that**
    (a) firms will use capital-intensive production methods, *ceteris paribus*.
    (b) virtually any combination of inputs would be economically efficient.
    (c) firms will employ labour-intensive production techniques.
    (d) there is a strong incentive to introduce labour-saving innovations.
    (e) Both (c) and (d) are correct.

*11. **Assume that a local garage employs 10 units of labour and 50 units of capital to produce 400 oil changes. Currently, the price of labour is $10 per unit and the price of capital is $5 per unit, and the MP_L equals 2 and the MP_K equals 6. Given these circumstances, the firm**
    (a) is both profit-maximizing and cost-minimizing.
    (b) should increase the use of both inputs.
    (c) could lower its production costs by decreasing labour input and increasing capital input.
    (d) could lower its production costs by increasing labour input and decreasing capital input.
    (e) should decrease the use of both inputs.

*12. If capital costs $8 per unit and labour costs $4 per unit, and a firm's marginal product of capital is 4 and the marginal product of labour is 8, this firm should

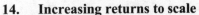

(a) employ more capital and labour.
(b) employ less capital and labour.
(c) employ more capital and less labour.
(d) employ less capital and more labour.
(e) not change its current factor use.

*13. Due to China's higher population density, the price of land (relative to the price of labour) is higher in China than in Canada. Consider Canadian and Chinese rice producers who have access to the same technologies. The Canadian firm will use the two inputs, land and labour, in such a way that its land–labour ratio is
(a) equal to that of the Chinese firm.
(b) lower than that of the Chinese firm.
(c) higher than that of the Chinese firm.
(d) equal to the relative prices of land and labour.
(e) indeterminable with information provided.

14. Increasing returns to scale
(a) means that output rises proportionately less than inputs, increasing per unit cost of production in the short run.
(b) means that output rises proportionately more than inputs, resulting in increasing per unit costs.
(c) means that output rises proportionately more than inputs, resulting in lower per unit costs in the long run.
(d) has the same meaning as increasing costs of production.
(e) None of the above.

15. Points below the long-run average cost curve
(a) may represent actual cost and production levels in the short run.
(b) represent less efficient cost levels than points on the long-run average cost curve.
(c) are attainable only when all factors are variable.
(d) represent unattainable cost levels.
(e) are attainable if the firm minimizes its costs according to the "principle of substitution."

Questions 16 to 20 refer to Figure 8-4, which depicts a firm's *LRAC* and selected *SRATC* curves.

Figure 8-4

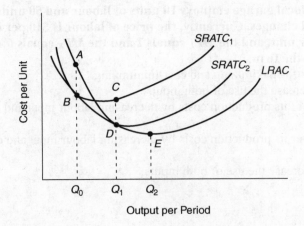

*16. If this firm is producing at point B, we could say that it
  (a) is maximizing its profits.
  (b) is minimizing the cost of producing Q_0.
  (c) can increase its profits by moving to point A.
  (d) can lower its costs by moving to point A.
  (e) would minimize total costs by moving to point E.

*17. The firm is currently producing at point A. If it increases its employment of labour, it will move toward
  (a) any point on $SRATC_2$.   (b) B.
  (c) C.   (d) D.
  (e) None of the above.

*18. The firm is currently producing at point B. An increase in its capital may be represented by
  (a) a movement to A.
  (b) staying at point B.
  (c) a movement to C.
  (d) an upward shift in the LRAC curve.
  (e) None of the above.

*19. A technological improvement can be characterized by
  (a) a movement either from A to B or from C to D.
  (b) a movement either from B to A or from D to C.
  (c) a shift from $SRATC_1$ to $SRATC_2$.
  (d) an upward shift in the LRAC curve.
  (e) a downward shift in the LRAC curve.

20. At output beyond Q_2 the firm is experiencing
  (a) diseconomies of scale.   (b) decreasing returns.
  (c) increasing costs.   (d) All of the above.
  (e) None of the above.

Appendix

Questions 21 to 23 refer to Figure 8-5, which shows several of a firm's isocost and isoquant curves.

Figure 8-5

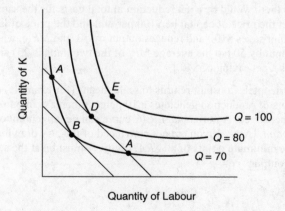

*21. A firm will minimize the costs of producing 80 units of output at point

    (a)   *A.*   (b)   *B.*
    (c)   *C.*   (d)   *D.*
    (e)   *E.*

*22. Suppose the firm is currently producing at point *B* and the price of labour increases. If the firm wants to minimize the cost of producing the same level of output, a possible input combination is at point

    (a)   *A.*   (b)   *B.*
    (c)   *C.*   (d)   *D.*
    (e)   *E.*

*23. Suppose the firm is currently producing at point *B* and the prices of both labour and capital increase by 25 percent. If the firm wants to minimize the cost of producing the same level of output, the firm's chosen input combination would be at point

    (a)   *A.*   (b)   *B.*
    (c)   *C.*   (d)   *D.*
    (e)   *E.*

Solutions

Chapter Review

1.(c) 2.(b) 3.(b) 4.(d) 5.(d) 6.(d) 7.(d) 8.(b) 9.(c) 10.(e) 11.(c) 12.(c) **Appendix:** 13.(c) 14.(c) 15.(a) 16.(b)

Short-Answer Questions

1.   Technical efficiency may be achieved with numerous combinations of inputs, requiring only that the same output cannot be obtained using a smaller *amount* of inputs. Economic efficiency, however, also takes input prices into account, requiring that the same output cannot be obtained using a smaller *value* of inputs. If production is not technically efficient, it cannot be economically efficient either, since using fewer inputs would reduce the value of inputs used. If the ratio of input prices changes, however, an entirely different technically efficient combination of inputs can now become the economically efficient combination.

2.   Output can be kept at the same level by reducing the amount of capital and increasing the amount of labour, but the cost of the extra labour needed to do this would be less than the amount saved by reducing capital. Thus there would be a net reduction in total costs for the same amount of output. [*Note:* For example, let the price of capital be \$100 per unit and the price of labour be \$30 per unit. If reducing capital by 1 unit saves \$100 and reduces output by 50 (the MP_K), while hiring two more units of labour increases output by 50 (so the average MP_L of the two units is 25) and costs \$60, output is unchanged and there is a net saving of \$40.]

3.   The *LRAC* curve is horizontal. Constant returns to scale means (for example) a 10 percent increase in the amount of all factors of production generates a 10 percent increase in output; so the average cost per unit of output is unchanged. A horizontal *LRAC* curve can be tangential to a *SRATC* curve only at the latter's *minimum point*. [*Note:* If you are not convinced of this, try drawing it.] So if the *LRAC* curve is horizontal, the minimum points of all *SRATC* curves must be at the same dollar value—in this case, at \$4 per unit of output.

4. The price consumers are willing to pay for a given amount of the good, and thus the total revenue received by a firm for its output, is determined by the demand curve for the good regardless of production costs. If the firm can produce the same quantity for a lower cost, total revenues are unchanged but total costs fall, so profits (the difference between total revenue and total cost) increase. Thus profits cannot be at a maximum if the costs of producing any given level of output are not minimized.

5. $LRAC$ equals total cost divided by quantity of output, or $[P_K(K) + P_L(L)]/Q$. For example, since it requires 5 units of capital at $20 each ($100) plus 100 units of labour at $4 each ($400) to produce 1000 units of Q, the $LRAC = \$500/1000 = \$0.50$ per unit. Applying this equation to all the units of output gives:

Q	$LRAC$	Q	$LRAC$	Q	$LRAC$
1 000	$0.50	4 000	$0.39	8 000	$0.41
2 000	$0.46	6 000	$0.35	10 000	$0.52

Increasing returns (to scale) causes decreasing $LRAC$, which occurs until $LRAC = \$0.35$ at $Q = 6000$. Further increases in output show $LRAC$ rising above $0.35—i.e., decreasing returns after $Q = 6000$. [*Note:* Since $Q = 6000$ is the lowest output level at which LRAC reaches its minimum, output of 6000 is the firm's minimum efficient scale.]

Exercises

1. (a) Method D is economically efficient, because it uses the least-cost combination of the three factors. Method A costs $285; B costs $315; C costs $260; and D costs $250.
    (b) Method A, which costs $310. (Method B now costs $390; C costs $340; and D costs $320.) Note that the increase in the relative price of lathe time caused the firm to substitute away from lathe time (i.e., from 70 hours in D to 25 hours in A) and use more of the other factors whose prices *relative to* lathe time have fallen.
    (c) Method B is technically inefficient since method D uses fewer units of *each* factor. Thus method B would not be economically efficient under any set of factor prices, since there would always be another method that used less of each factor than B, thereby producing the same output as B at a lower cost.

2. (a) Firm A is minimizing costs since, with combination 3, the ratio of the marginal products of capital and labour are equal to the ratio of their cost per unit of the factor employed (i.e., $MP_K/MP_L = 6/3 = 2$, and $P_K/P_L = 10/5 = 2$). The other combinations do not give this equality for Firm A.
    (b) At combination 2, Firm B has $MP_K/P_K = 5/10 = 0.5$, and $MP_L/P_L = 4/5 = 0.8$, so the extra output per marginal dollar spent on K is less than the extra output per marginal dollar spent on L. To be economically efficient it must use less K and more L, thereby raising the MP_K and lowering the MP_L. Combination 1 is economically efficient for Firm B, since $MP_K/P_K = 6/10 = 0.6$ and $MP_L/P_L = 3/5 = 6/10 = 0.6$. Similarly, Firm C would have to move from combination 4 to combination 3. With combination 4, Firm C has $MP_K/P_K = 10/10 = 1$ and $MP_L/P_L = 8/5 = 1.6$, so it should use less capital and more labour. At combination 3, Firm C has $MP_K/P_K = 14/10 = 1.4$, and $MP_L/P_L = 7/5 = 1.4$.

3. (a) $ATC_A = TC_A/Q = \$1\,000\,000/Q + 3$ and $ATC_B = TC_B/Q = \$500\,000/Q + 4$.
    For example, at $Q = 100\,000$, $ATC_A = \$1\,000\,000/100\,000 + 3 = 10 + 3 = 13$, and $ATC_B = \$500\,000/100\,000 + 4 = 5 + 4 = 9$.

Figure 8-6

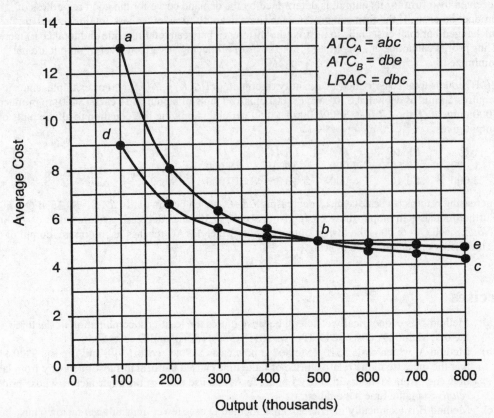

$ATC_A = abc$
$ATC_B = dbe$
$LRAC = dbc$

(b) Class B. With a Class A plant it would cost $2.2 million to produce 400 000 units, but only $2.1 million with a Class B plant.

(c) These total cost equations have the (unlikely) property that total costs continue to decrease regardless of how much output rises, so economies of scale occur over the entire range of output, from 1 to infinity. Each total cost curve is characterized by a fixed cost ($1 000 000 and $500 000, respectively) and constant marginal cost ($3 and $4, respectively). Since marginal cost is constant, marginal cost equals average variable cost. As output increases, average fixed cost continuously declines while average variable cost remains unchanged, so average total cost also continuously declines. That is, there is no increase in average variable cost to eventually offset the declining average fixed cost.

4. (a) Very long; downward; short; long. The new mining method represents a change in technology, which occurs over the very long run. A change in technology reduces both the short-run and the long-run costs of production, so both the long-run and the short-run cost curves shift downward (since the total cost of producing any given level of output, and so the average total costs per unit of output, falls).

(b) Labour productivity increased by roughly 67 percent (i.e., by two-thirds to be exact). Since 21 000 workers are 3/5 of 35 000 workers, this means that 3/5 of the number of workers employed in 1981 were able to produce the same total output in 1985. Thus productivity (per worker) increased to 5/3 of its original level or, equivalently, increased by two-thirds. [*Example:* If output is 525 000, the 35 000 workers produced 525/35 = 15 each. But 21 000 workers now produce 525/21 = 25 each. Output per worker increased by 25 − 15 = 10, which is two-thirds of the initial 15 per worker.]

(c) The losses with the erosion of monopoly power and the slump in the metal market made it necessary for Inco to invent a new technology that reduced costs in order to become profitable again. The necessity stimulated the invention.

Appendix Exercises

A1. **(a)**

Method	Δ Capital	Δ Labour	*MRS* of Capital for Labour (Δ*K*/Δ*L*)
A	—	—	—
B	+5	−22	−0.23
C	+10	−18	−0.56
D	+15	−16	−0.94
E	+18	−9	−2.00
F	+22	−6	−3.67

(b) **Figure 8-7**

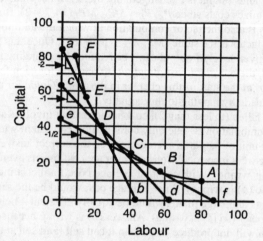

(c) For price combination 1, the relative price of labour to capital is $P_L/P_K = 1000/500 = 2$, so −2 is the slope of the isocost line. The MRS of capital for labour is −2 on the isoquant segment between methods D and E, implying that either method E or D could be used as the cost-minimizing method of producing 100 units of output. Note that using method D the total cost is $40(500) + 24(1000) = \$44\,000$, and using method E the total cost is $58(500) + 15(1000) = \$44\,000$. Thus the isocost line *ab* can be drawn tangential to the segment of the isoquant joining D and E. Now to find the isocost intercepts on the capital and labour axes: Dividing the total cost of \$44 000 by \$500 ($= P_K$) gives the maximum units of capital at point $a = 88$. Dividing \$44 000 by \$1000 ($= P_L$) gives the maximum units of labour at point $b = 44$. Following the same process for the other two price ratios you will find:

- combination 2 has a price ratio of 1 and a minimum isocost line *cd*, which implies method D should be used.
- combination 3 has a price ratio of 0.5 and a minimum isocost line *ef*, which implies that method B should be used.

A2. **(a)** One unit of capital and two units of labour. The slope of the isocost line is −1, intersecting both the capital and labour axes at 3.

(b) The slope of an isocost line is now −2, which yields a tangency with the isoquant representing 200 units of output at approximately two units of capital and two units of labour. The isocost line intersects the capital axis at 6, and the labour axis at 3.

(c) These isoquants indicate economies of scale. Take any factor mix such as two units each of capital and labour, which gives 200 units of output in (b), and double each to four units. Since factor prices are constant, doubling all factors serves to double total cost exactly. The combination of four units of each factor, however, lies above the isoquant representing 400 units of output. Therefore, doubling all factors results in more than double the output. A doubling of costs and a more than doubling of output implies that long-run average cost is decreasing.

Additional Multiple-Choice Questions

1.(a) 2.(b) 3.(b) 4.(a) 5.(c) 6.(c) 7.(e) 8.(c) 9.(e) 10.(c) 11.(c) 12.(d) 13.(c) 14.(c) 15.(d) 16.(b) 17.(d) 18.(a) 19.(e) 20.(d) **Appendix:** 21.(d) 22.(a) 23.(b)

Explanations for the Asterisked Multiple-Choice Questions

2.(b) The cost of a marginal unit of output using labour is $1/10 = $0.10, which is less than the cost of a marginal unit of output using capital = $2/5 = $0.40. The firm will reduce costs by using less capital and more labour. [For example, buying 2 fewer units of capital reduces costs by 2($2) = $4 and reduces output by $2(MP_K) = 2(5) = 10$. Buying 1 more unit of labour costs $1 and increases output by $MP_L = 10$. Thus output is unchanged, but there is a net change in costs of $1 – $4 = –$3.]

3.(b) Combination B minimizes costs since $P_K/P_L = MP_K/MP_L$ (14/7 = 2). But understand the economics—i.e., this is also the factor combination at which the additional output per (marginal) dollar spent on each factor is the same ($MP_K/P_K = MP_L/P_L$). Once this point is reached, the total cost of producing a given level of output can't be reduced by changing the mix of factors of production. In effect, the *marginal cost of output* is the same for each factor. [*Note:* See the second hint in *Hints and Tips* at the start of this chapter in the *Study Guide* for a numerical example of savings that can be made by moving to this equality.]

4.(a) Now that P_K/P_L has fallen (to less than 2), cost minimization involves substituting more capital for less labour than in combination B. The only combination consistent with this is combination A.

5.(c) Production costs per unit of output is average cost, so the correct answer is straightforward. But why are the other answers incorrect? Constant average cost means average cost and marginal cost are the same (so (e) is wrong). With constant average cost, total cost increases in proportion to the increase in output (so (d) is wrong). Since average cost would be the same regardless of the level of output, small plants and large plants would be equally efficient—neither would have an advantage over the other (so (a) is wrong). Answer (b) is wrong because it ignores the demand side of the market: a firm will not produce more than it can sell (and sell at a price which does not reduce profit).

7.(e) Increasing returns to scale means that higher output can be produced at lower average cost when *more of both* factors are used. The economies of scale will be achieved, therefore, by building larger plants (i.e., using both more capital and more labour). Note that (b) is not a correct answer, since increasing returns is a long-run attribute whereas changing technology is a very-long-run attribute.

8.(c) An increase in factor price increases (short-run and long-run) average cost at all levels of output, thereby shifting up the average (and marginal) cost curves. Even if it were the price of labour that increased and firms responded by increasing the capital–labour ratio in the long run, the long-run (as well as the short-run) average cost curve would still rise somewhat (so answer (d) is wrong). [*Note:* If you are unsure of this, ask yourself why the firm did not select its new capital–labour ratio <u>before</u> the rise in the price of labour.] Economies of scale are reflected in the <u>shape</u> of the firm's cost curves, not the <u>position</u> (so (a) is wrong), while technological improvement would shift the cost curves down, not up (so (e) is wrong). Answer (b) is wrong because (i) in the long run there are no fixed factors, (ii) the effect of different plant sizes is reflected in the <u>shape</u> of the <u>long-run</u> cost curve, and (iii) an increase in the firm's scale of operation (via an increase in plant size) can shift the <u>short-run</u> cost curves up <u>or</u> down depending on whether its production function exhibits decreasing or increasing *returns to scale*.

9.(e) Both technical and economic efficiency in production are <u>required</u> for cost minimization (so answers (a) and (b) are wrong), and the production function determines which combinations of factors are technically efficient (so (c) is wrong). Which of the technically efficient combinations of factors are also economically efficient depends on relative factor prices (so (d) is wrong). The maximum level of profits (answer (e)) is the only thing here that the firm does <u>not</u> need to know, since cost minimization is one of the conditions for profit maximization <u>regardless</u> of the <u>level</u> of profit.

11.(c) The extra output per marginal dollar spent on capital = $MP_K/P_K = 6/5 = 1.20$. The extra output per marginal dollar spent on labour = $MP_L/P_L = 2/10 = 0.20$. Since $MP_K/P_K > MP_L/P_L$, the garage can maintain the same output at a lower cost by using more of the factor that gives higher output per marginal dollar (capital) and less of the factor that gives lower output per marginal dollar (labour).

12.(d) This time you see that $MP_K/P_K = 4/8 = 0.5$ and $MP_L/P_L = 8/4 = 2$. Now $MP_K/P_K < MP_L/P_L$ and the situation is the reverse of Question 11, so the firm should use less capital and more labour.

13.(c) If they have access to the same technologies they would also have access to a common set of technically efficient combinations of inputs. The issue, therefore, is which of these combinations is economically efficient—i.e., which gives the lowest average cost per unit of output. If the relative price of land to labour is lower in Canada, the Canadian firm's economically efficient combination will be more land-intensive than in China—i.e., its land/capital ratio will be higher than in China. Note that, while the economically efficient combination for each country will be where its $MP_{Land}/MP_{Labour} = P_{Land}/P_{Labour}$, the corresponding ratio of <u>quantities</u> of land and labour used may be greater than, less than, or equal to the ratio of prices (so answer (e) is wrong).

16.(b) Since B is on the *LRAC* curve there is no other combination of factors, given their current prices, at which Q_0 can be produced for less cost. At point A the firm would be producing the same output but at a higher average cost (so (c) and (a) are incorrect). Point E gives the least possible *average* cost per unit of the <u>higher</u> output level of Q_2; also, a lower average for a greater number of units does not imply that <u>total</u> cost (*AC* times Q_2) would be less than at the lower output of Q_0 or Q_1 (so (e) is wrong). Nothing can be said about profits since the diagram gives no information about revenues, demand, and output price (so (a) is wrong).

17.(d) Employing more labour with the same capital will increase output along the same *SRATC* curve as point A; D is the only point on the diagram that is at a higher output and on the same *SRATC* curve.

18.(a) Capital (K) is the fixed factor of production for each short-run *ATC* curve. The $SRATC_2$ is the short-run average costs curve using <u>more capital</u> than on $SRATC_1$. The move from B to A is the only option in the answers that involves a move from $SRATC_1$ to $SRATC_2$.

19.(e) There is a tendency to answer this question by saying the *SRATC* curve will shift down—which it will. But since the *LRAC* curve is drawn for a given technology, a technological improvement will shift down all the *SRATC* curves *and* the *LRAC* curve. Since there is only one *LRAC* in the diagram, no two points in the diagram reflect a change in technology. Any movement from a point on $SRATC_1$ to a point on $SRATC_2$ is a response to using more capital (the fixed factor in each short run), not to a change in technology.

21.(d) Each *isoquant* shows all the combinations of capital (K) and labour (L) that yield a given quantity of output (70, 80, and 100, respectively). Each *isocost* line shows the various combinations of K and L that can be purchased for each given amount of total cost (and the current market prices of factors). The lowest attainable isocost line along $Q = 80$ is at point D. Note too that the isocost/isoquant <u>tangency</u> at point D is a diagrammatic representation of the cost-minimization condition $MP_L/MP_K = P_L/P_K$ (hence $MP_K/P_K = MP_L/P_L$).

22.(a) If P_L increases, the slope of the isocost curve (P_L/P_K) also increases. Since output is unchanged, the new isocost curve will be tangential to the same isoquant as point B, but at a steeper point (e.g., at point A), which reflects a higher *MRS* of capital for labour (consistent with maintaining $MRS = P_L/P_K$ after P_L/P_K increases).

23.(b) Since the *absolute* prices of both factors of production increase by the same percentage, their *relative* prices remain unchanged. The slope of the isocost curves remains unchanged, so the point on the $Q = 70$ isoquant at which $MRS = P_L/P_K$ also remains unchanged at B.

Competitive Markets

Chapter Overview

Market structure affects the degree to which individual firms have **market power**: the degree to which the individual firm can influence the price of its product. The less market power individual firms have, the more competitive the market structure. In **perfectly competitive markets**, firms produce a **homogeneous product** and are **price takers** with no market power at all. Firms in perfectly competitive markets have no need to actively engage in *competitive behaviour*, and would gain no advantage from doing so.

Profit-maximizing firms produce a level of output at which (a) price is at least as great as average variable cost, and (b) marginal cost equals marginal revenue. Since firms are price takers in perfectly competitive markets, their marginal revenue equals price. Thus, profit-maximizing firms in these markets equate marginal cost to price.

In the short run, firms will cease production entirely if revenues from the sale of output do not cover the variable costs of production but will continue to operate if revenue is above variable costs. This insight explains why some firms continue to employ less efficient, vintage technologies, and why some firms may continue to operate in declining industries even though they may be experiencing losses.

Perfect competition is also characterized by *freedom of entry and exit*. In the long run, profits or losses will lead to the entry or exit, respectively, of capital into or out of the industry. Freedom of entry and exit drives the competitive industry to a long-run equilibrium of zero profits, and results in the firm's production level corresponding to minimum average cost. Although firms will eventually exit the industry if revenues do not cover total costs of production, the speed of exit depends on the extent to which short-run fixed costs are divided into *sunk* and *non-sunk* costs.

LO LEARNING OBJECTIVES

After studying this chapter, you will be able to

1. state the difference between competitive behaviour and a competitive market.

2. list the four key assumptions of the theory of perfect competition.

3. derive a competitive firm's supply curve.

4. determine whether competitive firms are making profits or losses in the short run.

5. explain the role played by profits, entry, and exit in determining a competitive industry's long-run equilibrium.

Hints and Tips

The following may help you avoid some of the most common errors on examinations.

✓ Understand the difference between competitive market structure and competitive behaviour. There is a potential payoff to competitive *behaviour* only when the market structure is *not* perfectly competitive.

✓ Understand the very important difference between the condition that says the firm is doing the "best" it can do (i.e., maximizing profits) and the condition that determines how good is that best (i.e., how much profit it is making, if any). To do the best that it can do, the firm equates *marginal* cost and *marginal* revenue. To see how good the best is, the firm must compare *total* cost and *total* revenue.

✓ The way economics defines costs of production, and therefore profits, allows the theory to predict when and why firms will wish to enter or exit an industry. What could be earned in the firm's next-best alternative is an *implicit* cost of production. Consequently, positive economic profit in (for example) Industry A means that these firms are making a better return than firms in Industry B. This allows theory to predict that, in the long run, there will be a movement of firms out of Industry B and into Industry A. Conversely, negative economic profit in Industry A is an incentive for firms to exit Industry A and enter Industry B. Ultimately, these movements create a long-run equilibrium at zero economic profit in perfectly competitive industries. In perfect competition, therefore, the pursuit of profit eliminates economic profits (and losses) in the long run.

✓ Understand the market dynamics of how the behaviour of some firms affects the conditions under which the others operate. Even if all firms in an industry are making losses, they will not all leave the industry. As some leave, market forces drive up the price at which the remaining firms can sell their output. This process continues to the point where the remaining firms have no reason to leave (i.e., they make zero economic profit at the higher price).

Chapter Review

Market Structure and Firm Behaviour

Many students are surprised to hear that perfectly competitive firms do not actively engage in competitive behaviour; indeed, in later chapters you will find that competitive behaviour is a feature of market structures that are far from competitive. When reading this section, understand the link between lack of market power and lack of competitive behaviour, and the reason why perfectly competitive firms in particular do not engage in competitive behaviour.

1. **A perfectly competitive market structure is best described by firms that**
    (a) allocate a substantial share of their budget to advertising.
    (b) engage in cutthroat competition by denigrating each others' products.
    (c) are subjected to government controls ensuring fair competition.
    (d) do not actively advertise or undercut their competitors' prices.
    (e) can override the market forces of demand and supply.

2. **Which of the following characteristics of an industry is most conducive to competitive *behaviour* by firms?**
    (a)   A large number of firms exist in the industry.
    (b)   Individual firms can sell more by reducing price.
    (c)   A firm can affect its profits only by changing its own output or costs.
    (d)   All firms in the industry produce an identical product.
    (e)   All of the above.

The Theory of Perfect Competition

This section explains the conditions necessary for an industry to have a perfectly competitive market structure. It is because of these conditions that the individual firm faces a perfectly elastic demand curve (i.e., each firm is a price taker) even though the market demand curve is downward-sloping. Since the firm faces a perfectly elastic demand curve, its product price (or average revenue) is the same as its marginal revenue. In later sections, you will see that the necessary conditions also dictate that perfectly competitive firms make zero economic profit in the long run.

3. **The assumption that each firm in a perfectly competitive market is a price taker basically means that**
    (a)   market price is independent of the level of industry output.
    (b)   each firm's supply curve is perfectly elastic.
    (c)   the industry supply curve is perfectly elastic.
    (d)   the firm can take any price it wants to choose and still sell all its output.
    (e)   changes in the output of an individual firm do not affect the market price.

4. **Which one of the following characteristics of a market would you expect to be *inconsistent* with price-taking behaviour?**
    (a)   There are a large number of firms in the industry.
    (b)   Each firm's product is distinguishable from that of its competitors.
    (c)   Each firm's share of total industry output is insignificant.
    (d)   Each firm behaves as though it faces a perfectly elastic demand curve.
    (e)   Firms do not actively engage in competitive behaviour.

5. **A firm that faces a perfectly elastic demand curve has a**
    (a)   linear total revenue curve with a slope equal to the market price.
    (b)   horizontal total revenue curve.
    (c)   constant total revenue regardless of the level of output.
    (d)   total revenue curve shaped like an inverted U.
    (e)   negatively sloped total revenue curve.

6. **In a perfectly competitive market, each firm's demand curve is**
    (a)   the same as its average revenue curve.
    (b)   the same as its marginal revenue curve.
    (c)   a horizontal line drawn at the market price.
    (d)   All of the above.
    (e)   None of the above.

7. **The perfectly competitive firm will not increase its price above the price charged by other firms in the industry because**
   (a) there is freedom of entry and exit.
   (b) the other firms will react by reducing their prices.
   (c) it doesn't make enough profit to advertise how its product differs from that of its competitors.
   (d) consumers know the prices being charged by other firms for the same product.
   (e) it will increase its sales by reducing its price.

8. **In perfect competition, marginal revenue is**
   (a) the last dollar needed to make zero economic profit.
   (b) the last dollar needed to make maximum profit.
   (c) the change in revenue from selling an additional unit of output.
   (d) the extra revenue generated by a $1 change in price.
   (e) the revenue in excess of what can be earned in the next-best alternative.

Short-Run Decisions

Make sure you fully understand the general profit-maximizing condition (i.e., marginal cost equals marginal revenue), and the condition that must be satisfied if a firm is to produce anything at all in the short run (i.e., price at least equal to minimum average variable cost). The firm is in short-run equilibrium when it produces the output that maximizes its profit at a given price. Since profits are maximized at the output where $P = MC$, then the firm's MC curve (above minimum AVC) is also its short-run supply curve. Understand the reasoning behind Figure 9-8 in the text, which shows that a profit-maximizing firm may be making negative, zero, or positive profits in the short run. [*Note:* Students who have already read the rest of the chapter should note that the shut-down condition in this section implicitly assumes that all fixed costs are *sunk* costs. If you have not yet read the rest of the chapter, ignore this note.]

9. **If output is where marginal cost equals marginal revenue, then**
   (a) the last unit produced adds the same amount to costs as it does to revenue.
   (b) the firm is maximizing profits.
   (c) there is no reason to reduce or expand output, as long as TR is greater than or equal to TVC.
   (d) the difference between TR and TC is maximized.
   (e) All of the above.

10. **A profit-maximizing firm should shut down production and suffer a short-run loss equal to its fixed cost if**
   (a) average revenue is less than average variable cost.
   (b) average revenue is less than average total cost but greater than average variable cost.
   (c) total revenue is less than total cost but greater than total variable cost.
   (d) its economic profits are negative and smaller in absolute value than total fixed cost.
   (e) profits are negative.

11. **Should it decide to produce a positive output, any profit-maximizing firm should produce the output level for which**
   (a) the incremental change in revenue equals the incremental change in costs.
   (b) total revenue exceeds total costs.
   (c) average revenue equals average total costs.
   (d) average costs are minimized.
   (e) total revenue equals total costs.

12. **A perfectly competitive firm does not try to sell more of its product by lowering its price below the market price because**
   (a)   this would be considered unethical price chiselling.
   (b)   its competitors would not permit it.
   (c)   its demand is inelastic, so total revenue would decline.
   (d)   it can sell whatever it produces at the market price.
   (e)   consumers might believe this firm's product to be inferior, and therefore cease buying it.

13. **If it is worthwhile for a perfectly competitive firm to produce a positive output, the level of output at which it maximizes short-run profits is where**
   (a)   price equals average total cost.
   (b)   price equals short-run marginal cost.
   (c)   short-run marginal cost equals average total cost.
   (d)   marginal revenue equals average variable cost.
   (e)   price equals average variable cost.

14. **A firm producing a positive output level, covering variable costs but making a loss in the short run,**
   (a)   is not maximizing profits.
   (b)   should definitely shut down.
   (c)   should exit the industry.
   (d)   should either expand or contract its plant size.
   (e)   may nonetheless be doing the best that it can with respect to profits.

15. **The perfectly competitive firm's profits can be calculated as**
   (a) $(MR - ATC)Q$.   (b) $(P - ATC)Q$.
   (c) $(P - AVC - AFC)Q$.   (d) $(AR - ATC)Q$.
   (e)   All of the above.

16. **The short-run supply curve of a perfectly competitive firm is**
   (a)   its MC curve above minimum ATC.
   (b)   its demand curve, because it is a price taker.
   (c)   its MC curve above minimum MC.
   (d)   its MC curve above minimum AVC.
   (e)   its MC curve above minimum AFC.

Long-Run Decisions

Profits are a signal for resource allocation. If profits are positive (negative) firms will enter (exit) a perfectly competitive industry. If profits are zero, revenues are just covering opportunity cost, and there is no incentive for entry or exit. [*Note:* Always bear in mind that we are referring to economic profit, without which the theory could not make these predictions.] When the adjustment to long-run equilibrium requires exit, the *speed of exit* is affected by how fixed costs are distributed between *sunk* and *non-sunk* costs. Review the conditions for long-run equilibrium in perfect competition, and understand how they compare to the conditions for short-run equilibrium. After reading this section you should be able to understand its central lesson: how the pursuit of profits eliminates profits in an industry with freedom of entry. [*Note:* For students covering the long-run supply curve for a perfectly competitive industry, it is explained in *Additional Topics: The Long-Run Industry Supply Curve* on MyEconLab.]

17. **The existence of positive profits in a perfectly competitive industry**
    (a) is a signal for existing firms to lower their price.
    (b) is a signal for existing firms to maintain their plant size.
    (c) provides an incentive for new firms to enter the industry.
    (d) encourages all firms to expand their production levels.
    (e) signals firms to increase price.

18. **Long-run equilibrium in a perfectly competitive industry is characterized by**
    (a) each firm in the industry earning maximum attainable profits.
    (b) each firm in the industry making zero economic profits.
    (c) no firm desiring to enter or exit this industry.
    (d) no firm desiring to alter its plant size.
    (e) All of the above.

19. **Which of the following situations could occur in a short-run equilibrium but not in a long-run equilibrium?**
    (a) $P = AVC$.   (b) $P = MC$.
    (c) $P = SRATC$.   (d) $P = LRAC$.
    (e) $MR = MC$.

20. **Long-run economic profits will not exist in a perfectly competitive industry because**
    (a) new firms will enter the industry and eliminate them.
    (b) corporate income taxes eliminate profits.
    (c) competitive firms are too small to be profitable.
    (d) increasing costs will eliminate profits in the long run.
    (e) firms in this industry engage in cutthroat price cutting.

21. **If perfectly competitive firms are making losses in short-run equilibrium, the adjustment to long-run equilibrium**
    (a) is slower when it takes longer for capital to become obsolete.
    (b) is faster in industries that do not require significant investment in capital.
    (c) is faster if fixed costs are mainly non-sunk costs.
    (d) All of the above.
    (e) None of the above—the speed of exit will be the same in all industries making losses.

Short-Answer Questions

1. State whether the following statement is true or false, and explain your answer. "If the perfectly competitive firm is producing 200 units of output at a marginal cost of $8 and selling at a price of $12, profit is $800."

2. Explain why a perfectly competitive firm making losses in the short run may continue to produce, rather than temporarily cease production until other firms exit and price increases.

3.   Explain the difference between sunk and non-sunk fixed costs. Why should loss-making firms in industries with a high proportion of sunk fixed costs exit more slowly than firms in industries with a high proportion of non-sunk fixed costs?

4.   Explain the role of each of the following assumptions of perfect competition in making the firm's demand curve perfectly elastic.

      (a)   Each firm produces a small share of total industry output.

      (b)   Consumers know the prices charged by each firm and the nature of their products.

      (c)   All firms sell a homogeneous product.

5.   What is the role of freedom of entry and exit in the model of a perfectly competitive industry?

6.   Comment on the following statement. "The decline in the widget industry is attributable to its use of antiquated equipment and technology, which can be rectified by a government subsidy."

Exercises

1.   **Reading the Diagram**
      This exercise gives you practice in reading profit information from a firm's cost curves. Figure 9-1 depicts the cost structure of a hypothetical, profit-maximizing firm that operates in a perfectly competitive industry.
      Figure 9-1

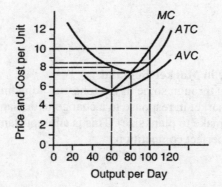

(a) Use the firm's cost structure to complete the following table.

If Market Price Is	$10.00	$7.50	$5.50
(i) profit-maximizing output is	100	80	60
At this output,			
(ii) total revenue is $P \times Q$			
(iii) total cost is $ATC \times Q$			
(iv) profit is (+ or −) $TR - TC$			
(v) marginal revenue is P			
(vi) marginal cost is MC			
(vii) average total cost is off ATC curve			
(viii) profit per unit is $AR - ATC$			

(b) Why is neither $10.00 nor $5.50 the long-run market price?

@ 7.50, MC = ATC

0 econ. profits

2. **Profit Maximization in the Short Run**

   The purpose of the following question is to determine (from raw data rather than diagrams) if a firm is maximizing profits and, if not, what adjustments it should make.

   Consider the following information regarding output levels, costs, and market price for two perfectly competitive firms operating in different industries. Each firm has an upward-sloping marginal cost curve.

   Firm A: output = 5000   total variable cost = $2500
            price = $1.00   total fixed cost = $2000
                                   marginal cost = $1.20

   Firm B: output = 5000   average total costs = $1.00
            price = $1.20   (and *ATC* is at the minimum)

   ⮡ ATC = MC = $1.00

	Firm A	Firm B

   (a) How much profit (or loss) is each firm making? _____ _____

   (b) Are these firms making *maximum* profits? Explain.   no   no

   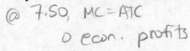
   ⮡ P = MC

   (c) Should each firm produce more, less, or the same output as currently? Explain.

   less   more

   b/c P<MC   b/c P>MC

3. **Adjusting to a Change in Market Demand**

   This exercise walks you through some of the long-run adjustments that take place in a perfectly competitive market in response to a change in demand (ignoring any adjustments that current firms may make to plant size). This is an important exercise for solidifying your understanding of perfect competition.

All firms in the gadget industry, as well as potential entrants, have the cost structure depicted in Panel (i) of Figure 9-2. Panel (ii) shows the industry's short-run supply curve S and the current market demand curve D.

Figure 9-2

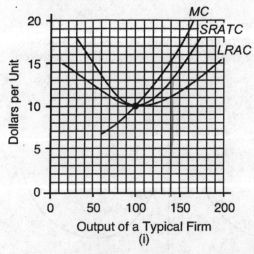
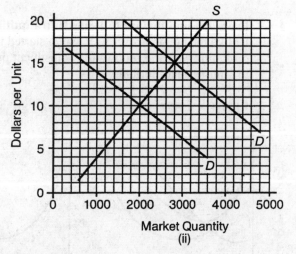

Output of a Typical Firm
(i)

Market Quantity
(ii)

(a) Before the increase in demand, what are equilibrium price and quantity in the gadget market? What is the output of each firm in this industry, and how much profit is each firm making?

$10 @ 2000 units

100

econ. profits 0 b/c at this P, MC=SRATC

(b) How many firms are operating in this industry? Is the industry in long-run equilibrium? Explain.

20

Yes b/c econ. profits 0

(c) Now suppose that the demand for gadgets shifts from D to D'. What are the new equilibrium market price and quantity in the short run?

$15 @ 2800 units.

(d) What happens to the quantity produced by each firm? What is each firm's short-run profit?

Increases →140

$15 x 140 units = $2100

average total cost to produce 140 units
P. $13 x 140 = $1820.
π = 2100 - 1820 = 280

(e) Explain what will happen to the industry short-run supply curve once sufficient time has elapsed for entry or exit to occur. Draw the new supply curve in Panel (ii).

Supply ↑   π > 0   new firms enter

(f) Once the new long-run equilibrium is established, what are the market price and quantity?

entry continues until long-run eqbm (zero econ profits)
occur at P=$10.
industry Q = 4000 (based on new D curve)

(g) What are the levels of output and associated profit of each firm in the new long-run equilibrium? How many firms are now in this gadget industry?

100 units/firm   40 firms
0 econ profits

4. From Disequilibrium to Long-Run Equilibrium

Unlike the previous exercise, which started in long-run equilibrium, this exercise starts in disequilibrium and follows the adjustment process through to short-run equilibrium and on to long-run equilibrium.

Figure 9-3

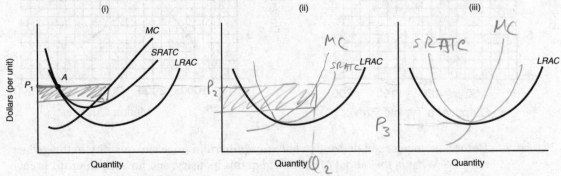

(a) The firm is initially at point A in Panel (i). Explain why the firm is making zero economic profit. Why is point A not even a short-run equilibrium?

AR = P = SRATC ∴ 0 econ profit   b/c MC≠P

(b) Explain what the firm would do to maximize short-run profit. Draw this situation in Panel (i) (showing price, quantity, and profit). Why is the result not a long-run equilibrium?

Increase output to Q_2, where P=MC

(c) What would the firm in Panel (i) do in the long run? Draw the result in Panel (ii). [*Hint:* How could the firm reduce costs of production?] Would other firms currently in the industry do the same? If no new firms entered, why is the result still not a long-run equilibrium for the industry?

- ↑ profit by ↑ plant size (using more capital)
∴ reduce costs of production
until plant size is that needed to reach min. LRAC
- all firms do so, so mc for all curves shift to right, ∴ est. new lower price, still not long run eqn b/c econ profits > 0

(d) How would the industry move to long-run equilibrium? Draw the resulting long-run equilibrium for the representative firm in Panel (iii).

New firms enter, shifting supply →
reducing price + profit
until profit=0, P=MC = min LRAC

5. The Very Long Run: The Impact of Technological Improvement

This exercise addresses the impact of a change in technology in a perfectly competitive market. There are only two vintages of technology, the old and the new. To keep Figure 9-4 tidy, only one set of cost curves is shown for the representative firm. The *LRAC* curves have not been drawn, but you should assume that minimum points on the *SRATC* curves shown are also the minimum points on the corresponding *LRAC* curves.

First we focus on Panels (i) and (ii), showing the situation before the new technology is invented. The cost structure of the representative firm is shown in Panel (i), and Panel (ii) shows the market demand curve (*D*) and the industry short-run supply curve (*S*).

Figure 9-4

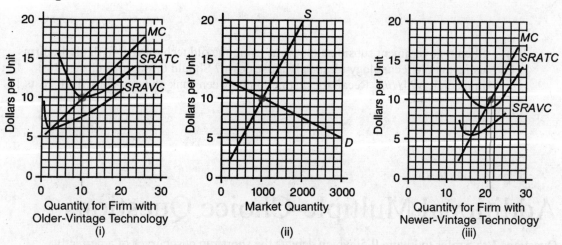

(a)   What are the industry's long-run equilibrium price and quantity? Draw the equilibrium price and quantity for the market and the firm.

$10,   1000

(b)   What is each firm's profit level in the long-run equilibrium? How many firms are in the industry?

zero   1000/10 = 100

(c)   Now focus on Panels (ii) and (iii). The new technology is invented, and any firms choosing to enter the industry have the cost structure shown in Panel (iii). Assume that existing firms do not adapt to the new technology, and only new firms have the cost structure in Panel (iii). Why will new firms enter the industry?

MC > SRATC ∴ econ profit >0
                      avg revenue > ATC

(d)   Next, assume that enough new firms have entered to bring the new firms to their long-run equilibrium, but the old firms are still using the old technology.
   (i)   What are the new long-run equilibrium price and quantity in the market? What has happened to the supply curve in Panel (ii)?

supply curve →

   (ii)   What are the output level and profit of firms using the new technology? Draw the price and quantity for the firm in Panel (iii).

(iii) What are the output level and profit of firms still using the old technology? Show this on Panel (i).

(iv) How many firms in the industry are using the new technology and how many are using the old, less efficient technology?

(e) Should government subsidize the firms using the old technology? Will all the firms using the old technology ultimately close down? Should these firms close down immediately? [*Hint:* Recall the distinction between sunk and non-sunk fixed costs.]

Additional Multiple-Choice Questions

Questions 1 to 8 refer to Figure 9-5, which depicts the short-run cost curves of a perfectly competitive firm.

Figure 9-5

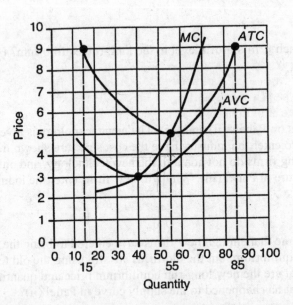

*1. If the current market price is $9, the profit-maximizing output of this firm is

(a) 15.
(b) 70.
(c) 55.
(d) 85.
(e) 40.

*2. At this output, total costs are equal to

(a) $135.
(b) $765.
(c) $630.
(d) $420.
(e) $350.

*3. The firm's total profit is equal to
(a) $210.
(b) $220.
(c) $280.
(d) $70.
(e) Indeterminable with data provided.

*4. Should the market price fall to $4, this firm will
(a) shut down immediately and make zero profit.
(b) shut down immediately and suffer a loss equal to its fixed costs.
(c) continue operating in the short run and suffer a loss that is less than its fixed cost.
(d) produce 55 units and make a loss equal to its total variable cost.
(e) produce 40 units and suffer a loss equal to its total fixed cost.

*5. This firm's maximum attainable profit level equals zero if
(a) the industry is in short-run equilibrium.
(b) the firm produces any output at which $MC = MR$.
(c) the market price is $5.
(d) the market price is $3.
(e) the market price is $7 and the firm produces 40 units of output.

*6. If all fixed costs are sunk costs, this firm would shut down production if the market price were below
(a) $5.
(b) $3.
(c) marginal cost.
(d) average total cost.
(e) Indeterminable with data provided.

*7. The short-run supply curve for this firm (assuming all fixed costs are sunk costs) is its
(a) marginal cost curve.
(b) marginal cost curve at or above $3.
(c) marginal cost curve at or above $5.
(d) ATC curve at or above $5.
(e) AVC curve at or above $3.

*8. With a market price of $6, an output of 60 units could be the firm's long-run profit-maximizing output if
(a) the firm expected price to rise in the future.
(b) its long-run average cost curve is minimized at 55 units of output.
(c) other firms were barred from entering this industry.
(d) this firm could not exit the industry.
(e) the firm was experiencing decreasing returns to scale.

*9. When all firms in a perfectly competitive industry are producing at minimum efficient scale and just covering costs,
(a) it is physically impossible for existing firms to increase output.
(b) new firms would enter, produce at minimum efficient scale, and also cover their costs.
(c) profits could be made only with larger plants.
(d) the industry is in long-run equilibrium.
(e) some firms will exit the industry.

*10. **Which of the following characteristics is true of a perfectly competitive industry that is subject to continuous technological change?**
   (a) Only plants of recent vintage and thus greater efficiency will operate.
   (b) The market price equals the minimum average total cost of the most efficient plants.
   (c) The market price equals the minimum average total cost of the least efficient plant still in use.
   (d) Plants with older technology will continue to produce if all fixed costs are non-sunk costs.
   (e) Any plant without the most recent and efficient technology will be closed.

11. **In which of the following situations should a profit-maximizing firm leave its output unaltered?**
   (a) $MR > MC$ and $TR > TC$.
   (b) $MR = MC$ and $TR > TVC$.
   (c) $MR > MC$ and $TR = TC$.
   (d) $MR < MC$ and $TR < TC$.
   (e) $MR = MC$ and $TR < TVC$.

12. **If a competitive industry faced a steady decrease in demand, economic theory predicts that in the long run**
   (a) firms will gradually leave the industry, thereby shrinking its productive capacity.
   (b) firms will modernize plant and equipment in order to increase efficiency.
   (c) existing firms will expand output levels as a means of recovering losses.
   (d) the industry will expand with newer, more efficient firms entering.
   (e) Both (b) and (d) are correct.

*13. **Suppose that the following data are observed for a perfectly competitive firm: output = 5000 units, market price = \$1, fixed costs = \$2000, variable costs = \$1000, and marginal cost = \$1.25. To maximize profits the firm should**
   (a) reduce output.
   (b) expand output.
   (c) shut down.
   (d) increase the market price.
   (e) not change output.

*14. **At its current level of output, a perfectly competitive firm's average variable cost is \$8, average total cost is \$10, and marginal cost is \$9. If the market price is \$10, this firm can increase profits by**
   (a) shutting down production.
   (b) decreasing output.
   (c) increasing output.
   (d) increasing the market price.
   (e) not changing output. This firm is at its profit-maximizing position.

*15. **If a perfectly competitive firm is producing where price equals average total cost and average total cost is greater than marginal cost, the firm should**
   (a) reduce output.
   (b) expand output.
   (c) shut down.
   (d) increase the market price.
   (e) not change output.

16. **If a perfectly competitive industry is in short-run equilibrium and each firm has $P > ATC$, then in the long run**
    (a) individual firms will increase their output.
    (b) new firms will enter the market.
    (c) factor prices must rise until $ATC = P$.
    (d) existing firms will continue to earn economic profits.
    (e) existing firms will acquire more capital and move to the upward-sloping portion of their *LRAC* curves.

*17. **A long-run competitive equilibrium is impossible if**
    (a) there are no barriers to entry.
    (b) all firms are producing where $P = ATC$.
    (c) accounting profits are always positive.
    (d) firms have downward-sloping *LRAC* curves at all levels of output.
    (e) all firms have U-shaped (or saucer-shaped) *LRAC* curves.

Questions 18 to 23 refer to the following diagram, which depicts cost curves for a firm in a perfectly competitive market.

Figure 9-6

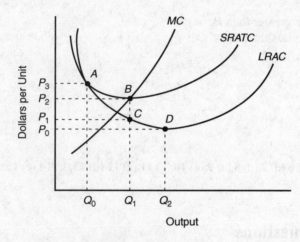

*18. **If this firm were producing at point *A*, it is**
    (a) maximizing profits.
    (b) minimizing the cost of producing Q_0.
    (c) in a short-run equilibrium.
    (d) in a long-run equilibrium.
    (e) not employing an efficient combination of capital and labour to produce Q_0.

*19. **If market price were P_2 and this firm were at point *B*, it**
    (a) should move to point *A* to maximize short-run profit.
    (b) should move to point *A* to maximize long-run profit.
    (c) is maximizing short-run profit.
    (d) will not want to change its capital in the long run.
    (e) is minimizing the long-run cost of producing Q_1.

*20. **If market price were initially P_2, this firm would eventually be in a long-run equilibrium at point**
    (a) *A*.   (b) *B*.
    (c) *C*.   (d) *D*.
    (e) None of the above.

*21. If market price were P_2,
    (a)   short run-profits would be maximized at point B.
    (b)   short-run profits would be zero.
    (c)   this firm will expand its capital.
    (d)   other firms will enter the industry.
    (e)   All of the above.

22. If factor prices in this industry were constant and market price is initially P_2, the long-run equilibrium will be
    (a)   at P_3 and Q_0.
    (b)   at P_2 and Q_1.
    (c)   at P_1 and Q_1.
    (d)   at P_0 and Q_2.
    (e)   Indeterminate with the information provided.

*23. If factor prices were to decrease as industry output increased and market price were initially P_2, the long-run equilibrium would be at
    (a) P_2 and Q_1.
    (b) P_1 and Q_1.
    (c) P_0 and Q_2.
    (d)   Some price greater than P_0.
    (e)   Some price less than P_0.

Solutions

Chapter Review

1.(d) 2.(b) 3.(e) 4.(b) 5.(a) 6.(d) 7.(d) 8.(c) 9.(e) 10.(a) 11.(a) 12.(d) 13.(b) 14.(e) 15.(e) 16.(d) 17.(c) 18.(e) 19.(a) 20.(a) 21.(d)

Short-Answer Questions

1.   False. Profit is calculated as $(P - ATC)Q$. Of the three items in this expression, you have information only on P and Q, but not on ATC. You know MC, but not ATC. [*Note:* You also know that the firm is not maximizing profit at this output. Since $P > MC$, additional units of output will add more to revenues than to costs, thereby increasing profits.]

2.   A perfectly competitive firm will continue to produce in the short run as long as revenues exceed total variable costs. Since the excess of revenues over total variable costs pays some of the fixed costs, short-run losses are less than total fixed costs. If the firm ceased to produce, it would have to pay all its fixed costs in the short run. By continuing to produce, therefore, it minimizes its short-run losses.

3.   Sunk fixed costs can never be recovered, while non-sunk fixed costs can be recovered (or avoided) if the firm shuts down. The firm minimizes losses by continuing to produce if its revenues exceed total variable costs plus non-sunk fixed costs. The greater the proportion of total fixed costs that are sunk costs, the smaller the revenues needed to cover variable plus non-sunk fixed costs and the longer the firm can minimize losses by not exiting.

4.   (a)   If a firm produces a small proportion of industry output, any increase in the individual firm's output will not be big enough to shift the market supply curve and alter the market equilibrium price.
    (b)   Consumers will not buy from a firm that raises its price if they know there are many other firms charging a lower price for the identical product.

(c) With a homogeneous product, there are no special attributes of one firm's product that are more attractive to some consumers than any other firm's product, so no consumer is willing to pay a price higher than that charged by other firms.

5. Firms in other industries are attracted by economic profits, and there is nothing to stop them from entering the industry making positive profit. The process of entry increases supply and reduces price and profits until there is no longer any incentive to enter—i.e., long-run equilibrium at zero economic profits is achieved. Conversely, there is nothing to prevent firms making economic losses from leaving the industry, thus reducing market supply and increasing price until there is no reason for further exit—i.e., again a long-run equilibrium at zero economic profits is achieved. Freedom of entry and exit ensures that the long-run equilibrium in a perfectly competitive industry is at zero profit.

6. This is an issue of cause and effect. Generally the use of antiquated equipment is an effect of the industry's decline, not a cause. When an industry is in decline, it is not profitable for firms to invest in new equipment and technology. A government subsidy merely extends the time that firms will stay in the declining industry, rather than allocating society's resources to produce goods and services that consumers demand.

Exercises

1. **(a)** (i)   100; 80; 60. (Where $P = MC$)
          (ii) $1000; $600; $330. (Total revenue = $P \times Q$)
          (iii) $850; $600; $480. (Total cost = $ATC \times Q$)
          (iv) $150; 0; –$150. (Profit = $TR - TC = (AR - ATC) \times Q$)
          (v) $10.00; $7.50; $5.50. ($MR = P$ in perfect competition)
          (vi) $10.00; $7.50; $5.50. ($MR = MC$ at profit-maximization)
          (vii) $8.50; $7.50; $8.00. (Read from the ATC curve at each Q)
          (viii) $1.50; 0; –$2.50. (Profit per unit = $AR - ATC$)

   (b) At $P = $10.00, profit (of $150) will cause firms to enter the industry. At $P = $5.50, losses (of $150) will cause exit of firms. In either case, the industry supply curve would shift until the long-run equilibrium price at which profit = zero is achieved (i.e., $P = $7.50).

2. **(a)** Firm A makes a profit of $TR - TC = $5000 - $4500 = $500. Firm B makes a profit of $TR - TC = (AR - ATC)Q = ($1.20 - $1.00)5000 = 1000.

   (b) No, for both firms. Neither firm is producing where $P = MC$. [*Note:* For Firm B, $MC = $1 because $ATC = MC$ at minimum ATC.]

   (c) Firm A should produce less output. At its current output, $P < MC$. Since P is constant for a perfectly competitive firm and MC is positively sloped, a decrease in output brings MC toward P. Firm B should produce more output. At its current output, $P > MC$ so additional units of output will add more to revenue than to cost, thereby increasing profit.

3. **Figure 9-7**

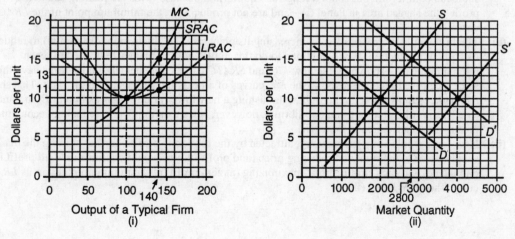

(a) $P = \$10$ and $Q = 2000$ units (at the intersection of D and S). Each firm produces 100 units of output (i.e., where $MC = MR = P = \$10$). Since at an output of 100 units average revenue (P) equals $SRATC$, profits are equal to zero.

(b) Divide industry output (2000) by firm output (100) to get 20 firms. Yes, this industry is in long-run equilibrium because the typical firm is making zero economic profit at the minimum point of its $LRAC$ curve. Not only are existing firms profit maximizing at the lowest attainable cost, but also there is no incentive for new firms to enter or existing firms to exit the industry.

(c) $P = \$15$ and $Q = 2800$ units (at intersection of D' and S).

(d) As market price increases from \$10 to \$15, each existing firm increases output along its MC curve from 100 to140 units (where $P = MC$ again). Each firm's total revenue is $\$15 \times 140 = \$2100$. The average total cost of producing 140 units is \$13, so total cost is $\$13 \times 140 = \$1820$. Short- run profit for each firm, therefore, is $\$2100 - \$1820 = \$280$.

(e) Since industry profits are positive, new firms will enter the industry. This entry shifts the industry short-run supply curve to the right, thereby lowering price.

(f) Entry continues until long-run equilibrium (i.e., zero profits) occurs at $P = \$10$ and industry $Q = 4000$ (the intersection of D' and S'). Because firms are profit-maximizing at zero profit again, there is no incentive for further entry.

(g) Each firm produces 100 units and earns an economic profit equal to zero, which is the same as the initial long-run equilibrium position of each firm in (a). The difference between the new long-run equilibrium and the initial long-run equilibrium is that there will be more firms in the industry—specifically, there will be 40 firms (4000/100) instead of 20 (2000/100).

4. **Figure 9-8**

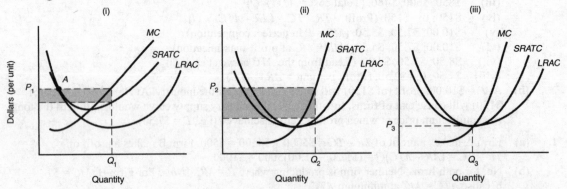

(a) Zero economic profit is made at A because $AR = ATC$. This is not even a short-run equilibrium, since at the price P_1 in Panel (i) of Figure 9-8 the firm is not producing where $P = MC$. [*Note:* Since the industry supply curve is the sum of firms' MC curves, and at A the firm is producing *off* its MC curve, then the total market quantity supplied would be *off* the market supply curve.]

(b) The firm will maximize short-run profit by increasing output to Q_1, where $P_1 = MC$. This is a short-run equilibrium but is not a long-run equilibrium because firms are making economic profit—the shaded area in Panel (i)—and are not producing at the minimum point of the $LRAC$ curve.

(c) The firm would increase profit by increasing its plant size (i.e., by using more capital) to reduce its costs of production. It will continue to do this until it has the plant size needed to reach minimum $LRAC$—shown by the new MC and $SRATC$ curves in Panel (ii). Other firms have the same incentive to reduce costs, so the MC curves of all existing firms shift to the right. This shifts the market supply curve to the right, establishing a new lower price at (for example) P_2 in Panel (ii). This is still not a long-run equilibrium, however, since existing firms are making economic profit—the shaded area in Panel (ii).

(d) New firms would enter the industry, attracted by the economic profits, further shifting the market supply curve to the right and reducing price (and profit). Entry would continue until all profit is eliminated, and each firm is profit-maximizing (at zero profit) at the minimum point on its $LRAC$ curve, shown in Panel (iii).

5.   Figure 9-9

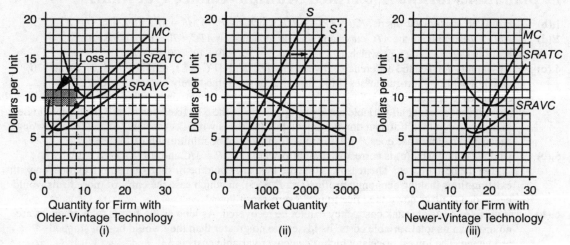

(a) $P = \$10$ and $Q = 1000$ units, where D and S intersect in Panel (ii).

(b)   Each firm produces 10 units of output at the minimum point of the *ATC* in Panel (i) and makes zero profit. Since industry output is 1000 and each firm produces 10, there are 100 firms in the industry (i.e., 1000/10 = 100).

(c)   A firm entering with the new technology faces the same price ($10) as the existing firms, and by producing 21 units—where $MR = MC = \$10$ for the new plant in Panel (iii)—it can make a positive profit because at this output, average revenue is greater than average total cost.

(d)   (i)   Entry will cease when profits of a potential entrant using the new technology are driven to zero. As the new firms enter, the market supply shifts to the right—to S' in Panel (ii)—until the demand and supply curves intersect at the zero-profit price of $9. At this price the industry produces 1400 units.

(ii)   In the new long-run equilibrium, each firm using the new technology is producing at minimum efficient scale—shown in Panel (iii)—which occurs at 20 units of output with $P = \$9$. Since $ATC = AR = \$9$ for the plants with new technology, they are now making zero profit.

(iii) For plants using the old technology, $P = MC = \$9$ at 8 units of output. Since $ATC = \$11$ and $AR = \$9$, the firm in Panel (i) makes a loss of $(ATC - AR) \times Q = (\$9 - \$11) \times 8 = \$16$.

(iv) Total output of the 100 firms using the old technology is (100×8) 800. Since industry output is 1400, the firms using the new technology are producing a total of $(1400 - 800)$ 600 units. Each firm produces 20 units, so there are $(600/20)$ 30 firms using the new technology.

(e)   No, the government should not subsidize the firms using the old technology. These firms will ultimately close down as their existing capital stock deteriorates, to be replaced by firms using the new technology and making more efficient use of resources. The firms should not close down immediately, however, if total revenue exceeds total variable costs plus *non-sunk* fixed costs. Under these circumstances they make smaller losses in the short run by continuing to produce than by shutting down immediately. Furthermore, assuming all fixed costs of the old technology are sunk costs, each firm using the old technology is using resources (i.e., total variable costs) valued at $(\$7 \times 8)$ $56 to produce output that the market values at $(\$9 \times 8)$ $72—i.e., greater than the value of resources.

Additional Multiple-Choice Questions

1.(b) 2.(d) 3.(a) 4.(c) 5.(c) 6.(b) 7.(b) 8.(c) 9.(d) 10.(b) 11.(b) 12.(a) 13.(a) 14.(c) 15.(b) 16.(b) 17.(d) 18.(b) 19.(c) 20.(d) 21.(e) 22.(d) 23.(e)

Explanations for the Asterisked Multiple-Choice Questions

1.(b)   Profits are maximized where $MC (> AVC) = MR$ which, at $(P =) MR = MC = \$9$, is at $Q = 70$.

2.(d)   At $Q = 70$, read up to the ATC curve and see that total costs $= ATC \times 70 = 6 \times 70 = \$420$.

3.(a)   Profit $(\pi) = (P - ATC) \times Q$, which, at $P = \$9$ and $Q = 70$, is $(9 - 6) \times 70 = \$210$.

4.(c)   At 70 units you see the difference between the ATC and AVC is \$1, telling you that TFC is \$70, which would be short-run losses if the firm shut down immediately (so (a) is wrong). If it continues to operate at a $P = \$4$ it minimizes losses producing 50 units (where $P = MC$); at this point revenues cover all variable costs <u>plus</u> a portion of the \$70 fixed costs, so it makes less losses in the short run than if it shut down immediately (so (b) is wrong). Answers (d) and (e) are wrong because in neither case does $P = MC$ so the firm will not be minimizing its losses.

5.(c)   Understanding why (c) is correct is straightforward (i.e., $P = MC$ and $AR = ATC$), but why is (a) not the <u>best</u> answer? The reason is that the industry could be in <u>short-run</u> equilibrium even with existing firms making <u>economic profits</u> (i.e., $P > \$5$), in which case the entry of more firms would be needed to drive down the price to its \$5 zero-profit level.

6.(b)   If all fixed costs are sunk costs, they cannot be recovered. As long as the firm's total revenues are no less than its total variable costs, its losses are no greater than they would be if it stopped producing. The lowest price at which it can cover variable costs is \$3.

7.(b)   Question 6 says that the firm will minimize losses by continuing to produce in the short run as long as price is at least \$3—the minimum average variable cost (AVC). Combine this with the perfectly competitive firm's profit-maximizing condition that $P = MC$, and you have explained the answer to Question 7.

8.(c)   At a price of \$6 and an output of 60, the firm is making profits that, with freedom of entry, would entice other firms to enter. Supply would increase and price would fall to \$5, where each firm would make zero profit producing 55 units of output at minimum average total cost. If other firms were barred from entering, market supply would not increase and price would remain at \$6—i.e., greater than average total cost—and profit could continue to be made. In this case, of course, the industry would not meet all of the conditions for perfect competition.

9.(d)   If perfectly competitive firms are making zero profit at minimum $LRAC$ (i.e., at minimum efficient scale, MES), price must equal minimum $LRAC$ and the industry must be in long-run equilibrium. If firms increased output, average cost would exceed price and losses would be made. Entry of new firms would increase supply and drive down price, again causing losses. Since firms are already at MES, larger plants would increase average cost, again creating losses. Since firms are not making losses, there is no reason for any firm to exit the industry.

10.(b)   Plants with old technology will continue to operate as long as revenues exceed variable plus non-sunk fixed costs (so (a) and (e) are wrong). A market price at the minimum ATC of the least efficient plant would create economic profits for firms with more efficient plants, attracting entry and reducing price (so (c) is wrong). If all fixed costs are non-sunk costs, plants with older technology will minimize losses by closing down and recovering their fixed costs (so (d) is wrong). Plants with the most efficient technology will continue to enter and drive down the market price to their zero-profit level—i.e., their minimum ATC (so (b) is correct).

13.(a)   The firm's average revenue (= price) of \$1 exceeds its average total cost of $(2000 + 1000)/5000 = \$0.60$, so it is making profit of $\$0.40 \times 5000 = \$2000$ and should not shut down. But it is producing at $P < MC$ (i.e., $\$1 < \$1.25$), so by reducing output the fall in costs exceeds the fall in revenues, thereby increasing profit.

14.(c)   The firm is producing where $P = ATC$ ($\$10 = \$10$), so is making zero profit. But it is also producing where $P > MC$ ($\$10 > \$9$), so profits would be increased by increasing output. [*Note:* Since $MC < ATC$, increasing output would reduce ATC below the \$10 price.]

15.(b)   If $P = ATC$ and $ATC > MC$, then it must be true that $P > MC$. Thus the firm is producing where $MR > MC$, so there are extra units of output it could produce that would add more to revenues than to costs, thereby increasing profit. [If you look at Figure 9-5 as an example, the firm would be producing $Q = 15$ at $P = \$9$ but the profit-maximizing output at that price is $Q = 70$.]

17.(d)   A continuously downward-sloping $LRAC$ means that a firm will always have economies of scale in production and can increase output without reaching a minimum point on its $LRAC$. It would be profitable for such a firm to keep reducing its costs by increasing output, even in the absence of an increase in market demand. Ultimately one firm would grow so large as to produce the whole market output. Answers (a), (b), and (e) are all conditions for long-run equilibrium in perfect competition, so are wrong for this question. Answer (c) is wrong because firms can have positive accounting profits yet zero economic profits because of the additional *implicit costs* included for the economic definition of profit (i.e., revenues in excess of opportunity costs).

18.(b) Since the firm is on its *LRAC* curve it is minimizing the costs of Q_0. Cost-minimization requires an economically efficient combination of factors, so (e) is wrong. Since there are more units of output at which $P_3 > MC$ it is producing insufficient output to maximize profit (i.e., it is not at $P = MC$, so (a) is wrong, and it is not even at a short-run equilibrium (answer (c)) let alone the long-run equilibrium of point *D* (answer (d)).

19.(c) At point *B*, $P_2 (=AR) = MC = SRATC$, so the firm is maximizing profits ($MC = MR$) in the <u>short-run</u> (although point *B* is not the long-run maximization point). Moving to point *A* would not change profits since $P_3 = SRATC$ (so (a) and (b) are wrong). And $P_3 (=MR) > MC$ so the incentive would be to increase output. Furthermore, at point *B* the firm's profit in the long run would be increased by *adding* more capital (so (d) is wrong) in order to reduce the *ATC* of producing Q_1 (so (e) is wrong). [To continue the story, move on to Questions 20 and 21.]

20.(d) At P_2, the firm can make economic profit in the long run by increasing its capital stock and producing more than Q_1, thereby reducing *LRAC* to make $P > LRAC$. The economic profit encourages entry into the industry, which further increases industry output and creates excess supply at P_2, forcing the price down. This process continues until *P* has fallen to where (i) existing firms can no longer reduce *LRAC* by further expanding capital stock (i.e., each has reached its capacity output), and (ii) there is no incentive for new firms to enter the industry since there are zero economic profits to be made (i.e., $P = LRAC$). These conditions are met at point *D*, where average total cost is at its minimum even for the long run.

21.(e) The reasoning process in the answer to Question 20 shows that all the options are true. Starting from point *B*, with maximum short-run profits at zero (answers (a) and (b)), existing firms expand capital stock (answer (c)) and new firms enter (answer (d)) until the long-run equilibrium is reached with each and every firm at point *D*.

23.(e) With no change in factor prices (as in Question 22), the long-run equilibrium would be at P_0 and Q_2. A decrease in factor prices, however, shifts down <u>both</u> the short-run <u>and</u> the long-run cost curves, so long-run equilibrium would occur at the lowest point (*minimum efficient scale*) on a new, lower long-run average cost curve, thus at a lower price than P_0.

10

Monopoly, Cartels, and Price Discrimination

LO **LEARNING OBJECTIVES**

After studying this chapter, you will be able to

1   explain why marginal revenue is less than price for a profit-maximizing monopolist.

2   understand how entry barriers can allow monopolists to maintain positive profits in the long run.

3   describe why firms would form a cartel to restrict industry output and how this would increase their profits.

4   explain how some firms can increase their profits through price discrimination.

Chapter Overview

In a **monopoly** market structure, a single firm faces the entire market demand curve. The monopoly maximizes profits by producing the output where *marginal revenue* equals *marginal cost*, just as competitive firms would do. A downward-sloping market demand curve, however, means that price must be reduced on all units of output in order to sell an additional unit. Unlike a firm in perfect competition, therefore, the monopolist's marginal revenue is less than price. As a result, while the most profitable output for a monopolist occurs where marginal revenue equals marginal cost (like the perfectly competitive firm), the fact that marginal revenue is less than price results in a price that exceeds marginal cost (unlike the situation for a perfectly competitive firm).

A monopoly does not necessarily earn positive profits, since profits depend on the relative magnitudes of price and average cost at the profit-maximizing output. In the long run, a monopoly can continue to make profits because there are **barriers to entry**, which can be natural barriers or created barriers. In the very long run, monopoly power can be threatened and eroded by the development of new substitute products, a process known as **creative destruction**.

The potential for profit provides an inducement for otherwise competitive firms to agree to limit output and jointly behave as a monopoly. A group of firms that make such agreements is called a **cartel**. Cartels are, however, unstable as there is an incentive for individual members to **cheat** on the agreement.

A monopolist may increase profits if it is able to practise **price discrimination**, whereby different prices are charged for the same product, and the price differences are not related to differences in costs of production. Discrimination can occur among different markets or among units of output. Price discrimination enables the firm to capture some (or in the extreme case, all) of the consumer surplus. It is possible, however, for price discrimination to actually increase consumer surplus at the same time as it increases the firm's profits.

Hints and Tips

The following may help you avoid some of the most common errors on examinations.

✓ Like perfect competition, the profit-maximizing condition for monopoly is $MR = MC$. Unlike perfect competition, where $P = MR$, for monopoly $P > MR$ at each quantity. So when the monopolist selects quantity produced on the basis of $MR = MC$, it charges $P > MC$. Understand how and why this difference comes about.

✓ Don't confuse this chapter with Chapter 16. In this chapter there is a comparison showing that a single-price monopoly creates deadweight loss in economic surplus relative to perfect competition. This conclusion is reached under the assumptions that (i) the two industry structures have the same cost curves (i.e., production functions), and (ii) there are no costs to society that are not paid by either the producers or the consumers of the product (i.e., there are no "negative externalities"). You will learn later (in Chapter 16) that these two assumptions often don't hold in the real world. Where they do hold, monopoly <u>may</u> generate more economic surplus than perfect competition. Even so, in most cases it can be said a single-price monopoly is being *less efficient than it <u>could be</u>*, even when it is *more efficient than perfect competition <u>would have been</u>*.

✓ In a cartel, the incentives facing the individual firm are different from the incentives facing the group as a whole. The incentives of the firm ultimately dominate unless there is some effective method of enforcing the cartel agreement.

✓ Price discrimination is not necessarily "bad," even for consumers. The different types of discrimination and the way they are used can have different implications for consumer surplus.

Chapter Review

A Single-Price Monopolist

After studying this section you should be able to explain the relationship between price and marginal revenue for a monopolist; solve for the monopolist's profit-maximizing output and associated profit level; explain how in the long run the monopoly can be sustained only by barriers to entry, which may be natural or created; and appreciate how the very-long-run process of creative destruction can erode monopoly power. When reading this section, contrast the monopoly equilibrium with that of perfect competition in terms of the *market efficiency* and *economic surplus* you encountered in Chapter 5.

1. **A fundamental feature of a monopolistic market is that the firm**
    (a)   can sell any quantity it desires at the current market price.
    (b)   can obtain any price for any quantity of output.
    (c)   faces a perfectly inelastic demand curve.
    (d)   faces the price and quantity trade-off dictated by market demand.
    (e)   must produce on its supply curve.

2. **For the single-price monopolist, the average revenue curve**
    (a) is a horizontal line drawn at the market price.
    (b) is the same as the market demand curve.
    (c) is the same as the marginal revenue curve.
    (d) has the same price intercept as the demand curve, but is twice as steep.
    (e) does not exist.

3. **If average revenue declines as output increases, marginal revenue must**
    (a) increase.
    (b) also decline and be less than average revenue.
    (c) also decline because it is equal to average revenue.
    (d) also decline and be greater than average revenue.
    (e) decline, but may be less than, equal to, or greater than average revenue.

4. **Since the profit-maximizing monopolist produces that output where marginal cost equals marginal revenue, we can conclude that**
    (a) $P = MC$.   (b) $P = MR$.
    (c) $P > MC$.   (d) $P < MR$.
    (e) $P > ATC$.

5. **A single-price monopoly is able to make positive profits only if the average total cost curve**
    (a) intersects the demand curve.
    (b) is tangent to the demand curve.
    (c) declines over a substantial portion of market demand.
    (d) lies above the marginal revenue curve.
    (e) lies above the demand curve.

6. **Which of the following is *not* a barrier to entry?**
    (a) Economies of scale.
    (b) Patent laws.
    (c) Long-run increasing average costs.
    (d) Large set-up costs.
    (e) Licensing.

7. **Natural barriers to entry**
    (a) include patent laws and exclusive franchises.
    (b) most commonly arise through economies of scale.
    (c) result from an increasing long-run average cost curve.
    (d) imply that small firms have lower ATC curves than larger firms.
    (e) must be sustained by government regulation.

8. **The process of "creative destruction" refers to**
    (a) the threat of price-cutting behaviour.
    (b) the inherent instability of cartels.
    (c) an early declaration of bankruptcy as a means of avoiding debts.
    (d) the takeover of a competitive industry by a monopoly.
    (e) the erosion of a monopoly's entry barriers through invention and innovation.

9. **Compared to a perfectly competitive industry with the same cost curves, a monopoly**
    (a) creates less economic surplus.
    (b) creates less deadweight loss.
    (c) creates market inefficiency.
    (d) is less profitable because it produces less output.
    (e) creates market inefficiency <u>and</u> less economic surplus.

Cartels as Monopolies

This section discusses the cartelization of a competitive industry. It establishes that, although cartels can maximize joint profits for a group of firms, there is an incentive for an individual member firm to cheat on the cartel. The key to this section is an understanding of the difference between the interests of cartel member firms as a group and the interests of an individual firm in the cartel (i.e., maximization of joint profits versus the profit of each firm individually).

10. **A cartel increases the industry's profits by**
    (a) fully capturing all economies of scale.
    (b) ceasing all active competitive behaviour with respect to price.
    (c) agreeing to sell all current output at an agreed-on fixed price.
    (d) decreasing industry output and thereby increasing market price.
    (e) agreeing to produce more but to sell at a higher price.

11. **Which of the following does *not* present an enforcement problem for a successful cartel?**
    (a) Entry of new firms.
    (b) Government restrictions on output.
    (c) Preventing cartel members from violating the agreed-on production level.
    (d) Convincing other firms to join the cartel.
    (e) Monitoring the output of cartel members.

12. **Economic theory predicts that cartels are inherently unstable because**
    (a) there is an incentive for individual firms to produce beyond their quota.
    (b) governments will invariably dismantle them.
    (c) although industry profits increase, the profits of individual firms decrease.
    (d) individual firms have an incentive to produce less than the restrictions imposed on them by the cartel.
    (e) the industry output that maximizes joint profits for the cartel tends to exceed that of a competitive market.

Price Discrimination

This section develops the theory of price discrimination, which is a particularly common and interesting feature of firms with market power. Focus on developing an understanding of when price discrimination is possible, how the firm practises discrimination among units of output and among market segments, and the implications for profits, efficiency, and consumer surplus. Understand why perfect price discrimination is the extreme version of discrimination among units of output, and how hurdle pricing is used as a way to get consumers to assign themselves to market segments.

13. **Among the following, which is the *best* example of price discrimination?**
    (a) Airfares are lower in spring and fall than in summer and in late December.
    (b) A telephone company charges lower rates for long-distance calls after midnight than during the day.
    (c) A local transit company allows senior citizens, the unemployed, and children to ride at reduced fares.
    (d) Public transportation systems often charge each individual according to the distance travelled.
    (e) A cinema charges lower prices on Tuesdays than on Fridays or Saturdays.

14. **Price discrimination is possible because**
    (a) different individuals are willing to pay different amounts for the same commodity.
    (b) each individual is willing to pay a different amount for each successive unit of the same commodity.
    (c) arbitrage is limited.
    (d) demand curves slope downward.
    (e) All of the above.

15. **When price discrimination does not increase output, it increases a monopoly's profits because it**
    (a) increases the willingness of households to pay for a good.
    (b) allows the firm to capture some consumer surplus.
    (c) allows the firm to exploit economies of scale more fully.
    (d) shifts the demand curve the firm faces.
    (e) reduces output.

16. **Perfect price discrimination implies that**
    (a) demand is perfectly elastic.
    (b) demand is perfectly inelastic.
    (c) supply is perfectly elastic.
    (d) the firm produces a lower output than it would as a single price monopolist.
    (e) the firm sells each unit at a different price and captures all consumer surplus.

17. **Which of the following is an example of a "hurdle"?**
    (a) Grocery stores located several blocks apart.
    (b) Many people must wait until retirement to get lower transit fares.
    (c) Lower hairstyling prices for children.
    (d) Having to stay at one's destination over a Saturday night to get lower airfares.
    (e) All of the above.

Short-Answer Questions

1. Why is marginal revenue less than price for a monopolist but equal to price for a perfectly competitive firm? Can you construct a numerical example?

2. Why will a single-price monopolist not operate on the inelastic portion of the demand curve?

3. Briefly argue the case that barriers to entry and monopoly profit in the short run are beneficial for society in the very long run.

4. Why is price discrimination more common for intangible services than for tangible goods?

5. Why is a single-price monopoly less economically efficient for society than a perfectly competitive industry with the same cost curves?

Exercises

1. **Equilibrium for a Single-Price Monopolist**
   Figure 10-1 shows the demand curve and cost curves of a single price monopolist.

   Figure 10-1

   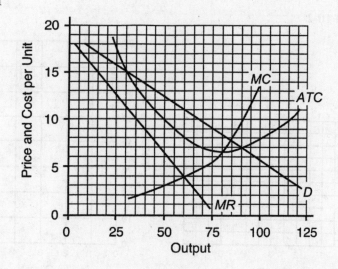

(a) At what output are the firm's profits at a maximum? _60_

(b) What is the price at this output? _$11_

(c) What is total revenue at this output? P×Q =$660

(d) What are the corresponding total costs? ATC×Q = $480

(e) What is the level of profits? Profit = (AR-ATC)×Q = $180

(f) What range of output would yield some positive profit? 30<Q<90

b/c ATC<D ∴ ATC<AR

2. Understanding the Revenue Curves

The objective of this exercise is to demonstrate that the output at which a monopolist's marginal revenue equals marginal cost is the output that maximizes the difference between its total revenue and total costs (i.e., profit). [*Note:* This exercise involves numerical calculations, and use of a spreadsheet can save time.]

The following data are taken from Solitary Inc., a fictitious monopolistic firm.

(a) Calculate Solitary Inc.'s total revenue (*TR*), marginal revenue (*MR*), marginal cost (*MC*), and profit to complete the table.

$TC×P \quad P_{i+1}-P_i \quad TC_{i+1}-TC_i$

Output	Total Cost	Price	Quantity Demanded	TR	MR	MC	Profit $TR-TC$
0	$20	$20	0	____			____
1	24	18	1	____	____ ____	____
2	27	16	2	____	____ ____	____
3	33	14	3	____	____ ____	____
4	43	12	4	____	____ ____	____
5	57	10	5	____	____ ____	____
6	75	8	6	____	____ ____	____

(b) Plot Solitary Inc.'s average revenue (*AR*), *MR*, and *MC* curves in Panel (i), and the *TC* and *TR* curves in Panel (ii).

Figure 10-2

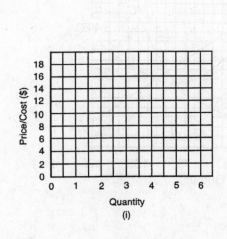

Quantity
(i)

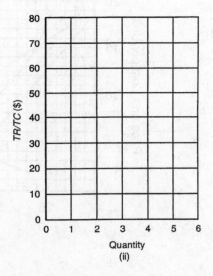

Quantity
(ii)

(c) What is the profit-maximizing output (whole units)? _MC=MR_

(d) At what price will the monopolist sell the product (whole units)? _price read from D-curve_

(e) What are the monopolist's economic profits? _____

(f) Are any of these answers different across the two diagrams? _____

3. A Natural Monopoly

Figure 10-3 shows the cost and revenue curves for a natural monopoly. [*Note:* In Chapter 12 you will learn why the cost curves for this type of monopoly are as shown in Figure 10-3.]

Figure 10-3

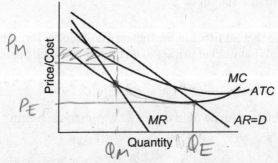

(a) Illustrate on the graph the price the profit-maximizing monopolist will set and the quantity that will be sold. (Label them P_M and Q_M.)

(b) Indicate monopoly profits by shading in the appropriate area.

(c) Suppose that the monopolist, to maximize economic surplus, sets price equal to marginal cost. Label the price P_E and the output Q_E. Would this output be sustainable in the long run? Explain. _NO b/c ATC > MC ∴ business is operating at a loss._

4. Cartel Behaviour

This exercise examines the implications of collusion by (otherwise perfectly competitive) firms that form a cartel to maximize joint profits.

The graph on the left of Figure 10-4 presents the cost structure for one of 100 identical firms in a perfectly competitive industry. On the right is the market demand curve and the industry supply curve. [*Note:* Recall that the supply curve of a perfectly competitive industry is the horizontal summation of the marginal cost curves of all firms in the industry.]

Figure 10-4

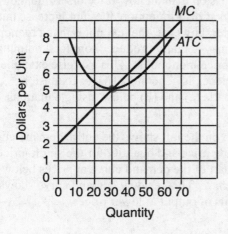

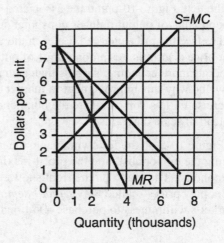

(a) Suppose that the industry is in long-run competitive equilibrium.

    (i) What is the market price and the corresponding quantity?

$5, 30/firm, 3000 total

    (ii) What is the output of each firm?

30

    (iii) What is the profit of each firm?

zero (LR eq'bm)

(b) Now suppose that all firms in the industry collude by forming a cartel to maximize joint profits. What market price and quantity maximize profits for the cartel?

$6, 2000 units

(c) What production quota would the cartel assign to each firm?

100 firms → 20 units

(d) What is the level of profits for each firm in the cartel if they abide by their quotas?

P = AR = $6
ATC = $5.50 ⟹ *20(0.50) = 10*

(e) Since the output of one firm is too small to affect price, what output would maximize the individual firm's profit at the cartel price? What would be the firm's profits? Does the firm have an incentive to "cheat" on its quota? Explain.

Behave as price taker → produce 40 units (where MC = MR = $6)
Profit = (AR - ATC) × 40 = 20 ∴ profit↑ ∴ incentive to cheat.

(f) Given your answer to (e), what is the incentive faced by every other firm in the cartel? Is this cartel likely to persist?

All have incentives. No unless there is punishment for cheating.

5. Discrimination Among Units of Output

In the text, Figure 10-6 and the associated discussion explain how price discrimination among units of output reduces consumer surplus if discrimination does not increase output and reduce the price charged. Later in the chapter, however, the text notes that a monopolist that price discriminates among units of output may actually produce more total output and generate more economic surplus than a single-price monopolist. This exercise examines how and why this improvement in market efficiency is generated. [*Note:* Extension Exercise E1 lets you calculate the numbers in parts (a) and (b) below, using equations instead of scale diagrams.]

In Figure 10-5 on the following page, the graph on the left shows the entire demand curve facing the monopolist, and the profit-maximizing price and quantity for the single-price monopolist. The graph on the right shows the part of the demand curve at prices below the monopoly price—called the *residual demand curve*. This residual demand curve shows the market's willingness to purchase additional units of output at lower prices.

For simplicity, marginal cost is assumed to be constant at all levels of output. This means that the marginal cost curve is also the average variable cost curve. The monopolist also has total fixed costs (not shown) of $100.   *MC=AVC*

Figure 10-5   *TFC*

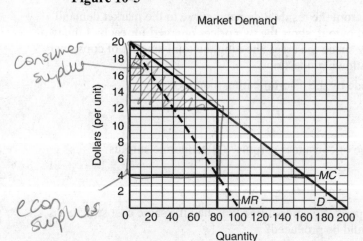
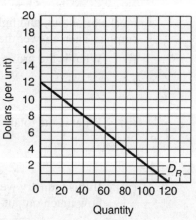

consumer surplus

econ surplus

(a)   From the diagram on the left:

(i)   What is the profit made by the single-price monopolist?

$$\text{Profit} = (AR - AVC)\,Q - TFC = (12-4)80 - 100 = 540$$

(ii)   Lightly shade the area of consumer surplus. What is the value of this consumer surplus? How much economic surplus is there?

(iii) In terms of the relationship between *MC* and *MR*, explain why the single-price monopolist would not produce more than 80 units of output.

After that, MC>MR ∴ cost to produce extra unit greater than the revenue it produces ∴ π ↓

(b)   Now assume that the monopolist can price discriminate by selling additional units of output at a lower price, without having to lower the price on the first 80 units sold. [*Note:* We assume that this monopolist will not charge more than two prices.] From the residual demand curve in the diagram on the right, calculate the following:

(i)   How much additional output will the discriminating monopolist produce, and what price will it charge? [*Hint:* Remember that the slope of the residual *MR* curve is twice the slope of the residual demand curve.]

$$M_{D_R} = -\tfrac{1}{10}$$
$$\therefore M_{MR_R} = -\tfrac{1}{20} \Rightarrow Y = -\tfrac{1}{20}Q + 12 \Rightarrow \text{intersects } MC=4 \text{ at } Q=40$$
price from D curve = $8

(ii)   How much extra profit does the monopolist make on the units of output sold at the lower price? [*Hint:* Remember you have already deducted all fixed costs when determining profit on the first 80 units of output. Don't deduct it twice!]

$$\$8 \times 40 - 4 \times 40 = 160$$

(iii)   What are the values of consumer surplus and economic surplus from these additional units of output?

(c)   Now transfer your findings from the residual demand curve to the market demand curve on the left. Show total output, show the two prices charged for each of the two blocks of output, and lightly shade the areas showing the total amount of consumer surplus. Then answer the following questions.

   (i)   What is the profit made by the discriminating monopolist?

   (ii)   What is the total value of consumer surplus? Of economic surplus?

   (iii)   If this industry were perfectly competitive (and had the same cost structure), how much output would be produced?

   (iv)   What would be the monopolist's profit if, instead of charging two prices, it sold all units of output at the lower price?

(d)   Has this firm benefitted from price discrimination? Explain.

(e)   Have consumers benefited from price discrimination? Explain.

(f)   Has society benefited from price discrimination? Explain.

(g)   In terms of *MC* and *MR*, explain why the firm is willing to produce more output when it can price discriminate than when it must charge a single price.

6.   **Perfect Price Discrimination: The Extreme of Discrimination Among Units of Output**
This exercise compares the equilibrium of the single-price monopolist to that of the perfect price discriminator.

For the monopoly in Figure 10-6, *AL* is the market demand curve, *EH* is both the *ATC* and the *MC* curve, and there are no fixed costs. [*Note:* These simplifying assumptions are consistent with the long-run cost curves of a constant-cost monopoly—i.e., the production function has neither increasing nor decreasing returns to scale.]

Figure 10-6

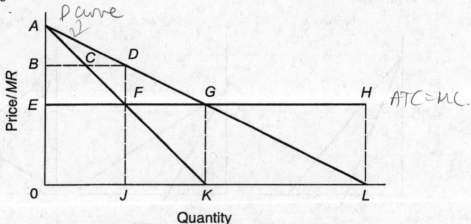

(a) Assume that the monopolist sets a single price and maximizes profits. Identify the following in terms of the letters in the above diagram:

   (i)   The monopoly price is ___OB___ and output is _OJ_ .

   (ii)   Consumer surplus at the monopoly price is __ABD__ .

   (iii) Economic surplus at the monopoly price is __AEFD__ .

   (iv) Economic profit at the monopoly price is _BDFE_ .

(b) Assume that a discriminating monopolist is able to obtain the maximum price that consumers are willing to pay for *each unit* of output. Answer the following questions.

   (i)   Prices range from ___OA___ to ___OE___ .

   (ii)   Output is __OK__ .

   (iii) Consumer surplus is ___O___ .

   (iv) Economic surplus is _AEG_ . } *same*

   (v)   Economic profit is _AEG_ . } b/c no fixed costs

7. **Price Discrimination Between Market Segments**

This exercise leads you through the analysis and implications of price discrimination between different segments of the market for a commodity (e.g., as when students are charged lower prices than other people). Assume that the firm and markets meet the necessary conditions for discrimination among markets, as explained in the text. [*Note:* A numerical question on this topic is given in Extension Exercise E2, using equations instead of scale diagrams and more deeply investigating the implications of elasticity.]

Figure 10-7 shows a profit-maximizing single-price monopolist charging the same price in two segments of the market. The market demand curve, $D_{A + B}$, is the horizontal summation of the demand curves of the two segments of the market, D_A and D_B. Demand in Segment B is more elastic than demand in Segment A.

Figure 10-7

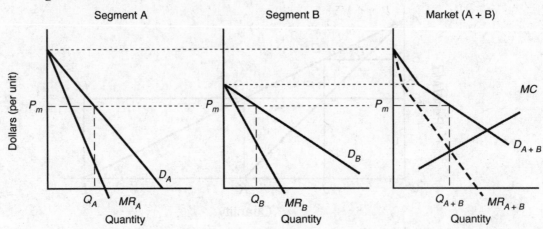

| Segment A | Segment B | Market (A + B) |

(a) Why are Q_{A+B} and P_M the profit-maximizing output and price for the single-price monopolist?

Q → MR=MC

P → read from D curve @ that Q

(b) If the monopolist now sells one less unit of output in Segment A and one more in Segment B,

(i) what happens to total costs of production? Explain.

unchanged b/c total Q doesn't change
A+B

(ii) what happens to price in each market segment? Why?

B: price ↓, move along D ↓
A: price ↑, move along D ↑

(iii) how does the revenue lost in Segment A compare with the revenue gained in Segment B? [*Hint:* Remember that *MR* is the revenue from one unit of output.]

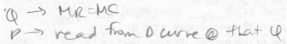

$MR_{A_i} < MR_{B_{i+1}}$

$MR_B > MR_A$ ∴ TR ↑ by $(MR_B - MR_A)$

(iv) what happens to profit? Explain. Will the firm make this transfer of sales?

Total cost unchanged, TR ↑ ⟹ π ↑
Yes.

(v) why will the firm not transfer sales from Segment B to Segment A?

B has more elastic demand $MR_B > MR_A$
A has less elastic demand   ∴ reduce revenue

(c) When will the firm stop transferring sales between segments? Explain why this is the profit-maximizing distribution of sales between the two segments. Draw this on the diagram. [*Hint:* Show sales and price in each segment, and link the segments to the market diagram to show the condition for profit maximization under price discrimination.]

MR same in both markets ⅃ equal to MC

MR=MC → profit-max output being produced

$MR_A = MR_B$ ⟹ current distribution of sales is
max-ng revenue

246 PART 4: MARKET STRUCTURE AND EFFICIENCY

(d) Comparing the situation in (c) with that in (a),

    (i)   have the *D* and *MR* curves in each market segment changed?

> *NO. → movement along curves.*

    (ii)   have the horizontally summed market *D* and *MR* curves changed?

> *NO b/c components are unchanged.*

    (iii)   has the firm's *MC* curve changed?

> *NO — unaffected by distribution of sales b/c it is derived from production fn*

    (iv)   has the firm's profit-maximizing level of output changed? Explain.

> *NO — MC & MR_A+B curves unchanged. So intersection is same*

    (v)   have total costs of production changed?

> *NO — costs & Q unchanged, so total costs of production unchanged.*

    (vi)   have profits changed? Explain.

> *Yes: Costs same, revenues ↑, so profits ↑.*

    (vii)   has economic surplus changed? Explain.

> *NO — b/c positions of ∧ curves are the same relevant*

Extension Exercises

These extension exercises analyze price discrimination using equations instead of scale diagrams.

In each question, the inverse equation is the correlation between quantity demanded and price, isolating price. It is simply the inverse of the causal equation for the demand function, $Q = a - bP$. In the inverse equation, the constant term (a/b) is the price–axis intercept of the demand curve, and the coefficient on Q (1/b) is the slope of the demand curve.

E1. **Price Discrimination Among Units of Output**
This is the same question as Exercise 5, except that you actually calculate the relevant numbers. Then you can return to Exercise 5 to complete the analysis. You should sketch your own diagrams as you go along, and/or check the diagram in Exercise 5.

The monopolist has constant $MC = 4$ for all units of output. Since *MC* is constant, $MC = AVC$. Total fixed costs (*TFC*) are $100.

(a) The single-price monopolist faces the following market demand function:

Causal equation: $Q = a - bP = 200 - 10P$
Inverse equation: $P = a/b - 1/bQ = 20 - 0.1Q$

    (i)   Calculate the profit-maximizing quantity and price. [*Hint:* The *MR* curve has the same price–axis intercept as the *D* curve and twice the slope.]

        (ii)   Calculate profits.

        (iii)   Calculate the value of consumer surplus. [*Hint:* The area under the demand curve and above the price charged is one-half of quantity purchased multiplied by the difference between price charged and the price–axis intercept.] Calculate the value of economic surplus.

(b)   The monopolist now decides to sell extra units of output at a lower price, without changing the price charged for the quantity calculated in part (a). The profit-maximizing price and quantity of these extra units is calculated from the part of the market demand curve below the price charged in (a)—called the *residual* demand curve. In the equations below, X is the quantity being sold at the higher price that you calculated in part (a).

Causal equation for residual demand curve: $Q = (200 - X) - 10P$

Inverse equation for residual demand curve: $P = (20 - X/10) - 0.1Q$

        (i)   How much additional output will the discriminating monopolist produce, and what price will it charge?

        (ii)   How much extra profit does the monopolist make on the units of output sold at the lower price? [*Hint:* Remember that you have already deducted all fixed costs. Don't deduct them twice!]

        (iii) What are the values of consumer surplus and economic surplus from these additional units of output?

Now return to Exercise 5 to complete the rest of the question.

E2. **Price Discrimination Among Markets**
The total market demand facing the monopolist consists of the demand in two separate markets, A and B—for example, non-students and students. [*Hint:* Recall that the market demand is the *horizontal* sum of individual demand so must be found by summing quantities, not prices!] The monopolist has a constant $MC = AVC = \$200$ and total fixed costs of $10\ 000$. [*Hint:* Before you start the question, sketch a copy of Figure 10-7 in Exercise 7, modified to show the MC curve as a horizontal line at \$200. Keep track of the numbers you calculate by putting them on your sketch.]

Algebraic Equations	Causal	Inverse
Market A	$Q_A = a - bP_A$	$P_A = a/b - 1/bQ_A$
Market B	$Q_B = c - dP_B$	$P_B = c/d - 1/dQ_B$
Total Demand	$Q_{A+B} = (a + c) - (b + d)P$	$P = (a + c)/(b + d) - 1/(b + d)Q_{A+B}$

This Question	Causal	Inverse
Market A	$Q_A = 1200 - 2P_A$	$P_A = 600 - 0.5Q_A$
Market B	$Q_B = 800 - 2P_B$	$P_B = 400 - 0.5Q_B$
Total Demand	$Q_{A+B} = 2000 - 4P$	$P = 500 - 0.25Q_{A+B}$

(a) Using the total demand function:

    (i)   Calculate the profit-maximizing price and quantity for the single-price monopolist. [*Hint:* Remember that the *MR* curve has the same price–axis intercept as the *D* curve, and twice the slope.]

    (ii)   How many units are sold in each market?

    (iii)   What are the point elasticities of demand in the two markets? Which market has the more-elastic demand?

    (iv)   Calculate the firm's profits.

(b) Now the monopolist price-discriminates between the two markets. [*Hint:* Remember that the profit-maximizing distribution of sales is where $MR_A = MR_B = MC$.]

    (i)   How many are sold in each market, and what prices are charged?

    (ii)   What are the profits?

(c) Comparing your results in section (b) to your results in section (a), what are the effects of price discrimination on

    (i)   total output and total production costs?

    (ii)   total spending in each market? What role do elasticities play here?

(iii)   total revenues and profits of the firm? Explain.

(iv)   price in the market with the more-elastic demand in part (a)? Price in the market with the less-elastic demand in part (a)?

Additional Multiple-Choice Questions

*1.   As long as marginal cost is positive, a profit-maximizing single-price monopolist will operate
(a)   on the elastic portion of the demand curve.
(b)   where demand is unit-elastic and total revenue is therefore at a maximum.
(c)   on the inelastic portion of the demand curve.
(d)   on any portion of the demand curve, depending on the supply curve.
(e)   where demand is perfectly inelastic.

*2.   A linear downward-sloping demand curve has a marginal revenue curve that is
(a)   also linear, with the same price intercept as the demand curve and half the quantity intercept.
(b)   the same as the average revenue curve.
(c)   horizontal at market price.
(d)   also linear, with half the slope of the demand curve.
(e)   Both (a) and (d) are correct.

*3.   In perfect competition, the industry short-run supply curve is the horizontal summation of the marginal cost curves (above *AVC*) of all of the firms in the industry. In monopoly, the short-run supply curve
(a)   is the single firm's marginal cost curve.
(b)   is the portion of the single firm's marginal cost curve that lies above average variable cost.
(c)   is the downward-sloping segment of the average total cost curve.
(d)   is the upward-sloping segment of the *MC* curve.
(e)   does not exist.

Questions 4 to 10 refer to Figure 10-8, which depicts the marginal cost curve of a monopoly and the market demand it faces.

Figure 10-8

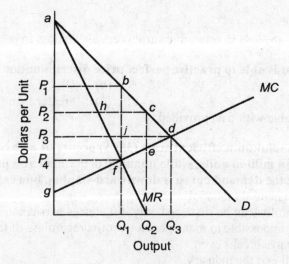

4. The monopolist's profit-maximizing output is
    (a) Q_1.
    (b) Q_2.
    (c) Q_3.
    (d) greater than Q_1 but less than Q_3.
    (e) Indeterminable with data provided.

5. The price set by the monopolist for the profit-maximizing output is
    (a) P_1.
    (b) P_2.
    (c) P_3.
    (d) P_4.
    (e) Indeterminable with data provided.

*6. The level of output that corresponds to maximum revenue is
    (a) Q_1.
    (b) Q_2.
    (c) Q_3.
    (d) greater than Q_3.
    (e) Indeterminable with data provided.

*7. Compared to the competitive market outcome, the single-price profit-maximizing monopoly reduces consumer surplus by the area
    (a) P_1bdP_3.   (b) P_2ac.
    (c) P_1bfP_4.   (d) P_1bjP_3.
    (e) bdf.

*8. Compared to the competitive market outcome, the single-price profit-maximizing monopoly reduces economic surplus by a deadweight loss equal to the area
    (a) P_1bdP_3.   (b) P_2ac.
    (c) P_1bfP_4.   (d) P_1bjP_3.
    (e) bdf.

*9. How much of the loss in consumer surplus generated by the single-price profit-maximizing monopoly remains part of economic surplus?
(a) P_1bdP_3
(b) P_2ac
(c) P_1bfP_4
(d) P_1bjP_3
(e) None of it—the loss in economic surplus equals the loss in consumer surplus.

*10. A monopolist that is able to practise perfect price discrimination will produce output
(a) Q_1.   (b) Q_2.
(c) Q_3.   (d) greater than Q_3.
(e) Indeterminable with data provided.

*11. Suppose a firm's minimum efficient scale (*MES*) occurs at an average total cost of \$4 and an output of 4 million units, while quantity demanded at a price of \$4 is 3 million units. Given that the demand curve is downward-sloping, one can conclude that
(a) the firm is a natural monopoly.
(b) the firm's profits can be sustained only if it creates barriers to entry.
(c) it is always impossible to make positive profits regardless of the output level.
(d) the firm always breaks even.
(e) the firm will exit the industry.

*12. Which of the following is *not* true of price discrimination among units of output?
(a) Output is generally larger than under a single-price monopoly.
(b) Any given level of output yields a larger total revenue than a single-price monopoly.
(c) To be successful, resale must be impossible or prevented.
(d) Lower-income individuals will always be charged lower prices.
(e) If discrimination does not increase output, consumer surplus decreases.

*13. If a firm can sell 10 units of output for \$15 each or 11 units at \$14 each, the additional revenue from selling the eleventh unit is
(a) \$14.   (b) \$4.
(c) \$15.   (d) \$154.
(e) \$1.

Questions 14 to 18 refer to Figure 10-9, which depicts the demand and supply facing an entire industry in Panel (i) and the cost structure for a typical firm in the industry in Panel (ii). Assume that each firm is identical and produces a small proportion of total market output.

Figure 10-9

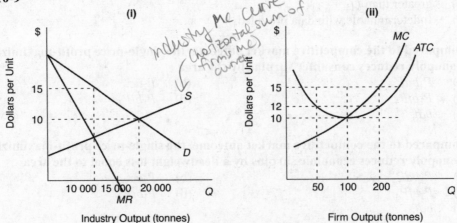

14. **If firms do not cooperate but behave as price takers, the market equilibrium price and quantity would be _____ and each firm's output and profit would be _____.**
    - (a) $15 and 10 000 tonnes; 200 tonnes and $600
    - (b) $15 and 10 000 tonnes; 100 tonnes and $500
    - (c) $10 and 20 000 tonnes; 100 tonnes and $1000
    - (d) $10 and 20 000 tonnes; 150 tonnes and $450
    - (e) $10 and 20 000 tonnes; 100 tonnes and zero

*15. **Now suppose that these firms cooperate with each other so as to maximize joint profits by forming a cartel. The market price and quantity are now**
    - (a) $15 and 10 000 tonnes.
    - (b) $15 and 15 000 tonnes.
    - (c) $15 and 20 000 tonnes.
    - (d) $10 and 20 000 tonnes.
    - (e) Indeterminable with data provided.

*16. **Suppose the cartel agreement reduces each firm's output by the same proportion as the reduction in industry output. An individual firm's output and profit under such an agreement would be**
    - (a) 50 tonnes and $250.
    - (b) 50 tonnes and $150.
    - (c) 50 tonnes and $0.
    - (d) 100 tonnes and $500.
    - (e) 100 tonnes and $300.

*17. **If an individual firm cheats on the cartel, it would produce _____ of output and make _____ profit.**
    - (a) 100 tonnes; $500
    - (b) 50 tonnes; $750
    - (c) 200 tonnes; $600
    - (d) 200 tonnes; $1000
    - (e) 100 tonnes; $300

*18. **The number of firms in this industry is**
    - (a) 100.
    - (b) 200.
    - (c) 500.
    - (d) 1000.
    - (e) Indeterminable from the data provided.

19. **Under perfect price discrimination**
    - (a) the firm captures all of the consumer surplus.
    - (b) each unit is sold at a different price (assuming a downward-sloping demand curve).
    - (c) the firm achieves more profit than it could with a single price.
    - (d) the firm produces the output that maximizes economic surplus.
    - (e) All of the above.

*20. **Suppose the elasticity of demand for electricity by residential customers of BC Hydro is 0.8 while that of industrial customers is 1.2. BC Hydro could practise price discrimination by charging**
    - (a) residential customers a higher price per kWh.
    - (b) industrial customers a higher price per kWh.
    - (c) the group with the larger quantity demanded a higher price per kWh.
    - (d) the group with the smaller quantity demanded a higher price per kWh.
    - (e) Insufficient data to determine.

21. **Price discrimination between two markets will result in**
    (a) equal marginal revenues across markets.
    (b) equal marginal costs across markets.
    (c) marginal revenue equal to marginal cost in each market.
    (d) a lower price in the market with the relatively more elastic demand.
    (e) All of the above.

22. **Hurdle pricing is generally used**
    (a) to prevent members of a cartel straying from the agreement.
    (b) to induce consumers to identify their different degrees of sensitivity to price.
    (c) as a barrier to entry.
    (d) to increase economies of scale.
    (e) to overcome diseconomies of scale.

Solutions

Chapter Review

1.(d) 2.(b) 3.(b) 4.(c) 5.(a) 6.(c) 7.(b) 8.(e) 9.(e) 10.(d) 11.(b) 12.(a) 13.(c) 14.(e) 15.(b) 16.(e) 17.(d)

Short-Answer Questions

1. The perfect competitor faced with a perfectly elastic demand curve does not have to lower price to sell more output, so the extra revenue on the marginal unit sold is its price. The monopolist, faced with a downward-sloping demand curve, must lower price on all units to sell an extra one. Thus the marginal revenue earned on the extra unit is the new lower price *minus* the reduction in revenue earned on all previous units (because of the fall in price). For example, if a monopolist selling 100 units at $20 each lowers price to $19.99 to sell the one-hundred-and-first unit, the extra revenue is $19.99 *minus* $0.01 on each of 100 units, = $19.99 − $1 = $18.99.

2. Profit maximization occurs at $MC = MR$, and MR is positive only on the elastic portion of the demand curve. So unless MC is negative (a highly unlikely case!), $MC = MR$ on the elastic portion of the demand curve.

3. Joseph Schumpeter argued that the expectation of profit is an incentive for research into and development of new technologies and new products, which are the main engines of economic growth, improved productivity, and higher living standards. Without this expectation, other firms would not have an incentive to "destroy" the market power of existing monopolies by "creating" new and better products (hence "creative destruction"). Similarly, existing monopolies would have less incentive for research and development since they would have less reason to protect themselves against new products and technologies developed by other firms.

4. Tangible goods can be subject to arbitrage—i.e., "middlemen" buying at the lower price and selling at a higher price. If there is significant arbitrage, the price-discriminating monopoly would be able to sell little at the higher price. But arbitrage is far more difficult, if not impossible, for intangible services. [For example, it is not possible for a young person to buy a haircut at a lower price and re-sell that haircut to an older person!]

5. The perfectly competitive industry produces to where price equals marginal cost—the condition for market efficiency. At this point, the value of the marginal unit equals the value of the resources used to produce it. But because the monopolist's price is greater than marginal revenue, and output is produced to where $MC = MR$, the monopolist does not produce some units of the good for which price exceeds marginal cost. That is, at $P > MC$, additional units having greater value than the resources needed to produce them are not produced.

Exercises

1. **(a)** 60. (Where $MC = MR$)
   (b) $11. (Read from the demand curve at $Q = 60$)
   (c) $660. (Price multiplied by quantity = 11×60)
   (d) $480. (Total cost = $ATC \times Q$ = $8(60) = $480)
   (e) $180. (Profit = $(AR - ATC)Q$ = $(11 - 8)60 = 180))
   (f) Output between 30 units and 90 units would create some profit, because over this range the ATC curve lies below the D curve so ATC is less than AR.

2. **(a)**

Output	TR	MR	MC	Profit
$0	$0			$–20
		$18	$4	
1	18			–6
		14	3	
2	32			5
		10	6	
3	42			9
		6	10	
4	48			5
		2	14	
5	50			–7
		–2	18	
6	48			–27

(b) **Figure 10-10**

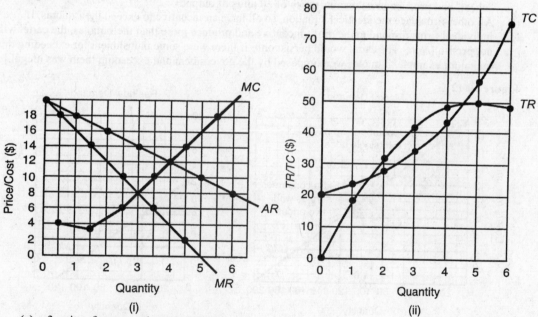

(i)

(ii)

(c) 3 units of output, where $MC = MR$.
(d) $14. (Price at 3 units of output, read from the demand curve.)
(e) At 3 units of output, TR is $42, TC is $33, and profits are $9.
(f) No, they are identical. In Panel (ii), the vertical distance between the TR and TC curves (i.e., the profit) is greatest at quantity of 3 units, and the total revenue and total cost at 3 units are $42 and $33, respectively.

3. **(a)** and **(b)** Figure 10-11

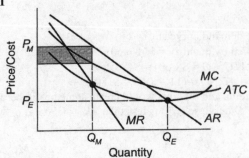

(c) No, it would not. At Q_E and P_E, where $P = MC$, the ATC exceeds the price so the business is operating at a loss and could not be sustained for long.

4. **(a)** (i) $5 and 3000 units, respectively. (Where the D and S curves intersect)
   (ii) 30 units. (Long-run competitive equilibrium occurs at the minimum point of the ATC curve.)
   (iii) zero profits. (This is the condition for long-run competitive equilibrium.)
   (b) $6 and 2000 units, respectively. (Where the market $MR = MC$)
   (c) In competitive equilibrium 3000 units were produced, with each firm producing 30 units, so there must be 100 firms in the industry. The cartel output of 2000 spread equally over 100 firms gives output of 20 per firm.
   (d) $10. At 20 units of output, $P = AR = \$6$ and $ATC = \$5.50$, so profit is $20(\$0.50) = \$10$.
   (e) The individual firm can behave as a price taker and maximize profit by producing 40 units (where the firm's $MC = MR = \$6$). The resulting profit level would be $(AR - ATC) \times 40 = (\$6 - \$5.50) \times 40 = \$20$. Since the individual firm can increase profit, it has an incentive to "cheat" and produce more than its quota of 20 units of output.
   (f) All other firms face the identical situation, so all have an incentive to exceed their quotas. If individual firms respond to the profit incentive and produce more than their quotas, the cartel will not persist. [*Note:* The cartel would persist only if there were some punishment for exceeding the quota; for example, if quotas were imposed by the government and exceeding them was illegal.]

5. **Figure 10-12**

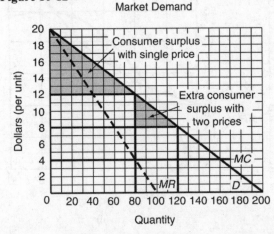

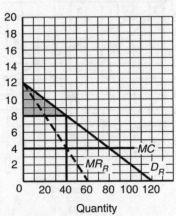

(a) (i) Profits are $(AR - AVC)Q - TFC = (\$12 - \$4)80 - \$100 = \$540$.
   (ii) Consumer surplus = area above $12 and below D curve = $1/2(20 - 12)80 = \$320$. Economic surplus is the area above the MC curve and below the D curve = $(12 - 4)80 + 1/2(20 - 12)80 = \$640 + \$320 = \$960$.
   (iii) Because $MC > MR$ above output of 80, each additional unit would add more to costs than it would add to revenues (i.e., $MC > MR$), thereby reducing profit.
   (b) (i) On the residual demand curve, $MC = MR = \$4$ at $Q = 40$. Price read from the demand curve = $8.

(ii) 40 units at \$4 each adds \$160 to costs. Selling for \$8 each adds \$8(40) = \$320 to revenues. The difference is \$160—the profits from these 40 units.

(iii) Consumer surplus = 1/2(12 − 8)40 = \$80. Economic surplus = (8 − 4)40 + 1/2(12 − 8)40 = \$160 + \$80 = \$240.

(c) (i) Profit on the 80 units (\$540) plus profit on the extra 40 units (\$160) = \$700.

(ii) Consumer surplus of \$320 on the first 80 units plus \$80 on the next 40 units = \$400. Economic surplus of \$960 on the first 80 units plus \$240 on the next 40 units = \$1200.

(iii) If the industry were perfectly competitive it would produce where $P = MC$, which is where MC (i.e., the equivalent of the long-run supply curve in perfect competition) cuts D at $Q = 160$ and $P = \$4$.

(iv) $TR − TVC − TFC = 120(\$8) − 120(\$4) − 100 = \$380$.

(d) Yes. Profits have increased by \$160 (i.e., the profits on the extra 40 units).

(e) Yes. Consumer surplus has increased by \$80.

(f) Yes. The firm's output is closer to the allocatively efficient level of 160 units, where $P = MC$.

(g) For the single-price monopoly to sell more, it must lower price on *all* units of output. If the firm is already producing at $MC = MR$, lowering the price on all units to sell more would reduce MR below MC on the extra units, thereby reducing profit. When the firm price discriminates among units of output, price is reduced only on the *additional* units of output. This creates a range where $MR > MC$ on extra units of output, so these extra units increase profit.

6. (a) (i) $OB; OJ$ (ii) ABD (iii) $ADFE$ (iv) $BDFE$

(b) (i) OA to OE (ii) OK   (iii) zero   (iv) AEG (v) AEG

[*Note:* In (b), answers (iv) and (v) are the same because there are no fixed costs. If there were fixed costs, profit under perfect price discrimination would be AEG <u>minus</u> the fixed costs.]

7. **Figure 10-13**

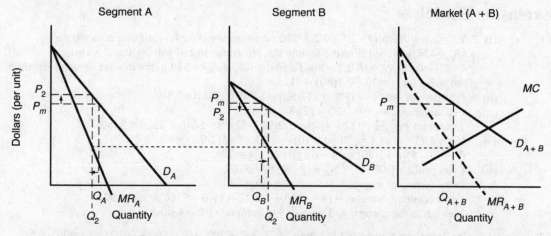

(a) The firm's market demand curve (D_{A+B}) is the horizontal sum of the demand curves of the two market segments. The single-price monopoly profit maximizes by producing where the firm's MR curve (MR_{A+B}) intersects the MC curve and charging the price, P_M, read from the market demand curve (D_{A+B}).

(b) (i) Total costs of production are unchanged because there is no change in output.

(ii) Price must be lowered in Segment B to sell more (i.e., a move down D_B). But since less is sold in Segment A, a higher price is charged in Segment A (i.e., a move up D_A).

(iii) Because the MR on the last unit sold in Segment A (read from MR_A) is less than the MR on the next unit sold in Segment B (read from MR_B), the revenue gained by selling one more unit in Segment B exceeds the revenue lost by selling one less unit in Segment A (i.e., $MR_B > MR_A$). Total revenue increases by the difference between the two marginal revenues.

(iv) Since total costs are unchanged and total revenue increases, profits increase. A profit-maximizing firm, therefore, will make this transfer of sales from Segment A to Segment B.

(v) If sales were transferred from the market with the more elastic demand (Segment B) to the market with the less elastic demand (Segment A), the revenue lost in Segment B would exceed the revenue gained in Segment A (since $MR_B > MR_A$), thereby reducing total revenues and reducing profits.

(c) When MR is the same in both markets, *and* equal to MC—i.e., $MR_B = MR_A = MC$ (as along the horizontal broken line in Figure 10-13). The $MR = MC$ condition says the profit-maximizing output is being produced. Equating the two MRs says that the distribution of sales between the two market segments is such as to maximize the revenue from that output. Any further transfer of sales will not increase revenues, and indeed will decrease revenues and profits.

(d) (i) No. The monopolist has moved to different points on the demand curves of the two market segments, but the curves themselves are unchanged.

    (ii) No. The two components of the overall demand curve (D_{A+B}) and MR curve (MR_{A+B}) are unchanged, so the sum of the components is unchanged.

    (iii) No. The MC curve is derived from the production function and the prices of factors of production, which are unaffected by a change in the distribution of sales.

    (iv) No. The MC curve is unchanged and the market MR_{A+B} curve is unchanged, so their intersection point (i.e., the profit maximizing level of output) is unchanged.

    (v) No. The cost curves are unchanged and total output is unchanged, so total costs of production are unchanged.

    (vi) Yes. Since total costs are unchanged but revenues have increased, profits have increased by the same amount as the increase in revenues.

    (vii) No. Economic surplus is the area under the market demand curve (D_{A+B}) and above the MC curve on Q_{A+B} units of output. This segmented-markets price discrimination has not changed any of these. [*Note:* Total consumer surplus is reduced, but it is more complicated to prove and you have not learned the required analytical tools.]

Extension Exercises

E1. (a) (i) $MR = a/b - 2(1/b)Q = 20 - 0.2Q$. The profit-maximizing level of output is where $MC = MR = \$4$. Substituting $\$4$ into the MR equation and solving for Q gives: $4 = 20 - 0.2Q$, $Q = 16/0.2 = 80$. To find price, put $Q = \$10$ in the inverse demand equation and solve for $P = 20 - 0.1(80) = \$12$.

    (ii) Profits $= TR - TVC - TFC = \$12(80) - \$4(80) - \$100 = \$540$.

    (iii) Consumer surplus $= 0.5(20 - 12)(80) = \$320$.
Economic surplus $= (12 - 4)80 + 1/2(20 - 12)80 = \$640 + \$320 = \$960$.

(b) (i) $MR = MC = 4$, so $4 = (20 - 80/10) - 0.2Q$, $Q = (12/0.2) = 40$.
$P = (20 - 8) - 0.1(40) = 12 - 0.1Q = 12 - 4 = \$8$.

    (ii) Extra profit $= (AR - AVC)Q = (8 - 4)40 = \$160$.

    (iii) Extra consumer surplus $= 0.5(12 - 8)(40) = \$80$.
Extra economic surplus $= (8 - 4)40 + 1/2(12 - 8)40 = \$160 + \$80 = \$240$.
Now go to the answers in Exercise 5 to complete the question.

E2. (a) (i) Profit maximizing output is where $MC = MR = 200$. $MR = 500 - 2(0.25)Q = 500 - 0.5Q$.
So $200 = 500 - 0.5(Q)$, $Q = 300/0.5 = 600$. $P = 500 - 0.25(600) = \$350$.

    (ii) $Q_A = 1200 - 2P_A = 1200 - 2(350) = 500$. $Q_B = 800 - 2P_B = 800 - 3(350) = 100$.

    (iii) Elasticity$_A = (P_A/Q_A)b = (350/500)2 = 1.4$.
Elasticity$_B = (P_B/Q_B)d = (350/100)2 = 7$ (i.e., more elastic than A).

    (iv) Profits $= TR - TVC - TFC = (AR - AVC)Q - TFC = (350 - 200)600 - 10\ 000 = \$80\ 000$.

(b) (i) $MR_A = MC = 200$, so $200 = 600 - Q_A$, $Q_A = 400$, $P_A = 600 - 0.5(400) = \$400$.
$MR_B = MC = 200$, so $200 = 400 - Q_B$, $Q_B = 200$, $P_A = 400 - 0.5(200) = \$300$.

    (ii) Profit $= TR_A + TR_B - TVC - TFC = 400(400) + 200(300) - 200(600) - 10\ 000 = \$90\ 000$.

(c) (i) No change in output, since sales of $400 + 200 =$ output of 600. If output does not change, total costs of production do not change.

    (ii) $TR_A = 400(400) = \$160\ 000$, a reduction of $\$15\ 000$ from the $500(350) = \$175\ 000$ without discrimination. $TR_B = 200(300) = \$60\ 000$, an increase of $\$25\ 000$ from the $100(350) = \$35\ 000$ without discrimination. The fall in spending in Market A is less than the increase in spending in Market B because the demand in A is less elastic than the demand in B. [*Note:* Had the elasticities of demand been equal, there would have been no change in total spending, revenues, and profits. Different elasticities of demand between segments is a *necessary condition* for profits to be increased by price discrimination among market segments.]

(iii) Total revenues increase by the increase in revenues from Market A ($25 000) *minus* the decrease in revenues from Market B ($15 000), for net increase of $10 000. Since output and, therefore, total costs of production are unchanged, the increase in revenues is an increase in profits.

(iv) Market B has the more-elastic demand (i.e., value 7 in (a) above), and price has fallen by $50 (from $350 to $300). Market A has the less-elastic demand (i.e., value 1.4 in (a) above), and price has increased by $50 (from $350 to $400).

Additional Multiple-Choice Questions

1.(a) 2.(a) 3.(e) 4.(a) 5.(a) 6.(b) 7.(a) 8.(e) 9.(d) 10.(c) 11.(a) 12.(d) 13.(b) 14.(e) 15.(a) 16.(b) 17.(c) 18.(b) 19.(e) 20.(a) 21.(e) 22.(b)

Explanations for the Asterisked Multiple-Choice Questions

1.(a) Figure 10-1 in the text illustrates that *MR* is negative on the inelastic portion of the demand curve. As long as *MC* is positive, therefore, the profit-maximizing condition $MC = MR$ can be reached only when *MR* is positive, which occurs only on the elastic portion of the demand curve.

2.(a) $MR = 0$ when price elasticity of demand is unity, which occurs at the midpoint of a linear demand curve.

3.(e) In previous chapters you had the supply curve as a unique (*ceteris paribus*) relationship between price and desired quantity supplied. It was also independent of the demand curve. The monopolist however has no such relationship. The intersection of *MC* and *MR* determines desired quantity supplied, and the price is then read from the demand curve. It may help if you think of the intersection of *MC* and *MR* as a single point on a diagram. Many different *MC* curves can be drawn intersecting *MR* at that point, and all will generate the same desired quantity and the firm will charge the same price (read from the same demand curve).

6.(b) Since $MR = 0$, Q_2 is at the midpoint of the linear demand curve, where price elasticity is unity. At higher prices demand is elastic, so an increase in price reduces total revenue. At lower prices demand is inelastic, so a decrease in price reduces total revenue.

7.(a) Compare the areas below the *D* curve and above the price charged. In competitive equilibrium at point *d* the price charged is P_3 and consumer surplus is adP_3. The monopoly maximizes profit at point *b*, charging price P_1 and generating consumer surplus of P_1ab. Subtract the latter from the former and get the fall in consumer surplus of P_1dbP_3.

8.(e) Economic surplus in perfect competition is the area *adg*. Economic surplus in monopoly is the area *abfg*. The latter is less than the former by the triangle *bdf*. Thus *bdf* is economic surplus that has "vanished"—i.e., the <u>deadweight loss</u> from monopoly. [*Note*: Please see the second item under *Hints and Tips* of this chapter. It tells you that *bdf* is the deadweight loss only if the *supply curve* for perfect competition is also the *MC* curve of the monopolist. You should return to review this answer after you have done Exercise 2 in Chapter 12 of this *Study Guide*.]

9.(d) In the answer to Question 7 above you found the fall in consumer surplus of P_1dbP_3. Economic surplus at Q_1 in monopoly is *abfg* (the area above *MC* curve and below *D* curve on Q_1 units of output). Thus the area P_1bjP_3 remains part of <u>economic</u> surplus even though it is part of the reduction in <u>consumer</u> surplus.

10.(c) With perfect price discrimination, each *P* is the *MR* for that unit of output (since *P* is not reduced on the other units in order to sell more), and the monopolist will continue to sell more and increase profit until $P (= MR) = MC$.

11.(a) Minimum efficient scale (the lowest point on the long-run average cost curve) is to the right of the demand curve, meaning that the firm will still have falling long-run average costs (attributable to economies of scale) even if it produces the entire output of the market. Such large economies of scale results in one firm serving the entire market.

12.(d) For price discrimination to be successful, firms must have market power; consumers must have different valuations of the product; there must be little or no arbitrage; and, for discrimination among market segments, the segments must have different price elasticities of demand. If these conditions are not met, price discrimination is not profit-maximizing regardless of the income level of consumers. Even where the conditions are met, it need not <u>always</u> be profit-maximizing to sell at lower prices to lower-income consumers. For example, discounts for seniors are based on age, not income.

13.(b) The price of the eleventh unit is $14. Revenue lost by lowering price by $1 on the previous 10 units = $10. The net increase in revenue (the *MR* of the eleventh unit) is $14 – $10 = $4.

15.(a) Maximum profit can be had by acting like a monopolist—i.e., where $MC = MR$ in the Panel (i), where S is the (horizontal) sum of all the individual firms' *MC* curves and so is the industry *MC* curve. This gives output of 10 000 tonnes and a price, read from the demand curve, of $15 per tonne.

16.(b) Following from Question 15 above, there is a 50 percent fall in industry output (i.e., from 20 000 to 10 000 tonnes). Thus each individual firm will cut its output by 50 percent, from 100 tonnes to 50 tonnes. At 50 tonnes *ATC* is $12 per tonne and P is $15 per tonne, giving each individual firm an economic profit of $(P - ATC)Q = (15 - 12)50 = \$150$.

17.(c) If all firms "cheated," the excess supply would reduce price and each firm would correspondingly reduce its profit-maximizing output until the market was back in competitive equilibrium at $P = \$10$ and $Q = 100$, each making zero economic profit since $P = ATC$. But if only one <u>individual</u> firm "cheats," its increase in output <u>alone</u> will be too small to affect the market price. Thus, price remains at $P = \$15$, and this firm will maximize profits at $P = MC = \$15$ with output of $Q = 200$. Economic profits for this firm would be $(AR - ATC)Q = (15 - 12)200 = \$600$.

18.(b) The number of firms can be found either by dividing the <u>competitive equilibrium</u> quantity in the market (20 000) by that for the firm (100), or by dividing <u>monopolistic</u> profit-maximizing industry output (10 000) by the output quota assigned to each firm (50). In both cases you get 200 firms. This also shows how the individual firm's "quota" is determined: take the profit-maximizing monopoly level of industry output (10 000), and divide by the number of firms in the industry (200) to get a cartel output of 50 per firm.

20.(a) In segmented markets, price-discrimination profits are maximized by charging the higher price in the market with the less-elastic demand curve. In this question the elasticity of demand of residential customers (0.8) is less than that of industrial customers (1.2), so the former will be charged a higher price than the latter (so (b) and (e) are wrong). Note that there is <u>nothing</u> to say which group has the larger or smaller total quantity demanded, so answers (c) and (d) are incorrect in the context of this analysis.

Imperfect Competition and Strategic Behaviour

11

Chapter Overview

Much of the production in the Canadian economy takes place in industries where firms cannot be considered either price takers or monopolists. These firms operate in an imperfectly competitive market framework that can be subdivided into two broad groups: those markets with a large number of relatively small firms and those with a small number of relatively large firms. **Concentration ratios**, which measure the fraction of total market sales controlled by the few largest sellers in a market, are used to help measure the amount of market power of oligopolistic firms, but these ratios have their weaknesses.

Monopolistic competition is characterized by many relatively small firms producing basically the same product, but each competing with the rest by producing a variant that is **differentiated** from others in some way. For example, there are many different characteristics to services such as convenience stores and restaurants. Monopolistic competition produces a wider variety of products but at a higher cost per unit than perfect competition.

Oligopolistic industries are characterized by a small number of firms, each of which accounts for a significant fraction of their industry's production. There can be vigorous interfirm competition in an oligopoly that results in a **non-cooperative outcome** as firms adopt **strategic behaviour** in an effort to increase their individual profits. The **cooperative outcome** results when firms maximize joint profits through **collusion**, which may be explicit or tacit. Oligopolistic industries generally have **entry barriers** into the industry that, as with a monopoly, may be natural or created. A fundamental issue in the role of oligopoly in the economy over time is whether an oligopolistic market structure is more conducive to innovation than other market structures.

Hints and Tips

The following may help you avoid some of the most common errors on examinations.

✓ Understand the properties of long-run equilibrium in monopolistic competition and, in particular, the reasons why the market structure dictates these properties. The lack of barriers to entry in monopolistic competition dictates long-run equilibrium at zero profit, which in turn means price equals *LRAC*. With a downward-sloping (albeit highly elastic) demand curve, tangency between the firm's demand and *LRAC* curves at zero profit must occur on the negatively sloped portion of the *LRAC*, where price exceeds marginal cost and each firm has excess capacity.

✓ A firm's strategic choices leading to a Nash equilibrium take into account the choices made by rival firms. Understand how to read these from a payoff matrix and how to construct the payoff matrix to show the outcomes for each set of choices.

✓ When studying oligopolies, recognize that each situation must be judged on its own merits (and demerits). The main challenge facing public policy toward oligopolistic market structures is not to prevent their existence, since many industries today require large firms in order to take full advantage of economies of scale. Nor is the challenge to prevent oligopolies from making profit, since the lure of profit can be a major driving force underlying innovation and "creative destruction," which benefit consumers and society in the long run. Rather, the challenge is to keep them competing rather than colluding.

✓ This chapter's *Additional Topics* on MyEconLab will further spur your interest in the extensive possibilities that exist in our world of imperfectly competitive markets. As with all *Additional Topics*, they make excellent reading even if not specifically assigned for your course.

Chapter Review

The Structure of the Canadian Economy

This section explains how imperfectly competitive market structures, which are the dominant types in modern economies, differ from the perfectly competitive and monopoly extremes. It also examines the nature and role of **concentration ratios**, and how issues regarding the practical definition of the relevant market can create problems in the use of concentration ratios as a measure of market power.

1. A concentration ratio is intended to measure
   (a) how much of an industry is concentrated in central Canada.
   (b) the number of firms in an industry.
   (c) how much production in a given market is controlled by a few firms.
   (d) how much of a given industry is concentrated in the hands of foreign-owned transnational corporations.
   (e) the proportion of an industry that concentrates on export markets.

2. **Neither the model of perfect competition nor that of monopoly provides a completely satisfactory description of the Canadian economy because there are significant sectors of the economy with**
    (a) many small firms that still have some price-setting ability.
    (b) only a few large firms.
    (c) many firms, but with a disproportionate amount of production concentrated in the hands of a few.
    (d) many small firms each selling a differentiated product.
    (e) All of the above.

3. **A concentration ratio that measures the proportion of Canadian production accounted for by the largest four firms in Canada may provide a misleading indicator of market power because**
    (a) the relevant market may be local instead of national.
    (b) the relevant market may be global instead of national.
    (c) the number four is arbitrarily chosen.
    (d) there may be only two firms in the industry.
    (e) the relevant market may be either local or global, instead of national.

4. **Which of the following is generally correct about Canadian <u>raw materials</u> industries?**
    (a) The high national concentration ratios reflect many firms, each with a small degree of market power.
    (b) The high national concentration ratios reflect few firms, each with a high degree of market power.
    (c) The low national concentration ratios reflect many firms, each with a small degree of market power.
    (d) The low national concentration ratios reflect few firms, each with a high degree of market power.
    (e) The high national concentration ratios reflect few firms, each with a low degree of market power.

What Is Imperfect Competition?

This section explains that, because a firm in an imperfectly competitive market structure faces a downward-sloping demand curve, it can choose both product variety and price. The outputs produced by the firms within such a market are similar enough to be the same "product," but dissimilar enough to be sold at different prices. The dissimilarities are what *differentiates* one firm's product from the others. Unlike the perfectly competitive firm, which is a price taker and not a price setter, the imperfectly competitive firm has some flexibility to *choose* its price and to choose how and when to *change* prices. The administrative costs of changing prices may cause some firms not to change price in response to *temporary* fluctuations in demand. Alternatively the prices of goods and services sold over the Internet may change very frequently because of the lack of administrative costs. This section also identifies the various ways that firms in imperfectly competitive markets can engage in non-price competition.

5. **Because firms in imperfectly competitive markets sell a differentiated product (such as Burger King and Harvey's hamburgers), each firm**
   (a) faces a downward-sloping demand curve.
   (b) has some ability to set its own price.
   (c) receives information on market conditions through changes in sales rather than changes in price.
   (d) tends to respond to temporary fluctuations in demand by changing output rather than price.
   (e) All of the above.

6. **In the sense used in this chapter, "choosing" prices means that prices are**
   (a) determined by international forces.
   (b) controlled by the government.
   (c) determined by market forces.
   (d) set by individual firms.
   (e) set by regulatory agencies such as marketing boards.

7. **Which of the following forms of *competitive behaviour* is observed in imperfectly competitive markets?**
   (a) Offering product guarantees.
   (b) Advertising.
   (c) Offering competing product standards.
   (d) Creating barriers to entry.
   (e) All of the above.

8. **Prices in imperfectly competitive markets typically change less frequently than do prices in perfectly competitive markets because in imperfectly competitive markets**
   (a) demand is more stable.
   (b) the prices of inputs change less frequently.
   (c) administrative costs of changing prices are higher.
   (d) supply is less elastic.
   (e) demand is more elastic <u>and</u> supply is less elastic.

Monopolistic Competition

Monopolistic competition has many small firms, each producing a differentiated product. Product differentiation gives some downward slope to a firm's demand curve, but the presence of the many close substitutes produced by the other firms in the industry makes each firm's demand curve highly elastic. The monopolistically competitive firm's short-run equilibrium is similar to that of a monopoly, but its long-run equilibrium (shown in Figure 11-2 in the text) differs from that of both monopoly and perfect competition. This section of the text concludes with an explanation of the excess capacity theorem and a review of the debate concerning its relevance.

9. **The excess capacity theorem in monopolistic competition**
   (a) means that firms will not be producing at minimum average total cost in the long-run equilibrium.
   (b) implies that the trade-off for product variety is a higher unit production cost.
   (c) arises because of the assumptions of freedom of entry and downward-sloping demand curves.
   (d) is a characteristic of long-run equilibrium in this market structure.
   (e) All of the above.

10. **An important feature that distinguishes monopolistic competition from perfect competition is that**
   (a) monopolistic competitors sell a differentiated product rather than a homogeneous one.
   (b) the monopolistic competitor's demand curve is the same as the market demand curve.
   (c) in long-run equilibrium, monopolistic competitors earn economic profits, whereas perfectly competitive firms do not.
   (d) there are important barriers to entry in monopolistic competition.
   (e) perfectly competitive firms maximize profits at $MC = MR$, while monopolistically competitive firms do not.

11. **Some economists have argued that monopolistic competition is inefficient because**
   (a) the long-run equilibrium of these firms is characterized by positive profits.
   (b) these firms over-invest in barriers to entry.
   (c) these firms produce an output less than that corresponding to the minimum point on the *LRAC* curve.
   (d) it produces a limited range of product variety.
   (e) these firms produce where $P = MR$.

12. **In long-run equilibrium, monopolistic competition differs from perfect competition because firms in monopolistic competition**
   (a) do not buy their inputs in competitive markets.
   (b) charge a price greater than marginal cost.
   (c) do not operate on the *LRAC* curve.
   (d) are protected by barriers to entry.
   (e) each has a high level of market power.

Oligopoly and Game Theory

This important section emphasizes that the fundamental difference between other market structures and oligopolistic markets is the widespread use of *strategic behaviour* by oligopolies, since each firm in an oligopoly is aware of and takes account of the interdependence between its decisions and the decisions of other firms in the industry. By explaining *payoff matrices* in the context of *game theory*, this section demonstrates the basic dilemma of oligopolistic firms—that although collusion would maximize joint profits, each firm may have an incentive to deviate from the cooperative outcome. Because of interdependence among the few large firms in the industry, such *non-cooperative behaviour* results in a Nash equilibrium where each firm has chosen its best strategy given the strategies adopted by the other firms. Thorough knowledge of this section is needed to properly understand the following section about how oligopolies act in practice.

13. **Which of the following best reflects the economic definition of *strategic behaviour* by an oligopolistic firm?**
   (a) It maximizes profit by producing where $MC = MR$.
   (b) It chooses to set price on the elastic portion of its demand curve.
   (c) It minimizes costs by producing on the *LRAC* curve.
   (d) It takes account of the reactions of other firms before offering a price discount.
   (e) All of the above, because they are all required for profit maximization.

14. **Collusive behaviour that sets each firm's output level in order to maximize joint profits in an oligopolistic industry will generally be effective over time only when**
    (a) the payoff matrix shows that each firm would otherwise have an incentive to increase output.
    (b) there would otherwise be a high degree of competition because there are many firms in the industry.
    (c) there is a way to enforce the output-restricting agreement.
    (d) the firms merge to become a monopoly.
    (e) the payoff matrix is symmetric for all firms.

15. **A non-cooperative (Nash) equilibrium among oligopolistic firms**
    (a) tends to be unstable because each firm has an incentive to cut price and increase output.
    (b) is the same outcome that a single monopoly firm would reach if it owned all of the firms in the industry.
    (c) results in each firm producing more than it would in a cooperative equilibrium but making less profit.
    (d) maximizes joint profits for the firms in the industry.
    (e) is characterized by each firm having an incentive to change its output.

16. **The equilibrium payoffs in the prisoners' dilemma**
    (a) represent a Nash equilibrium.
    (b) result from non-cooperative behaviour.
    (c) are such that no individual prisoner can do better by changing his/her plea.
    (d) All of the above.

Oligopoly in Practice

The section starts with a review of different types of collusive behaviour (*explicit* or *tacit*) and competitive behaviour. Even when price competition among the firms is limited or absent, each firm can attempt to increase its market share through different types of *non-price competition* and by trying to keep ahead of its rivals through innovation (i.e., by developing new products and production processes). There is then a review of different types of *firm-created* entry barriers (including brand proliferation, advertising, and the expectation of predatory pricing), which, along with natural barriers such as economies of scale (discussed in Chapter 10), prevent existing firms' profits from being eroded in the long run by new entrants. The section closes with an overview of the role of oligopolies in the economy; how they respond to changes in market conditions, what levels of profit they typically target, and whether/how they contribute to economic growth through innovation.

17. **Tacit cooperation among firms**
    (a) is a legally binding contract to collude.
    (b) is an explicit collusion agreement.
    (c) is an implicit understanding to cooperate in their joint interests.
    (d) is a stable agreement because no single firm can do better by violating the agreement.
    (e) can easily be distinguished from the effect of market forces.

18. **Which of the following methods of competition by an oligopolist best meets Joseph Schumpeter's criteria for "creative destruction"?**
    (a) Product innovation to increase market share.
    (b) Creating a larger market share by reducing price to destroy the market share of other firms.
    (c) Creating a higher market share by advertising the negative characteristics of competitors' products.
    (d) Providing more comprehensive warranties than its competitors.
    (e) Brand proliferation.

19. **Brand proliferation creates a barrier to entry by**
    (a) increasing variable costs of production for existing firms.
    (b) reducing the market share available to potential entrants.
    (c) preventing existing firms from fully exploiting economies of scale.
    (d) enabling new entrants to operate at minimum efficient scale.
    (e) increasing the sunk costs of entry into the industry.

20. **To the extent that some oligopolistic firms sometimes sell at below cost to deter potential new entrants, they are using a strategy described as**
    (a) non-maximizing behaviour.
    (b) predatory pricing.
    (c) competitive pricing.
    (d) non-price competition.
    (e) tacit cooperation.

21. **Economic profits can exist in an oligopolistic industry in the long run because of**
    (a) natural barriers to entry.
    (b) barriers created by existing firms.
    (c) barriers created by government policy.
    (d) economies of scale.
    (e) All of the above.

22. **In some markets, there may be room for only a few firms because**
    (a) of economies of scale.
    (b) the industry produces a homogeneous good.
    (c) individual firms face perfectly elastic demand curves.
    (d) each firm has an upward-sloping LRAC curve.
    (e) market demand is highly inelastic.

Short-Answer Questions

1. How do perfectly competitive and imperfectly competitive firms differ in their use of non-price competition? What is the reason for the difference?

2. How and why does long-run equilibrium in monopolistic competition differ from long-run equilibrium in perfect competition?

3. In many crime dramas on television the detectives question the suspects separately in different rooms, frequently offering special deals if one confesses. How is the situation faced by the suspects similar to that faced by oligopolists? How might the results of the detectives' strategy be affected if each suspect knows that the other's "family" will take revenge—and how can this principle extend to oligopolies?

4. If one oligopolist increases price and the others "follow" by increasing their prices too, is this evidence of tacit collusion? Explain.

Exercises

1. **Monopolistic Competition: Short-Run Equilibrium**
The following diagram shows selected cost and revenue curves facing a firm that is operating in a monopolistically competitive industry characterized by ease of entry, product differentiation, and a large number of firms.

Figure 11-1

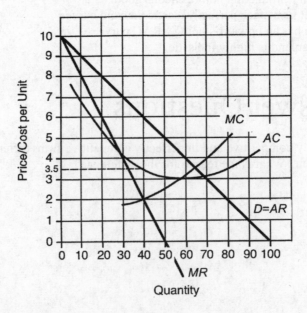

(a) What price will a profit-maximizing firm set? $6

(b) What are the associated profits? 6×40 ⇒ 240 revenue, TR − AC×Q = π

(c) Given that entry is relatively easy, is this a long-run equilibrium situation? Explain.

NO. Demand will ↓ until econ profit = 0

(d) Assume that the firm increases its advertising expenditures by a *fixed* amount (i.e., an amount unrelated to the level of output), thereby increasing its market share.

    (i) Which curves are affected, and how?

    Demand ↑
    AC ↑

    (ii) Will the increased sales result in higher profits?

    Depends on relative amounts of cost / revenue

    (iii) Is any resulting increase in profit sustainable in the long run? Explain.

    NO, again more firms will enter

    (iv) Would you expect to see monopolistically competitive firms spending large amounts on advertising? Explain.

    NO, b/c profits are short-lived.

2. **Monopolistic Competition: Long-Run Equilibrium**
This exercise examines the long-run equilibrium in monopolistic competition, and compares it to that in perfect competition.

(a) Draw a diagram in Figure 11-2 showing the long-run equilibrium of a firm in a monopolistically competitive industry.

Figure 11-2

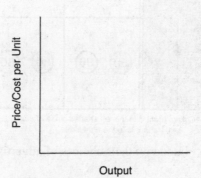

(b) Suppose that market demand for the product increases. Show the short-run effects on price, output, and profit for the firm. Explain.

(c) What will be the long-run effects of the increase in demand for this firm and for the industry as a whole?

(d) How does the long-run equilibrium illustrate the excess capacity theorem? Does this mean that society's resources are used less efficiently than in perfect competition? Explain.

3. Game Theory and Nash Equilibrium in a Duopoly

This exercise applies game theory to the choice of an advertising budget by the two large firms in the industry.

Suppose that each of two competitors, Pepsi and Coke, must select its own advertising expenditure. For simplicity, assume that there are only two sizes of advertising budgets: moderate and large. The relationship between advertising and profits for each firm, and for the two firms jointly, is presented in the payoff matrix in Figure 11-3. There are four possible combinations of budgets (the four cells in the payoff matrix). For each combination, Coke's profits are shown in the left circle of the cell and Pepsi's are in the right circle. [*Note:* You may wish to reread the caption to Figure 11-3 in the text to refresh your understanding of how to interpret the payoff matrix.]

Figure 11-3

Payoff Matrix (profit in millions of dollars)*

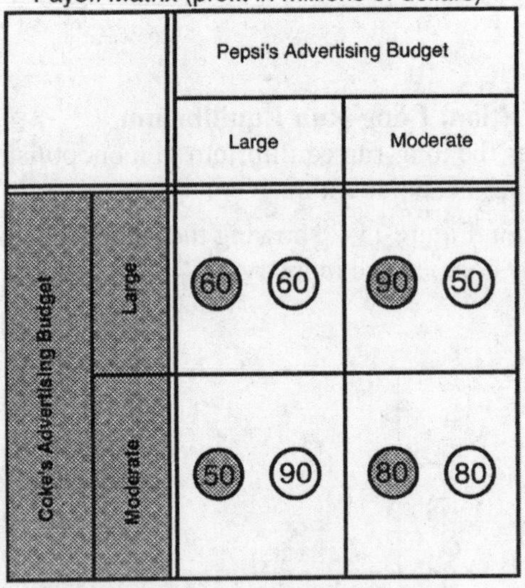

		Pepsi's Advertising Budget	
		Large	Moderate
Coke's Advertising Budget	Large	⓺⓪ ⓺⓪	⑨⓪ ⑤⓪
	Moderate	⑤⓪ ⑨⓪	⑧⓪ ⑧⓪

*Coke's profit is in the left shaded circle of each cell, Pepsi's is in the right circle

(a) If Pepsi and Coke colluded on their choices of advertising budgets, which would they select? Explain.

(b) Is the cooperative outcome in (a) likely to be stable? Explain.

(c) What is the non-cooperative outcome in this game? Is it likely to be stable? Explain.

(d) Is this a symmetric game? Explain.

4. **Game Theory and the Instability of a Multi-Firm Cartel**
In Chapter 10 you examined why, when a perfectly competitive industry forms a cartel to restrict output and increase profits, the incentives facing each individual firm are likely to cause the cartel to collapse. This exercise addresses the same issue but in a more rigorous way. While about neither monopolistic competition nor oligopoly, the exercise illustrates the pervasiveness of game theory.

The perfectly competitive industry is initially in long-run equilibrium, with each of many small firms producing 120 units of output and making zero profit at the equilibrium price of $6. The industry then forms a cartel and reduces output by assigning a quota of 80 units to each firm. The reduction in industry supply drives the market price to $10. Figure 11-4 shows the situation for one of these firms—call it Firm 1.

Figure 11-4

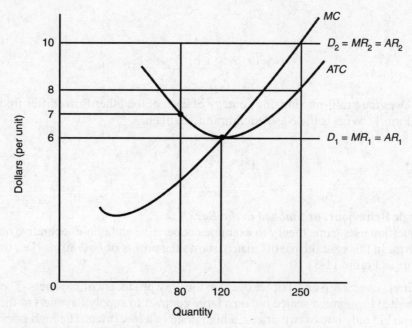

(a) If all other firms abide by their quotas, what is the profit of Firm 1 if
  (i) it abides by its quota?

  (ii) it ignores the quota and produces its profit-maximizing level of output?

(b) What is the best (i.e., profit-maximizing) strategy for Firm 1 in (a)? What happens to market price? Explain.

(c) If all other firms attempt to profit maximize by exceeding their quotas, what is the profit of Firm 1 if

    (i)   it abides by its quota?

    (ii)   it ignores the quota and produces its profit-maximizing level of output?

(d) What is the best (i.e., profit-maximizing) strategy for Firm 1 in (c)? What happens to market price? Explain.

(e) Construct a simple payoff matrix showing the profit of Firm 1 for each of the four cases in (a) and (c).

(f) Does the profit-maximizing strategy of each of the other firms differ from that of Firm 1? What is the Nash equilibrium? Explain.

5. **Strategic Behaviour, or *Stabbed in the Back!***
This question uses game theory to examine cooperative and non-cooperative outcomes for two firms. In this case the payoff matrix shows the profits of *both* firms (i.e., the same structure as Figure 11-3).

Two firms, EverSharp and TripleEdge, are the only producers of bayonets. They have each been invited to submit a sealed bid on a large contract to supply bayonets to the military. They can bid only one of two prices: a high price or a low price. The high price is expected to yield a profit of $10 million, while the low price will yield a profit of $7 million. If they both submit the same price, they will share the contract and the profits equally. If they bid different prices, the firm making the lower bid will get the entire contract.

(a) Construct the payoff matrix.

(b) What would be the outcome under cooperative behaviour? Explain.

(c) What would be the non-cooperative outcome under strategic behaviour? Explain.

6. ***Read All About It!***
Use the economic analysis developed in this and the previous chapters to discuss each of the following events described in newspaper headlines.

(a) "Prices of Petroleum Products Rise as OPEC Restricts Oil Supplies" (1974)
"Oil Prices Plummet with OPEC Price War" (1985)
"OPEC Ministers Unable to Agree on New Production Quotas" (1993)
"OPEC Maintains Discipline Over Production Levels" (1999)

(b) "GM Announces Price Hikes for 1992 Models; Ford and Chrysler Expected to Follow" (1991)

(c) "Personal Computer Price War Spurs Buying Spree" (1992)

(d) "Independent Gas Retailers Spur Price Wars in Southwestern Ontario" (1998)

(e) "Local Retailers Compete with Large Chains by Personalizing Service" (1999)

Additional Multiple-Choice Questions

*1. **An important prediction of monopolistic competition is that the long-run profit-maximizing output of the firm is**
(a) where price exceeds average total cost.
(b) less than the point at which average total cost is at a minimum.
(c) less than the point at which average total cost equals average revenue.
(d) less than the point at which marginal cost equals marginal revenue.
(e) where price equals marginal revenue.

Questions 2 and 3 refer to Figure 11-5.

Figure 11-5

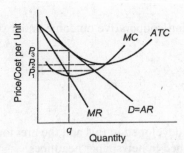

2. **The profit-maximizing firm in monopolistic competition will set its price equal to**
    (a) P_1.
    (b) P_2.
    (c) P_3.
    (d) minimum MC.
    (e) marginal cost.

3. **The situation described by price P_3 and output q is**
    (a) a long-run equilibrium in perfect competition since there are no economic profits.
    (b) a long-run equilibrium in monopolistic competition.
    (c) unstable; new firms will enter the industry to eliminate economic profits.
    (d) unstable; firms will exit because profits are zero.
    (e) not the profit-maximizing equilibrium for a monopolistic competitor.

*4. **Perfect competition differs from all other market structures in that perfectly competitive firms**
    (a) face negatively sloped demand curves.
    (b) sell an identical product and are price takers.
    (c) actively compete through various forms of non-price competition such as advertising.
    (d) choose their prices.
    (e) make zero profits in long-run equilibrium.

*5. **The key difference between oligopolists and firms that operate in all other market structures is that oligopolists**
    (a) are guaranteed long-run profits.
    (b) produce an identical product but choose their prices.
    (c) take explicit account of strategies of competing firms.
    (d) do not engage in strategic behaviour.
    (e) do not engage in tacit collusion.

6. **The cooperative, joint profit-maximizing outcome in oligopoly**
    (a) is a long-run equilibrium so long as there are barriers to entry.
    (b) will be unstable because each firm has an incentive to increase output.
    (c) results in market efficiency.
    (d) maximizes the output of each firm.
    (e) is an equilibrium so long as collusion is explicit as opposed to tacit.

*7. **Cooperation among oligopolistic firms that affects prices**
    (a) is an effective agreement because it is a legal contract.
    (b) results in a long-run joint profit-maximizing equilibrium and stability in the industry.
    (c) tends to break down through strategic behaviour.
    (d) is more likely the greater the number of firms in the industry.
    (e) is more likely the weaker are the industry's barriers to entry.

*8. **Advertising expenditures can create a barrier to entry by**
- (a) increasing costs for new entrants.
- (b) reducing the minimum efficient scale of production.
- (c) announcing to potential entrants the intention to engage in predatory pricing.
- (d) being a form of covert cheating on a collusive price-fixing agreement.
- (e) being a form of overt cheating on a collusive price-fixing agreement.

*9. **Which of the following would be covert cheating on a collusive agreement?**
- (a) Advertising.
- (b) Improving product quality.
- (c) Offering undisclosed discounts and rebates to special customers.
- (d) Improving coverage under warranties.
- (e) One firm reduces its published price.

*10. **According to the theory of monopolistic competition, a firm that lowers its price will**
- (a) gain some but not all buyers in the market due to product differentiation.
- (b) increase its profits.
- (c) gain all of the market due to the nature of the demand curve facing the firm.
- (d) not affect its profits.
- (e) induce other firms to raise their prices.

*11. **The notion that monopolistic competition is systematically inefficient is *invalid* because consumers benefit**
- (a) from lower prices.
- (b) from the availability of an increased variety of products.
- (c) from an increase in the quantity supplied of a good.
- (d) from products becoming more homogeneous.
- (e) from lower production costs.

12. **The long-run equilibrium of a monopolistically competitive firm has all of the following characteristics *except***
- (a) $P = ATC$.
- (b) $MR = MC$.
- (c) ATC is increasing.
- (d) $ATC >$ minimum average cost.
- (e) ATC curve is tangent to the demand curve.

*13. **Which of the following applies to *both* monopolistic competition and perfect competition?**
- (a) Firms produce a standardized product.
- (b) Non-price competition is common.
- (c) Absence of significant barriers to entry.
- (d) Each firm is a price taker.
- (e) Short-run equilibrium is characterized by zero profits.

*14. **By taking into account the expected reaction of their competitors, oligopolists are exhibiting**
- (a) tacit behaviour.
- (b) collusive behaviour.
- (c) cooperative behaviour.
- (d) non-cooperative behaviour.
- (e) strategic behaviour.

*15. **Which of the following statements about Nash equilibrium is *false*?**
   (a) A Nash equilibrium is an example of a non-cooperative equilibrium.
   (b) In a Nash equilibrium, all players are maximizing their payoffs given the current behaviour of the other players.
   (c) In a Nash equilibrium, all players are better off than they would be with any other combination of strategies.
   (d) A Nash equilibrium is self-enforcing.
   (e) Both (c) and (d) are false.

16. **Which of the following is *not* a characteristic of an oligopolistic market structure?**
   (a) Products of different firms may or may not be differentiated.
   (b) The price policies of the largest firm will have an impact on the price policies of other firms in the industry.
   (c) There is a relatively large number of sellers.
   (d) The concentration ratio is high.
   (e) The firms are price-setters.

*17. **Which of the following statements about oligopolistic behaviour is *false*?**
   (a) There is a wide range of oligopolistic behaviour.
   (b) Oligopoly prices will generally exceed marginal cost.
   (c) Oligopoly is the least desirable available market structure when minimum efficient scale output is large.
   (d) Oligopoly profits are likely to persist in the long run.
   (e) Oligopolists engage in strategic behaviour.

*18. **Predatory pricing**
   (a) refers to the impact of collusive behaviour on consumers.
   (b) can be difficult to distinguish from reactions to market forces.
   (c) can be used to establish a reputation to discourage entry.
   (d) refers to setting prices above minimum *LRAC*.
   (e) can establish the reputation to discourage entry *and* be difficult to distinguish from reactions to market forces.

19. **Consider an example of the prisoners' dilemma where two firms are making sealed bids on a contract and each firm is allowed to bid either $150 or $250. If both firms bid the same price, the job is shared equally and each firm earns half the value of its bid. Otherwise, the lowest bidder wins the contract and receives the full value of its bid. What is the cooperative outcome in this situation?**
   (a) Both firms bid $150.
   (b) Both firms bid $250.
   (c) One firm bids $150; the other bids $250.
   (d) There is no cooperative equilibrium in this situation.
   (e) Both bidding $150 *and* both bidding $250 are cooperative outcomes.

*20. **What is the Nash equilibrium in Question 19?**
   (a) Both firms bid $150.
   (b) Both firms bid $250.
   (c) One firm bids $150; the other bids $250.
   (d) There is no Nash equilibrium in this situation.
   (e) Both bidding $150 *and* both bidding $250 are both Nash equilibriums.

*21. **An individual firm in a perfectly competitive industry generally _____ engage in _____ competition because _____.**
  (a) does not; price; it captures a larger share of total market sales
  (b) does; price; it increases consumer demand for the firm's product
  (c) does not; non-price; it increases total costs without changing total revenues
  (d) does; non-price; it increases the firm's profits
  (e) does not; either price or non-price; it faces a perfectly elastic demand curve at the market price

*22. **By viewing a country as a firm, which of the following economic events is equivalent to what contributed to OPEC's decision in 1985 to eliminate oil production quotas as a form of explicit collusion (*Lessons from History 11-1*)?**
  (a) Entry of new firms into the industry.
  (b) Individual firms in the collusive agreement "cheated" on their quotas.
  (c) Innovation via more efficient new products and technologies.
  (d) Cooperative agreement on appropriate quotas could no longer be reached.
  (e) All of the above.

Solutions

Chapter Review

1.(c) 2.(e) 3.(e) 4.(e) 5.(e) 6.(d) 7.(e) 8.(c) 9.(e) 10.(a) 11.(c) 12.(b) 13.(d) 14.(c) 15.(c) 16.(d) 17.(c) 18.(a) 19.(b) 20.(b) 21.(e) 22.(a)

Short-Answer Questions

1. Because firms in imperfect competition sell differentiated products, each firm has the potential to increase its market share by using non-price competition to attract consumers away from competitors' products. [For example, restaurants advertise in newspapers.] Perfectly competitive firms, however, produce a homogeneous product, and each firm faces a perfectly elastic demand curve at the going market price. Each firm, therefore, chooses its own market share (by producing $P = MC$). Expenditures on non-price competition would have no effect on market share and would unnecessarily increase costs.

2. Monopolistically competitive firms differ from perfectly competitive firms in that the former produce differentiated products while the latter produce a homogeneous product. Product differentiation makes the monopolistic competitor's demand curve downward sloping (albeit highly elastic, because there are many close substitutes for each firm's product), while the perfect competitor's demand curve is perfectly elastic. The difference in demand curves causes two differences at long-run equilibrium. First, tangency between demand and $LRAC$ in long-run equilibrium (i.e., zero profit) occurs at less than minimum efficient scale (*MES*) in monopolistic competition but at *MES* in perfect competition. Unlike perfect competition, therefore, there is *excess capacity* at long-run equilibrium in monopolistic competition. Second, the negative slope of the demand curve in monopolistic competition means that MR is less than P. In contrast to perfect competition (where $MR = P$), therefore, when the monopolistically competitive firm profit maximizes at $MC = MR$, the resulting price exceeds MC.

3. The suspects face a prisoners' dilemma because jointly they can get a smaller punishment by not confessing, but each individually has an incentive to confess. Both confess, and each gets a bigger punishment than if they had cooperated and not confessed. Similarly, oligopolists facing the prisoners' dilemma can jointly earn greater profit by cooperating, but each individually has an incentive not to cooperate. Non-cooperative behaviour dominates, and each firm makes less profit than the cooperative level as a result. Returning to the suspects, if each knows that confession will result in an even more

severe punishment from the other's "family," the payoff changes and each has an incentive not to confess. The equivalent in oligopoly is when firms can make a credible threat to punish a firm that defects on the cooperative agreement (e.g., by matching any price reduction so the defector makes less profit instead of more). Without a credible threat to punish defectors, however, a collusive agreement is unlikely to last long.

4. One form of tacit collusion is for firms in an oligopoly to match the price changes of a "price leader." Just because we observed similar changes in price by oligopolistic firms, however, would not by itself be evidence of tacit collusion. All of the firms in the oligopoly could simply be reacting to the same changes in market forces.

Exercises

1. (a) $6.00. This is read from the demand curve at the output of 40, where $MC = MR$.
   (b) Profits $= (AR - AC) \times Q = (\$6.00 - \$3.50) \times 40 = \$100$.
   (c) No. This is not a long-run equilibrium situation, because profits will attract the entry of other firms. Entry reduces the market share of existing firms, thereby reducing profit.
   (d) (i) In this case advertising expenditures increase by a fixed amount, so the ATC curve rises because *fixed costs* increase. The MC curve will not change because the advertising cost is a fixed amount. To the extent that advertising is effective, the D and MR curves shift to the right.
       (ii) Profits may or may not increase in the short run, depending on whether the advertising increases total revenues by more than the increase in total costs. If the advertising does increase sales, profit will increase only if the increase in revenue exceeds the extra advertising costs *plus* the extra variable costs of production.
       (iii) No. Freedom of entry will ensure that profit is zero in long-run equilibrium.
       (iv) No. Even if advertising is effective in the short run, any increase in profit can be only *temporary* because profit is zero in long-run equilibrium. You will see monopolistically competitive owner-operated restaurants advertising in newspapers and even on radio, but they will not spend the large amounts that you see spent by oligopolies (e.g., TV advertising for automobiles and breakfast cereals).

2. (a) Long-run equilibrium is illustrated at price P_0 and output q_0 in Figure 11-6.

   Figure 11-6

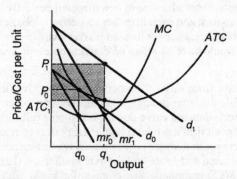

   (b) This firm will get a share of the increased demand for the industry's product, so its demand curve will shift to the right (d_1 in Figure 11-6). Because the associated MR curve also shifts to the right, the profit-maximizing output will increase (to q_1), price will increase (to P_1), and profit will rise from zero to equal the shaded area.
   (c) The positive profits will induce other firms to enter, thereby reducing the firm's market share. This is represented by a leftward shift in the firm's demand curve (and the associated MR curve) until it is again tangent to the average cost curve. Thus, output and price will decrease, and profit will again be zero.
   (d) The leftward shift of the downward-sloping demand curve eventually results in a tangency with the *downward-sloping* part of the ATC curve. This tangency occurs at an output that is less the output at which ATC is at its minimum point, so there is excess capacity. Just because ATC is not

at its minimum (where it would be in perfect competition) does not necessarily imply a less efficient use of society's resources. People want and are willing to pay for the product variety created by monopolistic competition. [For example, do you think consumers would prefer all restaurants to be identical and offer the same food?]

3. **(a)** Joint profits are maximized if both firms adopt moderate advertising budgets. In this case profits for each firm are $80 million, so that joint profits are $160 million.

   (b) No, the cooperative outcome of both firms adopting moderate budgets is unstable. Each firm can do better if it switches to a large budget while its competitor retains moderate expenditures. In the payoff matrix, a firm adopting a large budget would obtain profits of $90 million, while the competitor persisting with the moderate budget would receive $50 million.

   (c) The non-cooperative equilibrium obtains when each firm selects the large advertising budget. Note that this outcome results in the lowest joint profits. It is a Nash equilibrium, however, because neither firm can do better given the choice of its competitor.

   (d) Yes, this is a symmetric game because both "players" (Pepsi and Coke) face identical options (i.e., strategies) and have identical payoffs.

4. **(a)** (i) Profit $= (AR - ATC) \times Q = (\$10 - \$7) \times 80 = \$240$.

      (ii) It maximizes profit by producing 250 units (where P = MC), creating profits of $(\$10 - \$8) \times 250 = \$500$.

   (b) If all other firms abide by the quota, Firm 1's best strategy is to violate the quota and produce 250 units of output. With so many firms in the industry, the extra output of one firm is too small to have any effect on the market supply curve, so price remains unchanged at $10.

   (c) (i) If all other firms attempt to produce 250 units, there is excess supply in the market as a whole ($Q_D < Q_S$ at $10) and market price falls to the competitive equilibrium of $6. If Firm 1 abides by its quota, it makes a profit of $(AR - ATC) \times Q = (\$6 - \$7) \times 80 = -\$80$ (i.e., losses of $80).

      (ii) If Firm 1 also ignores the quota, it produces 120 units and makes zero profit at the competitive market price of $6—better than losses of $80.

   (d) If all other firms violate the quota, therefore, Firm 1's best strategy is to also violate the quota.

   (e) **Figure 11-7**

Profits Payoff Matrix for Firm 1

		Output of Firm 1	
		Quota	Exceed Quota
Output of Other Firms	Quota	$240	$500
	Exceed Quota	–$80	$0

   (f) No. This is a symmetric "game" in which the situation facing every firm is identical to that facing Firm 1. The strategies and payoffs to each strategy are identical across firms. Consequently, every firm will adopt the same strategy as Firm 1, which, as you have seen, is to violate the quota *regardless* of what other firms do. [*Note:* This makes violating the quota a *dominant strategy*.] The Nash equilibrium, therefore, is the competitive market equilibrium. As you see from Figure 11-7, there is no case in which any individual firm would want to abide by the quota. The cartel would fall apart.

5. **(a)** Here are the payoffs: if both firms bid high prices, they each get $5 million; if they both bid low, they each get $3.5 million; and if one firm bids high and the other low, the low bidder gets $7 million. See Figure 11-8 for the matrix.

Figure 11-8

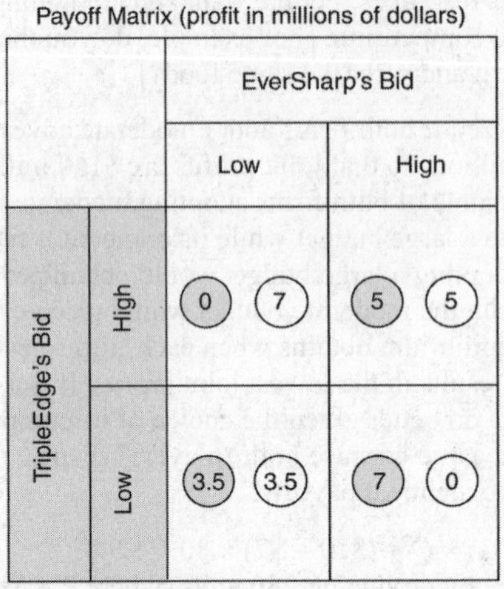

Payoff Matrix (profit in millions of dollars)

(b) Combined profits are greatest if they both submit a high price. Cooperative behaviour (through collusion) would yield each firm a profit of $5 million.

(c) In the non-cooperative outcome each firm submits a low bid, thereby sharing the $7 million contract and receiving $3.5 million each. This is the Nash equilibrium. Consider TripleEdge's (TE) strategic thinking. If EverSharp (ES) bids low, TE will get nothing if it bids high but will get $3.5 million if it too bids low. If ES bids high, TE receives $5 million if it too bids high but gets the entire contract of $7 million if it bids low. Regardless of what ES bids, therefore, it is in TE's best interest to bid low. A symmetric logic applies to ES's strategy.

6. (a) OPEC drastically restricted supply in 1974, eventually raising the price of oil above US$35 per barrel. A combination of factors including new entrants, innovative substitutes, and cheating by cartel members caused the price to drop in the 1980s to a low of $10 per barrel. In the early 1990s OPEC members were still unable to agree on enforceable output quotas, and the price of a barrel remained low. As of July 1999, OPEC had been able to increase the price per barrel of crude by 75 percent since the beginning of the year, to US$21.

(b) This is a classic example of strategic pricing behaviour by the "Big Three" U.S. automakers. It appears that Ford and Chrysler chose to follow the leader in setting their prices: a form of tacit collusion. Increased competition from transnational producers, however, has recently limited the ability of the Big Three to choose their own prices.

(c) This particular price war was triggered by the development of a 386 microprocessor by American Micro Devices that was compatible with Intel's, which, until then, had a virtual monopoly on the production of 386 chips. Intel responded by slashing prices. This is a good example of innovative pressures in oligopoly.

(d) The independent retailers were trying to increase their market share by offering lower prices. This is sometimes caused by market entry or by surplus production at the refinery. Brand-name retailers respond by matching or even undercutting prices, causing further price reductions (i.e., a "price war"). Price wars often result in temporary losses, until the war is over and prices return to their normal levels.

(e) This is an excellent example of non-price competition. Local retailers often cannot offer a good at the same low price as large chains that receive volume discounts on their purchases (e.g., Walmart). Thus, the local retailers were attempting to *differentiate* their product from that of the chains by offering more personal service.

Additional Multiple-Choice Questions

1.(b) 2.(c) 3.(b) 4.(b) 5.(c) 6.(b) 7.(c) 8.(a) 9.(c) 10.(a) 11.(b) 12.(c) 13.(c) 14.(e) 15.(c) 16.(c) 17.(c) 18.(e) 19.(b) 20.(a) 21.(e) 22.(e)

Explanations for the Asterisked Multiple-Choice Questions

1.(b) This is simply a statement of the *excess capacity theorem* in monopolistic competition. Absence of barriers to entry (and exit) means zero economic profits in the long run, which in turn means each individual firm's demand curve will eventually adjust to tangency with its *ATC* curve. Since the demand curve is downward-sloping, the point of tangency must be on the downward-sloping part of the *ATC*—i.e., at an output less than minimum *ATC*. [*Note:* Again, the definition of *capacity* in economics does not mean that the firm would be unable to produce more if it so wished. The economics definition is the output level at *minimum LRAC*.]

4.(b) Like monopolistic competition, perfect competition has no barriers to entry and therefore firms make zero profit in the long run. Because there are many firms all producing an identical (non-differentiated) product, the demand curve facing the individual firm in perfect competition is perfectly elastic. Since this means that the firm can sell as much as it wants to at the market price, any form of non-price competition would have no effect on production, sales, and profit. At worst it would be a waste of resources and at best a waste of time.

5.(c) In setting its own strategy, an oligopolist must take into account not only how it is affected by the current strategies of other firms, but also how the strategy it adopts may cause the other firms to change their strategies. This arises from the interdependency among the few large firms in an oligopolistic industry.

7.(c) While oligopolists may agree to cooperate by charging the same price, each one has an incentive to act strategically and "cheat" on the agreement by reducing price so as to increase its market share and its profits. This creates the conditions for the oligopoly to move to a Nash equilibrium where all firms "cheat" on the agreement (so answer (b) is wrong). Even if a credible threat of punishment maintained cooperation on price, the cartel would break down if technological innovation developed a new or more efficient product preferred by consumers. Answer (a) is wrong because a price-fixing agreement between firms does not need a legal contract, and in fact it is generally illegal in Canada; (e) is wrong because, without strong barriers to entry, other firms would enter and drive down price by increasing supply; (d) is wrong because it is even more difficult to reach agreement and to prevent "cheating" when there are more firms.

8.(a) Advertising expenditures raise potential entrants' costs of competing with existing firms by forcing the entrant with a low market share to spend heavily on advertising in order to make consumers aware of its own brand and to establish a brand image. Low sales combined with high average costs of production place the new entrant at a significant disadvantage relative to existing firms. Potential entrants are faced with the choice of (i) trying to sell at a higher price than their rivals, (ii) charging below cost and making losses for a significant period of time until they have established a large enough market share to take full advantage of economies of scale, or (iii) staying out of the market altogether. Answer (b) is wrong because the output level with the lowest average cost will not be reduced (and may well increase) by increasing average total cost; (c) is wrong because the advertising costs are themselves the barrier to entry and send no signal about industry intentions if entry does in fact occur; (d) and (e) are wrong because advertising is a form of *non-price* competition.

9.(c) *Covert* means concealed or disguised. There is nothing concealed about any of the tactics/strategic behaviour in answers other than (c).

10.(a) The negative slope of the monopolistic competitor's demand curve means quantity demanded increases as price falls (i.e., there are some new sales), while product differentiation implies that some consumers will not switch to a firm's product because they value the characteristics of other firms' products (so (a) is correct and (c) is wrong). What happens to profits depends on where the initial price is relative to the long-run equilibrium price (so (b) and (d) are wrong). If one firm lowering price induces a price change among *competing* firms, it would be a price fall rather than a price rise (so (e) is wrong).

11.(b) Average costs of production are higher in monopolistic competition than in perfect competition because monopolistically competitive firms do not produce at minimum efficient scale in long-run equilibrium. If firms' products were homogeneous, this would not be an efficient use of resources since fewer firms, each producing more output, could produce the same total output at a lower average cost and sell at a lower price. The very fact that firms' products are differentiated in monopolistic competition, however, is the reason why average costs are higher. If people prefer higher prices with more variety to lower prices with less (or no) variety, therefore, monopolistic competition is not inefficient.

13.(c) Individual firms in both market structures have zero economic profit in long-run equilibrium because of the *lack of barriers to entry*. Any short-run economic profits attract entry, which reduces price and market share until economic profit is zero and there is no more incentive to enter. As for the other (wrong) answers, (a) and (d) apply only to perfect competition, (b) does not apply to perfect competition even though it sometimes may be seen in monopolistic competition, albeit far less so than in oligopoly, and (e) applies to neither since there can be economic profits in short-run equilibrium.

14.(e) An oligopolist may be taking account of other firms' behaviour in answers (a) through (d), since what it chooses to do can be influenced by what other firms do. Answer (e) is the best answer, however, since the concept of "strategic" encompasses <u>all</u> cases where a firm's choice of action (i.e., its strategy) is affected by the behaviour of others.

15.(c) This answer recognizes that a cooperative equilibrium would be <u>more profitable</u> than a non-cooperative equilibrium; for example, in the cooperative equilibrium the *industry* could make maximum possible profits by all firms *jointly* producing the monopoly output and charging the monopoly price. As the text repeatedly emphasizes, however, a Nash equilibrium arises from non-cooperative behaviour (so (a) is not false) when each firm *individually* does not have the incentive to cooperate. It is self-enforcing precisely because no individual firm has an incentive to reduce output given the current behaviour of other firms (so (b) and (d) and (e) are not false statements).

17.(c) Only monopoly or oligopoly can produce the high levels of output per firm needed to take advantage of economies of scale that cause a high *MES*. Failure to exploit existing economies of scale would be an inefficient use of society's resources. Except where economies of scale are big enough to create a natural monopoly, oligopoly is the preferred market structure when *MES* is high, since oligopolistic firms have incentives to engage in both price and non-price competition. Most importantly, they have the incentive to compete by engaging in research and development, to create new and better products and more efficient production processes.

18.(e) A good example is Air Canada shortly after its merger with Canadian Airlines in 1999. Air Canada was *accused* of lowering its airfares to *cause a reduction* in competition by driving new smaller airlines out of the market. Air Canada, however, argued that it reduced fares *in response to* the increased competitive pressures from the entry of the new airlines. In some cases, therefore, the direction of cause-and-effect can be difficult to determine. In Air Canada's case, was its price reduction intended to *cause* a reduction in competition or was it the *effect* of an increase in competition?

20.(a) If Firm 1 bids $150, Firm 2 gets nothing if it bids $250 but $75 if it bids $150. If Firm 1 bids $250, Firm 2 will get only $125 if it also bids $250 but the whole $150 if it bids $150. Regardless of whether Firm 1 bids $150 or $250, therefore, Firm 2's payoff is bigger if it bids $150. Firm 1 is faced with exactly the same payoffs (i.e., this is a symmetric "game"), so in the non-cooperative outcome they both bid $150. Since either firm would be better off bidding $150 even if it knew the other would bid $250, both bidding $250 is not a Nash equilibrium.

21.(e) The firm's perfectly elastic demand curve means that it can sell *as much as it wants to* at the prevailing market price. Consequently, because of the perfectly elastic demand curve, the amount it is able to sell will be unaffected either by charging a lower price (which reduces average revenue) or by spending on non-price competition (which increases average total costs). In either case economic profits would fall.

22.(e) OPEC's quotas increased price and profits by reducing supply. The higher price of oil had several effects, as follows. It became profitable for petroleum firms to increase the exploration for and development of new oil supplies—i.e., the equivalent of "entry" into the industry. It created incentives to develop alternative energy sources—i.e., an increase in demand for alternatives in response to the increase in price of the substitute good, oil. It created incentives for producers of other goods to make more efficient use of oil in their production processes—i.e., an increase in the cost of a factor of production causing factor substitution and production innovation (e.g., the switch from low-compression automobile engines to the much more fuel-efficient high-compression engines in North America). The behaviour of OPEC members themselves was also affected, since higher prices made it more profitable to "cheat" by producing in excess of agreed quotas. All these effects are predictable from the microeconomic theory you have learned in this chapter.

Economic Efficiency and Public Policy

12

Chapter Overview

In the last three chapters you looked at different types of firms and industries individually. Now, in Chapter 12, you develop the basic analysis needed to <u>compare</u> these different types in terms of their relative "efficiency" for the economy and society as a whole. It is a very important chapter not only because it shows what this comparison implies for a broad approach to public policy, but also because it provides the platform from which Chapter 16 moves on to examine some specific situations where using this broad approach as the sole criterion for government intervention can be inappropriate and/or inadequate. Indeed, you will find situations where it simply can't address the issue at all. Consequently, you need to understand this chapter not only because of what it says about public policy but also to fully appreciate the issues and policies discussed in Chapter 16.

Economists distinguish between *productive efficiency* and *allocative efficiency*. **Productive efficiency** in an <u>industry</u> occurs when its total output is being produced at the lowest possible cost, for which two conditions must be met. First, every firm in the industry is on (rather than above) its long-run average cost curve. Second, the industry's total output is split among the firms in the industry such that the marginal cost of production is the same for all firms. Productive efficiency for the <u>economy as a whole</u> requires that all industries satisfy these two conditions and that the economy's resources are fully employed. Only then is the economy on its production possibilities boundary (which you first encountered in Chapter 1), so that increasing the production of one good can be done only by reducing the production of other goods. **Allocative efficiency** involves producing the best <u>mix</u> of products for society, which again requires that two conditions are satisfied. First, the economy must be productively efficient (i.e., on its production possibilities boundary, rather than inside it).

Second, it must be at the <u>specific point</u> on its production possibilities boundary where price equals marginal cost for every product. Only at this specific point are the economy's resources *efficiently allocated* across the multitude of goods and services to give the optimal amount of each one. [*Note:* Such an efficient allocation of the economy's resources is also called a *Pareto efficient* allocation.]

In Chapter 5 you used the concept of *market efficiency* to identify the level of output that maximizes total (economic) surplus in an individual market. Now, in Chapter 12, you will see that maximum total surplus in the individual market (i.e., the industry) is actually achieved when it is producing the output at which price equals marginal cost. Thus, the industry that achieves market efficiency is producing the level of output consistent with the condition for allocative efficiency in the economy as a whole. Consequently, although allocative efficiency in the economy requires that <u>all</u> firms and industries produce where price equals marginal cost, when any individual firm or industry is producing where its price equals its marginal cost we say it is producing <u>its own</u> *allocatively efficient* level of output. Since you understand more about firms' cost curves and profit-maximizing behaviour than you did in Chapter 5, therefore, the *allocatively efficient* level of output is now used instead of *market efficiency*. Also, this chapter breaks down total surplus into its <u>two</u> components, **consumer surplus** (which you first encountered in Chapter 6) and **producer surplus**; allocative efficiency is achieved when the <u>sum</u> of these two components is maximized, regardless of its <u>distribution</u> between the two.

Even when productive efficiency holds in all of the market structures you have studied, allocative efficiency holds only in perfect competition. Thus, the goal of allocative efficiency (often simply called economic efficiency) provides the rationale for government to promote competition. There are two broad types of policies designed to enhance allocative efficiency in monopolistic and imperfectly competitive markets: *economic regulation* and *competition policy*. Regulation of price and entry conditions are used in both monopolistic and oligopolistic market structures, with regulation of **natural monopolies** being a special case. Competition policy applies mainly to oligopolistic markets.

Canadian competition policy seeks to protect consumers by preventing exploitation of market power not justified by gains to international competitiveness or to efficiency via exploitation of economies of scale. Changes were made to the *Competition Act* in 2009 with these objectives in mind.

Hints and Tips

The following may help you avoid some of the most common errors on examinations.

✓ Economic (i.e., allocative) efficiency encompasses <u>both</u> the efficient use of resources to produce a given good or service <u>and</u> the mix of goods and services produced. The mix of output, or how resources are allocated among the different goods and services, should be the one that gives the most "value" to society.

✓ Comparisons of allocative efficiency between perfect competition and monopoly in this chapter generally assume that costs of production are the same in both market structures. Later in the text, however, the comparisons become more complex when economies of scale and externalities are introduced. Recognize this especially when you are revising this chapter after having read later chapters.

✓ *Extensions in Theory 12-2* in the text puts a broader perspective on this chapter's analysis of allocative inefficiency and market power. It explains the potential trade-off between (i) market power generating allocative inefficiency at <u>a point in time</u> while (ii) encouraging better products and lower prices <u>over time</u>. This trade-off is one of the links between Chapter 12 and some of the policy choices examined in Chapter 16.

✓ Understand the difference between average-cost pricing and marginal-cost pricing. Average-cost pricing regulation is generally aimed at controlling profits, while marginal-cost pricing seeks to promote allocative efficiency.

Chapter Review

Productive and Allocative Efficiency

Economic efficiency requires both **productive efficiency** and **allocative efficiency**; but, since productive efficiency is a prerequisite for allocative efficiency, economic efficiency and allocative efficiency mean the same thing. Productive efficiency for the firm requires that it use the least-cost method of producing its chosen output (i.e., is on its *LRAC* curve). Productive efficiency for the industry requires that all firms in the industry are productively efficient <u>and</u> that the marginal costs of production are equal for all firms in the same industry. Productive efficiency for the overall economy requires that all industries are productively efficient <u>and</u> the economy's resources are fully employed. All points on the economy's production possibilities boundary are productively efficient; any point inside the boundary is not, since more of one good can be produced without having to produce less of other goods. Allocative efficiency means that all of the economy's resources are allocated such that the combination of goods produced is the one which gives the maximum benefit to society. This in turn requires that the *marginal values* of all goods and services produced in the economy are equal to their respective *marginal costs*. Since price reflects the value of the marginal unit of a good to consumers, this condition can be restated as price equals marginal costs for all goods and services, which occurs at only one point on the production possibilities boundary. Since allocative efficiency also maximizes the sum of producer and consumer surplus, any firm or industry that does not produce its allocatively efficient level of output creates a *deadweight loss* in total economic surplus. This section demonstrates why perfect competition meets the criterion for allocative efficiency while monopoly and other market structures do not. The analysis is taken further in *Extensions in Theory 12-2*; although market power creates deadweight loss <u>at a point in time,</u> it may nevertheless benefit the economy and the consumer <u>over time</u> by generating better products and lower prices.

1. **The criterion that distinguishes allocative efficiency from productive efficiency is that**
    (a)   there are no unemployed resources.
    (b)   all firms are producing at the lowest attainable cost.
    (c)   prices are as low as possible.
    (d)   marginal value equals marginal cost.
    (e)   profits are maximized.

2. **If two firms are producing the same product at different marginal costs, then**
    (a)   a reallocation of output between the firms can lower the industry's total cost.
    (b)   neither firm is producing its output at the lowest attainable cost.
    (c)   some resources must be unemployed.
    (d)   one firm must be producing where *P* does not equal *MC*.
    (e)   one firm is not maximizing profits.

3. **Producer surplus is negative**
   (a)   when firms are not making any profit.
   (b)   on all units of output produced at anything other than minimum *LRAC*.
   (c)   when less than the allocatively efficient quantity is being produced.
   (d)   on units of output sold at a price less than marginal cost.
   (e)   if a firm is not using the least-cost method of production.

4. **Productive efficiency holds**
   (a)   when $P = MC$ for perfect competition.
   (b)   only for perfect competition and monopolistic competition where long-run profits are zero.
   (c)   for monopolies only when economies of scale are fully exploited.
   (d))   throughout the market economy if the objective of firms is to maximize profits.
   (e)   only when firms produce at the minimum point of the *LRAC* curve.

5. **A firm's producer surplus can be calculated as**
   (a)   profits.
   (b)   retained earnings.
   (c)   total revenue minus total costs.
   (d)   total revenue minus total variable costs.
   (e)   total revenue minus total fixed costs.

6. **The deadweight loss of monopoly is**
   (a)   its fixed cost.
   (b)   any negative profit due to temporary decreases in demand.
   (c)   the forgone surplus due to the allocatively inefficient monopoly output level.
   (d)   the cost of maintaining effective barriers to entry.
   (e)   the extra administrative costs of operating a large firm.

7. **If the whole economy were perfectly competitive and there were no externalities, allocative efficiency**
   (a)   would not be achieved because the market for a product does not take account of costs or benefits to people other than its consumers and producers.
   (b)   would be achieved through profit maximization at $MC = MR$, because $P = MR$ on a perfectly elastic demand curve.
   (c)   would not be achieved since perfectly competitive firms make zero profit in long-run equilibrium.
   (d)   would be achieved even if firms were not productively efficient.
   (e)   would not be achieved since producer surplus would not be maximized.

8. **What is the most *basic* reason why an unregulated profit-maximizing monopoly will not produce its allocatively efficient level of output?**
   (a)   Lack of competition means it does not need to be productively efficient.
   (b)   It does not produce where $MC = MR$.
   (c)   It need not produce at the minimum point on its long-run average cost curve.
   (d))   It faces a downward-sloping demand curve so $MR < P$.
   (e)   It makes economic profit in the long run.

9. **At its most general level, the term *market failure* refers to a situation where an industry**
    (a) fails to produce its profit-maximizing level of output.
    (b) does not produce where price equals its own marginal costs of production.
    (c) enables firms to make economic profits in the long run.
    (d) fails to produce the level of output at which price equals society's marginal cost.
    (e) makes economic losses due to lack of demand for the product.

Economic Regulation to Promote Efficiency

Here you develop an appreciation of the issues involved in government regulation of a natural monopoly and oligopolies. A *natural monopoly* arises when there are such large economies of scale that the most efficient use of society's resources can be achieved only when all output is produced by a single firm. Where this results in a continuously downward-sloping *LRAC* curve throughout the entire range of the demand curve (a *falling-cost* natural monopoly) a conflict arises because *MC* is less than *LRAC*. As usual, allocative efficiency is at the output level where $P = MC$, but since $MC < LRAC$ then allocative efficiency can be achieved only when the firm is making economic losses (i.e., $P = MC$ but $MC < LRAC$ so $P < LRAC$).

This section explains two types of price regulation, *average-cost pricing* and *marginal-cost pricing*, under which the natural monopoly would benefit society by exploiting more economies of scale than it would if it were unregulated. It also explains how a *two-part tariff* could resolve the conflict between allocative efficiency and economic losses. Nevertheless, there are complications: even where regulation of monopolies and large oligopolistic firms would obviously benefit society by increasing economic efficiency in the *short run*, there can be adverse *long-run* implications for investment and innovation. Following this discussion of the pros and cons of regulating large firms, the section closes with a brief mention of government interventions resulting from the 2008 financial crisis and the subsequent global recession. [*Note: Applying Economic Concepts 12-1* in the text provides a concise review of the topically important issue of government regulations in the Canadian banking system, and their implications for the trade-off between risk and confidence.]

10. **Average-cost pricing for a falling-cost natural monopoly results in**
    (a) zero profits.
    (b) allocative efficiency.
    (c) production at the optimal output.
    (d) $P = MC$.
    (e) *both* allocative efficiency *and* zero profits.

11. **The larger the minimum efficient scale of firms, *ceteris paribus*,**
    (a) the more likely a concentrated market will improve productive efficiency.
    (b) the greater the tendency toward natural monopoly.
    (c) the greater the advantages of large-scale production.
    (d) the smaller the number of firms in an industry.
    (e) All of the above.

12. **If a falling-cost natural monopoly is regulated to charge a price equal to marginal cost, the resulting level of output is**
    (a) allocatively efficient, and a positive profit is earned.
    (b) allocatively efficient, and the firm must be paid a subsidy or it will go out of business.
    (c) less than the allocatively efficient level, and profits are zero.
    (d) less than the allocatively efficient level, and negative profits are earned.
    (e) greater than the allocatively efficient level, and negative profits are earned.

13. **The main objective behind the regulation of natural monopolies such as public utilities is to**
    (a) guarantee consumers a low price.
    (b) have government ownership in key economic sectors.
    (c) achieve the advantages of large-scale production.
    (d) erect dependable and effective barriers to entry.
    (e) protect domestic industries from foreign competition.

14. **With a two-part tariff where one part sets $P = MC$, a regulated falling-cost natural monopoly can, in principle,**
    (a) cover fixed costs with the other part.
    (b) cover variable costs with the other part.
    (c) cover total costs with the $P = MC$ part and make economic profit from the other part.
    (d) make economic profit without being allocatively efficient.
    (e) still not simultaneously achieve productive efficiency, allocative efficiency, and economic profit.

15. **If demand for the product is increasing, how can average-cost pricing result in economic inefficiency in the long run?**
    (a) By encouraging entry it reduces the exploitation of economies of scale.
    (b) Quantity demanded and produced rises above the level where $P = MC$.
    (c) As the demand curve shifts to the right firms don't produce on the new curve.
    (d) In a falling-cost natural monopoly, the increase in demand increases price.
    (e) Preventing firms from making economic profits reduces the incentive for investment and innovation.

16. **In recent years, what has helped to reduce the market power of some natural monopolies?**
    (a) Technological change that facilitated creative destruction.
    (b) Investment that reduced costs by increasing the monopoly's productive capacity.
    (c) Technological change that increased competition by increasing economies of scale.
    (d) Technological change that reduced natural barriers to entry caused by economies of scale.
    (e) Technological change that *both* created new products *and* reduced natural barriers to entry.

17. **Practical problems with regulation of prices and profits include which of the following?**
    (a) Difficulty in accurately measuring *LRAC* and *MC* curves.
    (b) Preventing profit-maximization reduces the incentive for cost-minimization.
    (c) Lack of incentive for investment and innovation.
    (d) The opportunity costs of government resources used to monitor the regulated firms.
    (e) All of the above.

18. **Which of the following is *not* one of the forces encouraging deregulation and privatization in advanced industrial nations?**
    (a) The experience that many regulatory bodies serve to reduce competition rather than increase it.
    (b) The growing evidence that nationalized industries do not enhance productivity growth or allocative efficiency.
    (c) Increased pressures from world competition.
    (d) The conclusion that industrial performance improves when an oligopoly is replaced by a nationalized monopoly.
    (e) Private companies generate economic growth through invention and innovation.

19. **Contrary to their stated objectives, many regulatory agencies have pursued policies that**
    (a) protect the consumer.
    (b) reflect a concern for existing firms and limit the entry of potential competitors.
    (c) concern the trade-offs between domestic and foreign trade policy.
    (d) deal with work safety and environmental issues.
    (e) defend the market mechanism against monopoly control.

Canadian Competition Policy

This section gives you an appreciation of the historical development of competition policy in Canada and an understanding of its current structure and objectives. The two main challenges for competition policy created by continuing globalization are also reviewed.

20. **The objective of Canadian competition policy is to**
    (a) improve profits of Canadian firms by restricting foreign competition.
    (b) prevent unnecessary mergers and collusive practices.
    (c) give consumers more information about the differences between similar products.
    (d) subsidize Canadian firms so they can compete in world markets.
    (e) encourage firms to collude if, by doing so, they can increase profits.

21. **The lack of success in preventing mergers in Canada prior to 1986 was partly due to**
    (a) the inability of civil actions to cope with complex economic issues.
    (b) the standard of proof required by the criminal justice system.
    (c) the fact that the fines were rather small.
    (d) the reluctance of Canadian courts to assess economic evidence.
    (e) *both* the standard of proof required *and* the inability to meet this standard for complex economic issues.

22. **Which of the following was an important provision of the *Competition Act* of 1986?**
    (a) Advertising claims of product quality must be based on adequate tests.
    (b) Civil actions can be brought against firms using unfair trading practices.
    (c) The Competition Tribunal was disbanded.
    (d) Mergers were prohibited.
    (e) It prohibited both mergers and inaccurate advertising.

23. **In 2009 the Canadian federal government's objectives when considering reform of the 1986 *Competition Act* included which of the following?**
    (a) Make it easier for finance companies to form cartels.
    (b) Make it easier for finance companies to merge as long as they do not form a cartel.
    (c) Make it easier for firms with monopoly power to raise money for research and development by using restrictive pricing policies.
    (d) Make advertising more honest and informative.
    (e) Enforce average-cost pricing.

Short-Answer Questions

1. Why is productive efficiency a necessary condition for allocative efficiency?

2. State whether the following statement is true or false, and explain your answer. "Productive efficiency requires that, within an industry, output be allocated such that average costs of production are equal across firms."

3. Explain why the notion that perfect competition creates allocative efficiency is actually a theoretical ideal in the real world.

4. Why is there a conflict between profit and allocative efficiency in natural monopolies with continuously downward-sloping *LRAC* curves?

5. What is rate-of-return regulation, why is it used, and what problems does it give rise to?

6. What are the two main experiences that have led to skepticism about the need for and usefulness of direct control of oligopolistic firms? Briefly explain the economics.

7. On the one hand you are told that market power creates deadweight loss and allocative inefficiency. On the other you are told that market power gives firms the incentive for research and development that increases living standards. How can we reconcile these two arguments? [*Hint:* Refer to *Extensions in Theory 12-2* in the text.]

Exercises

1. **Allocative Efficiency and the Sum of Consumer and Producer Surplus**
   In Figure 12-1, *DD* is the market demand curve, and *DM* is the associated marginal revenue curve. The line *AN* is the supply curve for a competitive industry but also the marginal cost curve for a monopolist.

   Figure 12-1

   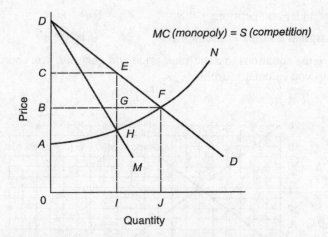

   (a) For perfect competition, what are the values of the following?

   (i) Equilibrium price is _____ and quantity is _____.
   (ii) Consumer surplus is _____.
   (iii) Producer surplus _____.
   (iv) The sum of producer and consumer surplus is _____.

   (b) For monopoly, what are the values of the following?

   (i) Equilibrium price is _____ and quantity is _____.
   (ii) Consumer surplus is _____.
   (iii) Producer surplus is _____.
   (iv) The sum of producer and consumer surplus is _____.

   (c) If the competitive industry is monopolized with no change in costs of production,

   (i) the deadweight loss from monopoly is _____.
   (ii) the surplus transferred from consumers to producers is _____.
   (iii) the reduction in consumer surplus is _____.
   (iv) the increase in producer surplus is _____.

(d) Given your answers in (c), briefly explain how you know that

    (i)   producer surplus must have increased.

    (ii)   the increase in producer surplus must be less than the fall in consumer surplus.

2. **Monopoly Versus Perfect Competition: Economies of Scale and Externalities**

This exercise demonstrates that monopoly need not be less allocatively efficient than perfect competition in all circumstances and teaches you to recognize the assumptions that underlie the standard comparison of allocative efficiency between the two types of industries. [*Note:* The exercise is not as long as it looks and is well worth the time required.]

In this exercise you examine the allocative efficiency of monopoly versus perfect competition when (i) there are negative externalities, and (ii) there are economies of scale in production. You can determine the price and quantity outcomes using the scale diagram of Figure 12-2 and/or the following algebraic equations:

Market demand: $Q_D = 200 - 10P$ (so $P = 20 - 0.1Q_D$)

Market supply under competition: $Q_S = 10P - 80$ (so $P = 0.1Q_S + 8$)

Equivalent marginal cost under monopoly: $MC = 0.1Q_S + 8$

Even if you use the equations to determine price and quantity, you should refer to the diagram to help you calculate surplus.

Figure 12-2

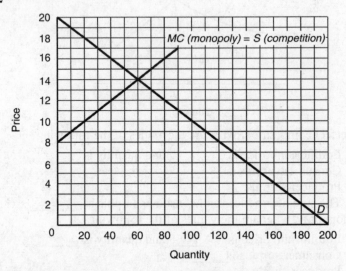

(a) Under perfect competition, what are the following values?

    (i)   Equilibrium price is _____ and equilibrium quantity is _____.

    (ii)   Consumer surplus is _____, producer surplus is _____, and total surplus is _____.

Now the industry is monopolized. [*Hint:* Recall that the monopolist's *MR* curve has the same price axis intercept as the demand curve and twice the slope.]

(b) If there is no change in costs, what is the monopolist's profit-maximizing price and quantity? Is the monopolist producing the allocatively efficient level of output? Explain. [*Note:* In your explanation, compare *P* with *MC* and also calculate the effect on total surplus.] [*Hint:* Producer surplus is total revenue minus total variable cost, and total variable cost is calculated as the area under the *MC* curve.]

(c) Now assume that there is a negative externality of $4 per unit of output. [*Hint:* The externality increases the marginal cost *to society* by $4 per unit but does not change the marginal cost curve that producers use to make their profit-maximizing decisions. Draw society's marginal cost curve by shifting the *MC* curve in Figure 12-2 vertically up by $4.]

    (i)   What is society's allocatively efficient level of output? Explain.

    (ii)   Compare and contrast the allocative efficiency of monopoly and competition when this externality is present. Explain.

    (iii)   Would your conclusions in (ii) change if the production or consumption of the good generated positive rather than negative externalities for society? Explain.

(d) This time there is no externality, but monopolization of the industry reduces the marginal cost of production by $6 per unit (by exploiting economies of scale).

    (i)   Draw the monopolist's new *MC* curve in Figure 12-2. Compare the prices and outputs of monopoly and competition.

    (ii)   Does consumer surplus change when this industry is monopolized? Does producer surplus change? Does total surplus change?

    (iii)   Which is more allocatively efficient, monopoly or perfect competition? Why?

    (iv)   Is the monopoly being as allocatively efficient as it could be? Explain.

3. **Regulatory Pricing in a Natural Monopoly**
This exercise reviews the implications of regulatory pricing for a falling-cost natural monopoly.

Figure 12-3 shows a market demand curve and a firm's cost structure. The cost structure is characterized by constant marginal cost (*MC*) and a large set-up cost so that long-run average cost (*LRAC*) is continuously declining.

Figure 12-3

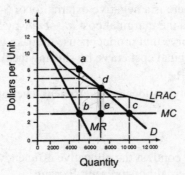

(a) What is the allocatively efficient level of output? Why?

    c → 10 000

(b) What are the unregulated monopolist's profit-maximizing price and quantity in this market? What is the associated profit level?

    5000 @ $8

(c) What is the resulting deadweight loss?

    abc

(d) Suppose that a regulatory agency attempted to induce this monopolist to produce the allocatively efficient output by restricting price to equal marginal cost. Would the agency be successful? Why or why not?

    P=MC < AC ∴ no, firm goes out of business

(e) As an alternative, suppose that the agency imposes average-cost pricing on the monopolist. What are the regulated price and the resulting quantity?

    P=ATC ⇒ $6, 7000 = Q

(f) Compare the profit and deadweight loss under average-cost pricing in (e) and under marginal-cost pricing in (d).

(g) How might the conflict between allocative efficiency and economic losses in a falling-cost natural monopoly be resolved using

(i) price discrimination by units of output?

(ii) a two-part tariff?

4. Perverse Regulations for Consumers

The text notes that regulation can sometimes be used to protect firms from competition, thereby creating market power rather than controlling it. An interesting example of this is seen in many cities, where the number of taxicabs is restricted. This exercise uses New York City as the example.

Before 1937 there was free entry into taxicab operation in New York City. In 1937, however, New York City passed a law freezing the number of taxicab licences (called medallions) at 11 797. (Taxicabs without medallions are not supposed to pick up people who hail cabs from the street.) When the law was passed, existing taxicab operators were granted a medallion by virtue of already being in the industry, and the price of obtaining a taxicab medallion from the city was near zero. The medallions became the private property of these operators, to use or sell as they pleased. New entrants had to purchase a medallion from an existing operator at whatever price the market determined. As demand for taxi services rose, the market value of a medallion rose, reaching $100 000 in December 1985. Many medallions are traded each year, with banks often giving mortgages for their purchase.

(a) Sketch a graph to illustrate why the price of medallions has increased over time. Why is the increase in market price likely to continue?

(b) If taxicab fares are set by the city (as is generally the case), and assuming the restriction on the number of taxicabs has no effect on the rates set, are consumers hurt by restricting the number of taxicabs?

(c) Why should new entrants be willing to pay such high prices to operate a taxicab?

(d) If the supply of medallions were to remain unchanged, would economic profit be made by

(i) new entrants?

       (ii) holders of medallions who had already paid off any loan they took out to purchase the medallions?

5. Impact of a Cost Increase: Monopoly Versus Perfect Competition

A perfectly competitive market is illustrated in the first graph in Figure 12-4, while a monopolistic market is presented in the second. Note that each market faces an identical demand curve.

Figure 12-4

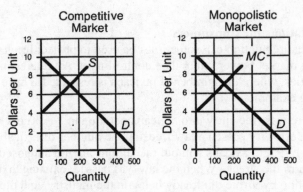

(a) What are the equilibrium levels of price and output in the perfectly competitive market? In the monopoly market?

(b) What shift in the monopolist's MC curve (relative to perfect competition) is required to have the levels of price and output the same in both market structures?

(c) Starting from the equilibrium situations depicted in (a), illustrate that both price and quantity would change by less in the monopolistic market than in the perfectly competitive market in response to an increase in marginal costs by $2 per unit of output.

6. Monopolization of a Competitive Industry

This exercise investigates the impact on consumer and producer surplus from the monopolization of an otherwise perfectly competitive industry. It is similar to Exercise 2 but does not investigate externalities and economies of scale. [*Note:* You can solve using either (or both) the equations or the scale diagrams in Figures 12-5 and 12-6.]

The demand curve for a product is $Q^d = 90\ 000 - 1000P$, where P (price) is expressed in dollars. In a competitive market, the supply curve is given by $Q^s = 2000P - 45\ 000$ (with supply being zero at $P \leq \$22.50$). Remember, the competitive supply curve is the horizontal summation of the firms' marginal cost curves above the minimum average variable cost (here, $22.50).

(a) Determine the equilibrium price and quantity of the product necessary for allocative efficiency. (Use the grid in Figure 12-5 or solve algebraically.)

(b) Indicate consumer and producer surpluses (total net benefits, in dollars) under allocative efficiency.

Figure 12-5

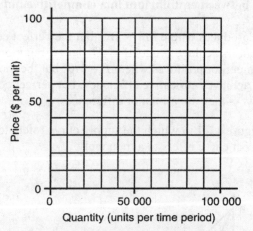

(c) Suppose that the market for this product were monopolized. The monopolist's counterpart to the competitive supply curve is $MC = 22.5 + 0.0005Q$. [*Note:* The *MC* curve you draw from this equation is identical to the *S* curve you drew in part (a).]. Determine the quantity that would be supplied by the monopolist and the market price. Indicate the associated consumer and producer surpluses on the grid in Figure 12-6.

Figure 12-6

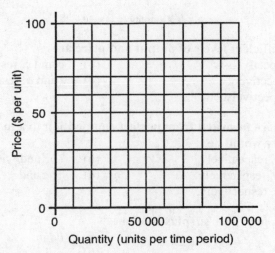

(d) Compare producer surplus, consumer surplus, and total net benefits (i.e., total surplus) in (c) with those obtained in (b).

Additional Multiple-Choice Questions

*1.   **A major difference between equilibrium in a competitive industry and a monopoly is that**
   (a)   the monopoly produces where $MR = MC$, but the perfect competitor does not.
   (b)   perfect competitors achieve productive efficiency, but monopolies do not.
   (c)   the perfect competitor produces where $P = MC$, but the monopoly does not.
   (d)   the monopoly achieves allocative efficiency, but perfect competition does not.
   (e)   All of the above—they are all major differences.

Questions 2 to 5 refer to Figure 12-7 in which the supply curve refers to a perfectly competitive industry and the marginal cost curve refers to a monopoly.

Figure 12-7

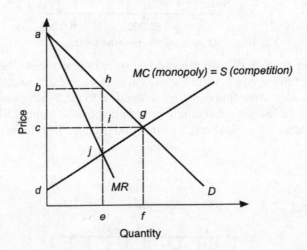

2.   **The allocatively efficient levels of output and price are**
   (a)   *e* and *b*, respectively.   (b)   *e* and *c*, respectively.
   (c)   *f* and *c*, respectively.   (d)   *f* and *a*, respectively.
   (e)   *e* and *d*, respectively.

3.   **If this industry were to switch from perfect competition to a monopoly, the changes in price and quantity would be**
   (a)   +*cb* and –*fe*, respectively.   (b)   –*bc* and –*fe*, respectively.
   (c)   +*db* and +*ef*, respectively.   (d)   +*dc* and +*ef*, respectively.
   (e)   +*ca* and –*fe*, respectively.

4.   **Under monopoly, producer surplus is area**
   (a)   *bdjh*.   (b)   *bdgh*.
   (c)   *cdg*.   (d)   *adj*.
   (e)   *adg*.

5.   **If price increases from *c* to *b*, and therefore quantity demanded is reduced from *f* to *e*, consumer surplus is reduced by area**
   (a)   *hig*.   (b)   *bcih*.
   (c)   *hjg*.   (d)   *bcgh*.
   (e)   *efgh*.

*6. **In unregulated markets, the condition for allocative efficiency is satisfied under only perfect competition because only this market structure results in**
   (a) long-run profits equal to zero.
   (b) $P = MC$.
   (c) complete freedom of entry and exit.
   (d) maximization of profits through cutthroat competition.
   (e) productive efficiency.

*7. **Productive efficiency requires that**
   (a) each firm produces its output at the lowest possible cost.
   (b) resources cannot be transferred out of an industry without reducing the industry's output.
   (c) the total cost of producing the industry's output is minimized.
   (d) marginal cost of production be equalized across all firms in the industry.
   (e) All of the above are required for productive efficiency in an industry.

*8. **Compared to unregulated monopoly, oligopoly is likely to be _____ allocatively efficient because _____.**
   (a) less; it creates less consumer surplus
   (b) more; it creates more consumer surplus
   (c) more; each firm producing at $MC = MR$ is closer to minimum efficient scale
   (d) more; it has greater incentive for innovation
   (e) less; it can make greater profit through collusive behaviour than non-cooperative behaviour

*9. **In reviewing a proposed merger, the main issue that the Competition Bureau should consider is**
   (a) the trade-off between productive efficiency and allocative efficiency.
   (b) the number of firms in the industry.
   (c) the concentration ratio of the largest six firms in the industry.
   (d) the extent to which the industry needs protection from foreign competition.
   (e) the possible cost reductions versus potential reduction in competition.

Questions 10 to 16 refer to Figure 12-8, which depicts a firm with a constant marginal cost curve and a declining long-run average cost (*LRAC*)

Figure 12-8

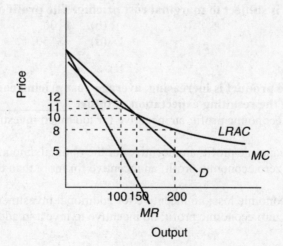

*10. The firm depicted above can be classified as
   (a)   a constant-cost natural monopoly.
   (b)   a declining-cost natural monopoly.
   (c)   an oligopoly.
   (d)   monopolistically competitive.
   (e)   perfectly competitive.

*11. If this firm were *not* subject to regulation, its output and profit would be
   (a)   100 units; $100.   (b)   150 units; $750.
   (c)   100 units; $700.   (d)   100 units; $12.
   (e)   200 units; $600.

*12. If this firm were *not* subject to regulation, the resulting deadweight loss would be
   (a)   zero.   (b) $100.
   (c) $350.   (d) $700.
   (e) $1000.

13. If this firm were subject to marginal cost price regulation, its output and profit would be
   (a)   100 units; $100.   (b)   100 units; $0.
   (c)   100 units; $700.   (d)   200 units; $0.
   (e)   200 units; –$600.

14. If this firm were subject to average cost price regulation, its output and profit would be
   (a)   100 units; $100.   (b)   150 units; $0.
   (c)   150 units; $750.   (d)   150 units; –$750.
   (e)   200 units; $0.

*15. The deadweight losses resulting from marginal-cost pricing and average-cost pricing are
   (a) $150 and $150, respectively.   (b) $100 and $150, respectively.
   (c) $0 and $125, respectively.   (d) $125 and $150, respectively.
   (e) $0 and $100, respectively.

*16. Suppose the firm is regulated by the following two-part tariff. If it produces 200 units, it is permitted to sell the first 100 units of output at whatever price it wishes, but any output after that is subject to marginal cost pricing. The profit of this firm would be
   (a) $0.   (b) $100.
   (c) $150.   (d)   –$150.
   (e)   –$600.

*17. If demand for the product is increasing, average-cost pricing can be _____ in the long run because the resulting expectation of future _____ creates _____.
   (a)   inefficient; economic profit; an incentive for too much investment in productive capacity.
   (b)   efficient; economic profit; an incentive for the optimal amount of investment.
   (c)   inefficient; zero economic profit; an incentive for more than the optimal amount of investment.
   (d)   efficient; economic loss; no incentive for additional investment.
   (e)   inefficient; zero economic profit; no incentive to invest in additional capital stock.

*18.   Rate-of-return regulation seeks to achieve the same result as _____ by creating
       _____, but has the drawback that it _____.
       (a)   marginal-cost pricing; allocative efficiency; is difficult to measure costs
       (b)   average-cost pricing; more competition; allows positive economic profit
       (c)   perfect competition; productive efficiency; creates economic losses
       (d)   marginal-cost pricing; monopolistic competition; ignores international competition
       (e)   average-cost pricing; zero economic profit; reduces incentives for cost minimization

*19.   Grolks are produced by an unregulated profit-maximizing monopoly with large
       economies of scale. If the Grolk monopoly could be broken up into so many small
       firms that it would become a perfectly competitive industry, which of the following
       comparisons would be true?
       (a)   Perfect competition would be more productively efficient than monopoly.
       (b)   Perfect competition would be more productively and allocatively efficient than
             monopoly.
       (c)   Monopoly could be more allocatively efficient than perfect competition, though not
             as allocatively efficient as possible for the monopoly.
       (d)   Total surplus would be greater under perfect competition than under monopoly.
       (e)   Since total surplus increases as allocative efficiency improves, perfect competition
             would have *both* greater total surplus *and* greater allocative efficiency.

*20.   Frangles are initially produced by a perfectly competitive industry in long-run
       equilibrium. Then all Frangle-producing firms are bought by one individual with no
       change to the production functions, the prices of inputs, and the number of plants
       (factories) producing Frangles. Output and pricing of Frangles, however, is now
       dictated by the new owner acting as a profit-maximizing monopolist. Which of the
       following is true as a result of this change?
       (a)   The conditions for productive efficiency are no longer satisfied because the plants do
             not now operate at minimum *LRAC*.
       (b)   In the absence of externalities, there is no change in the allocative efficiency of
             society's scarce resources to the production of Frangles.
       (c)   If positive externalities are present, allocative efficiency could improve.
       (d)   If negative externalities are present, allocative efficiency could improve.
       (e)   Regardless of whether or not there are any externalities, both productive and
             allocative efficiency will suffer.

*21.   Which of the following results when average-cost pricing is imposed on a monopoly?
       (a)   Accounting profits become negative.
       (d)   Buying gold-plated water coolers for executives does not reduce profitability.
       (c)   Allocative inefficiency in a natural monopoly but not in a regular monopoly.
       (d)   The resulting allocative inefficiency generates negative economic profits.
       (e)   Both (a) and (d) are correct.

*22.   (*Extensions in Theory 12-2* in the text) The deadweight loss of monopoly when
       compared to perfect competition
       (a)   is a dynamic concept that assumes increasing productivity from innovation.
       (b)   is a static concept that does not take account of incentives for future innovation.
       (c)   is a dynamic concept that takes account of incentives for future innovation.
       (d)   assumes that monopoly profits finance research and development.
       (e)   does not apply because all large firms are oligopolists.

Solutions

Chapter Review

1.(d) **2.**(a) **3.**(d) **4.**(d) **5.**(d) **6.**(c) **7.**(b) **8.**(d) **9.**(d) **10.**(a) **11.**(e) **12.**(b) **13.**(c) **14.**(a) **15.**(e). **16.**(e) **17.**(e) **18.**(d) **19.**(b) **20.**(b) **21.**(e) **22.**(b) **23.**(d)

Short-Answer Questions

1. The allocatively efficient combination of goods and services occurs at a specific point on the economy's production possibility boundary. If an industry is not productively efficient, the economy is not even on its production possibilities boundary. The industry's output could be produced using less resources, and the resources saved could then be used to produce more output.

2. False. The cost-minimizing criterion is that *marginal* costs are equal across firms in an industry. Assume Firm A's marginal cost of producing its last unit of output is $20 worth of resources while Firm B's marginal cost of producing one more unit of output is $14 worth of resources. Transferring the production of one unit of output from Firm A to Firm B would reduce resource cost by $6 with no change in industry output. This would happen regardless of whether Firm A's average total cost of production were less than, equal to, or greater than the average total cost of Firm B.

3. Very few industries are *perfectly* competitive in the real world. Some approximate perfect competition (e.g., monopolistic competition), but most are not even close (e.g., oligopolies and monopolies). Furthermore, even as an ideal, perfect competition would be neither productively nor allocatively efficient in industries with substantial economies of scale in production.

4. The conflict between profit and allocative efficiency in a natural monopoly stems from the relationship between marginal cost and long-run average cost ($LRAC$). If $LRAC$ is falling, marginal cost must be less than $LRAC$, so charging $P = MC$ (for allocative efficiency) means that average revenue is also less $LRAC$, thus generating losses. (If the firm is not a natural monopoly and $LRAC$ is rising, however, marginal cost must exceed $LRAC$. In this case at $P = MC$ the average revenue exceeds $LRAC$, thus generating profit.)

5. Rate-of-return regulation is profit regulation. Regulatory agencies may require firms to reduce price to achieve a "fair" level of profit (i.e., to approximate average cost pricing). It is often used because regulators do not have enough data to precisely determine demand and marginal cost curves. Average cost pricing, however, does not generate the allocative efficiency achieved by marginal cost pricing. Furthermore, average costs (and therefore profits) can be affected by inefficient operation and misleading accounting. Indeed, if firms are required to charge a price equal to average total cost (and earn zero profit), they have no incentive to reduce average costs by improving efficiency.

6. First, evidence shows that oligopolistic industries have created many new products and production methods, which contradicts the implication that such firms have no incentive for innovation because their profits are protected by significant barriers to entry. In fact, their actions would appear to be more consistent with inter-firm competition and existing firms innovating to protect themselves from adverse consequences of "creative destruction." Second, regulatory agencies often appeared to have protected existing firms from competition. This would be contrary to their supposed objectives of stimulating competition and improving the allocative efficiency of society's resources. Furthermore, even if the regulatory agencies had no direct negative impact, if they also had no direct positive impact there would still indirectly be a net loss to society since the resources used to run the agencies would be "wasted."

7. One statement says market power is bad for society while the other states that it is (or can be) good for society. These statements can be resolved by recognizing that each adopts a different time frame than the other. <u>Over time</u> the potential for economic profits gives firms with market power the incentive to invest in research and development, which has benefited consumers by generating new products and lower costs. This is part of the <u>process</u> by which such firms compete with one another over time; they seek to find the better products or production methods before other firms find them. <u>At a point in time,</u>

however, profit-maximizing firms produce at $P = MC$ in perfect competition but $MR = MC < P$ with market power. *But* if a firm with market power has responded to the profit incentive to innovate, its MC will be less than that for perfectly competitive firms without that incentive. Consequently, although firms with market power are not being as allocatively efficient <u>as they could be</u> at the point in time, they may still be more allocatively efficient than perfect competition <u>would have been</u>.

Exercises

1. **(a)** (i)   *B; J*
        (ii)   area *BDF* (The area under the demand curve and above price *B*)
        (iii) area *ABF* (The area above the supply curve and below the price)
        (iv)   area *ADF* (The area below the demand curve and above the supply curve)

    (b) (i)   *C; I*
        (ii)   area *CDE* (The area under the demand curve and above price *C*)
        (iii) area *ACEH* (The area above the *MC* curve and below the price)
        (iv)   area *ADEH* (The area below the demand curve and above the *MC* curve)

    (c) (i)   area *EFH*   (ii)   area *CBGE*.
        (iii) area *CEFB*   (iv)   area *CBEG* minus area *FGH*

    (d) (i)   Profits are higher at output *I* than at output *J*. Since fixed costs are constant by definition, the increase in profit must equal the increase in the excess of total revenue over total variable cost. Since producer surplus is also total revenue minus total variable costs, the increase in profit must equal the increase in producer surplus.
        (ii) Consumer surplus equals total surplus minus producer surplus. Since producer surplus increases but total surplus falls (by the amount of the deadweight loss), the increase in producer surplus must exceed the fall in consumer surplus.

2. **Figure 12-9**

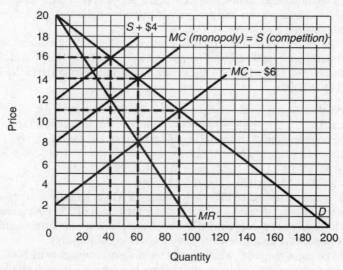

    (a) (i)   At the intersection of *D* and *S* (competition) in Figure 12-9, $P = \$14$ and $Q = 60$.
            consumer surplus $= 1/2(\$20 - \$14)60 = \$180$;
            producer surplus $= 1/2(\$14 - \$8)60 = \$180$;
            total surplus $= \$180 + \$180 = \$360$. [*Note:* The fact that consumer and producer surplus are equal is an "accident" of the specific demand and supply curves used in this exercise.]

    (b) Quantity $= 40$ and price $= \$16$. The output is *less than* the allocatively efficient level since $P > MC$ by ($\$16 - \$12$) $\$4$. There is a deadweight loss of $\$40$—i.e., $1/2(\$16 - \$14)(60 - 40) + 1/2(\$14 - \$12)(60 - 40)$. [*Note:* For those using equations, $MR = 20 - 0.2Q_D$ and $MC = 8 + 0.1Q_S$, so $MC = MR$ occurs at $Q = 12/0.3 = 40$ and, from the demand curve, $0 = 200 - 10P$, $P = 106/10 = \$16$.]

(c) The \$4 per unit negative externality shifts the marginal cost curve for society vertically up to $S + \$4$ in the figure. [*Note:* For those using equations, the social marginal cost curve equation is $MC_{SOCIAL} = 0.1Q_S + 12$.]

    (i) The allocatively efficient output for society is 40 units, where $P = MC_{SOCIAL} = \$16$. [*Note:* Set $MC = 0.1Q_S + 12$ equal to $P = 20 - 0.1Q_D$ and solve.]

    (ii) Perfect competition produces 20 units more than the social optimum of 40 units. Note that at the perfectly competitive output of 60 units, $P < MC_{SOCIAL}$ by \$4 (i.e., \$14 – \$18). In this example, monopoly is more allocatively efficient since it produces the 40 units at which $P = MC_{SOCIAL}$.

    (iii) Yes. A positive externality *reduces* the marginal cost to society as a whole, so competitive equilibrium would occur at less than the allocatively efficient output (i.e., at the intersection of the demand and supply curves $P = MC$ for producers and consumers of the good but $P > MC_{SOCIAL}$ for society as a whole). Since the monopoly produces even less than perfect competition, it would be even less allocatively efficient.

(d) Economies of scale shift the monopoly MC curve vertically down by \$6, to $MC - \$6$ in the figure. [*Note:* For those using equations, the new $MC = 0.1Q + 2$.]

    (i) In this example, monopoly profit maximizes at 60 units of output and a price of \$14—the same as in perfect competition without the economies of scale. [*Note:* Equate $MR = 20 - 0.2Q$ with $MC = 0.1Q + 2$ and solve.]

    (ii) Consumer surplus in this monopoly with economies of scale ($1/2(\$20 - \$14)60 = \$180$) is the same as in perfect competition without the economies of scale. Producer surplus increases from \$180 in perfect competition to \$540 in monopoly (($14 – \$8)60 + 1/2(\$8 – \$2)60$). Total surplus increases from \$180 + \$180 = \$360 in perfect competition to \$180 + \$540 = \$720 in the monopoly.

    (iii) This monopoly with economies of scale is more allocatively efficient than perfect competition without the economies of scale. Although this exercise is constructed to make price and output the same for both, total surplus is greater by \$360 in the monopoly. This arises because the economies of scale allow the monopoly to produce the same output using less resources than the perfectly competitive industry—obviously an improvement in efficiency for the economy as a whole.

    (iv) No. The monopoly could be more allocatively efficient by producing where its marginal cost equals price, at 90 units of output and a price of \$11. This would further increase total surplus by \$90 ($1/2(\$14 – \$8)30$), giving a total surplus of \$810 ($1/2(\$20 – \$11)90 + 1/2(\$11 – \$2)90$).

3. (a) The allocatively efficient level of output is 10 000 units, where $P = MC$. The value of the resources used to produce the ten-thousandth unit (i.e., the MC) equals the value that households place on the consumption of this unit (i.e., the price they are willing to pay).

    (b) When profit-maximizing at $MC = MR$, the unregulated monopoly produces 5000 units and charges $P = \$8$. Profit $= (AR - LRAC)Q = (\$8 - \$7)5000 = \$5000$.

    (c) area $abc = 1/2(\$8 - \$3)(10\ 000 - 5000) = \$12\ 500$.

    (d) At $P = MC$, output would be 10 000 units selling for \$3 per unit, for total revenues of \$30 000. Average cost, however, would be \$5 per unit, for total costs of \$50 000, generating losses of \$20 000. The regulatory agency would not be successful since the firm would eventually go out of business (unless the losses were offset by a government subsidy).

    (e) Price would be regulated at \$6, which would yield a market quantity of 7000 units.

    (f) Under average-cost pricing in (e), profits are zero but there is a deadweight loss of area $dec = 1/2(\$6 - \$3)(10\ 000 - 7000) = \$4500$. Marginal-cost pricing in (d) does not create any deadweight loss, but the firm is forced to incur an operating loss of \$20 000 and would eventually shut down.

    (g) (i) Discrimination by units of output would allow the firm to cover its costs by charging a higher price for some units of output. For example, it could charge a price of \$7 on the first 5000 units and \$3 on the next 5000, generating total revenues of $\$7(5000) + \$3(5000) = \$50\ 000$. Since it produces 10 000 at a $LRAC$ of \$5, total costs = total revenues = \$50 000. In this way the natural monopoly could produce the allocatively efficient level and make zero profit. [*Note:* The profit of $(\$7 - \$5)5000 = \$10\ 000$ on the first 5000 units exactly offsets the loss of $(\$5 - \$3)5000 = \$10\ 000$ on the second 5000 units.]

(ii)   The text gives the example of a two-part tariff when companies charge an initial "access" price (e.g., a hook-up fee to cover fixed costs). Applying the principle to this exercise, assume that the 10 000 units of output are sold to 2000 households. An access fee of $10 per household would generate the $20 000 in extra revenues that the firm needs to break even. This two-part tariff, therefore, would enable the monopoly to produce the allocatively efficient output without making losses.

4.   (a)   Figure 12-10 shows a vertical (perfectly inelastic) supply curve of medallions at the fixed amount of 11 797. The increase in demand between 1937 and 1985 increased the price of medallions from virtually zero (when there was unrestricted entry) to $100 000. Demand for taxicab rides, and therefore medallions, will likely continue to increase over time as population increases and as average income increases (under the reasonable assumption that a taxicab ride is a normal good).

Figure 12-10

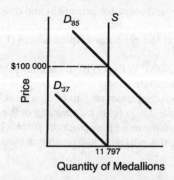

(b)   Yes. Consumers are hurt because the restriction on the number of taxicabs means they have to wait longer for a vacant taxicab, especially in peak periods.

(c)   Restricting the number of cabs increases the number of rides per day for each cab, thereby increasing the income of taxicab operators. New entrants are willing to pay the high prices in order to gain access to the future income stream.

(d)   (i)   No. As long as there were any (economic) profits to be made, the demand for medallions would continue to increase, raising their price, as people tried to enter the taxicab industry to reap the economic profit. The price would keep rising until entry gained access to only zero profit.

(ii)   No. The fact that the medallion holder is no longer making *direct* (or explicit) payments for the medallion does not mean that the economic cost of the medallion is now zero. The medallion could be sold and the market value of the medallion invested elsewhere. The income that could be earned from such an investment is an opportunity cost to the medallion holder (i.e., an implicit cost), and so is part of the economic cost of continuing to hold the medallion and operate the taxicab.

5.   (a)   **Figure 12-11**

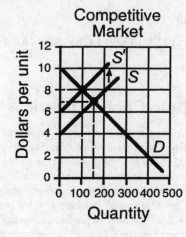

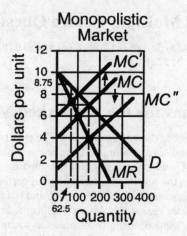

The initial equilibrium in perfect competition obtains at a price of $7 and a quantity of 150 units. The monopoly equilibrium is derived by first drawing the monopolist's marginal revenue curve (same price intercept and half the quantity intercept as the demand curve), which equals *MC* at an output of 100 units, implying a price of $8.

   (b)   The equilibrium in perfect competition obtains at a price of $7 and a quantity of 150 units. For these to be the profit-maximizing price and quantity of the monopolist, the market *MR* curve and the monopolist's *MC* curve must intersect at a quantity of 150. This requires (for a uniform shift) that *MC* be $3 lower per unit of output—for illustration, *MC''*.

   (c)   In the first graph, shift the supply curve a vertical distance of $2 to *S'*; the new equilibrium price is $8, and quantity is 100. In the second graph, shift the *MC* curve a vertical distance of $2 to *MC'*; equate *MR* and *MC'* to obtain the new profit-maximizing price of $8.75 and quantity of 62.5 (approximately). Thus both price and quantity change less in the monopoly situation.

6.   **(a)**   Set demand equal to supply and solve for price (45) and output (45 000). (See Panel (i) of Figure 12-12 below.)

   (b)   Consumer surplus is area (a) and producer surplus is area (b) in Panel (i); $1 012 000 and $506 250, respectively.

   (c)   Price is *h* and quantity is 27 000. In Panel (ii), consumer surplus is shown by the triangle *ehg*; producer surplus is the quadrangle *khgf*.

   (d)   Under competitive conditions, consumer surplus (*CS*) is more and producer surplus (*PS*) is less than under monopoly. For example, *CS* in (c) is the area *ehg* in Panel (ii), which is less than triangle (a) in Panel (i). Net benefits (consumer plus producer surplus) are less under monopoly. The amount of the reduction (the so-called deadweight loss) is shown by the triangle *ifg* in Panel (ii).

Figure 12-12

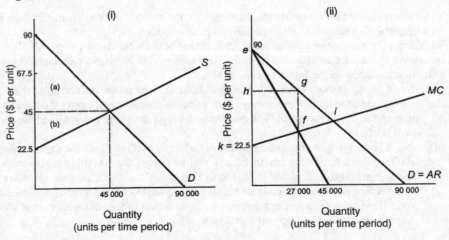

Additional Multiple-Choice Questions

1.(c) **2.**(c) **3.**(a) **4.**(a) **5.**(d) **6.**(b) **7.**(e) **8.**(d) **9.**(e) **10.**(b) **11.**(a) **12.**(c) **13.**(e) **14.**(b) **15.**(c) **16.**(b) **17.**(e) **18.**(e) **19.**(c) **20.**(d) **21.**(b) **22.**(b)

Explanations for the Asterisked Multiple-Choice Questions

1.(c)   First look at the wrong answers. The profit-maximizing perfect competitor produces at *MC* = *MR*, so (a) and (e) are wrong. All profit-maximizing firms seek productive efficiency to minimize the costs of producing their profit-maximizing output, so (b) is wrong. And (d) is wrong because it reverses the results for monopoly and perfect competition. Answer (c) is correct because (i) profit-maximization is where *MR* = *MC*, and (ii) the perfectly elastic demand curve of the perfect competitor means *P* = *MR*, so (iii) its profit-maximization point is where *P* = *MR* = *MC*.

6.(b)   All profit-maximizing firms produce where *MC* = *MR*, but only in perfect competition does *P* = *MR* (because the firm's demand curve is perfectly elastic). Only in perfect competition, therefore, does profit maximization result in $P = MC$ (the condition for allocative efficiency). In other market structures, the firm's downward-sloping demand curve means $P > MR$, so $P > MC$ when $MC = MR$.

7.(e) Answer (a) says each firm is on its *LRAC* curve, giving productive efficiency at the level of the firm. Answer (d) is the additional condition needed for productive efficiency in the industry. Answer (c) simply restates the definition of productive efficiency at the industry level, which in turn must imply (b) because, if it were possible for the industry to produce the same output using fewer resources, it could not have been productively efficient to start with.

8.(d) Each oligopolist will attempt to increase its market share at the expense of its competitors. One way to increase market share and profits is to produce a better product or use a more efficient production process to reduce costs and price. Each oligopolist, therefore, has a profit incentive to develop new products and innovative production technologies. The monopolist has no such competitors, and therefore has less incentive to innovate. [*Note:* A monopoly does not necessarily have no incentive at all to innovate; failure to do so may cause it to become a victim of "creative destruction."]

9.(e) Answer (a) is wrong because there is no such trade-off: if the industry is not productively efficient it can't be allocatively efficient. Answer (d) is wrong because the Competition Bureau's mandate is to do what is best for the consumer and the economy, <u>not</u> for the firms in an industry. Answers (b) and (c) may be indicators of the potential for a merger to reduce competition; these data are <u>inputs</u> into the *main* issue of whether consumers and society overall would benefit from a more efficient use of society's resources if the merger would allow greater exploitation of economies of scale.

10.(b) The firm is a falling-cost natural monopoly because the *LRAC* is everywhere declining (at least for all price-quantity combinations attainable given the constraint of the demand curve). It does not matter than *MC* is constant, because the definition is based on the shape of the *LRAC*.

11.(a) The firm maximizes profit at $MC = MR$, which is at $Q = 100$. The demand curve, from which the *MR* is derived, shows consumers are willing to pay $P = \$12$, for a *TR* of \$1200. The *LRAC* curve shows the cost to the firm is \$11 per unit, for *TC* of \$1100. Thus profit is $TR - TC = \$1200 - \$1100 = \$100$, or $(AR - LRAC)Q = (\$12 - \$11)100 = \$100$.

12.(c) The area of the deadweight loss triangle is $1/2(\$12 - \$5)(200 - 100) = 1/2(\$700) = \$350$.

15.(c) With marginal-cost pricing the firm produces 200 units of output, which is all units for which there is some surplus (i.e., all units for which $P > MC$). Since surplus is at its maximum, there is no deadweight loss. With average-cost pricing, the area of the deadweight loss triangle is $1/2(\$10 - \$5)(200 - 150) = 1/2(\$250) = \$125$.

16.(b) With marginal-cost pricing, output is 200 and the *LRAC* is \$8 *for each and every one of the 200 units*. The profit on the first 100 units is $(P - LRAC)100 = (\$12 - \$8)100 = \$400$. The loss on the next 100 units is $(\$8 - \$5)100 = \$300$. There is an overall profit of $\$400 - \$300 = \$100$.

17.(e) Profit-maximizing firms will not put money into investment if they can't get an acceptable rate of return. The "profit" that will be generated determines the rate of return. Average-cost pricing restricts firms to zero economic profit, thus reducing the incentive to invest by reducing the rate of return on some investments. If more investment in capital stock is required to increase output while remaining on the *LRAC* curve, then increasing output without such investment will put the firm <u>above</u> the *LRAC* curve. This is productively inefficient because the new output level is not being produced at its minimum possible average cost.

18.(e) A firm's cost curves are difficult (if not impossible) to measure by the regulatory agency, and costs in economics are *opportunity costs*, which include the rate of return the firm could have had elsewhere. The regulatory agency determines what would be a "reasonable" rate of return, so that setting $P = LRAC$ implies *zero economic profit* inclusive of this return. Regulating the firm to this rate of return, therefore, achieves the same result as *average-cost pricing*. As in Question 17 above, however, restricting the rate of return in this manner *reduces incentives to minimize costs*, whether by not undertaking investments that would enhance productive efficiency or by eliminating any profit "penalty" for unnecessary expenditures. [For example, putting gold-plated water coolers in executives' offices unnecessarily increases costs, but product price can then be increased to maintain the <u>percentage</u> rate of return on costs allowed by the regulatory agency.]

19.(c) The analysis underlying this question is done in Exercise 2, part (d). Here we compare a perfectly competitive industry to a monopoly with <u>lower costs</u>. The small firms in a perfectly competitive industry would therefore have higher average and marginal costs than the monopoly. In equilibrium, the perfectly competitive industry would be producing at minimum *LRAC* and at

$P = MC$, so being both productively efficient and allocatively efficient *relative to its own cost curves*. The monopoly would be productively efficient (a requirement for profit maximization), but not allocatively efficient *relative to its own cost curves* (since $P > MC = MR$). Nevertheless, even though it is $P > MC$, the monopoly could still be making better use of society's resources because of the economies of scale, since *its MC could be low enough* that it produced more than perfect competition at a lower price and by *using less resources*. So the monopoly would be more allocatively efficient and generate more total surplus than perfect competition, although not as allocatively efficient as it could be because its P exceeds *its own MC*. [*Note:* Here you see the trade-off that may be faced by an agency regulating mergers—i.e., less competition versus greater efficiency due to economies of scale.]

20.(d) The analysis underlying this question is done in Exercise 2, part (c). The question essentially states that we are comparing a perfectly competitive industry and a monopoly with the <u>same cost curves</u>. The actual condition for allocative efficiency is that price equals the marginal cost <u>to society</u>, which includes *externalities*—i.e., costs or benefits to people other than the consumers and producers of the product. If there are no externalities, $MC_{SOCIAL} = MC_{PRIVATE}$ (i.e., the MC to firms), so $P = MC_{PRIVATE}$ is the same as $P = MC_{SOCIAL}$ and the perfectly competitive industry produces the allocatively efficient output level (since $P = MC$) while a profit-maximizing monopoly produces less than the allocatively efficient level (since $P > MC$). Where there are positive externalities, even perfect competition produces less than the allocatively efficient level (since $P = MC_{PRIVATE} > MC_{SOCIAL}$). With *negative externalities*, however, $MC_{PRIVATE} < MC_{SOCIAL}$ so perfect competition produces more than the allocatively efficient amount. Since monopoly produces less, where $P > MC_{PRIVATE}$, it may well be producing closer to the allocatively efficient level than perfect competition.

21.(b) Average-cost pricing means the firm is restricted to zero economic profits, producing and selling at $(P=) AR = LRAC$. Accounting profits can be positive with zero economic profits, so (a) and (e) are wrong. Setting P (i.e., AR) $= LRAC$ means $P > MC$ so there is allocative inefficiency, and (c) is wrong for both a natural monopoly and a regular monopoly. Answer (d) is wrong because it directly contradicts the requirement for zero economic profits. Answer (d) is correct because average-cost pricing means that any increase in costs can be met by an equal increase in revenues, thus having no effect on profit and giving no incentive for the firm to seek productive efficiency. [*Note:* The resulting waste of resources has been described as the "gold-plated water cooler effect."]

22.(b) See the answer to Short-Answer Question 7 above.

13

How Factor
Markets Work

Chapter Overview

This chapter discusses the theory of how factor prices are determined in perfectly competitive factor markets. [*Note:* Imperfectly competitive factor markets are covered in Chapter 14.] As you might expect, equilibrium factor prices are determined by the forces of demand and supply in markets for factors of production.

The demand for a factor is a **derived demand**, since the demand for a factor is *derived from* the demand for the goods and services that it helps to produce. Thus derived demand provides the link between goods markets and factor markets: the market determination of the prices and quantities of goods and services determine the incomes of the factors that produce them. A firm's profit-maximizing quantity of a factor is where the additional cost of an extra unit of the factor (the **marginal factor cost**, or *MFC*) equals the extra revenue that the marginal unit of the factor generates (the **marginal revenue product**, or *MRP* of that unit). The *MRP* of the factor is the number of extra units of output it creates (the **marginal product**, or *MP* of the factor) multiplied by the extra revenue per unit (the **marginal revenue**, or *MR* of each extra unit of output). In perfectly competitive factor markets, the *MFC* is simply the market price of the factor.

The degree of responsiveness of the quantity of a factor demanded (supplied) to a change in its price is the **elasticity of factor demand (supply)**. Just like the elasticity of demand (supply) for a good or service, the elasticity of factor demand (supply) is the percentage change in quantity demanded (supplied) resulting from a percentage change in the factor's price. *Factor demand* will be more elastic the more slowly marginal productivity declines as output expands (i.e., the degree of diminishing returns to the factor), and the easier it is to substitute other factors for it. *Factor supply* to a particular industry or occupation is more elastic than its supply to the whole economy because one industry can bid units away from

LEARNING OBJECTIVES

After studying this chapter, you will be able to

1   discuss the size and functional distribution of income in Canada.

2   determine a profit-maximizing firm's demand for a factor of production.

3   examine the role of factor mobility in determining factor supply.

4   distinguish between temporary and equilibrium factor-price differentials.

5   discuss "economic rent" and how it relates to factor mobility.

other industries. The elasticity of supply to a particular use depends on **factor mobility**, which differs among different types of factors.

Differences in factor prices may be temporary or permanent. **Temporary differentials** will be eroded over time by factor mobility and the market forces of demand and supply. Permanent differentials, on the other hand, persist even when the factor markets are in equilibrium. These **equilibrium differentials** can persist between *different factors* due to their qualitative differences and the different costs of acquiring different skills. Furthermore, equilibrium differentials can persist for the *same factor in different uses*, as monetary compensation for non-monetary differences between jobs such as differences in risk, in flexibility of work hours, and in the overall pleasantness of the job. Pay-equity legislation may speed up the erosion of temporary wage differentials that are caused by discrimination but will encounter (and create) problems if it tries to eliminate equilibrium differentials that compensate for differences in the non-wage aspects of different jobs.

The total payment to a specific factor may be a combination of **transfer earnings** and **economic rent**. Transfer earnings is the minimum payment needed to keep the factor in its current use, and economic rent is the amount paid in excess of transfer earnings. How the total payment is distributed between transfer earnings and economic rent depends on the elasticity of factor supply (which in turn depends on the degree of mobility of the factor).

Hints and Tips

The following may help you avoid some of the most common errors on examinations.

✓ Understand that the condition for the firm's profit-maximizing amount of a factor to use is $MFC = MP \times MR$ (where MP is the marginal product of the factor and MR is the extra revenue per unit of output). When the firm is perfectly competitive in the product market, MR is the price of the product (p). When the firm is perfectly competitive in the factor market, MFC is the price of the factor (e.g., w for the wage rate of labour). So when the firm is perfectly competitive in both markets, $MFC = MP \times MR$ is the same as $w = MP \times p$.

✓ Don't be confused by terminology: the basic principle for deciding whether to hire another unit of a factor of production is the same as for whether to produce another unit of output—i.e., will it increase profits? If the extra revenue from producing another unit of output (MR) exceeds its extra cost (MC), the difference is an increase in profit <u>from that unit of output</u>—so produce it! Similarly, if the extra revenue from selling *all* the additional units of output produced by another unit of the factor (MRP) exceeds the extra cost of that factor (MFC), the difference is an increase in profit <u>from that unit of the factor</u>—so hire it!

✓ Don't confuse the different effects of a change in product price and a change in factor price on a perfectly competitive firm's demand for the factor. A change in the product price shifts the factor demand curve, while a change in the factor price causes a movement along its demand curve.

✓ Understand the difference between transfer earnings and economic rent. Economic rent is the amount that a factor earns in excess of what must be paid to prevent it from moving to another use (i.e., the excess over its transfer earnings). Just because a company executive, for example, is paid a huge salary does not necessarily mean that it is largely economic rent. If the executive could move to another company and get a similar salary, then it is largely transfer earnings.

Chapter Review

Income Distribution

Classical economists focused on the **functional distribution of income**, defined as the distribution of national income among the major factors of production (land, labour, capital). Modern economists, who are interested in income inequality between individuals, have concentrated on the **size distribution of income**. Lorenz curves show how much of (before-tax and after-tax) total income is accounted for by various proportions of the nation's families—i.e., in fairly simple terms, the curvature of the Lorenz curve illustrates the degree of income inequality. [*Note:* The *Applying Economic Concepts 13-1* box in the text gives some interesting and important information about rising income inequality in Canada and elsewhere, and some associated implications.]

1. **The functional distribution of income**
   - (a) emphasizes the function of income in attracting workers.
   - (b) is concerned with income distribution by socio-economic class.
   - (c) can be graphically shown by a Lorenz curve.
   - (d) shows income shares of factors of production.
   - (e) deals with the transfer earnings portion of total factor incomes.

2. **With complete equality of income distribution the Lorenz curve would be a**
   - (a) diagonal line.
   - (b) convex line.
   - (c) concave curve.
   - (d) single point.
   - (e) series of points below the diagonal.

The Demand for Factors

The profit-maximizing marginal decision rule says that a firm will hire a (variable) factor up to the point where the marginal cost of the factor is equal to the marginal revenue product of the factor ($MFC = MRP$). If $MFC < MRP$ for another unit of the factor, the difference is the firm's increase in profit from hiring that extra unit. The MRP has both a physical component and a dollar component. The physical component is the extra output generated by the marginal unit of the factor (MP), and the dollar component is the extra revenue the firm gets per extra unit of output (MR). Thus the profit-maximizing hiring condition can be expanded to $MFC = MP \times MR$.

   This chapter considers only firms that are perfect competitors in the factor market, with each firm facing a perfectly elastic factor supply curve so MFC equals the factor price (w). If the firm is perfectly competitive in the product market, it faces a perfectly elastic product demand curve so MR equals the product price (p). In the special case where the firm is perfectly competitive in both the factor and product markets, therefore, $MFC = MP \times MR$ can be rewritten as $w = MP \times p$. But if the firm is imperfectly competitive in the product market, it faces a downward-sloping product demand curve so $MR < p$ and p <u>cannot</u> replace MR.

   The MRP curve of a variable factor (for a given amount of the fixed factor) is the firm's derived demand curve for that factor. As more of the factor is hired when its price falls, the physical component (MP) of MRP falls due to diminishing returns to the variable factor. There is no change in the monetary component (MR) for the firm that is perfectly competitive in the product market, but MR falls for the imperfectly competitive firm since product price must fall if more output is to be sold. For a perfect competitor in the product market, therefore, there is only <u>one</u> reason why the MRP curve is negatively sloped, hence the slope of the MRP curve in these markets is also the slope of the MP curve. For an imperfect competitor in the product market, however, the slope of the *MRP* curve differs from the slope of the *MP* curve because there are <u>two</u> reasons for this negative relationship between factor price and the *quantity demanded* of the factor. The entire *MRP* curve will shift to the right (i.e., an increase in the firm's *demand* for the factor) if more of the fixed factor is added, if there is an improvement in technology, and if the firm's demand curve for the product increases.

This section also explains why technology determines the individual firm's elasticity of the factor demand curve, and identifies two influences on this elasticity. The section closes with an explanation of why the *market* demand curve for a specific factor is *less elastic* than the simple sum of all firms' demand curves for the factor. [*Note:* See Exercise 7 below for two additional determinants of a firm's elasticity of demand for a factor of production.]

3. **The marginal revenue product of a factor is**
    (a) the change in total revenue from selling the extra output produced by an additional unit of a factor.
    (b) the average product of the factor multiplied by product price.
    (c) the change in revenue from selling one more unit of output.
    (d) equal to the market price of the product that is produced by the factor.
    (e) its marginal product multiplied by the factor's price.

4. **The marginal product of labour is**
    (a) total output divided by total labour in use.
    (b) the change in output divided by the change in labour use.
    (c) total labour in use divided by total output.
    (d) the change in labour use divided by the change in output.
    (e) the cost of the factor divided by the extra output produced.

5. **A perfectly competitive, profit-maximizing firm hires a factor up to the point at which**
    (a) the factor's price equals its marginal revenue product.
    (b) the marginal cost of hiring the factor equals the additional revenue obtained from that factor's marginal contribution to output.
    (c) the factor's price equals its marginal product times the product's price.
    (d) All of the above.
    (e) Both (a) and (c), but not (b).

6. **Perfectly competitive, profit-maximizing firms that employ any factor until marginal revenue product equals the price of the factor will hire**
    (a) additional units of the factor if its price falls, other things being equal.
    (b) more of the factor if the price of the product it produces falls, other things being equal.
    (c) less of the factor if technology changes such that factor productivity rises, other things being equal.
    (d) additional units of the factor if the factor's price exceeds its marginal revenue product.
    (e) the same quantities of all factors.

7. **Which of the following explains why a profit-maximizing, competitive firm's demand curve for labour slopes downward? As the quantity of labour employed rises,**
    (a) the marginal product of labour eventually falls.
    (b) the firm's marginal revenue declines as output increases.
    (c) the marginal cost of hiring another unit of labour increases.
    (d) the price of the firm's product falls as that firm produces more.
    (e) as the firm's output rises, <u>both</u> its marginal revenue <u>and</u> its product price decline.

8. **If the quantity demanded of a factor of production decreases by 10 percent when its price increases by 8 percent, the elasticity of demand for the factor is**
   (a) −18.0.
   (b) 1.25 percent.
   (c) −0.80.
   (d) −2.00.
   (e) −1.25.

9. **Which of the following is true about the firm's demand for a factor of production?**
   (a) It is more elastic when it has to be used in fixed proportions with other factors.
   (b) It is more elastic the easier it is to substitute another factor for it.
   (c) It is less elastic the greater its share of total costs of production.
   (d) It is less elastic the greater its substitutability with alternative inputs.
   (e) It is more elastic the steeper the firm's *MRP* curve.

10. **Which of the following is likely to shift the demand curve for carpenters to the right?**
    (a) A decrease in carpenters' wages.
    (b) An increase in carpenters' wages.
    (c) An increase in the demand for residential construction.
    (d) A decrease in carpenters' marginal products at all levels of employment.
    (e) An increase in the price of wood as the supply of wood falls.

11. **The market demand curve for a factor of production is less elastic than the horizontal sum of individual (perfectly competitive) firms' *MRP* curves because**
    (a) as the individual firm hires more of the factor and produces more output, the price of output falls.
    (b) as all firms hire more of the factor, the price of the factor rises.
    (c) as all firms hire more of the factor, the factor's marginal product rises.
    (d) as all firms hire more of the factor and produce more output, the price of output falls.
    (e) None of the above—the market demand curve is *more elastic* than the sum of firms' *MRP* curves.

12. **The market demand curve for labour will shift to the left**
    (a) if improvements in technology increase labour's marginal product.
    (b) if firms increase the amount of capital they use.
    (c) if the prices of products fall.
    (d) if the wage rate of labour increases.
    (e) if hiring more labour reduces its marginal product.

The Supply of Factors

This section emphasizes that the supply of factors and the elasticity of the factor supply can be determined at three different levels of aggregation; for the economy as a whole, for a particular industry or occupation, and for one firm. The key determinant of supply elasticity is factor mobility within and among the three levels of aggregation. [*Note:* On *MyEconLab*, see an introduction to an interesting and topical policy issue in *Additional Topics: Does Government Support of Specific Industries Really Create Jobs?*]

13. **A highly mobile factor of production**
    (a) is one that shifts easily between uses in response to small changes in incentives.
    (b) has inelastic supply in most uses.
    (c) is one that possesses skills used by only one firm.
    (d) has a low market price at equilibrium.
    (e) will move easily between firms but not between industries.

14. **The elasticity of the supply of a factor will be lowest for**
    (a) factor movements between Ford Canada and Chrysler Canada.
    (b) factor movements between the steel industry and the automobile parts manufacturing industry.
    (c) doctors moving between countries.
    (d) carpenters moving between Brandon, Manitoba, and Winnipeg, Manitoba.
    (e) factors that are perfectly mobile between all uses.

15. **As a factor of production, agricultural land**
    (a) is considered to be highly immobile in both a physical and an economic sense.
    (b) is the only factor that is paid economic rents.
    (c) is mobile in an economic sense because it has many alternative uses as a factor of production.
    (d) is completely immobile because it cannot be moved.
    (e) ceases to be considered a factor of production if it is used for purposes other than farming.

16. **The labour force participation rate is**
    (a) the supply of labour.
    (b) the proportion of the population with jobs.
    (c) the proportion of the population willing to work.
    (d) the total number of hours that all individuals want to work.
    (e) the proportion of the workforce belonging to a labour union.

The Operation of Factor Markets

In a competitive factor market, equilibrium levels of factor employment and factor price are determined by the intersection of the demand and supply curves. The factor's total income is the factor price multiplied by the quantity employed. Differences in factor prices can be temporary **factor-price differentials** or **equilibrium differentials** that persist for long periods of time.

Temporary factor-price differentials are eroded over time as owners of factors choose the use that produces the greatest **net advantage**, allowing for both the monetary and non-monetary advantages of a particular employment. Mobility erodes the temporary differentials until there is **equal net advantage** among the various uses of the factor. Equilibrium differentials result from differences in the intrinsic and acquired characteristics of the factors, including differences in the skills of labour, and from the differences in the non-monetary aspects of jobs that create **compensating differentials** in factor prices. This section also reviews issues about policies to promote pay equity, particularly where they attempt to eliminate equilibrium differentials.

For a specific unit of the factor, the minimum payment needed to keep that unit in its current use is its **transfer earnings** (or transfer price, read from the factor supply curve). Any amount received in excess of transfer earnings is called **economic rent** (the difference between the supply curve and the actual price paid). Summing these for all employed units of the factor gives total transfer earnings and total economic rent paid to the factor. For example, if the market for the factor is in equilibrium, total transfer earnings is the area under the supply curve up to the equilibrium quantity, and total economic rent is the area above the supply curve but below the equilibrium factor price.

When the supply curve for a factor is perfectly inelastic (vertical), all earnings are economic rents since a perfectly inelastic supply curve implies that there are no alternative uses for this factor. When the supply curve for a factor is perfectly elastic (flat), all earnings are transfer income (there are no economic rents). When the supply curve for a factor is upward sloping, the total payment to the factor is partly transfer earnings and partly economic rent. The greater the mobility of the factor, the more elastic is its supply curve, so the share of the total payments to the factor that is transfer earnings increases while the share that is economic rent decreases.

17. **Which of the following will unambiguously increase the equilibrium wage rate of economists?**
    - (a) The demand curve for economists shifts to the left.
    - (b) Both the demand and supply curves for economists shift to the right.
    - (c) Both the demand and supply curves for economists shift to the left.
    - (d) The supply curve for economists shifts to the right.
    - (e) The demand curve for economists shifts to the right and the supply curve shifts to the left.

18. **Assume that a temporary differential exists such that wages in occupation *A* are higher than those in occupation *B*. According to the hypothesis of equal net advantage, we would expect**
    - (a) all non-monetary advantages to be equalized between the two occupations.
    - (b) workers to move from occupation *A* to occupation *B*.
    - (c) the wage differential to be eliminated as movers move from *B* to *A*.
    - (d) the wage differential to be long-lasting, particularly if workers are highly mobile.
    - (e) the non-wage advantages of occupation *B* to be unambiguously greater than those of occupation *A*.

19. **Equilibrium differentials in factor prices may reflect**
    - (a) intrinsic differences in factor characteristics.
    - (b) acquired differences in factor characteristics.
    - (c) non-monetary advantages in different uses of the factor.
    - (d) All of the above.
    - (e) Both intrinsic and acquired differences, but _not_ non-monetary advantages.

20. **Which of the following is *not* an example of an equilibrium differential in a factor price?**
    - (a) Land in downtown Toronto is more expensive than land in the suburbs.
    - (b) Wages in the Alberta construction trades are higher than elsewhere in the country because of a booming Albertan economy.
    - (c) Individuals working in isolated communities tend to be paid more than their counterparts in the more accessible cities.
    - (d) A dentist is paid more than a dental hygienist.
    - (e) Certain workers receive higher wages because of greater working hazards.

21. **Economic rent**
    - (a) refers exclusively to the income of landowners.
    - (b) is taxable under the income tax law, whereas transfer earnings are not.
    - (c) is earned only by completely immobile factors.
    - (d) is the excess of income over transfer earnings.
    - (e) refers exclusively to the income of capital.

22. **All payments to certain workers would be economic rent if**
    - (a) their supply curves were perfectly inelastic.
    - (b) they were perfectly mobile between alternative uses.
    - (c) their supply curves were upward sloping.
    - (d) firms' demand for their services were elastic.
    - (e) they were also part-owners of the firms they worked for.

23. **A politician who earns $150 000 and estimates she might have earned $100,000 in her occupation before she was elected is currently receiving**
    (a) economic rent of $150 000.
    (b) transfer payments of $150 000
    (c) economic rent of $100 000.
    (d) transfer payments of $50 000.
    (e) economic rent of $50 000.

Short-Answer Questions

1. Why will a firm hire more of a factor when marginal revenue product (*MRP*) exceeds marginal factor cost (*MFC*)? Why will it hire less when *MRP* < *MFC*? Why will it have hired the profit maximizing quantity when *MRP* = *MFC*?

2. Since a firm selling in a perfectly competitive product market can sell as much output as it wishes at the going market price, why is the firm's demand curve for labour negatively sloped? Why is this competitive industry's demand curve for labour negatively sloped? (In your answer, refer to the components of *MRP*.)

3. Assume that a firm is operating in perfectly competitive markets. In terms of the effect on labour's *MRP* at a constant wage rate, explain how and why the firm's demand curve for labour shifts when each of the following occurs.
    (i)   Technological change increases the productivity of labour.

    (ii) The firm buys more capital.

    (iii) The demand for the firm's product increases.

4. Firms A and B are located near each other and employ the same type of labour. Initially the jobs are identical except that Firm *A* has worse safety conditions than Firm *B* but pays an hourly wage rate that is $2 higher. Then Firm *B* introduces an employer-sponsored pension plan. Explain the economics of what happens next. What sort of differential is the $2 per hour?

5. What is the main thing that the following statement overlooks? "People with the same skills and characteristics should be paid the same wage rates."

6. Two firms have identical production functions. One sells in a perfectly competitive market while the other sells in an imperfectly competitive market. If the current prices charged in the two product markets are the same, will they have the same demand for labour curves? Explain why/why not.

Exercises

1.   The Firm's Demand Curve for a Factor
This exercise demonstrates that the law of diminishing returns yields a downward-sloping factor demand curve for a profit-maximizing firm selling its product in a perfectly competitive market. It also shows the conditions that cause shifts in the demand curve for the factor. (In this exercise, labour is the factor used.)

The following table shows three cases. Cases A and B have the same marginal product of labour (MP), but the product price (p) is lower in Case B than in Case A. Case C has the same product price as Case A, but MP differs from the other two cases.

Units of			Case A		Case B		Case C		
Labour	Output	*MP*	*p*	*MRP*	*p*	*MRP*	*MP*	*p*	*MRP*
1	50	50	$30	$1500	$27	$1350	60	$30	$1800
2	63	13	30	390	27	351	15	30	450
3	75	12	30	360	27	324	14	30	420
4	85	10	30	300	27	270	12	30	360
5	94	____	30	____	27	____	11	30	____
6	99	____	30	____	27	____	7	30	____

(a) Complete the table and plot all three *MRP* curves in Figure 13-1.

Figure 13-1

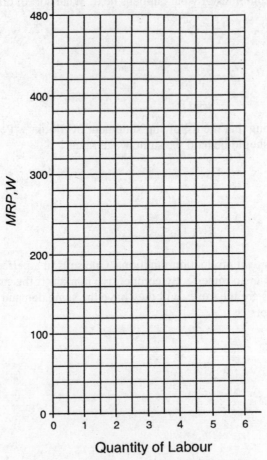

(b) Explain why the *MRP* curve slopes downward in all three cases.

(c) For Case A, what is the firm's demand for workers if the wage is $360? Explain your answer.

(d) For Case A, explain why the firm would hire more if the wage fell from $360 to $270. What is the new profit-maximizing amount of labour?

(e) For Case B, what is the firm's demand for workers if the weekly wage is $270? How does this quantity demanded compare with that for Case A in part (d)?

(f) Explain why the firm's demand for labour at every wage rate is less in Case B than in Case A.

(g) What effect does the lower product price in Case B have on the position and the slope of the demand curve for labour?

(h) For Case C, what is the firm's demand for labour when the weekly wage is $360? How does this value compare with that of Case A in part (c)?

(i) Explain why the firm's demand for labour at every wage is greater for Case C than for Case A.

2.   Economic Rent with Different Supply Curves
Given that *DD* is the demand curve for commercial aeroplane pilots and *W* is equilibrium monthly salary, draw the (linear) supply curves in Figure 13-2 for the following cases and briefly explain the economics of each case.

(a) None of the earnings is economic rent.

(b) All earnings are economic rent.

(c) Half of the earnings are economic rent.

Figure 13-2

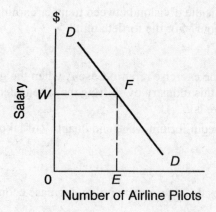

3. Transfer Earnings and Economic Rent

Figure 13-3 represents a labour market for a specific type of worker. The initial demand curve is L^D, but there are two possible supply curves, L^S_A (Case A) and L^S_B (Case B).

Figure 13-3

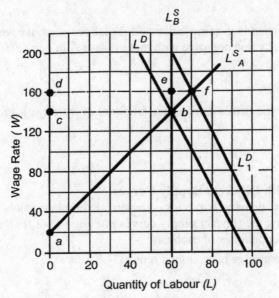

(a) What are the equilibrium values of W and L and the total payment to this factor in each case?

(b) What is the division of total payment to this factor between economic rent and transfer earnings in each case?

(c) For Case A, what is the division between transfer earnings and economic rent for the sixtieth unit of labour? For the fortieth unit?

The remaining parts of the exercise refer to Case A when the government attempts to increase employment in this industry by shifting the labour demand curve to the right (the new labour demand curve is L^D_1).

(d) What are the new equilibrium wage and quantity of labour demanded?

(e) By how much does the government policy increase economic rents in this market?

(f) How much of the increase in economic rents goes to labour that was employed before the policy was introduced?

4. Industry Demand and Allocation Among Firms

(a) A firm's demand for a factor of production is given by its marginal revenue product, and if the price of the factor is given, the quantity demanded can be determined as in Exercise 1. Using the *MRP* schedules for Firms *A* and *B* given here, determine the quantity of machines each will rent if the rental price is $8.

Quantity of Machines	MRP_A	MRP_B
10	10	8
20	9	6
30	8	4
40	7	2
50	6	0
60	5	0

Quantity of machines rented: Firm *A* _____; Firm *B* _____.

(b) A single firm may be able to take the rental price as given, but if *A* and *B* represent the *MRP* in two different industries and if the total number of machines available to these two industries is fixed, Industry *A* can acquire more machines only by bidding them away from Industry *B*. Assuming that the stock of machines available is 70, how should they be most efficiently allocated between the two industries?
Quantity of machines rented: Industry *A* _____; Industry *B* _____.

(c) You can show the result from (b) graphically by plotting the two *MRP* curves in the machine market represented by the graph below. The horizontal axis shows the 70 total machines available. The *MRP* of machines in Industry *A* is measured from the left-hand axis as usual. The *MRP* of machines in Industry *B* (plotted for you) is measured from the right-hand axis, which is why the curve is upward-sloping in the graph. Plot the *MRP* for Industry *A*, and determine the rental price where these two curves intersect. What is this price, and how are the machines allocated between the two industries?

Figure 13-4

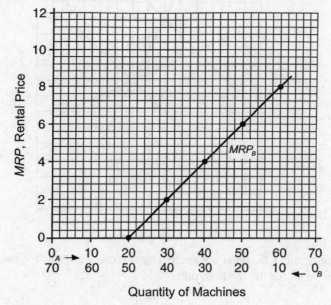

(d)   Suppose that the productivity of machines in Industry B rises because of technological improvements, and the new MRP schedule in B (MRP'_B) is as shown in the table below. Plot this curve on Figure 13-4, and determine the new equilibrium rental price and the allocation of machines between the two industries.

Quantity	MRP'_B
10	11
20	9
30	7
40	5
50	3

(e)   By how many machines does Industry B's MRP curve shift horizontally to the left? How many additional machines does Industry B rent? Explain why the number of machines B rents does not rise by as much as the MRP curve shifts to the left.

5.   **Competitive Factor Markets and Elasticity**
The demand and supply conditions in a competitive factor market are shown in Figure 13-5. Two possible demand scenarios are labelled D_1 and D_2. With an initial supply curve of S_0, the current equilibrium values of price and employment are 8 and 40, respectively.

Figure 13-5

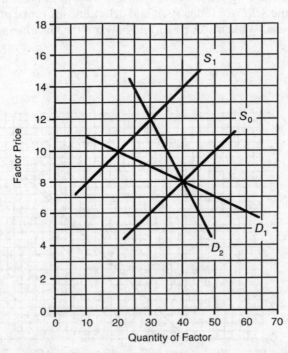

(a)   With supply curve S_0, what are current total factor earnings? What is the value of economic rents for the thirtieth unit?

(b) Suppose that the supply curve for the factor shifts up to the line labelled S_1. What are the new equilibrium values of price and employment for the two demand scenarios?

(c) Using midpoints between the new and old equilibrium values, calculate the elasticity of demand for each demand curve. Which demand curve is more elastic?

(d) Based on the elasticities you calculated in (c), answer each of the following questions (all else being equal). In each case give a brief explanation for your answer.

    (i) Which demand curve implies a lower elasticity of demand for the product that this factor produces?

    (ii) Which demand curve implies a higher degree of substitutability with other factors?

    (iii) Which demand curve implies larger increases in the factor's marginal productivity as less of the factor is used?

    (iv) Which demand curve implies lower total factor earnings at the new equilibrium situation compared with those at the initial equilibrium?

6. Regional Wage Differentials

There are two regional labour markets within a country, X and Y. Workers are equally qualified to perform the same type of job in either region. The cost of living is the same in the two regions, and workers have no non-monetary preferences with respect to the region in which they work and live. The initial situation in each labour market is shown in Figure 13-6, with equilibrium at point a in region X and at point h in region Y.

Figure 13-6

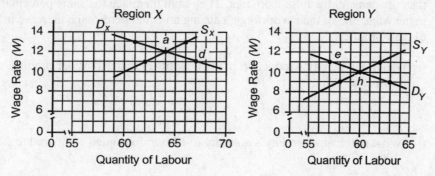

(a) Given the information provided, what type of wage differential exists between the two regions?

(b) In terms of the principle of net advantage, explain how and why labour mobility will create new equilibria (which might occur at points *d* and *e*).

7. **Influences on Elasticity of Factor Demand**

    In the text you discovered two influences on the firm's elasticity of demand for a factor (i.e., diminishing returns and substitutability between factors). In this exercise you discover two more, using labour as the example factor of production.

    (a) Alicia's firm and Henri's firm use the same type of labour, which is not substitutable with other factors of production, and have the same elasticity (slope) of demand for the final product. Their workers have the same wage rate, but wage payments are 80 percent of production costs for Alicia and only 7 percent for Henri. Then the wage rate increases by 10 percent.

    (i)   What is the percentage increase in total costs of production for Alicia? For Henri?

    (ii) Which one has the bigger percentage increase in the product price? Why?

    (iii) Which has the bigger reduction in quantity demanded of the product? Why?

    (iv) What happens to Henri's demand for labour compared to Alicia's? Why?

    (v)   What conclusion can you draw about the relationship between labour costs as a proportion of total costs, and the firm's elasticity of demand for labour?

    (b) Julie's firm and Fay's firms are identical in all respects except for the elasticity of demand for their (different) products. The demand for Fay's product is more elastic than the demand for Julie's product. They both then face the same percentage increase in the wage rate of their workforce, causing an equal percentage increase in the prices of their products.

    (i)   What will be Fay's reduction in the quantity demanded of her product, compared to Julie's? Why?

    (ii) What will happen to Fay's quantity of labour demanded compared to Julie's? Why?

    (iii) What conclusion can you draw about the relationship between elasticity of demand for the product and elasticity of demand for the factor of production?

Additional Multiple-Choice Questions

Use Figure 13-7 to answer Questions 1 and 2:

Figure 13-7

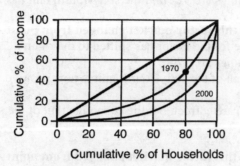

1. **The Lorenz curve for a hypothetical economy is given for two different years. Between 1970 and 2000,**
   - (a) the income distribution became less equal.
   - (b) the income distribution became more equal.
   - (c) the poverty rate rose.
   - (d) the poverty rate fell.
   - (e) the employment-income share of total income increased.

*2. **In 1970, the richest 20 percent of households received**
   - (a) twice as much income as the poorest 20 percent of households.
   - (b) as much income as the other 80 percent of households.
   - (c) twice as much income as the other 80 percent of households.
   - (d) half as much income as the other 80 percent of households.
   - (e) an indeterminate percentage of the total income of all households.

Questions 3 to 6 refer to Figure 13-8. The demand and supply curves apply to a competitive market for a factor of production. Point *A* is the initial market equilibrium situation; other points represent alternative equilibria caused by parallel shifts in either the demand curve or the supply curve, but *not* both.

Figure 13-8

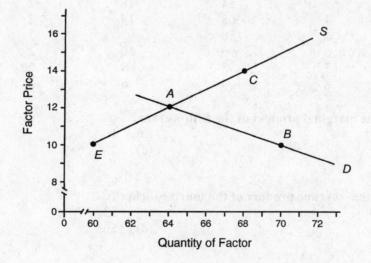

3.   At the initial equilibrium situation at point *A*,
      (a)   total income paid to the factor is $12.
      (b)   total factor earnings are $768.
      (c)   the economic rent of the sixty-fourth unit is zero.
      (d)   total factor earnings are $768 *and* the sixty-fourth unit has zero rent.
      (e)   total factor earnings are $12 *and* the sixty-fourth unit has zero rent.

*4.   If the equilibrium in this factor market changed from point *A* to point *B*, then
      (a)   the supply curve for the factor has shifted to the right.
      (b)   total factor earnings are $700.
      (c)   the economic rent of the sixty-fourth unit is now positive.
      (d)   All of the above.
      (e)   Both (a) and (b) are correct, but the economic rent of the sixty-fourth unit is now
             <u>negative</u>.

*5.   If the equilibrium in this factor market changed from point *A* to point *C*, then
      (a)   quantity supplied increased because the transfer price of the seventieth unit is $12.
      (b)   total factor earnings are lower at point *C* than at point *A*.
      (c)   total transfer payments for the initial 64 units of the factor increased.
      (d)   total economic rent for the initial 64 units of the factor increased.
      (e)   for the first total 64 units of the factor, the increase in economic rent equalled the
             decrease in transfer earnings.

*6.   Assuming an equilibrium factor price of $12,
      (a)   the sixtieth unit of the factor makes no economic rents.
      (b)   the economic rent of the sixtieth unit of the factor is $2.
      (c)   the transfer earnings of the sixtieth unit of the factor are $10.
      (d)   the economic rent of the sixtieth unit of the factor is $10.
      (e)   the sixtieth unit is paid $10 transfer earnings and $2 economic rent.

Questions 7 to 13 refer to the table below, which shows output at various levels of labour use and
the product price of the firm which sells in a perfectly competitive market.

Labour	Output	Marginal Product	Price
0	0	0	2
1	16	16	2
2	36	20	2
3	54	18	2
4	68	14	2
5	80	___	2
6	90	10	2
7	98	8	2
8	104	6	2

7.   What is the marginal product of the fifth worker?
      (a)   80.   (b)   16.
      (c)   12.   (d)   2.
      (e)   40.

*8.   The marginal revenue product of the fourth worker is
      (a) $108.   (b) $2.
      (c) $14.   (d) $68.
      (e) $28.

9. **The marginal revenue product of the seventh worker is**
   (a) greater than the *MRP* of the fourth worker.
   (b) equal to the *MRP* of the second worker.
   (c) less than the *MRP* of the eighth worker.
   (d) equal to $16.
   (e) equal to $2.

10. **Over the range of the second to the eighth worker, the value of the *MRP***
    (a) decreases due to diminishing marginal productivity.
    (b) remains constant at $2.
    (c) decreases because marginal revenue declines as more output is sold.
    (d) decreases because *both* marginal productivity *and* marginal revenue fall as output rises.
    (e) increases because total revenue product increases as more output is sold.

*11. **If the current wage rate per worker is $16, what is the profit-maximizing level of labour use?**
    (a) Five workers.   (b) Eight workers.
    (c) Seven workers.   (d) Six workers.
    (e) One worker.

*12. **If the firm's product price were to increase from $2 to $3, then**
    (a) the *MRP* curve would shift to the right.
    (b) at every level of employment, the value of *MRP* would decrease.
    (c) the firm would hire more workers, assuming the wage paid to workers did not change.
    (d) the wage rate would also have to increase by 50 percent.
    (e) the *MRP* would shift to the right and the firm would hire more workers if the wage rate did not change.

*13. **An increase in the wage rate would**
    (a) shift the *MRP* curve to the right.
    (b) cause the firm to hire more workers.
    (c) shift the *MRP* curve to the left.
    (d) necessarily lead to a decrease in the firm's product price.
    (e) None of the above.

*14. **Two firms have identical production functions using the same technology, the same fixed amount of capital, and the same type of labour. Firm *A* sells in a perfectly competitive product market, and Firm *B* sells in an imperfectly competitive product market. Which applies to their marginal revenue product curves for the variable factor, labour?**
    (a) The *MRP* curve is the demand for labour curve for Firm *A* but not Firm *B*.
    (b) The *MRP* curve is steeper for Firm *B* than for Firm *A* because Firm *B* sells its output at a higher price.
    (c) Their *MRP* curves are identical because they have the same production function.
    (d) The *MRP* curve for Firm *B* is the steeper one because it must lower price to sell more output.
    (e) The *MRP* curve for Firm *B* lies to the right of that for Firm *A* because marginal revenue is less than price for Firm *B*.

*15. Which of the following would be least likely to view most of the payment to a star basketball player as transfer earnings?
  (a)   The owners of the basketball team for which the star plays.
  (b)   The owners of a competing team.
  (c)   The star basketball player.
  (d)   The professional basketball industry.
  (e)   All of the above—they all think players are paid far more than they are worth.

*16. Equityville University implements a policy requiring that professors in economics be paid the same as professors in scrantomology. Then, government and business increase their demand for economists and reduce their demand for scrantomologists. Because of its pay-equity policy the university decides to leave its pay levels unchanged. If the university is to maintain its existing student–professor ratio, which of the following is most likely to happen to the average <u>quality</u> of the university's professors?
  (a)   It falls for economics and rises for scrantomology.
  (b)   It rises for economics and falls for scrantomology.
  (c)   It falls for both economics and scrantomology.
  (d)   It rises for both economics and scrantomology.
  (e)   It is unchanged for both economics and scrantomology, since the university's own demand and pay levels are unchanged.

*17. The market for a specific type of labour is currently in disequilibrium, with a wage greater than the equilibrium wage. As the market moves toward equilibrium, which of the following happens to *already employed* workers?
  (a)   Economic rent rises, and transfer earnings fall.
  (b)   Both economic rent and transfer earnings fall.
  (c)   Economic rent falls, and transfer earnings are unchanged.
  (d)   Economic rent rises, and transfer earnings rise.
  (e)   Both economic rent and transfer earnings are unchanged.

*18. If leisure is a normal good, how will an increase in the wage rate (i.e., the price of an hour's work) affect an *individual's* desired quantity supplied of hours worked?
  (a)   It will increase because the income and substitution effects work in the same direction for normal goods.
  (b)   It will increase because the labour-force participation rate will increase.
  (c)   It will increase because the opportunity cost of leisure has increased.
  (d)   It may increase or decrease, depending on the relative magnitudes of the income and substitution effects.
  (e)   It will increase because a rise in income increases the demand for normal goods.

Solutions

Chapter Review

1.(d) 2.(a) 3.(a) 4.(b) 5.(d) 6.(a) 7.(a) 8.(e) 9.(b) 10.(c) 11.(d) 12.(c) 13.(a) 14.(c) 15.(c) 16.(c) 17.(e) 18.(c) 19.(d) 20.(b) 21.(d) 22.(a) 23.(e)

Short-Answer Questions

1. When *MRP* > *MFC*, the extra revenues generated by another unit of the factor exceed the extra cost of the factor. Since the increase in revenues is greater than the increase in costs, profits will rise by the difference between *MFC* and *MRP*, so the profit maximizing firm will hire another unit of the factor. When *MRP* < *MFC*, the extra revenues generated by the last unit of the factor are less than the extra cost of the factor. Since the last unit of the factor adds more to costs than to revenues, it decreases profit by the difference, so the profit maximizing firm will want to get rid of (or lay off) the last unit of the factor. Since profits are increased by hiring more of the factor when *MRP* > *MFC* and by hiring less of the factor when *MRP* < *MFC,* profits must be at maximum when neither of these conditions apply—i.e., when *MRP* = *MFC*.

2. The firm's demand curve is its *MRP* curve of labour—i.e., the extra revenue generated as each extra worker is added to a fixed amount of capital. Since the firm sells in a perfectly competitive market, *MRP* = *MP* × *p*. Since *p* (the product price) does not change as the firm hires more workers and produces more output, the declining *MRP* as more workers are hired must be caused by a declining *MP*. The fall in *MP* is due to the law of diminishing marginal productivity—i.e., as more and more units of a variable factor are added to a fixed amount of other factors, the marginal product of the variable factor eventually falls. The competitive *industry's* demand curve for labour, however, is negatively sloped *not only* because each firm's *MP* falls as more labour is hired, *but also* because product price (*p*) falls when the output of the whole industry increases (i.e., the product's supply curve shifts to the right, causing excess supply and reducing the equilibrium price). The additional effect of the falling product price on *MRP* makes the perfectly competitive industry's demand curve for labour less elastic than the horizontal summation of the firms' *MRP* curves.

3. (i)   The firm's demand for labour is its *MRP* curve of labour, and *MRP* = *MP* × *p*. The firm profit maximizes at the prevailing market wage by hiring to where *MRP* = *w*. An increase in productivity increases *MP*, which increases *MRP* (i.e., shifts the firm's demand curve for labour). At the old level of hiring, *MRP* now exceeds *w*, and the firm profit-maximizes by hiring more labour.
    (ii) When the firm buys more capital, the variable factor, labour, has more of the fixed factor to work with and the *MP* of labour increases as a result. The rest of the answer is the same as in (i).
    (iii) The increase in demand for the product increases the product price, thereby shifting the *MRP* curve to the right (because *MRP* = *MP* × *p*). Now *MRP* exceeds *w* at the old level of hiring, and the firm profit-maximizes by hiring more labour. [*Note:* In all three cases the *MRP* at each level of employment increases, making *MRP* > *w* at the initial level of employment. In the first two cases the *physical* component of *MRP* increases, and in the third case the *monetary* component increases.]

4. Initially there is an *equilibrium differential* of $2 that *equalizes net advantage* by compensating for the higher risk in Firm A. [*Note:* It is also a *compensating differential* because it results solely from the difference in non-monetary aspects of jobs in the two firms.] When the pension plan is introduced, net advantage is no longer equalized across firms; it is now higher in Firm B than in Firm A. A *temporary differential* has been created. Workers will want to move from Firm A to Firm B, increasing labour supply and reducing the wage rate (by demand and supply) for Firm B while lowering labour supply and increasing the wage rate for Firm A. This will continue until a *new equilibrium differential* is established, where net advantage is again equalized. The new equilibrium differential will be more than $2 because the non-monetary advantages of Firm B now include *both* less risk *and* a better pension plan than Firm A.

5. This statement considers only the characteristics of the workers and not the characteristics of the jobs. Jobs with better non-monetary characteristics need to pay a lower wage rate to equalize net advantage. The pay-equity implication of the statement seeks to equalize wages regardless of net advantage. If wages were made equal, there would not be equal net advantage. Workers would want to leave firms with worse non-monetary conditions to join firms with better non-monetary conditions, since there would no longer be a compensating differential in wage rates. If the firms were prevented from paying different wage rates, they would likely re-establish equal net advantage by changing the non-monetary aspects of the job. Firms previously paying lower monetary wage rates because they provided better non-monetary conditions by, for example, spending more on job safety, likely would reduce safety expenditures. Workers who preferred more safety and lower wages to less safety and higher wages would be worse off than before.

6. No, they will not have the same demand for labour curves. The demand for labour curve is $MRP = MP \cdot MR$, and the MP component is the same for both firms because they have identical production functions. The perfectly elastic product demand curve for the perfect competitor means $P = MR$, but the downward-sloping product demand curve for the imperfectly competitive firm means $MR < P$. If they sell at the same price, therefore, at each quantity of labour the MR component for the imperfectly competitive firm is lower than for the perfect competitor, thus giving a lower MRP. Furthermore, the MRP has a *steeper slope* for the imperfectly competitive firm because, as it hires more labour to produce more output, <u>not only</u> does its MP decline (like the perfect competitor) <u>but also</u> its MR falls because it must lower price to sell more output (unlike the perfect competitor).

Exercises

1. **(a)** Case A: $MP = 9 \ (94 - 85)$ and $5 \ (99 - 94)$;
Case A: $MRP = 9 \times \$30 = \$270$ and $5 \times \$30 = \$150$;
Case B: $MRP = 9 \times \$27 = \$243$ and $5 \times \$27 = \$135$;
Case C: $MRP = 11 \times \$30 = \$330$ and $7 \times \$30 = \$210$.

Figure 13-9

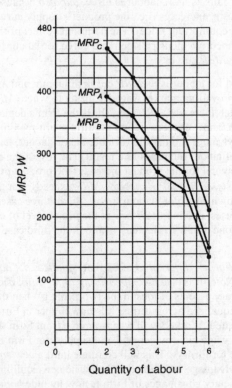

(b) As more labour is employed, marginal product falls; this is the law of diminishing returns (i.e., as more units of the variable factor are combined with a fixed amount of other factors, marginal product will eventually fall).

(c) For Case A, three units of labour are demanded. The firm maximizes profits at $MRP = w = \$360$ and $MRP = \$360$ for the third unit of labour.

(d) Three units of labour no longer represents a profit-maximizing situation since the MRP of the third unit of labour is $\$360$ while the wage rate is $\$270$. The firm will hire two more units of labour (a total of five), at which point $MRP = w = \$270$.

(e) For Case B, the firm will hire four units of labour, at which point $MRP = w = \$270$. This is one less unit of labour than in Case A because MRP is lower in Case B since the price of the product is less than in Case A.

(f) As noted for the specific case in (e), at each level of hiring the *MRP* of the marginal unit of labour is lower in Case B because the price (marginal revenue) per unit of output is lower ($27 versus $30).

(g) The demand curve for labour (i.e., the *MRP* curve) in Case B lies to the left of the demand curve in Case A (i.e., vertically below), because the product price is lower in Case B. The shift is not parallel because of diminishing *MP*. For example, by taking the $3 difference in price and multiplying by 13 (the MP of the second unit of labour), you see that the difference in *MRP* is $3 \times 13 = \$39$ (i.e., $390 – $351). For the fourth unit, however, the *MP* is 10 so the difference in *MRP* is $3 \times 10 = \$30$ (i.e., $300 – $270). Since the vertical distance between the two *MRP* curves declines as the number of units of labour increases, the *MRP* curve for Case B also has a flatter slope than the *MRP* curve for Case A.

(h) For Case C, the firm will hire four units of labour, which is one more than for Case A in part (c) at the same wage of $360. (See the answer to (i) below for the explanation.)

(i) The demand for labour at each wage rate is greater in Case C than in Case A, because the *MP* component of *MRP* at each level of hiring is greater in Case C. That is, even though both firms sell their product at the same price, the marginal productivity of each unit of labour is higher in Case C than in Case A.

2. (a) The supply curve is horizontal supply at *W*. Recall that economic rent is the difference between the lowest wage each worker will accept in this job (the transfer earnings component), which is read from the supply curve, and the wage actually received. A horizontal supply curve is the only one where there is no difference between the wage paid and the supply curve for *all* employed workers.

(b) The supply curve is vertical at *E*. This says that all the employed pilots would still be willing to work as pilots regardless of the wage paid. There is no transfer earnings component, so all earnings are economic rent.

(c) Total earnings of pilots is the area of the rectangle *OWFE*. Many non-linear supply curves could divide this area into two equal parts: half being transfer earnings and half being economic rent. The only linear supply curve to do this would be a diagonal line from *O* to *F*.

3. (a) In each case, $W = \$140$ and $L = 60$, so total factor payments are ($140 \times 60 =$) $8400.

(b) In Case A, economic rent is the area below the wage line and above the supply curve (area *abc* in the graph), which equals $1/2[(\$140 – \$20) \times 60] = 1/2(\$7200) = \$3600$. Transfer earnings equal total factor payments minus economic rent or, in this case, $8400 – $3600 = $4800. In Case B there is a perfectly inelastic supply curve, so all $8400 of factor payments are economic rent.

(c) At the wage of $140 the sixtieth unit of labour is *on* the supply curve L^S_A, so the whole $140 is transfer earnings. The fortieth unit is willing to work for $100 but is paid $140, so economic rent is $100 – $140 = $40.

(d) The new equilibrium wage and quantity at the intersection of L^S_A and L^D_1 are $160 and 70 units, respectively.

(e) Economic rents now equal area *adf* in the graph. Thus the increase in economic rent is area *bcdf*, which is area *bcde* ($20 \times 60 = \$1200$) plus area *efb* ($1/2(\$20 \times 10) = \$100$). Together they equal $1300.

(f) The 60 units of labour employed prior to the policy change receive area *bcde* in additional rents— i.e., the $1200 calculated in (e).

4. (a) The marginal cost of the factor is $8, so marginal factor cost = marginal revenue product = $8 (for profit maximization) and occurs at 30 machines for Firm *A* and 10 machines for Firm *B*.

(b) The industries will bid for the machines until *MRP* = the price of a machine for each and there is no excess demand or supply of machines—i.e., the total number of machines used must equal 70. To find the distribution of the 70 machines, therefore, you must find the point where *MRP*s are equal *and* the total number of machines is 70. This occurs when the price per machine is $6, with 50 machines allocated to Industry *A* and 20 to Industry *B*.

(c) The machines are allocated as explained in (b). The two *MRP* curves intersect at a rental price of $6, where Industry *A* rents 50 machines and Industry *B* rents 20. See Figure 13-10 for the plotted relationships.

(d) Comparing MRP_A in the first table with MRP'_B in the second table you see that $MRP_A = MRP'_B$ and total machines used = 70 when the equilibrium price per machine has risen from $6 to $7. Industry *A* rents 40 machines, and industry *B* rents 30.

Figure 13-10

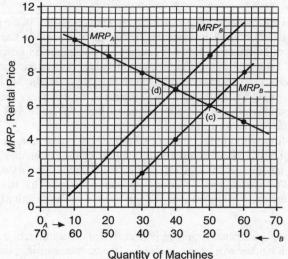

Quantity of Machines

(e) The *MRP* curve shifts to the left by about 15 machines. You can see this from the scale diagram, or you can compare the number of machines between the MRP'_B column and the MRP_B column at a common *MRP*. For example, at *MRP* of $7 the MRP'_B column gives 30 machines while the MRP_B column gives 15 machines (i.e., the midpoint between 8 and 6). Although Industry B's *MRP* curve shifts right by 15 machines, it uses only 10 more than initially (i.e., up from 20 to 30 machines) because the price per machine increases from $6 to $7. The rise in price occurs because Industry A is willing to pay a higher rental price ($7) to avoid losing all of the 15 extra machines that Industry B would want if the price remained at $6. Because of the rise in price, Industry B wants only 10 more machines (since MRP'_B = $7 at 30 machines, not at 35). [*Note:* What you see is nothing more than demand and supply at work. The change in Industry B's demand creates excess demand of 15 machines at the initial equilibrium price of $6. The excess demand pushes up price, which in turn reduces the quantity demanded by both industries, i.e., a movement *along* MRP_A and MRP'_B by industries A and B, respectively.]

5. **(a)** Total factor earnings are $320. The thirtieth unit is prepared to supply services for $6 but receives $8. Hence, economic rent is $2 for the thirtieth unit.

(b) For D_1, quantity is 20 and price per unit is $10. For D_2, quantity is 30 and price per unit is $12.

(c) Elasticity for $D_1 = 20/30 \times 9/2 = 3.00$; elasticity for $D_2 = 10/35 \times 10/4 = 0.71$. Clearly, D_1 has the higher elasticity.

(d) (i) D_2: A lower elasticity of demand for the product means a smaller increase in quantity demanded when the product's price falls, so the demand for factors also increases by less.

(ii) D_1: When the price of a factor rises (holding the prices of other factors constant), firms will want to use less of this factor and more of the factors whose prices did not rise. The greater the degree of substitutability between factors, the easier it is for firms to do this.

(iii) D_2: The question is another way of saying that the marginal product of the factor declines more rapidly as more of the factor is used, causing a bigger reduction in *MRP* and therefore requiring a bigger fall in factor price to achieve *MRP* = factor price at a higher level of employment—i.e., a steeper demand curve for the factor.

(iv) D_1: A rise in factor price reduces factor earnings if factor demand is elastic (and increases earnings if factor demand is inelastic). In part (c) you found D_1 to be elastic over the relevant range (and D_2 inelastic).

6. **(a)** There is a temporary differential of $2 per unit of labour since there are no non-monetary considerations, no differences in labour productivity, and no difference in the types of jobs available.

(b) Since there are no elements affecting net advantage other than the wage rate, workers will respond to the higher wage in Region X by moving from Y to X. As this migration takes place, the supply curve of labour in Region Y will shift to the left and the supply curve in Region X will shift to the right. Wages will rise in Y and fall in X. Migration from Y to X will continue until the wage differential is eliminated (wage = $11 in both regions). Net advantage will now be equalized across regions. The temporary differential is eliminated, and the equilibrium differential is zero.

7.　**(a)**　(i)　Alicia's production costs rise by 8 percent (= 10 percent of 80 percent) and Henri's by 0.7 percent (= 10 percent of 7 percent).

(ii)　Because the (percentage) rise in production costs is greater for Alicia than for Henri, *ceteris paribus,* she will also have a bigger (percentage) increase in her product price.

(iii)　Because of her bigger (percentage) increase in the product price, and because the two product demand curves have the same elasticity, Alicia will have a bigger (percentage) reduction in quantity of product demanded than Henri.

(iv)　Compared to Henri, Alicia's bigger (percentage) reduction in quantity demanded of the product means a bigger (percentage) fall in production, hence a bigger (percentage) fall in the quantity of labour she demands.

(v)　The greater the wage costs as a proportion of total costs of production, the greater the firm's elasticity of demand for labour.

(b)　(i)　Fay will face a bigger (percentage) reduction in quantity of product demanded, because hers is more sensitive to price (i.e., a more elastic demand curve) than Julie's.

(ii)　Compared to Julie, Fay's bigger (percentage) fall in product demand will, *ceteris paribus,* generate a bigger (percentage) fall in output and thus a bigger (percentage) fall in the amount of labour required to produce it.

(iii)　The greater the elasticity of demand for the firm's product, the greater the firm's elasticity of demand for a factor of production.

Additional Multiple-Choice Questions

1.(a) **2.**(b) **3.**(d) **4.**(d) **5.**(d) **6.**(e) **7.**(c) **8.**(e) **9.**(d) **10.**(a) **11.**(c) **12.**(e) **13.**(e) **14.**(d) **15.**(d) **16.**(a) **17.**(c) **18.**(d)

Explanations for the Asterisked Multiple-Choice Questions

2.(b)　Since you are looking for the share of the richest 20 percent, read up the vertical axis until you find the share going to the remaining 80 percent and subtract that share from 100. Since 50 percent of income goes to the bottom 80 percent of households, the remaining 50 percent goes to the top 20 percent of households.

4.(d)　The supply curve shifts to the right. Since the supply curve is upward sloping, the transfer earnings of the sixty-fourth unit (read from the new supply curve) will be less than the equilibrium wage rate at *B*. The difference is economic rent.

5.(d)　The first 64 workers are already working, and the supply curve shows that the sixty-fourth worker is willing to work in this job for a wage rate no less than $12, while the other 63 would work for less than $12. The first 63 workers, therefore, currently earn some economic rent—i.e., the difference between what they are paid ($12) and what the supply curve shows is the minimum wage necessary to keep them in their current jobs (i.e., their transfer earnings). An increase in their wage will simply add to this economic rent without changing their transfer earnings. That is, the extra earnings increase the area between the wage rate and the supply curve (i.e., their economic rent) without changing the area below the supply curve (i.e., their transfer earnings). The sixty-fourth worker currently earns only transfer earnings, but the extra earnings following an increase in the wage rate will be economic rent for this worker. [*Note:* Do not confuse *transfer payments* from government programs in answer (c) with *transfer earnings* from employment.]

6.(e)　Since the equilibrium price is $12, the applicable *D* and *S* curves are those drawn in the diagram intersecting at *A*. All units of the factor below the sixty-fourth earn some economic rent, ruling out answer (a). The sixtieth unit of the factor can be hired for $10 (at point *E* on the supply curve), so transfer earnings are $10 and answer (c) is correct. Since the sixtieth unit can be hired for $10 but is actually paid $12, economic rent is $2 and answer (b) is correct.

8.(e)　$MRP = MP \times p = 14 \times \$2 = \$28$ for the fourth worker.

11.(c)　The profit-maximizing level of hiring is where $MRP = w = \$16$. $MRP = MP \times p = \$16$ only for the seventh worker (i.e., $8 \times \$2$).

12.(e) An increase in the price of the product increases MRP at every level of employment, so answer (b) is incorrect. The increase in MRP at every level of employment means that the MRP curve shifts vertically up. Since the MRP curve is downward-sloping, a vertically upward shift is also a shift to the right, so answer (a) is correct. If the wage rate remains unchanged, the increase in MRP means $MRP > w$ at the previous level of employment, so the firm will want to hire more workers until $MRP = w$ again, so answer (c) is correct. The wage rate in the factor market is determined by the *market* demand and supply of the factor—i.e., by both the total supply of workers (over which this firm has no control) and the total demand for workers by *all* firms in *all* industries employing this type of worker. There is nothing at all in the question to tell us anything about this industry's supply curve of workers; it could be perfectly elastic, in which case the wage rate would not change. Answer (d) is clearly wrong.

13.(e) Since the firm is selling (good X) in a perfectly competitive product market, $MRP_L = VMP_L = MP_L \times P_x = MP_L \times 2$. The profit-maximizing (hence cost-minimizing) firm will hire labour to the point where $MFC_L = MRP_L$. A change in the wage rate <u>directly</u> affects the MFC_L curve, not the MRP_L curve. [*Note*: The higher wage rate would subsequently have an <u>indirect</u> (second-round) affect on the MRP_L curve if higher wages caused some firms to exit the industry, thereby increasing the market share of remaining firms. But firms would exit only if the higher wages created economic losses, so answer (a) would be correct if it said that the increase in wage rate <u>may</u> shift the MRP to the right; but, it says <u>would</u>, which is incorrect.]

14.(d) Having the same production functions means that the MP of the labour curve is the same for both firms, and the fixed amount of capital means this MP diminishes as more labour is hired. The demand for labour curve for each firm is its MRP ($= MP \times MR$). For the perfectly competitive firm the product price does not change as it sells more output, so $MR = P$, and diminishing MP is the sole reason why the MRP curve slopes downward. The imperfectly competitive firm, however, faces a negatively sloped demand curve for output so selling more means lowering price, making $MR < P$ with MR falling as output rises. For this firm, therefore, both MP <u>and</u> MR fall as it hires more labour to produce and sell more output. Since the MP curve is the same for both, the falling MR for the imperfectly competitive firm must mean that its MRP falls faster (i.e., the MRP curve is steeper) than for the perfectly competitive firm.

15.(d) Both team owners and the player know that the player can command a similar salary from another team, so view most of the salary as transfer earnings. If the star player were to leave basketball entirely, however, salary would fall substantially (i.e., earnings will be much lower in the next-best alternative). To the professional basketball industry, therefore, less of the player's salary is transfer earnings and most is economic rent (i.e., the amount in excess of transfer earnings).

16.(a) The increased demand for economists increases their wages/salaries elsewhere, causing some higher-quality economists to seek employment outside the university. Because it can't raise wages to induce them to stay, therefore, the university will have to lower its hiring standards to keep the same faculty size (needed to keep the student–professor ratio unchanged). For scrantomologists, however, the lower salary elsewhere will cause more to seek employment at the university. The university now has more applicants to choose from, so it can be more selective and raise its hiring standards for scrantomologists.

17.(c) At a wage above equilibrium the wage being paid to already employed workers (read from the demand curve) exceeds the minimum they are willing to accept (i.e., their transfer earnings, read from the supply curve), and this excess is economic rent. As the excess supply of labour in this disequilibrium pushes wages down the quantity hired is increased *along* the market demand curve, which is unchanged because the extra hiring is a response to a change only in the "price" of labour. The fall in the wage rate reduces the total earnings of already employed workers but does not change their transfer earnings since the supply curve is unchanged. All the reduction in their total earnings, therefore, is a reduction in their economic rent.

18.(d) The wage rate is the "price" of leisure. The increase in wage rate increases the opportunity cost of leisure, reducing the quantity of leisure demanded and increasing the quantity of labour supplied via the substitution effect (i.e., the response to the change in opportunity cost). At the same time, the higher wage increases the individual worker's income and so increases the purchasing power of income. Increased purchasing power increases the demand for normal goods, including leisure, via the income effect, so reducing the quantity of labour supplied. Since the two effects of the change in the "price" of leisure work in opposite directions, the net effect depends on the relative magnitudes of the two. If the substitution effect exceeds the income effect of the rise in wage, quantity of hours supplied will increase. If the income effect exceeds the substitution effect, quantity of hours supplied will decrease. [*Note*: In Chapter 6 you saw the income and substitution effects of a change in the price of a normal good worked in the *same direction*, but here you see them working in *opposite directions*. The reason is that an increase in the price of other goods *reduces* purchasing power, while an increase in the price of leisure (i.e., the wage rate) *increases* purchasing power.]

14

Labour Markets

Chapter Overview

In a competitive labour market, the forces of supply and demand set wages. **Differences in wages in competitive labour markets** will arise because some skills are more valued than others, because some jobs are more onerous and risky than others, because of varying amounts of human capital, and because of discrimination based on such factors as gender and race.

Two important non-competitive labour market situations are presented: a single employer with monopoly power in hiring labour (a **monopsonist**), and **a union acting as a monopolist** in supplying labour. In otherwise competitive labour markets, union actions tend to drive up wage rates but only at the cost of reducing employment. A monopsonist, however, tends to drive wages down below the competitive level and reduce employment, and union entry into such a monopsonistic labour market can generate higher wages and higher employment. A **legislated minimum wage** may also reduce employment in a competitive labour market but increase employment in a monopsonistic labour market.

This chapter also considers how **discrimination** affects wages and employment opportunities. Direct discrimination affects wages and employment opportunities in part by limiting labour supply in the better-paying occupations and by increasing it in less attractive occupations.

Union membership in Canada as a share of the labour force is about 30 percent. The **union goal** of increasing wages relative to those for non-union workers (thereby creating a **union wage premium**) can conflict with the goal of increasing employment of union members. The process by which unions and employers reach an agreement is known as **collective bargaining**. The chapter reviews the evidence about the effects of unions on wage rates and employment, and closes with a discussion of the implications of the shift in employment from manufacturing jobs to service-sector jobs.

LO **LEARNING OBJECTIVES**

After studying this chapter, you will be able to

1. explain wage differentials in both competitive and non-competitive labour markets.

2. describe the possible effects of legislated minimum wages.

3. discuss the trade-off that unions usually face between wages and employment.

4. explain why the trend away from manufacturing jobs and toward service jobs is not necessarily a problem for the economy as a whole.

Hints and Tips

The following may help you avoid some of the most common errors on examinations.

✓ The condition for a firm's profit-maximizing level of *employment* of a factor of production—that it hires to the point at which marginal factor cost equals marginal revenue product—is the same regardless of whether or not the firm has market power in the factor market. In a competitive labour market the wage rate equals the marginal factor cost, whereas in a monopsonistic labour market the wage rate is less than the marginal factor cost.

✓ Similarly, a monopsony faced with an effective minimum wage still profit-maximizes by hiring to where $MFC = MRP$. What the minimum wage does, however, is <u>change</u> the average and marginal factor cost curves (the AFC and MTC) of the monopsonist. Once you understand how, over a range of employment, imposing a minimum wage can <u>increase</u> the monopsonist's AFC yet simultaneously <u>decrease</u> its MFC, you are well on your way to understanding why the firm may hire more workers when the minimum is imposed.

✓ Don't be confused by the concept of economic rent; it is the same principle as economic profit but applies to factors of production rather than to firms. Economic rent is the excess over the payment required to keep the factor in its current use. For example, assume you would stay in your current job if your employer reduced your salary by $5000 but that you would move (i.e., transfer) to an alternative job if your current employer were to reduce your salary by more than $5000. The $5000 is your economic rent, and the rest of your salary is your transfer earnings.

✓ Be careful how you interpret data. Just because unionized workers on average have higher earnings than non-unionized workers does not necessarily mean that all the difference is attributable to unionization. Some of that earnings (or wage) difference would remain even without unions, if the characteristics of the workers and the jobs differed.

Chapter Review

Wage Differentials

Equilibrium wage differentials can exist in competitive labour markets due to differences in working conditions and other non-monetary differences, differences in innate skills of workers, and differences in the amount of investment in **human capital** (whether acquired through formal education or on-the-job training). Because people have some control over the amount of human capital they can acquire, part of the wage differentials attributable to human capital may also be temporary, but an equilibrium differential will remain because human capital is usually costly to acquire (particularly when acquired through more years of formal education). Wage differentials can also result from discrimination by characteristics such as gender or race. Discriminatory differentials are the wage differences that remain after the effects of all other factors have been taken into account. When wage discrimination results from the personal preferences of firm *owners or managers*, competitive market pressures will tend to reduce the differentials. When the discrimination results from the preferences of *customers*, however, the discriminatory wage differentials will remain until their attitudes change and/or government intervenes with anti-discriminatory legislation.

Wage differentials also occur in imperfect markets. The text discusses two types of imperfect labour market situations. On the demand side of the labour market, one firm may be a **monopsonist**, with sufficient market power to influence wage rates. On the supply side, labour supply may be regulated by a single seller (a union). A situation in which a monopsonist on the demand side faces a union on the supply side is called a **bilateral monopoly**. The effects of *unions* and *minimum wages* on employment differ depending on whether the demand side of the labour market is perfectly competitive or monopsonistic.

1. **Which of the following, by itself, would tend to generate a higher wage for worker *A* compared to worker *B*?**
   (a) Worker *A* has a job that is safer in terms of the chances of injury.
   (b) Worker *A*, of a particular ethnic heritage, has encountered more labour market discrimination.
   (c) Worker *B* has more years of formal education.
   (d) Worker *A* has obtained more on-the-job education than has *B*.
   (e) Both workers are accountants, but worker *B* has more knowledge of computer software than does *A*.

2. **All workers would receive the same wage if**
   (a) all workers were identical in terms of innate skills, human capital, and on-the-job education.
   (b) the non-monetary advantages and conditions of all jobs were identical.
   (c) all firms operated in competitive labour markets.
   (d) labour was supplied in perfectly competitive markets.
   (e) All of the above must apply.

3. **Which of the following is likely to influence the willingness of individuals to stay in school beyond the years of compulsory education?**
   (a) The earnings they could make in the labour market if they do not stay in school.
   (b) The expectation of higher incomes if they do stay in school.
   (c) Tuition fees and costs of attendance such as books and additional living costs.
   (d) The opportunity to have a greater choice of jobs that match their career preferences.
   (e) All of the above.

4. **If discrimination prevents a certain group of people from entering labour market *E* but not labour market *O*,**
   (a) the wage rate will be lower than the competitive level in both markets.
   (b) the labour supply curve is farther to the left than it would otherwise be, in both markets.
   (c) wage rates will tend to be higher in market *E* and lower in market *O* than they would be with no discrimination.
   (d) individuals in labour market *E* benefit only if the demand curve for labour is elastic.
   (e) individuals in labour market *O* will benefit from resulting higher wages if demand for labour in market *O* is inelastic.

5. **Assume that the owners of some firms in competitive product markets discriminate between equally qualified workers on the basis of gender and that this discrimination lowers the wage rate of women relative to men. Which of the following is likely to occur?**
   (a) Firms that do not discriminate will have higher costs of production.
   (b) Firms that do not discriminate will have higher product prices.
   (c) Firms that discriminate will pay for it in lower profits.
   (d) All of the above.
   (e) None of the above.

6. **If in January 2013 the demand for people with university degrees increased significantly relative to the demand for people with high-school diplomas, then the wage differential between the two groups in May 2013 would be which of the following (*ceteris paribus*)?**
   (a) An equilibrium differential.
   (b) Smaller than the differential that is expected to exist in May 2018.
   (c) A temporary differential.
   (d) Totally eliminated by May 2018.
   (e) Partly a temporary differential and partly an equilibrium differential.

7. **Where the supply curve of labour is upward sloping, the marginal cost curve of labour to the monopsonist**
   (a) is the same as the supply curve of labour.
   (b) is the same as the average cost curve of labour.
   (c) lies above the supply curve of labour.
   (d) lies below and parallel to the supply curve.
   (e) intersects the supply curve at the equilibrium wage.

8. **A firm that currently pays $16 per hour to each of its 10 workers discovers that it must pay $18 to get an eleventh worker. What is the marginal cost to the firm of obtaining the eleventh worker?**
   (a) $2.
   (b) $18.
   (c) $34.
   (d) $38.
   (e) $20.

9. **In the absence of a union, a monopsonist will employ labour to the point where**
   (a) demand equals supply.
   (b) the wage rate equals the marginal cost of the worker.
   (c) supply equals marginal revenue product of the worker.
   (d) marginal cost of the worker equals marginal revenue product of the worker.
   (e) the marginal cost of the worker equals the marginal cost of the product.

10. **In a bilateral monopoly, the effect of a union bargaining a higher wage than the monopsonist would pay in the absence of the union**
    (a) is to change the labour supply curve faced by the monopsonist.
    (b) may result in the monopsonist hiring more labour.
    (c) will always cause the monopsonist to reduce hiring of labour.
    (d) is to change the demand curve for labour of the monopsonist.
    (e) Both (a) and (b).

11. **A minimum wage is said to be *binding* or *effective* if**
    (a) it has been set by a union.
    (b) it is above the market wage that would otherwise prevail.
    (c) it is the lowest wage that allows a level of income above the poverty line.
    (d) all workers who desire employment at that wage are in fact employed.
    (e) all firms pay more than the minimum.

Labour Unions

Labour unions face an inherent conflict between the level of wages and the size of the union itself unless they face monopsonist employers or are able to increase the demand for labour using *featherbedding* practices. While there is some evidence that firms invest less when unions have the potential to *hold up* the firm and capture some of the returns to investment, there is no clear conclusion about the long-run impact on productivity.

12. **Evidence for Canada indicates that**
    (a) the growth in union membership was low in the immediate postwar era (late 1940s and early 1950s).
    (b) the growth in union membership was low in the 1980s and early 1990s.
    (c) unionization rates in the public sector are lower than those in the private sector.
    (d) unions have not been able to create a union wage premium.
    (e) unions have not lobbied for legislation that applies to all workers.

13. **Featherbedding practices by unions**
    (a) shift the supply curve of labour to the right.
    (b) if successful will increase employment.
    (c) increase the loss in employment of union members when union wage premiums are increased.
    (d) increase the productivity of all workers.
    (e) increase the productivity of unionized workers.

14. **The hold-up problem arises from**
    (a) the ability of unions to hold wages above market levels.
    (b) the ability of unions to capture some of the economic rent from installed capital.
    (c) the ability of a monopsony to hold employment below the competitive level.
    (d) the ability of a monopsony to hold *MRP* above the wage rate.
    (e) government holding the minimum wage above the free-market equilibrium level.

15. **Evidence for Canada indicates that**
    (a) unions have a substantial effect on both wage rates and employment.
    (b) unions decrease employment but have no effect on wage rates.
    (c) a significant union wage premium exists but the effect of unions on employment is unclear.
    (d) unions have no effect on either wage rates or employment.
    (e) featherbedding substantially increases employment in today's economy.

The "Good Jobs–Bad Jobs" Debate

"Good" jobs are characterized by high pay and job security while "bad" jobs are characterized by low wages with little job security and often little potential for advancement. In developed countries the manufacturing sector's share of total jobs has been falling and the service sector's share has been rising. It has been argued that, because the service sector contains a larger proportion of "bad" jobs than the manufacturing sector, the change in the relative importance of the two sectors in the job market has increased the overall share of "bad" jobs in the economy. In the context of this debate, and recognizing that by no means are all service-sector jobs "bad" jobs, the section reviews some of the issues and implications arising out of the shift from manufacturing-sector jobs to service-sector jobs.

16. **Which of the following provides support for the view that the continuing decline in manufacturing employment is not necessarily a problem?**
    (a) Despite the decline in manufacturing employment, real income per hour worked has continued to rise.
    (b) The decline in manufacturing employment is mainly due to the high level of unionization in that sector.
    (c) Productivity increases in the service sector have been overestimated.
    (d) The income elasticity of demand for services is falling.
    (e) The number of jobs in manufacturing has been falling, but their share of total jobs has been rising.

17. **Many "bad" jobs may not be as bad as they seem because**
    (a) although they pay low wages, they offer high job security.
    (b) they are generally unionized, and the unions protect the interests of the members.
    (c) they pay much more than the minimum-wage rate.
    (d) they provide valuable labour market experience for young workers.
    (e) they employ skilled workers displaced from the manufacturing sector.

Short-Answer Questions

1. Assume that there is a sudden increase in demand for people with master's degrees, which increases the difference in salaries between people with master's degrees and people with bachelor's degrees. Give a brief economic explanation for each of the following questions.

    (i) What effect would you expect this to have on university enrollment at the master's level?

    (ii) Over time, what would you expect to see happen to the difference in salaries?

    (iii) Would you eventually see the difference disappear?

2. Assume that a particular professional association argued that immigration should not be used to alleviate a shortage of qualified people in Canada because the qualification standards in other countries may be lower than in Canada. The Government of Canada responded that it would investigate the qualifications required in other countries and determine which were equivalent to Canadian qualifications. Immigrants with equivalent qualifications would be accredited to practise immediately upon arrival in Canada. The Canadian association, however, disagreed with this policy. What have you learned in this chapter that could explain why the association disagreed?

3. Why does the marginal cost of a factor of production exceed its average cost for a monopsony? Extend your reasoning to show the similarity between a monopsonist and a monopolist.

4. Explain the reasoning behind the following statement. "A minimum wage increases employment by a monopsony because it reduces the marginal cost of hiring additional workers."

5. Explain why a union of skilled workers, earning much more than the minimum wage, may have a selfish motive in pressuring the government to increase the minimum wage.

Exercises

1. **A Minimum Wage in a Competitive Labour Market**
    Draw a diagram showing the market demand and supply curves of unskilled workers. Label the equilibrium wage rate w_0 and the equilibrium employment L_0. The government then imposes a binding minimum wage (w_1). [*Note:* This exercise also applies to a union-imposed wage in a competitive labour market.]

    Your diagram:

    (a) Show the resulting level of employment (L_1). How much does employment fall as a result of the minimum wage? Would the employment level have fallen more if demand were less elastic? More elastic? What can you conclude about the relationship between the effect of an increase in the minimum wage and the elasticity of demand for low-wage workers?

(b) On your diagram, show the number of people who want jobs at the minimum wage (L_S). How much unemployment does the minimum wage create? [*Hint:* Unemployment is the difference between those who want to work and those who have jobs.] What is the relationship between the amount of unemployment created by the minimum wage and the elasticity of supply of people willing to work at low-wage jobs?

(c) Assume that there are 2000 people who are unemployed at the minimum wage in (b). Explain whether and why you agree or disagree with the following statement. "Eliminating the minimum wage will increase employment by 2000."

(d) Now assume that your diagram is for workers in a particular profession and their professional association has raised salaries above the equilibrium level *without* establishing a minimum wage. How has the professional association done this? How do you show its method in your diagram?

2.   A Monopsonist's Marginal Cost and Average Cost of Labour
This exercise demonstrates that the marginal cost of labour curve (*MC*) lies above the supply curve of labour in a non-parallel fashion. Columns 1 and 2 represent the supply-of-labour relationship for a monopsonistic employer.

(a) Fill in the values for total cost in column 3 and then calculate the marginal cost values in column 4.

(1) Quantity of Labour	(2) Wage Rate	(3) Total Cost	(4) Marginal Labour Cost
8	$10.00	$80.00	_____
9	10.50	_____	_____
10	11.00	_____	_____
11	11.50	_____	_____
12	12.00	_____	_____
13	12.50	_____	_____
14	13.00	_____	_____
15	13.50	_____	_____
16	14.00	_____	_____
17	14.50	_____	_____

(b) What is the *difference* between the wage rate and the marginal labour cost for the tenth worker? What is the *difference* for the fifteenth worker? Why does the difference increase?

(c) What is the slope of the marginal labour cost curve? What is the slope of the labour supply curve? What do you notice when you compare these slopes?

(d) Assume that the *MRP* of labour is $14.50. How many workers will the monopsonist hire? What wage rate will it pay? How many would be hired if this firm were perfectly competitive in the labour market? What wage rate would it pay?

3. **Competition, Monopsony, and a Union**
Referring to Figure 14-1, which represents the labour market in an industry, answer the following questions.

Figure 14-1

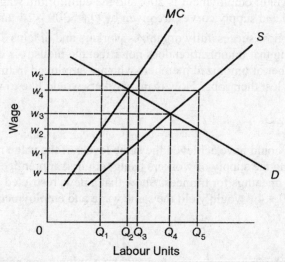

(a) If a competitive market prevailed, the equilibrium wage would be _____ and the amount of employment would be _____.

(b) If a wage-setting union enters this (competitive) market and establishes a higher wage at w_4, the amount of employment would be _____, and the amount of surplus labour unemployed would be _____. What would be the new labour supply curve facing employers?

(c) Assume that this market consists of a single large firm hiring labour in a local market. If the firm hired Q_1 workers, it would have to pay all workers the wage _____, but the marginal labour cost of the last person hired would be _____. Because the marginal revenue product of the last person hired (Q_1) is equal to _____, there is an incentive for the firm to continue hiring up to _____, at which the wage will be _____, the marginal labour cost will be _____, and the marginal revenue product will be _____. Compare this with the result in (a).

(d)   Suppose that a union now organizes in the monopsonist market and sets a wage at w_3. The amount of employment will be _____.

(e)   What happens to the labour supply curve when a union organizes this labour market, but instead of setting a high wage it excludes workers by stiff apprenticeship rules? Predict the effects.

Extension Exercises

These exercises use equations instead of diagrams to examine union-imposed wages.

E1.   A Union in a Competitive Labour Market
Suppose that there is a competitive market for workers in a particular industry. The equilibrium level of employment is 200, and the equilibrium wage rate (w) is $50. The labour demand and supply curves are given by $Q_D = 300 - 2w$ and $Q_S = 4w$, respectively.

(a)   A union now successfully organizes workers and obtains a wage rate of $60. Assuming that unionization does not affect the industry's demand curve, calculate the number of unionized members who are employed in this industry. How many workers lost their jobs? How many workers would like to work in this industry?

(b)   A union could have achieved the same levels of the wage rate and employment by restricting the supply of workers using required apprenticeship programs and/or reduced openings for trainees. Show that a new, restricted labour supply curve of $Q_S = -60 + 4w$ would yield the same wage and employment levels as in (a).

(c)   The reduction in employment caused by a union wage above the competitive level depends on the elasticity of labour demand. If the industry's demand curve for labour had been $Q_D = 200$, what would be the implied elasticity of labour demand? How many workers would have lost their jobs due to unionization? (Assume that the labour supply curve is $Q_S = 4w$.)

E2.   Union Wages and Mobility Between Labour Markets
There are two competitive labour markets in the economy of Arcadia. Market X has a labour demand function $L = 120 - 1/3w$ (i.e., $w = 360 - 3L$) and a labour supply function $L = 0.5w - 20$ (i.e., $w = 40 + 2L$), where w is the wage rate and L is the quantity of labour. Market Z has the same labour demand function as Market X, but its labour supply function is $L = 0.5w - 10$ (i.e., $w = 20 + 2L$).

(a)   Calculate the competitive equilibrium levels of w and L in each labour market.

(b) Suppose that a union imposes a wage of $162 in market Z. At the union wage, what is the quantity of labour demanded? The quantity of labour supplied? How many workers are displaced in this market?

(c) If all of the unemployed persons in (b) were to enter labour Market X, the supply curve of labour in X would become $L = 0.5w - 15$ (i.e., $w = 30 + 2L$). How many of the workers displaced from Market Z would find employment in Market X? What would happen to the wage in Market X?

Additional Multiple-Choice Questions

Questions 1 to 7 refer to Figure 14-2, which depicts a labour market for unskilled workers.

Figure 14-2

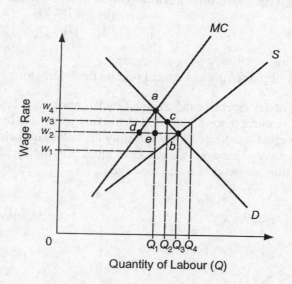

1. **If perfect competition existed in this market, the wage and quantity of employment would be**
   (a) w_4 and Q_1.
   (b) w_3 and Q_2.
   (c) w_1 and Q_1.
   (d) w_2 and Q_3.
   (e) w_2 and Q_4.

2. **If this market were monopsonistic, the firm would hire**
   (a) Q_1 workers.
   (b) Q_3 workers.
   (c) Q_2 workers.
   (d) Q_4 workers.
   (e) some quantity between Q_3 and Q_4 workers.

3. **A profit-maximizing monopsony would pay a wage of**
   (a) w_1.
   (b) w_3.
   (c) w_2.
   (d) w_4.
   (e) somewhere between zero and one half of $(w_1 + w_4)$.

*4. **If a minimum wage of w_2 is imposed on the monopsony, the supply curve of labour facing the firm becomes**

(a) $MC - S$.
(b) acb.
(c) w_2bS.
(d) w_2daMC.
(e) w_2dea.

5. **In this case, the minimum wage of w_2 would generate employment of**

(a) Q_1.
(b) Q_3.
(c) Q_2.
(d) Q_4.
(e)   less than Q_1.

6. **If a minimum wage of w_3 were imposed on the market, the monopsonist would hire**

(a) Q_2 workers.
(b)   more than Q_3 workers since the marginal cost of labour would fall.
(c) Q_4 workers because the demand for labour would shift to the right.
(d) Q_1 workers.
(e)   no workers.

*7. **With a minimum wage of w_3, total unemployment in this market would be**

(a) $Q_3 - Q_2$.
(b) $Q_4 - Q_3$.
(c) $Q_4 - Q_2$.
(d) $Q_4 - Q_1$.
(e)   zero.

Answer Questions 8 and 9 by referring to Figure 14-3 and the information below.

An economy consists of two competitive industries, X and Y, and a total labour force of 120 workers. Industry X requires more-highly skilled workers relative to Industry Y. Workers *within* each industry are equally productive, but differ by the colour of their eyes. Nine of the workers in each industry have green eyes, the rest have blue eyes. Industry X is now taken over by new owners, who don't trust any worker with green eyes.

Figure 14-3

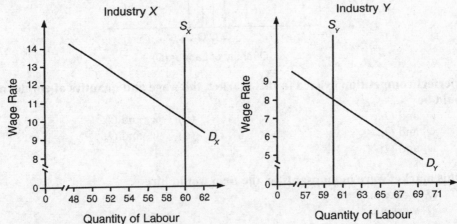

*8. **Before the new owners take possession of Industry X, the differential in the wage rate between the two industries**

(a)   represents "discrimination" by employers in Y, since the wage is $2 lower.
(b)   is a temporary differential of $2.
(c)   is an equilibrium differential of $2.
(d)   is $2, because employers in Industry X must be monopsonists.
(e)   is $2, because of the "mix" of green-eyed and blue-eyed workers in each industry.

*9. Now the new owners fire every green-eyed worker in Industry *X* but do not replace them with blue-eyed workers. If all green-eyed workers find jobs in Industry *Y*, then
   (a)   51 workers in *X* are paid $13 each.
   (b)   69 workers in *Y* are paid $5 each.
   (c)   the total income of all blue-eyed workers in *X* increases from $510 to $663.
   (d)   the total income of all workers in *Y* falls from $480 to $345.
   (e)   All of the above.

Questions 10 to 13 refer to the following table, which categorizes the four elements in the table according to the existence of market power, or lack of it, on the demand (buyer) and supply sides of the factor market. They are similar to Questions 1 to 7 above, but rely on your knowledge of the theory without using a diagram.

	Competitive Labour Demand	**Monopsony Buyer**
competitive labour supply	*element 1* competitive, competitive	*element 2* competitive, monopsonist
union labour supply	*element 3* union, competitive	*element 4* union, monopsonist

*10. Referring to the situation depicted by *element 1*, a minimum wage that is set above the competitive level will cause which of the following?
   (a)   Employment will increase.
   (b)   An excess demand for labour will be created.
   (c)   Some workers will lose their jobs in this industry.
   (d)   Fewer individuals will wish to offer their labour services to this industry.
   (e)   None of the above.

*11. Referring to the situation depicted by *element 2*, a monopsonist firm
   (a)   lowers both the wage rate and employment below their competitive levels.
   (b)   lowers the wage rate but not employment below their competitive levels.
   (c)   has the same employment level and the same wage as a competitive firm.
   (d)   raises the wage rate but decreases employment compared to their competitive levels.
   (e)   raises both the wage rate and employment above their competitive levels.

*12. Referring to the situation depicted by *element 3*, if a union negotiates a wage above the competitive level and the firms remain free to determine employment without any featherbedding, then
   (a)   employment in the industry will fall.
   (b)   employed workers will earn a lower wage rate than before.
   (c)   the reduction in employment equals the increase in unemployment.
   (d)   the industry's total payments to labour must increase.
   (e)   Both (a) and (d).

*13. Assume that a union is introduced into a monopsonistic labour market, creating a bilateral monopoly (*element 4* in the above table). Which of the following will happen when the union negotiates a higher wage with the monopsonist?
   (a)   Unemployment in the industry must increase.
   (b)   Employment must fall as a result of the higher wage.
   (c)   Both the wage rate and employment can increase over the monopsonistic outcome.
   (d)   Employment must remain lower than if the market were competitive on both the demand and supply sides of the market.
   (e)   Both (b) and (d).

*14. **An increase in the minimum wage may not result in a visible reduction in employment because of which of the following?**
    (a)   Rather than fire existing workers, firms may not replace them when they leave, quit, or retire.
    (b)   The increase in the minimum wage increases employment by monopsonistic firms.
    (c)   The wage bill for "McJobs" is a small proportion of firms' total production costs.
    (d)   The demand for low-wage workers is highly elastic.
    (e)   All of the above.

*15. **Which of the following is consistent with evidence on the average weekly earnings of non-unionized and unionized workers?**
    (a)   Non-unionized workers get approximately 82 percent of the average earnings of non-unionized workers.
    (b)   Non-unionized workers get approximately 82 percent of the average earnings of unionized workers in the same types of jobs.
    (c)   Non-unionized workers get approximately 82 percent of the average earnings of unionized workers with the same skills.
    (d)   On average, the presence of the union increases average wages by 10 percent to 15 percent.
    (e)   Both (a) and (d) are true.

*16. **"Efficiency wage theory" (explained in *Additional Topics: The Puzzle of Interindustry Wage Differentials in Canada* on *MyEconLab*) suggests that**
    (a)   competitive firms pay more than the competitive wage in order to induce workers to be more productive.
    (b)   transfer wages are very high if workers are paid more than the competitive wage.
    (c)   quit rates from jobs that pay more than the competitive wage are very high.
    (d)   wage rates across industries are always equalized.
    (e)   unions always increase workers' productivity.

Solutions

Chapter Review

1.(d) 2.(e) 3.(e) 4.(c) 5.(c) 6.(e) 7.(c) 8.(d) 9.(d) 10.(e) 11.(b) 12.(b) 13.(b) 14.(b) 15.(c) 16.(a) 17.(d)

Short-Answer Questions

1.   (i)   The difference in salaries now exceeds additional costs of obtaining a master's degree (including forgone earnings). Enrollment in master's programs will increase in response to the bigger wage differential.
    (ii)   As the supply of people with master's degrees increases, salaries for jobs needing a master's will be driven down by the market forces of demand and supply, reducing the differential.
    (iii)   No. Regardless of tuition fees, the extra time it takes to get a master's degree creates greater forgone earnings. The extra cost of a master's degree, therefore, means that an equilibrium differential will always remain.

2.   While it is possible that the professional association feels the policy will not be implemented carefully enough to properly determine whether someone has adequate qualifications (i.e., it has non-selfish motives), another explanation is possible. This chapter explains how a professional association, by restricting entry into its profession, reduces the available supply of qualified workers and thereby increases the average earnings of its members. Restricting the accreditation of qualified immigrants

would reduce entry into the profession in Canada, so it is possible that the professional association could have selfish motives for opposing the policy.

3. When the monopsonist increases the wage rate (the average cost of labour) to attract another worker, it increases the wage of *all* workers (in the absence of wage discrimination). The additional cost of the extra worker (the marginal cost), therefore, is the wage paid to that worker *plus* the increase in wages paid to all other workers. The similarity with the monopolist lies in the relationship between marginal and average, but for revenues rather than costs. When a monopolist reduces its product price (the average revenue) to sell another unit of output, it reduces the price of *all* units of output (in the absence of price discrimination). The marginal revenue generated by the additional unit of output is the price received for that unit *minus* the reduction in price on all other units.

4. When the minimum wage is imposed, the effective supply curve of labour facing the monopsonist becomes perfectly elastic at the minimum wage, until it meets the upward-sloping supply curve. Over the perfectly elastic range, the extra cost of hiring an additional worker is just the wage paid to that worker. Without the minimum, the wage to other workers must be increased to attract the new worker, so the extra cost of the additional worker is more than that worker's wage. Consequently, although the minimum wage does increase the average cost of labour to the monopsony, it actually *decreases* the *marginal cost* of hiring some additional workers. [*Note:* This is not an easy concept to grasp, since it seems intuitively contradictory. Refer to Figure 14-5 in the text, and assume that the minimum wage is set at w_0. The supply curve faced by the monopsonist becomes $w_0 E_0 A C$. For each extra worker between L_1 and L_0 the marginal cost is now w_0. Compare this to the *MC* without a minimum wage.]

5. An increase in the minimum wage can "trickle up" to higher wage levels in order to maintain the *differential* between the wage rate of skilled workers and the wage rate of unskilled workers earning the minimum wage. An increase in the minimum wage, therefore, can increase the wage rates of workers earning more than the minimum.

Exercises

1. **Figure 14-4**

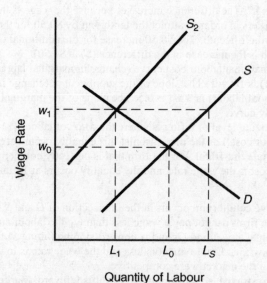

(a) When the minimum wage of w_1 is imposed in Figure 14-4, employment falls from L_0 to L_1. If demand were less elastic, the demand curve (through the equilibrium point w_0, L_0) would be steeper and L_1 would be farther to the right on the horizontal axis, giving a smaller reduction in employment. Conversely, a more elastic (flatter) demand curve would give a bigger reduction in employment. Conclusion: The less elastic the demand for unskilled low-wage labour, the smaller the reduction in employment caused by a minimum wage.

(b) Unemployment caused by the minimum wage is $(L_S - L_1)$. If S were more elastic (flatter), L_S would be farther to the right and the unemployment created by the minimum wage would be greater.

(c) Disagree. You have just seen that the increase in unemployment caused by the minimum wage is greater than the reduction in employment, because the quantity of labour *supplied* increases as the wage rate rises. If the minimum wage were eliminated, therefore, some of the 2000 unemployed would find jobs at the lower wage, but others would not want to work at that wage. In Figure 14-4, unemployment of $L_S - L_1$ (2000 in this question) would be eliminated, but employment would rise to L_0, not L_S.

(d) The professional association has raised salaries by restricting the supply of accredited labour to the profession. In the diagram, the restriction shifts the labour supply curve of accredited labour from S to S_2. Market forces would then establish the new "equilibrium" wage at w_1.

2. **(a)**

(1) Quantity of Labour	(2) Wage Rate	(3) Total Cost	(4) Marginal Labour Cost
8	$10.00	$80.00	Not applicable
9	10.50	94.50	$14.50
10	11.00	110.00	15.50
11	11.50	126.50	16.50
12	12.00	144.00	17.50
13	12.50	162.50	18.50
14	13.00	182.00	19.50
15	13.50	202.50	20.50
16	14.00	224.00	21.50
17	14.50	246.50	22.50

(b) The difference for the tenth worker is $15.50 - $11.00 = $4.50. For the fifteenth worker it is $20.50 - $13.50 = $7. The difference increases because the wage is increased by $0.50 for the previous nine workers in order to attract the tenth, but by $0.50 for the previous *fourteen* workers in order to attract the fifteenth. The $0.50 increase for the additional $(14 - 9 =)$ 5 workers is an extra $2.50, which is the increase in the difference ($7 - $4.50).

(c) The slope of the marginal labour cost curve (change in marginal labour cost divided by change in quantity of labour) is $1/1 = 1$. The slope of the supply curve (change in wage rate divided by change in quantity of labour) is $0.5/1 = 0.5$. The slope of the marginal cost curve is twice the slope of the supply curve.

(d) The profit-maximizing level of hiring is where the MRP of labour ($14.50 in the question) equals the marginal labour cost. For the monopsonist this equality occurs at 9 units of labour hired, requiring a wage rate of $10.50. For the firm that is perfectly competitive in the factor market, marginal labour cost *is* the wage rate, and the equality occurs at 17 units of labour hired and a wage rate of $14.50.

3. **(a)** w_3; Q_4. Competitive equilibrium occurs at the intersection of D and S.

(b) Q_2; $Q_5 - Q_2$. Since firms cannot pay a wage less than w_4, the labour supply curve facing the industry is horizontal at w_4 up to Q_5 and is upward-sloping (along S) for wages greater than w_4.

(c) w; w_2; w_5; Q_2; w_1; w_4; w_4. Employment is less and the wage rate is lower than in (a).

(d) Q_4—the same as if the market were competitive.

(e) Labour supply is restricted, so the supply curve shifts leftward. Market forces will establish a new "equilibrium" at a higher wage and lower employment than in the competitive market.

Extension Exercises

E1. **(a)** Substituting $w = 60$ into the demand equation, we obtain an employment level of 180. Twenty workers lost their jobs. At $w = 60$, 240 individuals wish to work in this industry.

(b) Equating the new supply equation with the demand equation and solving gives $w = 60$ and employment of 180, which is the same result as in (a).

(c) The new demand curve is perfectly inelastic; changes in the wage rate have no effect on the quantity of labour demanded. As a result, the union could increase the wage by any amount without loss of jobs.

E2. **(a)** For Market X, equilibrium is found by setting $360 - 3L = 40 + 2L$ and solving. This gives $L = 64$ and $w = \$168$. For Market Z, $L = 68$ and $w = \$156$.

(b) At the union wage, the quantity of labour demanded is 66 while the quantity of labour supplied is 71. Unemployment is therefore 5, and employment in Market Z would be two fewer than under competitive conditions.

(c) The supply curve in X now has become $w = 30 + 2L$ (or $L = 0.5w - 15$ instead of $L = 0.5w - 10$). Setting $D = S$ and solving, $L = 66$ and $w = 162$. Thus, two of the unemployed workers from Z would find employment in X, and the wage in X would fall to \$162 from \$168.

Additional Multiple-Choice Questions

1.(d) 2.(a) 3.(a) 4.(c) 5.(b) 6.(a) 7.(c) 8.(c) 9.(e) 10.(c) 11.(a) 12.(a) 13.(c) 14.(e) 15.(e) 16.(a)

Explanations for the Asterisked Multiple-Choice Questions

4.(c) Since the firm cannot pay a wage less than w_2, the firm can hire up to Q_3 units of labour without raising wages, after which it must increase wages along the supply curve to attract more workers.

7.(c) Unemployment is the difference between the number working (Q_2) and the number who want to work (Q_4). Note that, relative to the competitive equilibrium (Q_3), only part of this unemployment ($Q_3 - Q_2$) is caused by a reduction in employment. The rest ($Q_4 - Q_3$) is an increase in the quantity of labour supplied, as more people want to work at the higher wage.

8.(c) There are no forces here to create a temporary differential. The \$2 is the equilibrium differential between the higher-skilled workers in Industry X and the lower-skilled workers in Industry Y.

9.(e) The nine green-eyed workers move out of Industry X, shifting the vertical supply curve from 60 to 51 on the horizontal axis. Now demand equals supply at a wage of \$13 (read from the demand curve of Industry X in the diagram). Total income of the 51 blue-eyed workers in Industry X increases from $\$10 \times 51 = \$510$ to $\$13 \times 51 = \$663$. The addition of the nine green-eyed workers from Industry X shifts the vertical supply curve in Industry Y from 60 to 69. Now demand equals supply at a wage of \$5 (read from the demand curve of Industry Y in the diagram). Total income in Industry Y falls from $\$8 \times 60 = \$480$ to $\$5 \times 69 = \$345$.

10.(c) This is a standard competitive market demand-and-supply application of a price floor first seen in Chapter 5, where the minimum wage set above the competitive equilibrium level is a binding price floor. Quantity demanded of labour falls (moving up the negatively sloped demand curve), and this reduction in quantity demanded is the loss of jobs. [*Note:* In Figure 14-2, w_3 would be the minimum wage above the competitive level w_2, with Q_3 minus Q_2 being the resulting loss of jobs. The rise in excess supply of labour is Q_4 minus Q_2, which exceeds the loss in jobs because excess supply is the sum of reduced quantity demanded *and* increased quantity supplied.]

11.(a) As with firms that are competitive in the labour market, the profit-maximizing monopsonist will hire to the point where $MC = MRP$ for the marginal worker. Unlike the firm in the competitive market, however, the monopsonist faces an upward-sloping supply of labour curve and must increase the wage rate for <u>all</u> workers to attract the marginal worker. Consequently, the monopsonist's MC of the marginal worker *exceeds* that worker's wage rate by the extra wages paid to the other workers. Therefore, $MC = MRP$ occurs at a higher MRP and so at a lower level of employment than the competitive level. On an upward-sloping supply curve, this lower level of employment can be achieved by a lower wage rate. Thus both employment and the wage rate are less than their competitive levels. [*Note:* In Figure 14-2, $MC = MRP$ at a, for employment of Q_1, which requires w_1 wage rate.]

12.(a) As with the binding minimum wage in Question 10 above, the union's wage rate bargained above the competitive level reduces employment along the industry's demand for labour curve. While total payments to workers who *remain employed* at the higher wage do increase (so (b) is wrong), what happens to the industry's *total payment to labour* (i.e., its *wage bill*) depends on the elasticity of labour demand between the competitive wage rate and the bargained rate (so (d) is wrong). Total payment to labour falls if demand is elastic and rises if demand is inelastic. Note too that, as in Question 10 above, the increase in unemployment exceeds the reduction in employment (so answer (c) is wrong). [*Note:* The absence of featherbedding implies that the union and employer are bargaining solely on wage rates, not on *both* wage rates *and* employment, so the demand curve determines employment once the wage is set.]

13.(c)　As with any binding minimum wage, the *effective* supply curve facing employers becomes horizontal (i.e., perfectly elastic) at that wage until employment reaches the market supply curve of labour. Along the horizontal portion the monopsonist now does *not* have to increase the wage rate to attract more workers, so *MC equals* wage. For some workers, therefore, their *MC* actually <u>falls</u> from *MC* > market wage to *MC* = bargained wage. This fall in *MC* makes *MC* < *MRP* for more workers, so it is profitable for the monopsonist to *increase* employment. The higher union wage means the monopsonist's <u>profits</u> fall because *average* cost of labour is higher, but the increase in hiring is the firm's response to the lower *marginal* cost, which *minimizes* that fall in profits. [*Note:* Answers containing the word *must* are wrong because the effects of the union on employment and unemployment (i.e., excess supply of labour) differ depending on the specific wage rate that is negotiated. This is best shown with reference to Figure 14-2. If the union bargains a wage of w_2, the monopsonist's profit-maximizing employment rises from Q_1 to the competitive level, Q_3, and there is no excess supply of labour. If the bargained wage is w_3, employment rises from Q_1 to Q_2, but there is also excess supply of Q_4 minus Q_2 (because more labour is supplied at the higher wage). If the bargained wage is w_4, employment remains unchanged at Q_1 but there is even greater excess supply. If the bargained wage is above w_4, employment actually falls below Q_1 and excess supply is even higher.]

14.(a)　Answer (a) is correct because although unemployment <u>in the future</u> may rise because the number of positions available for minimum-wage workers has fallen, this loss in the future would not be <u>visibly</u> caused by the higher minimum wage. Answer (c) is wrong because "McJobs" are at or near minimum-wage levels. For McJobs, then, minimum-wage labour is more likely to be a high proportion of a firm's total cost, making the demand for minimum-wage labour more elastic. An elastic demand for labour (as in wrong answer (d)) will cause <u>more</u> layoffs and unemployment than an inelastic demand. Answer (b) is wrong because the theory in this chapter says only that the monopsony will hire more workers when there is a minimum wage than when there is not: It doesn't say that <u>increases</u> in the minimum wage will <u>further</u> increase employment.

15.(e)　Refer to the fourth tip in *Hints and Tips* for this chapter. As noted in the text, 82 percent is the raw data in 2008 comparing unionized and non-unionized workers. It says that unionized workers get roughly a 22 percent earnings premium $(100 - 82)/82 = 0.22$. But when the data are adjusted (i.e., compensated) for differences in skills and jobs, the 22 percent premium falls to a compensated earnings premium of 10 percent to 15 percent. The rest of the 22 percent premium is due to differences in (average) skills and types of jobs. [For example, some jobs may have a higher wage to compensate for poorer or more risky working conditions.]

16.(a)　The competitive equilibrium is the transfer wage that workers can earn elsewhere (so answer (b) is wrong). Paying a higher wage than this increases the workers' incentive to be more productive in order to retain the higher-paying job (so (a) is correct). Similarly, workers have an incentive not to quit, because they will be able to earn less elsewhere (so (c) is wrong). Answer (d) is wrong because, in efficiency wage theory, some workers are paid the competitive equilibrium wage while other, similar workers are being paid the higher efficiency wage. Answer (e) is wrong because this theory says it is the higher wage that increases productivity, not necessarily a union. Indeed, workers receiving the higher efficiency wage potentially have less to gain from unionization than other workers.

Interest Rates and the Capital Market

15

Chapter Overview

This chapter focuses on **physical capital** as a factor of production, and the links between the markets for physical and **financial capital**. The *purchase price* of capital depends on the **present value** of the future earnings it is expected to generate. The present value is the amount that would need to be invested today at the market interest rate to generate the same future earnings, and is calculated as the future earnings **discounted** using the market interest rate.

An individual firm will **invest** in additional physical capital as long as the present value of the future earnings it will generate exceeds its purchase price. The future earnings are the stream of the capital good's marginal revenue products (*MRP*s) expected to be received by the firm. Since the profit-maximizing firm's optimal capital stock is negatively related to the rate of interest, other things constant, and since changes in a *stock* of capital is a *flow* of investment, then both the firm's and the aggregate economy's demand for investment are also negatively related to the interest rate. Changes in interest rates cause a movement along this demand curve for investment, while anything else that changes the expected future stream of *MRP*s shifts the investment demand curve. Although firms invest in *physical capital*, such as computers and machinery, the **investment demand curve** is expressed as a *demand for financial capital* since (i) the only way to sum different investments in different types of real capital is to add their financial values, and (ii) firms need financial capital to "purchase" their investments in physical capital. The interest rate is the "price" firms pay for this financial capital.

Household **saving** (equals income minus current spending) is the key component of the annual *supply of financial capital* available to meet firms' demand for financial capital needed for investment. The current *flow* of savings changes households' *stock of assets*, which in turn represent the accumulation of past

LO **LEARNING OBJECTIVES**

After studying this chapter, you will be able to

1   describe how the capital market brings together the borrowing decisions of firms with the lending decisions of households.

2   compute the present value of an asset that delivers a stream of future benefits.

3   explain why the demand for investment is negatively related to the interest rate.

4   explain why the supply of saving is positively related to the interest rate.

5   understand how the equilibrium interest rate is determined and why it changes over time.

saving. Major determinants of household saving are current and expected future income and the interest rate. Since the interest rate represents households' opportunity cost (or "price") of spending now rather than in the future, the positively sloped supply curve of savings is plotted against the interest rate. In the economy's market for financial capital, therefore, the equilibrium real interest rate is determined by the intersection of the investment demand curve and saving supply curve. Changes in the equilibrium level of the interest rate are caused by economic forces that shift these curves, creating excess demand or supply of financial capital and a return to a new equilibrium at another interest rate.

Hints and Tips

The following may help you avoid some of the most common errors on examinations.

✓ Don't let the equations used to calculate present value make you lose sight of the underlying logic. If you feel yourself getting confused or lost, ask yourself a question like "If I invest $100 today at a 10 percent rate of interest, what will I have in one year's time?" The answer ($110) is the future value (i.e., the equivalent of the firm's expected *MRP*) and the amount you would need to invest today ($100) is its present value (at the 10 percent interest rate). The text goes through this way of thinking in detail, and it is well worth your while to spend time on it.

✓ Although you will learn some new terminology about the working of the capital market, don't lose sight of the fact that most of the analysis is an application of what you learned in Chapter 3 about competitive demand and supply. Like any application of competitive demand and supply, the key elements to understand are (i) what "other things" are held constant along a demand or supply curve of financial capital, and (ii) how do changes in these "other things" shift the curves? Most of the rest of the analysis follows from these.

✓ Don't lose sight of opportunity cost. The opportunity cost of consuming more in the future (i.e., saving money now) is the resulting fall in current consumption. The opportunity cost of current consumption (i.e., spending now) is the resulting reduction in future consumption. A change in interest rates changes the opportunity costs.

✓ Understand the link between the firm's <u>stock</u> of capital and the <u>flow</u> of investment. The flow of investment is what brings firms' actual capital stock to the desired level. Actual can be less than desired (thus stimulating investment) either because (i) old capital has "worn out" (i.e., depreciation) and needs replacing, or because (ii) changes in economic conditions make some investment projects profitable which previously were not profitable (e.g., a fall in the interest rate, improved technology, or expectations of a future increase in output and sales).

✓ Understand the link between the household's <u>stock</u> of assets and the <u>flow</u> of saving—think of the link between the amount of money in your bank account (your stock of assets) and the amounts you deposit into it or withdraw from it (your flow of saving, positive for deposits and negative for withdrawals). Your *flows* of deposits and withdrawals change the *stock* of money in your account. The deposits into the account are <u>your</u> equivalent of the firm investing to increase its capital stock.

Chapter Review

A Brief Overview of the Capital Market

This section explains how firms' demand for **financial capital** is *derived* from their demand for **physical capital**, and identifies the various ways that firms can raise financial capital. Capital markets connect firms' borrowing decisions with households' lending (i.e., saving) decisions, which jointly determine the **rate of interest** (i.e., the "price" of capital). The supply of financial capital that ultimately flows from households' savings is often lent to firms through *financial intermediaries* such as commercial banks. In normal times these flows run smoothly, but there were severe disruptions in the financial crisis of 2007–2008. [*Note:* Learn more about the financial crisis from *Additional Topics: The U.S. Housing Collapse and the Financial Crisis of 2007–2008* on *MyEconLab*.]

1. **Financial intermediaries play an important role because**
   (a) without them, households would not save.
   (b) without them, firms would not borrow.
   (c) they can pool households' savings to make large loans to firms.
   (d) they are better than households at assessing risk.
   (e) Both (c) and (d).

2. **The main *economic* difference between a firm's input of physical capital and its input of labour is that**
   (a) physical capital is tangible whereas labour services are intangible.
   (b) the stock of physical capital provides a flow of services even after it has been paid for.
   (c) a firm's addition to physical capital is an investment, but a worker's addition to human capital is not.
   (d) the capital stock is a fixed factor that cannot be varied in the long run.
   (e) labour provides services but physical capital does not.

Present Value

The **present value** of the future stream of marginal revenue products (*MRP*s) from a piece of capital equipment determines the **maximum price** the firm is willing to pay for that piece of capital. A dollar received now is worth more than a dollar received in the future, since the current dollar can earn interest and be worth more than one dollar in the future. A future stream of payments (i.e., the stream of *MRP*s from a piece of capital equipment), therefore, must be **discounted** by the market interest rate to determine its present value. Present value is negatively related to the market interest rate: the higher the market interest rate, the lower the present value of a future stream of payments. The present value is positively related to the size of each year's *MRP*, to the number of years over which an *MRP* is received, and to the proportion of the total stream received in earlier rather than later years.

3. **If the interest rate is *i*, the present value of *R* dollars received a year from now is**
   (a) Ri.
   (b) $R/(1 + i)$.
   (c) R/i.
   (d) $i/(1 + R)$.
   (e) i/R.

4. If $100 is invested today at an interest rate of 10 percent per year, and the interest is reinvested each year, the $100 will be worth $200 after 7.2 years. If the market interest rate is 10 percent, the present value of $10 000 to be received in 8 years' time is
    (a) one-eighth of $10 000.
    (b) less than $5000.
    (c) one-tenth of $10 000.
    (d) $1000.
    (e) $7200.

5. The present value of a capital asset will increase if
    (a) the *MRP* values per period decrease.
    (b) a greater proportion of *MRP* values are received farther into the future.
    (c) the interest rate decreases.
    (d) the purchase price of the capital asset decreases.
    (e) the wage rate of labour increases.

6. An investment of $100 today at an annual interest rate of 10 percent will be worth $110 in one year's time. If you re-invest that $110 at 10 percent it will be worth $121 after another year. Consequently, if the market interest rate is 10 percent, then the present value of a stream of payments that pays you $110 after one year and another $121 after two years is
    (a) $100.
    (b) $110.
    (c) $200.
    (d) $221.
    (e) $231.

Investment Demand

A firm will increase profits by purchasing another unit of physical capital as long as the present value of the future stream of its *MRP*s exceeds the purchase price. Thus a firm reaches its **optimal capital stock** when the purchase price equals the present value of the future stream of *MRP*s of the marginal unit of capital. An increase in the firm's desired physical capital *stock* requires a *flow* of new investment in physical capital, which in turn requires a *flow* of additional financial capital to purchase it. **Technological change,** an increase in the market price of the firm's product, and a *fall in the interest rate* all increase the present value of the stream of *MRP*s, thereby increasing the firm's optimal capital stock and its demand for financial capital.

The negative relationship between the interest rate and this demand for financial capital needed for investment, other things being constant, is the firm's **demand curve for financial capital**, or its **demand curve for investment**. The sum of all firms' demand curves for financial capital is the **economy's aggregate demand curve for financial capital**, which is its **investment demand curve**. Anything that shifts firms' demand curves for financial capital and investment also shifts the economy's aggregate demand for financial capital and investment in the same direction. [*Note:* The text implicitly makes the simplifying assumption that capital does not "wear out," so that all investment is "net investment"—i.e., investment that changes the firm's total stock of physical capital. In reality capital does wear out over time, and some investment will be "replacement investment"—i.e., investment needed to keep the firm's capital stock unchanged. This *Study Guide* also adopts the text's simplifying assumption.]

7. If *PV* equals the present value of the annual stream of receipts from a machine into the future, *PP* equals its purchase price, and *i* equals the interest rate, then a capital good should be purchased if
    (a) $PV \times i < PP$.
    (b) $PV/PP < i$.
    (c) $PV/i > PP$.
    (d) $PV > PP$.
    (e) $PV/(1+i) < PP$.

8. **Which of the following *causes* the demand curve for investment to shift to the right?**
   (a) More capital is accumulated.
   (b) The interest rate decreases.
   (c) Technology improves physical capital productivity.
   (d) Diminishing returns to physical capital occur.
   (e) Both (b) and (c).

9. **The higher the interest rate (all other things being equal),**
   (a) the more investment projects will be profitable, so investment demand increases.
   (b) the lower a firm's optimal capital stock and the lower its investment.
   (c) the higher the present value of the income stream generated by a specific investment project.
   (d) the greater the shift in the firm's demand for financial capital curve.
   (e) the bigger the inward shift in the economy's investment demand curve.

10. **The economy's overall demand curve for investment is negatively related to the interest rate because, other things being equal,**
    (a) the economy's demand for investment is the sum of all firms' demands for investment.
    (b) as the economy expands because more firms start up, there will be more investment at any given interest rate.
    (c) a fall in the rate of interest increases the future values of *MRP*s.
    (d) an individual firm's investment demand is negatively related to the rate of interest.
    (e) Both (a) and (d).

The Supply of Saving

The economy's supply of financial capital per period is the *flow* of households' savings, which alters their total *stock* of financial assets. The main determinants of how much a household decides to save in a particular period are current income, expected future income, and the interest rate. The rate of interest is the opportunity cost of current spending—i.e., the price of spending now rather than in the future. Thus economists draw the supply curve of financial capital as a negative relationship between dollars saved and the interest rate. An increase in the interest rate increases savings, while a decrease in the interest rate reduces savings. Changes in current income and in expected future income change savings at each level of the interest rate, thus shifting the supply curve of financial capital.

11. **Which of the following shifts the supply curve of savings to the right?**
    (a) An increase in expected future income.
    (b) A fall in the interest rate.
    (c) A rise in the interest rate.
    (d) An increase in current income.
    (e) Both (a) and (c).

12. **The supply curve of savings is positively sloped because**
    (a) an increase in the interest rate increases the amount of future consumption forfeited for each dollar of current consumption.
    (b) an increase in current income increases saving.
    (c) an increase in firms' demand for capital increases the interest rate.
    (d) households save more as the cost of saving increases.
    (e) lower expected future income reduces current saving.

Investment, Saving, and the Interest Rate

The demand for investment and the supply of savings jointly determine the interest rate (i.e., the "price" of capital) at the equilibrium flow of savings and investment. As with the price of any good in a perfectly competitive market, the interest rate is exogenous to the individual household and the individual firm but endogenous within the market as a whole. The relevant interest rate is the **real interest rate**, which is the nominal rate adjusted for inflation. The equilibrium interest rate changes if either the investment demand curve or the savings supply curve shifts. This section explains the causes of such shifts and how the market for financial capital moves to a new equilibrium as a result. The major causes of increases in the savings supply curve are income growth, population growth, and government policies to increase desired saving: the tax treatment of RRSPs and TFSAs are government policies, although it is debatable as to how much these policies actually increase the *total* amount of savings. The major causes of increases in the investment demand curve are population and income growth, technological change, and policies to encourage investment. Finally, the chapter reviews long-run trends in the capital market, noting in particular that the total capital stock has increased steadily over time even though the flow of investment has been quite volatile and without any clear trend in the interest rate.

13. **Given the linkages between the nominal interest rate, the real interest rate, and the inflation rate, which of the following is the most accurate prediction?**
    (a)   A high nominal interest rate creates a high real interest rate.
    (b)   A high inflation rate creates a high real rate of interest.
    (c)   A low nominal interest rate creates a high real interest rate.
    (d)   A low inflation rate creates a high real rate of interest.
    (e)   A high nominal interest rate and an even higher inflation rate create a negative real rate of interest.

14. **Other things being equal, an increase in current income in the economy**
    (a)   increases the supply of savings and the equilibrium interest rate.
    (b)   increases the equilibrium capital stock and reduces the interest rate.
    (c)   reduces the interest rate, but the effect on the equilibrium capital stock is uncertain.
    (d)   increases the interest rate, but the effect on the equilibrium capital stock is uncertain.
    (e)   increases the equilibrium capital stock, but the effect on the interest rate is uncertain.

15. **Which of the following is expected to increase the economy's investment demand, other things being equal?**
    (a)   An expected increase in the future stream of *MRP*s.
    (b)   An increase in population.
    (c)   An increase in average household income.
    (d)   A reduction in the corporate income-tax rate.
    (e)   All of the above.

16. **Tax deductions for retirement savings in Registered Retirement Savings Plans (RRSPs)**
    (a)   reduce the opportunity cost of future consumption.
    (b)   shift the supply curve of savings to the right.
    (c)   cause a transfer of savings from regular savings accounts to tax-deductible savings accounts.
    (d)   All of the above.
    (e)   Both (b) and (c), but not (a).

Short-Answer Questions

1.   Why do economists treat the interest rate, not the purchase price, as the "price" of capital?

2.   If there is no inflation, $100 can buy the same in one year's time as it can buy today. Under these circumstances, is the present value of $100 in one year's time less than $100? Explain.

3.   Why should profit-maximizing firms compare the purchase price of physical capital to the present value of the stream of *MRP*s rather than to the simple sum of future values?

4.   Why is the historical path of the interest rate in Canada much more volatile than the historical path of the capital stock?

5.   If a firm does not borrow money to invest in new machinery but instead pays for it out of undistributed profits (i.e., profits not distributed to shareholders), does the market interest rate play any part in determining the firm's desired amount of investment?

Exercises

1.   **Practise Using Present Value and Annuity Tables**
      (a)   Here you consider a *one-time payment*. Fill in the blanks using Table 15-1 (the table of present values (*PV*) at the end of this *Study Guide* chapter) or your calculator.

This many dollars	in *t* years	has this *PV*	at *i*
10	5	_____	6%
100	50	$60.80	
1000	_____	3.00	12%
_____	6	4.56	14%

(b) Now you consider a *stream of payments*. In each row of the table below "this many dollars" is received each year for *t* years into the future. Refer to Table 15-2 at the end of this *Study Guide* chapter.

This many dollars	in each of *t* years	has this *PV*	at *i*
10	5	_____	6%
100	50	$3919.60	_____
1000	_____	8304.00	12%
_____	6	38.89	14%

2. **The Firm's Profit-Maximizing Capital Stock**

This exercise illustrates the relationships among the various components of the present value formula, $PV = MRP/(1+i)$, and the desired capital stock.

The Base Case

At a current interest rate of 10 percent, Acme Machine Shop maximizes profits with a capital stock of 20 machines. It is considering the purchase of another machine that costs $500. The financial manager estimates that the additional machine will generate $545 in additional net income one year from now.

(a) By making the appropriate substitutions, write the algebraic expression for the present value of this incremental capital good.

(b) Using Table 15-1 or your calculator, calculate the magnitude of the present value to the nearest dollar. Should the financial manager recommend that Acme expand its capital stock (invest) by one?

The investment decision in part (b) may change if economic conditions change or if the financial manager revises her forecasts. We outline three cases below.

Case 1: Variations in the interest rate, *i*

(c) If the interest rate had been 8 percent rather than 10 percent, would the financial manager have made a different recommendation? Explain.

(d) What can you conclude about the effect of an interest rate decrease on the present value of a capital asset? About the relationship between interest rates and the desired capital stock?

Case 2: A change in expected net receipts, *MRP*

Suppose Acme's financial manager revises her forecast of net revenues to $555 instead of $545.

(e) Assuming an interest rate of 10 percent, would the financial manager now recommend a capital stock of 21?

(f) What do you conclude about the effect of an increase in *MRP* and the present value of a capital good? About the relationship between net expected receipts and the desired capital stock?

Case 3: A change in the timing of receipts, *t*

As in Case 2, the financial manager is convinced that net revenues will be $555. Now, however, she forecasts that they will be received after two years instead of one year.

(g) If the interest rate were 10 percent, would the financial manager recommend the purchase of the machine? What have you concluded about the relationship between present value and the timing of net receipts?

3. **Present Value and the Time Distribution of *MRPs***

Three firms (Firms *A*, *B*, and *C*) are each considering whether to invest in a machine that will yield returns (*MRPs*) for three years. At the end of the three-year period the machine will be worthless. Because of the types of businesses that they operate, the stream of returns differs for the three firms, as shown below. The market interest rate is 10 percent.

Years	Firm *A*		Firm *B*		Firm *C*	
Hence	*MRP*	*PV*	*MRP*	*PV*	*MRP*	*PV*
1	2000		1000		4000	
2	2000		1000		1000	
3	2000		4000		1000	

(a) For each firm, what is the sum of future values of the three-year stream of *MRPs*?

(b) Fill in the *PV* columns for each firm using Table 15-1 and then determine which firms will buy the machine if the purchase price is
  (i) $5000? Why?

  (ii) $4800? Why?

  (iii) $4700? Why?

(c) From your findings in (b), what conclusion can you draw?

(d) If the purchase price is $5000, Firm *B* would purchase the machine if the resale (or scrap) value of the machine after three years is expected to be _____.

4. **Present Value and Investment in Human Capital**
    This problem applies the present value concept to investment in human capital (introduced in Chapter 14). Firms will "invest" in their workers in order to increase future productivity and profits. In this case a baseball team is considering hiring a player, Eddy Grant.

    Eddy Grant has had an illustrious career in professional baseball playing for the Mudville Mustangs. He is approaching the end of his baseball career, and his performance has recently deteriorated. Jimmy McKennett, the general manager of the Grover Griffens, believes that Grant has two good years left. With the proper coaching and sports therapy, McKennett believes that Grant can increase the Griffens' revenues through larger TV royalties and greater attendance at home games. To persuade him to leave the Mustangs, Grant wants an initial $500 000 at the beginning of the 2012 season, and a two-year contract that guarantees a salary of $1 000 000 at the end of the 2012 season plus another $1 500 000 at the end of the 2013 season.

    McKennett estimates that Grant's extra therapeutic care and coaching will cost $100 000 per year of the contract. McKennett also estimates that Grant will increase the team's stream of revenues by $1 800 000 at the end of the 2004 season and $1 700 000 at the end of the 2013 season. The annual interest rate over the two seasons is expected to be 6 percent.

    (a) Using Table 15-1, calculate the present value of the total costs associated with hiring Grant.

    (b) Providing that McKennett's estimates of the stream of revenues are based on the best possible information, should the Griffens offer Grant the two-year contract that he seeks? Explain.

5. **Investment in Physical Capital and Rates of Return**
    Moosejay Printing Company is analyzing a proposal to purchase equipment estimated to provide $15 000 in labour savings annually and cost $1000 in maintenance a year. It calculates a 10-year economic life of the equipment and $10 000 salvage at the end of the tenth year. If the purchase price of the equipment is $75 000, should Moosejay expand its current capital stock if it wants a minimum rate of return of 14 percent? [*Hint:* If the present value of the revenue flows calculated at an interest rate of 14 percent is greater than the purchase price, then the rate of return on the equipment must be greater than 14 percent. Use Table 15-2 for the *PV* of the constant annual amounts and Table 15-1 for the *PV* of the salvage value.]

6. **Equilibrium in the Financial Capital Market**
    For each of the following, other things being constant, determine whether the economy's equilibrium interest rate and the equilibrium level of savings and investment would increase, decrease, or change in an uncertain direction. In each case explain the reason for your answer. [*Hint:* Sketch a demand and supply diagram to determine the effect of each change separately, then compare the predicted directions of change in equilibrium values.]

(a) The government reduces tax allowances on firms' investment costs and households' Registered Retirement Savings Plan contributions.

(b) The current income of the average household increases.

(c) Expected future incomes of households increase, and their tax allowances on RRSPs increase.

(d) Expected future income of the average household increases, and population increases because there is more immigration.

Additional Multiple-Choice Questions

*1. **The present value of $100 received one year from now is**
(a) more than $100 if the interest rate is positive.
(b) more than $107 if the interest rate is more than 7 percent.
(c) $106 if the interest rate is 6 percent.
(d) All of the above.
(e) None of the above.

2. **If the interest rate is 5 percent, the present value of $500 received two years from now is**
(a) $453.51.   (b) $525.
(c) $467.19.   (d) $551.25.
(e) $510.

3. **The formula for the present value of $10 received three years from now and an interest rate of 10 percent is**
(a) $10/(0.1)^3$.   (b) $10/3(1.1)$.
(c) $(1.1)^3/$10$.   (d) $10/(1.1)^3$.
(e) $10^3/(1.1)^3$.

Questions 4 to 8 refer to the following data concerning a machine. You can find the answers directly from the *PV* equation using a calculator or spreadsheet, or by using Table 15-1 at the end of this *Study Guide* chapter. [*Note:* Using Table 15-1 may not give the exact answers because of rounding, but they will be close enough to identify the correct answers to the questions.]

A business can buy a machine that yields net revenue of $1000 at the end of the first year and $2000 at the end of the second year, after which the machine falls apart and thus has no scrap value.

4.	If the rate of interest is 10 percent, the present value of the $1000 received one year hence is equal to
(a)	$900.
(b)	$990.
(c)	$909.
(d)	$100.
(e)	$1100.

*5.	If the rate of interest in both years is 10 percent, the *total* present value of the machine over the two-year period is
(a)	$2562.
(b)	$3000.
(c)	$2727.
(d)	$3520.
(e)	$3300.

*6.	Assuming an interest rate of 10 percent, the firm will buy this machine if its purchase price is
(a)	less than or equal to $2562.
(b)	greater than $2561 but less than $2727.
(c)	equal to $2727.
(d)	equal to $3000.
(e)	equal to $3500, which is 110 percent of $1000 plus 120 percent of $2000.

*7.	The interest rate that generates a total present value of net revenue flows for this machine of $2487 is
(a)	15 percent.
(b)	12 percent.
(c)	8 percent.
(d)	14 percent.
(e)	24.87 percent.

*8.	If the interest rate was 12 percent and the purchase price was $3000, what would the first year's net revenue (before discounting) have to be to warrant purchasing this machine? Continue to assume that the net revenue in the second year remains at $2000.
(a)	$893.
(b)	$1256.
(c)	$1406.
(d)	$1574.
(e)	$3360.

*9.	The _____ is the rate of interest and the _____ distant the payment date, the lower will be the present value of a future payment.
(a)	higher; more
(b)	higher; less
(c)	lower; more
(d)	lower; less
(e)	Any of the above, depending on the purchase price.

10.	The firm's investment demand curve shows
(a)	the relationship between interest rates and present value.
(b)	an asset's present value after one year.
(c)	how the firm's desired level of investment varies with changes in *MRP*.
(d)	how the firm's *MRP* changes with the interest rate.
(e)	how the firm's desired level of investment varies with the interest rate.

*11.	In the very long run, the investment demand curve shifts to the right as
(a)	diminishing returns to capital set in.
(b)	technological improvements increase the productivity of capital.
(c)	the interest rate decreases.
(d)	the supply of savings falls.
(e)	the present value of capital falls.

*12. Suppose you lend me $100 and I agree to repay you $112 in a year's time (principal plus interest). During the year, however, the average price of goods in the economy rises by 5 percent. Your real rate of return on your loan to me is therefore

(a)   17 percent.   (b)   12 percent.

(c)   7 percent.   (d)   5 percent.

(e)   −5 percent.

*13. The flow of household saving is greater the _____ and the _____.

(a)   greater is current income; lower is the interest rate

(b)   smaller is expected future income; smaller is current income

(c)   higher is the interest rate; smaller is expected future income

(d)   higher is the interest rate; smaller is current income

(e)   greater is *MRP* of physical capital; greater is the accumulated stock of physical capital

*14. Other things being equal, an increase in population

(a)   increases the equilibrium interest rate and capital stock.

(b)   increases the equilibrium capital stock and reduces the interest rate.

(c)   reduces the interest rate, but the effect on the equilibrium capital stock is uncertain.

(d)   increases the interest rate, but the effect on the equilibrium capital stock is uncertain.

(e)   increases the equilibrium capital stock, but the effect on the interest rate is uncertain.

Solutions

Chapter Review

1.(e) 2.(b) 3.(b) 4.(b) 5.(c) 6.(c) 7.(d) 8.(c) 9.(b) 10.(e) 11.(d) 12.(a) 13.(e) 14.(e) 15.(e) 16.(e)

Short-Answer Questions

1.   First, firms use financial capital to purchase physical capital, and the interest rate is the cost of financial capital. Second, there are many different types of physical capital with many different purchase prices (e.g., a new computer and a big truck), so the term *physical capital* actually refers to a composite of all types of physical equipment. The interest rate *per dollar of financial capital* invested is the cost that is common to all types of physical capital and to all purchase prices (e.g., a jet aircraft or a long-distance truck).

2.   Yes. Although the purchase price of a good remains unchanged if there is no inflation, $100 in one year's time *includes interest*, so less than $100 would have to be saved today. So for anything that costs $1 per unit in both years, you have to give up *less than* 100 units of it today in order to get 100 units in a year's time.

3.   Because the purchase price can be invested either in the machine or in a financial asset that pays interest. If the firm can earn more from the financial asset than from the machine, it will maximize profits by investing the purchase price of the machine in a financial asset even if the future value of *MRP*s exceed the machine's purchase price. Only if the *present value* of the machine's *MRP*s exceeds its purchase price is it profit maximizing to invest in the machine rather than in the financial asset.

4.   Population growth, growth in household income, and improvements in technology shift both the investment demand curve and the savings supply curve of financial capital to the right. An increase in investment demand increases the equilibrium capital stock and increases the interest rate. An increase in savings supply increases the equilibrium capital stock but reduces the interest rate. Both shifts increase the capital stock, but whether the rate of interest rises or falls (or remains unchanged) depends

on the relative magnitudes of the shifts. This explains why Canada has experienced a clear and continuing upward trend in its capital stock but with no associated trend in interest rates.

5. Yes it does—for the reason explained in the answer to Question 3 above. The firm has the choice of investing in physical capital or in a financial asset that pays interest. Even though the firm that uses undistributed profits does not have an explicit *direct cost* of interest payments on borrowed money, the interest that *could have been earned* from the financial asset is the implicit *opportunity cost* of investing in physical capital.

Exercises

1. (a) Row 1: The *PV* of \$1 = \$0.747, so the *PV* of \$10 = \$7.47.
        Row 2: The *PV* of \$1 = 60.8/100 = \$0.608; $i = 1\%$, $t = 50$.
        Row 3: The *PV* of \$1 = 3/1000 = \$0.003; $i = 12\%$, $t = 50$.
        Row 4: The *PV* of \$1 in the sixth year at 14% = \$0.456, so the number of dollars to be received in 6 years' time must be \$4.56/0.456 = \$10.
    (b) Row 1: The *PV* of \$1 = \$4.212, so the *PV* of \$10 = \$42.12.
        Row 2: The *PV* of \$1 = 3919.6/100 = \$39.196; $i = 1\%$, for $t = 50$ years.
        Row 3: The *PV* of \$1 = 8304/1000 = \$8.304; $i = 12\%$, for $t = 50$ years.
        Row 4: The *PV* of \$1 per year for 6 years at 14% = \$3.889, so the number of dollars received per year must be \$38.89/3.889 = \$10.

2. (a) $PV = \$545/(1.1)$.
    (b) *PV* is equal to \$495. Since this value is less than the machine's purchase price, the financial manager would not recommend its purchase.
    (c) Yes, the present value of the net income flow is now \$504 (to the nearest dollar). Since the present value of the income stream is greater than the purchase price of \$500, Acme's profits would increase if it bought this machine.
    (d) There is a negative relationship between *PV* and *i*. When the interest rate falls (from 10 percent to 8 percent), the present value of a capital asset increases (from \$495 to \$504 for Acme). A decrease in the interest rate increases the desired capital stock (from 20 to 21 for Acme).
    (e) Yes, since the *PV* of expected net revenue of \$555 is \$504 (at an interest rate of 10 percent), and \$504 is greater than the machine's purchase price of \$500.
    (f) There is a positive relationship between *PV* and *MRP*. An increase in net expected receipts (*MRP*) increases the desired capital stock (via an increase in *PV* which makes capital expansion profitable).
    (g) No, since the $PV = \$555/(1.1)^2 = \$458$ is less than the \$500 purchase price. Comparing the answers in parts (e) and (g), we clearly see that the present value of receiving \$555 one year from now is greater than the present value of receiving \$555 two years from now. Thus, the longer the time until the revenue is received, the lower the present value today.

3.

Years Hence	Firm *A* MRP	Firm *A* PV	Firm *B* MRP	Firm *B* PV	Firm *C* MRP	Firm *C* PV
1	2000	1818	1000	909	4000	3636
2	2000	1652	1000	826	1000	826
3	2000	1502	4000	3004	1000	751

    (a) The total dollar value of the *MRP* streams is \$6000 for all three firms.
    (b) [*Note:* The answers here use Table 15-1. Because Table 15-1 is rounded to three decimal places, your spreadsheet calculations may be slightly different.]
        (i) Firm *C* will buy the machine. It is the only firm for which the stream of payments has a *PV* > \$5000 (*PV* = \$5213).
        (ii) Firms *A* and *C*. Both have *PV* > \$4800. (For Firm *A*, *PV* = \$4972.)
        (iii) All three. They all have *PV* > \$4700. (*PV* for Firm *B* = \$4739.)

(c) The greater the proportion of the total value of *MRP*s expected to be received further into the future, the lower the present value and therefore the lower the purchase price the firm is willing to pay.

(d) Firm *B* would need a *PV* of $5000 instead of $4739. To raise Firm *B*'s *PV* by ($5000 − $4739) $261, the resale value must be $261/0.751 = $347.54.

4. **(a)** The stream of total costs consists of the initial $500 000 payment, the wages in both of the two years ($1 000 000 and $1 500 000), and the $100 000 training cost each year. So the present value of costs is $PV = \$500\ 000 + \$1\ 100\ 000/(1.06) + \$1\ 600\ 000/(1.06)^2 = \$2\ 961\ 730$. [*Note:* Using the approximate numbers from Table 15-1 gives $500 000 + $1 100 000(0.943) + $1 600 000(0.89) = $2 961 300.]

(b) Yes, since the present value of the expected net receipts is greater than the present value of the total costs. In this case, the *PV* of receipts is $\$1\ 800\ 000/(1.06) + \$1\ 700\ 000/(1.06)^2 =$ $3 211 107. [*Note:* Using the approximate numbers from Table 15-1 gives $1 800 000(0.943) + $1 700 000(0.89) = $3 210 400.]

5. Yes, since the present value of the savings and salvage value is greater than the purchase price. At 14 percent, the *PV* of the net savings plus the salvage value is ($15 000 − $1000) × 5.216 (according to Table 15-2) plus $\$10\ 000/(1.14)^{10}$. This sum is equal to $75 724 ($73 024 + $2700). Since the *PV* is greater than $75 000, Moosejay should invest in this machine. Note too that since the *PV* of net savings is greater than the purchase price, the rate of return must be greater than 14 percent. [*Note:* In fact, the rate of return is 14.3 percent.]

6. **(a)** Firms' after-tax costs of investment increase, shifting the investment demand curve to the left and reducing the equilibrium interest rate and the equilibrium flow of financial capital (i.e., the equilibrium level of saving and investment). Households' opportunity cost of saving increases, which shifts the supply curve of savings to the left and increases the equilibrium interest rate but reduces the equilibrium flow of financial capital. The combined effect of the two reduces the equilibrium flow of financial capital but the effect on the interest rate is uncertain—it depends on the relative magnitudes of the shifts in the demand and supply curves.

(b) The increase in current income shifts the supply curve of savings to the right. The increase in current income also increases demand for goods and services, shifting the investment demand curve to the right. Both work to increase the equilibrium flow of financial capital, but have opposing effects on the rate of interest. Thus the net effect on the equilibrium interest rate is uncertain.

(c) The increase in expected future income shifts the supply of savings left, while the improved tax allowances shift it to the right. If the net shift is to the left, the equilibrium interest rate rises and equilibrium flow of financial capital falls. If the net shift is to the right, the reverse happens.

(d) The increase in population shifts the investment demand curve to the right, increasing both the equilibrium interest rate and the equilibrium flow of financial capital. The effect on the savings supply curve, however, is uncertain. The increase in expected future incomes of the average household shifts the savings supply curve to the left (increasing the equilibrium interest rate and reducing the equilibrium flow of financial capital), but the increase in population shifts it to the right (reducing the equilibrium interest rate and increasing the equilibrium flow of financial capital). If the net effect is a leftward shift of the supply curve, the combined effect of the increase in demand and decrease in supply increases the equilibrium interest rate but the effect on the equilibrium level of savings and investment is uncertain because it depends on the relative magnitudes of the shifts in demand and supply. If the net effect is a rightward shift of the supply curve, the combined effect increases the equilibrium level of savings and investment but the effect on the equilibrium interest rate is uncertain.

Additional Multiple-Choice Questions

1.(e) 2.(a) 3.(d) 4.(c) 5.(a) 6.(a) 7.(b) 8.(d) 9.(a) 10.(e) 11.(b) 12.(c) 13.(c) 14.(e)

Explanations for the Asterisked Multiple-Choice Questions

1.(e) This question makes sure you understand the basic principle of *discounting*. Unless the interest rate is zero, any money to be received in the future has a *lower* value in the present, since money invested today returns a higher value in the future. For example, $94.34 invested today at an annual interest rate of 6 percent will be worth $94.34(1.06) = $100 in one year's time, so that $100 is worth $100/1.06 = $94.34 today.

5.(a) Using the equation, $PV = \$1000/1.1 + \$2000/(1.1)^2 = \$909 + \$1653 = \$2562$. [Using Table 15-1, $PV = 1000(0.909) + 2000(0.826) = 909 + 1652 = \$2561$.] The reasoning is (i) investing $909 today at a 10 percent interest rate is worth ($909 + $91) $1000 in one year's time, and (ii) investing $1653 today at 10 percent is worth $1653(1.1) = $1818 in one year's time, which when reinvested at 10 percent gives $1818(1.1) = $2000 after another year. The sum of the two PVs ($909 + $1653) is $2562.

6.(a) The firm will not pay *more* than the $2562 determined above, since it can get the *same future payments* by investing $2562 in (for example) a financial asset paying 10 percent annual interest. At a purchase price of $2562 it can get the same future payments as the financial asset, so the firm is indifferent between the two. At a purchase price of less than $2562 it can get the same future payments as the financial asset *for a lower cost*, so giving a rate of return in excess of 10 percent. [*Note:* Here we assume that the future payments from the machine are known with certainty, so there is no difference in "risk" between the machine and the financial asset.]

7.(b) Using Table 15-1, at 12 percent, $PV = 1000(0.893) + 2000(0.797) = 893 + 1594 = \$2487$.

8.(d) Using Table 15-1, at 12 percent, $3000 = \$X(0.893) + 2000(0.797) = \$X(0.893) + 1594$. So $\$X = (3000 - 1594)/0.893 = 1406/0.893 = \$1574$. Since the PV of net revenue in the first year must be $1406 and the PV per dollar is $0.893, the number of dollars earned in the first year must be $1406/0.893.
Using the PV equation, $3000 = \$X/1.12 + 2000/(1.12)^2 = \$X/1.12 + 1594$. So $\$X/1.12 = 3000 - 1594 = \$1406$, hence $\$X = 1406(1.12) = \$1574$.

9.(a) If you want to have $1000 in the future, a higher <u>interest rate</u> means you need to invest less today to get it (i.e., a lower present value). If you want the $1000 in the <u>more distant</u> future 20 years hence, rather than in 10 years time, then again you need to invest less today to get it (i.e., a lower present value).

11.(b) Technology is fixed in two of the analytical time periods used: the short run and the long run. The very long run refers to the period over which technology changes and more investment goes hand-in-hand with improvements in production technology that increase the quantity of output per unit of capital input. Answer (a) is wrong because diminishing returns is a short-run concept with fixed capital stock and fixed technology. Changes in the interest rate do not shift the investment demand curve but move along it, so (c) is wrong. Similarly, a fall on the supply of savings would increase the equilibrium interest rate along the investment demand curve rather than shift it, so (d) is wrong.

12.(c) Because of the 5 percent inflation, $105 of the $112 is needed to buy what $100 would have bought last year. This leaves you with additional spending power of only $7—i.e., a real rate of interest of 7 percent (12 percent nominal rate minus 5 percent inflation). [*Note:* This formula actually gives a very close approximation of the real interest rate. The exact formula recognizes that the extra $7 has less *purchasing power* this year than did $7 last year because of inflation. With the 5 percent inflation rate, therefore, the exact real rate of interest is $7/$105 = 6.67 percent.]

13.(c) You have three elements in the answers: current income, expected future income, and the interest rate. Saving is positively related to the interest rate and current income, and negatively related to expected future income. So greater saving results from a higher interest rate, from greater current income, and from a smaller expected future income. The only answer that is not inconsistent with at least one of these is (c).

14.(e) An increase in population increases the economy's current income, which affects both the demand and supply curves. The demand curve for capital shifts right, increasing the equilibrium capital stock and interest rate. The supply curve of capital shifts to the right too, increasing the equilibrium capital stock but reducing the equilibrium interest rate. Thus the equilibrium capital stock increases (because both predict this effect), but the effect on the equilibrium interest rate is uncertain because the two shifts predict opposing changes in the interest rate. What happens to the equilibrium interest rate, therefore, depends on the relative magnitudes of the two shifts. If the demand shift dominates, the interest rate rises. If the supply shift dominates, the interest rate falls. If the two shifts are equal, the interest rate remains unchanged.

Table 15-1 Present Value of $1.00 to Be Received in a Future Year (i.e., a one-time payment)

$$PV = \frac{1}{(1+i)^n}$$

[*Note:* Numbers rounded to three decimal places.]

	Market Rate of Interest									
Years Hence (*n*)	1%	2%	4%	5%	6%	8%	10%	12%	14%	15%
1	0.990	0.980	0.962	0.952	0.943	0.926	0.909	0.893	0.877	0.870
2	0.980	0.961	0.925	0.907	0.890	0.857	0.826	0.797	0.769	0.756
3	0.971	0.942	0.889	0.864	0.840	0.794	0.751	0.712	0.675	0.658
4	0.961	0.924	0.855	0.823	0.792	0.735	0.683	0.636	0.592	0.572
5	0.951	0.906	0.822	0.784	0.747	0.681	0.621	0.567	0.519	0.497
6	0.942	0.888	0.790	0.746	0.705	0.630	0.564	0.507	0.456	0.432
7	0.933	0.871	0.760	0.711	0.665	0.583	0.513	0.452	0.400	0.376
8	0.923	0.853	0.731	0.677	0.627	0.540	0.467	0.404	0.351	0.327
9	0.914	0.837	0.703	0.645	0.592	0.500	0.424	0.361	0.308	0.284
10	0.905	0.820	0.676	0.614	0.558	0.463	0.386	0.322	0.270	0.247
11	0.896	0.804	0.650	0.585	0.527	0.429	0.350	0.287	0.237	0.215
12	0.887	0.788	0.625	0.557	0.497	0.397	0.319	0.257	0.208	0.187
13	0.879	0.773	0.601	0.530	0.469	0.368	0.290	0.229	0.182	0.163
14	0.870	0.758	0.577	0.505	0.442	0.340	0.263	0.205	0.160	0.141
15	0.861	0.743	0.555	0.481	0.417	0.315	0.239	0.183	0.140	0.123
16	0.853	0.728	0.534	0.458	0.394	0.292	0.218	0.163	0.123	0.107
17	0.844	0.714	0.513	0.436	0.371	0.270	0.198	0.146	0.108	0.093
18	0.836	0.700	0.494	0.416	0.350	0.250	0.180	0.130	0.095	0.081
19	0.828	0.686	0.475	0.396	0.331	0.232	0.164	0.116	0.083	0.070
20	0.820	0.673	0.456	0.377	0.312	0.215	0.149	0.104	0.073	0.061
21	0.811	0.660	0.439	0.359	0.294	0.199	0.135	0.093	0.064	0.053
22	0.803	0.647	0.422	0.342	0.278	0.184	0.123	0.083	0.056	0.046
23	0.795	0.634	0.406	0.326	0.262	0.170	0.112	0.074	0.049	0.040
24	0.788	0.622	0.390	0.310	0.247	0.158	0.102	0.066	0.043	0.035
25	0.780	0.610	0.375	0.295	0.233	0.146	0.092	0.059	0.038	0.030
26	0.772	0.598	0.361	0.281	0.220	0.135	0.084	0.053	0.033	0.026
27	0.764	0.586	0.347	0.268	0.207	0.125	0.076	0.047	0.029	0.023
28	0.757	0.574	0.333	0.255	0.196	0.116	0.069	0.042	0.026	0.020
29	0.749	0.563	0.321	0.243	0.185	0.107	0.063	0.037	0.022	0.017
30	0.742	0.552	0.308	0.231	0.174	0.099	0.057	0.033	0.020	0.015
40	0.672	0.453	0.208	0.142	0.097	0.046	0.022	0.011	0.005	0.004
50	0.608	0.372	0.141	0.087	0.054	0.021	0.009	0.003	0.001	0.001

Table 15-2 Present Value of $1.00 Received Each Year for n Years (i.e., a stream of payments)

$$PV = \frac{1}{(1+i)^1} + \frac{1}{(1+i)^1} + \cdots + \frac{1}{(1+i)^n}$$

[*Note:* Numbers rounded to three decimal places.]

Years Hence (n)	1%	2%	4%	5%	6%	8%	10%	12%	14%	15%
1	0.990	0.980	0.962	0.952	0.943	0.926	0.909	0.893	0.877	0.870
2	1.970	1.942	1.886	1.859	1.833	1.783	1.736	1.690	1.647	1.626
3	2.941	2.884	2.775	2.723	2.673	2.577	2.487	2.402	2.322	2.283
4	3.902	3.808	3.630	3.546	3.465	3.312	3.170	3.037	2.914	2.855
5	4.853	4.713	4.452	4.329	4.212	3.993	3.791	3.605	3.433	3.352
6	5.795	5.601	5.242	5.076	4.917	4.623	4.355	4.111	3.889	3.784
7	6.728	6.472	6.002	5.786	5.582	5.206	4.868	4.565	4.288	4.160
8	7.652	7.325	6.733	6.463	6.210	5.747	5.335	4.968	4.639	4.487
9	8.566	8.162	7.435	7.108	6.802	6.247	5.759	5.328	4.946	4.772
10	9.714	8.983	8.111	7.722	7.360	6.710	6.145	5.650	5.216	5.019
11	10.368	9.787	8.760	8.306	7.877	7.139	6.495	5.988	5.453	5.234
12	11.255	10.575	9.385	8.863	8.384	7.536	6.814	6.194	5.660	5.421
13	12.134	11.343	9.986	9.394	8.853	7.904	7.103	6.424	5.842	5.583
14	13.004	12.106	10.563	9.899	9.295	8.244	7.367	6.628	6.002	5.724
15	13.865	12.849	11.118	10.380	9.712	8.559	7.606	6.811	6.142	5.847
16	14.718	13.578	11.652	10.838	10.106	8.851	7.824	6.974	6.265	5.954
17	15.562	14.292	12.166	11.274	10.477	9.122	8.022	7.120	6.373	6.047
18	16.398	14.992	12.659	11.690	10.828	9.372	8.201	7.250	6.467	6.128
19	17.226	15.678	13.134	12.085	11.158	9.604	8.365	7.466	6.550	6.198
20	18.046	16.351	13.590	12.462	11.470	9.818	8.514	7.469	6.623	6.259
21	18.857	17.011	14.029	12.821	11.764	10.017	8.649	7.562	6.687	6.312
22	19.660	17.658	14.451	13.163	12.042	10.201	8.772	7.645	6.743	6.359
23	20.456	18.292	14.857	13.489	12.303	10.371	8.883	7.718	6.792	6.399
24	21.234	18.914	15.247	13.799	12.550	10.529	8.985	7.784	6.835	6.434
25	22.023	19.523	15.622	14.094	12.783	10.675	9.077	7.843	6.873	6.464
26	22.795	20.121	15.983	14.375	13.003	10.810	9.161	7.896	6.906	6.591
27	23.560	20.707	16.330	14.643	13.211	10.935	9.237	7.943	6.935	6.514
28	24.316	21.281	16.663	14.898	13.406	11.051	9.307	7.984	6.961	6.534
29	25.066	21.844	16.984	15.141	13.591	11.158	9.370	8.022	6.983	6.551
30	25.808	27.306	17.292	15.373	13.765	11.258	9.247	8.055	7.003	6.566
40	32.835	27.355	19.793	17.159	15.046	11.925	9.779	8.244	7.105	6.642
50	39.196	31.424	21.482	18.256	15.762	12.234	9.915	8.304	7.133	6.661

Market Failures and Government Intervention

16

Chapter Overview

This is the first of three chapters that consider the role of government in a market economy. This chapter reviews the benefits and costs of government intervention in the market economy. The formal defence of the market economy refers to the concept of allocative efficiency developed in Chapter 12. The informal defence is based on three attributes of free markets: flexibility and automatic coordination of decentralized decision making; stimulus for innovation and growth; and decentralization of economic power.

Several sources of market failure that might be addressed by government policy are identified. Such failures occur when there are divergences between **private and social costs or benefits** (e.g., **externalities** and **public goods**), or **information asymmetries** (e.g., **moral hazard** and **adverse selection**). These sources of market failure provide an economic justification for considering remedial government action. Government intervention in free markets may also be required when a social goal other than economic efficiency is not achieved by the market system (e.g., a more equal distribution of income).

Government policies and actions impose costs as well as benefits. There are **direct** resource costs incurred by government expenditures on goods and services, and there are **indirect costs** that are imposed on those who are regulated as well as on third parties. The indirect costs result from changes in the costs of production, from the costs of compliance, and from **rent seeking** behaviour. The costs of government intervention, as well as the possibility that the government action may fail, must be balanced against the benefits of government intervention to determine whether and to what degree government intervention to correct market failures is warranted. For example, will the bailout of financial institutions in the financial crisis of 2007–2008 create expectations of future bailouts, which in turn may encourage more-risky investments and assets than otherwise (i.e., behavioural change as a case of a "moral hazard")?

Hints and Tips

The following may help you avoid some of the most common errors on examinations.

✓ Recognize that the criterion for allocative efficiency used in this chapter has the same underlying principle as the one you used in Chapter 12 (i.e., marginal benefit equals marginal cost), but it is *broadened* to cover markets in which there are additional costs and benefits to persons other than the producers and consumers of the specific product.

✓ In the section on market failures, don't let your personal views of what constitutes a "just society" obstruct your understanding of the economic analysis. First, the conditions for market failure are meant to be used as a *benchmark* to help identify the *important* cases. Second, society will make tradeoffs between economic efficiency and broader social goals. The economic analysis of market failure and allocative efficiency does <u>not</u> say that any such tradeoffs that reduce allocative efficiency should be avoided. Rather, the analysis helps you better identify the potential tradeoffs and make *better informed* choices.

✓ Many new definitions and concepts are introduced in this chapter, which are very important for a proper appreciation of economic analysis and its implications for public policy. You need to understand these concepts and their implications to put the analysis you learned in previous chapters into its appropriate context and perspective.

Chapter Review

Basic Functions of Government

The "minimal" role of government is the protection of individuals from others and the establishment and enforcement of property rights. Economic prosperity has seldom been achieved without governments being able to effectively perform these functions, and a growing share of assistance to developing countries has been directed at building the institutions needed to do this. One of the challenges facing international aid to developing countries is the potential conflicts between helping governments maintain a *monopoly of violence* and encouraging a political structure within which governments will not abuse that monopoly but rather use it to protect individual rights and promote social justice.

1. **Citizens can safely conduct their economic activities when government**
   (a) plays no role in the economy.
   (b) violently competes with other organizations for economic control.
   (c) determines the allocation of society's resources.
   (d) provides law and order and enforces property rights.
   (e) owns all private property.

The Case for Free Markets

This section goes beyond the "formal defence" of free markets based on allocative efficiency introduced in Chapters 5 and 12 to review the arguments that constitute the "informal defence" of market economies. For each component of the informal defence, the workings of a decentralized market system are contrasted with the difficulties and problems arising in a more centrally planned system.

2. **Independent decisions in a market economy are coordinated by**
   (a) marketing boards.
   (b) the pursuit of profit.
   (c) allocative efficiency.
   (d) the price system.
   (e) opportunity cost.

3. **Which of the following is required for a market economy to function?**
   (a) Enforcement of contractual obligations.
   (b) Well-defined property rights.
   (c) Reasonable protection of private property from theft.
   (d) All of the above.
   (e) Both (a) and (c), but not (b).

4. **Which of the following is part of the "formal defence" of free markets?**
   (a) Allocative efficiency.
   (b) Decentralization of economic power.
   (c) Stimulus for innovation and economic growth.
   (d) Automatic coordination of decentralized decisions.
   (e) None of the above—they are all part of the "informal defence."

5. **One of the most important features of the price system is**
   (a) long-term stability of prices and output.
   (b) its ability to respond quickly and automatically to changing demand and supply conditions.
   (c) the assurance that government will not tax consumers and producers.
   (d) that it solves the problem of scarcity and provides abundance for all.
   (e) that it provides an equitable distribution of income.

Market Failures

This section defines "market failure" strictly in terms of failure to achieve allocative efficiency. Four major situations of market failure are considered: market power; externalities; non-rivalrous and non-excludable goods; and asymmetric information. Market power can result from economies of scale causing few firms in the industry; from firms having some ability to set prices because they sell differentiated products; and from new products or production processes that give the innovating firms at least temporary monopoly power. Numerous new definitions and new concepts are introduced, and the potential conflict between allocative efficiency at a point in time and encouraging economic growth over time is highlighted. After reading this section you should be able to define and provide examples of each source of market failure, to understand the implications for allocative efficiency, and to identify the type and level of government intervention that could (in principle) be warranted. [*Note:* The term *tragedy of the commons* is often used to refer to the private sector's excessive use of common-property resources, ignoring the resulting social costs.]

6. *Market failure* **is the general term used to describe situations in which**
   (a) nothing is produced.
   (b) there is persistent excess demand or supply.
   (c) the allocatively efficient outcome is not achieved.
   (d) there is an undesirable distribution of income in the economy.
   (e) markets fail to create economic profit.

7. **The fundamental objective of government policy toward market power is to**
   (a)   eliminate the market power of oligopolies.
   (b)   destroy the barriers to entry of a natural monopoly.
   (c)   increase market power to create greater incentives for innovation.
   (d)   prevent the abuse of market power.
   (e)   give firms a greater share of total economic surplus.

8. **When people who neither produce nor consume a specific good are adversely affected by it, economists say that**
   (a)   there is adverse selection.
   (b)   there are negative externalities.
   (c)   there is a free-rider problem.
   (d)   private costs exceed social costs.
   (e)   society is in danger of a moral hazard.

9. **In a perfectly competitive market, the presence of _____ results in _____ the allocatively efficient level of output.**
   (a)   positive economic profits; more than
   (b)   negative externalities; less than
   (c)   no externalities; less than
   (d)   any externality, positive or negative; more than
   (e)   positive externalities; less than

10. **Which of the following is the *best* example of the free-rider problem?**
    (a)   A municipal bus service with a policy of not charging senior citizens.
    (b)   A local cinema that charges youths a lower price than adults.
    (c)   A university professor who receives the benefits of a contract negotiated by the faculty union but does not pay union dues.
    (d)   A student who attends university for free because of a scholarship.
    (e)   A person who visits the Museum of Civilization only when there is no admission fee.

11. **Which of the following is the *best* example of a good that is excludable and non-rivalrous in consumption?**
    (a)   Pay-per-view television.   (b)   The cod fishery.
    (c)   A lighthouse.   (d)   Police protection.
    (e)   A radio broadcast.

12. **Externalities essentially create**
    (a)   non-excludability in consumption.
    (b)   non-rivalry in consumption.
    (c)   a divergence between private and social costs.
    (d)   the free-rider problem.
    (e)   asymmetric information.

13. **Suppose my bicycle is fully insured and as a consequence I don't bother locking it. This is an example of**
    (a)   adverse selection.   (b)   moral hazard.
    (c)   the market for lemons.   (d)   a common property resource.
    (e)   the free-rider problem.

14. **Winnipeg's flood-control system, which protects all people within its boundaries, is an example of**
    (a) a negative externality.   (b) an information asymmetry.
    (c) a common property resource.   (d) a public good.
    (e) Okun's "leaky bucket."

15. **Which of the following is the best example of a public good in a classroom?**
    (a) A pencil.
    (b) A student's notes.
    (c) A copy of the textbook.
    (d) The temperature in the room.
    (e) Anything that is provided free by the government.

16. **Adverse selection arises from a situation in which**
    (a) the managers of corporations pursue goals other than profits.
    (b) the values of consumers and producers differ.
    (c) one party to a transaction has more information than the other party.
    (d) the government selects the wrong form of intervention for correcting a market failure.
    (e) a firm's owners are not the firm's managers.

17. **A positive externality would probably result from**
    (a) a discharge of a toxic waste into the St. Lawrence River.
    (b) a newly painted house.
    (c) the dumping of garbage on a seldom-used country road.
    (d) cigarette smoking.
    (e) a loud radio at a public beach.

Broader Social Goals

This section recognizes that society may prefer to sacrifice some allocative efficiency in order to achieve broader social goals. The discussion focuses on social preferences relating to (i) the distribution of income; (ii) public rather than private provision of some goods or services; (iii) government responsibility for the protection of individuals from others and from themselves; (iv) social obligations that individuals should not be allowed to avoid even by mutually advantageous trades; and (v) long-term economic growth. This is a non-technical section, but is important for giving perspective to the economic theory you have learned.

18. **The Government of Canada requires that all employed Canadians save for their retirement through the Canada Pension Plan. This is an example of**
    (a) social responsibility.   (b) paternalism.
    (c) allocative efficiency.   (d) moral hazard.
    (e) adverse selection.

19. **Redistribution of income conflicts with the goal of allocative efficiency because**
    (a) it invariably changes incentives.
    (b) redistribution is essentially a negative externality.
    (c) recipients overstate their marginal benefits and providers overstate their marginal costs.
    (d) some recipients are not legitimately needy.
    (e) it creates a moral hazard problem.

20. **Preventing mutually advantageous trades whereby individuals in a democracy could sell their electoral votes to others is generally viewed as**
    (a) encouraging social responsibility.
    (b) preventing adverse selection.
    (c) a way to increase allocative efficiency.
    (d) creating a moral hazard.
    (e) a way to reduce asymmetric information.

Government Intervention

Just as there are benefits from government attempts to correct market failures, so too there are costs. Consequently, it is neither possible nor efficient to correct <u>all</u> market failures, nor is it always efficient to do nothing. There are different views among economists as to whether the level of government intervention spurred by the financial crisis of 2007–2008 was appropriate or excessive; it prevented large-scale collapse of the financial system in several countries, but to what extent should firms have been held responsible for the results of their own excessive risk-taking? This section also explains some of the *tools* of government intervention, the *costs* (direct and indirect) of intervention, and various reasons why government interventions/programs can *fail to achieve their potential*. It closes with an important principle that should be followed when evaluating government interventions: a principle that may well be ignored in many a policy debate between political parties and among pressure groups.

21. **Efficient government intervention requires that**
    (a) the costs of government enforcement be zero.
    (b) the marginal benefits of intervention be just equal to the marginal costs of intervention.
    (c) intervention should continue until all negative externalities have been eliminated.
    (d) there be no productivity losses in the private sector as a result of government intervention.
    (e) all intervention be self-financing.

22. **Which of the following can the government use to correct market failure?**
    (a) Taxes and/or subsidies.
    (b) Rules and regulations restricting market activity.
    (c) Public provision of goods and services.
    (d) Restructuring incentives.
    (e) All of the above.

23. **In practice, assessing the benefits and costs of a proposed government program is difficult because**
    (a) the effects of the program may be difficult to determine.
    (b) many benefits and costs occur in the distant future.
    (c) some costs and benefits are difficult, perhaps impossible, to quantify.
    (d) All of the above.
    (e) Both (a) and (b) are correct, but not (c).

24. **Rent seeking behaviour refers to**
    (a) the conversion of owner-occupied housing to rental housing.
    (b) activities by individuals seeking favourable government actions.
    (c) consumers seeking low-rent housing.
    (d) actions in former socialist countries to convert public housing to private ownership.
    (e) firms that avoid the fixed costs of plant and equipment by leasing instead of buying.

25.   **Which of the following best describes the concept of "rational ignorance"?**
  (a)   A person decides that the opportunity cost of forgone earnings outweighs the benefits of a university education.
  (b)   Government deliberately chooses to hide the true costs of a policy from voters.
  (c)   Individuals decide that the costs of understanding the complexities of a policy are not worth the benefits of such understanding.
  (d)   A firm chooses to inflate its profit statement to increase the value of its shares on the stock market.
  (e)   A lecturer has an excellent understanding of economic theory but ignores real-world political constraints.

Short-Answer Questions

1.   Under what circumstances do private costs differ from social costs? Explain how and why these differences affect the allocatively efficient output of a good or service.

2.   Why will the private sector not produce a public good? If a private firm can prevent people from consuming a non-rivalrous good if they do not pay for it, will the firm produce the allocatively efficient amount of the good?

3.   People in business generally cannot buy insurance against bankruptcy. As an executive of a large insurance company, use the concept of adverse selection to explain why you do not provide such insurance.

4.   Why does income redistribution through the tax-transfer system create allocative inefficiency? Does this mean that income redistribution programs should be abandoned?

5.   State whether the following statement is true or false, and explain your answer in terms of public choice theory. "A democratically elected government will increase its likelihood of remaining in power after the next election if it eliminates programs that benefit few voters in order to reduce taxes paid by the vast majority of voters."

Exercises

1. **Externalities**

This exercise focuses on how the profit-maximizing free-market outcome differs from the optimal outcome for society when social costs are not the same as private costs. [*Note:* Exercise 2 in Chapter 12 also compares the allocative efficiency of monopoly and competition when there are externalities.]

Figure 16-1 illustrates a competitive market in which the production process emits pollutants on neighbouring residences. The market demand curve is D. MC_P represents the private marginal costs of production (i.e., the competitive industry supply curve), and MC_E represents the marginal external costs to local residents from pollution.

Figure 16-1

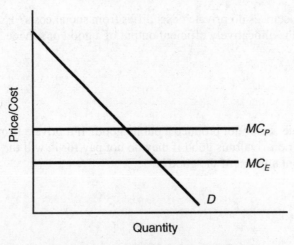

(a) Identify the free-market output, and label it X in the figure.

(b) Derive the social marginal cost curve, and label it MC_S. Explain how you derived it.

(c) Indicate on the graph the socially optimal output level (label it Z).

(d) Explain why it would be inefficient to reduce emissions in this market to zero.

(e) Suppose this market is monopolized. Draw the monopoly output, and compare it to the optimal output Z. What can you conclude about the allocative efficiency of monopoly versus competition in this case?

(f)   Would your conclusion about the allocative efficiency of monopoly versus competition change if the industry in Figure 16-1 created a positive rather than a negative externality? Explain.

2.   **Public Goods**
Mr. Maple and Mr. Oak have cottages in a particular wooded retreat. Access to both cottages is by way of the same two-kilometre private road. All maintenance costs of the road are paid for by these two individuals. The individual demand curves (i.e., marginal benefit curves) for road quality of Mr. Oak and Mr. Maple are shown in the graphs. The marginal cost of increasing quality is shown as *MC*. (We assume that "zero" quality implies that the road is barely passable.)

Figure 16-2

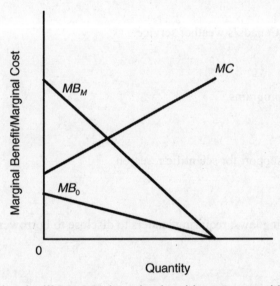

(a)   What quality level will Mr. Maple maintain without any consideration for Mr. Oak? Similarly, what quality would Mr. Oak maintain without considering his neighbour?

(b)   How would you illustrate the social demand for road quality? Use the graph.
[*Hint:* Review the discussion of Figure 16-2 in the text.]

(c)   Given the costs of road improvements as shown, would the optimal quality level represent an improvement in road quality compared to the level maintained by Mr. Maple alone?

(d)   What would be the maximum price per unit of quality that Mr. Oak would be willing to pay for the level of road quality given by (c)? Would he necessarily pay this maximum?

3. **Classification of Market Failures**

For each of the government programs or regulations cited, identify what type of market failure or social objective might be used as a rationale for government intervention. Briefly explain your choice.

(a) National defence.

(b) Pollution control regulations.

(c) Public health insurance programs.

(d) Environment Canada's weather service.

(e) Student loan programs.

(f) Government support for scientific research.

(g) Truth-in-lending laws, requiring lenders to disclose to borrowers the true rate of interest.

(h) Minimum wage legislation.

(i) Quotas limiting the number of fish that may be caught.

(j) Municipal zoning regulations.

(k) Mandatory employment insurance policies.

4. **Costly Government Intervention**

The following diagram depicts a market's marginal private benefit (*MPB*) curve, which gives the *incremental* private gain ($P - MC$) to consumers and producers as output is increased. Also shown is the marginal damage (*MD*) curve, which refers to pollution costs from incremental increases in production. These damages are external to the consumers and producers of this product; that is to say, they are negative externalities imposed on third parties.

Figure 16-3

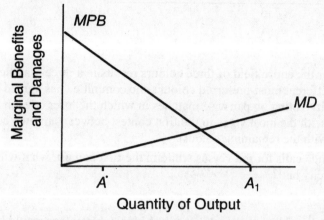

(a) With no government intervention, what level of output would obtain in this market? Why?

(b) From society's point of view, what is the optimal output level? Explain.

(c) Suppose that the government has faulty information on the precise shape of the *MD* curve and limits the output to level *A**. At *A**, is society better off or worse off than in a no-intervention situation? Explain.

Extension Exercises

E1. A Problem with Democracy

This exercise is an application of Arrow's impossibility theorem which, although not discussed in the text, gives an interesting perspective on potential difficulties of coming to efficient policy decisions in a democracy.

A small community is in the process of repainting city hall. The citizens have decided that only one colour will be used and have narrowed the potential colours down to a choice of red, white, or blue. To choose one colour from among the three, a committee of three individuals has been selected. Each of the committee members has a personal preference ranking of the alternatives as indicated in the following schedule (where 1 indicates the most preferred and 3 indicates the least preferred).

Individual Preference Rankings

Committee Member

Colour	A	B	C
Red	1	3	2
White	2	1	3
Blue	3	2	1

Since a vote over the entire field of three colours results in a three-way tie (each committee member has a different most-preferred colour), the committee has agreed to select the winning colour by majority voting on pairwise matches in which the loser of each match is eliminated (i.e., the colour with the most votes in the first contest between any two colours proceeds to a second contest with the remaining colour).

(a) If the agenda calls for red versus white in the first contest, what will ultimately be the colour of city hall?

(b) If the first round had pitted white against blue, what colour would have been chosen from the three?

(c) If the first round had matched red against blue, what colour would city hall have been painted?

E2. Property Rights and the Coase Theorem

[*Note:* This question is based on *Additional Topics: Externalities and the Coase Theorem* on MyEconLab. Before doing it, ask your instructor if this topic is covered in your course.]

Mr. Bookworm and Mr. Blaster live in adjacent condominium apartments separated by a thin dividing wall. Blaster likes playing loud music, the sound of which penetrates through the dividing wall and disturbs Bookworm. Blaster values listening to loud music at $900 and Bookworm values silence at $700.

(a) **Case 1:** The cost of soundproofing the dividing wall is $500 if Bookworm does it and $300 if Blaster does it.

    (i) What is the efficient outcome for this problem?

    (ii) Will this outcome be achieved if Blaster has the legal right to make noise? If Bookworm has the legal right to silence? Explain your answers.

(b) **Case 2:** Repeat question (a), but this time assume the costs of soundproofing are reversed (i.e., $300 for Bookworm and $500 for Blaster).

(c) Repeat Question (a), but this time assume the cost of soundproofing is $1200 if Blaster does it and $1000 if Bookworm does it.

(d) Now the problem changes. Blaster values playing loud music at $1000. The noise bothers all 100 residents of the building equally, to the value of $20 each. The cost of soundproofing is $2500 regardless of who does it. There are no transaction costs of the 100 residents meeting and deciding what to do. In this case, what is the efficient outcome? Will it be achieved if Blaster has the legal right to play loud music? Explain your answer.

Additional Multiple-Choice Questions

1.   **The likely result in a market economy if the government taxed away all profits would be**
     (a)   a more rapid shift of resources to expanding industries.
     (b)   the removal of the most important incentive for resource allocation.
     (c)   improved market signals and responses.
     (d)   improved information about temporary shortages and surpluses.
     (e)   enhanced efficiency in resource allocation.

2.   **Which of the following is *not* an argument for increased reliance on markets for the allocation of resources?**
     (a)   The market system coordinates millions of independent economic decisions automatically.
     (b)   Profits in a market economy provide a stimulus for innovation and growth.
     (c)   Markets function best when there are external benefits from consumption or production.
     (d)   Market forces provide an effective means of adapting to changing economic conditions.
     (e)   In a market system relative prices reflect relative costs.

3.   **If a tonne of newspaper costs $350 to produce and in the process causes $10 worth of pollution damage to the environment,**
     (a)   the private cost is $360 per tonne.
     (b)   the social cost is $10 per tonne and the private cost is $350 per tonne.
     (c)   the private cost is $350 per tonne and the social cost is $340 per tonne.
     (d)   the social cost is $360 per tonne and the private cost is $350 per tonne.
     (e)   the social cost is $10 per tonne and the private cost is $360 per tonne.

*4.   **If there are costly negative externalities associated with an economic activity and that activity is carried out until the private marginal benefit equals the private marginal cost,**
     (a)   this activity should be subsidized.
     (b)   the social marginal net benefit is positive.
     (c)   private costs exceed social costs.
     (d)   too many resources are being allocated to this activity.
     (e)   output of this activity should increase.

*5. **The presence of external benefits associated with production implies that**
  (a) private output exceeds the socially optimal output.
  (b) private output is less than the socially optimal output.
  (c) private output corresponds to the socially optimal output.
  (d) Any of the above, depending on the relative magnitude of social and private benefits.
  (e) Any of the above, depending on whether social benefits exceed external benefits.

*6. **A market economy is unlikely to provide a sufficient amount of a public good such as national defence because**
  (a) national defence does not benefit everyone to the same degree.
  (b) private firms produce national defence less efficiently than does the government.
  (c) consumers are poorly informed about the benefits of national defence.
  (d) it is impossible to withhold national defence from people who don't pay for it.
  (e) private firms would profit from exaggerating the dangers faced by the general public.

7. **Which one of the following would not be a source of inefficient market outcomes?**
  (a) Externalities.
  (b) Public goods.
  (c) Profits and losses.
  (d) Information asymmetries.
  (e) Moral hazard.

*8. **A Vancouver resident who drives a car to work rather than taking public transportation**
  (a) is reducing the free-rider problem.
  (b) is likely to be creating a negative externality.
  (c) creates a situation in which private cost is likely to exceed social cost.
  (d) is contributing to efficient resource allocation.
  (e) is not using a public good and so should get a tax rebate.

*9. **Competitive markets are unlikely to produce an efficient amount of a public good because**
  (a) of non-excludability in consumption.
  (b) private firms are likely to make more profits than are socially undesirable.
  (c) these goods should be consumed until the marginal benefit is zero.
  (d) of rivalry in consumption.
  (e) of moral hazard by private firms.

*10. **Private markets will always underprovide public goods because**
  (a) private markets will never provide goods at a price of zero.
  (b) of the positive externalities associated with these goods.
  (c) of the negative externalities associated with these goods.
  (d) the private marginal cost is less than the social marginal cost.
  (e) private markets will never provide goods that they know the government will provide.

*11. **Optimal public good provision is the level at which**
  (a) the cost of providing an extra unit of the good is equal to each consumer's marginal benefit from the extra unit.
  (b) the cost of providing an extra unit of the good is equal to the sum of all consumers' marginal benefits for that unit.
  (c) the cost of providing an extra unit of the good is equal to the price of the good.
  (d) the marginal benefit of each consumer for the last unit of the good produced is zero.
  (e) voters are satisfied that an adequate amount of the good is being produced.

*12. It is inefficient for the government to charge a price for consuming a good, such as weather forecasts, because
(a)   too many forecasts will be produced.
(b)   the price cannot be set to cover all research costs.
(c)   no one will be willing to pay for these forecasts.
(d)   the marginal cost of providing this information to another consumer is zero.
(e)   too few forecasts will be provided.

*13. Moral hazard exists when one party to a transaction
(a)   has more information than the other party.
(b)   has the incentive and ability to shift costs onto another party.
(c)   is threatened by a hostile takeover.
(d)   does not realize that it is creating negative externalities.
(e)   commits illegal activities because prison sentences are too low.

*14. Suppose some people derive a positive benefit from a public good but others receive a negative benefit. This public good should be produced if
(a)   the sum of everyone's marginal benefit is positive.
(b)   the sum of all the positive marginal benefits equals marginal cost.
(c)   the sum of individual valuations is maximized.
(d)   the sum of everyone's marginal benefit is at least as great as marginal cost.
(e)   those with negative benefits can be excluded from consuming the good.

*15. Tax exemptions for private pension plan contributions represent government intervention through
(a)   government provision of a public good.   (b)   redistribution.
(c)   regulation.   (d)   changing economic incentives.
(e)   paternalism.

*16. Examples of indirect costs of government intervention include all of the following *except*
(a)   expenditures by special interest groups to gain preferential tax treatment.
(b)   the salaries of tax lawyers employed by many Canadian corporations.
(c)   the time spent by Canadians completing income tax returns.
(d)   the government's administrative costs of collecting income tax revenue.
(e)   costs of complying with the goods and services tax.

17. Attempts by lobbyists to influence the government's subsidy to the shipbuilding industry represent
(a)   external costs.
(b)   market power by the government.
(c)   rent seeking.
(d)   moral hazard.
(e)   adverse selection.

*18. Resource allocation on the principle of one-person-one-vote will generally be _____ because the intensity of preferences is _____.
(a)   efficient, accounted for
(b)   efficient, not accounted for
(c)   inefficient, accounted for
(d)   inefficient, not accounted for

*19. **Which of the following best describes the cause of overfishing in Canada's offshore fisheries?**
    (a) Fishing has depleted fish stocks, leading to smaller catches.
    (b) The private marginal cost incurred by fishers is less than the social marginal cost.
    (c) A trend toward healthy diets increased the demand for fish.
    (d) Canadian governments explicitly encourage fishing through subsidies to fishers.
    (e) Fishing is a non-rivalrous activity.

*20. **The market for "lemons" (i.e., bad cars) is an example of market failure due to**
    (a) public goods.
    (b) externalities.
    (c) monopoly power.
    (d) asymmetric information.
    (e) pursuit of social goals other than allocative efficiency.

*21. **Arthur Okun's comparison of the economy to a "leaky bucket" refers to the**
    (a) loss of efficiency due to imperfect competition in the economy.
    (b) forgone tax revenues resulting from an inefficient tax system.
    (c) costs involved in the regulation of the economy.
    (d) the efficiency costs involved in the redistribution of income.
    (e) the reduction in tax revenues due to tax evasion.

Solutions

Chapter Review

1.(d) 2.(d) 3.(d) 4.(a) 5.(b) 6.(c) 7.(d) 8.(b) 9.(e) 10.(c) 11.(a) 12.(c) 13.(b) 14.(d) 15.(d) 16.(c) 17.(b) 18.(b) 19.(a) 20.(a) 21.(b) 22.(e) 23.(d) 24.(b) 25.(c)

Short-Answer Questions

1.   Private and social costs differ when there are externalities to the production or consumption of a good—i.e., when people other than the producers and consumers of the good get benefits from it or bear part of the full cost of producing it. The allocatively efficient output occurs where $P = MC_{SOCIAL}$, but profit-maximizing firms consider only the private cost component of social costs when making their output decisions. Even perfect competition, producing where $P = MC_{PRIVATE}$, produces more than the allocatively efficient output when there are negative externalities (which make $MC_{PRIVATE} < MC_{SOCIAL}$), and produces less than the allocatively efficient output when there are positive externalities (which make $MC_{PRIVATE} > MC_{SOCIAL}$).

2.   A public good is both non-excludable (i.e., people can't be prevented from consuming it even if they do not pay for it) and non-rivalrous (i.e., one person's consumption of the good does not reduce the amount available for others to consume). The non-excludability property means that private producers would get no revenue and make losses equal to the costs of production. If a non-rivalrous good is excludable, however, private firms can make people pay for it and so make profits. Since the marginal cost of additional consumption of a non-rivalrous good is zero, however, the allocative efficiency condition is $P = MC = 0$. Private firms charging a positive price will therefore provide less than the allocatively efficient amount of the good.

3.   There is *asymmetric information* since firms know their own risk of bankruptcy better than do insurance companies. Bankruptcy insurance would be taken out by firms with a high risk of going bankrupt, and this process of *adverse selection* would drive up insurance premiums to where only firms with the *highest* risk of bankruptcy would take out the insurance. The only way for the insurance company to avoid making losses would be to charge a premium at least equal to what they would pay these highest-risk firms when

they went bankrupt. Since the firms would "lose" as much from paying the premium as they would from going bankrupt, they would not insure. [*Note:* Health insurance companies, for example, make their profit by insuring *both* high-risk *and* low-risk people. One part of the premiums of the low-risk people helps to pay the claims from high-risk people, and the other part is profit.]

4. The higher tax rates needed to finance the benefit payments reduce taxpayers' opportunity cost of leisure (i.e., the after-tax wage rate), reducing their incentive to work. The benefit payments also reduce the recipients' incentive to work, so there is less income generated in the overall economy. Nevertheless, if income redistribution to assist low-income households is a social objective, the inefficiencies resulting from lower incentives to work and produce income can be seen as an acceptable cost of achieving this broader social objective and not as a reason to abandon income redistribution.

5. False. Because the costs are spread over so many taxpayers, the tax savings *per taxpayer* would be too small to affect taxpayers' voting behaviour. Payments to the program's individual beneficiaries, however, are much larger than the cost to the individual taxpayer—i.e., large enough to have an impact on voting patterns. A government that eliminates the program runs the risk of losing the votes of beneficiaries without gaining votes from taxpayers.

Exercises

1. **(a)** The competitive free-market output is X in Figure 16-4, where $P = MC_P$ at the intersection of the industry demand and supply curves.

Figure 16-4

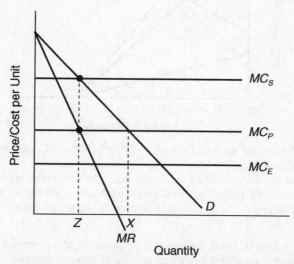

(b) See graph: $MC_S = MC_P + MC_E$. The MC_S curve is obtained by vertical summation of MC_P and MC_E curves.

(c) Society's optimal output is Z, where price equals the marginal social cost—i.e.,
$P = MC_S = MC_P + MC_E$.

(d) For all units of output below Z, the marginal benefit (indicated by the price people are willing to pay for the good) exceeds the marginal social cost. Reducing output below Z certainly would reduce pollution, but the cost to society from having less of the good to consume would exceed the benefits of having less pollution.

(e) A monopoly maximizes profit where $MR = MC_P$. Since the monopolist faces a linear, downward-sloping demand curve, the MR curve is as depicted in Figure 16-4. The intersection of the monopolist's MR and MC_P occurs at an output closer to the optimal output Z than is the competitive output X. Thus a monopoly is more allocatively efficient than a competitive market in this particular case. [*Note:* As drawn, the diagram shows that the intersection of MC_P and MR is exactly at Z, but this is not necessary. The monopoly is the more allocatively efficient as long as its output is *closer* to Z than is the competitive output.]

(f) Yes. If MC_E were a positive externality, then MC_S would equal MC_P *minus* MC_E (since a benefit is a "negative" cost). The MC_S line would be below the MC_P line in the figure, and the allocatively efficient output would be *greater* than the competitive industry output X. The competitive industry would *underproduce* relative to the social optimum, and the monopoly would underproduce by even more.

2. (a) Mr. Maple will maintain the quality level Q_M at the intersection of his MB_M curve and the MC curve. At this point Mr. Maple is investing in quality to the point where the extra cost of the marginal unit of quality equals his extra benefit. Mr. Oak would not invest at all in road quality, since his MB_O curve does not intersect the MC curve at a positive level of quality. That is, for Mr. Oak, the marginal cost of road quality is everywhere greater than the marginal benefit.

(b) Add the MB curves vertically to get MB_{M+O} in Figure 16-5. This is the total willingness to pay (i.e., demand) curve of Mr. Maple and Mr. Oak jointly.

Figure 16-5

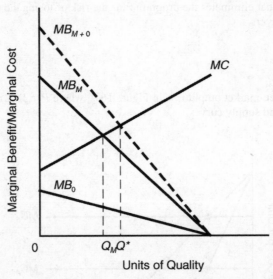

(c) Yes, because quality would increase from Q_M to Q^*, where the MC intersects MB_{M+O} to the right of the MB_M intersection with MC.

(d) The maximum that Mr. Oak would be willing to pay is the area under his MB_O curve up to Q^* units of quality—i.e., the sum of his marginal benefit from each unit of quality up to Q^*. Whether he would actually pay this maximum would, of course, depend on the specific cost-sharing arrangement on which he and Mr. Maple agreed.

3. (a) National defence is a public good. Adding to the population of a country does not diminish the extent to which each citizen is protected by a given amount of national defence.

(b) Pollution is an external cost; it is borne by people who neither consume nor produce the polluting good.

(c) Asymmetric information. Until the advent of publicly provided health insurance, it was difficult for the elderly to purchase health insurance because insurance companies were aware of the problem of adverse selection (i.e., they feared that only those who knew themselves to be bad risks would buy health insurance).

(d) Providing weather information is a public good—once the information is available, it is neither excludable nor rivalrous.

(e) Student loan programs are designed to increase the general educational level in society (in part a public good) and, to the extent that they reduce the immediate financial burden of going to college, should contribute to a more equitable distribution of income (a social objective).

(f) It can be argued that the knowledge gained from scientific research provides public goods (e.g., cures for various diseases) and that without government subsidies the socially optimal amount of research would not be done.

(g) Information asymmetry. Financial institutions are far more likely than the average borrower to know the true rate of interest. For example, borrowing $1000 to be repaid in 12 monthly instalments of $100 gives a total interest *payment* of $200, or 20 percent of the amount borrowed. The annual interest *rate*, however, is much higher than 20 percent because the monthly payments mean that not all of the $1000 is borrowed for the <u>whole year</u>.

(h) Minimum wage legislation is a form of price floor. Proponents usually argue that it will achieve a more equitable distribution of income and that it is a means of protecting some individuals (workers) from others (employers).

(i) External cost. Fish are a common-property resource (i.e., non-excludable). Overfishing by current generations endangers the future stock of fish, imposing a cost on future generations that is not taken into account by current generations.

(j) Externalities. Zoning laws that regulate such things as lot size, noise, and certain types of activities (such as fraternities in a residential area) are meant to reduce external costs.

(k) Paternalism. Individuals may not save enough on their own to cover unexpected bouts of temporary unemployment.

4. **(a)** The free market would result in output A_1 since this output corresponds to $MPB = 0$, which implies that total private benefits are at a maximum. Each unit below A_1 adds to total private benefits because $MPB > 0$; similarly, each unit above A_1 decreases total private benefits. The damage to third parties is part of the social cost but not the private cost, so will not be taken into consideration by producers.

(b) The social optimum is where the MPB and MD curves intersect, at output A_0 in Figure 16-6. For units of output in excess of A_0 the incremental cost to society exceeds the incremental benefit.

Figure 16-6

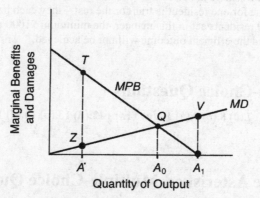

(c) At output A^* society is worse off than at output A_1. By increasing output to A_0 society would gain a net benefit of area ZTQ (i.e., the increase in total benefits to producers, A^*TQA_0, minus the increase in external damages, A^*ZQA_0). A further increase from A_0 to A_1 would occur at a net cost of area QVA_1 (i.e., the increase in external damages, A_0QVA_1, minus the increase in benefits to producers, A_0QA_1). As long as area ZTQ exceeds area QVA_1—which it does in Figure 16-6—the net increase in benefits on units A^* to A_0 exceeds the net increase in costs on units A_0 to A_1, so society is better off at A_1 than at A^* (by the difference between areas ZTQ and QVA_1).

Extension Exercises

E1. **(a)** Blue. Both A and C prefer red to white, so red will proceed to the second contest against blue. Both B and C prefer blue to red, so blue would be the ultimate winner.

(b) Red. White would win the first round, and red would win over white in the second round.

(c) White.

E2. **(a)** **(i)** The efficient (least cost) solution is for Blaster to soundproof the wall, since the $300 cost for Blaster is less than the $500 cost if Bookworm soundproofs, and both are less than the values of noise and silence to Blaster and Bookworm, respectively.

(ii) If Blaster has the right to make noise, Bookworm will be willing to pay Blaster up to $500 to soundproof, and they will agree on a mutually advantageous trade (e.g., Bookworm pays Blaster $350 to soundproof). If Bookworm has the right to silence, Blaster will have to soundproof and pay for it himself. Regardless of who owns the "property right," therefore, the efficient outcome will be achieved.

(b) The efficient (least cost) solution is for Bookworm to soundproof. If Blaster owns the property right, Bookworm will pay. If Bookworm owns the property right, Blaster will pay via a mutually advantageous trade.

(c)   (i)   Since the costs of soundproofing exceed the value of silence to Bookworm and the value of noise to Blaster, neither will be willing to pay for soundproofing. Since Blaster values noise more than Bookworm values silence, the efficient (least cost) outcome is for Blaster to make noise and for Bookworm to live with it.

      (ii)   If Blaster has the right to make noise, Bookworm will be unwilling to pay Blaster the $900 minimum needed to persuade Blaster to remain silent, so the noise continues. If Bookworm has the right to silence, Blaster will be willing to pay enough to persuade Bookworm to live with the noise, and they will agree on a mutually advantageous trade (e.g., Blaster pays Bookworm $750 to let him keep playing his music). Again, the efficient outcome is achieved regardless of who owns the property right.

(d) Since each resident values Blaster's silence at $20, their combined valuation of Blaster remaining silent is $20(100) = $2000—i.e., twice the value of the noise to Blaster. The efficient outcome is for Blaster to stop playing his loud music. Since the residents can easily meet and decide what to do, it seems that they would be willing to contribute, say, $12 each to give Blaster $1200—more than enough to compensate him for the loss of his noise. An individual resident, however, could recognize that his contribution alone will make no difference to the outcome (since the total willingness to pay of the remaining 99 residents is still well in excess of $1000). This resident would have an incentive to tell the others that Blaster's music does not bother him at all, thereby introducing the *free-rider* problem! What is true for one resident is true for the rest—they each have an incentive to take a free ride. If more than 50 residents act in this manner, the minimum $1000 needed to compensate Blaster will not be raised and the efficient outcome will not be achieved.

Additional Multiple-Choice Questions

1.(b) **2.**(c) **3.**(d) **4.**(d) **5.**(b) **6.**(d) **7.**(c) **8.**(b) **9.**(a) **10.**(a) **11.**(b) **12.**(d) **13.**(b) **14.**(d) **15.**(d) **16.**(d) **17.**(c) **18.**(d) **19.**(b) **20.**(d) **21.**(d)

Explanations for the Asterisked Multiple-Choice Questions

4.(d) The profit-maximizing condition for the private sector is to carry out the activity (i.e., produce) to where $MB_{PRIVATE} = MC_{PRIVATE}$, ignoring any externalities (so answer (c) is wrong). The *socially efficient* level of output, however, is where $MB_{SOCIAL} = MC_{SOCIAL}$—i.e., where $MB_{SOCIAL} = MC_{PRIVATE}$ **plus** *net negative externalities*. If, as the question states, there are such negative externalities, the level of output at which the private-sector condition is met will be where $MB_{SOCIAL} < MC_{SOCIAL}$. Thus the marginal net benefit for society to the last unit(s) of output is negative, meaning too much is being produced (so answers (a), (b), and (e) are wrong). Because production takes resources, producing too much means using too many resources (answer (d) is right).

5.(b) The socially optimal output occurs when $P = MC_{SOCIAL}$. When external benefits (i.e., positive externalities) are present, $MC_{PRIVATE}$ exceeds MC_{SOCIAL}—and even perfectly competitive firms will produce only to where $P = MC_{PRIVATE}$. Allocative efficiency would require an increase in supply to reduce price below that at which $P = MC_{PRIVATE}$, which in turn would reduce profits. Profit-maximizing firms, therefore, will produce less than the allocatively efficient amount in this case.

6.(d) A public good is both non-excludable and non-rivalrous. Non-excludable means a person can't be prevented from consuming it even if he/she does not pay for it, thus creating a *free-rider* problem. Consumers are highly unlikely to pay for something if they can get it free. A private firm in the economy would make losses if anyone could consume the good without paying for it; it would mean the firm was, in essence, giving the good away at zero price.

8.(b) There are two possible causes of a negative externality in this question. First, driving to work rather than taking public transit creates more pollution. Second, additional automobiles on the highway at rush hour reduce the speed of *all* automobiles, thus increasing the time it takes all people on the highway to drive to work. The extra time taken by others is a negative externality of the additional automobiles using the highway.

9.(a) This is the same question as Question 6 above, except that it uses the specific *economic terminology*. Thus the answer is the same as Question 6—i.e., because of non-excludability competitive markets will not produce the good at all regardless of what the socially efficient amount is.

10.(a) Again this is due to the non-excludability property of a public good. Since people can't be prevented from consuming it even though they choose not to pay for it, private markets will not be willing to provide goods at a price of zero.

11.(b) Since a public good is non-rivalrous (as well as non-excludable), many people benefit from consuming the same unit of the good. The marginal benefit from that unit, therefore, is the sum of the marginal benefits of *all* of these consumers. This is the reason why the demand (i.e., marginal benefit) curve for a non-rivalrous good is the *vertical* summation of individual demand curves (unlike the *horizontal* summation for a rivalrous good).

12.(d) This highlights the non-rivalrous property, whereby one person consuming the good does not reduce the amount available for consumption by others. The marginal cost of anyone consuming the good is therefore zero, and the rule for efficient allocation is to produce to where $P = MC$, which in turn means the efficient amount is where price is zero. [*Note:* Private firms may produce a non-rivalrous good if it is excludable but will charge a price greater than zero, so less than the efficient amount will be consumed. The government would be doing the same if it too charged a positive price.]

13.(b) Why is answer (a) not also correct? Asymmetric information is the *reason* why people have the ability to shift costs to another party, but moral hazard is a *result*. While moral hazard requires asymmetric information, not all cases of asymmetric information result in moral hazard. For example, adverse selection in answer (d) is not the same as moral hazard, but it too requires asymmetric information.

14.(d) Again, maximization occurs where the marginal costs and marginal benefits are equalized. In this case it is the costs and benefits to society as a whole, not just to the individual producers and consumers of a specific product. As long as the <u>extra</u> benefit to society exceeds the <u>extra</u> cost to society, there will be a <u>net benefit</u> to society if the additional unit(s) of the product is (are) produced.

15.(d) Since (for example) Registered Retirement Savings Plan (RRSP) contributions are tax-deductible, each dollar contributed causes less than a dollar reduction in disposable (after-tax) income because taxes paid are also reduced. The opportunity cost of each dollar contributed (i.e., saved), therefore, is less than a one-dollar reduction in spending on current consumption. The reduction in the opportunity cost of saving increases the incentive to save.

16.(d) The definition of indirect costs of government intervention given in the text is the costs imposed on firms and households <u>over and above</u> the taxes that must be paid by government to finance its policies. Answers (a), (b), (c), and (e) all refer to such costs that are incurred by the private sector. Answer (d), on the other hand, refers to costs that are directly paid out of tax revenues and will be identified as such in the government's budget.

18.(d) Assume three students (1, 2, and 3) have to share one carton of ice cream, and the flavour can be vanilla or chocolate. Students 1 and 2 each value vanilla at $1 more than chocolate, but Student 3 values chocolate at $3 more than vanilla. The efficient outcome is to buy chocolate, since it has a total net value of $1 more than vanilla. Under a one-person-one-vote system, however, Students 1 and 2 would be majority vote for vanilla. [*Note:* The difference in intensity of preferences means that Student 3 would be willing to pay $1.10 to each of the other students in order to get chocolate, and all three would have higher utility than if vanilla were chosen. Students 1 and 2 each would have a net gain of $0.10 and Student 3 would have a net gain of $0.80—i.e., $3, –$1.10, –$1.10.]

19.(b) Answer (a) is a consequence of overfishing, not the cause. Since the fish caught by one fisher (and eaten by one consumer) cannot be caught by another fisher (or eaten again by other consumers), fishing is a rivalrous activity so answer (e) is wrong. Answers (c) and (d) may have shifted demand and supply curves of fish, but even bigger shifts have been seen, for example, in the market for personal computers without adverse results. The fundamental reason for overfishing (i.e., a reduction in the stock of fish below the level necessary for regeneration) is that the costs incurred by future generations, although part of the social cost, are *not* part of the private costs of current fishers. [*Note:* Because the oceans' fish are not the "private property" of anyone, nobody in the private sector has the incentive to limit catches to protect *future* profits.]

20.(d) In the used-car market, if there were perfect information, then the differences in prices of used cars would far more accurately reflect their true differences in quality. With asymmetric information, however, the person buying from a used-car dealer will be willing to pay a price reflecting only the <u>probability</u> that the item may be of good quality and not a lemon. Note that this also has a feedback effect; sellers of higher-quality items will be more likely to avoid used-car dealers and sell privately for a price that better reflects its real value. This reduces the proportion of higher-quality automobiles sold by used-car dealers, increasing the probability of consumers getting a lemon from them.

21.(d) Practically all forms of government activity have costs, even including programs designed simply to redistribute income from one section of the population to another. There are administrative costs (e.g., civil servants' time) to redistributive tax-transfer programs, but the main "leak" comes from the impact on incentives. Taking income from the "rich" and giving it to the "poor" generally reduces the earnings incentives of <u>both groups</u>. The rich pay a higher tax rate than otherwise, thereby reducing the return on additional gross earnings. The poor will lose some of the transfer as earnings rise, thereby reducing their return to additional earnings too. [*Note:* The resulting economic inefficiency does <u>not</u> necessarily mean that the program should not be undertaken. That decision depends also on society's values and objectives. Nevertheless, the economic analysis improves the information on which society bases its decision, and may even influence the design of the program so as to reduce the "leakage."]

The Economics of Environmental Protection

17

Chapter Overview

The previous chapter identified several types of market failure that might be addressed by government policy. This chapter is devoted to a discussion of environmental externalities and government policies to address them.

Pollution is viewed as a negative externality. In going about their daily business, firms and households sometimes make decisions that harm the environment. This results in inefficiencies because decision makers fail to take account of these external costs, thereby creating a divergence between *private* and *social* costs and benefits. Government intervention is designed to induce decision makers to **internalize the externality**.

The allocatively efficient level of pollution is generally not zero; rather, it is the level at which the marginal cost of abatement is just matched by the marginal damage of the pollution. This chapter compares the relative merits of several forms of pollution controls: *direct controls*, such as the setting of standards, and *indirect controls*, such as **emissions taxes** and **tradable emissions permits**. Further, while it demonstrates that the two types of indirect controls have the same effect *in principle*, it also recognizes that they have different implications *in practice*.

The chapter then reviews the nature of the global warming problem and the Kyoto Protocol, which is aimed at reducing the world's greenhouse gas (GHG) emissions. There is a readable and highly intelligible breakdown of the potential for using various methods to reduce GHG emissions, including (i) reducing world output and consumption, (ii) reducing the amount of energy used per unit of output, and (iii) reducing the amount of GHG emissions per unit of energy used. [*Note:* The *Additional Topics* section on MyEconLab gives examples of market-based pollution controls and the *political issues* that arise.]

LO **LEARNING OBJECTIVES**

After studying this chapter, you will be able to

1. explain how an externality can be internalized, and how this can lead to allocative efficiency.

2. understand why direct pollution controls are often inefficient.

3. describe how market-based policies, such as emissions taxes and tradable pollution permits, can improve economic efficiency.

4. discuss some basic facts about greenhouse gases and global climate change and the associated economic challenges.

Hints and Tips

The following may help you avoid some of the most common errors on examinations.

✓ The discussion of pollution control is cast in terms of abatement instead of the level of pollution, so be careful not to misinterpret the implications. An *increase* in abatement is a *reduction* in pollution.

✓ Understand that the criterion for efficiency must take into account the cost of pollution abatement as well as the cost of pollution.

✓ Understand that the reduction in the firm's costs of polluting is its benefit from pollution abatement. For example, the *costs* of emissions taxes or pollution permits are the firm's *benefits* from abatement, because by reducing pollution the firm pays less pollution tax or can get revenues from the sale of its pollution permits.

✓ A thorough understanding of the different ways of reducing greenhouse gases will make the subsequent discussion about global warming much easier to comprehend. To help you in this, pretend that you are trying to lose weight. You can do this by (i) reducing your caloric intake by eating less, (ii) reducing your caloric intake by changing the type of food you eat, or (iii) rerouting more calories away from body fat by doing more exercise (and even increasing your caloric intake). In terms of global warming these translate into reducing GHG emissions by (i) reducing world production, (ii) reducing the amount of energy used in the production process, or (iii) generating the same (or even more) GHG but reducing the amount that escapes into the atmosphere.

Chapter Review

The Economic Rationale for Regulating Pollution

Pollution is a negative externality of production, raising the marginal social cost (MC_S) of output above the marginal private cost (MC_P) by the amount of the marginal external cost (MEC). Allocative efficiency is achieved at the level of output where the price of the good (which reflects its marginal benefit) equals MC_S. Firms will not take account of the MEC component, however, unless the cost of the externality is **internalized**, making it part of the firm's MC_P. The text then moves to an analysis of pollution abatement. The optimal amount of pollution abatement occurs where the marginal cost of abatement equals the marginal benefit from the reduction in pollution. As long as there is some cost of pollution abatement, whether it be the direct cost of resources used to reduce pollution or the loss in benefits from having less output available for consumption, the optimal amount of pollution abatement is less than the amount that would eliminate pollution entirely. Even though the optimal amount of pollution abatement is not easily determined, however, there is a direct relationship between the optimal amount of abatement and the *magnitude* of the negative impact of pollution. For example, the greater the negative effect of greenhouse gases and global warming than the greater is the MEC and the greater is the optimal amount of abatement.

1. **A profit-maximizing competitive firm**
   (a) always produces in excess of the output that is allocatively efficient.
   (b) always generates pollution as a byproduct of production.
   (c) produces more than the allocatively efficient output when it ignores external costs associated with its production.
   (d) automatically considers external costs in making production decisions.
   (e) internalizes all external costs.

2. **A commodity's allocatively efficient output is that quantity at which**
   (a) all marginal costs, private plus external, equal all marginal benefits, private plus external.
   (b) external costs are minimized.
   (c) the social benefit of the last unit of output is just equal to its external cost.
   (d) all externalities are eliminated.
   (e) marginal private cost equals marginal benefit.

3. **Achieving the optimal level of pollution is problematic because**
   (a) the private sector will not voluntarily take account of external costs.
   (b) the marginal cost and marginal benefit of abatement are not usually observable.
   (c) methods to regulate pollution and the enforcement of regulations are not perfect.
   (d) the social costs of pollution may occur in the future.
   (e) All of the above.

4. **If steel is produced in a competitive world market and the production of steel generates external costs, profit maximization in steel production will result in**
   (a) too much steel at too high a price.
   (b) too little steel at too low a price.
   (c) too much steel at too low a price.
   (d) too little steel at too high a price.
   (e) the socially efficient output of steel, but at too low a price.

Pollution-Control Policies

This section analyzes three methods of pollution abatement: direct controls, emissions taxes, and tradable emissions permits ("cap-and-trade"). You should be able to discuss the relative merits of these methods and why direct controls are generally less efficient than the two market-based methods (except, perhaps, if the policy objective were to *totally* eliminate the designated type of pollution). Understand the problems that arise even with the market-based approaches, and the differences that arise in principle and in practice.

5. **Direct controls aimed at reducing pollution are not productively efficient because**
   (a) the marginal cost of abatement is not equalized across all firms.
   (b) unlike emissions taxes, they generate no revenue for the government.
   (c) they cannot achieve the socially optimal amount of abatement.
   (d) they change firms' short-run cost curves but not their long-run cost curves.
   (e) they prevent firms from operating at minimum efficient scale.

6. **A firm currently emitting pollutants would have an incentive to reduce emissions if**
   (a) an emissions tax per unit of discharge were imposed.
   (b) private citizens were able to sue for pollution damages.
   (c) it were forced to purchase emissions permits.
   (d) a tax on output were designed to internalize the externality.
   (e) any of the above actions were taken.

7. **Which of the following is true of an emissions tax per unit of pollution?**
   (a) The tax is an addition to the firm's marginal cost of production.
   (b) The tax is the firm's marginal benefit from pollution abatement.
   (c) The tax internalizes the marginal external cost of pollution.
   (d) All of the above.
   (e) Only (a) and (c) are true.

8. **A common problem with the successful use of emissions taxes is that**
   (a) information on external costs is not always available for setting tax rates.
   (b) they do not provide appropriate incentives for pollution reduction.
   (c) firms will generally not reduce emissions to zero.
   (d) the government must also specify the means by which firms are to abate pollution.
   (e) some firms will still pollute more than others.

9. **Tradable emissions permits in a cap-and-trade system**
   (a) are, in effect, equivalent to creating a market for "bads."
   (b) can achieve the same resource allocation as emissions taxes.
   (c) are cost-effective in that, for a given amount of abatement, the total cost of abatement is minimized.
   (d) provide an example of how markets themselves can be used to correct market failures.
   (e) All of the above.

10. **Which of the following is true of the market for a fixed supply of tradable pollution permits?**
    (a) For every unit of pollution abated, the firm requires one more pollution permit.
    (b) An increase in the price of pollution permits increases the firm's marginal cost of abatement.
    (c) Firms with high abatement costs sell permits to firms with low abatement costs.
    (d) Profits are maximized when the marginal cost of abatement equals the market price of a pollution permit.
    (e) Improvements in abatement technology shift the market demand for permits to the right.

11. **Opponents of tradable pollution permits have argued that**
    (a) pollution is a social responsibility, not a private one.
    (b) emissions taxes are more effective because the resulting reduction in emissions is easier to predict.
    (c) by selling permits the government is condoning crimes against society.
    (d) direct controls are more effective because pollution is easy to measure.
    (e) permit sales require a mutual coincidence of wants.

12. **If there is uncertainty about firms' marginal costs of pollution abatement, then**
    (a)   a unit emissions tax gives a known amount of pollution abatement.
    (b)   economists can still accurately predict the market price of an emissions permit.
    (c)   emissions taxes will raise firms' production costs by more than cap-and-trade.
    (d)   emissions taxes and a cap-and-trade system are extremely close policy substitutes.
    (e)   cap-and-trade will give a known amount of pollution abatement but emissions taxes will not.

The Economic Challenge of Global Climate Change

This section focuses on the atmospheric pollution and resulting global warming and climate change due to emissions of greenhouse gases (GHG). It reviews the basic facts of the problem and explains the economic, political, and scientific challenges. GHG are a *negative externality* of production and consumption, but with the special property of being global in nature. When one country (or group of countries) emits GHG it affects the atmosphere of all countries. With many countries spilling GHG into the atmosphere, emission abatement by one country alone will have little effect, if any, on overall global warming and climate change. The nature, shortcomings, and impact of the **Kyoto Protocol** (2006–2012) are presented, as is the more recent (2011) UN-sponsored meeting to reach a legally binding agreement by 2015 for implementation by 2020.

The text splits the creation of greenhouse gases into three components: the amount of GHG created per unit of energy consumed, the amount of energy consumed per unit of GDP, and the number of units of GDP produced. These are used to classify the methods for large-scale emissions reduction. One method is large-scale *substitution* away from fossil fuels, likely requiring a major technological change if "clean" energy is to be generated cheaply. Another is *emissions prevention*, which continues to use "dirty" fossil-fuel energy but captures and stores the GHG before they can escape into the environment—an expensive proposition given current technology.

The last parts of this highly topical and informative chapter review (i) the political problems of developing a global policy in a world with both developed and developing countries, (ii) the failure of Canada to reduce its carbon emissions let alone meet its target Kyoto reductions, and (iii) the requirements for an *effective* future policy with both private-sector and public-sector involvement.

13. **The growing concentration of greenhouse gasses is a problem because it will potentially**
    (a)   reduce crop yields in some parts of the world.
    (b)   reduce the world's fresh-water supplies.
    (c)   create volatile weather patterns.
    (d)   All of the above.
    (e)   Both (b) and (c), but not (d).

14. **The biggest share of the burden of climate change is likely to be carried by**
    (a)   countries with the highest greenhouse gas emissions.
    (b)   taxpayers under an emissions tax system.
    (c)   firms under a cap-and-trade system.
    (d)   developing countries.
    (e)   developed countries.

15. **Greenhouse-gas emissions are**
    (a) a positive externality of energy production and use.
    (b) a national problem requiring a national solution.
    (c) adequately controlled by the Kyoto Protocol.
    (d) a bigger problem for equatorial climates than for subarctic climates.
    (e) a negative externality of energy production and use.

16. **The Kyoto Protocol was an agreement to reduce emissions of greenhouse gases by using**
    (a) emissions taxes.
    (b) a cap-and-trade system.
    (c) an international system of direct control standards.
    (d) a system of transfers from developed to developing nations.
    (e) a system of subsidies to polluting firms as a means of encouraging them to invest in abatement technology.

17. **Which of the following poses a major problem for reducing global warming?**
    (a) There is an upward trend in world population.
    (b) Currently-available technology is unable to increase "clean" energy on a scale needed to curtail global warming.
    (c) Carbon capture and storage is expensive.
    (d) People will continue to increase their *per capita* income.
    (e) All of the above.

18. **Which of the following poses a major problem for reducing global warming that is specific to reducing the greenhouse-gas intensity of energy use (GHG/Energy)?**
    (a) There is an upward trend in world population.
    (b) Currently-available technology is unable to increase "clean" energy on a scale needed to curtail global warming.
    (c) Carbon capture and storage is expensive.
    (d) People will continue to increase their per capita income.
    (e) Both (b) and (c).

19. **In international negotiations on curbing greenhouse gas emissions, developing countries argue that**
    (a) developed countries caused the problem, so they should fix it.
    (b) they will cut production if they get free imports from developed countries.
    (c) they must cut their own emissions as an example to voters in developed countries.
    (d) their economic growth will do little to increase world greenhouse-gas emissions.
    (e) their greenhouse gases will affect only them, not the rest of the world.

20. **Most economists agree that**
    (a) GHG emissions can easily be reduced in the near future.
    (b) policies enacted by Europe and North America alone will be sufficient to reverse global warming.
    (c) tackling climate change requires a global policy.
    (d) higher living standards in developing countries will reduce average family size enough to reverse global warming.
    (e) carbon capture and storage will be such a profit-maximizing strategy for private firms that no other government actions or interventions will be needed.

21. Canada's policies on climate change in the wake of the Kyoto Protocol
(a) were largely ineffective.
(b) efficiently internalized the full costs of pollution.
(c) were largely a public information and awareness exercise.
(d) All of the above.
(e) Both (a) and (c), but not (b).

Short-Answer Questions

1. How do emissions taxes and tradable pollution permits "internalize" negative externalities of pollution, and why does this lead to less pollution?

2. Comment on the economics of the following statement. "Direct controls are preferable to tradable pollution permits because direct controls can force the biggest polluters to do the most cleaning up."

3. What is misleading about the argument that environmental protection reduces overall welfare by reducing output and employment?

4. Present an economic argument in favour of financing the costs of garbage collection and disposal by charging households a fixed price per bag of garbage rather than by using property taxes. What possible disadvantages may arise? [*Hint*: See *Additional Topics: Charging for Garbage by the Bag* on MyEconLab.]

5. "Emissions taxes would give firms a big incentive to invest in research and development, and provide enough clean energy to substantially reduce greenhouse gas (GHG) emissions." Explain how and why private-sector firms would respond to this policy. What else might be needed, and why?

6. The countries that adopted the Kyoto Protocol were responsible for only about one-third of global greenhouse gas (GHG) emissions. In a world of free trade, examine the possible relationships between (i) the number of countries signing an agreement to tax carbon emissions, (ii) the size of the tax, and (iii) the degree of carbon leakage. [*Note:* In the context used here, *carbon leakage* is the increase in carbon emissions by some countries in response to reductions in emissions in other countries.]

Exercises

1. **Compensating for Negative Externalities**
   The following schedule gives the relationship between output and total production costs for a perfectly competitive firm. As the firm expands output, it releases pollutants into a river, which adversely affects local households. The amounts required to compensate the households at different levels of output are shown in the external cost column. The private and external costs are the same for all firms in the industry.

Output (units per week)	Total Private Cost	Total External Cost
1	500	100
2	550	225
3	620	365
4	710	515
5	820	675
6	1050	845
7	1450	1025

   (a) Complete the following table. [*Hint:* Don't forget that social costs are the sum of private costs and external costs.] You may wish to sketch the resulting marginal and average cost curves (private and social) in a diagram.

Output (units per week)	Average Private Cost (AC_p)	Marginal Private Cost (MC_p)	Average Social Cost (AC_s)	Marginal Social Cost (MC_s)
1	_____		_____	
2	_____	_____	_____	_____
3	_____	_____	_____	_____
4	_____	_____	_____	_____
5	_____	_____	_____	_____
6	_____	_____	_____	_____
7	_____	_____	_____	_____

(b)   If this firm were producing 7 units of output per week, how much revenue would be required to cover its private costs? How much revenue would be required to cover the social costs?

(c)   What is the long-run equilibrium price and the output of this firm in the absence of pollution controls?

(d)   Assume now that firms in this industry are required to pay compensation to the households, equal to the external costs.
   (i)   What is the new long-run equilibrium price?

   (ii)   In this example, what happens to the long-run equilibrium output of the firm? What happens to the output of the industry? Explain.

2.   **Emissions Taxes**
This exercise investigates the tax required to induce firms to internalize an externality. In the text, the external cost per unit of output is assumed constant (see Figure 17-1 in the text). In this problem, however, the marginal external cost is an increasing function of the level of output. [*Note:* Parts of this question are repeated in Extension Exercise E1, where you solve using equations instead of a scale diagram.]

Figure 17-1 below shows the demand curve (*D*) facing the perfectly competitive gadget industry, which is also the marginal benefit (*MB*) curve of gadgets. The industry's private marginal production cost (*MCP*) is constant at $10 per unit of output, but the marginal external cost (*MEC*) increases with output. These external costs arise because production in the gadget industry releases pollutants into the air. Answer the following questions and give brief explanations for your answers.

Figure 17-1

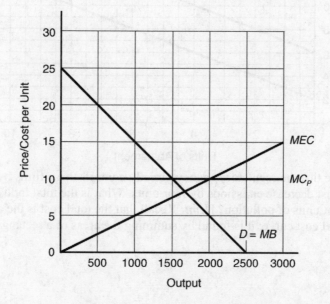

(a) What is the profit-maximizing output of the gadget industry in the absence of any pollution controls? What is the marginal external cost of pollution at this level of output?

(b) Graph the marginal social cost curve (label it MC_S). What is the allocatively efficient output of gadgets? How does this differ from the profit-maximizing output in (a)? Why does it differ?

(c) What tax per gadget would cause firms in the gadget industry to produce the allocatively efficient level of output?

(d) Why would firms still be maximizing profits at this output? [*Hint:* What happens to the MC_P curve when the tax is imposed?]

3. **Direct Controls, Emissions Taxes, and Tradable Emissions Permits**
Figure 17-2 shows the marginal cost curves of pollution abatement for an industry consisting of two firms, Firm A and Firm B. (For simplicity, assume that there is no fixed cost associated with abatement). The regulatory agency has determined that the level of pollution emissions must decrease by a total of eight units. Assume that the amount of pollution in this industry is readily measurable.

Figure 17-2

(a) Suppose that the regulatory agency directly controls these firms by ruling that each firm must decrease emissions by four units. What is the total industry cost of abating the eight units of pollution? [*Hint:* Recall that the total cost is the area under the marginal cost curve; it is found by summing the areas of a rectangle and a triangle.]

(b) Instead of using direct controls, suppose that the regulatory agency imposes a tax of $8 per unit of emissions. Draw the abatement marginal benefit curve (MB) in the diagram. What is the level of abatement of each firm?

(c) What is the total cost of abatement for the industry when the emissions tax is imposed?

(d) Now consider the effect of the introduction of a system of tradable emissions permits. Specifically, suppose that the agency rules that each firm must abate emissions by four units, but that either firm can reduce this by any amount so long as it can induce the other firm to increase its abatement by an offsetting amount. What would be the resulting level of abatement by each firm? Explain.

(e) What is the total abatement cost for each firm and for the industry as a whole under the system of tradable emissions permits? Compared to the costs using direct controls in (a), what is the net saving for the industry? For Firm A? For Firm B? How are the net savings per firm shown on your diagram?

4. **Inefficiency of Emission Standards**
   In Question 3 the inefficiency of a common standard was related to differences in the marginal costs of abatement. The same problems can arise when the marginal costs of abatement are the same but marginal benefits differ. For the purposes of this exercise it is assumed that the marginal benefits of reducing automobile emissions of carbon monoxide are lower in rural areas than in urban areas.

   Figure 17-3 shows two firms that emit pollutants. Each firm has access to the same abatement technology and costs, giving them identical marginal cost of abatement curves (MCA). Firm R is located in a rural area whereas Firm U is located in an urban area. As a consequence, the marginal benefit of abatement for Firm R (MBR) is lower than for Firm U (MBU). Explain why a common standard set at A_0 units of abatement for each firm will, in general, not be allocatively efficient. Also show the allocatively efficient level of abatement for each firm.

Figure 17-3

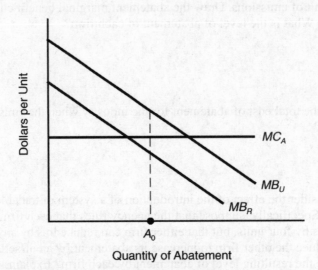

Quantity of Abatement

5. **Practical Problems of Global Emissions Abatement?**
    Climate change is a global problem needing a global remedy. Building on the text's
    analysis, this question investigates an emissions abatement policy in a global setting. It uses
    a tax per unit of carbon emissions (t) as the policy, but similar arguments apply to a cap-
    and-trade policy. [*Note:* The fact that carbon emissions are not the only cause of global
    warming is recognized but ignored in this exercise.]

    (a) In principle, what is the economic reasoning that explains how a carbon emissions
         tax (t) will reduce greenhouse gases?

    (b) If the marginal cost of abatement is high given current technology, what does your
         answer in (a) imply about the tax per unit of emissions?

    (c) If the vast majority of carbon emissions were produced by developed countries in the
         West, and if all these countries imposed a high unit tax on emissions, would there be
         a very large reduction in greenhouse gases in these countries? Explain.

    (d) If the greenhouse gas emissions in the countries in the West fell substantially as a
         result of the tax, would world emissions also fall substantially?

    (e) How would developing countries likely respond to political pressures to impose the
         emissions tax? Why?

(f)   Can you think of how to avoid the problems you have come across so far in this question?

Extension Exercise

E1.   Compensating for Negative Externalities

Here you use equations rather than scale diagrams to calculate the values for Exercise 2. Having done these calculations you should review the answers to both this exercise and Exercise 2.

The demand curve facing the perfectly competitive gadget industry is given by

$$Q = 2500 - 100P$$

where Q is output and P is the price per unit of output. Marginal production costs in the gadget industry are constant at $10 per unit of output, and marginal external costs of pollution are estimated to be an increasing function of output, according to the following equation:

$$MEC = 0.005Q$$

(a)   Calculate the profit-maximizing output of the gadget industry in the absence of any pollution controls. What is the marginal external cost of pollution at this level of output?

(b)   Using the marginal social cost (MC_S) and the marginal benefit (MB) curve equations for gadgets, calculate the socially optimal level of output. [*Hint:* Replace P with MB in the demand equation and isolate MB.]

(c)   Calculate the tax per gadget that would cause firms in the gadget industry to produce the allocatively efficient level of output.

Additional Multiple-Choice Questions

1.   If incremental costs of pollution abatement increase with increasing levels of abatement, the optimal
  (a)   pollution level is the minimum attainable.
  (b)   level of pollution reduction is the amount at which the marginal benefit of abatement equals the marginal cost.
  (c)   pollution level is necessarily zero.
  (d)   amount of abatement is zero.
  (e)   pollution level is that at which all external costs have been eliminated.

Questions 2 to 5 refer to Figure 17-4, which depicts the marginal benefit (*MB*) and marginal cost (*MC*) of pollution abatement.

Figure 17-4

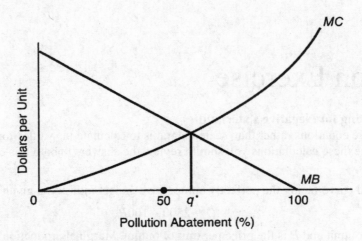

2. **The marginal benefit of pollution abatement**
   (a) is the value of reducing pollution damages.
   (b) increases as *MB* shifts rightward.
   (c) declines as the level of abatement increases.
   (d) is equivalent to a demand curve for pollution control.
   (e) All of the above.

3. **The economically efficient amount of pollution abatement is**
   (a) the level at which the marginal benefit of abatement equals the marginal cost.
   (b) 100 percent, since that maximizes the gains from pollution control.
   (c) zero.
   (d) dependent on the external costs of pollution, which are not given in the graph.
   (e) impossible to determine without additional information about the type of pollution.

*4. **New findings of adverse health effects or other damages from this pollutant will**
   (a) shift the marginal cost curve rightward.
   (b) shift the marginal benefit curve rightward.
   (c) shift both the marginal benefit curve and the marginal cost curves rightward.
   (d) have no effect on either the marginal benefit curve or the marginal cost curve.
   (e) decrease the optimal abatement level.

*5. **Other things being equal, an improvement in pollution control technology**
   (a) shifts the *MC* curve rightward, increasing the optimal level of pollution control.
   (b) shifts the *MC* curve leftward, decreasing the optimal level of pollution control.
   (c) shifts both the *MC* and *MB* curves rightward.
   (d) shifts *MB* rightward, increasing the optimal level of pollution control.
   (e) will not affect either of the curves in this diagram.

6. **With multiple firms emitting pollutants, economic efficiency requires that**
   (a) all emitters reduce pollution by the same percentage.
   (b) marginal costs of abatement be equal for all emitters.
   (c) all emitters reduce pollution by the same absolute amount.
   (d) there be zero emissions.
   (e) firms reduce emissions in proportion to their size.

*7. The requirement that all pollution sources adopt a specific pollution-control technique when there are many methods for controlling a certain type of pollution
  (a)   is likely to be the most efficient way to achieve a certain amount of pollution abatement.
  (b)   is likely to be less efficient than either emissions taxes or tradable emissions permits in achieving a given amount of abatement.
  (c)   is more efficient the more divergent the abatement costs of different firms.
  (d)   eliminates the need for monitoring and enforcement by the regulatory agency.
  (e)   is likely to minimize total costs of achieving a given level of abatement in the industry.

8. Which of the following is *not* true of direct pollution controls?
  (a)   They minimize total abatement costs for a given level of pollution.
  (b)   They slow down the adoption of improved abatement technology.
  (c)   They are costly to monitor and enforce.
  (d)   They often specify the method of abatement to be used.
  (e)   They result in different marginal costs of abatement across firms.

*9. When we say that a firm has internalized an externality, we mean
  (a)   production takes place indoors.
  (b)   production occurs without any external damage.
  (c)   the firm takes into account all costs associated with production.
  (d)   the firm is complying with all regulatory standards.
  (e)   pollution has been eliminated.

10. Complete abatement would be optimal only if
  (a)   the marginal benefit of abatement is always positive.
  (b)   the marginal benefit of abatement were positive and constant.
  (c)   the marginal benefit of abatement were positive and increasing.
  (d)   the marginal cost of abatement were zero.
  (e)   the marginal cost of abatement exceeded the marginal benefit.

*11. If the plastics industry has been disposing of its wastes free of charge, government regulation to ensure a more efficient use of resources would affect the industry's output and product price in which of the following ways?
  (a)   Both output and price would decrease.
  (b)   Output would decrease, but there would be no change in price.
  (c)   Output would be unchanged, but price would increase.
  (d)   Price would increase and output would decrease.
  (e)   There would be no change in either price or output.

*12. Internalizing a production externality will
  (a)   shift the demand curve for the good to the left.
  (b)   shift the supply curve (*MC* for a monopoly) for the good to the left.
  (c)   shift both the demand and supply curves to the left.
  (d)   increase the size of external costs.
  (e)   have no effect on either demand or supply.

*13. Which of the following is *not* an example of a direct pollution control?
  (a)   Bans on household fireplaces in some cities.
  (b)   Automobile pollution controls.
  (c)   A fee per bag of garbage collected.
  (d)   A requirement that scrubbers be installed on factory chimneys.
  (e)   Laws against littering.

*14. **If polluting firms are required to pay for pollution permits, overall economic welfare will**
- (a) fall, because higher production costs will reduce output and employment.
- (b) increase, because the market for permits will create new economic surplus.
- (c) increase, because a negative externality is internalized into private costs of production.
- (d) increase, because forcing firms to pay for their emissions gives them an incentive to re-evaluate their production methods and reduce costs of production.
- (e) Both (c) and (d).

*15. **Which of the following best describes the effect of the Kyoto Protocol?**
- (a) It has been successful because all countries with high GHG emissions signed on.
- (b) It has been less successful than it appeared because a substantial portion of the world-wide reduction in GHG was unrelated to Kyoto.
- (c) It has been highly successful because the signatory countries reduced their GHG emission by the targeted 5 percent.
- (d) It spurred Canada into setting strict controls that substantially reduced the amount Canada's GHG emissions.
- (e) It internalized the costs of a positive externality.

*16. **In a cap-and-trade system,**
- (a) the permit price is the "cap," and pollution is "traded."
- (b) total permitted emissions are the "cap," and permits are "traded."
- (c) the total face value of the permit is the "trade," and its market value is the "cap."
- (d) the tax rate per unit of emissions is the "cap," and emissions are "traded."
- (e) sales tax revenues are acquired from each "trade," but the government "caps" the total tax revenues that it can receive.

*17. **Reductions in the energy intensity of GDP (*Energy/GDP*) are _____ to achieve the necessary reductions in world greenhouse-gas emissions because _____.**
- (a) likely; technological change to reduce energy intensity is ongoing
- (b) unlikely; world GDP will be falling
- (c) unlikely; they will be more than offset by increases in world GDP
- (d) likely; the economic growth of developing countries can be curtailed
- (e) unlikely; the emissions-prevention approach will be greater than the energy substitution approach

*18. **In international negotiations on curbing greenhouse-gas emissions, developed countries argue that**
- (a) their citizens will be unwilling to vote for costly actions to curb emissions if they perceive developing countries as getting a "free ride."
- (b) they do not have sufficient public funds to give huge clean-energy subsidies to developing countries.
- (c) curbing emissions requires world commitment, or production will move to lower-cost countries still using low-cost "dirty" energy.
- (d) without clean energy, developing countries will soon be responsible for more emissions than developed countries.
- (e) All of the above.

*19. **A system that puts a price on greenhouse-gas emissions would be _____ because it would _____.**
   (a) beneficial; provide an incentive to use cleaner energy
   (b) detrimental; make cleaner energy more competitive
   (c) detrimental; it would affect the *emissions* but not the *production* of GHG
   (d) beneficial; create revenues for government to finance research for cleaner forms of energy
   (e) Both (a) and (d).

*20. **The *short-run* impact of a carbon tax on greenhouse-gas (GHG) emissions is likely to be**
   (a) substantial even without using capture and storage.
   (b) modest if the supply of clean energy is quite inelastic.
   (c) substantial if the demand for carbon-based energy is highly inelastic.
   (d) minimal if the tax is on *emissions* rather than on *production* of GHG.
   (e) greater than the long-run impact on GHG emissions.

Solutions

Chapter Review

1.(c) 2.(a) 3.(e) 4.(c) 5.(a) 6.(e) 7.(d) 8.(a) 9.(e) 10.(d) 11.(c) 12.(e) 13.(d) 14.(d) 15.(e) 16.(b) 17.(e) 18.(e) 19.(a) 20.(c) 21.(e)

Short-Answer Questions

1. Emissions taxes and tradable pollution permits make each unit of pollution a direct cost to the firm, increasing the marginal private costs per unit of pollution and thereby increasing the marginal cost per unit of output. When firms profit-maximize by producing where $MC_{PRIVATE} = MR$, the $MC_{PRIVATE}$ now more closely approximates the MC_{SOCIAL}. For a given MR, the increase in $MC_{PRIVATE}$ (by the marginal cost of pollution) reduces the profit-maximizing level of output and thereby reduces the amount of pollution.

2. This statement is incorrect for two reasons. First, the total amount of pollution abatement can be the same with both methods, since there is no reason why the pollution permitted by tradable permits should be any more or less than the amount permitted by direct controls. Second, permits will not be traded unless the trade is mutually beneficial. Take two firms as an example. The permit price received by the selling firm must be no less than the firm's costs of paying for further abatement, and the price paid by the buying firm must be no greater than its costs of further abatement. Both firms gain, and society gains because the total value of resources used to achieve a given amount of abatement is minimized. This leaves more resources available for the production of "goods," accompanied by a reduction in "bads" equal to the reduction that could have been achieved using direct controls.

3. The argument is misleading because it fails to acknowledge the fact that negative externalities also reduce society's welfare by increasing the amount of "bads." Eliminating a "bad" has the same effect on overall welfare as creating the welfare-equivalent amount of a "good." Even if pollution abatement reduces output and employment, which is by no means necessarily the case especially in the long run, it does not reflect an overall reduction in welfare but rather a change in the mix of "goods" being "produced." The elimination of a "bad" is in itself the creation of a "good."

4. Property taxes do not vary with the number of bags of garbage the household produces, so the MC per bag is zero to the household (although not to society). A charge per bag, however, creates a positive MC for the household and internalizes the negative externality. This creates an incentive to reduce the bags of garbage, whether by creating less garbage in total or by disposing of it through other methods,

such as recycling. Unfortunately the tax creates an incentive to dispose by other methods, which can also create problems if such other methods are not environmentally friendly. For example, if people avoid the cost per bag by dumping their garbage in public parks then not only does the garbage still have to be collected and disposed of, but in the interim other people get an additional negative externality from the reduction in their enjoyment of the garbage-filled public parks.

5. Firms providing clean energy would increase profit by <u>not</u> paying the energy tax. This potential for higher profit is the private-sector's incentive to invest in research and development to find and adopt "clean" energy. Also, higher consumer prices resulting from the tax gives incentives for consumers to economize on their use of "dirty" energy in favour of "clean" energy. But the text notes that private-sector incentives may well be insufficient to cause the amount of technological change needed for the necessary fall in GHG emissions to occur and/or occur soon enough. The private-sector response to incentives may be hampered by (i) uncertainty about the size of the payoff, (ii) whether clean energy technology could be patented by firms that discovered and/or developed it, and (iii) whether the rest of the world would honour patent rights even if the new energy sources could be patented. The text, therefore, also argues for active government polices to develop and promote new technologies. Revenues from an emissions tax (or from the sale of emissions permits) can fund research by private-sector firms, universities, and government itself.

6. If the signatory countries produced a large proportion of world GHG emissions, a small tax per unit of carbon emissions could raise substantial funds for government policies to promote research and development into clean energy. A large unit tax would not only provide more funds for research and development, but also give more incentive for the use of existing "clean" energy technologies. There would be little carbon leakage if all countries adopted the same tax rate. But problems arise if, as with Kyoto, *relatively few* countries signed on. In this case the high tax in signatory countries could cause substantial carbon leakage to non-signatory countries because more production would move to those countries where "dirty" energy was cheaper (as long as free trade allowed the goods produced elsewhere to be sold in the signatory countries). Only a truly global policy could avoid the problem of carbon leakage.

Exercises

1. **(a)**

Output (units per week)	Average Private Cost (AC_p)	Marginal Private Cost (MC_p)	Average Social Cost (AC_s)	Marginal Social Cost (MC_s)
1	500		600	
		50		175
2	275		387.50	
		70		210
3	207		328.33	
		90		240
4	178		306.25	
		110		270
5	164		299	
		230		400
6	175		315.83	
		400		580
7	207		353.57	

Figure 17-5

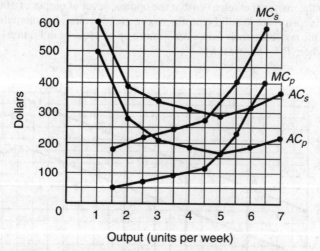

Output (units per week)

(b) $1450 (price of $207.14 per unit); $2475 (price of $353.57 per unit).

(c) Price of $164, producing 5 units per week. (This is where price = minimum AC_p, the point at which profits are zero.)

(d) (i) Price of $299 (where price = minimum AC_s, which is the new minimum AC_p now that the external cost is "internalized" by the compensation payments.

(ii) In this particular example, the long-run output of the firm will remain at 5 units. Industry output will fall, however, since the rise in price will reduce total quantity demanded by consumers. There will be fewer firms in the industry.

2. **Figure 17-6**

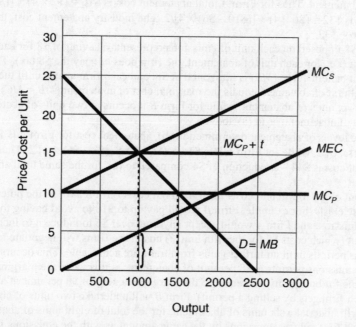

Output

(a) Profit-maximizing output is 1500 gadgets, where $MB = MC_P$. Marginal external cost at output of 1500 is $7.50 (read from the MEC curve).

(b) See Figure 17-6 for the MC_S curve; it is the MEC curve plus the constant $10 marginal private cost (MC_P) at each level of output. The allocatively efficient output is 1000 gadgets—a reduction of 500 gadgets. This output satisfies the allocative efficiency condition that price (which is also the marginal benefit to consumers of the one-thousandth gadget) equals marginal social cost.

(c) The optimal tax is $5 per gadget, read from the *MEC* curve at the *allocatively efficient output* of 1000 gadgets. [*Note:* Since marginal external cost varies with the level of output, the tax is calculated as the marginal external cost at the optimal level of output of 1000 gadgets.]

(d) Firms in the industry would still be profit-maximizing because, by internalizing the external cost of pollution, the tax shifts each firm's MC_P curve up to $MC_P + t$ in Figure 17-6. Each firm profit-maximizes where $P = MC_P + t = \$15$.

3. **Figure 17-7**

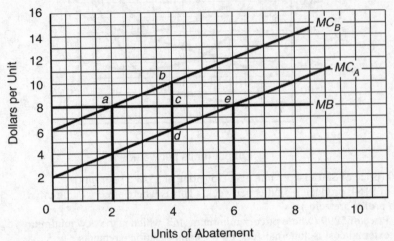

(a) Each firm abates four units, so the marginal abatement costs for Firms *A* and *B* are $6 (at point d) and $10 (at point b), respectively. Since there are no fixed costs to abatement, total abatement cost for each firm is given by the area under its abatement marginal cost curve, measured up to its level of abatement. Thus for Firm *A* total abatement cost is $16 = (\$2 \times 4) + [(\$6 - \$2) \times 4]/2$; for Firm *B* it is $32 = (\$6 \times 4) + [(\$10 - \$6) \times 4]/2$. The industry abatement cost, therefore, is $48 = \$16 + \$32$.

(b) A tax of $8 imposed on each unit of emissions represents a saving of $8 for each unit of abatement (i.e., for each unit of abatement, the firm does *not* pay the $8 tax). Thus the marginal abatement benefit curve (*MB*) is horizontal at $8, and each firm abates until the savings from an additional unit of abatement equals the marginal cost of abatement (*MB* = *MC*). For Firm *A* this occurs at six units of abatement, while for Firm *B* it occurs at two units of abatement (for a total of 8 units of abatement, as in (a) above).

(c) Given the levels of abatement determined in (b), abatement cost for Firm *A* is $30 = (\$2 \times 6) + [(\$8 - \$2) \times 6]/2$, while for Firm *B* it is $14 = (\$6 \times 2) + [(\$8 - \$6) \times 2]/2$. Thus industry abatement cost is $44—a reduction of $4 compared to (a), for the same total amount of abatement.

(d) Abatement of the fourth unit costs Firm *A* $6 but costs Firm *B* $10; so the potential for gains from trade exists. For example, Firm *B* would pay up to $10 to avoid having to abate the fourth unit of emission, and Firm *A* would accept anything over $6 to induce it to increase its level of abatement (which costs $7 for the fifth unit). Thus, these firms will negotiate to buy and sell emissions permits until no further gains from trade are achievable. This occurs when the market price of emissions permits is $8 per unit of abatement; at this value the marginal abatement cost is the same for both firms, and equal to the marginal benefit of $8 per unit of abatement (i.e., the price each firm gets by selling a permit). Firm *B* will undertake two units of abatement and Firm *A* will undertake six units of abatement, for the total of eight units of abatement.

(e) Since each firm reduces emissions by the same amount as with the emissions tax in (b) above, the total cost of the eight units of abatement is also the same—i.e., $44, which is $4 less than with direct controls in (a). The total cost for Firm *A* is $14, consisting of the cost of six units of abatement = $(\$2 \times 6) + [(\$8 - \$2) \times 6]/2 = \$12 + \$18 = \$30$ <u>minus</u> the $16 received from Firm *B* for the sale of two emissions permits. This total is $2 less than the $16 cost with direct controls in (a). Firm *A*'s net saving of $2 is shown by the area of the triangle *cde* in Figure 17-7. The total cost for Firm *B* is $30, consisting of the cost of two units of abatement = $(\$6 \times 2) + [(\$8 - \$6) \times 2]/2 = \$12 + \$2 = \$14$, <u>plus</u> the $16 paid to Firm *A* for the two emissions permits. This total is $2 less than the $32 cost with direct controls in part (a). Firm *B*'s net saving of $2 is shown by the area of the triangle *abc* in Figure 17-7.

4. **Figure 17-8**

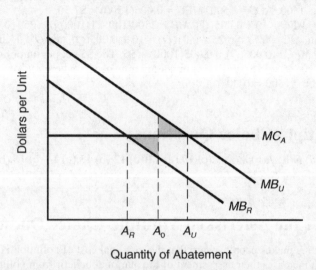

Refer to Figure 17-8. Since Firm *R* is the low marginal benefit firm, it follows that at A_0, $MBR < MB_U$ and neither firm is abating to where its marginal cost of abatement equals its marginal benefit. Society would gain if Firm *U* abated more and Firm *R* abated less. The optimal abatement levels are given as A_R and A_U, where the marginal benefit curve intersects the marginal cost curve for each firm. For each unit abated by Firm *U* between A_0 and A_U the marginal benefit exceeds the marginal cost, and society gains by the difference. For each unit of abatement between A_0 and A_R for Firm *R*, the marginal cost exceeds the marginal benefit, and society gains by the difference when this abatement is *not* done. The total gain to society (i.e., the increase in allocative efficiency) is represented by the sum of the shaded areas in Figure 17-8.

5. **(a)** It is profit-maximizing for polluting firms to pay to reduce emissions as long as the marginal cost of doing so is less than the emissions tax ($MC < t$).

(b) The tax per unit of emissions (t) would have to be high if abatement were to be a better alternative for firms than paying the tax. If it were not, firms would soon reach the point where $MC > t$ and further abatement would be more costly than paying the tax. The high tax would be passed along to consumers in the form of high prices.

(c) The discussion of Equation 17-1 in the text shows that there would be only a very large reduction by these countries if (i) they had the ability/technology to use much less energy per unit of output (i.e., by reducing *(GHG/Energy)* × *(Energy/GDP)*) or (ii) they substantially reduced their output (*GDP*). If energy per unit of output were not reduced, effect of the tax would be substantially higher prices for consumers with little change in emissions (at least in the short run).

(d) Likely not, for two important reasons. First, other high-population countries (e.g., China and India) would increase emissions as a result of their own development and economic growth. Second, higher costs in the Western countries with the emissions tax could induce substitution by outsourcing production to countries (again, such as China and India) where "dirty" energy costs are lower without an emissions tax.

(e) Developing countries may well ignore pressures to impose an emissions tax because (i) it would not be in their own interest economically, and (ii) politically it would be viewed as unfair when their *per capita* standard of living is far less than that of developed countries (which are mainly responsible for global warming to date).

(f) Develop new technology to reduce emissions from current energy sources and/or discovery of new sources of low-cost "clean" energy. If "clean" energy is not also low cost, it will not be able to compete with "dirty" energy from low-cost carbon-rich coal deposits in numerous countries. These countries, and others, may well be unwilling (or unable) to switch from "dirty but cheap" to "clean and expensive."

Extension Exercise

E1. **(a)** For profit maximization, $MC_P = MR$ (= P in perfect competition). Thus $Q = 2500 - 100(10) = 2500 - 1000 = 1500$. At $Q = 1500$, $MEC = 0.005(1500) = \$7.50$.

(b) $MC_S = MC_P + MEC = 10 + 0.005(Q)$. $MB = 2500/100 - 1/100(Q) = 25 - 0.01(Q)$. For the socially optimal output, $MC_S = MB$. So $25 - 0.01(Q) = 10 + 0.005(Q)$, and $Q = 15/0.015 = 1000$.

(c) At $Q = 1000$, $MEC = 0.005(Q) = 0.005(1000) = \$5$. The \$5 tax per unit of output increases MC_P to $MC_P + t = 10 + 5 = \$15$. Profit maximization now occurs where $MC_P + t = P$. So $Q = 2500 - 100(15) = 2500 - 1500 = 1000$.

Additional Multiple-Choice Questions

1.(b) **2.**(e) **3.**(a) **4.**(b) **5.**(a) **6.**(b) **7.**(b) **8.**(a) **9.**(c) **10.**(d) **11.**(d) **12.**(b) **13.**(c) **14.**(e) **15.**(b) **16.**(b) **17.**(c) **18.**(e) **19.**(e) **20.**(b)

Explanations for the Asterisked Multiple-Choice Questions

4.(b) The health finding makes people aware that the marginal cost of pollution is higher than they had realized, which increases their assessment of the marginal benefit from pollution abatement—i.e., a rightward shift in the marginal benefit of abatement curve.

5.(a) Improvements in control technology reduce the costs of abatement—a rightward shift in the MC of abatement curve.

7.(b) This requirement would be even less efficient than direct controls that simply specify how much abatement each firm should undertake. For some firms it may well be more efficient to use techniques other than the specific one required. Profit-maximizing firms would choose the least-cost (i.e., most efficient) methods for themselves, and taxes or tradable permits would allow the equalization of marginal costs of abatement across firms.

9.(c) By internalizing the externality, the firms' marginal private cost would be made equal to the marginal social cost. Their profit-maximizing strategy, therefore, would be consistent with marginal social cost (i.e., marginal cost = marginal benefit for society as a whole).

11.(d) A more efficient use of resources would be achieved by having the firm internalize the costs of waste disposal, rather than by having society bearing the costs at no cost to the firm. Marginal private cost would be made equal to marginal social cost. An increase in marginal private cost would reduce the profit-maximizing output (thereby increasing the price) at which marginal cost would equal marginal revenue.

12.(b) "Internalizing" the production externality means that production costs previously borne by other people (hence a negative externality such as pollution) are now borne by the producing firms. The demand curve for the product is unaffected, but the firm's extra costs of production are reflected in a vertically upward shift in the MC curve—i.e., the MC for each unit of output has increased. An increase in MC means that firms will be willing to supply less at each P, so a vertically upward shift of the MC (or supply) curve is also a leftward shift in the curve. [*Note:* This relationship holds for all positively sloped curves; an upward shift is also an inward (leftward) shift.]

13.(c) The bag fee for garbage removal is just like an emissions tax (rather than a direct control). It increases the marginal cost of garbage disposal for households, giving them an incentive to reduce the amount of garbage. The marginal benefit for each bag of garbage *not* put out for disposal is the bag fee saved.

14.(e) By internalizing the negative externality (pollution), the private market will allocate society's resources to better reflect their true marginal cost to society as a whole, thereby improving allocative efficiency (answer (c)). And if the permit cost causes firms to avoid the resulting higher production costs by using cheaper "clean" production methods, this too is a welfare improvement for society (answer (d)).

15.(b) Answer (a) not only is factually incorrect (even the U.S. did not sign on), but also "success" should be measured by the reduction in emissions, not the number of signatories. While answer (c) is factually correct, much of the reduction in GHG emissions was attributable to reduced output in recessions (so answer (b) is correct), and GHG emissions increased again when output subsequently increased. Answer (d) is factually incorrect, as Canada tried to rely on voluntary actions by producers and consumers—i.e., a "policy" that did not work. Answer (e) is incorrect because (i) pollution is a negative (not a positive) externality and (ii) the resulting market price of the pollution permits was far too low to internalize the true costs of the negative externalities of GHG emissions.

16.(b) Since producers (in principle) can generate only the permitted level of emissions, the permits specify the maximum permitted emissions (which, when all the permits are taken together, is the "cap" on emissions). The permits are traded at their market price, and the "face value" is not a "price" but the permitted number of units of emissions (so (c) is wrong). Firms for which the cost of reducing emissions is less than the market price of the permits will not buy permits, while those for which the cost of reducing emissions exceeds the price will buy permits. So the permit price is indirectly the price paid to pollute, and that price is determined by the demand for and supply of permits. The latter specifies the total cap on emissions and is the total number of permitted units of emissions (so answer (a) is wrong). Answers (d) and (e) are incorrect because they refer to a tax per unit of emissions, not a cap-and-trade system.

17.(c) The correct answer to this question lies in the analysis of future trends in the text's section on *Energy Use, GDP, and Greenhouse-Gas Emissions*. It argues that world GDP will continue to rise (so answer (b) is wrong), if for no other reason than the growth of developing countries will increase both GDP and energy use (so answer (d) is inconsistent). The net effect is that while technology may reduce the energy per unit of GDP, this reduction *per unit* will be more than outweighed by growth in the number of units of world GDP. For example, a 10 percent reduction in energy use per unit of GDP (consistent with answer (a)) will not reduce total emissions if GDP grows by more than 10 percent (as answer (c) states). Finally, both approaches in answer (e) are ways of reducing the GHG intensity of energy, not the energy intensity of GDP referred to in this question.

18.(e) On the one hand developing countries say, "Developed countries made the mess so why should we pay for it by keeping our living standards below theirs?" On the other hand, developed countries say (or imply), "It's a world problem needing world commitment, but not at the expense of falling living standards for us!" While there is general agreement on (c) and (d), the political issues in how to address the problems must still be resolved.

19.(e) Making producers pay the price for emitting GHG internalizes (at least part of) the negative externality, thereby giving them an incentive to use cleaner energy. The latter is beneficial (answer (a)), so answers (b) and (c) are false. The price paid to governments, whether in the form of revenues from a carbon tax or from the sales of pollution permits in cap-and-trade, can be used for research by government directly and/or as subsidies for private-sector research (as in answer (d)).

20.(b) The short-run impact of a carbon tax will depend on willingness and ability to shift to other, cleaner forms of energy. If the short-run supply of "clean" energy is quite inelastic, the ability to shift will be restricted even if the willingness is there. The carbon tax will increase the demand for "clean" energy (a substitute for "dirty" energy), but inelastic supply will generate higher prices with little increase in quantity supplied. In the longer-run the supply of clean energy should be less inelastic, allowing a bigger increase in the quantity of clean energy used (than in the short run).

18

Taxation and Public Expenditure

LEARNING OBJECTIVES

After studying this chapter, you will be able to

1 describe the main taxes in use in Canada.

2 explain why a tax can lead to allocative inefficiency.

3 discuss the concept of fiscal federalism in Canada.

4 describe Canada's major social programs.

5 consider the costs and benefits of government intervention in the economy.

Chapter Overview

This chapter addresses how taxation and government expenditures affect the allocation of resources and distribution of income. The importance of this discussion is underlined by the fact that, in 2011, government tax revenues at the federal, provincial, and local levels were about 40 percent of the value of Canada's national output (GDP).

While the main purpose of the tax system is to raise revenue, tax policy is also a powerful device for income redistribution, whereby the distribution of after-tax income is altered through the **progressivity** of the income-tax system. Personal and corporate income taxes, excise and sales taxes, as well as property taxes are the primary sources of tax revenue in Canada.

Evaluation of the tax system involves the consideration of **efficiency** and **equity** for the entire system, rather than simply for specific taxes within the system. The concept of equity is discussed by assessing two principles in taxation: *ability-to-pay* and *benefits received*. Taxation involves both a **direct burden** and an **excess burden**. An efficient tax system raises a given amount of tax revenue while minimizing the resulting excess burden. For a given amount of tax revenue, efficiency and progressivity can be altered by changing the mix of the various taxes used.

Public expenditure in Canada includes the provision of goods and services, including interest paid on the government debt, and **transfer payments** to individuals, firms, and other levels of government. *Fiscal federalism* refers to the idea that the three layers of government (federal, provincial, and municipal) should coordinate their spending plans and have a mechanism for **intergovernmental transfers**. A large share of total government expenditures in Canada is made on the major social programs: education, health care, income-support programs, employment insurance, and retirement benefits. The *combination of tax programs and expenditure programs* in Canada is progressive overall, and so narrows the inequalities in income created by the market. Finally, while some types of government intervention can complement and potentially improve on a free-market outcome, it is also the case that intervention has sometimes been ineffective or counterproductive. Consequently, there is room for disagreement as to the *appropriate* level of government activity and intervention.

Hints and Tips

The following may help you avoid some of the most common errors on examinations.

✓ Understand the difference between marginal and average income tax rates. The average tax rate is total income tax paid as a percentage of total income. The marginal tax rate is the *change* in income taxes paid as a percentage of the *change* in income.

✓ The progressivity of the tax system depends on what happens to the average tax rate as income increases. The tax system is progressive if the average tax rate increases with income, regressive if the average tax rate decreases with income, and proportional if the average tax rate is the same at all income levels.

✓ The "clawback" rate on a benefit is the reduction in the benefit per additional dollar of other income. For example, the Guaranteed Income Supplement for low-income seniors falls by $0.50 per $1 of other income received—i.e., it has a 50 percent clawback rate.

Chapter Review

Taxation in Canada

After reading this section, you should understand the roles of the tax system in raising revenue, redistributing income, and affecting resource allocation. You should also be able to distinguish between progressive and regressive taxes, and discuss the general taxes used in Canada. Make sure that you understand the difference between the marginal tax rate and the average tax rate; this distinction is at the core of the definition of tax progressivity.

1. **In Econoland each individual's taxable income is total income minus a basic personal amount of $10 000. The tax paid is 20 percent of taxable income regardless of the level of taxable income. Econoland, therefore, has a _____ income tax system.**
   (a) regressive   (b) proportional
   (c) progressive   (d) lump-sum
   (e) value-added

2. **What is one reason why Canada's federal corporate income tax is levied on accounting profits and not on economic profits? [*Hint:* See *Extensions in Theory 18-1* in the text.]**
   (a) Taxing economic profits would be more regressive than taxing accounting profits.
   (b) It makes no difference which is taxed since the tax rate is constant.
   (c) Taxing accounting profits provides greater stimulus for investment.
   (d) The tax authorities cannot measure economic profits in practice.
   (e) Taxing accounting profits has no effect on firms' prices, whereas taxing economic profit would cause price increases.

3. **"Tax brackets" refer to the different**
   (a) types of taxes an individual must pay.
   (b) taxation of individuals according to the number of dependants they have.
   (c) marginal tax rates applied to different ranges of income.
   (d) objectives of taxes such as redistribution, resource re-allocation, or pure revenue raising.
   (e) levels of tax payments.

4. **Which of the following statements concerning the GST/HST is *false*?**
   (a) It changes the relative prices of all taxed goods and services.
   (b) It is a value-added tax.
   (c) It does not discourage saving.
   (d) It is applied at the same rate in all Canadian provinces.
   (e) Its regressivity is reduced through a system of exemptions and refundable tax credits.

5. **Because the "rich" typically live in more expensive houses than the "poor," the rich pay more in property taxes. Theory, therefore, leads us to the conclusion that Canadian property taxes as a percentage of household incomes are**
   (a) proportional.   (b) highly progressive.
   (c) mildly progressive.   (d) Any of the above.
   (e) mildly regressive.

6. **If the amount of tax paid increases as income rises, the tax is**
   (a) proportional.   (b) progressive.
   (c) regressive.   (d) a negative income tax.
   (e) All of the above.

7. **If the income tax is progressive, the marginal tax rate must be**
   (a) less than the average tax rate.
   (b) the same as the average tax rate.
   (c) greater than the average tax rate.
   (d) continuously increasing with income.
   (e) constant.

8. **Which of the following is true of the Canadian tax system?**
   (a) The GST tax credit reduces the regressivity of the sales tax.
   (b) Income taxes increase the rate of return on savings.
   (c) Property taxes are progressive because they increase as wealth increases.
   (d) Exempting food purchases from GST makes the tax more regressive.
   (e) The GST/HST is an excise tax.

Evaluating the Tax System

This section reviews the two criteria used for evaluating the tax system: equity and efficiency. Make sure that you understand the differences between vertical and horizontal equity, and between the direct and excess burdens of taxation.

9. **Horizontal equity refers to**
   (a)   the distribution of income between eastern and western Canada.
   (b)   the treatment of individuals with identical incomes but different circumstances.
   (c)   the treatment of households of similar composition but with different incomes.
   (d)   the flat-rate tax scheme.
   (e)   changes in the marginal tax rate across income levels.

10. **The central idea behind the Laffer curve is that as tax rates increase**
   (a)   the tax base will increase.
   (b)   a tax revolt by taxpayers will be ignited.
   (c)   more economic activity will go unreported so as to evade income taxation.
   (d)   tax revenue will reach a maximum and then decline as tax rates continue to increase.
   (e)   the size of the government increases.

11. **According to the benefit principle of taxation,**
   (a)   the amount of taxes paid should be equal across income groups.
   (b)   taxes should be paid according to the benefits that taxpayers derive from public expenditure.
   (c)   there should be no user charges for government services.
   (d)   the greater one's income, the greater the benefit generally received from public expenditures.
   (e)   the economy benefits most when the government maximizes its tax revenue.

12. **Vertical equity in a tax system**
   (a)   refers to the way in which GST is calculated at each stage of production.
   (b)   focuses on comparisons of taxes paid by taxpayers with different incomes.
   (c)   is often used to support regressive taxation.
   (d)   refers to attempts to tax monopoly power by a surtax on firms that have undergone vertical mergers.
   (e)   refers to the relationship between federal and provincial income taxes.

13. **The excess burden of a tax**
   (a)   equals the total amount of tax paid.
   (b)   refers to the amount of tax paid by consumers.
   (c)   starts when the slope of the Laffer curve becomes negative.
   (d)   measures the administrative cost of raising tax revenue.
   (e)   measures the allocative inefficiency of the tax.

14. **An efficient tax system is defined as one that**
   (a)   does not redistribute income.
   (b)   imposes taxes only on goods with elastic demand curves.
   (c)   minimizes the excess burden for any given amount of tax revenue.
   (d)   eliminates the excess burden of taxation.
   (e)   eliminates the direct burden of taxation.

Public Expenditure in Canada

After reading this section you will have a better appreciation of the extent of the activities of the public sector in the Canadian economy and be able to explain the economic logic of the distribution of government responsibilities within the system of fiscal federalism. You will also be able to outline Canada's various social programs.

15. **Which of the following categories takes the biggest share of total public spending in Canada?**
    (a) Transfer payments to individuals.
    (b) Interest on the national debt.
    (c) Defence spending.
    (d) Health, education, and social services.
    (e) Environmental protection.

16. **Which of the following is true of the combined total paid by the federal government to the provincial governments under the Canada Health Transfer (CHT) and the Canadian Social Transfer (CST)?**
    (a) It is calculated as one-half of the amount that each province spends on health and social assistance.
    (b) Provincial governments can spend the money as they wish.
    (c) It equals the total amount of transfer payments that each province is allowed to make to individual households.
    (d) It equals the amount of provincial income taxes collected by the federal government for each province.
    (e) It equalizes the per capita tax revenue of each province.

17. **Which of the following is *not* considered one of the five pillars of Canadian social policy?**
    (a) Retirement benefits.
    (b) Employment insurance.
    (c) Government expenditure on goods and services.
    (d) Health care.
    (e) Income support.

18. **The term *poverty trap* is used to refer to**
    (a) low-paying jobs.
    (b) low-paying jobs with high tax rates.
    (c) low-income housing.
    (d) income-support programs that do not provide an adequate standard of living.
    (e) tax-and-transfer incentives that discourage individuals from increasing their pre-tax income.

19. **Under the equalization payments program, the federal government**
    (a) equalizes the tax revenue of each province.
    (b) transfers money to provinces with below-average taxation capacity.
    (c) transfers tax revenue to provinces to ensure a reasonably equal educational expenditure per student across the country.
    (d) ensures that each province taxes income at the same average tax rate.
    (e) provides equal unconditional grants to each province.

20. **Advocates of having private hospitals in Canada argue which of the following?**
    (a) The system already has one tier for the rich and another for the poor.
    (b) People should be allowed to pay for immediate treatment if they wish.
    (c) High-income people bypass waiting lists by paying for treatment in the U.S.
    (d) The overall system would be improved by reducing the flow of trained health professionals from Canada to the U.S.
    (e) All of the above.

Evaluating the Role of Government

This section offers a brief discussion of the broad arguments for and against increasing the size of the public sector relative to the private. It also provides a commentary on the scope of government activity and the evolution of policy.

21.   **In his book *The Affluent Society*, John Kenneth Galbraith argued that**
    (a)   modern economies have enough wealth to provide all people with an adequate standard of living.
    (b)   the value of a marginal dollar spent by government is less than the value of a marginal dollar spent by the private sector.
    (c)   redistribution of income generates aggregate affluence.
    (d)   the Canadian economy has sufficient resources to eliminate the poverty line as defined by Statistics Canada.
    (e)   the marginal utility of public goods is higher than that for private goods.

Short-Answer Questions

1.   How and why are corporate and personal income taxes integrated in Canada?

2.   What is the argument supporting the idea that reducing the corporate income tax rate may cause a more rapid growth in average living standards? How would the argument change if taxes were levied on economic profits rather than on accounting profits? [*Hint:* See *Extensions in Theory 18-1* in the text.]

3.   What is the argument behind the idea that the direct burden of taxation is not a cost to society as a whole?

4.   First, using the concept of the excess burden of a tax, present an argument in favour of having higher sales taxes on basic necessities than on other goods. Then present an argument against this proposition.

5.   Comment on the following statement. "Because university graduates generally earn significantly higher incomes than others, student tuition fees should cover a much larger proportion of the costs of post-secondary education than currently is the case."

6. What is the difference between an absolute and a relative standard of "poverty"?

Exercises

1. **Tax Progressivity**
   (a) The table that follows shows the amount of tax paid by four individuals in four different income categories under each of three tax regimes: *A*, *B*, and *C*. Indicate whether and why each regime is proportional, regressive, or progressive.

TAX PAID BY INCOME LEVEL
Income Level

Tax	$10 000	$20 000	$40 000	$60 000
A	$1000	$2000	$4000	$6000
B	800	1400	2600	3600
C	400	1200	3000	5600

Tax regime *A* is _____ because _____.

Tax regime *B* is _____ because _____.

Tax regime *C* is _____ because _____.

   (b) Taking all taxes together $(A + B + C)$, is the overall tax system progressive, regressive, or proportional? Why?

2. **Excess Burden**
   This exercise illustrates the relationship between elasticity of demand and the excess burden of a tax, using the demand curves for Goods *A* and *B* in Figure 18-1. [*Note:* The demand equations for Goods *A* and *B*, respectively, are $Q_A = 40 - P_A$ and $Q_B = 60 - 2P_B$.]

Figure 18-1

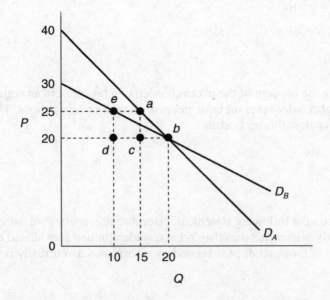

(a) Suppose that the price of each good is initially $20. By inspection of the above graph, which good has the more elastic demand at a price of $20? Explain.

(b) Suppose that a tax of $5 per unit is imposed on each good, raising the price to $25. Calculate the direct burden of the tax in each market.

(c) What areas illustrate the excess burden in each market? Calculate the value of the excess burden for each good. How is the excess burden related to the elasticity of demand?

3. **The Negative Income Tax**
    The following is an example of the negative income tax that the text discusses in *Applying Economic Concepts 18-1*.

    (a) Suppose that a negative income tax provides a $5000 guaranteed income for a family, with a 50 percent marginal tax rate on earnings. Complete the table. [*Note:* A negative value of income tax is the benefit received, and after-tax income equals earnings plus benefits minus any positive income tax paid.]

(A) Before-Tax Earnings	(B) Income Tax (−$5000 + 0.5A)	(C) After-Tax Income (A − B)
$ 0	−$5 000	$5 000
2 000	−$4 000	_____
5 000	_____	7 500
7 000	_____	_____
10 000	_____	_____
12 000	_____	_____

(b) The following version of the negative income tax was part of a 1970 experiment in Manitoba. Suppose that a family of five earns $90 a week in income and receives $15 a week in cash from the government (1970 dollars). If earnings fall to $50, the family will receive $43 a week from the government, and if there are no earnings, the family will receive $78 a week from the government. Complete the table and calculate the implicit marginal rate of taxation on earnings.

Earnings	Change in Earnings	Cash Transfer	Change in Cash Transfer	Marginal Rate of Taxation
$ 0		$78		
50	_____	43	_____	_____
90	_____	15	_____	_____

4. Sales Taxes

This exercise compares four structures of sales tax when applied to a commodity that has four stages of production. The following schedule presents the purchases and sales at each stage. [*Note:* In the first three stages, sales are to other firms. In the last stage (i.e., retail) the sales are to consumers.]

Production Stage	Purchases from Other Firms	Sales to Other Firms/Customers
Primary	$ 0	$ 1 000
Manufacturing	1 000	4 000
Wholesale	4 000	6 000
Retail	6 000	10 000

(a) A retail sales tax (RST), as used in the United States, imposes the tax only when the good is sold to consumers. If the RST is 6 percent of the *retail* value, what is total tax revenue?

(b) The federal goods and services tax (GST) in Canada taxes the full value at each stage, but all taxes paid on purchases from other firms are deducted from the amount remitted to the government at each stage. With a GST tax rate of 6 percent, what is the net tax paid at each stage, and what is total tax revenue? [*Note:* The federal GST rate in 2012 is 5 percent, but the combined federal plus provincial sales tax rates (or the HST rates in some provinces) are generally almost three times this.]

(c) A value added tax (VAT), as used in the United Kingdom, taxes the increase in value at each stage. If the tax rate is 6 percent, what is the tax liability at each stage and what is total tax revenue?

(d) What is the difference between the VAT and the GST?

(e) The Manufacturers Sales Tax, which the GST replaced in Canada, taxes the value of sales at the manufacturing stage. [*Note:* The MST applied only to goods (and not to services) manufactured in Canada—a fact that is ignored in this question.] If an MST must guarantee the same total tax revenue as the GST in part (b), what is the required tax rate for the MST?

Additional Multiple-Choice Questions

1. **The fact that the tax rates needed to provide a similar level of public goods and services vary with the tax base is the basis of justification for which of the following programs?**
    - (a) Provincial social assistance.
    - (b) Equalization payments.
    - (c) The Canada Health Transfer.
    - (d) The Canada Pension Plan.
    - (e) Income support programs.

2. **If "rich" people and "poor" people smoke the same amount, a sales tax on cigarettes is regressive because**
    - (a) everyone spends the same proportion of income on cigarettes.
    - (b) the demand for cigarettes is inelastic.
    - (c) the tax paid per person represents a larger proportion of a poor person's income.
    - (d) the rich are better informed about the health hazards of smoking.
    - (e) the poor pay more taxes.

*3. **If a tax takes the same amount of money from everyone regardless of individual income, the tax is**
    - (a) vertically equitable.
    - (b) proportional.
    - (c) regressive.
    - (d) horizontally inequitable.
    - (e) progressive.

*4. **If an individual has an average tax rate of 30 percent and a marginal tax rate of 50 percent, an additional $100 of income would imply additional tax payments of**
    - (a) $50.
    - (b) $30.
    - (c) $80.
    - (d) $20.
    - (e) Indeterminable without knowing the individual's income level.

*5. **A major objective underlying tax deferral plans is to**
    - (a) influence how the government spends its tax revenues.
    - (b) increase an individual's lifetime tax payments.
    - (c) create incentives for taxpayers to behave in specific ways.
    - (d) reduce the need for intergovernmental transfers.
    - (e) increase current tax revenues at the expense of lower future tax revenues.

*6. **The more elastic is demand, the greater will be the**
    - (a) tax revenue raised from a given excise tax.
    - (b) horizontal equity of a particular tax.
    - (c) progressivity of a tax.
    - (d) excess burden of a tax.
    - (e) direct burden of a tax.

7. **The determination of whether a tax is regressive, proportional, or progressive is based on a comparison of the amount of tax paid at different levels of income with the**
    - (a) tax base.
    - (b) value of the item being taxed.
    - (c) taxpayer's income.
    - (d) distribution of income.
    - (e) level of government expenditures.

*8. **A marginal tax rate of 58 percent on taxable income of $200 000 implies that**
(a) a person with $200 000 of taxable income pays $116 000 in taxes.
(b) the tax system is progressive.
(c) the tax system is vertically equitable.
(d) a dollar of income above $200 000 increases one's tax liability by $0.58.
(e) the average tax rate exceeds 58 percent.

9. **Which of the following is the best example of a tax deferral program?**
(a) Registered Retirement Savings Plans.
(b) Old Age Security.
(c) Provincially funded health care.
(d) Guaranteed Income Supplement.
(e) Employment Insurance.

*10. **Which of the following is *not* an example of government transfer payments to individuals?**
(a) Salaries of government employees.
(b) Canada Pension Plan payments.
(c) Unemployment insurance benefits.
(d) Child tax credits.
(e) Workers' Compensation payments.

*11. **Decentralization of government economic activity can be justified by all but which of the following?**
(a) Regional preferences.
(b) Income redistribution efforts.
(c) Particular local needs for public expenditure.
(d) Diseconomies of scale in program administration.
(e) Responsiveness to changing preferences.

*12. **Which of the following statements is a reasonable economic argument for some subsidization of post-secondary education?**
(a) All of the benefits of a university education accrue to the student in the form of a higher lifetime income.
(b) It is vertically equitable that all taxpayers pay to educate individuals who will earn above-average incomes.
(c) Charging the full cost of education would deter many children from low-income families from continuing their education.
(d) There are external benefits to the entire nation from a better-educated population.
(e) Both (c) and (d) are correct.

*13. **Which of the following is likely to occur if the qualification period for employment insurance were shortened to 10 weeks in some regions?**
(a) The scheme would tend to become a subsidy for seasonal employment.
(b) Provincial and municipal governments would create make-work schemes to provide employment for 10 weeks.
(c) The rate of labour turnover would increase.
(d) Labour mobility toward occupations and locations with more stable employment prospects would be discouraged.
(e) All of the above.

*14. **Which of the following is *not* true of Canadian benefit programs for the elderly?**
    (a)   RRSPs are a means of deferring taxes to the retirement years when one's marginal tax rate may be lower.
    (b)   Canada Pension Plan payments are made to individuals who contributed to the plan during their working lives.
    (c)   Old Age Security is paid to all Canadians over 65 years of age, with a tax clawback.
    (d)   The Guaranteed Income Supplement is a demogrant paid to Canadians over age 65.
    (e)   Canada Pension Plan contributions are shared equally by employees and their employers.

*15. **Which of the following is true of a relative definition of the poverty line?**
    (a)   It is based on the market prices of basic necessities.
    (b)   Economic growth can, in principle, eliminate poverty entirely.
    (c)   As average household income in the economy rises, the poverty line rises.
    (d)   The poverty line is defined as the level of welfare benefits available.
    (e)   It is defined as full-time earnings at the minimum wage, and so is measured relative to that minimum wage.

Solutions

Chapter Review

1.(c) 2.(d) 3.(c) 4.(a) 5.(e) 6.(e) 7.(c) 8.(a) 9.(b) 10.(d) 11.(b) 12.(b) 13.(e) 14.(c) 15.(d) 16.(b) 17.(c) 18.(e) 19.(b) 20.(e) 21.(e)

Short-Answer Questions

1.   Individual shareholders receive income-tax credits for the amount of corporate income taxes already paid by the firms on dividends. The purpose is to avoid double-taxation of this income (i.e., once through corporate taxes and again through personal income taxes).

2.   The main argument is that the tax on accounting profits reduces the return on investment in new physical capital, thereby slowing the adoption of new technology and reducing productivity growth, which in the long run causes slower growth in average living standards. If the tax were on economic profits, maximizing before-tax profits would still maximize after-tax profits. Unlike the tax on accounting profits, therefore, the tax on economic profits would have no effect on the profit-maximizing decisions of firms (including prices, output, employment, and long-run investment choices). [*Note:* Whether or not economic profits would be the better tax base in theory, precise identification by the tax authorities of the opportunity costs necessary to calculate economic profits would be technically impossible.]

3.   The tax revenues received by government are used to finance government programs, thereby transferring resources within the economy. For example, governments provide public goods that benefit society as a whole, but that would not be produced by the private sector. [*Note:* Part of the deadweight loss in surplus that measures the excess burden of a tax may be offset by surplus created from government provision of public goods.]

4.   Because the demand curves for basic necessities are generally highly inelastic, there is only a small reduction in equilibrium quantity as a result of the tax. This in turn means that the resulting deadweight loss is small—i.e., a small excess burden of the tax. On the other hand, because a high proportion of the income of low-income households is spent on basic necessities, such a tax structure would be highly regressive.

5. The major argument in favour of raising tuition fees is that post-secondary education is an investment in human capital. Since the return on this investment accrues to graduates in the form of higher earnings, the costs should not be paid by others (especially low-income taxpayers). The arguments against high tuition fees are made on efficiency and equity grounds. The efficiency argument is that higher education generates positive externalities for society as a whole. Students paying the full cost would not internalize these externalities, resulting in less than the optimal level of post-secondary education for society as a whole. The equity argument is that high fees would make post-secondary education affordable only by people from higher-income households.

6. An absolute standard is based on the level of income needed to purchase the goods and services required to achieve a specific minimum standard of living (e.g., food, clothing, and shelter). A relative standard defines the poverty level as a percentage of the average income of households (e.g., Statistics Canada's low-income cutoffs, or LICOs). In principle, it is possible to entirely eliminate poverty as defined by an absolute standard. With a relative standard, however, some households will always be classed as "in poverty," since an increase in average income will automatically increase the income level at which the poverty line is drawn.

Exercises

1. (a) Tax regime A is proportional because the average tax rate is constant as income increases. Regime B is regressive because the average tax rate falls as income increases. Regime C is progressive because the average tax rate increases as income increases.
    (b) The combined average tax rates are 22 percent at \$10 000 (2200/10 000 = 0.22), 23 percent at \$20 000 (4600/20 000 = 0.23), 24 percent at \$40 000 (9600/40 000 = 0.24), and 25.3 percent at \$60 000 (15 200/60 000 = 0.253). The tax system is slightly progressive, since the average tax rate increases slightly with income.

2. (a) Recall from Chapter 4 that $\eta = (1/\text{slope}) \times (P/Q^D)$. Since these demand curves have the same quantity demanded at a price of \$20, the difference in their elasticities is determined by the difference in their slopes. The demand curve for Good B has the relatively steeper slope, so demand for A is more elastic than for B.
    (b) As depicted in Figure 18-1, when a tax of \$5 per unit increases the price to \$25, quantity demanded of Good A is reduced to 15 units while that for B is reduced to 10 units. The direct burdens are 5(15) = \$75 for Good A and 5(10) = \$50 for Good B (i.e., the tax per unit multiplied by the quantity demanded of each).
    (c) The excess burden is area abc for Good A and area ebd for Good B. These values are (5)(20 − 10)/2 = \$25 for B and (5)(20 − 15)/2 = \$12.50 for A. The excess burden is greater for the commodity with the relatively more elastic demand (i.e., Good B).

3. (a) Column B: −\$5000; −\$4000; −\$2500; −\$1500; 0; +\$1000.
        Column C: \$5000; \$6000; \$7500; \$8500; \$10 000; \$11 000.
    (b)

Earnings	Change in Earnings	Cash Transfer	Change in Cash Transfer	Marginal Rate of Taxation
\$ 0		\$78		
	\$50		\$35	35/50 = 0.7 (70%)
50		43		
	\$40		\$28	28/40 = 0.7 (70%)
90		15		

$$\text{Marginal tax rate} = \frac{\Delta \text{ Transfer}}{\Delta \text{ Earnings}} = 0.70 \text{ (i.e., 70\%)}$$

4. (a) The RST is imposed on sales of \$10 000 at the retail level. Thus total tax revenue is 6 percent of \$10 000 = \$600.
    (b) Net tax paid at the primary stage is \$60 = 0.06 × \$1000. At the manufacturing stage it is \$180 = (0.06 × \$4000) − \$60. At the wholesale stage it is \$120 = (0.06 × \$6000) − \$180 − \$60. Finally, at

the retail stage the net tax paid is $240 = (0.06 \times \$10\ 000) - \$120 - \$180 - \$60$. Total tax revenue from all four stages is $600 = \$60 + \$180 + \$120 + \$240$.

(c) Value added at the primary stage is $1000, so tax payments here are $60. At the manufacturing stage, value added is $3000 ($4000 – $1000), so taxes here are $180. The value added of wholesalers is $2000, so taxes here are $120. Finally, the value added by retailers is $4000, so tax payments at the retail level are $240. The total is $600.

(d) There is no difference—the GST is a VAT.

(e) Sales at the manufacturing level are $4000, and the government must collect $600 in tax revenue. This requires an MST tax rate of $(\$600/\$4000) \times 100 = 15\%$.

Additional Multiple-Choice Questions

1.(b) 2.(c) 3.(c) 4.(a) 5.(c) 6.(d) 7.(c) 8.(d) 9.(a) 10.(a) 11.(b) 12.(e) 13.(e) 14.(d) 15.(c)

Explanations for the Asterisked Multiple-Choice Questions

3.(c) The tax paid is a smaller and smaller proportion of total income as income rises, thus giving a lower and lower average tax rate (i.e., the tax is regressive, so (b) and (e) are wrong). The tax would be horizontally equitable (so answer (d) is incorrect) in the sense that people with the same income would pay the same tax, but vertically inequitable (so answer (a) is wrong) since people with higher incomes would pay a lower average tax rate.

4.(a) The *change* in tax payments as income *changes* is determined by the marginal tax rate (not the average tax rate, which is the proportion of total income paid in taxes). Thus if income changes by $100 the tax payments change by 50 percent of $100 = $50.

5.(c) The tax deferral plan described in the text is Registered Retirement Savings Plans (RRSPs), which increases incentives to save for retirement. Use the example of a person with a marginal tax rate of 40 percent contributing $1000 to an RRSP this year. This year's income taxes fall by 40 percent of $1000 = $400. When $1000 is withdrawn from the plan some years in the future, taxes of 40 percent of $1000 = $400 would be payable on the $1000. Note also that, as a result of deferring the $400 tax to a later year, there are two aspects of RRSPs that can actually increase lifetime after-tax income. First, if the individual is in a lower marginal tax bracket when the $1000 is withdrawn (as may well be the case after retiring from work), less than $400 tax will be paid on that $1000. For example, if the marginal tax rate has fallen from 40 percent to 30 percent, only $300 of tax will be paid on the $1000—a net saving of $100. Second, interest earned on the $1000 while in the plan is also taxable only when withdrawn, so the plan holder can actually earn extra interest on these deferred taxes too. [*Note:* Canada/Quebec Pension Plan (C/QPP) contributions are also tax deductible, but unlike voluntary RRSP contributions they are compulsory.]

6.(d) Figure 18-2 in the text illustrates that the more elastic demand curve gives a bigger percentage reduction in quantity demanded for a given increase in price caused by the tax, which generates less tax revenue (i.e., a smaller direct burden) and more deadweight loss (i.e., a greater excess burden).

8.(d) This is a reminder that the marginal tax rate shows only the change in tax paid per dollar of additional income. Since the question does not state what marginal tax rates apply to other income ranges, there are no implications for vertical equity (answer (b)) or progressivity (answer (c)), or for any specific value of the average tax rate (so answers (a) and (e) are wrong).

10.(a) Salaries of government employees are paid in exchange for services provided. Government transfer payments, however, are defined as payments that are *not* made in exchange for any good or service (as is the case for the benefits from the programs in answers (b) through (e)).

11.(b) Centralization of government is needed to redistribute income across regions. The obvious example is income transfers made by the (centralized) federal government from provinces with high average incomes to provinces with low average incomes. [*Note:* Do not take answer (d) as a necessary characteristic of big government. Recall from your analysis of firm productivity and cost curves that "bigness" can actually increase productivity through economies (not diseconomies) of scale.]

12.(e)   Answer (d) makes general reference to positive social externalities from a higher-educated population, while (c) recognizes that subsidies may be desirable to compensate for imperfections in the intertemporal capital market (i.e., student's difficulties in borrowing against their expected future incomes). Answer (a) is wrong because it refers only to the private benefits of those getting educated and so gives no rationale for subsidies. Answer (b) is wrong because it is internally inconsistent, in that people with below-average income subsidizing those with above-average incomes is vertically <u>inequitable</u> (rather than vertically equitable).

13.(e)   Assuming 10 weeks of work at weekly wages of $W gave eligibility for 20 weeks of benefits at 55 percent of W, the total income from employment would be $10(W) + (0.55)(20)W = 21W$. That gives an effective return to employment of a little more than twice the market rate (i.e., 21 weeks worth of earnings for 10 weeks worked). Such an increase in the return to 10 weeks of work would effectively subsidize regular seasonal employment where jobs last 10 weeks or more (answer (a)). This in turn would be an incentive for more people to seek seasonal jobs rather than full-year jobs (answers (c) and (d)). Furthermore, since Employment Insurance is a federal government program in Canada, other levels of government could reduce their own spending (and/or increase their tax revenues) by creating 10-week jobs to transfer people from their programs (e.g., welfare) to Employment Insurance.

14.(d)   A demogrant is a program that pays the same amount to all eligible individuals regardless of income. The Guaranteed Income Supplement (GIS) is paid only to *low-income* Canadians over age 65, and even then payments are reduced by 50 cents for each dollar of other income. It is, therefore, *not* a demogrant. The answer to Question 5 above shows why (a) is correct. The other answers are true because the programs are specifically designed to do what the answers say.

15.(c)   A relative standard defines the poverty level as a percentage of the average income of households (e.g., Statistics Canada's low-income cutoffs, or LICOs). With any reasonable distribution of income, therefore, some households will always be classed as "in poverty," since an increase in average income (e.g., via economic growth) will automatically increase the income level at which the poverty line is drawn. While welfare authorities and minimum wage legislators may use the poverty line to help them determine the level of benefits, there is no *necessary* relationship to the poverty line. Furthermore, full-time minimum wage earnings are the same for different individuals with different family sizes, whereas a poverty line will vary by family size.

33

The Gains from International Trade

Chapter Overview

This chapter explains how international trade makes possible a higher average standard of living for a country. A country benefits from buying goods abroad at a lower cost. A country is said to have **absolute advantage** in the production of a particular commodity when it can produce more of the good with a given amount of resources than can other countries. A country has a **comparative advantage** in producing a good when it has a lower opportunity cost in production than other countries. The **gains from trade** do not depend on absolute advantage, but rather on comparative advantage. Even if a country has an absolute advantage in the production of all goods, both trading partners can share in the gains from trade.

Comparative advantage can be attributed to differences in exogenous considerations such as factor endowments and climate. Today, there is widespread acceptance by economists that comparative advantage may also be acquired. International trade encourages countries to specialize in the production of goods where they have a comparative advantage as opposed to the costly product diversification associated with self-sufficiency. The gains from trade are likely to be even greater when countries can achieve economies of scale or benefit from **learning-by-doing**.

When transportation costs are insignificant, a traded good will sell at the same price in all countries—this is the so-called *law of one price*. This price is referred to as the world price.

The division of the gains from trade between two countries depends on the **terms of trade**, which refers to the ratio of the index of prices of exported goods to the index of prices of imported goods. The terms of trade determine the quantity of imported goods that can be obtained per unit of exported good.

LO LEARNING OBJECTIVES

After studying this chapter, you will be able to

1 explain why the gains from trade depend on the patterns of comparative advantage.

2 understand how factor endowments and climate can influence a country's comparative advantage.

3 describe the law of one price.

4 explain why countries export some goods and import others.

Hints and Tips

The following may help you avoid some of the most common errors on examinations.

✓ Gains from trade do *not* depend on *absolute* advantage. They depend only on *comparative* advantage. Comparative advantage promotes production specialization and gains from international trade. Consider, for example, a two-country, two-product world where one country has an absolute advantage in the production of both products. Even in this situation, both countries could still gain from specialization and international trade—the country with the absolute advantage in the production of both goods should specialize in the production and export of the good in which it has the *greater absolute advantage*, and the country with the absolute disadvantage in the production of both goods should specialize in the production and export of the good in which it has the *smaller absolute disadvantage*.

✓ The above implies that the basis for trade in not differences in *efficiency* between countries (absolute advantage) but rather differences in *opportunity costs* between countries (comparative advantage). The opportunity cost of one good is measured by the forgone output of another good. In terms of a diagram, opportunity cost is measured by the slope of the country's production possibilities boundary.

✓ The law of one price determines the pattern of international trade. A country will export a particular good if its equilibrium price under autarky is below the international price and will import it if its equilibrium price under autarky is above the international price.

✓ The *terms of trade* determine how the gains from trade are divided between trading partners. The terms of trade are measured by the ratio of the price of exports to the price of imports. In other words, the terms of trade represent the opportunity cost of obtaining a particular good in the international market.

Chapter Review

The Gains from Trade

After studying this section, you should recognize that international trade among countries involves basically the same principles of exchange that apply to trade among individuals. With trade, people (regions) can specialize in what they do well and satisfy other needs by trading. You will also learn that although gains from trade can occur even when production is fixed, further gains arise when nations specialize production in goods for which they have a comparative advantage. Comparative advantage arises from differences in production opportunity costs, which are determined by factor endowments and climate, but also by changing human skills and experience in production. Comparative advantages can be acquired—e.g., as a result of government policy—and they can also change. Therefore, comparative advantages should be viewed as being *dynamic* rather than *static*.

1. **Country X has an absolute advantage over Country Y in the production of widgets if**
   (a) more resources are required in X to produce a given quantity of widgets than in Y.
   (b) a given amount of resources in X produces more widgets than the same amount of resources in Y.
   (c) relative to Y, more widgets can be produced in X with fewer resources.
   (d) relative to Y, fewer widgets can be produced in X with fewer resources.
   (e) None of the above.

2. **If, given the same amount of inputs, Canadian farmers produce 2 tonnes of rice per hectare while Japanese farmers produce 1 tonne of rice per hectare, we can be certain that**
    (a) Canada will export rice to Japan.
    (b) Canada has a comparative advantage in rice production.
    (c) Canada has an absolute advantage in rice production.
    (d) Japanese rice farmers must be paid twice as much as Canadian farmers.
    (e) Japan should not produce any rice.

3. **Comparative advantage is said to exist whenever**
    (a) one country can produce a given level of output with fewer resources compared to another country.
    (b) a given amount of resources produces more output in one country compared to another.
    (c) one country has an absolute advantage over another country in the production of all goods.
    (d) different countries have different opportunity costs in production.
    (e) two countries are of different sizes.

4. **If there are two countries, *A* and *B*, and two goods, *X* and *Y*, and if *A* has a comparative advantage in the production of *X*, it necessarily follows that**
    (a) *A* has an absolute advantage in the production of *X*.
    (b) *B* has an absolute advantage in the production of *X*.
    (c) *A* has a comparative disadvantage in the production of *Y*.
    (d) *B* has an absolute advantage in the production of *Y*.
    (e) *B* has a comparative disadvantage in the production of *Y*.

5. **Which of the following is *not* a source of comparative advantage?**
    (a) Factor endowments.
    (b) Climate.
    (c) Country size.
    (d) Acquiring human capital.
    (e) None of the above.

6. **Gains from specialization can arise when**
    (a) countries have different opportunity costs in production.
    (b) there are economies of scale in production.
    (c) experience gained via specialization lowers cost through learning by doing.
    (d) trading partners have a different comparative advantage.
    (e) All of the above.

7. **Free trade within the European Union (EU) led to**
    (a) each member country specializing in specific products (e.g., furniture, cars).
    (b) a large increase in product differentiation and intra-industry trade, with countries tending to specialize in subproduct lines (e.g., office furniture, household furniture).
    (c) no perceptible alteration in production patterns.
    (d) less trade among EU members.
    (e) less product diversity.

8. **Economies of scale and learning by doing are different because**
   (a) one refers to an increase in variable costs and the other to a decrease.
   (b) economies of scale refer to a movement along the long-run average cost curve, whereas learning by doing shifts the long-run average cost curve.
   (c) economies of scale affect variable costs, but learning by doing affects only fixed costs.
   (d) learning by doing affects profits but not costs.
   (e) economies of scale affect costs, whereas learning by doing affects revenue.

9. **According to the Hecksher-Ohlin theory,**
   (a) resource-rich countries benefit the most from trade.
   (b) different opportunity costs across countries can be explained by differences in factor endowments.
   (c) different opportunity costs across countries can be explained by differences in production functions.
   (d) low-wage countries gain the most from trade.
   (e) countries with similar opportunity costs can gain the most from trade.

10. **The concept of dynamic comparative advantage is best characterized by**
    (a) the importance of factor endowments in determining trade patterns.
    (b) changes in a country's terms of trade due to depletion of natural resources.
    (c) acquiring new areas of specialization through investment in human capital.
    (d) changes in a country's variable costs due to economies of scale.
    (e) greater specialization in resource-intensive industries.

The Determination of Trade Patterns

After reading this section, you will understand the law of one price and its implications for a country's imports and exports. Make certain that you understand the relationship between a country's comparative advantage and its no-trade price.

After studying this section you should also be able to explain that the *terms of trade*, defined as the ratio of the index of export prices to the index of import prices, indicate how the gains from trade are divided between buyers and sellers. Changes in the terms of trade lead to changes in a country's consumption possibilities. You will also be able to distinguish an improvement in the terms of trade from a deterioration.

11. **The "law of one price" refers to**
    (a) the idea that international cartels collude to charge a single price.
    (b) federal statutes that regulate firms to charge the same price domestically and globally.
    (c) the idea that when transportation costs are insignificant, a product will tend to have the same price worldwide.
    (d) the international trade principle that export products cannot be subject to price discrimination.
    (e) the assumption that average costs of production are equal in all countries.

12. **A single world price of oil is likely to exist if**
    (a) oil can be transported easily from one country to another.
    (b) each country produces all of its domestic consumption.
    (c) all governments restrict exports of oil.
    (d) demand for oil is the same in all countries.
    (e) the cost of producing oil is the same in each country.

13. **Canada is a major exporter of nickel because at the world price**
    (a) Canadian quantity demanded exceeds Canadian quantity supplied.
    (b) Canadian quantity supplied exceeds Canadian quantity demanded.
    (c) the quantity of nickel demanded by Canadians exceeds domestic production.
    (d) Canada mines more nickel than any other country.
    (e) domestic consumption and production are the same as they would be in the "no-trade" equilibrium.

14. **The terms of trade**
    (a) refer to the quantity of imported goods that can be obtained for a given amount of money.
    (b) are measured by the product between the price of exports and the price of imports.
    (c) determine the division of the gains from trade.
    (d) are determined by the federal government.
    (e) None of the above.

15. **A rise in export prices as compared to import prices is considered a favourable change in the terms of trade since**
    (a) one can export more per unit of imported goods.
    (b) employment in export industries will increase.
    (c) one can acquire more imports per unit of exports.
    (d) total exports will increase.
    (e) All of the above.

16. **Due to a labour strike by port workers, it is expected that this year beef exports will fall by 10 percent in the small country of Tacuarembó. As a result,**
    (a) the international price of beef will fall.
    (b) the international price of beef will rise.
    (c) the domestic price of beef will fall in Tacuarembó.
    (d) Tacuarembó's supply curve for beef will shift to the left.
    (e) Tacuarembó's supply curve for beef will shift to the right, *and* the domestic price of beef will fall.

Short-Answer Questions

1. Distinguish between a country's constant cost production possibilities curve, the terms of trade, and its consumption possibilities curve.

2. Draw a rough diagram that illustrates a country importing a good for which the world price is below the domestic non-trade price of that good. What is the role of comparative advantage in this analysis?

3. Draw a rough diagram that illustrates a small country exporting a good for which the world price is above the domestic non-trade price of that good. Suppose now that a technological improvement takes place in the industry producing this good. Show the impact of this technological improvement in your diagram. What will be the impact of this technological improvement on both the domestic and international price of this good?

4. Identify the likely source of comparative advantage in each of the following trade relationships:

   (a) Canada exports apples to Honduras, and Honduras exports bananas to Canada.

   (b) Venezuela exports oil to Cuba, and Cuba exports medical services to Venezuela.

   (c) Canada exports financial services to China, and China exports shoes to Canada.

5. Explain the fact that while Canada exports cars to the U.S., the U.S. also exports cars to Canada.

Exercises

1. **Comparative and Absolute Advantage**
   This exercise provides basic production data and requires you to calculate the opportunity cost of production. It then draws out the distinction between absolute and comparative advantage and the implications for trade.

   For each of the following scenarios, determine the opportunity costs of producing each good in each country, and indicate in which commodity each country should specialize its production with trade.

   (a) One unit of resources can produce:

	Radios	Cameras		The opportunity costs are	
				1 Radio	1 Camera
Japan	2	4	Japan	_____	_____
Indonesia	3	1	Indonesia	_____	_____

   Japan should specialize in the production of _____.
   Indonesia should specialize in the production of _____.
   Japan has an absolute advantage in the production of _____.
   Indonesia has a comparative advantage in the production of _____.

(b) One unit of resources can produce:

	Radios	Cameras		The opportunity costs are	
				1 Radio	*1 Camera*
Japan	2	4	Japan	_____	_____
Indonesia	1	3	Indonesia	_____	_____

Japan should specialize in the production of _____.
Indonesia should specialize in the production of _____.
Indonesia has a comparative advantage in the production of _____.

(c) One unit of resources can produce:

	Radios	Cameras		The opportunity costs are	
				1 Radio	*1 Camera*
Japan	2	4	Japan	_____	_____
Indonesia	1	2	Indonesia	_____	_____

Japan should specialize in the production of _____.
Indonesia should specialize in the production of _____.

(d) Which scenario demonstrates that absolute advantage is not a sufficient condition for trade to occur? Explain.

(e) Which scenario suggests why a nation as technologically advanced as Japan can gain from trading with other countries with lower wages? Explain.

2. **Opportunity Cost and Terms of Trade**

Countries *A* and *B* each currently produce both watches and dairy products. Assume that Country *A* gives up the opportunity to produce 100 litres of dairy products for each watch it makes, and *B* could produce one watch at a cost of 200 litres of dairy products.

(a) The opportunity cost of making watches (in terms of dairy products) is lower in Country _____.

(b) The opportunity cost of making dairy products (in terms of watches) is lower in Country _____.

(c) Country *B* should specialize in _____ and let Country *A* produce _____.

(d) The terms of trade (the price of one product in terms of the other) would be somewhere between _____ and _____ litres of dairy products for one watch.

3. **The Terms of Trade**

The following table provides data on the index of merchandise export prices and the index of merchandise import prices for a hypothetical economy.

Year	Index of Export Prices	Index of Import Prices	Terms of Trade
2009	100.6	98.6	_____
2010	103.3	102.3	_____
2011	157.1	135.6	_____
2012	176.6	157.9	_____
2013	205.4	200.7	_____

(a) Using the definition of the terms of trade that involves indexes, complete the table by calculating the terms of trade to one decimal place.

(b) What does an increase in the terms of trade signify?

(c) Would you classify the change in the terms of trade from 2010 to 2011 as favourable to this economy? Explain.

4. **The Production Possibility Curve and Trade**
The following table provides hypothetical data on the productivity of a single unit of resource in producing wheat and microchips in both Canada and Japan.

	One Unit of Resources Produces	
	Wheat (tonnes)	**Microchips**
Canada	50	20
Japan	2	12

(a) Which country has an absolute advantage in the production of wheat? Of microchips?

(b) What is the opportunity cost of producing a tonne of wheat in Canada? In Japan?

(c) Which country has a comparative advantage in the production of wheat? Of microchips?

(d) Suppose that Canada is endowed with 2 units of this all-purpose resource while Japan is endowed with 10 units. Draw each country's production possibility boundary on the following grids. (Assume constant costs.)

Figure 33-1

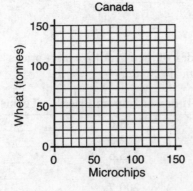
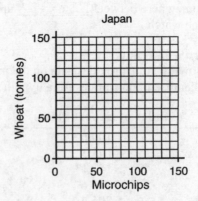

(e) Suppose that prior to trade, each country allocated half of its resource endowment to the production of each good. Indicate the production and consumption points of each country in the graphs (for simplicity, assume that these are the only two countries in the world).

(f) What is world output of each good?

(g) Indicate the production points of each country after trade, and determine world production levels.

(h) Suppose that the terms of trade are one microchip for one tonne of wheat and that Canada consumes as much wheat after trade as it did before trade. Indicate the post-trade consumption points of each country and each country's imports and exports.

(i) If the terms of trade changed to two microchips for one tonne of wheat, which country would benefit? Explain.

5. **Imports and Exports**
Figure 33-2 depicts Canadian domestic supply and demand curves, S_C and D_C, respectively, for a commodity in a market for which Canada is assumed to face a fixed world price.

Figure 33-2

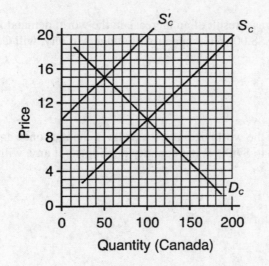

(a) At a world price of $5, Canadian producers sell _____ units, while Canadian consumers purchase _____ units. Canada therefore (imports/exports) _____ units of this commodity.

(b) If the world price increased from $5 to $12 per unit (assuming there was no tariff), Canadians would consume _____ units but produce _____ units. Thus Canada would (import/export) _____ units.

(c) Should domestic supply shift to S'_C while the world price remains at $12, domestic production would now be _____ units and domestic consumption _____ units. Canada would therefore be an (importer/exporter) of _____ units.

6. **Imports and Exports**

The table below shows the Canadian domestic demand schedule and the domestic supply schedule for widgets.

Price of Widgets	Quantity of Widgets Demanded (thousands)	Quantity of Widgets Supplied (thousands)
$10.00	1 000	10 000
9.50	1 500	9 000
9.00	2 000	8 000
8.50	2 500	7 000
8.00	3 000	6 000
7.50	3 500	5 000
7.00	4 000	4 000
6.50	4 500	3 000
6.00	5 000	2 000
5.50	5 500	1 000
5.00	6 000	0

(a) What are the equilibrium price and the equilibrium quantity of widgets under autarky?

(b) Suppose now that Canada—a relatively small producer of widgets—engages in international trade and that the world price of widgets is $6.00. What quantity of widgets, if any, will Canada export or import?

(c) Suppose that as a result of an increase in the world demand for widgets the world price rises to $8.00. What quantity of widgets, if any, will Canada now export or import?

(d) Suppose that the world demand for widgets changes once again causing the world price to drop to $7.00. What quantity of widgets, if any, will Canada now export or import?

7. **Comparative Advantage and Specialization in Production**
   Italy and France produce only two goods, wine and wool, using a single input, labour. An Italian worker in an eight-hour day can produce 100 bottles of wine or 100 bales of wool, while a French worker can produce 75 bottles of wine or 25 bales of wool in an eight-hour day.

   (a) In the absence of trade, what is the opportunity cost in Italy and in France of producing one unit of wine?

   (b) If trade is opened up between the two countries, in which product will each of the countries specialize? Explain your answer.

   (c) Suppose that labour productivity in both wine and wool production in France doubles. How does this change your answer in (b)? Explain.

   (d) If mutually advantageous trade occurs between Italy and France, what will be the range of the international terms of trade between bales of wool and bottles of wine? Explain.

Extension Exercises

E1. Production and Consumption Possibility Curves
   The Republic of Canelones produces only two goods, wool and lumber. Given the current level of technology, one unit of resources can produce either one unit of wool or two units of lumber in this small country. Canelones has a total resource endowment of 1000 units.

   (a) What is the opportunity cost of producing one unit of lumber in Canelones? Of producing one unit of wool?

   (b) In a carefully labelled diagram, draw this country's production possibility curve measuring the quantity of lumber on the horizontal axis. What information does the slope of the production possibility curve give you? If Canelones is currently producing 800 units of lumber, how many units of wool might it be producing as well? Identify this point on your production possibility curve (point *A*).

(c) What is the consumption possibility curve of this country under autarky?

(d) Now Canelones starts trading in the world market where one unit of wool exchanges for four units of lumber. What good will this country sell (export) in the international market? Explain.

(e) Assuming that Canelones continues producing the output combination at point *A*, draw in your diagram the new consumption possibility curve. Given the new consumption possibilities open to this country, how many units of wool will Canelones end up consuming if it chooses to consume 1600 units of lumber? Identify this point on your consumption possibility curve (point *B*).

(f) Suppose now that Canelones changes its production bundle according to its comparative advantage. What combination of wool and lumber will it produce? Identify this point on your production possibility curve (point *C*).

(g) Given the new consumption possibilities open to this country, how many units of wool will Canelones end up consuming if it chooses to continue consuming 1600 units of lumber? Identify this point on your consumption possibility curve (point *D*).

The following exercise examines the tendency toward specialization with trade when production is characterized by increasing opportunity costs (i.e., production possibility curve is concave). A review of *Extensions in Theory 33-1: The Gains from Trade More Generally* will help you answer this exercise.

E2. International Trade and Opportunity Cost
The graph in Figure 33-3 depicts a country's production possibility curve between wool and lumber. Prior to trade, the country is producing and consuming at point *R*, which involves 10 units of wool and 10 units of lumber. Due to large increases in construction activity in this economy, the country now decides that it wishes to consume 14 units of lumber.

Figure 33-3

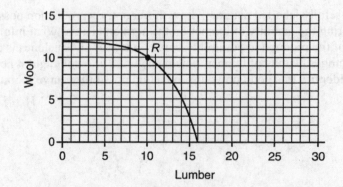

(a) How much wool must this country give up to obtain the additional four units of lumber in a no-trade environment? Explain.

(b) Suppose that the terms of trade in international markets are one unit of wool for two units of lumber. Assuming that production remains at point R, how much wool would the country have to give up to obtain the additional four units of lumber if it engages in international trade? Explain.

Additional Multiple-Choice Questions

1. **In a two-country and two-good model, gains from trade would not exist if**
   (a) one country had an absolute advantage in the production of both goods.
   (b) a given amount of resources produced more of both goods in one country.
   (c) one country was endowed with far more resources than the other.
   (d) the countries had the same opportunity costs in the production of both goods.
   (e) only one country had a comparative advantage in the production of one good.

2. **Which of the following statements is *not* true about opportunity cost?**
   (a) Equal opportunity costs for pairs of commodities between two countries lead to gains from trade.
   (b) Opportunity costs depend on relative production costs.
   (c) Differences in opportunity costs across countries can enhance total output of both goods through trade and specialization.
   (d) Comparative advantage can be expressed in terms of opportunity costs.
   (e) Opportunity cost can be read as the slope of a tangent to a country's production possibility curve.

*3. **If production of each unit of wool in Country A implies that beef production must be decreased by four units, while in Country B each additional unit of beef decreases wool output by four units, the gains from trade**
   (a) are maximized if Country A specializes in wool production and Country B in beef.
   (b) are maximized if Country A specializes in beef production and Country B in wool.
   (c) are maximized if Country A allocates 80 percent of its resources to wool and the remainder to beef, while Country B does the opposite.
   (d) are maximized if Country A allocates 20 percent of its resources to wool and the remainder to beef, while Country B does the opposite.
   (e) cannot be realized because opportunity costs in the two countries are the same.

4. **The gains from specialization and trade depend on the pattern of _____ advantage, not _____ advantage.**
   (a) absolute; comparative
   (b) monetary; non-monetary
   (c) absolute; reciprocal
   (d) comparative; absolute
   (e) size; cost

*5. **By trading in international markets, countries**
- (a) can consume beyond their production possibility boundary.
- (b) will always produce the same commodity bundle as before trade.
- (c) can produce outside of their production possibility boundary.
- (d) must choose one of the intercepts on the production possibility boundary, indicating complete specialization.
- (e) always produce and consume the same bundle of commodities.

Questions 6 to 11 refer to the data in the following table. You will find it useful to first calculate the opportunity costs of production for each commodity in each country.

	One Unit of Resource Can Produce	
Country	Lumber (bd m)	Aluminum (kg)
Australia	4	9
Canada	9	3
Brazil	3	2

*6. **Considering just Australia and Canada,**
- (a) Australia has an absolute advantage in lumber.
- (b) Australia has an absolute advantage in aluminum.
- (c) There are no possible gains from trade.
- (d) Canada should specialize in aluminum production.
- (e) Australia has a comparative advantage in lumber.

*7. **Considering just Canada and Brazil,**
- (a) Brazil has an absolute advantage in lumber.
- (b) Brazil has a comparative advantage in aluminum.
- (c) Canada has an absolute advantage in only one commodity.
- (d) there are no possible gains from trade.
- (e) None of the above.

*8. **Considering just Australia and Brazil,**
- (a) Australia has an absolute advantage in lumber and Brazil in aluminum.
- (b) Australia has an absolute advantage in aluminum and Brazil in lumber.
- (c) Australia has a comparative advantage in lumber and Brazil in aluminum.
- (d) Australia has an absolute advantage in lumber and a comparative advantage in aluminum.
- (e) Australia has a comparative advantage in both lumber and aluminum.

*9. **In Brazil, the opportunity cost of 1 kg of aluminum is**
- (a) 0.67 bd m of lumber.
- (b) 0.87 bd m of lumber.
- (c) 1.25 bd m of lumber.
- (d) 1.50 bd m of lumber.
- (e) 1.30 bd m of lumber.

*10. **In Australia, the opportunity cost of 1 bd m of lumber is**
- (a) 2.25 kg of aluminum.
- (b) 0.44 kg of aluminum.
- (c) 0.36 kg of aluminum.
- (d) 3.60 kg of aluminum.
- (e) 3.00 kg of aluminum.

*11. In Canada, the opportunity cost of 1 kg of aluminum is
    (a)   0.33 bd m of lumber.
    (b)   2.70 bd m of lumber.
    (c)   3.0 bd m of lumber.
    (d)   3.33 bd m of lumber.
    (e)   1.50 bd m of lumber.

12. For a country with one important export commodity such as coffee or oil,
    (a)   a rise in the commodity's price will improve the country's terms of trade.
    (b)   a fall in the commodity's price is a favourable change in its terms of trade.
    (c)   its terms of trade will improve only if it is able to increase the quantity of exports.
    (d)   its terms of trade will improve only if world demand for its exports is inelastic.
    (e)   its terms of trade improve only if the prices of imports decrease.

Use the following diagram to answer Questions 13 and 14.

Figure 33-4

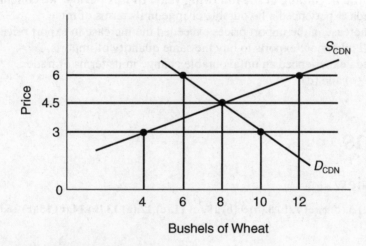

Bushels of Wheat

*13. At a world price of $3, Canada will
    (a)   produce 4 million bushels of wheat.
    (b)   consume 10 million bushels of wheat.
    (c)   import 6 million bushels of wheat.
    (d)   consume more wheat than it produces.
    (e)   All of the above are correct.

*14. If the world price remains at $3, while the Canadian demand for wheat increases, the primary result would be
    (a)   an increase in the Canadian production of wheat.
    (b)   an increase in the price of wheat in Canada.
    (c)   a decrease in Canadian wheat exports.
    (d)   an increase in wheat imports into Canada.
    (e)   a decrease in quantity supplied by Canadian producers.

*15. At a world price of $4.50, Canada will
    (a)   import 8 million bushels of wheat.
    (b)   consume 8 million bushels of wheat.
    (c)   import <u>and</u> consume 8 million bushels of wheat.
    (d)   produce 8 million bushels of wheat.
    (e)   produce <u>and</u> consume 8 million bushels of wheat.

*16. At a world price of $6.00, Canada will
- (a) import 6 million <u>and</u> consume 12 million bushels of wheat.
- (b) import 6 million <u>and</u> consume 6 million bushels of wheat.
- (c) export 6 million <u>and</u> consume 6 million bushels of wheat.
- (d) produce 6 million <u>and</u> consume 6 million bushels of wheat.
- (e) export 12 million bushels of wheat.

*17. If the world price remains at $6.00, while the Canadian supply increases, the primary result would be
- (a) a decrease in the price of wheat in Canada.
- (b) an increase in the Canadian consumption of wheat.
- (c) a decrease in Canadian wheat imports.
- (d) a decrease in the quantity demanded by Canadian consumers.
- (e) an increase in Canadian wheat exports.

*18. Suppose that Canada's terms of trade changed from 97.0 at the beginning of one year to 105.1 at the beginning of the following year. In this period, we conclude that
- (a) Canada experienced a favourable change in its terms of trade.
- (b) the increase in the import prices exceeded the increase in export prices.
- (c) it will take more exports to buy the same quantity of imports.
- (d) Canada experienced an unfavourable change in its terms of trade.
- (e) Both (c) and (d).

Solutions

Chapter Review

1.(b) 2.(c) 3.(d) 4.(c) 5.(c) 6.(e) 7.(b) 8.(b) 9.(b) 10.(c) 11.(c) 12.(a) 13.(b) 14.(c) 15.(c) 16.(c)

Short-Answer Questions

1. A constant cost production possibilities curve reflects the possible combinations of the production (and consumption) of two goods in a closed economy with a given endowment of resources. The two intercepts in a production possibilities diagram indicate the maximum production (consumption) levels if only one of the goods was produced. The slope of the production possibilities boundary indicates the opportunity costs of reallocating resources in order to increase the production of one good by decreasing the production of another. The terms of trade line reflects the relative price that one good can be traded for another. The relative price is constant and so the terms of trade line is linear. With constant costs, countries tend to completely specialize in production of one good (in a two-good world). The consumption possibilities curve is the line at which a country, specializing in one good, can consume some of the other good at the world's terms of trade. Hence, a country is able to consume combinations of two goods that are beyond its production possibilities curve.

2. Your rough sketch should resemble Figure 33-6 in the text. A country imports the goods of its trading partners because its opportunity costs are higher than the world price. The country will satisfy its total demand by importing goods from abroad at the lower world price. Some domestic production will occur, however. Since its domestic opportunity costs are higher than the world price, the country has a comparative disadvantage.

3. Your rough sketch should resemble Figure 33-5 in the text. A country exports this good to its trading partners because its opportunity cost is lower than the world price. The country will produce in excess of what is required to satisfy the domestic demand at the world price and sell the rest in the world market. Technological improvement will allow this country to produce any quantity of this good

at a lower cost than before, and thus the supply curve will shift down and to the right (i.e., the domestic supply will increase). Since this is a small country—i.e., a price-taker in the world market—the international price will not be affected by this country's increase in the production of this good. Therefore, the domestic price will not be affected either.

4. **(a)** In both cases, the most likely source of comparative advantage might be climatic differences.
   (b) In the case of Venezuela's exports of oil to Cuba, the most likely source of comparative advantage might be differences in natural resource endowments. In the case of and Cuba's exports of medical services to Venezuela, the most likely source of comparative advantages might be differences in human capital endowments.
   (c) In the case of Canada's exports of financial services to China, the most likely source of comparative advantage might be difference in technology and human capital endowments. In the case of China's exports of shoes to Canada, the most likely source of comparative advantage is differences in unskilled labour endowments.

5. This is the result of the existence of imperfectly competitive markets. Two basic assumptions of perfectly competitive markets are (i) there is a large number of firms, and (ii) these firms produce a homogeneous—i.e., undifferentiated—good. However, even if the assumption of a large number of producers were to be satisfied, only a few markets, if any, would satisfy today the latter strong assumption of producing an undifferentiated product. Indeed, virtually all of today's manufactured consumer goods are produced in a vast array of differentiated product lines. And it is this proliferation of differentiated products that allows different countries to specialize in different subproduct lines and to trade with one another—i.e., creating what is known as intra-industry trade.

Exercises

1. **(a)** Japan: 1 radio costs 2 cameras; 1 camera costs 1/2 radio.
   Indonesia: 1 radio costs 1/3 camera; 1 camera costs 3 radios.
   Japan should produce cameras. Indonesia should produce radios.
   Japan has an absolute advantage in the production of cameras.
   Indonesia has a comparative advantage in radios.
   (b) Japan: 1 radio costs 2 cameras; 1 camera costs 1/2 radio.
   Indonesia: 1 radio costs 3 cameras; 1 camera costs 1/3 radio.
   Japan should produce radios. Indonesia should produce cameras.
   Indonesia has a comparative advantage in cameras.
   (c) Japan: 1 radio costs 2 cameras; 1 camera costs 1/2 radio.
   Indonesia: 1 radio costs 2 cameras; 1 camera costs 1/2 radio.
   Japan should produce both and Indonesia should produce both. There would be no gains from trade.
   (d) Case (c) shows that even though Japan has an absolute advantage in producing both goods, no trade will occur because relative prices (or opportunity costs of production) are identical to those in Indonesia.
   (e) Case (b) shows that even though Japanese workers are more productive in both industries (and therefore can expect to earn more than Indonesian workers), mutually beneficial trade can still occur if each country exports the good for which it has a comparative advantage.

2. **(a)** *A*.
   (b) *B*.
   (c) dairy products; watches
   (d) 100; 200

3. **(a)** Terms of Trade: 102.0; 101.0; 115.9; 111.8; 102.3.
   (b) An increase in the terms of trade means that fewer exports are required to pay for a given amount of imports.
   (c) The terms of trade changed from 101.0 to 115.6; this was a favourable change in terms of trade for this economy. It cost fewer exports to buy the same imports; or, for the same exports this economy received more imports.

4.   **(a)**   Canada has an absolute advantage in both goods.
     (b)   Canada: 0.4; Japan; 6.0.
     (c)   Wheat: Canada; Microchips: Japan.
     (d)   **Figure 33-5**

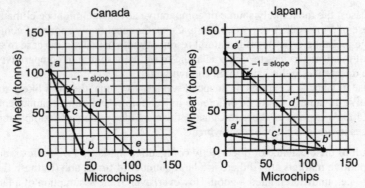

Canada's production possibility boundary is denoted *ab*, and Japan's is *a'b'*.

     (e)   Canada would be producing and consuming 50 tonnes of wheat and 20 microchips (point *c* in the diagram), and Japan would be producing and consuming 10 tonnes of wheat and 60 microchips (point *c'*).
     (f)   Assuming that these are the only countries making up the world, total output of wheat is 60 tonnes and world production of microchips is 80 units.
     (g)   Each country specializes in the commodity in which it has a comparative advantage. Thus Canada specializes completely in wheat production (see point *a*), and Japan specializes completely in microchip production (see point *b'*). World output is now 100 tonnes of wheat and 120 microchips.
     (h)   Terms of trade equal to one tonne of wheat for one microchip mean that Canada can trade from its production point *a* to any point on its consumption possibility curve *ae*, which has a slope of −1, representing the terms of trade. Similarly, Japan can trade from point *b'* to any point on its consumption possibility curve *b'e'*. Since it was assumed that Canada consumes the same amount of wheat both before and after trade, its consumption bundle is represented by point *d*, which contains 50 units of each good. Therefore, Canada is exporting 50 tonnes of wheat in return for imports of 50 microchips. Japan, having exported 50 microchips to Canada, has 70 remaining for its own consumption. When this is combined with its 50 tonnes of wheat imports, Japan consumes at point *d'*.
     (i)   The terms of trade lines in the graphs would become flatter with a slope of −1/2. Thus Canada's consumption possibilities would increase (the new terms of trade line rotates outward on point *a*), while Japan's decrease (the new terms of trade line rotates inward on point *b'*). Thus Canada would get a larger share of the gains from trade.

5.   **(a)**   50; 150; imports; 100
     (b)   80; 120; exports; 40
     (c)   20; 80; importer; 60

6.   **(a)**   Equilibrium price: $7.00; Equilibrium quantity: 4000 thousand.
     (b)   Canada will produce 2000 thousand and consume 5000 thousand widgets at the world price of $6.00. Hence, Canada will import 3000 thousand widgets to satisfy its domestic demand.
     (c)   Canada will produce 6000 thousand and consume 3000 thousand widgets at the world price of $8.00. Hence, Canada will export 3000 thousand widgets.
     (d)   Canada will produce 4000 thousand and consume 4000 thousand widgets at the world price of $7.00. Canada will produce just enough to satisfy the domestic demand and thus will neither export nor import widgets.

7. **(a)** In the absence of trade, the opportunity cost of one unit of wine is one bale of wool in Italy and one-third of a bale of wool in France.

(b) The opportunity cost of one unit of wine is lower in France than in Italy and thus France has a comparative advantage in the production of wine. Therefore, Italy has a comparative advantage in the production of wool. Indeed, the opportunity cost of one bale of wool is one unit of wine in Italy and three units of wine in France.

(c) There will be no change to the answer above. If labour productivity increases in the same proportion in the wine and wool industries in France, the opportunity cost of producing either good doesn't change.

(d) Since Italy has a comparative advantage in the production of wool, it will specialize in the production of wool and will export wool to France in exchange for wine. Before trade takes place, Italian wool producers would exchange one bale of wool for one unit of wine. Therefore, they will engage in trade if they can obtain from France more than one unit of wine for each bale of wool.

In turn, before trade takes place, French wine producers would exchange three units of wine for one bale of wool. Therefore, they will engage in trade if they can obtain from Italy one bale of wool for less than three units of wine.

$\rightarrow$ 1 Wool < 1 Wine < 3 Wool

Extension Exercises

E1. **(a)** The opportunity cost of producing one unit of lumber is 0.5 units of wool, while the opportunity cost of producing one unit of wool is two units of lumber in Canelones.

(b) The slope of the production possibility curve indicates the opportunity cost of producing an additional unit of lumber. Since Canelones must allocate 400 units of resources to produce 800 units of lumber, the remaining 600 units of resources will produce 600 units of wool—it will produce at point *A*.

Figure 33-6

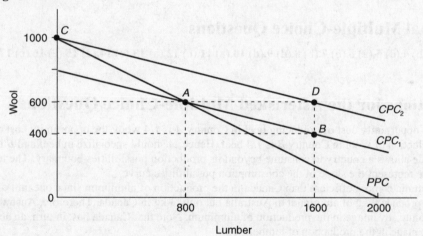

(c) In autarky, the consumption possibility curve coincides with the production possibility curve.

(d) The opportunity cost of producing one unit of wool is two units of lumber in Canelones, while the opportunity cost of obtaining one unit of wool in the international market is four units of lumber. Canelones has a comparative advantage in the production of wool and thus it will export wool and import lumber.

(e) The slope of the consumption possibility curve is now 0.25—flatter than the slope of the production possibility curve, which is 0.5. If Canelones continues to produce at point *A*—800 units of lumber and 600 units of wool—while now consuming 1600 units of lumber, then it will have to import 800 units of lumber—thus exporting 200 units of wool given that one unit of wool exchanges for four units of lumber in the world market. Therefore, it will now consume a combination of 400 units of wool and 1600 units of lumber (point *B*).

(f) Since Canelones has a comparative advantage in the production of wool, it will specialize in the production of wool. Moreover, since opportunity costs are constant, Canelones will produce only wool and import from the world market any quantity of lumber it will consume. Therefore, it will produce 1000 units of wool and 0 of lumber (point *C*).

(g) Canelones will need to export 400 units of wool to be able to import the 1600 units of lumber it desires to consume. Therefore, it will consume a combination of 600 units of wool and 1600 units of lumber (point *D*).

E2. **(a)** Five units. This requires a movement along the production possibility boundary from point *R* to point *A* in Figure 33-7.

Figure 33-7

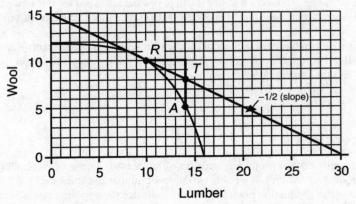

(b) Two units. The terms of trade line has a slope of –1/2 and is tangent to the production possibility curve at *R*. Thus, the economy can export two units of wool in return for imports of four units of lumber. This is represented by a movement from point *R* to point *T* on the graph.

Additional Multiple-Choice Questions

1.(d) **2.**(a) **3.**(b) **4.**(d) **5.**(a) **6.**(b) **7.**(b) **8.**(d) **9.**(d) **10.**(a) **11.**(c) **12.**(a) **13.**(e) **14.**(d) **15.**(e) **16.**(c) **17.**(e) **18.**(a)

Explanations for the Asterisked Multiple-Choice Questions

3.(b) The opportunity cost of producing beef in Country *A* is 1/4 wool; the opportunity cost of the production of wool in Country *B* is 1/4 beef. Hence, *A* should specialize in beef and *B* in wool.

5.(a) Trade allows a country to consume beyond its production possibilities boundary. The terms of trade represent the slope of the consumption possibilities curve.

6.(b) Australia is more efficient than Canada in the production of aluminum since one unit of resources can produce 9 kg of aluminum in Australia but only 3 kg in Canada. Therefore, Australia has an absolute advantage in the production of aluminum. Note that Canada has, in turn, an absolute advantage in the production of lumber.

7.(b) The opportunity cost of producing 1 kg of aluminum in Brazil is 1.5 bd m of lumber, while in Canada it is 3 bd m of lumber. Hence, Brazil has a comparative advantage in the production of aluminum.

8.(d) Relative to Brazil, Australia has an absolute advantage in the production of both lumber and aluminum since it can produce both goods more efficiently than Brazil; however, the opportunity cost of producing aluminum in Australia is 4/9 bd m of lumber, while in Brazil it is 1.5 bd m of lumber. Hence, Australia has a comparative advantage in the production of aluminum.

9.(d) The table indicates that Brazil can produce either 3 bd m of lumber or 2 kg of aluminum with one unit of resources. Hence, the opportunity cost of producing 1 kg of aluminum in Brazil is 1.5 bd m of lumber.

10.(a) The table indicates that Australia can produce either 4 bd m of lumber or 9 kg of aluminum. Hence, the opportunity cost of 1 bd m of lumber is 2.25 kg of aluminum.

11.(c) In Canada, one unit of resources can produce either 9 bd m of lumber or 3 kg of aluminum. Therefore, the opportunity cost of 3 kg of aluminum is 9 bd m of lumber and the opportunity cost of 1 kg of aluminum is 3 bd m of lumber.

13.(e) Since the intersection of the domestic demand for and supply of wheat is above the world price of $3, this country has a comparative disadvantage in wheat. It would produce 4 bushels of wheat and satisfy the total demand of 10 bushels by importing 6 bushels at the world price of $3. Hence, trade allows the country to consume more wheat than it produces.

14.(d) Since the domestic price is determined by the world price, the domestic price of wheat will also remain unchanged at $3 a bushel. The quantity supplied by domestic producers will also remain unchanged at 4 bushels, but the quantity demanded at the price of $3 a bushel will increase. Therefore, Canada will import more wheat to satisfy this increase in demand.

15.(e) Since the intersection of the domestic demand for and supply of wheat is at the world price of $4.50, the domestic quantity supplied of wheat will be just sufficient to satisfy the domestic quantity demanded and thus wheat will be neither imported into Canada nor exported abroad.

16.(c) Since the intersection of the domestic demand for and supply of wheat is below the world price of $6.00, this country has a comparative advantage in wheat. It would produce 12 bushels of wheat, satisfy the total domestic demand of 6 bushels, and export the other 6 bushels at the world price of $6.00. Hence, trade allows the country to produce more wheat than it consumes.

17.(e) Assuming Canada is a price-taker in the world market for wheat, the increase in the Canadian supply of wheat—i.e., a shift to the right of the domestic supply curve—will not affect the world price of wheat (i.e., the world price will remain at $6.00). However, a larger quantity of wheat will now be produced in Canada at the world price of $6.00 and, since the domestic quantity demanded will not change, a larger quantity of wheat will be exported.

18.(a) Canada's terms of trade improved. Canada can buy the same amount of imports with fewer exports at the beginning of the following year.

34

Trade Policy

Chapter Overview

This chapter examines the ways in which a government may intervene in markets to restrict international trade and demonstrates the resulting consequences. **Protectionist trade policy** usually takes one of two forms: **tariffs** that serve to raise import prices, and **non-tariff barriers**—such as **import quotas** or **voluntary export restrictions**—that serve to reduce import quantities.

Free trade maximizes world output and average living standards. Arguments for protection may rest on objectives other than maximizing average living standards, such as reducing fluctuations in national income or promoting economic diversification. Protectionism may also be advanced by a large country as a means of gaining a favourable improvement in the terms of trade, and thereby increasing national income. Several invalid but widely employed arguments for protection are also discussed.

Since its inception in 1947, The **General Agreement on Trade and Tariffs** (GATT) has served to substantially reduce tariffs through a series of multilateral negotiations. The final round of trade agreements under GATT, the Uruguay Round, concluded in 1994 with an agreement in several important areas that served to promote more liberal trade. GATT was replaced by the **World Trade Organization** (WTO) in 1995.

There has been a sharp increase in the number and extent of regional trade-liberalizing agreements such as **free trade areas**, **customs unions**, and **common markets** since the early 1990s. The **North American Free Trade Agreement** (NAFTA) is the world's largest and most successful free trade area and the European Union is the world's largest and most successful common market. These regional agreements bring about efficiency gains through **trade creation** but may also lead to efficiency losses from **trade diversion**.

Hints and Tips

The following may help you avoid some of the most common errors on examinations.

✓ Do not confuse some valid arguments for protection with the so-called fallacious arguments.

✓ In order to analyze the effects of tariffs and quotas, refresh your understanding of the concepts of consumer surplus, producer surplus, and deadweight loss. Consumer surplus is the difference between the value that consumers place on a product and the payment they make to buy that product (Section 6.3 of the text) while producer surplus is the difference between the price that a producer receives and the lowest amount that the producer would be willing to accept for the sale of that product (Section 12.1 of the text).

✓ Learn the distinguishing features of a free trade area, a customs union, and a common market.

✓ Learn some of the major features of NAFTA, including "national treatment," dispute settlement, and trade diversion and creation.

Chapter Review

Free Trade or Protection?

After reading this section, you should be able to discuss the benefits and costs of protectionism versus freer international trade. You should begin to understand some of the valid arguments for trade policy that restricts trade and to recognize the invalid arguments for protection.

1. **Which of the following statements is *not* true of free trade?**
   (a) Free trade leads to a maximization of world output.
   (b) Free trade maximizes world living standards.
   (c) Free trade always makes each individual better off.
   (d) Free trade can increase the average income in a country.
   (e) Free trade encourages countries to specialize in production.

2. **The infant industry argument for tariffs is**
   (a) only appropriate for industries where there are no economies of scale.
   (b) an example of dynamic comparative advantage.
   (c) theoretically valid if a new producer can sufficiently reduce average costs as output increases in the future.
   (d) a proposal to earmark tariff revenues to finance daycare facilities for infants.
   (e) most applicable in developing countries because of their relative abundance of unskilled labour.

3. **Protection against low-wage foreign labour is an invalid protectionist argument because**
   (a) free trade benefits everyone.
   (b) the gains from trade depend on comparative, not absolute, advantage.
   (c) when the foreign country increases its exports to us, their wages will rise.
   (d) the terms of trade are necessarily equal for low-wage and high-wage countries.
   (e) low-wage labourers are necessarily less productive.

4. **If the objective of a government is to maximize national income, which of the following is the *least* valid reason for using tariff protection?**
   (a) To protect against unfair subsidization of foreign firms by their governments.
   (b) To protect against unfair low wages paid to foreign labour.
   (c) To protect newly developing industries.
   (d) To protect against dumping of foreign produced goods.
   (e) To improve the country's terms of trade.

5. **Which of the following is *not* a fallacious protectionist argument?**
   (a) Buy Canadian, and both the money and the goods stay at home.
   (b) Trade cannot be mutually advantageous if one of the trading partners is much larger than the other.
   (c) Too many imports lower Canadian living standards as our money is sent abroad.
   (d) A foreign firm, temporarily selling in Canada at a much lower price than in its own country, threatens the Canadian industry's existence.
   (e) A high-wage country such as Canada cannot effectively compete with a low-wage country such as Mexico.

6. **The main purpose served by a country's exports is**
   (a) to contribute toward the accumulation of foreign reserves.
   (b) to increase the country's GDP.
   (c) to increase the standard of living of its population.
   (d) to allow for higher levels of domestic consumption.
   (e) to provide the resources to purchase imports.

Methods of Protection

This section discusses protectionist trade policies that directly raise the price of imports or directly reduce the quantity of imports. A tariff or an import duty is a tax on imported goods. Quotas and voluntary export restrictions (VERs) restrict the quantity of an imported product. The chapter analyzes the "deadweight" loss of tariffs and quotas/VERs. Various trade-remedy laws and non-tariff barriers are also discussed.

7. **Which of the following is an effect of imposing a tariff on an imported good?**
   (a) The domestic price of the imported product increases.
   (b) The quantity of domestic production increases.
   (c) The government receives customs revenues.
   (d) Domestic producers earn more because of increases in the domestic price and domestic production.
   (e) All of the above.

8. **Which of the following is an effect of imposing quotas and/or VERs on imported goods?**
   (a) Unlike tariffs, they lower domestic prices.
   (b) They decrease domestic production and consumption.
   (c) The deadweight loss for them is greater than that for an equivalent tariff.
   (d) All importers refuse to sell to the country that imposed the quotas.
   (e) In the case of VERs, the domestic government provides subsidies to exporters.

9. **Countervailing duties are attempts to maintain "a level playing ground" by**
   (a) retaliating against foreign tariffs.
   (b) raising or lowering tariffs multilaterally.
   (c) establishing a common tariff wall around a customs union.
   (d) assessing tariffs that will offset foreign government subsidies.
   (e) subsidizing exports.

10. **Which of the following statements about non-tariff barriers to trade (NTBs) is *incorrect*?**
    (a) The use of NTBs has been discontinued throughout the world.
    (b) The misuse of antidumping practices constitutes an increasingly important NTB.
    (c) Countervailing duties have become a covert method of protection.
    (d) Most NTBs are ostensibly levied for trade remedy purposes but end up being protectionist.
    (e) Environmental and labour standards can be used as disguised NTBs.

11. **Which of the following motivations for dumping can be of permanent benefit to the buying country?**
    (a) Predatory pricing.
    (b) Cyclical stabilization of sales.
    (c) Enabling foreign producers to achieve lower average costs and therefore price.
    (d) Altering the terms of trade.
    (e) All of the above.

Current Trade Policy

After reading this section you will have a better appreciation of the issues in multilateral, regional, and bilateral trade negotiations, and be able to discuss the important highlights of the NAFTA and its impact on the Canadian economy.

12. **Which of the following is an example of trade diversion?**
    (a) A government promotes diversification of a country's industries.
    (b) Liberalized trade encourages industries to specialize in subproduct lines.
    (c) NAFTA encourages more trade between low- and high-wage countries.
    (d) NAFTA encourages Canada to switch imports from low-wage non-member countries to Mexico.
    (e) Publicized trade disputes divert attention from the gains from trade.

13. **A common market includes all but which of the following?**
    (a) Tariff-free trade among members.
    (b) A common trade policy with the rest of the world.
    (c) Rules of origin.
    (d) Free movement of labour.
    (e) Free movement of capital.

14. **The countries in a free trade area**
    (a) impose no tariffs on one another's goods.
    (b) each have an independent tariff structure with the rest of the world.
    (c) do not permit the free movement of labour across their borders.
    (d) do not have a common monetary policy.
    (e) All of the above.

15. **Which of the following was *not* one of the features of NAFTA?**
    (a) Elimination of all tariffs between the U.S. and Canada by 1999.
    (b) Elimination of countervailing duties between the U.S. and Canada.
    (c) Exemption of cultural industries.
    (d) Continuance of quotas to support provincial supply management schemes.
    (e) Provision for national treatment for most service industries.

16. **Which of the following was *not* an outcome of the Uruguay Round (1994) of GATT negotiations?**
    (a) Major trade liberalization in agriculture.
    (b) Replacement of the GATT with the World Trade Organization (WTO).
    (c) A new dispute settlement mechanism.
    (d) Reduction in world tariffs by approximately 40 percent.
    (e) All of the above.

Short-Answer Questions

1. **Sketching the Effects of Various Trade Policies**
    Case 1: Demand Restriction
    Figure 34-1 illustrates a country's demand and supply curves of commodity Z.

    (a) According to the diagram, what are equilibrium values of price and quantity in a free market?

    (b) Now, the government restricts importers to purchasing only half the quantity demanded at each price. Draw the new demand curve in Figure 34-1. What are the new equilibrium values for price and quantity?

    Figure 34-1

    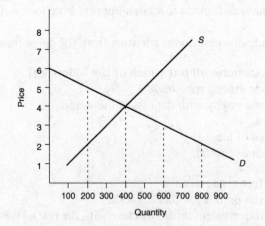

    Case 2: A Tariff
    Figure 34-2 illustrates the domestic demand and supply curves of commodity V. The key assumption in this question is that the foreign (world) supply curve is horizontal at a world price of $2 for V.

Figure 34-2

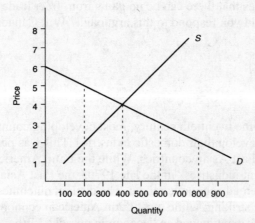

(a)   At the world price, what is the total quantity of domestic supply? Domestic demand? What is the quantity of imports of V from foreign producers?

(b)   Now, the government imposes a tariff of $1 per unit of V such that the domestic price (with the tariff) increases to $3/unit. Sketch this result, and estimate from the diagram what is the change in the quantity of imported V.

Case 3: A Quota

Figure 34-3 illustrates the domestic demand and supply curves of commodity U. The world supply curve is horizontal at a price of $2 per unit of U. Now, the government wants to impose an import quota on commodity U of 300 units. The quota must satisfy domestic excess demand. Sketch this policy and indicate the new domestic price level of commodity U.

Figure 34-3

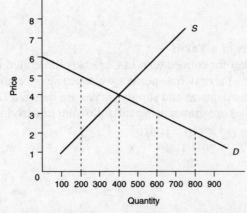

2.   Explain briefly the economic considerations that explain why reductions in trade restrictions in agricultural products have been difficult to achieve.

3. A non-economist observes that wages in Mexico are considerably lower than wages in Canada, and concludes that there can be no gains from freer trade with Mexico. As an economist, how would you respond to this argument? Will Canada be able to export goods to Mexico? Explain.

4. In the second half of the twentieth century, most developing countries adopted protectionist policies in order to develop their domestic industries. This was particularly the case among Latin American and East Asian countries. While the Latin American countries were still protecting their "infant industries" in the late 1970s, the East Asian countries had moved toward an export-oriented economic model. The distinct outcomes of these two different paths were also quite striking: while most Latin American economies remained stagnant, East Asian economies experienced an "economic miracle." What factors might have contributed to the realization of these two different economic outcomes?

5. Do you agree with the following statement about trade? "When Canada imposes a tariff on an import, the government will earn tariff revenues; further, some Canadians will be better off and some will be worse off. The losses, however, will exceed the gains (including tariff revenues as a gain)." Provide an explanation using a demand-supply diagram.

Exercises

1. **The Economic Effects of a Tariff**
    The hypothetical market for canned tuna in Canada is illustrated in Figure 34-4, where the foreign supply curve (S_f) is drawn as perfectly elastic (i.e., horizontal) at the world price of $1.00, and the domestic demand and supply curves are denoted D_C and S_C, respectively.
    The domestic curves are drawn using the following underlying algebraic equations:

    Domestic demand: $D_C = 340 - 100P$
    Domestic supply: $S_C = 20 + 100P$

Figure 34-4

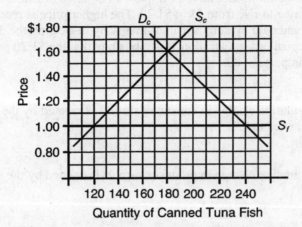

(a)   Under free trade, what is the quantity of tuna consumed in Canada, the quantity supplied by Canadian producers, and the quantity supplied by foreign producers to Canadian consumers?

(b)   Suppose that a 20 percent tariff is imposed such that the new imported price on tuna is $1.20. Calculate the consequent changes in domestic consumption, domestic production, and imports. Why is the change in imports greater than the change in domestic production?

(c)   With the imposition of the 20 percent tariff on imported tuna, what is the quantitative change in consumer surplus? You might refer to Figure 34-1 in the text.

(d)   With the imposition of the 20 percent tariff on imported tuna, what is the quantitative change in producer surplus? You might refer to Figure 34-1 in the text.

(e)   What is the change in tariff revenue?

(f)   What is the "deadweight" loss to Canada?

2.   **The Economic Effects of a Quota**
Consider the canned tuna case outlined in Question 1. Now the government wishes to impose an import quota rather than a tariff. The domestic demand and supply curves are those in Question 1, and the world price (without trade restrictions) is $1.

You learned in Question 1(b) that a world price of $1.20 (including the 20 percent tax) resulted in a quantity of imports into Canada of 80 cans (220 – 140). Along with domestic supply, imports satisfied total domestic demand for canned tuna.

(a) The government imposes an import quota of 80 units of canned tuna and allows the domestic price to rise from \$1 to \$1.20. The higher price is received by foreign producers and paid by domestic consumers. By inspecting the diagram or using the algebraic equations in Question 1, demonstrate that the \$1.20 price for canned tuna generates imports of 80.

(b) What quantitative change in consumer surplus is created by the introduction of the quota on canned tuna?

(c) What quantitative change in producer surplus is created by the introduction of the quota?

(d) What is the deadweight loss to Canada?

(e) How does this deadweight loss compare to that in Question 1?

3. **Impact of Free Trade and Government Subsidies**
    Consider the following information: (i) corn production in the U.S. accounts for about 40 percent of world output and close to 70 percent of all corn exports; (ii) American corn producers receive close to \$10 billion a year in government subsidies; (iii) in Mexico, the domestic price of corn was significantly higher than its world price at the outset of the NAFTA negotiations; and (iv) U.S. corn exports to Mexico have zero tariff after January 1, 2008.

    (a) Draw a rough diagram that illustrates the situation in the Mexican corn market at the outset of the NAFTA negotiations. Show in your diagram the new domestic corn price when all tariffs are eliminated.

    (b) Show in your diagram the effect of the change in domestic price on both the consumer surplus and the producer surplus.

    (c) What role, if any, do U.S. government subsidies play in this outcome? What possible actions could the Mexican government undertake under NAFTA?

Extension Exercises

E1. Improving the Terms of Trade

Suppose the country of Gill constitutes a large buyer of widgets. For simplicity, we will assume Gill represents the entire world demand. Production, however, takes place by both domestic and foreign firms. Gill's monetary unit is the dollar ($).

Gill's (and world's) demand curve is $Q_D = 1200 - 200P$
Gill's domestic supply is $Q_S{}^G = 100P$

Foreign supply is $Q_S{}^F = 300P$. [*Note:* The foreign supply is no longer horizontal, as was the case for Exercise 1.]

Total supply (domestic plus foreign): $Q_S{}^T = 400P$

(a) Under free trade, what are the equilibrium values of world price and quantity demanded?

(b) At this world price, what is the level of Gill's consumption, imports, and production of widgets?

(c) Gill's government now seeks to improve its terms of trade by imposing a tariff on imported widgets. Suppose it levies a tariff of $2 per imported widget. Prove that the new foreign supply curve changes to $Q_S{}^F = -600 + 300P$. [*Hint:* What is the net price received by foreigners after paying the tariff?]

(d) What is the new world price? What are Gill's new levels of consumption, imports, and production of widgets?

(e) What price per widget do foreign firms receive after the tariff is imposed? What price per widget do domestic suppliers receive?

E2. The Impact of Government's Protectionist Policy

The table below shows the Republic of Atlantida's domestic demand schedule and domestic supply schedule for widgets, where price is in dollars per unit and quantities are in thousands of units per month. Suppose that the world price of widgets is $5 per unit. Atlantida is a very small country that takes the world price as given (constant).

Price ($)	10	9	8	7	6	5	4
Quantity demanded (000s)	0	2	4	6	8	10	12
Quantity supplied (000s)	12	10	8	6	4	2	0

(a) In the absence of international trade, what is this country's equilibrium price and equilibrium quantity of widgets? In a neat and clearly labelled diagram, draw the Republic of Atlantida's domestic demand curve and domestic supply curve and indicate this equilibrium (point A).

(b) Suppose now that this country starts trading with the rest of the world. Given that the international price of widgets is $5, will this country become an importer or an exporter of widgets? How many widgets will this country import or export? In your diagram, draw the international supply (or demand) curve for widgets and show the quantity demanded and the quantity domestically supplied after this country starts trading in the international market.

(c) The government of Republic of Atlantida wants this industry to grow and, to that end, introduces a subsidy to domestic producers of $4 per widget produced. In your diagram, show the change caused by the introduction of this subsidy to the equilibrium of part (b) above. How many widgets will domestic producers supply now? How many widgets will Atlantida import or export now?

(d) The government is considering alternative methods to facilitate the growth of the domestic widget industry and decides now to impose an import tariff of $2 per widget. In your diagram, show the change caused by the introduction of this tariff to the equilibrium of part (b) above. How many widgets will domestic producers supply now? How many widgets will Atlantida import or export now?

Additional Multiple-Choice Questions

*1. **Which of the following trade practices is *not* specifically designed as a device to promote protectionism?**
    (a)   Tariffs.   (b)   Voluntary export restrictions.
    (c)   Countervailing duties.   (d)   Import quotas.
    (e)   Costly customs procedures.

2. **Which of the following national objectives is a valid argument for some degree of protectionism?**
    (a)   Concentration of national resources in a few specialized products.
    (b)   Increases in average incomes.
    (c)   Diversification of a small economy in order to reduce the risk associated with cyclical fluctuations in world prices.
    (d)   Ability of domestic firms to operate at minimum efficient scale.
    (e)   Maximization of the national standard of living.

*3. **A large country may favourably alter its terms of trade by restricting domestic**
    (a)   demand and thereby reduce the price of imports for domestic consumers.
    (b)   demand and thereby reduce the price of imports received by foreign producers.
    (c)   supply and thereby reduce the price of imports for domestic consumers.
    (d)   supply and thereby reduce the price of imports for domestic consumers.
    (e)   demand and supply and thereby reduce imports.

4. **_____ serve to raise a country's standard of living only to the extent that they raise national income to permit the purchase of more _____.**
    (a)   Tariffs; imports   (b)   Exports; imports
    (c)   Imports; strategic subsidies   (d)   Imports; non-traded goods
    (e)   Exports; domestically produced goods

5. **A large country, accounting for a significant share of world demand for an imported product, can increase its national income by**
    (a)   encouraging domestic production.
    (b)   restricting domestic demand for the product, thereby decreasing its price and improving its terms of trade.
    (c)   imposing import quotas on the product.
    (d)   subsidizing imports of the good, thereby monopolizing world consumption.
    (e)   negotiating voluntary export restrictions.

*6. **The problem with restricting imports as a means of reducing domestic unemployment is that**
    (a)   it merely redistributes unemployment from import-competing industries to our export industries when trading partners retaliate.
    (b)   Canadians would rather do without than have to buy Canadian-produced goods.
    (c)   our import-competing industries are not labour-intensive.
    (d)   our import-competing industries are always fully employed.
    (e)   it will also reduce exports when the economy is in equilibrium.

7. **Which of the following is *not* true of the EU's Common Agricultural Policy (CAP)?**
   (a) The CAP has led to agricultural surpluses in the EU.
   (b) The CAP has turned the EU from a net importer in many agricultural products to self-sufficiency.
   (c) The CAP leads the EU to heavily subsidize its agricultural exports.
   (d) The CAP benefits agricultural producers in less developed countries.
   (e) Quotas that support the CAP are being replaced with tariff equivalents.

8. **The principle of national treatment that is embedded in the NAFTA means that Canada could, for example, introduce any product standards it likes, so long as**
   (a) they apply only to Canadian-produced goods.
   (b) the standards are no more stringent than those existing in either Mexico or the United States.
   (c) they apply equally to Canadian-, Mexican- and American-produced goods sold in Canada.
   (d) they apply only to Canadian exports.
   (e) they apply only to Canadian imports.

*9. **A major effect of a tariff is to**
   (a) redistribute income from consumers to domestic producers and the government.
   (b) allow consumers to benefit at the expense of domestic producers.
   (c) discourage domestic production.
   (d) encourage consumers to buy more of the good.
   (e) reduce government revenues.

10. **A free trade agreement**
    (a) must include rules of origin.
    (b) eliminates the need for customs controls on the movement of goods.
    (c) allows for free cross-border movement of labour.
    (d) erects a common tariff wall against non-member countries.
    (e) always contributes more to trade diversion than to trade creation

11. **Which of the following is *not* a feature of the NAFTA?**
    (a) A common regime for antidumping and countervailing duties.
    (b) The principle of national treatment.
    (c) A dispute-settlement mechanism.
    (d) An accession clause whereby other countries may join.
    (e) A reduction in the barriers to trade in both goods and services among member countries.

Questions 12 to 18 refer to Figure 34-5, which illustrates the domestic demand and supply curves for a commodity as well as a horizontal world supply curve (P_w) at a constant price of $6/unit.

Figure 34-5

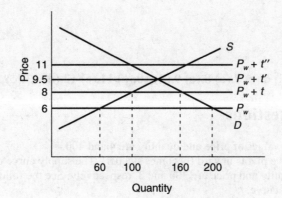

*12. At a world price of $6, imports of this commodity into the domestic economy are
   (a)   200.   (b)   160.
   (c)   140.   (d)   60.
   (e)   40.

*13. If a tariff of $2 is levied against imports of this commodity, domestic consumption and production would be
   (a)   200 and 60, respectively.   (b)   160 and 60, respectively.
   (c)   200 and 100, respectively.   (d)   160 and 100, respectively.
   (e)   160 and 40, respectively.

*14. Given a tariff of $2, government tariff revenue would be
   (a) $120.   (b) $320.
   (c) $200.   (d) $1280.
   (e) $800.

*15. The tariff has _____ imports of this commodity by _____ units.
   (a)   reduced; 80   (b)   reduced; 40
   (c)   reduced; 100   (d)   increased; 40
   (e)   increased; 60

*16. The deadweight loss of the tariff is
   (a) $400.   (b) $120.
   (c) $80.   (d) $160.
   (e) $2.

*17. If a tariff of $3.50 is instead levied against imports of this commodity, government tariff revenue would be
   (a) $0.   (b) $45.
   (c) $130.   (d) $195.
   (e) $455.

*18. If a tariff of $5.00 is instead levied against imports of this commodity, domestic production would be
   (a)   0.   (b)   100.
   (c)   130.   (d)   160.
   (e)   None of the above.

Solutions

Chapter Review

1.(c) 2.(c) 3.(b) 4.(b) 5.(d) 6.(e) 7.(e) 8.(c) 9.(d) 10.(a) 11.(c) 12.(d) 13.(c) 14.(e) 15.(b) 16.(a)

Short-Answer Questions

1. **Case 1**
    (a) The equilibrium values of price and quantity are 4 and 400.
    (b) The demand curve pivots inward (becomes steeper). The supply curve doesn't change. The new equilibrium quantity and price are 300 and 3, respectively. See the following table that describes the new demand curve.

Price	Quantity
5	100
4	200
3	300
2	400

    Case 2
    (a) At a world price of $2, domestic supply is 200 while quantity demanded is 800. Imports are therefore 600.
    (b) Draw a horizontal line at price equals $3. At this higher price, which includes the $1 tariff, the quantity supplied is 300 and the quantity demanded is 600. Therefore, imports have fallen to 300.

    Case 3
    An import quota of 300 can be achieved if the government allows the world price to increase to $3. Hence, draw a horizontal line at $3. Your diagram should indicate that domestic supply is 300 and the excess domestic demand of 300 is satisfied by a quota of 300 on imports.

2. Your explanation should discuss the unwillingness of governments to eliminate their supply-management policies. These have been a key feature of Canadian agricultural policy both at the federal and provincial level. The policies have been implemented mainly to stabilize farm income and protect domestic farmers from volatile price swings in international markets. They also serve to increase export competitiveness by subsidizing domestic production. The Canadian federal government has attempted to protect Canadian farmers by imposing quotas on imports or by levying tariffs.

3. Gains from trade are not determined by difference in absolute costs but rather by difference in opportunity costs. Freer trade with a low-wage country such as Mexico will bring about a relocation of resources in Canada from unskilled labour-intensive to skilled labour-intensive industries. After a period of adjustment, therefore, Canada will end up importing unskilled labour-intensive goods from Mexico and exporting skilled labour-intensive goods to Mexico.

4. The "infant industry argument" justifies the introduction of protectionist measures when the government wants to foster the development of new industries with potential for economies of scale or learning by doing. This was the intention of both Latin American and East Asian countries when they first introduced these policies in the second half of the twentieth century. In both groups of countries the objective was to protect their industries from foreign competition while they were growing up and to gradually relax the level of protection as they became more competitive. This was what the East Asian governments did to a large extent—gradually reducing the level of protection in order to provide an incentive for firms to improve their degree of competitiveness in the international market. Latin American governments, on the contrary, continued protecting their industries beyond the "infant" stage, thus providing the wrong incentive for firms to become complacent and inefficient.

5. The world price is P_w, and thus initially the domestic price is equal to the world price. The domestic quantity supplied is Q_S^1 and the domestic quantity demanded is Q_D^1, and thus imports are $Q_D^1 - Q_S^1$. When a tariff (t) is introduced, the domestic price becomes equal to the world price plus the tariff ($P_d = P_w + t$). Now the domestic quantity supplied is Q_S^2 and the domestic quantity demanded is Q_D^2, and thus imports are now reduced to $Q_D^2 - Q_S^2$. This is shown in Figure 34-6.

Figure 34-6

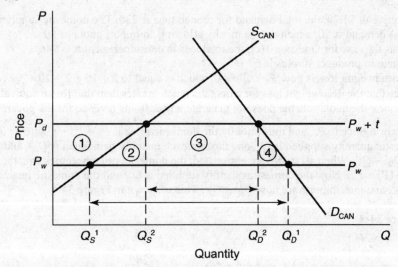

When the tariff is introduced and the domestic price increases, consumer surplus decreases. In the diagram, the decrease in consumer surplus is represented by the summation of the areas ① + ② + ③ + ④. At the same time, the increase in price causes the producer surplus to increase. In the diagram, the increase in producer surplus is represented by the area ①. The net loss between producers' gains and consumers' losses is thus represented by the sum of the areas ② + ③ + ④. However, since government tariff revenues are not a loss to society (area ③), the net welfare loss to society ("deadweight loss") is represented by the summation of the areas ② + ④.

Exercises

1. **(a)** Canadian production is 120; Canadian consumption is 240; and imports are 120.
    (b) Domestic production rises by 20; domestic consumption falls by 20; and imports fall by 40. Imports fall by more than domestic production rises due to the decline in total quantity demanded.

Figure 34-7

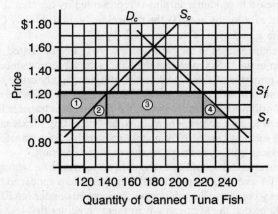

Quantity of Canned Tuna Fish

(c) There is a loss in consumer surplus equal to the total area ① + ② + ③ + ④. This is equal to a loss of $46. [*Hint:* Add the area of the rectangle of areas ① + ② + ③ = $0.20 × 220 to the area of the triangle (④), which equals 0.5[0.20 × 20].

(d) There is a gain in producer surplus equal to ①. This is equal to a gain of 6.

(e) There is an increase in tariff revenue equal to the area of ③, which is equal to $0.2 × 80 = 16.

(f) The deadweight loss is ② + ④, which is equal to 2 + 2 = 4.

2. **(a)** At a price of $1.20, the total demand for canned tuna is 220. The domestic supply is 140. Hence, excess demand is 80, which can be met by allowing an import quota of 80.

(b) As was the case for Question 1(c), the total loss in consumer surplus is $46.

(c) The gain in producer surplus is 6.

(d) The deadweight loss is now ② + ③ + ④, which is equal to 2 + 16 + 2 = 20.

(e) Notice that the deadweight loss for a quota is much greater than that for an equivalent tariff. This is because the quota scheme does not generate any customs revenue for the government (area ③).

3. **(a)** The world price is P_w, and thus initially the domestic price is $P_d = P_w + t$, where t is the tariff. The domestic quantity supplied is Q_S^1 and the domestic quantity demanded is Q_D^1, and thus imports are $Q_D^1 - Q_S^1$. When all tariffs are eliminated, the domestic price becomes equal to the world price ($P_d = P_w$). Now the domestic quantity supplied is Q_S^2 and the domestic quantity demanded is Q_D^2, and thus imports are now $Q_D^2 - Q_S^2$. This is shown in Figure 34-8.

Figure 34-8

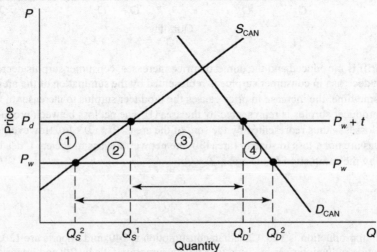

(b) When the tariff is eliminated and the domestic price falls to P_w, consumer surplus increases. In the diagram, the increase in consumer surplus is represented by the summation of the areas ① + ② + ③ + ④. At the same time, the fall in price causes the producer surplus to decrease. In the diagram, the decrease in producer surplus is represented by the area ①. Since government tariff revenues also decrease by the area ③, the net welfare gain to society ("deadweight gain") is represented by the summation of the areas ② + ④.

(c) If U.S. government subsidies to the corn sector were to be eliminated, corn production would significantly drop in the U.S. Given that the U.S. is the largest producer and exporter of corn in the world, the elimination of these subsidies would most likely cause a significant increase in the world price of corn. Therefore, these subsidies are responsible for the maintenance of an artificially low world price and represent, in the first place, a transfer from U.S. taxpayers to U.S. corn producers and to corn consumers worldwide—including Mexican consumers. Second, these U.S. government subsidies are also ultimately responsible for a transfer from Mexican corn producers to Mexican corn consumers, as shown in the diagram.

The U.S. government subsidies to the corn sector could be seen as unfair trade practice under both NAFTA and WTO regulations. Therefore, there appear to be grounds for the Mexican government to levy countervailing duties on corn imports under NAFTA. Why hasn't it done so? One reason might be that the Mexican government perceives that levying countervailing duties on corn imports has the potential of triggering a trade war with the U.S. with potentially enormous negative effects on the Mexican economy given its trade dependence with the U.S. A second reason might be that, since corn is an important staple in Mexico and low corn prices contribute to maintaining low wages, the Mexican government might have decided to pursue an industrial development strategy at a cost to the sector of small agricultural producers.

Extension Exercises

E1. **(a)** Equating total supply to demand, we obtain $P = \$2$ and a total quantity demanded of 800 widgets.

(b) At a world price of $2, total demand is 800 widgets and domestic supply is 200 (100×2). Hence, foreign supply is $600 = 300 \times 2$. This value represents the quantity of widget imports into Gill.

(c) The price received by foreigners after paying the tariff of $2 per unit is $P - 2$. Substituting this value into the world supply equation, we obtain $Q_S{}^F = 300(P - 2)$ or $-600 + 300P$.

(d) The imposition of the tax has the effect of shifting the world supply upward. Equating the new total supply curve ($-600 + 400P$) with demand, we obtain a new world equilibrium price of $3 and new quantity demanded of 600 widgets. Domestic production at the higher price increases to 300. Foreign supply (and imports) declines to 300.

(e) Domestic producers receive $3 per widget; however, foreign firms receive a lower net price than before. They receive $1 net after paying a $2 tariff.

E2. **(a)** Equilibrium is established at the price level at which the quantity demanded is equal to the quantity supplied. The table shows that at $P = \$7$ the quantity demanded and the quantity supplied are equal at $Q = 6000$ per month.

Figure 34-9

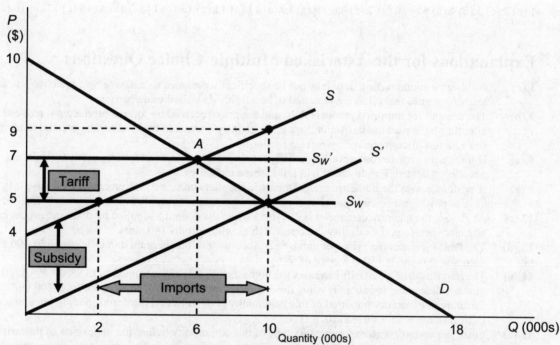

(b) Since Atlantida is a small country and takes the international price as given, the domestic price for widgets will fall to the international level of $5. Therefore, the quantity domestically supplied will fall while the quantity demanded will rise, and thus the excess domestic demand will be satisfied through imports.

The table below also shows that at $P = \$5$, the quantity demanded is 10 000, while the quantity domestically supplied is 2000 per month. Therefore, Atlantida will import 8000 widgets per month.

(c) As shown in Figure 34-9 and the table below, at $P = \$5$ domestic producers will supply 10 000 widgets now (since with the subsidy they will receive a price of $9), a quantity equal to the quantity demanded at this price. Therefore, 100 percent of the domestic demand will be satisfied with domestic production and imports will be zero.

Price ($)	10	9	8	7	6	5	4
Quantity demanded (000s)	0	2	4	6	8	10	12
Quantity supplied without subsidy (000s)	12	10	8	6	4	2	0
Quantity supplied with subsidy (000s)	20	18	16	14	12	10	8

(d) The tariff increases the domestic price by $2. Therefore, the international supply curve now is perfectly elastic at $P = \$7$. Therefore, as shown in Figure 34-9 and the table above, at $P = \$7$, the quantity demanded is 6000 and the quantity domestically supplied is also 6000 per month. Therefore, 100 percent of the domestic demand will be satisfied with domestic production and imports will be zero.

Additional Multiple-Choice Questions

1.(c) **2.**(c) **3.**(b) **4.**(b) **5.**(b) **6.**(a) **7.**(d) **8.**(c) **9.**(a) **10.**(a) **11.**(a) **12.**(c) **13.**(d) **14.**(a) **15.**(a) **16.**(c) **17.**(a) **18.**(c)

Explanations for the Asterisked Multiple-Choice Questions

1.(c)   Although a counteracting duty may not be specifically designed as a device for protectionism, the textbook argues that it has the potential to be a thinly disguised trade barrier.

3.(b)   The demand for imported products falls, and the price received by foreign producers is reduced after they have paid the tariff/unit; hence, the country's terms of trade have the potential to increase since import prices received by foreign producers fall.

6.(a)   If foreigners impose countervailing tariffs, export industries in the domestic economy will be adversely affected. Employment will fall in these industries.

9.(a)   A tariff increases the domestic price. Domestic suppliers gain, but consumers lose because they have to pay higher prices. The government gains by receiving tariff revenue.

12.(c)   At $P = \$6$, the quantity demanded is 200 units while the quantity supplied by domestic producers is 60 units; therefore, the quantity imported of this commodity is 140 units.

13.(d)   The tariff increases the price per unit by $2. According to the diagram domestic supply is 100 and domestic demand is 160 at a price of $8.

14.(a)   The imposition of a $2 tariff increases the domestic price of this commodity to $8. At $P = \$8$, the quantity demanded is 160 units while the quantity supplied by domestic producers is 100 units; therefore, the quantity imported of this commodity is 60 units and the corresponding government tariff revenue is $\$2 \times 60 = \$120$.

15.(a)   Since this country was importing 140 units of this commodity before the imposition of the tariff and is now importing only 60 units, the tariff has contributed to reduce imports of this commodity by 80 units.

16.(c)   As the textbook explains, the deadweight loss of a tariff is the sum of the areas of two triangles— one under the supply curve and one under the demand curve. The area of each is $40, and so the deadweight loss is $80.

17.(a)   If a tariff of $3.50 is levied against the import of this commodity, then the domestic price will be $9.50—equal to the market price under autarky. The quantity domestically supplied, therefore, will be equal to the quantity demanded, and thus imports will be zero and so will be the government tariff revenue.

18.(c)   A tariff that increases the domestic price of an imported commodity beyond the autarky market equilibrium price is ineffective since at the latter price imports are already zero. Therefore, the price of the commodity would be $9.50, and the quantity domestically produced would be 130.